Voices of Christianity
A GLOBAL INTRODUCTION

Voices of Christianity
A GLOBAL INTRODUCTION

REBECCA MOORE

San Diego State University

Boston   Burr Ridge, IL   Dubuque, IA   Madison, WI   New York   San Francisco   St. Louis
Bangkok   Bogotá   Caracas   Kuala Lumpur   Lisbon   London   Madrid   Mexico City
Milan   Montreal   New Delhi   Santiago   Seoul   Singapore   Sydney   Taipei   Toronto

Higher Education

VOICES OF CHRISTIANITY: A GLOBAL INTRODUCTION
Published by McGraw-Hill, a business unit of The McGraw-Hill Companies, Inc., 1221 Avenue of the Americas, New York, NY, 10020. Copyright © 2006 by The McGraw-Hill Companies, Inc. All rights reserved. No part of this publication may be reproduced or distributed in any form or by any means, or stored in a database or retrieval system, without the prior written consent of The McGraw-Hill Companies, Inc., including, but not limited to, in any network or other electronic storage or transmission, or broadcast for distance learning.

Some ancillaries, including electronic and print components, may not be available to customers outside the United States.

This book is printed on acid-free paper.

1 2 3 4 5 6 7 8 9 0 FGR/FGR 0 9 8 7 6 5

ISBN 0-07-287043-5

Vice president and Editor-in-chief: *Emily Barrosse*
Publisher: *Lyn Uhl*
Senior sponsoring editor: *Jon-David Hague*
Editorial coordinator: *Allison Rona*
Permissions coordinator: *Frederick T. Courtright*
Senior marketing manager: *Zina Craft*
Production editor: *Mel Valentin*
Manuscript editor: *Thomas Briggs*
Design manager/Cover designer: *Kim Menning*
Interior designer: *Valerie Brewster*
Art editor: *Robin Mouat*
Photo research coordinator: *Brian Pecko*
Senior production supervisor: *Rich DeVitto*
Typeface: *10/13 Berkeley Book*
Compositor: *TBH Typecast, Inc.*
Printer: *Quebecor-Fairfield*

Credits: The credits section for this book begins on page 449 and is considered an extension of the copyright page.

Library of Congress Cataloging-in-Publication Data

Voices of Christianity: a global introduction / Rebecca Moore.
     p. cm.
  Includes bibliographical references and index.
  ISBN-13: 978-0-07-287043-5 (alk. paper)
  ISBN-10: 0-07-287043-5 (alk. paper)
    1. Church history—Sources.   I. Moore, Rebecca, 1951–
BR141.V65 2005
270—dc22

2005054379

www.mhhe.com

Table of Contents

Part Two

The Enlightenment • The Authority of Reason • A Reasonable God • The Authority of Scripture • Women in the Bible • The Authority of Experience • Pietism: The Experience of the Holy Spirit • Romanticism: The Authority of Feeling • Mysticism: The Truth of Experience • The Philokalia • The Authority of Tradition • Episcopal Infallibility • Conclusions

Part Three   311

CHAPTER SIX
Missions and Inculturation: Singing The Lord's Song in a New Key   313

Christianity in the New World • "Christian" Holidays? • The Virgin of Guadalupe • Christianity in North America • Old World Missions • South Asian Christianity and the Acts of Thomas • Christian Fiction • Slave Christianity • Africa for Christ • Go Tell It on the Mountain! • Modern African Christianity • Conclusions

CHAPTER SEVEN
Voices for the Future   379

Liberalism, Fundamentalism, and Neo-Orthodoxy • *Shaking the Foundations* • *Christian Existentialism* • *A World Come of Age* • *Christianity and Non-Christian Religions* • *Vatican Council II* • *The Ecumenical Movement* • *Pentecostal Christianity* • *Liberation Theology in Latin America* • *Liberation Theology in North America* • *Feminist Theology* • *Liberating the Planet* • *Conclusions*

Invitation

Dear Reader,

I decided to write this introduction as a letter because it really serves as an invitation: an invitation to read. While an introduction sets the stage and helps create a sense of expectation within the reader, it is also more formal, and sometimes more alienating, than a letter. A letter is more intimate, more informal, and, I hope, more inviting. And that is exactly what I would like to do in this letter: invite you to learn about Christianity by reading an assortment of Christian texts.

This anthology has two purposes. First and foremost, it tells the story of Christian history through primary documents. Primary sources are the original words and writings of historical figures. They may be public records, letters, diaries, journals, or other kinds of writings. In the case of Christianity and the readings in this book, these primary documents may be sermons, commentaries, arguments, poems, liturgies, hymns, analyses, or other types of writing—like letters, for instance. Thus, this book provides an overview of 2000 years of Christian history from a variety of perspectives and in many different ways. By the time we get to "the end," we will have a good sense of how Christianity developed, what the key beliefs and practices of Christians are, and why there is so much diversity in the world's single largest religion.

The second purpose of this book is to provide the tools needed to read primary sources. I hear many students complain that they do not understand what they read. Sometimes teachers fail to give students sufficient guidance to help them through difficult texts. I am convinced, however, that with enough preparation, students can read and comprehend a wide variety of primary source materials. This book is designed to demystify the reading process and to help us approach *any* reading assignment, not just the ones in this anthology.

Reading involves not just mastering the words but somehow making sense of the words and then "getting" the meaning of the words all put together. This "getting it" is not something innate or inborn; it is something that is learned. Some are fortunate to learn it early, and some never learn it. Good readers have mastered a number of techniques—consciously or unconsciously—that help them persevere when the going gets rough. This book supplies a method for reading, analyzing, and comprehending a number of different styles of writing. While we learn about Christianity, we will also be learning how to approach texts that are radically different from what is written today.

For example, I will discuss genres, a fine French word meaning "kind," or sort or type. A genre is simply a category. Music genres include jazz, rock, heavy metal, rap, the blues, and country. Fiction genres encompass science fiction, for example, and mysteries, romances, Westerns, children's literature, and much more. Each genre has its own rules: romance novels follow a certain formula that is different from the formula for Westerns. Similarly, the rules for writing sermons are different from those governing letters, or poems, or Bible commentaries. If we know what the genre is, we know what to expect. This knowledge helps with comprehension because we are already bringing some understanding to the text we are reading.

It also helps to know who wrote something, and why, and when. Our social and cultural contexts definitely affect how we understand things. Someone who is in a bitter child custody dispute, for example, will see the nature of marriage differently than will someone who is happily married. The writers represented in this book are no different. They are engaged in conversations with other Christians and with society at large. If we know the historical or theological setting, we have a better chance of following the conversation. This book therefore discusses the contexts of the readings to help create a preunderstanding of what each writer feels is at stake.

And yes, a great deal was at stake for the writers of the following texts. They were writing about important issues—in some instances, with life-and-death consequences, or even with what they perceived to be eternal-life-and-eternal death consequences. Christians have rarely played supporting roles on the stage of world history. Rather, they have been deeply engaged in debates, arguments, and apologetics, that is, persuasion. A great deal was at stake for these writers, and if we know this, we can begin to appreciate what they are trying to say.

Reading requires imagination. Although it may seem that the words on the page are merely black-and-white symbols, this is far from the case. The words on the page are windows onto the heart and mind and soul of the writer. When we remember that flesh and blood wrote these squiggly lines—and that the writers believed they had a compelling reason to do so—we begin to understand reading for what it really is: a dialogue between writer and reader.

When I began this letter, I thought perhaps I should start with "Dear Readers"— the plural. Although reading seems to be a solitary pursuit, it is far from it. In the olden days, when books and literacy were rare, books were read aloud. The word *lecture* comes from the Latin root *legere,* which means "to read." Texts were read out loud, and usually read to more than one person. The letters of Paul, for example, were written to churches in the Mediterranean and were intended to be read to the entire group. "I solemnly command you by the Lord that this letter be read to all of them," Paul concluded his first letter to the Thessalonians (5:27). In the New Testament letter to the Colossians, similar evidence of this kind of reading appears: "And when this letter has been read among you, have it read also in the church of the Laodiceans; and see that you read also the letter from Laodicea" (4:16). In the convents and monasteries of the Middle Ages, the nuns and monks ate their meals while listening to someone reading from scripture or from theological works. Throughout the day, they would stop their tasks, go to chapel, and read or recite the psalms. Today we tend to understand what we have read much better when we have a chance to discuss the reading with others: "Is this what he really means?" "I thought she was saying something else." In many respects, then, reading is a collective process, a method of dialogue and engagement that is never solitary.

At the same time, there is a privacy to reading that is undeniable. The dialogue that occurs between writer and reader takes place, initially at least, in one's own mind. There is an "I–Thou" relationship, in the words of Martin Buber, a "you 'n' me" connection that excludes the rest of the world. The writer is first speaking to *me,* and *I* am the one to process those words through my own experiences, abilities, and insights. Once I digest the words, I make them my own: I comprehend, that is, I grasp, what is being said; I get it. And then I check it out with others to see if I got it right or if my own opinions distorted what I thought I saw.

Of course, with religious texts, there is yet another dimension: the realm of the transcendent and the divine; the province of God. This adds a challenge to readers because we must continuously make judgments about whether the writer is expressing her own opinion or is channeling in some way for the divine. This is an especially difficult question when reading scripture. Yet whether we believe that the text presents merely human reflections or divinely inspired revelations, we can still ask the same questions: What is being said? How is it being said? What argument is being made? What evidence is given in support of the argument? Who is the opposition, and what is their argument? In other words, we can read religious texts with the same critical mind that we bring to other texts. While the subject matter differs, our method can usually, though not always, remain the same. We ask questions of the text just as we would ask questions of the person sitting next to us, because it was a person—whether divine or human is beyond our knowledge—who wrote the text.

There is a further complication in a compilation such as this, which contains selections rather than entire works. We are always entering in the middle of the conversation. We're not sure what was said before we came in, and we don't know how the conversation will continue once we leave. The best approach to reading these selections resembles one we might take when we go into a room and the party has already started. Rather than barging in, we usually get the lay of the land: check out what's going on, who's doing the talking, and where the food is; and when we join a group, we usually listen to see what the subject matter is before we jump in with our own comments.

Listening to the author is one way to manage difficult texts. Sometimes, however, our thoughts interfere with our ability to understand. We might be preoccupied with how exhausted we are, or how bored we are, or how hungry we are. Or our thoughts might be a bit more critical: Who does this guy think he is? He's wrong wrong wrong! Who ever heard of something so [pick one: weird, strange, bizarre, ridiculous, blasphemous]?!? These latter thoughts are certainly preferable to the former because they indicate an engagement with the text. But if we can manage the self-discipline (having gotten enough food and sleep before reading), it is even better to try to listen to the author to understand what is being said.

And so this invitation to you, my singular reader. The thesaurus provides a number of synonyms for the word *invite*: tempt, encourage, incite, attract, provoke, induce. These are all colorful verbs that describe exactly what I hope to do in this book. I want to tempt you to pick up this book, open it up, and read. I also hope to encourage you to persevere despite occasional difficulties. I plan to do more than merely encourage you or be a cheerleader on the sidelines. By presenting historical background, contextual information, genre discussions, and reflection questions, I would like to induce you to approach these texts knowing that you are well prepared to understand and appreciate what you are reading. The writers in this book can be provocative; they may incite admiration or ire. All of them write from a profound commitment to Christianity, however. Even when we may disagree with what they are saying, we can respect the depth of their belief and attempt to understand why they believe what they do.

Augustine of Hippo (354–430) was sitting in a garden, agonizing over the course of his life, when he heard children playing a game. They were chanting "*tolle lege; tolle lege*," which means "take up and read." Augustine picked up a Bible and read a verse, and it changed his life. I invite you to pick up this book and read it to catch a few glimpses of the incredibly rich treasury of texts that make up the Christian tradition.

Sincerely,

Rebecca Moore

Rebecca Moore

P.S. to Teachers:
The difficulty inherent in developing a collection of readings is the selection process: Which writers should be included? This anthology takes a different approach.

The purpose of this book is to introduce readers to the vast history and diversity of Christianity, particularly its theology, rather than provide samplings of various key figures. Most compilations attempt to provide a buffet menu of readings, with little tastes of everything. This collection differs greatly from the buffet model. If we stick with the food analogy, perhaps we can consider each chapter a full-course dinner comprising specific types of cuisine. When we are finished with each meal, we will have a pretty good idea of what we just ate and digested.

I did not invent this approach to "reading Christianity." I learned the value of struggling through complete primary sources at Marquette University, in Milwaukee, Wisconsin. I have had the good fortune to be raised a Protestant (in the home of a United Methodist minister and his wife), to attend a Catholic graduate school (and Jesuit at that!), and to work for two years with a mentor who is an Orthodox monk. My small-"c" catholic background created a lasting appreciation for the variety of beliefs and practices that exists within Christianity. That richness can only be grasped by engaging with texts and their writers at some length.

This explains why some writers are "missing" and others are included in their place. My goal is not to cover the Top Fifty Writers of Christianity. Rather, my goal is to help readers understand and appreciate the concerns and passions of various Christians throughout history. Those concerns led to the development of doctrines that are taught today, as well as some that were abandoned by orthodoxy. This book is structured to engage readers in the various conversations that Christians have had over key issues through the centuries, and to give them the tools necessary to do so successfully. If readers follow the conversation as it develops from chapter to chapter, a clear outline of Christian thought emerges.

Since all of us who teach introductory courses in Christianity have certain imperatives about what must be covered, however, free access to a comprehensive Web site accompanies this text: www.mhhe.com/voices1e. The site provides links to primary and secondary sources, to bibliographies, and to articles and pictures, in order to broaden and enrich the readings included in the anthology itself. Used with supplementary Internet items as appropriate, this text is designed to be textbook and anthology in a single volume.

I invite your feedback, suggestions, and comments so that the conversation begun in these pages may continue.

Acknowledgments

My deepest thanks go to Jon-David Hague at McGraw-Hill for proposing this project in the first place, for being patient with me throughout the delays, and for believing in what we were doing. Indeed, all of the staff at McGraw-Hill have been extremely helpful, especially Allison Rona and Mel Valentín. I appreciate their care and attention to the project. I also thank copyeditor extraordinaire Tom Briggs for his excellent eye, and ear, for editing.

I would also like to express my sincere gratitude to the many anonymous readers whose comments and insights made this a much better book. Fortunately, they are now willing to be identified, and so I thank the following: Lisa Driver (Valparaiso University), Thomas Ferguson (Manhattan College), Constance Furey (Indiana University, Bloomington), Michelle A. Gonzalez (Loyola Marymount University), David G. Hunter (Iowa State University), William Madges (Xavier University), Nicolae Roddy (Creighton University), Lynn Ross-Bryant (University of Colorado, Boulder), Dan R. Stiver (Hardin-Simmons University), and Valarie Ziegler (DePauw University). These reviewers suggested readings, translations, clarifications, and corrections that improved the final product. Any errors or omissions remain my full responsibility.

The idea of doing a reader that provides complete texts and chapters, rather than "sound bites" of selections, came from the faculty in theology at Marquette University. While there are many people I would like to thank, I will mention only two by name: Dr. Kenneth G. Hagen, who reviewed several chapters for me even while engrossed in his own writing project; and Father Alexander Golitzin, who gave me an appreciation for Orthodox Christianity.

Many thanks go to the supportive faculty and staff in the Department of Religious Studies at San Diego State University. I also appreciate the assistance of Dr. E. Nick Genovese, from the Department of Classics and Humanities.

Although listed last, the people who endured the most during this process were, of course, members of my family: my husband, Fielding McGehee III, and my father, John V Moore. My mother, Barbara C. Moore, died while this book was in progress. This is one of life's little ironies, since she is the one who taught me about Christianity in the first place.

INVITATION TO
Part One

PART ONE reveals just how rapidly Christianity developed during the first five centuries of the Common Era. It traces the transformation of a small, apocalyptic movement popular among some Palestinian Jews into an international organization with power and authority throughout the Roman Empire.

CHAPTER ONE begins by looking at the historical and theological context in which Jesus and his movement emerge. It briefly surveys the history of Israelite religion, the ancestor of both Judaism and Christianity, and discusses the composition of biblical texts. It closely examines key passages of the Christian Old Testament—what Jews would call the Hebrew Bible, or Tanakh—that the followers of Jesus turned to in order to understand their Lord. Chapter One also looks at the first-century Judean environment into which Jesus was born, as well as at his teaching and at the scholarly study of his teachings. It then describes the impact of Paul, the apostle to the Gentiles (that is, to non-Jews), whose letters make up the majority of the New Testament and greatly contribute to all subsequent Christian theology.

CHAPTER TWO concentrates on the extremely fruitful period of church and doctrinal development during the first five centuries after Jesus' death. While Christian practices differed from place to place, the two primary practices of the early church were baptism and communion. Christian beliefs also differed from place to place, and the nature of Jesus and his relationship to God was hotly debated. In order to clarify what was "correct" Christian doctrine regarding Jesus, a number of church councils developed creeds and faith statements that spelled out official church teaching.

PART ONE concludes with the fall of the western Roman Empire and sets the stage for the myriad theological developments that occur in the Middle Ages.

	587/6 B.C.E. → Babylonians destroy first temple in Jerusalem
Persians capture Babylon ←	**539**
	c. 515 → Second temple built
Persian Empire falls to Alexander the Great (from Macedonia) ←	**330**
	301 → Alexandrian Empire falls to Ptolemy Dynasty (from Egypt)
Ptolemy Dynasty falls to Seleucid Dynasty (from Syria) ←	**201**
	168–52 → Civil war in Judea
Hasmonean Dynasty rules (Hellenistic Jews) ←	**152**
	63 → Roman conquest of Judea, all the Land of Israel
Herod I the Great (from Idumea; nominally Jewish) ←	**37**
	4 → Death of Herod I; rule transferred to his sons
Jesus of Nazareth born ←	**c. 4 B.C.E.**
	6 C.E. → Roman governors (procurators) rule Judea, Samaria, Galilee; various descendants of Herod I have oversight
Pontius Pilate appointed procurator ←	**26/7**
	c. 30 → Jesus executed by Romans
Execution of Peter and Paul in Rome ←	**c. 64**
	66 → First Jewish War begins
Second temple in Jerusalem destroyed by Romans ←	**70**
	73 → First Jewish War ends with fall of fortress at Masada
Persecution of Christians by Emperor Domitian (r. 81–96) ←	**c. 95**

CHAPTER ONE

The Jewish Roots of Jesus, Paul, and Christianity

Literary Sources for Understanding Jesus

While Christianity claims Jesus Christ as its central figure, its history neither begins nor ends with his life, death, and resurrection. Jewish beliefs and traditions, and the struggle of Jews against their Roman rulers during the first century C.E., provide the context in which Jesus was born. (Chapter Two examines the Greek and Roman context in which subsequent Christian doctrine develops.) The story of Jesus that appears in the New Testament of the Bible is really just a small part of this sacred text for Christians. The four Gospels that describe Jesus' earthly life—Matthew, Mark, Luke, and John—take up less than a quarter of the New Testament, and still less of the entire Bible, which for Christians includes an Old Testament and a New Testament.

A number of literary sources exist that set the scene for Jesus' arrival on the world stage. First, of course, is the Bible, with its Old Testament, which relates the story of the Israelites, and the New Testament, which relates the story of first-century Jews and of Jesus and his followers. Other texts—such as the Dead Sea Scrolls and the Pseudepigrapha—illuminate the religious framework further by revealing the diversity of Jewish thought in Jesus' day. All of these texts broaden our understanding of who Jesus was.

A Semitic tribe of nomads known as the Israelites wrote the first and largest part of the Bible. The Israelites, who are the religious ancestors of Christians and Muslims as well as of Jews, compiled a collection of scrolls. This collection ultimately formed a body of Jewish scripture called Tanakh, an acronym for Torah (the first five books of the Bible); Neviim (the Prophets); and Ketuvim (the Writings). Protestant Christians know Tanakh as the Old Testament, while Catholic and Orthodox Christians include ancient Jewish texts written in Greek, as well as the Tanakh, in their Old Testament. Biblical scholars use the term *Hebrew Bible* for the texts accepted as authoritative by Jews, to provide a neutral, all-inclusive phrase for the writings three major world religions hold sacred. Muslims dub Jews and Christians "people of the Book," and in essence they are correct in labeling the Hebrew Bible *the* book, since all three faiths base subsequent holy texts upon it. Jews have the Talmud, Christians have the New Testament, and Muslims have the Qur'an.

The Hebrew Bible chronicles the fortunes of the Israelites. It uses poems, legends, prophetic oracles or sayings, prayers, hymns, dialogues, sermons, and other literary genres to show the ups and downs of a particular people and their relationship with their god. It describes the heroic men and women who were faithful to the one god of their tribe, as well as the less-than-heroic ones who were faithless. Though not a history book, the Hebrew Bible does recount historical events, and two of these events profoundly influenced Israelite religion and the creation of the Hebrew Bible. The first was the eighth-century B.C.E.* Assyrian invasion that led to the fall of the northern kingdom of the Israelites—called Israel. Rather than deal with troublemakers in their own land, the Assyrians deported thousands of Israelites, particularly those in positions of political, economic, and religious leadership. A second disaster occurred with the fall of the southern kingdom, Judah, to the Babylonians in the sixth century B.C.E. Like the Assyrians before them, the Babylonians deported thousands of Israelites to Babylon. In 587 the Babylonians destroyed the Israelite temple in Jerusalem. This was extremely traumatic because all religions of the ancient Near East, including Israelite religion, shared a belief that their national deities had specific places, or thrones, where their power resided. For the Israelites, that place was the temple in Jerusalem. With the temple destroyed, the Israelites asked themselves: Where is our God, Where can we worship God?

In exile in Babylon, the Israelites came up with an answer. Now called Jews, or Judahites, because of their origin in Judah (Yehuda), they gathered together the religious stories and traditions of their people. They considered their long history of conflict with foreigners who did not believe in their deity but worshiped other gods and goddesses. They turned to collections of oracles of prophets for inspiration and hope. They were guided in part by a contemporary prophet named Ezekiel, whose vision of God's throne leaving the temple in Jerusalem gave them hope that God was present in their exile. The Jewish community compiled and edited a set of scrolls that traced their encounters with a god whose name was so sacred it was never spoken aloud. The editors arranged the scrolls somewhat chronologically: from narratives of the creation of the world and the lives of early ancestors; through stories of kings, queens, and prophets; to the present. They also ordered the scrolls in terms of theological importance. Thus, the first five books of the Hebrew Bible—called the Torah by Jews and the Pentateuch by Christians—come first because they were the most important.

Jews returned to the land of Judah later in the sixth century B.C.E. and rebuilt their temple in Jerusalem. Because this was the second temple that had been constructed, the Judaism of that period, and up to its destruction in 70 C.E., has been called Second Temple Judaism. During the period dating from Alexander the Great (356–323 B.C.E.), the Jews faced enemies and invasions on several fronts: from the Greeks under Alexander; from the Ptolemies of Egypt; from the Seleucids of Syria; and

---

* B.C.E. is the acronym for "Before Common Era," the equivalent of B.C., or "Before Christ." C.E., or "Common Era," is the term scholars use for A.D., "Anno Domini." Biblical scholars employ B.C.E. and C.E. as a way of being inclusive of researchers of different faiths.

▦ Judaic Religions

Over the past twenty-five years, scholars have debated the proper terminology for identifying the religion of the "Judahites"—those people who had been exiled to Babylon in the sixth century B.C.E. and who subsequently returned to the land of Judah in the centuries following. Are they Jews? Judahites? Judeans, after the Greek, and then English, transliteration of the Hebrew word *Yehudim*? And can we even call their religion "Judaism," since it differs from contemporary Rabbinic Judaism? The influential American Jewish scholar Jacob Neusner observes that there was no single type of Judaism in first-century Judea; rather, there were various "Judaisms." Others have called the religion of those who believed in the God of Israel "Second Temple Judaism," because it mixed elements of both Israelite religion and later Judaism. In the nineteenth century, Christian theologians called this "Late Judaism," by which they implied that Judaism ended with the coming of Christianity. Today some scholars call this complex of religious practices "Early Judaism," which expresses the view that they are not yet what we would call normative Judaism.

As study of this period continues, it becomes apparent that old labels are not always accurate—and yet new labels can be confusing. For example, "Judaism" during the centuries before and after the turn of the Common Era was not so much a religion as a cultural complex of beliefs, practices, and traditions that claimed descent from the ancestral customs of the Israelites. In this view, "Judaism" is an alternative to "Hellenism," a competing system of beliefs, practices and traditions that claimed descent from the customs of ancient Hellas, that is, Greece. When we refer to "Judaism," however, we tend to think of it in its modern form. What language should historians use to describe all the people who believed in the God of Israel in the centuries just before and just after the turn of the Common Era?

This book is published at a time when terms and labels are in great flux. Some scholars argue, for example, that the very idea of "religion" began in the third and fourth centuries. This text will continue to use the language that has been commonly accepted, although it will also introduce one new term—"Judaic religions"—to better describe all of the different practices of what has been called "Second Temple Judaism." "Judaic religions" encompasses and renders more accurately the great diversity of beliefs and traditions that existed in first-century Palestine, which contained the regions of Idumea, Judea, Samaria, and Galilee. It also includes the religions practiced in the Diaspora—that is, outside the Land of Israel—by Egyptian, Babylonian, and other Jews. "Judaic religions" also takes in the various movements that proclaimed Jesus as their messiah and savior, yet also claimed to be the descendants of biblical Israel. Finally, "Judaic" suggests that all of these groups are *somewhat* Jewish, or *sort of like* Judaism, rather than asserting their complete orthodoxy or manifestation as Judaism as we know it today.

in 63 B.C.E., from the Romans under the general Pompey. They also faced tyranny from within their own ranks—most notably, the Hasmonean dynasty of priestly rulers (152–63 B.C.E.), who first liberated the Jews from their Seleucid rulers and then oppressed their countrymen and -women under a corrupt temple priesthood.

The two centuries before the birth of Jesus served as the crucible in which many religious works emerged and new types of Judaic religions arose. A number of Judaic texts surfaced in this time that do not appear in the Hebrew Bible. Some were written in Greek, the language of learning and culture in the Mediterranean inherited from Alexander the Great and his successors. Their late arrival on the religious scene, as well as their Greek rather than Hebrew origins, made them suspect in terms of credibility and authority. Some were the writings of anonymous Jews, which reflected influences outside of Israelite religion. Still others came from the hearts of Jews living outside of Jerusalem and practicing alternative forms of Judaic religions. This last group, sometimes identified as Essenes, comprised ascetic monastic Jews who lived on the shores of the Dead Sea. In addition to maintaining traditional or orthodox Jewish scriptures, such as the Prophets, the Qumran community (named after its location at Khirbet Qumran) also wrote its own sacred texts. These writings, called the Dead Sea Scrolls, were found there by accident in 1947.

It has taken decades to translate and publish these ancient Jewish writings, in part because of the fragmentary nature of the scrolls—they were in bits and pieces—and in part because of scholarly and professional envy. What the materials reveal is a strand of Judaism that anticipated a holy war that would be fought in heaven between the "sons of light" and the "sons of darkness." God had acted in history, on earth, in the previous centuries of Israelite religion, and the Hebrew Bible documented this divine activity. But the time had come, according to the Qumran writings, for God and God's angels to fight the enemy, Satan and Satan's forces, in heaven. These Jews expected an other-worldly savior to lead God's army against Satan's army. Some writings suggest that the angel Michael—who would be leading God's troops—might be the savior. The Dead Sea Scrolls depict a type of religion that was apocalyptic, a type that anticipated a climactic cosmic battle in which, eventually, the good guys would win. Upon that victory, God would rule on earth and would be the king, just as God had been king of Israel in its earliest days.

During this same period—from about 200 B.C.E. to 200 C.E.—another set of writings surfaced from Jews who had been influenced by Persian religion. Sometimes these texts are called Inter-Testamental Literature because they were written more or less between the time the latest book of the Old Testament and the latest book of the New Testament were written. Sometimes they are called "Pseudepigrapha," which means "fake or false writings." They earned this name because they purport to be written by biblical figures like Moses and Abraham and even Adam. In a sense, these texts could be titled "The Further Adventures of . . . ," with heroes of the Old Testament figuring prominently. These books vividly describe a world vastly different from that of the Hebrew Bible. Whereas the latter is grounded, literally, in the land of Canaan, the Pseudepigrapha turn heavenward, reporting dreams, visions, and celestial travel—a realm in which angels, archangels, demons, and Satan figure prominently. What appears important in these "revelations" is what is going on behind the scenes, up above. Like the Dead Sea Scrolls, the Pseudepigrapha are apocalyptic literature that turn attention away from the earth and toward heaven. That is where the action is; it is where history will be made in the future.

A final ancient literary source for understanding Jesus is the New Testament. Although Christians usually start with this scripture, the New Testament actually reinterprets and retells many of the stories and themes that precede it in the Hebrew Bible, the Dead Sea Scrolls and the Pseudepigrapha. To begin with the New

The Apocalypse

When we think of the apocalypse, images of rivers of blood, plagues of locusts, and other global disasters come to mind. These mental pictures reflect some of the imagery that appears in the last book of the Christian New Testament, the book of Revelation, which is also known as the Apocalypse of John. But *apocalypse* simply means "revelation" in Greek, and there were many revelatory texts written in the period 200 B.C.E.–200 C.E. Apocalypse came to be understood as a literary genre in which heavenly journeys, angelic visitations, and vivid dreams disclosed unknown truths. While some revelations were bloody and violent, others unveiled heavenly cities and perfect worlds.

Apocalyptic literature marked a theological shift in the thinking of many Jews. Instead of God acting on earth and dealing with the chosen people—the Israelites—in historical events, God now acted in heaven, the site of a celestial battle between the forces of good and evil. While the cosmic war would also be waged on earth, the outcome would be determined strictly in heaven. People thus had to choose sides and decide whether they were on the side of light or the side of darkness.

Sometimes this final war is described as an eschatological conflict. *Eschatology* means the "doctrine of last things," that is, the doctrine of our future destiny. There may be a day of judgment, a time of reward or punishment, or, as the book of Revelation says, "a new heaven and a new earth." But Jesus always spoke of the end of the *age* (eon), that is, the present evil times. When this age ended, a new and improved age would begin under God's reign. Thus, when we speak of eschatology, we speak of this turning point in time. It may come about through a climactic, apocalyptic battle; or it may come silently, like a thief in the night. In either case, in the apocalyptic view, things will be radically different, on earth and in heaven.

Christianity emerged, in part, from the Judaic traditions that prophesied a heavenly battle between good and evil, and that preached an imminent Judgment Day in which God would right the wrongs of this world and redeem those who had already died, or were currently suffering, because of their faithfulness to the God of Israel.

Testament and then go back to the Old Testament is a bit like reading the ending of a book before its beginning. The New Testament brims with references to Jewish scripture, practices, and theology—everything from Sabbath to sacrifice. Some Jewish scholars claim that the New Testament is, in fact, a Jewish text: just one of many that came out of the period of great diversity occurring within Judaism between 200 B.C.E. and 200 C.E. The writers of the New Testament certainly knew Jewish scripture, including the legends of the Pseudepigrapha, and they used it to interpret the meaning and significance of Jesus' life.

Thinking About Scripture

The texts just noted—Tanakh (or Hebrew Bible, or Old Testament), Dead Sea Scrolls, Pseudepigrapha, and New Testament—are, or were, sacred to members of their religious communities, but not necessarily to all readers. Each of us brings a discrete worldview into our reading of any text, but especially of sacred texts. Thus, a Hindu reading a New Testament account of Jesus comes away with a different understanding of Jesus than does a Christian—just as Mohandas K. Gandhi did. Gandhi founded his movement of nonviolent resistance to British colonialists in India in part on the teachings of Jesus. A feminist who reads the story of Jesus' encounters with women may well explain those stories differently than a conservative Christian, a Buddhist, or an atheist. The concept of worldview helps explain these differences, for a worldview captures all of the beliefs, opinions, presuppositions, and prejudices we bring to our reading. When we read ancient texts, our modern worldview collides with the worldview in the text, as we attempt to make sense of what we are reading.

How, then, should we read scripture? It may come as a surprise, but the more literally we read it, the better we will understand. That means reading the stories in the Bible *as stories* rather than as history, or science, or theology. This kind of reading pays close attention to plot and to character development. It ignores the succeeding layers of interpretation and doctrine that have gathered around the texts and focuses on the stories themselves. What does the text actually, or literally, say? This may be hard for some readers to do because for many these are not "just" stories, and the Bible is not "just" any book. The genre of literature called "scripture" invests significant and even transcendent meaning in writings and makes them holy. If we drop a novel or a cookbook on the floor, we pick it up and dust it off. If we drop a Bible on the floor, however, we may experience a sense of guilt or violation. A student in a New Testament class once asked me if it was okay to write in his Bible and, specifically, to use a highlighter. I could understand his concern. Out of a large collection of Bibles that I own, I write in just one, which I use for teaching and study. Christians call the Bible the "Word of God," and the "Good Book," which indicates the sense of reverence they feel toward this particular book. Jews have this same feeling of respect for their scripture. On the Sabbath, when the Torah scroll is removed from the ark, people stand, and as the scroll circulates through the congregation, worshipers may touch a scarf or prayer shawl to the scroll and then kiss it. Muslims feel similarly about the Qur'an, their scripture, and believe that it cannot be translated from Arabic, the language in which it was originally recited by the prophet Muhammad. Other world religions have sacred texts as well and share this reverence for the stories that reveal something of the divine and of the nature and destiny of humankind.

Thus, most readers approach scripture differently than they do other kinds of writing. And religious believers have still more at stake because certain scriptures make up their identity as human beings. With all this noted, it is important to reiterate the value of reading the Bible in a scholarly, nonconfessional way. (By "nonconfessional," I mean temporarily setting aside one's religious beliefs for the purpose of seeing the text in a new light.) Obviously, this is not the only way to read sacred texts, nor is it even the most common. But it is the most useful in seeing how Christian doctrine developed. Marcus Borg, a contemporary Protestant theologian, calls it "reading the Bible again for the first time."

Jewish Concepts in Christian Theology

Christianity begins not with the birth of Jesus but with the creation of the world. It was at creation—in the very beginning—that a huge disaster occurred, which is described in the first three chapters of the very first book of the Bible: Genesis. Most Christians read these chapters as depicting the disruption of God's wonderful world—and everything in it—by an act of human disobedience. As a result of this act, the first man and the first woman, and all of their descendants, were cursed and were doomed to die. This story provides the central reason for God's divine son to come to earth. In a nutshell, Jesus, the Son of God, came to release human beings from the consequences of this prehistoric catastrophe.

It is important to note, however, that the predominant Christian interpretation of Genesis 1–3 as describing creation and a "fall" from that creation is not the only way the story of Adam and Eve can be read. Jews read this as a story that describes God's gift of freedom to people: the freedom to make bad choices, but freedom nonetheless. Muslims, and even other Christians, also read this story differently. In the Qur'an, for example, Adam and Eve are not blamed, but rather Satan, the tempter, is cursed and exiled from God's realm. According to Irenaeus (c. 120/140–200/203), a Christian bishop in Lyon, France, God knew that Adam and Eve were moral infants, and God's plan had always been a developmental one. We begin our lives as children, and it is only through growing up that we become adults. God intended Jesus Christ to be the perfect model of adulthood and fully expected the first humans to eat from the tree of knowledge—just as we would expect toddlers to eat cookies left on the coffee table.

Christianity developed a theology of loss and failure, however, from the story of Adam and Eve. Humans lost their original perfection, most Christians would argue. We can look around today and see that the world seems less than perfect. Human activity frequently seems to tend toward evil rather than good. The garden story offers an explanation, an etiology, for the origin of human behavior in general, and human sin in particular.

The creation accounts in Genesis 1–3 also provide a more hopeful theology, however. Genesis 1 states that God created the world and, not once but several times, said that it was "good." This indicates God's interest in the earth around us. It also invests worldly things with a divine nature. If God made the planet and everything in it, then surely humans should value them. Genesis demonstrates that God deliberately created this world and intended it to be home for plants, animals, and humans. Since God also created the waters and the skies, they too contain something of the divine. Christians thus find both an optimistic theology of creation from the book of Genesis and a pessimistic theology of human nature.

The Reading

The book of Genesis is the first book in the Bible, for Christians and Jews alike, and is widely known throughout the world. The first three chapters describe the creation of the world and the first human beings. Some interesting questions emerge if we read what follows as mythology or legend, rather than as science or history. Try reading the chapters a number of different ways: How would a scientist interpret these stories? What about a feminist? A Hindu or Native American who has their own creation stories? A Christian Fundamentalist? How do *you* think the chapters should be read?

Questions to Consider

1. Why are there two creation stories in Genesis (1:1–2:3 and 2:4–25)? What are some possible explanations for this? How would you explain the different names used for the divine in chapter 1 (God) and chapters 2 and 3 (LORD God)?

2. Examine God's instructions to Adam about the various trees and fruits in the garden. How are they relayed by Eve to the serpent? How does the serpent interpret them? What is lost in the translation? What is added?

3. Who is telling the truth about the tree of knowledge: God or the serpent? (See Genesis 2:15–17; 3:4–5, 3:22–24.) What do you make of this?

4. What is the difference between the tree of knowledge and the tree of life in these stories? Figuratively, or metaphorically, how would you describe the difference?

5. If we read the stories in Genesis as legends, or "just-so stories," that explain the origin of the way things are, what questions of origins do they answer? Think of this as "Genesis Jeopardy," and come up with the questions that the stories are answering. Example: Why are women called "women"? Genesis 2:23 has the answer. Or, Why do we observe the Sabbath? Genesis 2:2–3 explains why.

6. How do the creation stories in Genesis compare with stories of origin in other religions and cultures? What, if anything, makes them different?

Genesis 1–3*

1 In the beginning when God created the heavens and the earth, the earth was a formless void and darkness covered the face of the deep, while a wind from God swept over the face of the waters. Then God said, "Let there be light"; and there was light. And God saw that the light was good; and God separated the light from the darkness. God called the light Day, and the darkness he called Night. And there was evening and there was morning, the first day.

And God said, "Let there be a dome in the midst of the waters, and let it separate the waters from the waters." So God made the dome and separated the waters that were under the dome from the waters that were above the dome. And it was so. God called the dome Sky. And there was evening and there was morning, the second day.

And God said, "Let the waters under the sky be gathered together into one place, and let the dry land appear." And it was so. God called the dry land Earth, and the waters that were gathered together he called Seas. And God saw that it was good. Then God said, "Let the earth put forth vegetation: plants yielding seed, and fruit trees of every kind on earth that bear fruit with the seed in it." And it was so. The earth brought forth vegetation: plants yielding seed of every kind, and trees of every kind bearing fruit with the seed in it. And God saw that it was good. And there was evening and there was morning, the third day.

And God said, "Let there be lights in the dome of the sky to separate the day from the night; and let them be for signs and for seasons and for days and years, and let them be lights in the dome of the sky to give light upon the earth." And it was so. God made the two great lights—the greater light to rule the day and the lesser light to rule the night—and the stars. God set them in the dome of the sky to give light upon the earth, to rule over the day and over the night, and to separate the light from the darkness. And God saw that it was good. And there was evening and there was morning, the fourth day.

And God said, "Let the waters bring forth swarms of living creatures, and let birds fly above the earth across the dome of the sky." So God created the great sea monsters and every living creature that moves, of every kind, with which the waters swarm, and every winged bird of every kind. And God saw that it was good. God blessed them, saying, "Be fruitful and multiply and fill the waters in the seas, and let birds multiply on the earth." And there was evening and there was morning, the fifth day.

And God said, "Let the earth bring forth living creatures of every kind: cattle and creeping things and wild animals of the earth of every kind." And it was so. God made the wild animals of the earth of every kind, and the cattle of every kind, and everything that creeps upon the ground of every kind. And God saw that it was good. Then God said, "Let us make humankind in our image, according to our likeness; and let them have dominion over the fish of the sea, and over the birds of the air, and over the cattle, and over all the wild animals of the earth, and over every creeping thing that creeps upon the earth." So God created humankind in his image, in the image of God he created them; male and female he created them. God blessed them, and God said to them, "Be fruitful and multiply, and fill the earth and subdue it; and have dominion over the fish of the sea and over the birds of the air and over every living thing that moves upon the earth." God said, "See, I have given you every plant yielding seed that is upon the face of all the earth, and every tree with seed in its fruit; you shall have them for food. And to every beast of the earth, and to every bird of the air, and to everything that creeps on the earth, everything that has the breath of life, I have given every green plant for food." And it was so. God saw everything that he had made, and indeed, it was very good. And there was evening and there was morning, the sixth day.

2 Thus the heavens and the earth were finished, and all their multitude. And on the seventh day God finished the work that he had done, and he rested on

---

* All Bible verses in Chapter One come from the New Revised Standard Version of the Bible.

the seventh day from all the work that he had done. So God blessed the seventh day and hallowed it, because on it God rested from all the work that he had done in creation.

These are the generations of the heavens and the earth when they were created. In the day that the LORD* God made the earth and the heavens, when no plant of the field was yet in the earth and no herb of the field had yet sprung up—for the LORD God had not caused it to rain upon the earth, and there was no one to till the ground; but a stream would rise from the earth, and water the whole face of the ground—then the LORD God formed man from the dust of the ground, and breathed into his nostrils the breath of life; and the man became a living being. And the LORD God planted a garden in Eden, in the east; and there he put the man whom he had formed. Out of the ground the LORD God made to grow every tree that is pleasant to the sight and good for food, the tree of life also in the midst of the garden, and the tree of the knowledge of good and evil. A river flows out of Eden to water the garden, and from there it divides and becomes four branches. The name of the first is Pishon; it is the one that flows around the whole land of Havilah, where there is gold; and the gold of that land is good; bdellium and onyx stone are there. The name of the second river is Gihon; it is the one that flows around the whole land of Cush. The name of the third river is Tigris, which flows east of Assyria. And the fourth river is the Euphrates.

The LORD God took the man and put him in the garden of Eden to till it and keep it. And the LORD God commanded the man, "You may freely eat of every tree of the garden; but of the tree of the knowledge of good and evil you shall not eat, for in the day that you eat of it you shall die." Then the LORD God said, "It is not good that the man should be alone; I will make him a helper as his partner." So out of the ground the LORD God formed every animal of the field and every bird of the air, and brought them to the man to see what he would call them; and whatever the man called every living creature, that was its name. The man gave names to all cattle, and to the birds of the air, and to every animal of the field; but for the man there was not found a helper as his partner.

So the LORD God caused a deep sleep to fall upon the man, and he slept; then he took one of his ribs and closed up its place with flesh. And the rib that the LORD God had taken from the man he made into a woman and brought her to the man. Then the man said, "This at last is bone of my bones and flesh of my flesh; this one shall be called Woman, for out of Man this one was taken." Therefore a man leaves his father and his mother and clings to his wife, and they become one flesh. And the man and his wife were both naked, and were not ashamed.

3 Now the serpent was more crafty than any other wild animal that the LORD God had made. He said to the woman, "Did God say, 'You shall not eat from any tree in the garden'?" The woman said to the serpent, "We may eat of the fruit of the trees in the garden; but God said, 'You shall not eat of the fruit of the tree that is in the middle of the garden, nor shall you touch it, or you shall die.'" But the serpent said to the woman, "You will not die; for God knows that when you eat of it your eyes will be opened, and you will be like God, knowing good and evil."

So when the woman saw that the tree was good for food, and that it was a delight to the eyes, and that the tree was to be desired to make one wise, she took of its fruit and ate; and she also gave some to her husband, who was with her, and he ate. Then the eyes of both were opened, and they knew that they were naked; and they sewed fig leaves together and made loincloths for themselves.

They heard the sound of the LORD God walking in the garden at the time of the evening breeze, and the man and his wife hid themselves from the presence of the LORD God among the trees of the garden. But the LORD God called to the man, and said to him, "Where are you?" He said, "I heard the sound of you in the garden, and I was afraid, because I was naked; and I hid myself." He said, "Who told you that you were naked? Have you eaten from the tree of which I commanded you not to eat?" The man said, "The woman whom you gave to be with me, she gave me fruit from the tree, and I ate." Then the LORD God said to the woman, "What is this that you have done?" The woman said, "The serpent tricked me, and I ate."

The LORD God said to the serpent, "Because you have done this, cursed are you among all animals and among all wild creatures; upon your belly you shall go, and dust you shall eat all the days of your life. I will put enmity between you and the woman, and be-

---

* The Hebrew Bible uses a sacred acronym for the name of God: YHWH. Bible translators use the euphemism LORD to indicate this holy word, which in Jewish practice must not be pronounced.

tween your offspring and hers; he will strike your head, and you will strike his heel."

To the woman he said, "I will greatly increase your pangs in childbearing; in pain you shall bring forth children, yet your desire shall be for your husband, and he shall rule over you."

And to the man he said, "Because you have listened to the voice of your wife, and have eaten of the tree about which I commanded you, 'You shall not eat of it,' cursed is the ground because of you; in toil you shall eat of it all the days of your life; thorns and thistles it shall bring forth for you; and you shall eat the plants of the field. By the sweat of your face you shall eat bread until you return to the ground, for out of it

you were taken; you are dust, and to dust you shall return."

The man named his wife Eve, because she was the mother of all living. And the LORD God made garments of skins for the man and for his wife, and clothed them. Then the LORD God said, "See, the man has become like one of us, knowing good and evil; and now, he might reach out his hand and take also from the tree of life, and eat, and live forever"— therefore the LORD God sent him forth from the garden of Eden, to till the ground from which he was taken. He drove out the man; and at the east of the garden of Eden he placed the cherubim, and a sword flaming and turning to guard the way to the tree of life.

The story of the human race would look fairly bleak if the story ended with the expulsion of the first humans from the garden. But the story of creation does not end with the "fall" or with our exile from paradise, but rather continues by revealing God's later acts of redemption. The rest of the story as given in the Hebrew Bible shows that time and again God saves the Israelites. Sometimes God saves through miracles, as when separating the waters of the Red Sea so that the Israelite slaves could escape their Egyptian masters. Sometimes God acts through historical events, punishing the Israelites for their idolatry by allowing foreign armies to invade and take them captive. Sometimes God works by speaking through the words of prophets, or in wind or fire. The principle way God redeems the Israelites, however, is through covenants—that is, by making agreements with them. This is another theological concept that Christians adopted from Jewish scripture. A covenant is essentially a contract that binds two parties together by stipulating what each party promises to do. We see one of the earliest covenants in Genesis between God and Noah, the survivor of a great flood. The first seven verses specify human obligations in the covenant; the next ten verses outline God's part of the bargain.

Genesis 9:1–17

God blessed Noah and his sons, and said to them, "Be fruitful and multiply, and fill the earth. The fear and dread of you shall rest on every animal of the earth, and on every bird of the air, on everything that creeps on the ground, and on all the fish of the sea; into your hand they are delivered. Every moving thing that lives shall be food for you; and just as I gave you the green plants, I give you everything.

"Only, you shall not eat flesh with its life, that is, its blood. For your own lifeblood I will surely require a reckoning: from every animal I will require it and from human beings, each one for the blood of another, I will require a reckoning for human life. Whoever sheds the blood of a human, by a human shall that person's blood be shed; for in his own image God made humankind.

"And you, be fruitful and multiply, abound on the earth and multiply in it."

Then God said to Noah and to his sons with him, "As for me, I am establishing my covenant with you and your descendants after you, and with every living creature that is with you, the birds, the domestic animals, and every animal of the earth with you, as many as came out of the ark. I establish my covenant with you, that never again shall all flesh be cut off by the waters of a flood, and never again shall there be a flood to destroy the earth." God said, "This is the sign of the covenant that I make between me and you and every living creature that is with you, for all future generations: I have set my bow in the clouds, and it shall be a sign of the covenant between me and the earth. When I bring clouds over the earth and the bow is seen in the clouds, I will remember my covenant that is between me and you and every living creature of all flesh; and the waters shall never again become a flood to destroy all flesh. When the bow is in the clouds, I will see it and remember the everlasting covenant between God and every living creature of all flesh that is on the earth." God said to Noah, "This is the sign of the covenant that I have established between me and all flesh that is on the earth."

Later in Genesis, God makes a covenant with Abram (Genesis 17), changing his name to Abraham. God promises to give Abraham and his descendants the land of Canaan, and guarantees that Abraham and his wife, Sarah, will be the ancestors of a multitude of nations. In return, Abraham must circumcise himself and all the males of his household. "Throughout your generations every male among you shall be circumcised when he is eight days old, including the slave born in your house. . . . Any uncircumcised male who is not circumcised in the flesh of his foreskin shall be cut off from his people; he has broken my covenant" (Genesis 17:12, 14). God's promise to Abraham seemed slightly impossible, however, since Sarah was past menopause. Yet Abraham believed in God's promise, and God delivered: Sarah got pregnant with Isaac, Abraham's second son after Ishmael. Abraham's belief in God's promises, despite all evidence to the contrary, became a key part in subsequent Christian theology, as did the story of Adam and Eve in the garden.

Three more covenants are important to mention, since Christians rely on them as well. The covenant God makes with Moses and the Israelites at Mount Sinai (Exodus 19–20) is central for Jews even today. At Mount Sinai (or Mount Horeb, as it is located in the book of Deuteronomy), God gives the Israelites the Ten Commandments (Exodus 20:1–17), which scholars call the "Decalogue," or "Ten Sayings." At the holy mountain, God gives additional commandments for the Israelites to observe in order to create a holy people. "You shall be holy, for I the LORD your God am holy," God instructs Moses to tell the Israelite congregation (Leviticus 19:2):

> Speak to the people of Israel and say to them: I am the LORD your God. You shall not do as they do in the land of Egypt, where you lived, and you shall not do as they do in the land of Canaan, to which I am bringing you. You shall not follow their statutes. My ordinances you shall observe and my statutes you shall keep, following them: I am the LORD your God. You shall keep my statutes and my ordinances; by doing so one shall live: I am the LORD. (Leviticus 18:2–5)

By keeping the commandments, the Israelites are fulfilling their contractual obligations to God. They are differentiating themselves by their unique practices from the people occupying the land. More importantly, though, the commandments keep them mindful of God's goodness and graciousness. Obeying God's orders is not really an option, given the fact that the entire Israelite nation agreed to do exactly that in return for receiving God's favor. Yet it is this question of observing the commandments—or the law, as it is rendered in the original Greek of the New Testament—that becomes an issue for Jesus' earliest disciples.

With the Davidic covenant, God promises King David that a dynasty of kings will descend from his line. The prophet Nathan informs David, "Your house and your kingdom shall be made sure forever before me; your throne shall be established forever" (2 Samuel 7:16). Although David had sinned by having an adulterous affair—and by arranging for the death of his lover's husband—his descendants would rule a realm that united the northern kingdom, Israel, with the southern kingdom, Judah. Moreover, David's son Solomon would build a magnificent temple to house the ark of the covenant. Speaking through Nathan, God says of Solomon: "I will be a father to him, and he shall be a son to me. When he commits iniquity, I will punish him. . . . But I will not take my steadfast love from him" (2 Samuel 7:14–15). The ark was a container that was supposed to hold the original set of commandments given by God in the covenant made with Moses. The Davidic covenant was also important for first-century Jews because it created the expectation that an earthly king descended from David would eventually return to kick out the Roman oppressors and rule a united Judah. This kingly figure—called "messiah," which literally means "anointed one"—would restore the independence of the Jews and bring about justice and righteousness on earth. Jesus' early followers considered Jesus anointed by God, and called him messiah as well: Jesus the Messiah, or in Greek, Jesus the Christ (Jesus the Anointed One). The definition of messiah will become a point of contention in first-century Jewish and Christian relations.

A final covenant that appears in Jewish scriptures that Christians found significant is the new covenant that God promises to the prophet Jeremiah. Jeremiah provides words of hope to the inhabitants of Judah after the fall of Jerusalem, when he writes:

> The days are surely coming, says the LORD, when I will make a new covenant with the house of Israel and the house of Judah. It will not be like the covenant that I made with their ancestors when I took them by the hand to bring them out of the land of Egypt—a covenant that they broke, though I was their husband, says the LORD. But this is the covenant that I will make with the house of Israel after those days, says the Lord: I will put my law within them, and I will write it on their hearts; and I will be their God, and they shall be my people. No longer shall they teach one another, or say to each other, "Know the LORD," for they shall all know me, from the least of them to the greatest, says the LORD; for I will forgive their iniquity, and remember their sin no more. (Jeremiah 31:31–34)

Jeremiah's words reveal several key themes found in the Hebrew Bible. First is the centrality of the exodus from Egypt, a divine act that revealed God's love to the Israelites, and to their descendants the Jews. Second is the centrality of the law, or the commandments, in Jewish theology. But there is a difference in Jeremiah: rather than giving the law in writing, as it had appeared in Torah, God will now "write it on their hearts." This action indicates God's forgiveness for the past sins of the Israelites. Some Christians interpret Jeremiah to mean that God's previous covenants with the Israelites have been abrogated, that is, revoked or annulled. But in the very next verse, Jeremiah makes it plain that this is not the case. He says that if the moon and the stars were no longer to light up the night, or the oceans were ever to cease roaring, then and only then would the Israelites and their children cease to be a nation:

> If the heavens above can be measured, and the foundations of the earth below can be explored, then I will reject all the offspring of Israel because of all they have done, says the LORD. (Jeremiah 31:37)

The implication is that since neither the heights of heaven nor the depths of earth can be measured, God will never abandon the chosen ones.

We can see how important the concept of covenant is to Jewish theology. From the earliest covenants with Noah and Abraham, to the covenants made with the Israelites through Moses and David, and on to Jeremiah's proclamation of a new covenant, Jewish history speaks of the primacy of covenant for understanding the relationship Jews have with God. Subsequent Christians adopt and appropriate this theology of covenant, explaining it in a new way, however, in light of their attempt to understand the nature and identity of Jesus.

Another key theme in Israelite religion that Christians take up is that of sacrifice. Like their ancient contemporaries the Egyptians, the Babylonians, and the Greeks, the Israelites worshiped their deity primarily through acts of sacrifice. The earliest sacrifice mentioned in the Bible is the story in Genesis 4 of Cain and Abel, Adam and Eve's sons. Cain presents an offering to the Lord of his crops, since he is a farmer; Abel brings the "fat portions" of some of his first lambs, since he is a shepherd. God preferred Abel's offering to Cain's, and in a rage, Cain kills his brother Abel. The presentation of "first fruits," whether of crops or animals, was a sacrifice in ancient religions in which the deity was thanked for sustaining the people. Other sacrifices might repay vows people made to the deity.

The book of Leviticus specifies a number of sacrifices to be made in order to atone for sin. The deity described in the Hebrew Bible is eminently practical: in addition to providing the Israelites with commandments for living holy lives, God also provides them the remedy for returning to holiness when they fail to be holy— whether through sin, or defilement, or other means. Recognizing humanity's fallibility, particularly in the area of sin (perhaps remembering the unfortunate garden incident), God supplies rituals, practices, and most especially sacrifices to make things right and restore things and people to their original holiness. Leviticus 17, for example, explains when sacrifices are supposed to occur and how animals are to be slaughtered. A vital ritual is atonement, that is, reconciling humans with God, or making them one: "at-one-ment." Leviticus 16 details a number of atonement rituals, a different one for individual sins, for those of the leaders or priests, and for the people as a whole. One element of the atonement ritual is selection of a scapegoat to bear the sins of the people.

> Then Aaron shall lay both his hands on the head of the live goat, and confess over it all the iniquities of the people of Israel, and all their transgressions, all their sins, putting them on the head of the goat, and sending it away into the wilderness by means of someone designated for the task. The goat shall bear on itself all their iniquities to a barren region; and the goat shall be set free in the wilderness. (Leviticus 16:21–22)

The people of Israel were supposed to atone for all their sins once a year. Throughout the year, numerous other sacrifices—thanksgiving offerings, peace offerings, offerings to fulfill vows or to observe milestones like marriages or births—occurred in the temple in Jerusalem. But the Day of Atonement, called Yom Kippur, was the holiest day in the year for the Israelites then, and for Jews today.

While all of the religions in the ancient Near East practiced a sacrificial form of worship, Jews were forced to rethink exactly what sacrifice meant when they lived in exile in Babylon. With their temple in Jerusalem destroyed, an alternative institution called the synagogue arose. The synagogue was a community center in which Jews could meet, gather, pray, and read and discuss scripture. Although the return to Judea brought about a reconstructed temple, the synagogue system continued to exist both outside Judea—in the Diaspora—and within Judea. We can see evidence for both institutions existing in the New Testament. What also occurred, however, was a continuing questioning or reinterpretation of the nature of sacrifice by Jews. How could Jews living outside of Judea, hundreds or thousands of miles from the temple, make their offerings to God? The prophets had said that sacrifices and feast days were not really what God had wanted; rather, it was pure hearts and righteous deeds. The Dead Sea Scrolls indicate the existence of Jews in Judea itself who seemed to have abandoned a sacrificial system and practiced purity and piety without the benefit of the temple. The Community Rule of the Qumran group states explicitly that blood sacrifices are unnecessary for atonement:

> They shall atone for guilty rebellion and for sins of unfaithfulness that they may obtain loving-kindness for the Land without the flesh of holocausts and the fat of sacrifice. And prayer rightly offered shall be as an acceptable fragrance of righteousness, and perfection of way as a delectable free-will offering. (1QS, *Community Rule,* IX)

Other Jewish texts, compiled after—though perhaps written before—the destruction of the second temple of Jerusalem in 70 C.E. had already begun to redefine sacrifice in new, nonbloody ways: as study of Torah, worship, prayer, and acts of loving-kindness. Certainly, the desolation of the holiest place on earth for the second time in history caused further reexamination of sacrifice and led to the nonsacrificial system of Rabbinic Judaism we know today.

Christianity also emerged as a nonsacrificial religion in the first century. It doesn't take too much imagination to recognize the amazement that Gentile (non-Jewish) converts to Christianity must have felt when they heard that blood sacrifices were no longer required. Sacrifice turns up as a significant theme in the New Testament. The missionary Saint Paul, for instance, discusses it quite a bit. He answers questions early Christians had about whether it was okay to eat meat sacrificed to idols (1 Corinthians 8). He states that God put forth Jesus "as a sacrifice of atonement by his blood" (Romans 3:25) that necessitated only a belief in the efficacy of that final sacrifice. The book of Hebrews, which is an extended sermon, goes into great detail about sacrifice and the end of the practice of blood sacrifices effected by Jesus' sacrificial death. The last book in the New Testament, Revelation, depicts a slain lamb as the hero and champion of persecuted Christians. The idea of a sacrificial lamb originated in Israelite tradition, in the story of Moses and the exodus. The Israelites were to slaughter lambs and place the blood on the doorposts of their houses so that the Angel of Death would not harm those inside. The Jewish festival of Passover—in which lambs were sacrificed at the Temple—commemorated this miracle in Jewish history. Christians, however, retold the traditional Passover story with a new twist, calling Jesus the Passover lamb.

The Israelite practice of sacrifice, therefore, is redefined by both Jews and Christians in the first century. Sacrifice is transformed from a practice of using animal blood (or other items such as fruits and grains) into a practice of personal piety (Judaism) or a practice of belief in a divine sacrifice (Christianity). In all cases—Jewish, Christian, pagan—however, the purpose of sacrifice was generally the same—namely, to regain oneness, or to reconcile with the deity or deities.

Another theme running through the Hebrew Bible that emerges in early Christianity is the "Day of the Lord." This appears to be a sort of judgment day, or time of reckoning, announced by the prophets. The prophet Amos, for example, warns those who welcome the Day of the Lord: "It is darkness, not light; as if someone fled from a lion, and was met by a bear; or went into the house and rested a hand against the wall and was bitten by a snake" (Amos 5:18–19). Joel proclaims the nearness of the Day of the Lord, "a day of darkness and gloom, a day of clouds and thick darkness" (Joel 2:2). The early Christian community also awaited a Day of the Lord, but expected it to include Jesus' triumphant return, as well as a final judgment. Jesus himself speaks about a day of judgment, on which it would be better to be dead than alive.

A final concept in Jewish theology that we find transformed in Christian theology is that of kingship. As noted previously, the Davidic covenant promised a dynasty of kings flowing from David's line. This king was the anointed one, the messiah, who was a political figure. Some apocalyptic Jews, however, understood the messiah to be a cosmic savior: perhaps an angel or heavenly being, perhaps a wise teacher. For Jesus' followers to call him the anointed one, therefore, was puzzling. What kind of messiah was he? A king? A savior? A sacrificial lamb? A prophet or priest? At the very least, they claimed that he descended from the line of David and that he indeed fulfilled God's promise to David for a successor. Jews have long debated Christians over this issue, arguing that because the messiah was to usher in an age of peace, justice, and righteousness, the messiah could not have come, given the state of the world we live in. Christians, in turn, have argued that God, through Jesus, changed the meaning of messiah, and that Jews don't get it when they argue otherwise. What it really comes down to is different interpretations of the meaning of messiah. Since it is an interpretive issue, dependent on one's hermeneutics or worldview, both sides can muster believable arguments. To claim that one side or the other is blind ignores the dynamics of the dispute and, moreover, attacks the one arguing rather than the argument itself. What *is* certain is that the followers of Jesus appropriated the term *messiah* and applied it to their leader.

Varieties of First-Century Judaic Religions

As noted previously, a number of beliefs and practices come under the umbrella "Judaic religions." Jesus engages in debates with the Pharisees; he comes into conflict with the Sadducees; one of his followers is known as a Zealot; there is Paul, a Diaspora Jew from Tarsus; and there is the mysterious figure of John the Baptist, an ascetic Jew who preaches in the wilderness and baptizes Jews in the Jordan River. The New Testament does not mention Essenes by name, but some scholars have argued that John the Baptist might have been an Essene, given his life of renunciation and his rejection of the Jerusalem temple. Surely his proclamation of "a baptism of repentance for the forgiveness of sins" (Mark 1:4) bypasses the sacrificial system of atonement for sin offered by the temple priests.

It is necessary to recognize that Jews in the first century were living under Roman occupation. This means they had to deal with foreigners politically, economically, and culturally. The group that appeared to collaborate most closely with the Romans were the Sadducees, the party of temple priests and their families. The religious conservatives of their day, the Sadducees believed that the only religious authority that existed was the written Torah. This belief bolstered their role in the priestly system, which controlled the riches of the temple. The Sadducees tended to be wealthy, so cooperation with the invader helped to maintain their power base. Sometimes they were aligned with the Herodians, the party of King Herod, who along with his sons were nominal rulers of Palestine with the consent of the Romans.

The Zealots took the opposite stance, violently opposing Roman rule. Although the New Testament indicates that one of Jesus' disciples was called Simon the Zealot (Luke 6:15; Acts 1:13), there is little evidence that Zealots existed before the First Jewish War in 66–73 C.E., a generation after Jesus' death. Zealots were essentially first-century terrorists, murdering collaborators—that is, other Jews—and generally harassing Roman rulers with acts of resistance.

The group with which Jesus apparently had the most contact, and the most conflict, was the Pharisees. They seem to be plotting against him in all the Gospels, planning ways to trip him up, challenging his interpretation of the law, and criticizing his actions. It is fair to say that the Pharisees come across as the bad guys in the Gospels. This is somewhat ironic given the fact that a number of scholars believe

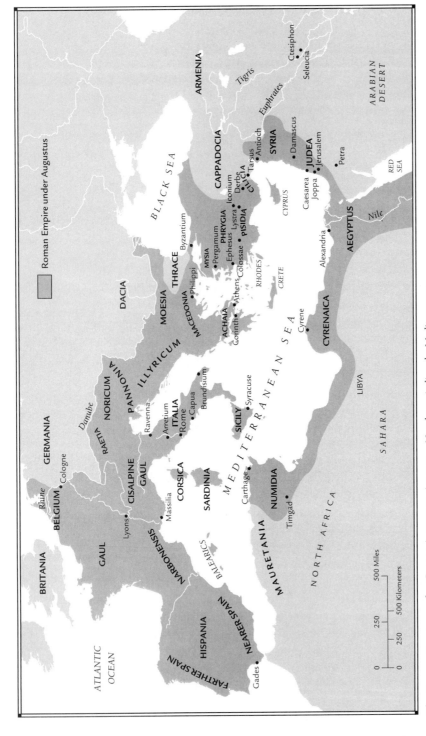

The Roman Empire under Caesar Augustus, 4 B.C.E.   *Nearly encircling the Mediterranean Sea, the Roman Empire was larger even than that of Alexander the Great and included much of the territory Alexander had conquered.*

that Jesus himself may have been a Pharisee. The Pharisees thought that the holiness code of the Hebrew Bible, which originally had been intended for the priestly class, ought to be observed by all faithful Jews. In effect, they democratized the practices that traditionally had been reserved for priests alone. But within Pharisaism there were divisions. Regarding the commandment "Remember the Sabbath, to keep it holy," the Pharisees wondered what it meant in practical terms. Did it mean no cooking? No cleaning? Did it mean that you could or could not feed your livestock? Could you save a life? Conservative interpreters of the law tended to prohibit almost any activity on the Sabbath, while the liberals took a broader view: it was okay, in their opinion, to do good deeds on the Sabbath.

Jesus' battles with the Pharisees appear odd in light of the fact that he himself was Jewish and followed Jewish customs. He was circumcised on the eighth day, like all good Jewish males (Luke 2:21); apparently, he had a bar mitzvah when he was twelve (Luke 2:42–47); and his father, a carpenter, undoubtedly trained Jesus in his craft (Mark 6:3; Matthew 13:55). Jesus demonstrates a thorough knowledge of Jewish scripture and practices, even though he challenges both at times. In the Gospels, Jesus sometimes takes a liberal view of the law but other times embraces a strict view.

That the Pharisees are the bad guys in the Gospels, and that a Zealot anachronistically appears in the life of Jesus, may reflect the time in which the Gospels were written. The Gospels were probably composed after the destruction of the Jewish temple in Jerusalem in 70 C.E. Without a temple, the priestly class of Sadducees vanished overnight (though some types of Jewish biblical literalists continue to exist today). Those Jews who had been practicing their religion in the synagogues, who were familiar with what scripture—the Law (Torah) and the Prophets (Neviim)— had to say, and who believed that holiness belonged to all Jews, and not just certain classes, survived. These were the Pharisees, who were instrumental in developing a posttemple, postsacrificial form of Judaism. The followers of Jesus were in conflict with the Pharisees for disciples and for the right to claim that they were the "true" Jews. Some of the animosity we find between Jesus and Jews in the New Testament may reflect later conflicts, while some incidents—such as Jesus' reinterpretation of Torah—may be historical.

Four more first-century Jewish groups deserve mention. The first group, the am ha-eretz, or "people of the land," were the ordinary folks whom Jesus encountered in his work. They may have observed the Sabbath, or not; they may have gone to the temple once a year for sacrifices; they probably observed certain agricultural festivals. But they were not scrupulously observant of the law, unlike the Pharisees. A second group comprised the Samaritans, a group of Jews who rejected Mount Zion in Jerusalem as the only holy site for Judaism, and instead claimed Mount Gerizim in the city of Shechem in Samaria for their holy temple. The Pharisees and Sadducees did not consider the Samaritans to be legitimate Jews, although certainly the Samaritans then, as today, claimed full Jewish heritage.

A third Jewish group was made up of Jesus' followers, who considered themselves followers of "the Way," or followers of the "Nazarene." Both Jewish and Christian scholars today argue that Christianity started as a sect within Judaism, hence its inclusion here as a first-century Judaic religion. Jesus' immediate disciples and the leaders of the church in Jerusalem were Jews by birth, and continued to consider themselves Jews who believed in Jesus as the messiah promised by God. I have somewhat anachronistically been calling these people Christians, but that is not how they would have identified themselves. The early followers of Jesus saw themselves as part of a new movement within the context of their Jewish heritage. Scholars identify this group as the "Jesus Movement." I will also use this term to describe followers of "the Way." Later, they considered themselves members of the church, a body called out of, and apart from, the world. The "Christian" label was used by outsiders to describe people in the movement. It was probably not until the second century that followers of "the Way" identified themselves as Christians. For example, Ignatius of Antioch (d. c. 107) said, "It is not that I want merely to be called a Christian, but actually to be one. Yes, if I prove to be one, then I can have the name" (Romans 3). Ignatius proved himself worthy of the name by being martyred in Rome sometime during the reign of Emperor Trajan (r. 98–117).

A final group, and by far the largest group of first-century Jews, was that of the Diaspora—that is, Jews living outside the land of Judea. Some scholars estimate that one in ten residents of the Roman Empire was Jewish. Thriving Jewish communities existed in Egypt, Rome, and Babylon (today's Iraq). To put it into perspective, large

▨ Jews or Judeans?

Some have argued that the Greek word *Ioudaioi* should be translated as "Judeans" rather than "Jews," especially in the Gospel of John. They suggest that this is a geographic, rather than a religious, identity. This is a reasonable translation of the words inscribed upon Jesus' cross: "King of the Judeans" (Mark 15:26; Luke 23:38; John 19:19; Matthew's gospel says, "King of Israel," 27:42). Since the Romans saw Jesus as a political, rather than a religious, threat, they likely identified him as political leader—thus, King of the Judeans. In contrast, the leader of the "Jews," a religious designation, would be someone from the priestly class, one of the Sadducees who collaborated with Roman rule.

The earlier Gospels do not use the word *Ioudaioi* very often, and most of the references occur during Jesus' trial before Pilate. But John's Gospel depicts Jesus in constant conflict with "the Jews," especially the Pharisees. The expression "the Jews/Judeans" occurs more than 60 times in John, in contrast to its appearance 5, 6, and 3 times in Matthew, Mark, and Luke, respectively. This is one reason biblical scholars believe John's Gospel was written at the end of the first century, when tensions were high between the followers of Jesus and those in control of the synagogues.

communities of Jews were well established in Europe, North Africa, and Southwest Asia at the time of Jesus. The apostle Paul was one such Diaspora Jew, and probably the most influential person in Christianity next to Jesus.

Paul the Convert

The story of Paul appears in the letters he wrote to churches he established throughout the Mediterranean. The book called Acts, or Acts of the Apostles, also describes Paul's adventures as a missionary. And to be sure, Paul did lead an adventurous life. Born and raised a Jew, he called himself a Pharisee. Initially, he persecuted the early followers of Jesus, believing they were blaspheming the God of Israel. But a religious experience caused Paul, originally called Saul, to reverse directions. Acts describes this event in dramatic terms:

> Now as he was going along and approaching Damascus, suddenly a light from heaven flashed around him. He fell to the ground and heard a voice saying to him, "Saul, Saul, why do you persecute me?" He asked, "Who are you, Lord?" The reply came, "I am Jesus, whom you are persecuting. But get up and enter the city, and you will be told what you are to do." (Acts 9:3–6)

Paul is blinded for three days, and his companions, who also hear the voice, are amazed. A disciple in Damascus, Ananias, has a vision in which Jesus tells him to take Paul in. Ananias does so, places his hands on Paul's eyes, "and immediately something like scales fell from his eyes, and his sight was restored." What is most incredible, however, is Paul's about-face, because he begins to preach in the synagogues, claiming that Jesus is the Son of God. This is the same guy who a week before had been roughing up fellow Jews for saying the same thing.

Acts gives two accounts of Paul's miraculous conversion (Acts 9 and 22). Paul himself, however, describes events differently in his personal letters. In 2 Corinthians, he speaks of himself in the third person, saying:

> I know a person in Christ who fourteen years ago was caught up to the third heaven—whether in the body or out of the body I do not know; God knows. And I know that such a person—whether in the body or out of the body I do not know; God knows—was caught up into Paradise and heard things that are not to be told, that no mortal is permitted to repeat. (2 Corinthians 12:2–4)

In Galatians, he simply states "that the gospel that was proclaimed by me is not of human origin; for I did not receive it from a human source, nor was I taught it, but I received it through a revelation of Jesus Christ" (Galatians 1:11b–12). He goes on to say that this revelation occurred "so that I might proclaim him among the Gentiles." In other words, Paul received a revelation that told him to preach about Jesus to Gentiles, non-Jews, rather than to other Jews. Prior to this, the majority of Jesus' followers were Jews. Paul's commission to spread the word to non-Jews, however, dramatically altered the movement, and ultimately laid the groundwork for the differentiation between Judaism and Christianity.

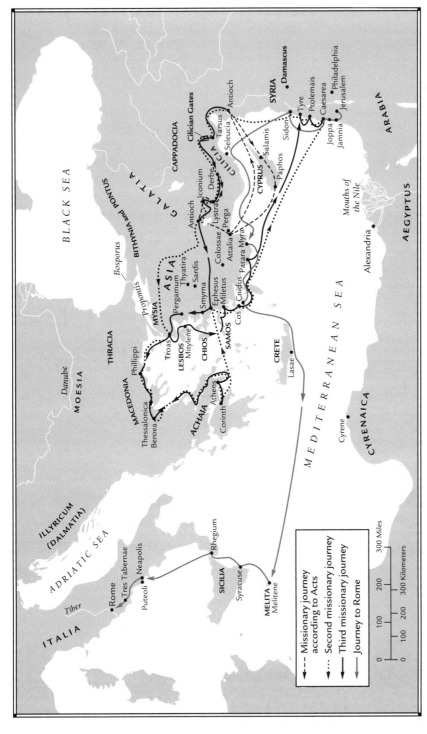

Paul's missionary journeys. Paul preached the gospel to Jews and Gentiles alike in the course of travels that took him to Syria, Asia Minor, Macedonia, Greece, Cyprus, Crete, and Italy.

The question of whether Gentiles had to observe Jewish law in order to be part of the covenant with Israel divided the early church. Jewish Christians, like Jesus' disciple Peter and Jesus' brother James, were completely observant, or "torah-true" in their behavior, yet also believed that Jesus was the Messiah, and the Son of God. Gentile Christians, however, like some of the early converts discussed in Acts, did not observe the commandments, although they confessed Jesus as their lord and savior. Acts 15 describes a meeting church leaders had and the decision they made about Gentile observance of Jewish law.

> For it has seemed good to the Holy Spirit and to us to impose on you [Gentiles] no further burden than these essentials: that you abstain from what has been sacrificed to idols and from blood and from what is strangled and from fornication. If you keep yourselves from these, you will do well . . . (Acts 15:28–29)

The meeting in Jerusalem resulted in the edict that Gentiles should not eat anything designated for other deities (idols), that they should follow the Jewish dietary rule of not eating meat with blood in it, which strangling the animal would permit. In short, Gentiles were supposed to eat kosher, in accordance with Jewish law. And Gentiles should be moral in areas of sexual behavior. Paul again presents a different account of what occurred, however. In his letter to the Galatians, he says that church leaders at the Jerusalem conference divided up the mission territory: Paul would continue to proselytize* the Gentiles, while James and Peter and those in Jerusalem would evangelize Jews. They would not impose any requirements upon Gentile Christians, neither circumcision nor diet. Paul mentions this because Peter's subsequent behavior contradicted the agreement. Paul believed that Jewish and Gentile Christians entered into a new covenant established by Jesus' death in exactly the same way: by belief in Jesus, rather than by observance of the original covenant requirements. Paul's views eventually prevailed, which dramatically changed the face of the Jesus Movement and the early church. What began as a small sect within Judaism became a major religion within the Gentile world: Christianity.

We know much about the early church—its concerns, disputes, and practices—from letters that Paul wrote to the churches he established in the Mediterranean. Although these letters are now considered scripture, that is, sacred writings, Paul probably wrote them with more worldly concerns in mind. That is why they are called "occasional letters"—he wrote them in response to specific occasions, or questions, new Christians had for him. Since most had come from a pagan background, they had questions about morality, about marriage, about church practices, about

---

*"Proselytize" comes from the word *proselyte,* which was what Gentile converts to Judaism were called in the Roman Empire. Gentiles who attended synagogue and were observant—but who were not circumcised if they were men—were called "God-fearers." Many of these Gentiles who had great admiration for and commitment to Judaism eventually converted to Christianity.

beliefs. The letters do not reveal a unified church with clearly stated doctrines, but rather a number of churches attempting to clarify both doctrinal and practical questions. This explains why Paul sometimes seems to offer contradictory advice. If the problem is one of antinomianism—or "lawlessness," or too much freedom—as in the church at Corinth, then he emphasizes the value of the law. If the problem is too much law, as in the church at Galatia, then he emphasizes freedom. Addressing the divisions at Corinth, he recommends love as the solution. Addressing divisions at Philippi, he advises obedience. His letters also reveal a great deal about himself and how people perceived him. Some thought he was weak, or lacked authority in church matters; some said his letters were great, but in person he was somewhat disappointing; others claimed that their baptism by Paul made them superior to those baptized by others. All in all, Paul's letters provide glimpses of a movement in great flux and of an institution creating itself.

Because Paul was educated as a Jew and studied under the rabbis, he was extremely familiar with Jewish scripture. His writings show how conversant he was with the Law and the Prophets, as he used biblical figures and prophetic language to build convincing arguments against his opponents. For example, he turned to Abraham as the model of faith, since Abraham believed in God's promises before God had actually delivered on them. He picked Adam, the first man, and the one who introduced sin and death into the world, to contrast with Jesus, the last man, who forgives sin and eradicates death. He quoted various prophets to justify his position on observing Jewish law. His thought was steeped in Jewish tradition, although he interpreted that heritage in a new and creative manner.

Letters make up the majority of New Testament texts, with Paul's letters taking the most prominent place. They indicate that Paul had a classical Hellenistic education, as well as training in Jewish scripture, for they reveal a sophisticated rhetorical style and a knowledgeable, probably native, use of Greek. Clearly, however, we are missing some of Paul's writings, since he alludes to them in the letters we do possess. It also seems unlikely that, given his energy and enthusiasm, he would have written only a handful of letters over a missionary career that spanned at least two decades. The letters of Paul that do appear in the New Testament follow a particular format, one that he learned as an educated Jew living in the Roman Empire and modified for his own uses:

> Sender
> Addressee (usually a church)
> Greeting
> Thanksgiving
> Body (the reason he is writing, usually beginning with "I want you to know" or "I do not want you to be uninformed")
> Moral exhortation (ethical instructions, usually beginning "I beseech you" or "I appeal to you")
> Travelogue (where Paul is planning to travel)

Greetings
Doxology and/or benediction

We can see this format, for example, in the letter to the Galatians, which begins:

> Paul, an apostle . . . and all the members of God's family who are with me,
>   [sender]
> To the churches of Galatia: [addressee]
> Grace to you and peace from God our Father and the Lord Jesus Christ . . .
>   [greeting]

Of course, Paul doesn't always follow his own formula, and the Galatians letter is a good example because it lacks a thanksgiving. Instead, Paul writes, "I am astonished that you are so quickly deserting the one who called you in the grace of Christ and are turning to a different gospel" (1:6).

Paul's letters are among the oldest Christian writings available and are the oldest writings in the New Testament—although traditions and sayings of Jesus are clearly older. That is why we begin with Paul's writings rather than the Gospels: because they come so early in Christian history, and because the teachings they contain provide an interpretive lens through which the writers of the Gospels view Jesus. They do not tell the story of the earthly Jesus, but instead indicate how people understood Jesus after his death and resurrection. Paul did not know Jesus, and neither did his converts, but their experiences and discussions shaped later interpretations of the "good news" or gospel that Paul preached.

The Reading

Paul's first letter to the Thessalonians is the oldest book in the New Testament. Thessalonica was an important city in Greece located on a major Roman highway. Paul wrote to the Thessalonian church in the early 50s, and his letter reveals a great deal about the congregation: its past practices and its present concerns. The Thessalonian church was made up of pagan converts who had little or no understanding of Judaism or of Christianity. The letter also says a lot about how Paul treated his infant congregations and dealt with their questions. It shows the connection between ethics, or how one should live, and the beliefs of Christians.

Although many Christians hear bits and pieces of scripture each Sunday at church, few actually sit down and read the texts the way they were written or intended to be read. In the case of Paul's letters, they were sent to the church and designed to be read out loud at a service so that all could hear them and discuss the contents. Sometimes the letters were then sent on to other churches; sometimes they were copied and preserved. In any case, they lacked chapter and verse numbers, paragraphing, and even punctuation. I have preserved the chapter numbers but have eliminated verse numbers in order to facilitate reading the text as a letter, not as tiny fragments. Reading out loud may help in understanding difficult passages. Since Paul wanted the letter to be read out loud, an oral reading is entirely appropriate.

Questions to Consider

1. Try to identify the letter parts in 1 Thessalonians, using the list provided above.

2. What is Paul's tone in addressing the Thessalonians? What words or expressions does he use to communicate with them? What is his relationship with them?

3. How do we know that the Thessalonians were pagans before becoming Christians? What clues does the text provide?

4. What is bothering the Thessalonians? Are there some things, or "occasions," that Paul seems to be addressing? (*Hint:* look at chapter 4 in the letter.)

5. What does this letter say about Christians' expectation regarding Christ's return to earth?

6. How does Paul relate this expectation to ethics, or how Christians should live?

7. What, if anything, do we know about Jesus' own teachings from this letter?

1 Thessalonians

1 Paul, Silvanus, and Timothy, to the church of the Thessalonians in God the Father and the Lord Jesus Christ: Grace to you and peace. We always give thanks to God for all of you and mention you in our prayers, constantly remembering before our God and Father your work of faith and labor of love and steadfastness of hope in our Lord Jesus Christ. For we know, brothers and sisters beloved by God, that he has chosen you, because our message of the Gospel came to you not in word only, but also in power and in the Holy Spirit and with full conviction; just as you know what kind of persons we proved to be among you for your sake. And you became imitators of us and of the Lord, for in spite of persecution you received the word with joy inspired by the Holy Spirit, so that you became an example to all the believers in Macedonia and in Achaia.

For the word of the Lord has sounded forth from you not only in Macedonia and Achaia, but in every place your faith in God has become known, so that we have no need to speak about it. For the people of those regions report about us what kind of welcome we had among you, and how you turned to God from idols, to serve a living and true God, and to wait for his Son from heaven, whom he raised from the dead—Jesus, who rescues us from the wrath that is coming.

2 You yourselves know, brothers and sisters, that our coming to you was not in vain, but though we had already suffered and been shamefully mistreated at Philippi, as you know, we had courage in our God to declare to you the gospel of God in spite of great opposition. For our appeal does not spring from deceit or impure motives or trickery, but just as we have been approved by God to be entrusted with the message of the gospel, even so we speak, not to please mortals, but to please God who tests our hearts.

As you know and as God is our witness, we never came with words of flattery or with a pretext for greed; nor did we seek praise from mortals, whether from you or from others, though we might have made demands as apostles of Christ. But we were gentle among you, like a nurse tenderly caring for her own children. So deeply do we care for you that we are determined to share with you not only the gospel of God but also our own selves, because you have become very dear to us. You remember our labor and toil, brothers and sisters; we worked night and day, so that we might not burden any of you while we proclaimed to you the gospel of God. You are witnesses, and God also, how pure, upright, and blameless our conduct was toward you believers. As you know, we dealt with each one of you like a father with his children, urging and encouraging you and pleading that you lead a life worthy of God, who calls you into his own kingdom and glory.

We also constantly give thanks to God for this, that when you received the word of God that you heard from us, you accepted it not as a human word but as what it really is, God's word, which is also at work in you believers. For you, brothers and sisters, became imitators of the churches of God in Christ Jesus that are in Judea, for you suffered the same things from your own compatriots as they did from the Jews, who killed both the Lord Jesus and the prophets, and drove us out; they displease God and oppose everyone by hindering us from speaking to the Gentiles so that they may be saved. Thus they have constantly been filling up the measure of their sins; but God's wrath has overtaken them at last. As for us, brothers and sisters, when, for a short time, we were made orphans by being separated from you—in person, not in heart—we longed with great eagerness to see you face to face. For we wanted to come to you—certainly I, Paul, wanted to again and again—but Satan blocked our way. For what is our hope or joy or crown of boasting before our Lord Jesus at his coming? Is it not you? Yes, you are our glory and joy!

3 Therefore when we could bear it no longer, we decided to be left alone in Athens; and we sent Timothy, our brother and co-worker for God in proclaiming the gospel of Christ, to strengthen and encourage you for the sake of your faith, so that no one would be shaken by these persecutions. Indeed, you yourselves know that this is what we are destined for. In fact, when we were with you, we told you beforehand that we were to suffer persecution; so it turned out, as you know. For this reason, when I could bear it no longer, I sent to find out about your faith; I was afraid that somehow the tempter had tempted you and that our labor had been in vain.

But Timothy has just now come to us from you, and has brought us the good news of your faith and love. He has told us also that you always remember us kindly and long to see us—just as we long to see you. For this reason, brothers and sisters, during all our distress and persecution we have been encouraged about you through your faith. For we now live, if you continue to stand firm in the Lord. How can we thank God enough for you in return for all the joy that we feel before our God because of you? Night and day we pray most earnestly that we may see you face to face and restore whatever is lacking in your faith. Now may our God and Father himself and our Lord Jesus direct our way to you. And may the Lord

make you increase and abound in love for one another and for all, just as we abound in love for you. And may he so strengthen your hearts in holiness that you may be blameless before our God and Father at the coming of our Lord Jesus with all his saints.

4 Finally, brothers and sisters, we ask and urge you in the Lord Jesus that, as you learned from us how you ought to live and to please God (as, in fact, you are doing), you should do so more and more. For you know what instructions we gave you through the Lord Jesus. For this is the will of God, your sanctification: that you abstain from fornication; that each one of you know how to control your own body in holiness and honor, not with lustful passion, like the Gentiles who do not know God; that no one wrong or exploit a brother or sister in this matter, because the Lord is an avenger in all these things, just as we have already told you beforehand and solemnly warned you. For God did not call us to impurity but in holiness. Therefore whoever rejects this rejects not human authority but God, who also gives his Holy Spirit to you.

Now concerning love of the brothers and sisters, you do not need to have anyone write to you, for you yourselves have been taught by God to love one another; and indeed you do love all the brothers and sisters throughout Macedonia. But we urge you, beloved, to do so more and more, to aspire to live quietly, to mind your own affairs, and to work with your hands, as we directed you, so that you may behave properly toward outsiders and be dependent on no one.

But we do not want you to be uninformed, brothers and sisters, about those who have died, so that you may not grieve as others do who have no hope. For since we believe that Jesus died and rose again, even so, through Jesus, God will bring with him those who have died. For this we declare to you by the word of the Lord, that we who are alive, who are left until the coming of the Lord, will by no means precede those who have died. For the Lord himself, with a cry of command, with the archangel's call and with the sound of God's trumpet, will descend from heaven, and the dead in Christ will rise first. Then we who are alive, who are left, will be caught up in the clouds together with them to meet the Lord in the air; and so we will be with the Lord forever. Therefore encourage one another with these words.

5 Now concerning the times and the seasons, brothers and sisters, you do not need to have anything written to you. For you yourselves know very

well that the Day of the Lord will come like a thief in the night. When they say, "There is peace and security," then sudden destruction will come upon them, as labor pains come upon a pregnant woman, and there will be no escape! But you, beloved, are not in darkness, for that day to surprise you like a thief; for you are all children of light and children of the day; we are not of the night or of darkness. So then let us not fall asleep as others do, but let us keep awake and be sober; for those who sleep at night, and those who are drunk get drunk at night. But since we belong to the day, let us be sober, and put on the breastplate of faith and love, and for a helmet the hope of salvation. For God has destined us not for wrath but for obtaining salvation through our Lord Jesus Christ, who died for us, so that whether we are awake or asleep we may live with him.

Therefore encourage one another and build up each other, as indeed you are doing. But we appeal to you, brothers and sisters, to respect those who labor among you, and have charge of you in the Lord and admonish you; esteem them very highly in love because of their work. Be at peace among yourselves. And we urge you, beloved, to admonish the idlers, encourage the faint hearted, help the weak, be patient with all of them. See that none of you repays evil for evil, but always seek to do good to one another and to all. Rejoice always, pray without ceasing, give thanks in all circumstances; for this is the will of God in Christ Jesus for you.

Do not quench the Spirit. Do not despise the words of prophets, but test everything; hold fast to what is good; abstain from every form of evil. May the God of peace himself sanctify you entirely; and may your spirit and soul and body be kept sound and blameless at the coming of our Lord Jesus Christ. The one who calls you is faithful, and he will do this. Beloved, pray for us. Greet all the brothers and sisters with a holy kiss. I solemnly command you by the Lord that this letter be read to all of them. The grace of our Lord Jesus Christ be with you.

Gospel Formation

Paul's letters say a great deal about the early churches and what they were thinking and doing. They say much less about Jesus: who he was and what he taught. Paul was not interested in Jesus of Nazareth; what was important to him was why Christ died and for whom, rather than how Christ lived. The Gospels, however, written long after Paul's letters, fill in the human side of Jesus' life. It is important to recall, however, that a generation or two elapsed between Jesus' death and the composition of the Gospels, and so they reveal a number of developments within the early church in addition to the teachings of Jesus.

There is much debate among biblical scholars about who wrote the Gospels—Matthew, Mark, Luke, and John—as well as when they were written, for whom, and why. Although a small minority of scholars believes the Gospels were written during Jesus' lifetime, and a larger minority believes they were written prior to 70 C.E., most mainstream biblicists believe they were composed during or after the First Jewish War. For a long time, Christians believed that Matthew was the oldest gospel, and that was the reason it appeared first. But nineteenth-century biblical scholars began to examine the Gospels and their composition in more critical ways, looking at how different writers used Jesus' parables and sayings, how they depicted his healings and exorcisms, how they reported what Jesus said when he died, and when his disciples found an empty tomb. These historical-critical studies, as they were called, highlighted a number of interesting facts. First, it became clear that Mark was the first gospel written, because Matthew and Luke had taken whole chunks from it, as well as stylistic elements, and incorporated them into their own gospels. The author of Luke actually admits in the very first chapter that there were a number of different gospels:

> Since many have undertaken to set down an orderly account of the events that have been fulfilled among us, just as they were handed on to us by those who from the beginning were eyewitnesses and servants of the word, I too decided, after investigating everything carefully from the very first, to write an orderly account for you, most excellent Theophilus, so that you may know the truth concerning the things about which you have been instructed. (Luke 1:1–4)

Scholars also noticed that Matthew and Luke included almost identical sayings of Jesus that did not appear in Mark or John. They hypothesized that a sayings gospel existed, which they called "Q," short for *Quelle,* or "source," in German. The Q gospel has never been found, and some now question whether this is the best explanation for the similarities between Luke and Matthew. Some argue that Luke took Matthew and rewrote it to fit the needs of a Lukan audience. The Q gospel nevertheless seems to be well accepted, despite its hypothetical existence.

Most biblical scholars would also agree that John's gospel was written last, probably around the end of the first century. Even so, parts of John may predate the other gospels. Raymond E. Brown, one of the best-known scholars on John, argues that John was composed over a period of decades and that at least five versions of the gospel existed prior to its final form. Others disagree with Brown's analysis. What everyone can agree on is that John's gospel radically differs from the other three. Matthew, Mark, and Luke are called the Synoptic Gospels (synoptic meaning "seen together") because they are the most similar. They show Jesus speaking in short sayings and parables, acting in a very human manner, and preaching a coming reign of God. John's gospel, on the other hand, paints a picture of a mystical Jesus who speaks in similes and metaphors, claims to have come down from heaven, and says he will return to his Father. Rather than speaking in snappy one-liners, Jesus in John speaks in long discourses, sermons, and prayers. In contrast to the other three Gospels, he does not have a last supper with his disciples, but rather washes their feet the night before he is killed. John quotes Jesus saying things like "I am the bread of life," and "I am the true vine," and "I am the good shepherd." These "I Am" statements indicate a number of metaphors by which John's community understood the significance of Jesus. They appear only in John's gospel.

How do we account for the differences in the gospel accounts of Jesus' life? Some would assert that different people saw the same events and were just describing them differently. Since the Gospels were written long after Jesus' death, however, it is unlikely that his disciples or other eyewitnesses composed them, although John, or the "beloved disciple" may have written part of John's gospel. Furthermore, the disciples were not present at the inner sanctum of the Sanhedrin—an assembly of the political and religious leaders in Jerusalem—or at Pilate's court where Jesus was tried, so those events were imaginatively reconstructed. This is not to say that the

▦ From Oral Tradition to Written Gospel: Hypothetical Stages in the Gospels' Historical Development

New Testament scholars employ a variety of critical methods to discover the processes by which originally oral traditions about Jesus gradually evolved into written form. Historical and literary analysis of the Gospels suggests that they developed over a relatively long period (c. 30–100 C.E.), undergoing several discrete stages of growth. The following list provides a hypothetical reconstruction of events and movements leading to the Gospels' creation.

DATE   EVENT OR DEVELOPMENT

I. Period of Exclusively Oral Traditions

30 C.E.	Oral preaching by Jesus in Galilee, Samaria, and Judea
30–33 C.E.	Crucifixion
30–50 C.E.	Oral preaching about Jesus by Aramaic-speaking disciples in Galilee, Samaria, Judea, and neighboring regions; formation of the first Christian community at Jerusalem, led by Peter, John, and James; formation of additional Aramaic-speaking communities throughout Palestine; development of a second major Christian center at Antioch in Syria
40–60 C.E.	Missionary tours of Paul and associates; establishment of new, larger Gentile, Greek-speaking churches in Asia Minor and Greece

II. Period of Earliest Written Documents

50–70 C.E.	Oldest surviving Christian documents (Paul's letters to Gentile congregations) composed; collection of Jesus' sayings, in Greek (the Q document) compiled; possible collection of Jesus' miraculous works, the Signs Gospel (later incorporated into the Gospel of John); possible first edition of the Gospel of Thomas (like Q, a Sayings Gospel)

III. The Jewish Revolt Against Rome and the Appearance of the First Canonical Gospel

66 C.E.	Outbreak of the Jewish War
66–70 C.E.	Mark's "wartime" Gospel composed, relating Jesus' suffering to that of his persecuted followers
70 C.E.	Roman destruction of Jerusalem, the Temple, and the original Christian center

IV. Production of New, Enlarged Editions of Mark

80–90 C.E.	Composition of Matthew and Luke, who use Mark and Q as their primary sources (plus their individual special sources, respectively M and L)

V. Production of New Gospels Promoting an Independent (Non-Synoptic) Tradition

90–100 C.E.	Composition of the Gospel of John, incorporating the older Signs Gospel; second edition of the Gospel of Thomas, incorporating the older Thomas sayings collection

Gospels are not based on factual accounts or traditions that were gathered and maintained by Jesus' followers. These traditions might have been compilations of miracle stories or healings, or collections of sayings. While some historians claim that Jesus' disciples were literate and that collections of Jesus materials were written relatively early in the first century, perhaps even during his lifetime, most think that Jesus materials were transmitted orally for many years before they were written down. Arguing for the literacy of simple fishermen and other rural people seems somewhat dubious.

There are other ways to account for differences in the Gospels, however. One explanation looks at the authors and audiences of the Gospels, considering what the author knew about Judaism and Judea, what kind of Greek the author was writing in, and how the author presents Jesus. If Jesus was a teacher of the law, as he appears in Matthew, then it is likely that Matthew was writing for a predominantly Jewish audience. Mark portrays a human Jesus who hungers, angers, and suffers, and so scholars deduce that Mark's audience may have been undergoing persecution at the hands of the Romans. Perhaps Mark was writing in Rome for a Gentile audience, though some would now argue for a Syrian or even Galilean origin for this gospel. John's gospel reflects a period of great conflict between Jews and Jesus' followers. In the 90s C.E., Jews expelled Jesus' followers from the synagogues: Jesus makes this prediction in John 16:2. Is this prophecy remembered, or is it current history retrojected (superimposed) into the past? In either case, it is clear that John presents Jesus in much greater conflict with Jewish authorities than do the other Gospels.

Another way to understand why the Gospels are so different—and yet so similar at the same time—is to read them as theological reflections rather than as biographies of Jesus. The Gospels represent the efforts of different communities of Jesus' disciples to understand who Jesus was and what he did. We see these differences in the names and titles various writers use for Jesus. Luke, for example, calls Jesus "Savior" in both the gospel and in Acts, which Luke also wrote; John, the only other gospel to use this title, uses it only once. Matthew, Mark and John call Jesus "Rabbi," which means "teacher" in Hebrew, but Luke does not use this title. Only Matthew calls Jesus "Immanuel," or "God with us." These titles tell us a great deal about the Gospels and their audiences. "Rabbi" would indicate a Jewish audience that would appreciate Jewish traditions. "Savior" would be a term familiar to pagan, or non-Jewish, cultures. "Rabbi" indicates a belief in Jesus as a Jewish teacher or authority. "Savior" points to a more exalted, even divine figure. Because the Gospels were written at different times, in different places, and for different audiences, they reproduce those differences. In some respects, they say more about the authors writing them than they do about Jesus, but they say much about Jesus as well.

The Historical Jesus

In the early twentieth century, Albert Schweitzer (1875–1965) wrote *The Quest of the Historical Jesus,* in which he analyzed nineteenth-century depictions of Jesus.

Schweitzer is best known as a medical missionary to Africa, but before he turned to medicine, he was a concert organist, a Bach specialist, and a biblical scholar. Schweitzer discussed the ways in which scholars had sought to understand Jesus: from giving his miracles rationalistic explanations, to portraying him as a super-nice guy (sort of a 1960s flower child), to presenting his teachings as moral proverbs. They had attempted to find a Jesus grounded in history, rather than one developed in subsequent theology or philosophy. Schweitzer himself believed that the Gospels depicted Jesus as an eschatological prophet, that is, one proclaiming the coming end of the age and the arrival of God's kingdom. Nevertheless, he concluded that historical Jesus studies say more about their authors than about Jesus and that Jesus of Nazareth would remain an enigma.

Although historical Jesus studies have surpassed nineteenth-century efforts in their sophistication, Schweitzer's conclusions may be as true today as they were when he wrote them. While a number of New Testament scholars have expressed skepticism over the possibility of accessing any sort of actual history from the Gospels—arguing instead that the texts are revealed truths rather than history as we know it—two great waves of historical Jesus studies occurred in the twentieth century. If we count nineteenth-century analyses as the first wave, the second wave occurred in the 1950s, amid doubt over the historicity of the Gospels. In response to German theologians and French existentialists who doubted that the Gospels provided much more than a proclamation calling Christians to action, biblical scholars in the United States and Europe attempted to recover a credible Jesus of history. This second wave was a relatively small blip on the academic radar screen, however. The discovery of ancient Jewish texts like the Dead Sea Scrolls, coupled with the discovery of some ancient Christian texts in Egypt in the 1940s, helped create a third wave of historical studies, as did the creation of the Jesus Seminar. The Jesus Seminar, convened in 1985, gathered New Testament scholars together for the purpose of publicizing historical research on Jesus. One of the more controversial, and most interesting, things the Seminar did was to assess each and every saying attributed to Jesus in the Gospels, and rate whether he actually said it. While other scholars decried this method of ranking authenticity, the Seminar achieved exactly what it intended: it put historical Jesus studies on the map and in popular bookstores, with titles like *The Five Gospels, The Complete Gospels,* and *The Gospel of Jesus.*

Historical Jesus studies attempt to differentiate between what Jesus actually did and said, and what was attributed to him later on by the early church. For example, did Jesus really refer to himself as a "son of man," or was this a title later followers gave to him? Was he actually called the messiah during his lifetime, or only after his death? Some scholars distinguish between the two visions of Jesus by saying one is "the historical Jesus" and the other "the risen Christ," or "the earthly Jesus" and "the post-Easter Christ." These terms indicate the belief in a difference, and even a disjunction, between Jesus of Nazareth and Jesus the Christ, since the resurrection caused Jesus' disciples to reevaluate everything they'd ever known and thought about him before his death. Other scholars, however, argue for continuity between the two, since an oral culture would tell and re-tell stories of Jesus in the present tense, and not dramatically depart from existing traditions.

The Synoptic Gospels (Mark, Matthew, Luke) seem to present more historical materials than does John. One reason scholars believe this is that Jesus appears more human and worldly, less divine and other-worldly, than in John's gospel. He expresses exasperation with his disciples and criticizes his family. The Synoptic writers even include uncomplimentary things about Jesus, such as noting his reputation as a "glutton and a drunkard" (Matthew 11:18–19; Luke 7:33–35), and the fact that he is unable to perform a miracle (Mark 6:1–5), and that he is somewhat rude to a non-Jew (Mark 7:24–30). Would writers say negative things about their hero if they weren't true? The Synoptics also provide numerous sayings of Jesus, memorable even to non-Christians because of their wisdom:

> Judge not, lest ye be judged.
> Do unto others as you would have done unto you.
> Go the second mile.
> Turn the other cheek.
> Don't hide your light under a bushel.

Jesus' parables also reveal a man familiar with agricultural life and its problems. Jesus talked about weeds and wheat, about birds eating seeds, about day laborers looking for agricultural work, about a woman who made bread dough, about looking for oil in the middle of the night, and about taxes and robbery. He spoke of everyday things in parables—short stories that made comparisons between daily life and what he said about the kingdom of God. Many of his parables began with the words "The kingdom of God is like . . ." or, in Matthew's gospel, "The kingdom of Heaven is like . . ." because Jesus planned to compare God's rule with what actually happens on earth. While his parables show good people, dishonest people, and foolish people, they all show that the realm of God reverses the status quo and upsets human expectations of what is right and what is wrong.

Because the parables show Jesus talking about God's coming rule on earth, New Testament scholars believe that Jesus' main message—at least in the Synoptic Gospels—was about the "kingdom of God." This kingdom was not like the worldly kingdom with which people were familiar. On the contrary, it would be a kingdom of "nuisances and nobodies" in the words of theologian John Dominic Crossan. Children, women, and poor people would be first to sit at the table. Everyone would eat together (eating being a major theme in all of the Gospels), would share, and would live in some sort of equality. The current order in which wealth and privilege were rewarded would be overturned, and the nobodies would inherit the earth. The song Mary sings in Luke's gospel when she learns of her pregnancy anticipates this great reversal:

> [God] has shown strength with his arm; he has scattered the proud in the thoughts of their hearts. He has brought down the powerful from their thrones, and lifted up the lowly; he has filled the hungry with good things, and sent the rich away empty. (Luke 1:51–53)

The question that arises is whether this kingdom would be on earth or in heaven. Did Jesus mean that everything would be changed in this life, in this world? Or did he mean that things would change in an afterlife? Or, as later Christian writers believed, that things would change after a final cosmic battle between God and Satan? There seems to be general agreement that Jesus expected a reversal in history, in earthly life. This would be in accord with the Jewish expectation that the Messiah would usher in a period of peace and justice in the world. The Gospels do report Jesus describing some sort of judgment day, or Day of the Lord, and this evidence persuaded Schweitzer and others that Jesus preached an eschatological message: the end of the present evil age was near; the forces of *this* world—namely, Satan and his princes—would pass away very soon, so that God would rule. Nevertheless, God's rule would occur on earth, not only in heaven, just as Jesus taught the disciples how to pray:

> Father, hallowed be your name. Your kingdom come. Give us each day our daily bread. And forgive us our sins, for we ourselves forgive everyone indebted to us. And do not bring us to the time of trial. (Luke 11:2b–4)

The Gospel of Mark

Mark is the oldest gospel in the New Testament, although it may not be the oldest ever written because not all gospels were included in the New Testament, as we shall see in the next chapter. Matthew was the most popular gospel in the early church, hence its inclusion at the beginning of the New Testament. Mark was thought to be a cheap copy, perhaps an abbreviated summary, of the better gospels, but the belief that it originated from stories told by the disciple Peter—said to have founded the church in Rome—obviously made it worth including. Mark is a strange, even a mysterious, gospel, with an extremely human Jesus dealing with extremely human disciples.

Mark has several unique elements, which have helped persuade biblical scholars that it is the oldest gospel in the New Testament. First, Mark makes a secret of Jesus' identity until chapter 8. This "messianic secret" can be seen when Jesus tells people, as well as demons and spirits, not to go around saying who he is. Second, when Jesus is revealed to be the Messiah, he is not a kingly figure, but a messiah who must suffer. Third, Mark tends to combine stories. The "Markan sandwich" does exactly that: it sandwiches one story in the middle of another. For example, when Jesus is on his way to heal the daughter of one of the leaders of the synagogue (5:22–24), he heals a bleeding woman when she touches him (5:24b–34) and then continues on his way to heal the little girl (5:35–43).

Finally, Mark is distinct in having not one, not two, but *three* endings. The most ancient copies of Mark that we have end rather abruptly in 16:8: "So they went out and fled from the tomb for terror and amazement had seized them; and they said nothing to anyone, for they were afraid." There is one copy of Mark that contains 16:9:

And all that had been commanded them they told briefly to those around Peter. And afterward Jesus himself sent out through them, from east to west, the sacred and imperishable proclamation of eternal salvation.

Then there are a few later versions of Mark that continue the story beyond verse 8 and parallel other gospel accounts of Jesus' resurrection. While the longer ending may be more satisfying to readers familiar with the other renditions, the shorter—and probably original—ending is more interesting, and certainly more provocative: Where was Jesus? Why did the women say nothing? Why were they afraid? Obviously, the women who found the empty tomb did, in fact, say something; otherwise, their story would not have been told, and there would be no Christianity. The absence of Jesus, and the terror at his absence, was something later Gospel writers either knew nothing about or ignored.

The Reading

The Gospel of Mark, which is the next reading, was selected for several reasons. First, it is the oldest gospel, and subsequent writers take elements from it to create new gospels. Second, and related to its antiquity, it represents an early interpretation of Jesus' life and purpose, in which he is a wonder-worker and healer, an exorcist and prophet, but also a messiah who must suffer. Third, Jesus is still connected to his Jewish roots. Although Jewish religious authorities constantly oppose Jesus, the Pharisees are somewhat more sympathetically portrayed. Fourth, it is the shortest canonical gospel—which means the shortest gospel in the New Testament, with just sixteen chapters.

As with the reading from Genesis 1–3, it is best to read the Gospel of Mark straight through as a story we have never heard before, about people we have never met. This way we can begin to see stylistic elements and themes that the author uses to tell the story.

Questions to Consider

1. How would you describe the character of Jesus in Mark's gospel? What about the character of the disciples? Jesus' family? What is the relationship between Jesus and the disciples, and his family?

2. What evidence is there in Mark that would indicate that the Messiah is a human, suffering figure? What evidence is there that the Messiah is a strong, heavenly figure?

3. Are the Romans depicted sympathetically in Mark? What about the Jews? What was the historical context of the creation of Mark that might explain these characterizations?

4. Review the narrative in which Jesus dies: Mark 15:16–41. Note that it is Roman soldiers who torture, mock, and execute Jesus. Now read the narratives

of Jesus' death in the other gospels: Matthew 27:27–55; Luke 23:26–44; and John 19:16b–37. How are these accounts similar? How are they different? What do these differences say about the theological views of the authors?

5. Whom do you think Mark was writing for? Who was his audience? Whom do you think his readers might identify with?

The Gospel of Mark

1 The beginning of the good news of Jesus Christ, the Son of God. As it is written in the prophet Isaiah, "See, I am sending my messenger ahead of you, who will prepare your way; the voice of one crying out in the wilderness: 'Prepare the way of the Lord, make his paths straight,'" John the baptizer appeared in the wilderness, proclaiming a baptism of repentance for the forgiveness of sins. And people from the whole Judean countryside and all the people of Jerusalem were going out to him, and were baptized by him in the river Jordan, confessing their sins. Now John was clothed with camel's hair, with a leather belt around his waist, and he ate locusts and wild honey. He proclaimed, "The one who is more powerful than I is coming after me; I am not worthy to stoop down and untie the thong of his sandals. I have baptized you with water; but he will baptize you with the Holy Spirit."

In those days Jesus came from Nazareth of Galilee and was baptized by John in the Jordan. And just as he was coming up out of the water, he saw the heavens torn apart and the Spirit descending like a dove on him. And a voice came from heaven, "You are my Son, the Beloved; with you I am well pleased." And the Spirit immediately drove him out into the wilderness. He was in the wilderness forty days, tempted by Satan; and he was with the wild beasts; and the angels waited on him.

Now after John was arrested, Jesus came to Galilee, proclaiming the good news of God, and saying, "The time is fulfilled, and the kingdom of God has come near; repent, and believe in the good news." As Jesus passed along the Sea of Galilee, he saw Simon and his brother Andrew casting a net into the sea—for they were fishermen. And Jesus said to them, "Follow me and I will make you fish for people." And immediately they left their nets and followed him. As he went a little farther, he saw James son of Zebedee and his brother John, who were in their boat mending the nets. Immediately he called them; and they left their father Zebedee in the boat with the hired men, and followed him.

They went to Capernaum; and when the Sabbath came, he entered the synagogue and taught. They were astounded at his teaching, for he taught them as one having authority, and not as the scribes. Just then there was in their synagogue a man with an unclean spirit, and he cried out, "What have you to do with us, Jesus of Nazareth? Have you come to destroy us? I know who you are, the Holy One of God." But Jesus rebuked him, saying, "Be silent, and come out of him!" And the unclean spirit, convulsing him and crying with a loud voice, came out of him. They were all amazed, and they kept on asking one another, "What is this? A new teaching—with authority! He commands even the unclean spirits, and they obey him." At once his fame began to spread throughout the surrounding region of Galilee.

As soon as they left the synagogue, they entered the house of Simon and Andrew, with James and John. Now Simon's mother-in-law was in bed with a fever, and they told him about her at once. He came and took her by the hand and lifted her up. Then the fever left her, and she began to serve them.

That evening, at sundown, they brought to him all who were sick or possessed with demons. And the whole city was gathered around the door. And he cured many who were sick with various diseases, and cast out many demons; and he would not permit the demons to speak, because they knew him.

In the morning, while it was still very dark, he got up and went out to a deserted place, and there he prayed. And Simon and his companions hunted for him. When they found him, they said to him, "Everyone is searching for you." He answered, "Let us go on to the neighboring towns, so that I may proclaim the message there also; for that is what I came out to do." And he went throughout Galilee, proclaiming the message in their synagogues and casting out demons.

A leper came to him begging him, and kneeling he said to him, "If you choose, you can make me clean." Moved with pity, Jesus stretched out his hand and touched him, and said to him, "I do choose. Be made clean!" Immediately the leprosy left him, and he was made clean. After sternly warning him he sent him away at once, saying to him, "See that you say nothing to anyone; but go, show yourself to the priest, and offer for your cleansing what Moses commanded, as a testimony to them." But he went out and began to proclaim it freely, and to spread the word, so that Jesus could no longer go into a town openly, but stayed out in the country; and people came to him from every quarter.

2 When he returned to Capernaum after some days, it was reported that he was at home. So many gathered around that there was no longer room for them, not even in front of the door; and he was speaking the word to them.

Then some people came, bringing to him a paralyzed man, carried by four of them. And when they could not bring him to Jesus because of the crowd, they removed the roof above him; and after having dug through it, they let down the mat on which the paralytic lay. When Jesus saw their faith, he said to the paralytic, "Son, your sins are forgiven." Now some of the scribes were sitting there, questioning in their hearts, "Why does this fellow speak in this way? It is blasphemy! Who can forgive sins but God alone?" At once Jesus perceived in his spirit that they were discussing these questions among themselves; and he said to them, "Why do you raise such questions in your hearts? Which is easier, to say to the paralytic, 'Your sins are forgiven,' or to say, 'Stand up and take your mat and walk'? But so that you may know that the Son of Man has authority on earth to forgive sins"—he said to the paralytic—"I say to you, stand up, take your mat and go to your home." And he stood up, and immediately took the mat and went out before all of them; so that they were all amazed and glorified God, saying, "We have never seen anything like this!"

Jesus went out again beside the sea; the whole crowd gathered around him, and he taught them. As he was walking along, he saw Levi son of Alphaeus sitting at the tax booth, and he said to him, "Follow me." And he got up and followed him. And as he sat at dinner in Levi's house, many tax collectors and sin-

ners were also sitting with Jesus and his disciples—for there were many who followed him. When the scribes of the Pharisees saw that he was eating with sinners and tax collectors, they said to his disciples, "Why does he eat with tax collectors and sinners?" When Jesus heard this, he said to them, "Those who are well have no need of a physician, but those who are sick; I have come to call not the righteous but sinners."

Now John's disciples and the Pharisees were fasting; and people came and said to him, "Why do John's disciples and the disciples of the Pharisees fast, but your disciples do not fast?" Jesus said to them, "The wedding guests cannot fast while the bridegroom is with them, can they? As long as they have the bridegroom with them, they cannot fast. The days will come when the bridegroom is taken away from them, and then they will fast on that day. No one sews a piece of unshrunk cloth on an old cloak; otherwise, the patch pulls away from it, the new from the old, and a worse tear is made. And no one puts new wine into old wineskins; otherwise, the wine will burst the skins, and the wine is lost, and so are the skins; but one puts new wine into fresh wineskins."

One Sabbath he was going through the grain fields; and as they made their way his disciples began to pluck heads of grain. The Pharisees said to him, "Look, why are they doing what is not lawful on the Sabbath?" And he said to them, "Have you never read what David did when he and his companions were hungry and in need of food? He entered the house of God, when Abiathar was high priest, and ate the bread of the Presence, which it is not lawful for any but the priests to eat, and he gave some to his companions." Then he said to them, "The Sabbath was made for humankind, and not humankind for the Sabbath; so the Son of Man is lord even of the Sabbath."

3 Again he entered the synagogue, and a man was there who had a withered hand. They watched him to see whether he would cure him on the Sabbath, so that they might accuse him. And he said to the man who had the withered hand, "Come forward." Then he said to them, "Is it lawful to do good or to do harm on the Sabbath, to save life or to kill?" But they were silent. He looked around at them with anger; he was grieved at their hardness of heart and said to the man, "Stretch out your hand." He stretched it out, and his hand was restored. The Pharisees went out and immediately conspired with the Herodians against him, how to destroy him.

Jesus departed with his disciples to the sea, and a great multitude from Galilee followed him; hearing all that he was doing, they came to him in great numbers from Judea, Jerusalem, Idumea, beyond the Jordan, and the region around Tyre and Sidon. He told his disciples to have a boat ready for him because of the crowd, so that they would not crush him; for he had cured many, so that all who had diseases pressed upon him to touch him. Whenever the unclean spirits saw him, they fell down before him and shouted, "You are the Son of God!" But he sternly ordered them not to make him known.

He went up the mountain and called to him those whom he wanted, and they came to him. And he appointed twelve, whom he also named apostles, to be with him, and to be sent out to proclaim the message, and to have authority to cast out demons. So he appointed the twelve: Simon (to whom he gave the name Peter); James son of Zebedee and John the brother of James (to whom he gave the name Boanerges, that is, Sons of Thunder); and Andrew, and Philip, and Bartholomew, and Matthew, and Thomas, and James son of Alphaeus, and Thaddaeus, and Simon the Cananaean, and Judas Iscariot, who betrayed him.

Then he went home; and the crowd came together again, so that they could not even eat. When his family heard it, they went out to restrain him, for people were saying, "He has gone out of his mind." And the scribes who came down from Jerusalem said, "He has Beelzebul, and by the ruler of the demons he casts out demons." And he called them to him, and spoke to them in parables, "How can Satan cast out Satan? If a kingdom is divided against itself, that kingdom cannot stand. And if a house is divided against itself, that house will not be able to stand. And if Satan has risen up against himself and is divided, he cannot stand, but his end has come. But no one can enter a strong man's house and plunder his property without first tying up the strong man; then indeed the house can be plundered."

"Truly I tell you, people will be forgiven for their sins and whatever blasphemies they utter; but whoever blasphemes against the Holy Spirit can never have forgiveness, but is guilty of an eternal sin"—for they had said, "He has an unclean spirit."

Then his mother and his brothers came; and standing outside, they sent to him and called him. A crowd was sitting around him; and they said to him, "Your mother and your brothers and sisters are outside, asking for you." And he replied, "Who are my mother and my brothers?" And looking at those who sat around him, he said, "Here are my mother and my brothers! Whoever does the will of God is my brother and sister and mother."

4 Again he began to teach beside the sea. Such a very large crowd gathered around him that he got into a boat on the sea and sat there, while the whole crowd was beside the sea on the land. He began to teach them many things in parables, and in his teaching he said to them: "Listen! A sower went out to sow. And as he sowed, some seed fell on the path, and the birds came and ate it up. Other seed fell on rocky ground, where it did not have much soil, and it sprang up quickly, since it had no depth of soil. And when the sun rose, it was scorched; and since it had no root, it withered away. Other seed fell among thorns, and the thorns grew up and choked it, and it yielded no grain. Other seed fell into good soil and brought forth grain, growing up and increasing and yielding thirty and sixty and a hundredfold." And he said, "Let anyone with ears to hear listen!"

When he was alone, those who were around him along with the twelve asked him about the parables. And he said to them, "To you has been given the secret of the kingdom of God, but for those outside, everything comes in parables; in order that 'they may indeed look, but not perceive, and may indeed listen, but not understand; so that they may not turn again and be forgiven.'"

And he said to them, "Do you not understand this parable? Then how will you understand all the parables? The sower sows the word. These are the ones on the path where the word is sown: when they hear, Satan immediately comes and takes away the word that is sown in them. And these are the ones sown on rocky ground: when they hear the word, they immediately receive it with joy. But they have no root, and endure only for a while; then, when trouble or persecution arises on account of the word, immediately they fall away. And others are those sown among the thorns: these are the ones who hear the word, but the cares of the world, and the lure of wealth, and the desire for other things come in and choke the word, and it yields nothing. And these are the ones sown on the good soil: they hear the word and accept it and bear fruit, thirty and sixty and a hundredfold."

He said to them, "Is a lamp brought in to be put under the bushel basket, or under the bed, and not on the lampstand? For there is nothing hidden, except to be disclosed; nor is anything secret, except to come to light. Let anyone with ears to hear listen!"

And he said to them, "Pay attention to what you hear; the measure you give will be the measure you get, and still more will be given you. For to those who have, more will be given; and from those who have nothing, even what they have will be taken away."

He also said, "The kingdom of God is as if someone would scatter seed on the ground, and would sleep and rise night and day, and the seed would sprout and grow, he does not know how. The earth produces of itself, first the stalk, then the head, then the full grain in the head. But when the grain is ripe, at once he goes in with his sickle, because the harvest has come."

He also said, "With what can we compare the kingdom of God, or what parable will we use for it? It is like a mustard seed, which, when sown upon the ground, is the smallest of all the seeds on earth; yet when it is sown it grows up and becomes the greatest of all shrubs, and puts forth large branches, so that the birds of the air can make nests in its shade." With many such parables he spoke the word to them, as they were able to hear it; he did not speak to them except in parables, but he explained everything in private to his disciples.

On that day, when evening had come, he said to them, "Let us go across to the other side." And leaving the crowd behind, they took him with them in the boat, just as he was. Other boats were with him. A great windstorm arose, and the waves beat into the boat, so that the boat was already being swamped. But he was in the stern, asleep on the cushion; and they woke him up and said to him, "Teacher, do you not care that we are perishing?" He woke up and rebuked the wind, and said to the sea, "Peace! Be still!" Then the wind ceased, and there was a dead calm. He said to them, "Why are you afraid? Have you still no faith?" And they were filled with great awe and said to one another, "Who then is this, that even the wind and the sea obey him?"

5 They came to the other side of the sea, to the country of the Gerasenes. And when he had stepped out of the boat, immediately a man out of the tombs with an unclean spirit met him. He lived among the tombs; and no one could restrain him any more, even with a chain; for he had often been restrained with shackles and chains, but the chains he wrenched apart, and the shackles he broke in pieces; and no one had the strength to subdue him. Night and day among the tombs and on the mountains he was always howling and bruising himself with stones.

When he saw Jesus from a distance, he ran and bowed down before him; and he shouted at the top of his voice, "What have you to do with me, Jesus, Son of the Most High God? I adjure you by God, do not torment me." For he had said to him, "Come out of the man, you unclean spirit!" Then Jesus asked him, "What is your name?" He replied, "My name is Legion; for we are many." He begged him earnestly not to send them out of the country. Now there on the hillside a great herd of swine was feeding; and the unclean spirits begged him, "Send us into the swine; let us enter them." So he gave them permission. And the unclean spirits came out and entered the swine; and the herd, numbering about two thousand, rushed down the steep bank into the sea, and were drowned in the sea. The swineherds ran off and told it in the city and in the country. Then people came to see what it was that had happened. They came to Jesus and saw the demoniac sitting there, clothed and in his right mind, the very man who had had the legion; and they were afraid. Those who had seen what had happened to the demoniac and to the swine reported it. Then they began to beg Jesus to leave their neighborhood. As he was getting into the boat, the man who had been possessed by demons begged him that he might be with him. But Jesus refused, and said to him, "Go home to your friends, and tell them how much the Lord has done for you, and what mercy he has shown you." And he went away and began to proclaim in the Decapolis how much Jesus had done for him; and everyone was amazed.

When Jesus had crossed again in the boat to the other side, a great crowd gathered around him; and he was by the sea. Then one of the leaders of the synagogue named Jairus came and, when he saw him, fell at his feet and begged him repeatedly, "My little daughter is at the point of death. Come and lay your hands on her, so that she may be made well, and live." He went with him.

And a large crowd followed him and pressed in on him. Now there was a woman who had been suffering from hemorrhages for twelve years. She had endured much under many physicians, and had spent all that she had; and she was no better, but rather grew worse. She had heard about Jesus, and came up behind him in the crowd and touched his cloak, for she said, "If I but touch his clothes, I will be made well." Immediately her hemorrhage stopped; and she felt in her body that she was healed of her disease. Immediately aware that power had gone forth from him, Jesus turned about in the crowd and said, "Who touched my clothes?" And his disciples said to him, "You see the crowd pressing in on you; how can you say, 'Who touched me?'" He looked all around to see who had done it. But the woman, knowing what had happened to her, came in fear and trembling, fell down before him, and told him the whole truth. He said to her, "Daughter, your faith has made you well; go in peace, and be healed of your disease."

While he was still speaking, some people came from the leader's house to say, "Your daughter is dead. Why trouble the teacher any further?" But overhearing what they said, Jesus said to the leader of the synagogue, "Do not fear, only believe." He allowed no one to follow him except Peter, James, and John, the brother of James. When they came to the house of the leader of the synagogue, he saw a commotion, people weeping and wailing loudly. When he had entered, he said to them, "Why do you make a commotion and weep? The child is not dead but sleeping." And they laughed at him. Then he put them all outside, and took the child's father and mother and those who were with him, and went in where the child was. He took her by the hand and said to her, "Talitha cum," which means, "Little girl, get up!" And immediately the girl got up and began to walk about (she was twelve years of age). At this they were overcome with amazement. He strictly ordered them that no one should know this, and told them to give her something to eat.

6 He left that place and came to his hometown, and his disciples followed him. On the Sabbath he began to teach in the synagogue, and many who heard him were astounded. They said, "Where did this man get all this? What is this wisdom that has been given to him? What deeds of power are being done by his hands! Is not this the carpenter, the son of Mary and brother of James and Jesus and Judas and Simon, and are not his sisters here with us?" And they took offense at him. Then Jesus said to them, "Prophets are not without honor, except in their hometown, and among their own kin, and in their own house." And he could do no deed of power there, except that he laid his hands on a few sick people and cured them. And he was amazed at their unbelief.

Then he went about among the villages teaching. He called the twelve and began to send them out two by two, and gave them authority over the unclean spirits. He ordered them to take nothing for their journey except a staff; no bread, no bag, no money in their belts; but to wear sandals and not to put on two tunics. He said to them, "Wherever you enter a house, stay there until you leave the place. If any place will not welcome you and they refuse to hear you, as you leave, shake off the dust that is on your feet as a testimony against them." So they went out and proclaimed that all should repent. They cast out many demons, and anointed with oil many who were sick and cured them.

King Herod heard of it, for Jesus' name had become known. Some were saying, "John the baptizer has been raised from the dead; and for this reason these powers are at work in him." But others said, "It is Elijah." And others said, "It is a prophet, like one of the prophets of old." But when Herod heard of it, he said, "John, whom I beheaded, has been raised." For Herod himself had sent men who arrested John, bound him, and put him in prison on account of Herodias, his brother Philip's wife, because Herod had married her. For John had been telling Herod, "It is not lawful for you to have your brother's wife." And Herodias had a grudge against him, and wanted to kill him. But she could not, for Herod feared John, knowing that he was a righteous and holy man, and he protected him. When he heard him, he was greatly perplexed; and yet he liked to listen to him. But an opportunity came when Herod on his birthday gave a banquet for his courtiers and officers and for the leaders of Galilee. When his daughter Herodias came in and danced, she pleased Herod and his guests; and the king said to the girl, "Ask me for whatever you wish, and I will give it." And he solemnly swore to her, "Whatever you ask me, I will give you, even half of my kingdom." She went out and said to her mother, "What should I ask for?" She replied, "The head of John the baptizer." Immediately she rushed back to the king and requested, "I want you to give me at once the head of John the Baptist on a platter." The king was deeply grieved; yet out of regard for his oaths and for the guests, he did not want to refuse her. Immediately the king sent a soldier of the guard with orders to bring John's head. He went and beheaded him in the prison, brought his head on a platter, and gave it to the girl. Then the girl gave it to her mother. When his disciples heard about it, they came and took his body, and laid it in a tomb.

The apostles gathered around Jesus, and told him all that they had done and taught. He said to them, "Come away to a deserted place all by yourselves and rest a while." For many were coming and going, and they had no leisure even to eat. And they went away in the boat to a deserted place by themselves. Now many saw them going and recognized them, and they hurried there on foot from all the towns and arrived ahead of them. As he went ashore, he saw a great crowd; and he had compassion for them, because they were like sheep without a shepherd; and he began to teach them many things. When it grew late, his disciples came to him and said, "This is a deserted place, and the hour is now very late; send them away so that they may go into the surrounding country and villages and buy something for themselves to eat." But he answered them, "You give them something to eat." They said to him, "Are we to go and buy two hundred denarii worth of bread, and give it to them to eat?" And he said to them, "How many loaves have you? Go and see." When they had found out, they said, "Five, and two fish." Then he ordered them to get all the people to sit down in groups on the green grass. So they sat down in groups of hundreds and of fifties. Taking the five loaves and the two fish, he looked up to heaven, and blessed and broke the loaves, and gave them to his disciples to set before the people; and he divided the two fish among them all. And all ate and were filled; and they took up twelve baskets full of broken pieces and of the fish. Those who had eaten the loaves numbered five thousand men.

Immediately he made his disciples get into the boat and go on ahead to the other side, to Bethsaida, while he dismissed the crowd. After saying farewell to them, he went up on the mountain to pray. When evening came, the boat was out on the sea, and he was alone on the land. When he saw that they were straining at the oars against an adverse wind, he came towards them early in the morning, walking on the sea. He intended to pass them by. But when they saw him walking on the sea, they thought it was a ghost and cried out; for they all saw him and were terrified. But immediately he spoke to them and said, "Take heart, it is I; do not be afraid." Then he got into the boat with them and the wind ceased. And they were utterly astounded, for they did not understand about the loaves, but their hearts were hardened.

When they had crossed over, they came to land at Gennesaret and moored the boat. When they got out of the boat, people at once recognized him, and rushed about that whole region and began to bring the sick on mats to wherever they heard he was. And wherever he went, into villages or cities or farms, they laid the sick in the marketplaces, and begged him that they might touch even the fringe of his cloak; and all who touched it were healed.

7 Now when the Pharisees and some of the scribes who had come from Jerusalem gathered around him, they noticed that some of his disciples were eating with defiled hands, that is, without washing them. (For the Pharisees, and all the Jews, do not eat unless they thoroughly wash their hands, thus observing the tradition of the elders; and they do not eat anything from the market unless they wash it; and there are also many other traditions that they observe, the washing of cups, pots, and bronze kettles.) So the Pharisees and the scribes asked him, "Why do your disciples not live according to the tradition of the elders, but eat with defiled hands?" He said to them, "Isaiah prophesied rightly about you hypocrites, as it is written, 'This people honors me with their lips, but their hearts are far from me; in vain do they worship me, teaching human precepts as doctrines.' You abandon the commandment of God and hold to human tradition."

Then he said to them, "You have a fine way of rejecting the commandment of God in order to keep your tradition! For Moses said, 'Honor your father and your mother'; and, 'Whoever speaks evil of father or mother must surely die.' But you say that if anyone tells father or mother, 'Whatever support you might have had from me is Corban' (that is, an offering to God)—then you no longer permit doing anything for a father or mother, thus making void the word of God through your tradition that you have handed on. And you do many things like this."

Then he called the crowd again and said to them, "Listen to me, all of you, and understand: there is nothing outside a person that by going in can defile, but the things that come out are what defile." When he had left the crowd and entered the house, his disciples asked him about the parable. He said to them, "Then do you also fail to understand? Do you not see that whatever goes into a person from outside cannot defile, since it enters, not the heart but the stomach, and goes out into the sewer?" (Thus he declared all foods clean.) And he said, "It is what comes out of a person that defiles. For it is from within, from the human heart, that evil intentions come: fornication, theft, murder, adultery, avarice, wickedness, deceit, licentiousness, envy, slander, pride, folly. All these evil things come from within, and they defile a person."

From there he set out and went away to the region of Tyre. He entered a house and did not want anyone to know he was there. Yet he could not escape notice, but a woman whose little daughter had an unclean spirit immediately heard about him, and she came and bowed down at his feet. Now the woman was a Gentile, of Syrophoenician origin. She begged him to cast the demon out of her daughter. He said to her, "Let the children be fed first, for it is not fair to take the children's food and throw it to the dogs." But she answered him, "Sir, even the dogs under the table eat the children's crumbs." Then he said to her, "For saying that, you may go—the demon has left your daughter." So she went home, found the child lying on the bed, and the demon gone. Then he returned from the region of Tyre, and went by way of Sidon towards the Sea of Galilee, in the region of the Decapolis.

They brought to him a deaf man who had an impediment in his speech; and they begged him to lay his hand on him. He took him aside in private, away from the crowd, and put his fingers into his ears, and he spat and touched his tongue. Then looking up to heaven, he sighed and said to him, "Ephphatha," that is, "Be opened." And immediately his ears were opened, his tongue was released, and he spoke plainly. Then Jesus ordered them to tell no one; but the more he ordered them, the more zealously they proclaimed it. They were astounded beyond measure, saying, "He has done everything well; he even makes the deaf to hear and the mute to speak."

8 In those days when there was again a great crowd without anything to eat, he called his disciples and said to them, "I have compassion for the crowd, because they have been with me now for three days and have nothing to eat. If I send them away hungry to their homes, they will faint on the way—and some of them have come from a great distance." His disciples replied, "How can one feed these people with bread here in the desert?" He asked them, "How many loaves do you have?" They said, "Seven." Then he ordered the crowd to sit down on the ground; and he took the seven loaves, and after giving thanks he broke them and gave them to his disciples to distribute; and they distributed them to the crowd. They had also a few small fish; and after blessing them, he ordered that these too should be distributed. They ate and were filled; and they took up the broken pieces left over, seven baskets full. Now there were about four thousand people. And he sent them away.

And immediately he got into the boat with his disciples and went to the district of Dalmanutha. The Pharisees came and began to argue with him, asking him for a sign from heaven, to test him. And he sighed deeply in his spirit and said, "Why does this generation ask for a sign? Truly I tell you, no sign will be given to this generation." And he left them, and getting into the boat again, he went across to the other side. Now the disciples had forgotten to bring any bread; and they had only one loaf with them in the boat. And he cautioned them, saying, "Watch out—beware of the yeast of the Pharisees and the yeast of Herod." They said to one another, "It is because we have no bread." And becoming aware of it, Jesus said to them, "Why are you talking about having no bread? Do you still not perceive or understand? Are your hearts hardened? Do you have eyes, and fail to see? Do you have ears, and fail to hear? And do you not remember? When I broke the five loaves for the five thousand, how many baskets full of broken pieces did you collect?" They said to him, "Twelve." "And the seven for the four thousand, how many baskets full of broken pieces did you collect?" And they said to him, "Seven." Then he said to them, "Do you not yet understand?"

They came to Bethsaida. Some people brought a blind man to him and begged him to touch him. He took the blind man by the hand and led him out of the village; and when he had put saliva on his eyes and laid his hands on him, he asked him, "Can you see anything?" And the man looked up and said, "I can see people, but they look like trees, walking." Then Jesus laid his hands on his eyes again; and he looked intently and his sight was restored, and he saw everything clearly. Then he sent him away to his home, saying, "Do not even go into the village."

Jesus went on with his disciples to the villages of Caesarea Philippi; and on the way he asked his disciples, "Who do people say that I am?" And they answered him, "John the Baptist; and others, Elijah; and still others, one of the prophets." He asked them, "But who do you say that I am?" Peter answered him, "You are the Messiah." And he sternly ordered them not to tell anyone about him.

Then he began to teach them that the Son of Man must undergo great suffering, and be rejected by the elders, the chief priests, and the scribes, and be killed, and after three days rise again. He said all this quite openly. And Peter took him aside and began to rebuke him. But turning and looking at his disciples, he rebuked Peter and said, "Get behind me, Satan! For you are setting your mind not on divine things but on human things."

He called the crowd with his disciples, and said to them, "If any want to become my followers, let them deny themselves and take up their cross and follow me. For those who want to save their life will lose it, and those who lose their life for my sake, and for the sake of the gospel, will save it. For what will it profit them to gain the whole world and forfeit their life? Indeed, what can they give in return for their life? Those who are ashamed of me and of my words in this adulterous and sinful generation, of them the Son of Man will also be ashamed when he comes in the glory of his Father with the holy angels."

9 And he said to them, "Truly I tell you, there are some standing here who will not taste death until they see that the kingdom of God has come with power." Six days later, Jesus took with him Peter and James and John, and led them up a high mountain apart, by themselves. And he was transfigured before them, and his clothes became dazzling white, such as no one on earth could bleach them. And there appeared to them Elijah with Moses, who were talking with Jesus. Then Peter said to Jesus, "Rabbi, it is good for us to be here; let us make three dwellings, one for you, one for Moses, and one for Elijah." He did not know what to say, for they were terrified. Then a cloud overshadowed them, and from the cloud there came a voice, "This is my Son, the Beloved; listen to him!" Suddenly when they looked around, they saw no one with them any more, but only Jesus. As they were coming down the mountain, he ordered them to tell no one about what they had seen, until after the Son of Man had risen from the dead. So they kept the matter to themselves, questioning what this rising from the dead could mean.

Then they asked him, "Why do the scribes say that Elijah must come first?" He said to them, "Elijah is indeed coming first to restore all things. How then is it written about the Son of Man, that he is to go through many sufferings and be treated with contempt? But I tell you that Elijah has come, and they did to him whatever they pleased, as it is written about him."

When they came to the disciples, they saw a great crowd around them, and some scribes arguing with them. When the whole crowd saw him, they were immediately overcome with awe, and they ran forward to greet him. He asked them, "What are you arguing about with them?" Someone from the crowd answered him, "Teacher, I brought you my son; he has a spirit that makes him unable to speak; and whenever it seizes him, it dashes him down; and he foams and grinds his teeth and becomes rigid; and I asked your disciples to cast it out, but they could not do so." He answered them, "You faithless generation, how much longer must I be among you? How much

longer must I put up with you? Bring him to me." And they brought the boy to him. When the spirit saw him, immediately it convulsed the boy, and he fell on the ground and rolled about, foaming at the mouth. Jesus asked the father, "How long has this been happening to him?" And he said, "From childhood. It has often cast him into the fire and into the water, to destroy him; but if you are able to do anything, have pity on us and help us." Jesus said to him, "If you are able!—All things can be done for the one who believes." Immediately the father of the child cried out, "I believe; help my unbelief!" When Jesus saw that a crowd came running together, he rebuked the unclean spirit, saying to it, "You spirit that keeps this boy from speaking and hearing, I command you, come out of him, and never enter him again!" After crying out and convulsing him terribly, it came out, and the boy was like a corpse, so that most of them said, "He is dead." But Jesus took him by the hand and lifted him up, and he was able to stand. When he had entered the house, his disciples asked him privately, "Why could we not cast it out?" He said to them, "This kind can come out only through prayer."

They went on from there and passed through Galilee. He did not want anyone to know it; for he was teaching his disciples, saying to them, "The Son of Man is to be betrayed into human hands, and they will kill him, and three days after being killed, he will rise again." But they did not understand what he was saying and were afraid to ask him.

Then they came to Capernaum; and when he was in the house he asked them, "What were you arguing about on the way?" But they were silent, for on the way they had argued with one another who was the greatest. He sat down, called the twelve, and said to them, "Whoever wants to be first must be last of all and servant of all." Then he took a little child and put it among them; and taking it in his arms, he said to them, "Whoever welcomes one such child in my name welcomes me, and whoever welcomes me welcomes not me but the one who sent me."

John said to him, "Teacher, we saw someone casting out demons in your name, and we tried to stop him, because he was not following us." But Jesus said, "Do not stop him; for no one who does a deed of power in my name will be able soon afterward to speak evil of me. Whoever is not against us is for us. For truly I tell you, whoever gives you a cup of water to drink because you bear the name of Christ will by no means lose the reward.

"If any of you put a stumbling block before one of these little ones who believe in me, it would be better for you if a great millstone were hung around your neck and you were thrown into the sea. If your hand causes you to stumble, cut it off; it is better for you to enter life maimed than to have two hands and to go to hell, to the unquenchable fire. And if your foot causes you to stumble, cut it off; it is better for you to enter life lame than to have two feet and to be thrown into hell. And if your eye causes you to stumble, tear it out; it is better for you to enter the kingdom of God with one eye than to have two eyes and to be thrown into hell, where their worm never dies, and the fire is never quenched. For everyone will be salted with fire. Salt is good; but if salt has lost its saltiness, how can you season it? Have salt in yourselves, and be at peace with one another."

10 He left that place and went to the region of Judea and beyond the Jordan. And crowds again gathered around him; and, as was his custom, he again taught them. Some Pharisees came, and to test him they asked, "Is it lawful for a man to divorce his wife?" He answered them, "What did Moses command you?" They said, "Moses allowed a man to write a certificate of dismissal and to divorce her." But Jesus said to them, "Because of your hardness of heart he wrote this commandment for you. But from the beginning of creation, 'God made them male and female.' 'For this reason a man shall leave his father and mother and be joined to his wife, and the two shall become one flesh.' So they are no longer two, but one flesh. Therefore what God has joined together, let no one separate." Then in the house the disciples asked him again about this matter. He said to them, "Whoever divorces his wife and marries another commits adultery against her; and if she divorces her husband and marries another, she commits adultery."

People were bringing little children to him in order that he might touch them; and the disciples spoke sternly to them. But when Jesus saw this, he was indignant and said to them, "Let the little children come to me; do not stop them; for it is to such as these that the kingdom of God belongs. Truly I tell you, whoever does not receive the kingdom of God as a little child will never enter it." And he took them up in his arms, laid his hands on them, and blessed them.

As he was setting out on a journey, a man ran up and knelt before him, and asked him, "Good Teacher, what must I do to inherit eternal life?" Jesus said to him, "Why do you call me good? No one is good but God alone. You know the commandments: 'You shall not murder; You shall not commit adultery; You shall not steal; You shall not bear false witness; You shall not defraud; Honor your father and mother.'" He said to him, "Teacher, I have kept all these since my youth." Jesus, looking at him, loved him and said, "You lack one thing; go, sell what you own, and give the money to the poor, and you will have treasure in heaven; then come, follow me." When he heard this, he was shocked and went away grieving, for he had many possessions. Then Jesus looked around and said to his disciples, "How hard it will be for those who have wealth to enter the kingdom of God!"

And the disciples were perplexed at these words. But Jesus said to them again, "Children, how hard it is to enter the kingdom of God! It is easier for a camel to go through the eye of a needle than for someone who is rich to enter the kingdom of God." They were greatly astounded and said to one another, "Then who can be saved?" Jesus looked at them and said, "For mortals it is impossible, but not for God; for God all things are possible." Peter began to say to him, "Look, we have left everything and followed you." Jesus said, "Truly I tell you, there is no one who has left house or brothers or sisters or mother or father or children or fields, for my sake and for the sake of the good news, who will not receive a hundredfold now in this age—houses, brothers and sisters, mothers and children, and fields with persecutions—and in the age to come eternal life. But many who are first will be last, and the last will be first."

They were on the road, going up to Jerusalem, and Jesus was walking ahead of them; they were amazed, and those who followed were afraid. He took the twelve aside again and began to tell them what was to happen to him, saying, "See, we are going up to Jerusalem, and the Son of Man will be handed over to the chief priests and the scribes, and they will condemn him to death; then they will hand him over to the Gentiles; they will mock him, and spit upon him, and flog him, and kill him; and after three days he will rise again."

James and John, the sons of Zebedee, came forward to him and said to him, "Teacher, we want you to do for us whatever we ask of you." And he said to them, "What is it you want me to do for you?" And they said to him, "Grant us to sit, one at your right hand and one at your left, in your glory." But Jesus said to them, "You do not know what you are asking. Are you able to drink the cup that I drink, or be baptized with the baptism that I am baptized with?" They replied, "We are able." Then Jesus said to them, "The cup that I drink you will drink; and with the baptism with which I am baptized, you will be baptized; but to sit at my right hand or at my left is not mine to grant, but it is for those for whom it has been prepared." When the ten heard this, they began to be angry with James and John. So Jesus called them and said to them, "You know that among the Gentiles those whom they recognize as their rulers lord it over them, and their great ones are tyrants over them. But it is not so among you; but whoever wishes to become great among you must be your servant, and whoever wishes to be first among you must be slave of all. For the Son of Man came not to be served but to serve, and to give his life a ransom for many."

They came to Jericho. As he and his disciples and a large crowd were leaving Jericho, Bartimaeus son of Timaeus, a blind beggar, was sitting by the roadside. When he heard that it was Jesus of Nazareth, he began to shout out and say, "Jesus, Son of David, have mercy on me!" Many sternly ordered him to be quiet, but he cried out even more loudly, "Son of David, have mercy on me!" Jesus stood still and said, "Call him here." And they called the blind man, saying to him, "Take heart; get up, he is calling you." So throwing off his cloak, he sprang up and came to Jesus. Then Jesus said to him, "What do you want me to do for you?" The blind man said to him, "My teacher, let me see again." Jesus said to him, "Go; your faith has made you well." Immediately he regained his sight and followed him on the way.

11 When they were approaching Jerusalem, at Bethphage and Bethany, near the Mount of Olives, he sent two of his disciples and said to them, "Go into the village ahead of you, and immediately as you enter it, you will find tied there a colt that has never been ridden; untie it and bring it. If anyone says to you, 'Why are you doing this?' just say this, 'The Lord needs it and will send it back here immediately.'" They went away and found a colt tied near a door, outside in the street. As they were untying it, some of the bystanders said to them, "What are you doing, untying the colt?" They told them what Jesus had said; and they allowed them to take it. Then they brought the colt to Jesus and threw their cloaks on it; and he sat on it. Many people spread their cloaks on the road, and others spread leafy branches that they had cut in the fields. Then those who went ahead and those who followed were shouting, "Hosanna! Blessed is the one who comes in the name of the Lord! Blessed is the coming kingdom of our ancestor David! Hosanna in the highest heaven!"

Then he entered Jerusalem and went into the temple; and when he had looked around at everything, as it was already late, he went out to Bethany with the twelve. On the following day, when they came from Bethany, he was hungry. Seeing in the distance a fig tree in leaf, he went to see whether perhaps he would find anything on it. When he came to it, he found nothing but leaves, for it was not the season for figs. He said to it, "May no one ever eat fruit from you again." And his disciples heard it.

Then they came to Jerusalem. And he entered the temple and began to drive out those who were selling and those who were buying in the temple, and he overturned the tables of the money changers and the seats of those who sold doves; and he would not allow anyone to carry anything through the temple. He was teaching and saying, "Is it not written, 'My house shall be called a house of prayer for all the nations'? But you have made it a den of robbers." And when the chief priests and the scribes heard it, they kept looking for a way to kill him; for they were afraid of him, because the whole crowd was spellbound by his teaching.

And when evening came, Jesus and his disciples went out of the city. In the morning as they passed by, they saw the fig tree withered away to its roots. Then Peter remembered and said to him, "Rabbi, look! The fig tree that you cursed has withered." Jesus answered them, "Have faith in God. Truly I tell you, if you say to this mountain, 'Be taken up and thrown into the sea,' and if you do not doubt in your heart, but believe that what you say will come to pass, it will be done for you. So I tell you, whatever you ask for in prayer, believe that you have received it, and it will be yours. Whenever you stand praying, forgive, if you have anything against anyone; so that your Father in heaven may also forgive you your trespasses." Again they came to Jerusalem.

As he was walking in the temple, the chief priests, the scribes, and the elders came to him and said, "By what authority are you doing these things? Who gave you this authority to do them?" Jesus said to them, "I will ask you one question; answer me, and I will tell you by what authority I do these things. Did the baptism of John come from heaven, or was it of human origin? Answer me." They argued with one another, "If we say, 'From heaven,' he will say, 'Why then did you not believe him?' But shall we say, 'Of human origin'?"—they were afraid of the crowd, for all regarded John as truly a prophet. So they answered Jesus, "We do not know." And Jesus said to them, "Neither will I tell you by what authority I am doing these things."

12 Then he began to speak to them in parables. "A man planted a vineyard, put a fence around it, dug a pit for the wine press, and built a watchtower; then he leased it to tenants and went to another country. When the season came, he sent a slave to the tenants to collect from them his share of the produce of the vineyard. But they seized him, and beat him, and sent him away empty-handed. And again he sent another slave to them; this one they beat over the head and insulted. Then he sent another, and that one they killed. And so it was with many others; some they beat, and others they killed. He had still one other, a beloved son. Finally he sent him to them, saying, 'They will respect my son.' But those tenants said to one another, 'This is the heir; come, let us kill him, and the inheritance will be ours.' So they seized him, killed him, and threw him out of the vineyard. What then will the owner of the vineyard do? He will come and destroy the tenants and give the vineyard to others. Have you not read this scripture: 'The stone that the builders rejected has become the cornerstone; this was the Lord's doing, and it is amazing in our eyes'?"

When they realized that he had told this parable against them, they wanted to arrest him, but they feared the crowd. So they left him and went away. Then they sent to him some Pharisees and some Herodians to trap him in what he said. And they came and said to him, "Teacher, we know that you are sincere, and show deference to no one; for you do not regard people with partiality, but teach the way of God in accordance with truth. Is it lawful to pay taxes to the emperor, or not? Should we pay them, or should we not?" But knowing their hypocrisy, he said to them, "Why are you putting me to the test? Bring me a denarius and let me see it." And they brought one. Then he said to them, "Whose head is this, and whose title?" They answered, "The emperor's." Jesus said to them, "Give to the emperor the things that are the emperor's, and to God the things that are God's." And they were utterly amazed at him.

Some Sadducees, who say there is no resurrection, came to him and asked him a question, saying, "Teacher, Moses wrote for us that 'if a man's brother dies, leaving a wife but no child, the man shall marry the widow and raise up children for his brother.' There were seven brothers; the first married and, when he died, left no children; and the second married her and died, leaving no children; and the third likewise; none of the seven left children. Last of all the woman herself died. In the resurrection whose wife will she be? For the seven had married her." Jesus said to them, "Is not this the reason you are wrong, that you know neither the scriptures nor the power of God? For when they rise from the dead, they neither marry nor are given in marriage, but are like angels in heaven. And as for the dead being raised, have you not read in the book of Moses, in the story about the bush, how God said to him, 'I am the God of Abraham, the God of Isaac, and the God of Jacob'? He is God not of the dead, but of the living; you are quite wrong."

One of the scribes came near and heard them disputing with one another, and seeing that he answered them well, he asked him, "Which commandment is the first of all?" Jesus answered, "The first is, 'Hear, O Israel: the Lord our God, the Lord is one; you shall love the Lord your God with all your heart, and with all your soul, and with all your mind, and with all your strength.' The second is this, 'You shall love your neighbor as yourself.' There is no other commandment greater than these." Then the scribe said to him, "You are right, Teacher; you have truly said that 'he is one, and besides him there is no other'; and 'to love him with all the heart, and with all the understanding, and with all the strength,' and 'to love one's neighbor as oneself,'—this is much more important than all whole burnt offerings and sacrifices." When Jesus saw that he answered wisely, he said to him, "You are not far from the kingdom of God." After that no one dared to ask him any question.

While Jesus was teaching in the temple, he said, "How can the scribes say that the Messiah is the son of David? David himself, by the Holy Spirit, declared, 'The Lord said to my Lord, "Sit at my right hand, until I put your enemies under your feet."' David himself calls him Lord; so how can he be his son?" And the large crowd was listening to him with delight.

As he taught, he said, "Beware of the scribes, who like to walk around in long robes, and to be greeted with respect in the marketplaces, and to have the best seats in the synagogues and places of honor at banquets! They devour widows' houses and for the sake of appearance say long prayers. They will receive the greater condemnation." He sat down opposite the treasury, and watched the crowd putting money into the treasury. Many rich people put in large sums. A poor widow came and put in two small copper coins, which are worth a penny. Then he called his disciples and said to them, "Truly I tell you, this poor widow has put in more than all those who are contributing to the treasury. For all of them have contributed out of their abundance; but she out of her poverty has put in everything she had, all she had to live on."

13 As he came out of the temple, one of his disciples said to him, "Look, Teacher, what large stones and what large buildings!" Then Jesus asked him, "Do you see these great buildings? Not one stone will be left here upon another; all will be thrown down." When he was sitting on the Mount of Olives opposite the temple, Peter, James, John, and Andrew asked him privately, "Tell us, when will this be, and what will be the sign that all these things are about to be accomplished?" Then Jesus began to say to them, "Beware that no one leads you astray. Many will come in my name and say, 'I am he!' and they will lead many astray. When you hear of wars and rumors of wars, do not be alarmed; this must take place, but the end is still to come. For nation will rise against nation, and kingdom against kingdom; there will be earthquakes in various places; there will be famines. This is but the beginning of the birth pangs.

"As for yourselves, beware; for they will hand you over to councils; and you will be beaten in synagogues; and you will stand before governors and kings because of me, as a testimony to them. And the good news must first be proclaimed to all nations. When they bring you to trial and hand you over, do not worry beforehand about what you are to say; but say whatever is given you at that time, for it is not you who speak, but the Holy Spirit. Brother will betray brother to death, and a father his child, and children will rise against parents and have them put to death; and you will be hated by all because of my name. But the one who endures to the end will be saved.

"But when you see the desolating sacrilege set up where it ought not to be (let the reader understand), then those in Judea must flee to the mountains; the one on the housetop must not go down or enter the house to take anything away; the one in the field must not turn back to get a coat. Woe to those who are pregnant and to those who are nursing infants in those days! Pray that it may not be in winter. For in those days there will be suffering, such as has not been from the beginning of the creation that God created until now, no, and never will be. And if the Lord had not cut short those days, no one would be saved; but for the sake of the elect, whom he chose, he has cut short those days.

"And if anyone says to you at that time, 'Look! Here is the Messiah!' or 'Look! There he is!'—do not believe it. False messiahs and false prophets will appear and produce signs and omens, to lead astray, if possible, the elect. But be alert; I have already told you everything. But in those days, after that suffering, the sun will be darkened, and the moon will not give its light, and the stars will be falling from heaven, and the powers in the heavens will be shaken. Then they will see 'the Son of Man coming in clouds' with great power and glory. Then he will send out the angels, and gather his elect from the four winds, from the ends of the earth to the ends of heaven.

"From the fig tree learn its lesson: as soon as its branch becomes tender and puts forth its leaves, you know that summer is near. So also, when you see these things taking place, you know that he is near, at the very gates. Truly I tell you, this generation will not pass away until all these things have taken place. Heaven and earth will pass away, but my words will not pass away.

"But about that day or hour no one knows, neither the angels in heaven, nor the Son, but only the Father. Beware, keep alert; for you do not know when the time will come. It is like a man going on a journey, when he leaves home and puts his slaves in charge, each with his work, and commands the doorkeeper to be on the watch. Therefore, keep awake—for you do not know when the master of the house will come, in the evening, or at midnight, or at cockcrow, or at dawn, or else he may find you asleep when he comes suddenly. And what I say to you I say to all: Keep awake."

14 It was two days before the Passover and the festival of Unleavened Bread. The chief priests and the scribes were looking for a way to arrest Jesus by stealth and kill him; for they said, "Not during the festival, or there may be a riot among the people."

While he was at Bethany in the house of Simon the leper, as he sat at the table, a woman came with an alabaster jar of very costly ointment of nard, and she broke open the jar and poured the ointment on his head. But some were there who said to one another in anger, "Why was the ointment wasted in this way? For this ointment could have been sold for more than three hundred denarii, and the money given to the poor." And they scolded her. But Jesus said, "Let her alone; why do you trouble her? She has performed a good service for me. For you always have the poor with you, and you can show kindness to them whenever you wish; but you will not always have me. She has done what she could; she has anointed my body beforehand for its burial. Truly I tell you, wherever the good news is proclaimed in the whole world, what she has done will be told in remembrance of her."

Then Judas Iscariot, who was one of the twelve, went to the chief priests in order to betray him to them. When they heard it, they were greatly pleased, and promised to give him money. So he began to look for an opportunity to betray him.

On the first day of Unleavened Bread, when the Passover lamb is sacrificed, his disciples said to him, "Where do you want us to go and make the preparations for you to eat the Passover?" So he sent two of his disciples, saying to them, "Go into the city, and a man carrying a jar of water will meet you; follow him, and wherever he enters, say to the owner of the house, 'The Teacher asks, Where is my guest room where I may eat the Passover with my disciples?' He will show you a large room upstairs, furnished and ready. Make preparations for us there." So the disciples set out and went to the city, and found everything as he had told them; and they prepared the Passover meal.

When it was evening, he came with the twelve. And when they had taken their places and were eating, Jesus said, "Truly I tell you, one of you will betray me, one who is eating with me." They began to be distressed and to say to him one after another, "Surely, not I?" He said to them, "It is one of the twelve, one who is dipping bread into the bowl with me. For the Son of Man goes as it is written of him, but woe to that one by whom the Son of Man is betrayed! It would have been better for that one not to have been born."

While they were eating, he took a loaf of bread, and after blessing it he broke it, gave it to them, and said, "Take; this is my body." Then he took a cup, and after giving thanks he gave it to them, and all of them drank from it. He said to them, "This is my blood of the covenant, which is poured out for many. Truly I tell you, I will never again drink of the fruit of the vine until that day when I drink it new in the kingdom of God." When they had sung the hymn, they went out to the Mount of Olives.

And Jesus said to them, "You will all become deserters; for it is written, 'I will strike the shepherd, and the sheep will be scattered.' But after I am raised up, I will go before you to Galilee." Peter said to him, "Even though all become deserters, I will not." Jesus said to him, "Truly I tell you, this day, this very night, before the cock crows twice, you will deny me three times." But he said vehemently, "Even though I must die with you, I will not deny you." And all of them said the same.

They went to a place called Gethsemane; and he said to his disciples, "Sit here while I pray." He took with him Peter and James and John, and began to be distressed and agitated. And he said to them, "I am deeply grieved, even to death; remain here, and keep awake." And going a little farther, he threw himself on the ground and prayed that, if it were possible, the hour might pass from him. He said, "Abba, Father, for you all things are possible; remove this cup from me; yet, not what I want, but what you want." He came and found them sleeping; and he said to Peter, "Simon, are you asleep? Could you not keep awake one hour? Keep awake and pray that you may not come into the time of trial; the spirit indeed is willing, but the flesh is weak." And again he went away and prayed, saying the same words. And once more he came and found them sleeping, for their eyes were very heavy; and they did not know what to say to him. He came a third time and said to them, "Are you still sleeping and taking your rest? Enough! The hour has come; the Son of Man is betrayed into the hands of sinners. Get up, let us be going. See, my betrayer is at hand."

Immediately, while he was still speaking, Judas, one of the twelve, arrived; and with him there was a crowd with swords and clubs, from the chief priests, the scribes, and the elders. Now the betrayer had given them a sign, saying, "The one I will kiss is the man; arrest him and lead him away under guard." So when he came, he went up to him at once and said, "Rabbi!" and kissed him. Then they laid hands on him and arrested him. But one of those who stood near drew his sword and struck the slave of the high priest, cutting off his ear. Then Jesus said to them, "Have you come out with swords and clubs to arrest me as though I were a bandit? Day after day I was with you in the temple teaching, and you did not arrest me. But let the scriptures be fulfilled." All of them deserted him and fled. A certain young man was following him, wearing nothing but a linen cloth. They caught hold of him, but he left the linen cloth and ran off naked.

They took Jesus to the high priest; and all the chief priests, the elders, and the scribes were assembled. Peter had followed him at a distance, right into the courtyard of the high priest; and he was sitting with the guards, warming himself at the fire. Now the chief priests and the whole council were looking for testimony against Jesus to put him to death; but they found none. For many gave false testimony against him, and their testimony did not agree. Some stood up and gave false testimony against him, saying, "We heard him say, 'I will destroy this temple that is made with hands, and in three days I will build another, not made with hands.'" But even on this point their testimony did not agree. Then the high priest stood up before them and asked Jesus, "Have you no answer? What is it that they testify against you?" But he was silent and did not answer. Again the high priest asked him, "Are you the Messiah, the Son of the Blessed One?" Jesus said, "I am; and you will see 'the Son of Man seated at the right hand of the Power,' and 'coming with the clouds of heaven.'" Then the high priest tore his clothes and said, "Why do we still need witnesses? You have heard his blasphemy! What is your decision?" All of them condemned him as deserving death. Some began to spit on him, to blindfold him, and to strike him, saying to him, "Prophesy!" The guards also took him over and beat him.

While Peter was below in the courtyard, one of the servant-girls of the high priest came by. When she saw Peter warming himself, she stared at him and said, "You also were with Jesus, the man from Nazareth." But he denied it, saying, "I do not know or understand what you are talking about." And he went out into the forecourt. Then the cock crowed. And the servant-girl, on seeing him, began again to say to the bystanders, "This man is one of them." But again he denied it. Then after a little while the bystanders again said to Peter, "Certainly you are one of them; for you are a Galilean." But he began to curse, and he swore an oath, "I do not know this man you are talking about." At that moment the cock crowed for the second time. Then Peter remembered that Jesus had said to him, "Before the cock crows twice, you will deny me three times." And he broke down and wept.

15 As soon as it was morning, the chief priests held a consultation with the elders and scribes and the whole council. They bound Jesus, led him away, and handed him over to Pilate. Pilate asked him, "Are you the King of the Jews?" He answered him, "You say so." Then the chief priests accused him of many things. Pilate asked him again, "Have you no answer? See how many charges they bring against you." But Jesus made no further reply, so that Pilate was amazed.

Now at the festival he used to release a prisoner for them, anyone for whom they asked. Now a man called Barabbas was in prison with the rebels who had committed murder during the insurrection. So the crowd came and began to ask Pilate to do for them according to his custom. Then he answered them, "Do you want me to release for you the King of the Jews?" For he realized that it was out of jealousy that the chief priests had handed him over. But the chief priests stirred up the crowd to have him release Barabbas for them instead. Pilate spoke to them again, "Then what do you wish me to do with the man you call the King of the Jews?" They shouted

back, "Crucify him!" Pilate asked them, "Why, what evil has he done?" But they shouted all the more, "Crucify him!" So Pilate, wishing to satisfy the crowd, released Barabbas for them; and after flogging Jesus, he handed him over to be crucified.

Then the soldiers led him into the courtyard of the palace (that is, the governor's headquarters); and they called together the whole cohort. And they clothed him in a purple cloak; and after twisting some thorns into a crown, they put it on him. And they began saluting him, "Hail, King of the Jews!" They struck his head with a reed, spat upon him, and knelt down in homage to him. After mocking him, they stripped him of the purple cloak and put his own clothes on him. Then they led him out to crucify him. They compelled a passer-by, who was coming in from the country, to carry his cross; it was Simon of Cyrene, the father of Alexander and Rufus.

Then they brought Jesus to the place called Golgotha (which means the place of a skull). And they offered him wine mixed with myrrh; but he did not take it. And they crucified him, and divided his clothes among them, casting lots to decide what each should take. It was nine o'clock in the morning when they crucified him. The inscription of the charge against him read, "The King of the Jews." And with him they crucified two bandits, one on his right and one on his left. Those who passed by derided him, shaking their heads and saying, "Aha! You who would destroy the temple and build it in three days, save yourself, and come down from the cross!" In the same way the chief priests, along with the scribes, were also mocking him among themselves and saying, "He saved others; he cannot save himself. Let the Messiah, the King of Israel, come down from the cross now, so that we may see and believe." Those who were crucified with him also taunted him.

When it was noon, darkness came over the whole land until three in the afternoon. At three o'clock Jesus cried out with a loud voice, "Eloi, Eloi, lema sabachthani?" which means, "My God, my God, why have you forsaken me?" When some of the bystanders heard it, they said, "Listen, he is calling for Elijah." And someone ran, filled a sponge with sour wine, put it on a stick, and gave it to him to drink, saying, "Wait, let us see whether Elijah will come to take him down." Then Jesus gave a loud cry and breathed his last. And the curtain of the temple was torn in two, from top to bottom. Now when the centurion, who stood facing him, saw that in this way he breathed his last, he said, "Truly this man was God's Son!"

There were also women looking on from a distance; among them were Mary Magdalene, and Mary the mother of James the younger and of Joses, and Salome. These used to follow him and provided for him when he was in Galilee; and there were many other women who had come up with him to Jerusalem.

When evening had come, and since it was the day of Preparation, that is, the day before the Sabbath, Joseph of Arimathea, a respected member of the council, who was also himself waiting expectantly for the kingdom of God, went boldly to Pilate and asked for the body of Jesus. Then Pilate wondered if he were already dead; and summoning the centurion, he asked him whether he had been dead for some time. When he learned from the centurion that he was dead, he granted the body to Joseph. Then Joseph bought a linen cloth, and taking down the body, wrapped it in the linen cloth, and laid it in a tomb that had been hewn out of the rock. He then rolled a stone against the door of the tomb. Mary Magdalene and Mary the mother of Joses saw where the body was laid.

16 When the Sabbath was over, Mary Magdalene, and Mary the mother of James, and Salome bought spices, so that they might go and anoint him. And very early on the first day of the week, when the sun had risen, they went to the tomb. They had been saying to one another, "Who will roll away the stone for us from the entrance to the tomb?" When they looked up, they saw that the stone, which was very large, had already been rolled back. As they entered the tomb, they saw a young man, dressed in a white robe, sitting on the right side; and they were alarmed. But he said to them, "Do not be alarmed; you are looking for Jesus of Nazareth, who was crucified. He has been raised; he is not here. Look, there is the place they laid him. But go, tell his disciples and Peter that he is going ahead of you to Galilee; there you will see him, just as he told you." So they went out and fled from the tomb, for terror and amazement had seized them; and they said nothing to anyone, for they were afraid.

The Shorter Ending of Mark

And all that had been commanded them they told briefly to those around Peter. And afterward Jesus himself sent out through them, from east to west, the sacred and imperishable proclamation of eternal salvation.

The Longer Ending of Mark

Now after he rose early on the first day of the week, he appeared first to Mary Magdalene, from whom he had cast out seven demons. She went out and told those who had been with him, while they were mourning and weeping. But when they heard that he was alive and had been seen by her, they would not believe it. After this he appeared in another form to two of them, as they were walking into the country. And they went back and told the rest, but they did not believe them. Later he appeared to the eleven themselves as they were sitting at the table; and he upbraided them for their lack of faith and stubbornness, because they had not believed those who saw him after he had risen. And he said to them, "Go into all the world and proclaim the good news to the whole creation. The one who believes and is baptized will be saved; but the one who does not believe will be condemned. And these signs will accompany those who believe: by using my name they will cast out demons; they will speak in new tongues; they will pick up snakes in their hands, and if they drink any deadly thing, it will not hurt them; they will lay their hands on the sick, and they will recover."

So then the Lord Jesus, after he had spoken to them, was taken up into heaven and sat down at the right hand of God. And they went out and proclaimed the good news everywhere, while the Lord worked with them and confirmed the message by the signs that accompanied it.

Conclusions

The first century saw several major changes within what we have broadly called Judaic religion. The war against Rome, and the consequent destruction of the temple in Jerusalem, led to the demise of the Sadducees—the group aligned with Rome and the temple—and the ascendancy of the Pharisees. In addition, a new movement arose in which a self-proclaimed messiah had risen from the dead, according to his followers. This movement included Gentiles, and it seemed to abandon observance of Jewish traditions. Members of the movement also reinterpreted the scriptures and identified this messiah as a suffering servant rather than a kingly figure. They even redefined traditional ideas about resurrection.

The concept of resurrection—the bodily rising from the dead—was a relatively late development in Jewish theology. Even the New Testament reveals on-going debate within first-century Jews over resurrection, with Pharisees believing in it and Sadducees denying it. Those who did accept the idea of resurrection believed that the people of Israel would be raised all at once, corporately, and not singly. Ezekiel 37 suggests this scenario, when the prophet preaches to a field of dry bones, and they begin to take shape, to reknit themselves, become muscled and covered with skin, and lie there as human beings. It takes the breath of God to fully animate them, but that breath repopulates an entire nation. When Jesus' followers claimed that he alone rose from the dead—bodily, that is, not as a disembodied spirit or ghost—Jewish listeners were skeptical. Jesus' disciples, however, thought that his resurrection signaled the beginning of a general resurrection of all believers in the near future. This expectation is clear in Paul's letter to the Thessalonians, who were concerned about those who had died before the general resurrection occurred.

In addition to reinterpreting theological concepts, like resurrection, and Jewish scripture to explain their messiah, Christians redefined Jewish festivals and holy days. Because Jesus had died during the Jewish festival of Passover, members of the early church observed the events of that "holy week" each year during Passover. Indeed, the Gospels' account of Jesus' last week on earth may well have come from ancient liturgies in which Christians recalled the saving events of their savior's life, death, and resurrection. Another Jewish holy day that Christians adapted was that of Pentecost, which occurs fifty days after Passover. In Judaism, Pentecost celebrates the giving of Torah by God to the Israelites and their descendants, the Jews. It is a day of thanksgiving for the gift of the law and the covenant. In Christianity, Pentecost celebrates the gift of the Holy Spirit to the disciples. Observed fifty days after Easter, it recognizes the "birthday" of the church, since the disciples begin a missionary movement after their experience of the Holy Spirit.

The less Christianity drew from its Jewish roots in the thoroughly Hebrew persons of Jesus and Paul, the more antagonistic Christians became toward Jews. Later Christian writings magnify and enlarge the conflicts between Jesus and Jewish religious authorities depicted in the Gospels. Part of the quarrel is rhetorical, that is, exaggerated to persuade readers that Christianity is the true heir to biblical prophecies. Part of the quarrel reflects competition between Christians and Jews for members of church and synagogue. A number of people—should we call them Christians? Jews?—were observing the Sabbath in synagogue and also celebrating the Lord's Day in church. In other words, later texts amplify the level of actual discord.

This disconnect between Christianity and Judaism led, in part, to the development of Christian anti-Judaism over the ages, and even Christian anti-Semitism, which was a form of racial and ethnic discrimination. For these reasons, Christians in the twentieth century attempted to recover Jesus' Jewish roots, especially in light of Christian responsibility for the Holocaust during World War II. One scholar, Willis Barnstone, has translated the Gospels and the book of Revelation in a way that retains the Hebrew names and words that would have been used in Jesus' day. Thus, Jesus is Yeshua; John the Baptist is Yohanan the Dipper; and Natzaret, Galil, and Yarden are Nazareth, Galilee, and Jordan, respectively. Barnstone explains in his introduction that he wanted to frame the Jewish identity of the main figure of the covenant, Jesus, and his family and followers. "The disappearance of Yeshua's Jewish identity dumbfounds common sense and history," he writes, "but alas, this illusion has remained dominantly at the center of Christian reception of the New Covenant."

To dispel the illusion, this chapter concludes with the first nineteen verses of Mark in Barnstone's translation. It is an appropriate reminder of the Jewish sources of Christian theology; it is also a significant point of departure, however, because Christianity begins to move away from its Jewish origins and toward a predominantly Gentile worldview.

Mark 1:1–19

1 The beginning of the Gospel of Yeshua the mashiah, son of God.

2 As it is written in Yeshayah the prophet:

> Look, I send my messenger ahead of you,
>   and he will prepare your road;
> 3 a voice of one crying out in the desert:
>   "Prepare the way of Adonai and make
>   his paths straight."

4 Yohanan the Dipper appeared in the desert, preaching an immersion of repentance for the remission of sin. 5 The whole land of Yehuda and all the people of Yerushalayim came out to him and were being immersed by him in the Yarden river and confessing their sins. 6 Clothed in camel hair, Yohanan wore a belt of hide around his waist, and he ate locusts and wild honey. 7 He preached, saying,

> After me will come one more powerful
>   than I am of whom I am not fit to
>   stoop down and untie the strap of his
>   sandals.

8 I immersed you in water, but he will
    immerse you in holy spirit.

9 And it happened in those days that Yeshua came from Natzeret in the Galil and was immersed in the Yarden by Yohanan. 10 And as soon as he came out of the water, he saw the skies torn open and the spirit like a dove descending on him. 11 And there came a voice out of the skies:

> You are my son whom I love.
> With you I am well pleased.

12 And at once the spirit drove him out into the desert. 13 He was in the desert forty days, tested by Satan, and he was among the wild beasts, and the angels attended him.

14 After Yohanan was arrested, Yeshua came into the Galil preaching the gospel of God, 15 and saying,

> The hour is fulfilled and the kingdom of
>   God is near.

Repent and believe in the good news

16 And as Yeshua went by the Sea of the Galil, he saw Shimon and his brother Andreas casting nets into the sea, for they were fishermen, 17 and Yeshua said to them,

> Come follow me, and I will make you
> fishers of people.

18 And at once they dropped their nets and followed him.

19 And going on a little farther he saw Yaakov the son of Zavdai and his brother Yohanan in their boat mending their nets. 20 And at once he called them, and leaving their father Zavdai in the boat with the hired hands, they followed him.

Sources for Selections

Barnstone, Willis. *The New Covenant, Commonly Called the New Testament.* Vol. I. New York: Riverhead Books, 2002.

The Holy Bible. New Revised Standard Version. New York: Oxford University Press, 1989.

Additional Resources

Aland, Kurt, ed. *Synopsis of the Four Gospels.* English edition. n.c.: United Bible Society, 1982.

Borg, Marcus. *Reading the Bible Again for the First Time.* San Francisco: HarperSanFrancisco, 2002.

Brown, Raymond E. *The Gospel According to John.* 2 vols. New York: Doubleday, 1966–70.

Crossan, John Dominic. *Jesus: A Revolutionary Biography.* San Francisco: HarperSanFrancisco, 1994.

Funk, Robert, W., Roy W. Hoover, and the Jesus Seminar. *The Five Gospels.* New York: Macmillan, 1993.

Ignatius of Antioch. *Letter to the Romans.* In *Early Christian Fathers.* Trans. Cyril C. Richardson. New York: Macmillan, 1970.

Neusner, Jacob. *First Century Judaism in Crisis: Yohanan ben Zakkai and the Renaissance of Torah.* Nashville, Tenn.: Abingdon, 1975.

Segal, Alan F. *Paul the Convert: The Apostolate and Apostasy of Saul the Pharisee.* New Haven, Conn.: Yale University Press, 1990.

———. *Rebecca's Children: Judaism and Christianity in the Roman World.* Cambridge, Mass.: Harvard University Press, 1986.

Films

The Gospel According to St. Matthew. Directed by Pier Paolo Pasolini, 1964.

The Greatest Story Ever Told. Directed by George Stevens, 1965.

Jesus Christ, Superstar. Directed by Norman Jewison, 1973.

Jesus of Montreal. Directed by Denys Arcand, 1990.

Jesus of Nazareth. Directed by Franco Zeffirelli, 1976.

The Last Temptation of Christ. Directed by Martin Scorsese, 1988.

The Passion of the Christ. Directed by Mel Gibson, 2004.

The Prince of Egypt. Directed by Brenda Chapman, Steve Hickner, and Simon Wells, 1998.

The Ten Commandments. Directed by Cecil B. De Mille, 1956.

	c. 4 B.C.E. → Jesus of Nazareth born
Jesus executed by Romans ○—	**c. 30 C.E.**
	c. 64 → Execution of Peter and Paul in Rome
First Jewish War begins ○—	**66**
	70 → Second temple in Jerusalem destroyed by Romans
First Jewish War ends with fall of fortress at Masada ○—	**73**
	c. 95 → Persecution of Christians by Emperor Domitian (r. 81–96)
Martyrdom of Ignatius, Bishop of Antioch ○—	**c. 107**
	c.165 → Martyrdom of Justin Martyr, early Christian apologist
Martyrdom of Perpetua and Felicity ○—	**c. 203**
	c. 225 → Death of Tertullian, North African theologian who coined term "Trinity"
Persecution of Christians by Emperor Decius (r. 249–251) ○—	**c. 250–51**
	c. 251–52 → Cyprian, Bishop of Carthage, oversees readmittance of "lapsed" Christians into church after Decian persecution
Death of Origen, Egyptian theologian, after tortures in Decian persecution ○—	**c. 254**
	303–4 → Persecution of Christians by Emperor Diocletian (r. 284–305)
Constantine's dream and victory at Milvian Bridge ○—	**312**
	313 → Edict of Milan, which makes Christianity legal in Roman Empire
Council of Nicea ○—	**325**
	330 → Constantine moves capital of Empire to Constantinople
Council of Constantinople ○—	**381**
	431 → Council of Ephesus
Council of Chalcedon ○—	**451**
	410 → Sack of Rome by Visigoths
Last western emperor deposed ○—	**476**

CHAPTER TWO

The Early Church
DIVERSITY, DIVISION, AND DOMINION

The central figure of Christianity, Jesus of Nazareth, was a martyr, executed by Roman authorities who considered him a threat to the Roman Empire. By the end of the first century, many of Jesus' followers had also been martyred, and still more would face torturous executions in the future. Within three hundred years, however, Christianity moved from the margins of the empire to the centers of power. By 410 C.E., when Rome fell to invaders from northern Europe, the Christian Church in the western empire was the strongest, wealthiest, and best organized political institution left standing. In Constantinople to the east, a Greek-speaking church dominated political, cultural, and intellectual life for centuries, even after the conquest by Muslim forces.

The journey from the church of the martyrs to the church of the empire saw internal as well as external struggles. As missionaries from Judea traveled east to Syria, south to Arabia, west to Ethiopia and Egypt, and north to Turkey and into Europe, different local practices and beliefs developed. Questions arose as a result: When should Easter be celebrated? What kind of bread should be used in communion? What writings were sacred? And, most importantly, who, exactly, was Jesus the Christ, and what, exactly, had he done to save humanity? Conflicts grew out of different cultures and mores. The eastern church spoke Greek; the western church, Latin. Sacred texts in Coptic did not spread outside of their origin in Egypt. Some communities in the east held the book of Revelation in great esteem; those in the Roman west considered it an incendiary anti-imperial tract.

Thus, in the first five centuries of Christianity, numerous theological and practical issues were resolved, either by force, by fiat, or by church council. In subsequent centuries, Christians would ask new questions, and new conflicts would surface. By the end of the fifth century, however, a normative, or orthodox, Christianity emerged that confessed belief in a divine Son of God, both fully human and fully divine, who was a coequal member of a trinitarian deity.

Church of the Martyrs

The earliest Christians understood themselves within a Jewish context. They were Jews who believed that Jesus was the anointed one prophesied in the scriptures. As the Jesus Movement spread around the Mediterranean basin, however, more Gentiles than Jews proclaimed that "Jesus is Lord." When Gentiles assumed the leadership of local churches, Christianity began to abandon its Jewish roots. The First Jewish War (66–73 C.E.) also contributed to this separation by encouraging Christians to disavow their ties to the rebellious Jews in Judea. Other forces were at work as well, including clashes between Christians and Roman authorities over civic and religious observances.

The first martyrdom after that of Jesus recorded in the New Testament—the death of Stephen, an apostle in the early church—occurs at the hands of a group of Jews angered at his condemnation of them. Paul's letters describe his own experiences of torture, imprisonment, and flight. As early as the 60s, Christians began to come into conflict with Roman authorities. At that time, the emperor Nero blamed Christians for burning the city of Rome, a fire to which he undoubtedly contributed. Later Christian tradition states that Peter and Paul died during the persecution by Nero.

The word *martyr* itself means "witness" in Greek. Though today we may assume that the most righteous believer would die rather than abandon God, the deed was uncommon in the ancient world. One of the earliest accounts of martyrdom appears in the second book of the Maccabees in the Catholic and Orthodox Old Testament. During a Jewish rebellion against a corrupt Jewish priesthood, a mother and her seven sons are brought before the king and asked to renounce their faith (2 Maccabees 7). The first son is tortured horribly but dies in his faith. Each son is tortured in turn, with the mother encouraging each to remain faithful. Finally, she herself is killed. This kind of faithfulness was unheard-of in the ancient world, where deities were plentiful, and no one's lord required absolute fidelity. A laissez-faire attitude prevailed in which many religions existed and were tolerated.

The one thing that was intolerable, however, was refusal to pay homage to the "genius" of the Roman emperor. Most emperors claimed to be divine and commissioned narratives to be composed that detailed miraculous births and infancies. Making a sacrifice to the emperor's genius (his divine spirit) was really a patriotic, rather than religious, duty, rather like reciting the Pledge of Allegiance to the flag today. But early Christians viewed this as sacrificing to a pagan idol, and for them, the time of sacrifices and idol worship was over. If only a few people had resisted, it would not have been a problem; but as the number, and influence, of Christians grew, authorities faced the prospect of widespread resistance to Roman rule—an intolerable situation.

Jews had long been exempt from certain civic duties under Roman rule, because these duties always had religious implications. Thus, Jewish citizens did not have to enter the military or serve in public office, although they could if they liked; they also did not have to pay certain taxes that supported pagan civic functions. Government officials respected anything old, and Jews had an ancient pedigree that legitimated exemption from ordinary duties. Many Roman citizens even attended Jewish sabbath services and observed Jewish law. Those attendees were called "God-fearers"; males who also were circumcised were called "proselytes" and, according to rabbinic tradition, were considered fully and completely Jewish. Christian missionaries recruited among the God-fearers with some success, although they had the greatest impact on pagans, that is, Gentiles or non-Jews. As long as Christianity was seen as part of Judaism, Christians too could skip the most onerous public tasks. But when Christianity pulled away from Judaism, it lost its protection and was seen as something new, and worse, something unpatriotic. The refusal to perform sacrifices—a small but defiant "no" to anything that appeared to be idolatry—had major consequences. Christians were executed by facing fire, wild animals, or gladiators in huge arenas. This was a form of public entertainment, as well as political propaganda, that communicated a clear message about the danger of disloyalty to empire.

Persecution was far from systematic or organized, however, in the first two and a half centuries of Christianity. Instead, episodes occurred sporadically across the empire—sometimes in the east in Turkey, sometimes in the west in France, sometimes in the south in North Africa. Correspondence between Pliny the Younger, the governor of Pontus and Bithynia (111–113), and the emperor Trajan indicates an unwillingness to seek out Christians, but an equal unwillingness to let them off the hook once they came to the attention of authorities. It was only under the reigns of the emperors Decius (249–251) and Diocletian (284–305) that anti-Christian sentiment became widespread, full-blown, and well organized. Even then, Christians could avoid making actual sacrifices by presenting proof that they had, frequently with forged documents. Some fled or went into hiding. It was not tens of thousands who were martyred, but rather tens of thousands who watched many hundreds bear witness to their faith by facing torture and death rather than denying their god. Popular history and mass media have inflated our perspective on martyrdom in the early church.

The New Testament has contributed to this impression by relating accounts of persecution in the letters of Paul, later writings of the early church, and the book of Revelation. The Apocalypse of John, also known as Revelation, appears to have been written during a time when the church was persecuted in the first century. Written by a man named John, from the island of Patmos where he had been exiled "because of the word of God and the testimony of Jesus," Revelation depicts Rome as a great beast and presupposes the martyrdom of Christians. In Revelation 6, for example, a heavenly lamb that is opening the wax seals on a gigantic scroll removes the fifth one so that the narrator—John of Patmos—has a vision of Christian martyrs.

> When he opened the fifth seal, I saw under the altar the souls of those who had been slaughtered for the word of God and for the testimony they had given; they cried out with a loud voice, "Sovereign Lord, holy and true, how long will it be before you judge and avenge our blood on the inhabitants of the earth?" They were each given a white robe and told to rest a little longer, until the number would be complete both of their fellow servants and of their brothers and sisters, who were soon to be killed as they themselves had been killed. (Revelation 6:9–11)

Biblical scholars do not agree on when Revelation was written, with some placing it in the Neronian persecution (64–65 C.E.) and others placing it in the Domitian persecution (95–96 C.E.). In either case, the visions and dreams of the author were intended to provide hope to an embattled community, just as the Gospel of Mark targeted a persecuted group.

A body of literature called "martyrologies" arose that related the heroic and horrifying tales of honor, torture, death, and glory. The format usually included a first-person narrative by the martyr, explaining his or her desire to share in Christ's sufferings, or leave this life for the greater one awaiting. An account of the execution itself would follow, written by an observer of the (usually) miraculous events. Thus, Bishop Polycarp of Smyrna (69–155), who was burned at the stake, turned golden, appearing to onlookers to resemble bread baking in the oven. The flames did not consume his body, and so he was stabbed to death. So much blood flowed from the wound that it put out the fire. The body was burned, and then Christian onlookers took up his bones,

> more precious than costly stones and more valuable than gold, and laid them away in a suitable place. There the Lord will permit us, so far as possible, to gather together in joy and gladness to celebrate the day of his martyrdom as a birthday, in memory of those athletes who have gone before, and to train and make ready those who are to come hereafter. (*The Martyrdom of Polycarp*)

The Reading

One of the most vivid narratives of martyrdom is "The Passion of Saints Perpetua and Felicity," which describes the deaths of several Christians in Carthage around 203 C.E. Perpetua is a young noblewoman who, despite her father's pleas and the existence of her still-nursing two year-old son, refuses to renounce God and sacrifice to the emperor. Felicity, another young woman, miraculously gives birth prematurely so that she can die with her fellow Christians. The account makes it quite clear that neither had to die: other Christians visit them in prison, and even the jailer is converted. But Perpetua has several dreams and visions, including one about her dead brother Dinocrates, which convince her that she is making the right decision. Her narrative is followed by that of Saturus, who describes his vision of angels. Finally, an anonymous observer relates the details of the deaths of Felicity and Perpetua.

It is important to recall that martyrologies follow a rather strict genre formula. Their purpose is to evoke sympathy and admiration for the victim, and to give glory to God for the courage demonstrated. Moreover, they give proof to the truth of the Christians' claims, for who would be willing to die such an awful death were their future in heaven not assured?

Vocabulary note: The word *catechumens* appears in the third paragraph of the reading. A catechumen was essentially a Christian-in-training—someone who was learning the teachings of the faith, but who probably had not yet been baptized or taken communion. Perpetua and Felicity and their friends were all catechumens, which apparently made them more vulnerable to arrest and imprisonment. The process of joining the church was rather long, taking between one and three years. Baptism, as well as the celebration of the first communion, was usually held the night before

Easter, on Holy Saturday. Thus, some of the martyrs described in this account were not even full-fledged Christians when they met their deaths. The word *deacon* also appears in Perpetua's account. A deacon was a church official appointed to serve or help other Christians.

Questions to Consider

1. What type of person is Perpetua? What is her status? Her personality?

2. What type of person is Felicity? What is her status? Her personality?

3. How do you interpret Perpetua's dream of the bronze ladder? What about the dream in which she sees herself as a man?

4. Perpetua has two visions or dreams about her brother Dinocrates. How does she herself interpret these visions? What role does her martyrdom play for Dinocrates?

5. How would martyrdom be different, or more difficult, for women than for men at that time?

6. What do you think of Perpetua's character? Do you like her? Would you want to be friends with her?

7. Does Perpetua seem to know scripture? What authority does she rely on to support her beliefs?

The Passion of Saints Perpetua and Felicity

PROLOGUE

1. If ancient examples of faith kept, both testifying the grace of God and working the edification of man, have to this end been set in writing, that by their reading as though by the showing of the deeds again, God may be glorified and man strengthened; why should not new witnesses also be so set forth which likewise serve either end? Yea, for these things also shall at some time be ancient and necessary to our sons, though in their own present time (through some reverence of antiquity presumed) they are made of but slight account. But let those take heed who judge the one power of the Holy Spirit according to the succession of times; whereas those things which are later ought for their very lateness to be thought the more eminent, according to the abundance of grace appointed for the last periods of time. For In

the last days, says the Lord, I will pour my spirit upon all flesh, and their sons and daughters shall prophesy; and upon my servants and upon my handmaids I will pour forth of my spirit; and the young men shall see visions, and the old men shall dream dreams [Acts 2:17, see also Joel 2:28].

We also therefore, by whom both the prophecies and the new visions promised are received and honored, and by whom those other wonders of the Holy Spirit are assigned unto the service of the Church, to which also was sent the same Spirit administering all gifts among all men, according as the Lord hath distributed unto each [1 Corinthians 7:17]—do of necessity both write them and by reading celebrate them to the glory of God; that no weakness or failing of faith may presume that among those of old time only was the grace of divinity present, whether in martyrs or in revelations vouchsafed; since God ever works that which He has promised, for a witness to them that believe not and a benefit to them that believe. Wherefore we too, brethren and dear sons, declare to you likewise that which we have heard and handled [1 Corinthians 15:1?]; that both you who were present may call to mind the glory of the Lord, and you who now know by hearing may have communion with those holy martyrs, and through them with the Lord Jesus Christ, to whom is glory and honor for ever and ever. Amen.

2. There were apprehended the young catechumens, Revocatus and Felicity his fellow servant, Saturninus and Secundulus. With them also was Vibia Perpetua, nobly born reared in a liberal manner, wedded honorably; having a father and mother and two brothers, one of them a catechumen likewise, and a son, a child at the breast; and she herself was about twenty-two years of age. What follows here shall she tell herself; the whole order of her martyrdom as she left it written with her own hand and in her own words.

PERPETUA'S ACCOUNT

3. When, she said, we were still under legal surveillance and my father was liked to vex me with his words and continually strove to hurt my faith because of his love: Father, said I, Do you see (for examples) this vessel lying, a pitcher or whatsoever it may be? And he said, I see it. And I said to him, Can it be called by any other name than that which it is? And he answered, No. So can I call myself nought other than that which I am, a Christian.

Then my father angry with this word came upon me to tear out my eyes; but he only vexed me, and he departed vanquished, he and the arguments of the devil. Then because I was without my father for a few days I gave thanks unto the Lord; and I was comforted because of his absence. In this same space of a few days we were baptized, and the Spirit declared to me, I must pray for nothing else after that water save only endurance of the flesh. After a few days we were taken into prison, and I was much afraid because I had never known such darkness. O bitter day! There was a great heat because of the press, there was cruel handling of the soldiers. Lastly I was tormented there by care for the child.

Then Tertius and Pomponius, the blessed deacons who ministered to us, obtained with money that for a few hours we should be taken forth to a better part of the prison and be refreshed. Then all of them going out from the dungeon took their pleasure; I suckled my child that was now faint with hunger. And being careful for him, I spoke to my mother and strengthened my brother and commended my son unto them. I pined because I saw they pined for my sake. Such cares I suffered for many days; and I obtained that the child should abide with me in prison; and straightway I became well and was lightened of my labor and care for the child; and suddenly the prison was made a palace for me, so that I would sooner be there than anywhere else.

4. Then said my brother to me: Lady my sister, you are now in high honor, even such that you might ask for a vision; and it should be shown you whether this be a passion or else a deliverance. And I, as knowing that I conversed with the Lord, for Whose sake I had suffered such things, did promise him nothing doubting; and I said: Tomorrow I will tell you. And I asked, and this was shown me.

I beheld a ladder of bronze, marvelously great, reaching up to heaven; and it was narrow, so that not more than one might go up at one time. And in the sides of the ladder were planted all manner of things of iron. There were swords there, spears, hooks, and knives; so that if any that went up took not good heed or looked not upward, he would be torn and his flesh cling to the iron. And there was right at the ladder's foot a serpent lying, marvelously great, which lay in wait for those that would go up, and frightened them that they might not go up. Now Saturus went up first (who afterwards had of his own free will given up himself for our sakes, because it was he who had edified us; and when we were taken he had not been there). And he came to the ladder's head; and he turned and said: Perpetua, I await you; but see that serpent bite you not. And I said: it shall not hurt me, in the name of Jesus Christ. And from beneath the ladder, as though it feared me, it softly put forth its head; and as though I trod on the first step I trod on its head. And I went up, and I saw a very great space of garden, and in the midst a man sitting, white-headed, in shepherd's clothing, tall milking his sheep; and standing around in white were many thousands. And he raised his head and beheld me and said to me: Welcome, child. And he cried to me, and from the curd he had from the milk he gave me as it were a morsel; and I took it with joined hands and ate it up; and all that stood around said, Amen. And at the sound of that word I awoke, yet eating I know not what of sweet.

And at once I told my brother, and we knew it should be a passion; and we began to have no hope any longer in this world.

5. A few days after, the report went abroad that we were to be tried. Also my father returned from the city spent with weariness; and he came up to me to cast down my faith saying: Have pity, daughter, on my grey hairs; have pity on your father, if I am worthy to be called father by you; if with these hands I have brought you unto this flower of youth—and I have preferred you before all your brothers; give me not over to the reproach of men. Look upon your brothers; look upon your mother and mother's sister; look upon your son, who will not endure to live after you. Give up your resolution; do not destroy us all together; for none of us will speak openly against men again if you suffer aught.

This he said fatherly in his love, kissing my hands and groveling at my feet; and with tears he named me, not daughter, but lady. And I was grieved for my father's case because he would not rejoice at my passion out of all my kin; and I comforted him, saying: That shall be done at this tribunal, whatsoever God shall please; for know that we are not established in our own power, but in God's. And he went from me very sorrowful.

6. Another day as we were at meal we were suddenly snatched away to be tried; and we came to the forum. Therewith a report spread abroad through the parts near to the forum, and a very great multitude gathered together. We went up to the tribunal. The others being asked, confessed. So they came to me. And my father appeared there also, with my son, and would draw me from the step, saying: Perform the Sacrifice; have mercy on the child. And Hilarian the procurator—he that after the death of Minucius Timinian the proconsul had received in his room the right and power of the sword—said: Spare your father's grey hairs; spare the infancy of the boy. Make sacrifice for the Emperors' prosperity. And I answered: I am a Christian. And when my father stood by me yet to cast down my faith, he was bidden by Hilarian to be cast down and was smitten with a rod. And I sorrowed for my father's harm as though I had been smitten myself; so sorrowed I for his unhappy old age. Then Hilarian passed sentence upon us all and condemned us to the beasts; and cheerfully we went down to the dungeon. Then because my child

had been used to being breastfed and to staying with me in the prison, straightway I sent Pomponius the deacon to my father, asking for the child. But my father would not give him. And as God willed, no longer did he need to be suckled, nor did I take fever; that I might not be tormented by care for the child and by the pain of my breasts.

7. A few days after, while we were all praying, suddenly in the midst of the prayer I uttered a word and named Dinocrates; and I was amazed because he had never come into my mind save then; and I sorrowed, remembering his fate. And straightway I knew that I was worthy, and that I ought to ask for him. And I began to pray for him long, and to groan unto the Lord. Immediately the same night, this was shown me.

I beheld Dinocrates coming forth from a dark place, where were many others also; being both hot and thirsty, his raiment foul, his color pale; and the wound on his face which he had when he died. This Dinocrates had been my brother in the flesh, seven years old, who being diseased with ulcers of the face had come to a horrible death, so that his death was abominated of all men. For him therefore I had made my prayer; and between him and me was a great gulf, so that either might not go to the other. There was moreover, in the same place where Dinocrates was, a font full of water, having its edge higher than was the boy's stature; and Dinocrates stretched up as though to drink. I was sorry that the font had water in it, and yet for the height of the edge he might not drink.

And I awoke, and I knew that my brother was in travail. Yet I was confident I should ease his travail; and I prayed for him every day till we passed over into the camp prison. (For it was in the camp games that we were to fight; and the time was the feast of the Emperor Geta's birthday.) And I prayed for him day and night with groans and tears, that he might be given me.

8. On the day when we abode in the stocks, this was shown me.

I saw that place which I had before seen, and Dinocrates clean of body, finely clothed, in comfort; and the font I had seen before, the edge of it being drawn to the boy's navel; and he drew water thence which flowed without ceasing. And on the edge was a golden cup full of water; and Dinocrates came up and began to drink therefrom; which cup failed not. And being satisfied he departed away from the water and began to play as children will, joyfully.

And I awoke. Then I understood that he was translated from his pains.

9. Then a few days after, Pudens the adjutant, in whose charge the prison was, who also began to magnify us because he understood that there was much grace in us, let in many to us that both we and they in turn might be comforted. Now when the day of the games drew near, there came in my father to me, spent with weariness, and began to pluck out his beard and throw it on the ground and to fall on his face cursing his years and saying such words as might move all creation. I was grieved for his unhappy old age.

10. The day before we fought, I saw in a vision that Pomponius the deacon had come hither to the door of the prison, and knocked hard upon it. And I went out to him and opened to him; he was clothed in a white robe ungirdled, having shoes curiously wrought. And he said to me: Perpetua, we await you; come. And he took my hand, and we began to go through rugged and winding places. At last with much breathing hard we came to the amphitheatre, and he led me into the midst of the arena. And he said to me: Be not afraid; I am here with you and labor together with you. And he went away. And I saw much people watching closely. And because I knew that I was condemned to the beasts I marveled that beasts were not sent out against me. And there came out against me a certain ill-favored Egyptian with his helpers, to fight with me. Also there came to me comely young men, my helpers and aiders. And I was stripped naked, and I became a man. And my helpers began to rub me with oil as their custom is for a contest; and over against me saw that Egyptian wallowing in the dust. And there came forth a man of very great stature, so that he overpassed the very top of the amphitheatre, wearing a robe ungirdled, and beneath it between the two stripes over the breast a robe of purple; having also shoes curiously wrought in gold and silver; bearing a rod like a master of gladiators, and a green branch whereon were golden apples. And he besought silence and said: The Egyptian, if shall conquer this woman, shall slay her with the sword; and if she shall conquer him, she shall receive this branch. And he went away. And we came nigh to each other, and began to buffet one another. He tried to trip up my feet, but I with my heels smote upon his face. And I rose up into the air and began so to smite him as though I trod not the earth. But when I saw that there was yet delay, I joined my hands, setting finger against finger of them. And I caught his

head, and he fell upon his face; and I trod upon his head. And the people began to shout, and my helpers began to sing. And I went up to the master of gladiators and received the branch. And he kissed me and said to me: Daughter, peace be with you. And I began to go with glory to the gate called the Gate of Life.

And I awoke; and I understood that I should fight, not with beasts but against the devil; but I knew that mine was the victory.

Thus far I have written this, till the day before the games; but the deed of the games themselves let him write who will.

SATURUS' ACCOUNT

11. And blessed Saturus too delivered this vision which he himself wrote down.

We had suffered, he said, and we passed out of the flesh, and we began to be carried towards the east by four angels whose hand touched us not. And we went not as though turned upwards upon our backs, but as though we went up an easy hill. And passing over the world's edge we saw a very great light; and I said to Perpetua (for she was at my side): This which the Lord promised us; we have received His promise. And while we were being carried by these same four angels, a great space opened before us, as it had been a [sic] having rose trees and all kinds of flowers. The height of the trees was after the manner of the cypress, and their leaves sang without ceasing. And there in the garden were four other angels, more glorious than the rest; who when they saw us gave us honor and said to the other angels: Lo, here are they, here are they: and marveled. And the four angels who bore us set us down trembling; and we passed on foot by a broad way over a plain. There we found Jocundus and Saturninus and Artaxius who in the same persecution had been burned alive; and Quintus, a martyr also, who in prison had departed this life; and we asked of them where were the rest. The other angels said to us: Come first, go in, and salute the Lord.

12. And we came near to a place, of which place the walls were such, they seemed built of light; and before the door of that place stood four angels who clothed us when we went in with white raiment. And we went in, and we heard as it were one voice crying Sanctus, Sanctus, Sanctus, without any end. And we saw sitting in that same place as it were a man, white-headed, having hair like snow; youthful of countenance; whose feet we saw not. And on his right hand and on his left, four elders; and behind them stood many other elders. And we went in with wonder and

stood before the throne; and the four angels raised us up and we kissed him, and with his hand he passed over our faces. And the other elders said to us: Stand you. And we stood, and gave the kiss of peace. And the elders said to us: Go you and play. And I said to Perpetua: You have that which you desire. And she said to me: Yes, God be thanked; so that I that was glad in the flesh am now more glad.

13. And we went out, and we saw before the doors, on the right Optatus the bishop, and on the left Aspasius the priest and teacher, being apart and sorrowful. And they cast themselves at our feet and said: Make peace between us, because you went forth and left us thus. And we said to them: Are not you our Father, and you our priest, that you should throw yourselves at our feet? And we were moved, and embraced them. And Perpetua began to talk with them in Greek; and we set them apart in the pleasure garden beneath a rose tree. And while we yet spoke with them, the angels said to them: Let these go and be refreshed; and whatsoever dissensions you have between you, Put them away from you each for each. And they made them to be confounded. And they said to Optatus: Correct your people; for they come to you as those that return from the games and wrangle concerning the parties there. And it seemed to us as though they would shut the gates. And we began to know many brothers there, martyrs also. And we were all sustained there with a savor inexpressible which satisfied us. Then in joy I awoke.

NARRATIVE OF MARTYRDOM

14. These were the glorious visions of those martyrs themselves, the most blessed Saturus and Perpetua, which they themselves wrote down. But Secundulus by an earlier end God called from this world while he was yet in prison; not without grace, that he should escape the beasts. Yet if not his soul, his flesh at least knew the sword.

15. As for Felicity, she too received this grace of the Lord. For because she was now gone eight months (being indeed with child when she was taken) she was very sorrowful as the day of the games drew near, fearing lest for this cause she should be kept back (for it is not lawful for women that are with child to be brought forth for torment) and lest she should shed her holy and innocent blood after the rest, among strangers and malefactors. Also her fellow martyrs were much afflicted lest they should leave behind them so good a friend and as it were their fellow-traveler on the road of the same hope. Wherefore with joint and united groaning they poured out their prayer to the Lord, three days before the games. Incontinently after their prayer her pains came upon her. And when by reason of the natural difficulty of the eighth month she was oppressed with her travail and made complaint, there said to her one of the servants of the keepers of the door: You that thus make complaint now, what wilt you do when you are thrown to the beasts, which you didst contemn when you would not sacrifice? And she answered, I myself now suffer that which I suffer, but there another shall be in me who shall suffer for me, because I am to suffer for him. So she was delivered of a daughter, whom a sister reared up to be her own daughter.

16. Since therefore the Holy Spirit has suffered, and suffering has willed, that the order of the games also should be written; though we are unworthy to finish the recounting of so great glory, yet we accomplish the will of the most holy Perpetua, nay rather her sacred trust, adding one testimony more of her own steadfastness and height of spirit. When they were being more cruelly handled by the tribune, because through advice of certain most despicable men he feared lest by magic charms they might be withdrawn secretly from the prison house, Perpetua answered him to his face: Why do you not allow us to take some comfort, seeing we are victims most noble, namely Caesar's, and on his feast day we are to fight? Or is it not your glory that we should be taken out thither fatter of flesh? The tribune trembled and blushed, and gave order that they should be more gently handled, granting that her brothers and the rest should come in and rest with them. Also the adjutant of the prison now believed.

17. Likewise on the day before the games, when at the last feast which they call Free they made (as far as they might) not a Free Feast but a Love Feast,* with like hardihood they cast these words at the people; threatening the judgment of the Lord, witnessing to the felicity of their passion, setting at nought the curiosity of those that ran together. And Saturus said: Is not tomorrow sufficient for you? Why do you favorably behold that which you hate? You are friends

---

* Apparently in Roman, as with modern, custom, the condemned were allowed a choice of food. The martyrs used the opportunity to celebrate an Agape, or Christian Love Feast.

today, foes tomorrow. Yet mark our faces diligently, that you may know us again on that day. So they began all to go away thence astonished; of whom many believed.

18. Now dawned the day of their victory, and they went forth from the prison into the amphitheatre as it were into heaven, cheerful and bright of countenance; if they trembled at all, it was for joy, not for fear. Perpetua followed behind, glorious of presence, as a true spouse of Christ and darling of God; at whose piercing look all cast down their eyes. Felicity likewise, rejoicing that she had borne a child in safety, that she might fight with the beasts, came now from blood to blood, from the midwife to the gladiator, to wash after her travail in a second baptism. And when they had been brought to the gate and were being compelled to put on, the men the dress of the priests of Saturn, the women the dress of the priestesses of Ceres, the noble Perpetua remained of like firmness to the end, and would not. For she said: For this cause came we willingly unto this, that our liberty might not be obscured. For this cause have we devoted our lives, that we might do no such thing as this; this we agreed with you. Injustice acknowledged justice; the tribune suffered that they should be brought forth as they were, without more ado. Perpetua began to sing, as already treading on the Egyptian's head. Revocatus and Saturninus and Saturus threatened the people as they gazed. Then when they came into Hilarian's sight, they began to say to Hilarian, stretching forth their hands and nodding their heads: You judge us, they said, and God you. At this the people being enraged besought that they should be vexed with scourges before the line of gladiators (those namely who fought with beasts). Then truly they gave thanks because they had received somewhat of the sufferings of the Lord.

19. But He who had said Ask and you shall receive [John 16:24] gave to them asking that end which each had desired. For whenever they spoke together of their desire in their martyrdom, Saturninus for his part would declare that he wished to be thrown to every kind of beast, that so indeed he might wear the more glorious crown. At the beginning of the spectacle therefore himself with Revocatus first had ado with a leopard and was afterwards torn by a bear on a raised bridge. Now Saturus detested nothing more than a bear, but was confident already he should die by one bite of a leopard. Therefore when he was being given to a boar, the gladiator instead who had bound him to the boar was torn asunder by the same beast and died after the days of the games; nor was Saturus more than dragged. More-

over when he had been tied on the bridge to be assaulted by a bear, the bear would not come forth from his den. So Saturus was called back unharmed a second time.

20. But for the women the devil had made ready a most savage cow, prepared for this purpose against all custom; for even in this beast he would mock their sex. They were stripped therefore and made to put on nets; and so they were brought forth. The people shuddered, seeing one a tender girl, the other her breasts yet dropping from her late childbearing. So they were called back and clothed in loose robes. Perpetua was first thrown, and fell upon her loins. And when she had sat upright, her robe being rent at the side, she drew it over to cover her thigh, mindful rather of modesty than of pain. Next, looking for a pin, she likewise pinned up her disheveled hair; for it was not meet that a martyr should suffer with hair disheveled, lest she should seem to grieve in her glory. So she stood up; and when she saw Felicity smitten down, she went up and gave her hand and raised her up. And both of them stood up together and the (hardness of the people being now subdued) were called back to the Gate of Life. There Perpetua being received by one named Rusticus, then a catechumen, who stood close at her side, and as now awakening from sleep (so much was she in the Spirit and in ecstasy) began first to look about her; and then (which amazed all there), When, forsooth, she asked, are we to be thrown to the cow? And when she heard that this had been done already, she would not believe till she perceived some marks of mauling on her body and on her dress. Thereupon she called her brother to her, and that catechumen, and spoke to them, saying: Stand fast in the faith, and love you all one another; and be not offended because of our passion.

21. Saturus also at another gate exhorted Pudens the soldier, saying: So then indeed, as I trusted and foretold, I have felt no assault of beasts until now. And now believe with all your heart. Behold, I go out thither and shall perish by one bite of the leopard. And immediately at the end of the spectacle, the leopard being released, with one bite of his he was covered with so much blood that the people (in witness to his second baptism) cried out to him returning: Well washed, well washed. Truly it was well with him who had washed in this wise. Then said he to Pudens the soldier: Farewell; remember the faith and me; and let not these things trouble you, but strengthen you. And therewith he took from Pudens' finger a little ring, and dipping it in his wound gave it back again

for an heirloom, leaving him a pledge and memorial of his blood. Then as the breath left him he was cast down with the rest in the accustomed place for his throat to be cut. And when the people besought that they should be brought forward, that when the sword pierced through their bodies their eyes might be joined thereto as witnesses to the slaughter, they rose of themselves and moved, whither the people willed them, first kissing one another, that they might accomplish their martyrdom with the rites of peace. The rest not moving and in silence received the sword; Saturus much earlier gave up the ghost; for he had gone up earlier also, and now he waited for Perpetua likewise. But Perpetua, that she might have some taste of pain, was pierced between the bones and shrieked out; and when the swordsman's hand wandered still (for he was a novice), herself set it upon her own neck. Perchance so great a woman could not else have been slain (being feared of the unclean spirit) had she not herself so willed it.

O most valiant and blessed martyrs! O truly called and elected unto the glory of Our Lord Jesus Christ! Which glory he that magnifies, honors and adores, ought to read these witnesses likewise, as being no less than the old, unto the Church's edification; that these new wonders also may testify that one and the same Holy Spirit works ever until now, and with Him God the Father Almighty, and His Son Jesus Christ Our Lord, to Whom is glory and power unending for ever and ever. Amen.

The deaths of Christians in the arenas—though not the arenas themselves—came to an abrupt halt in 313 C.E. The Roman emperor Constantine (c. 272–337) had a dream, or so legend tells us, of a military victory under the banner of the cross. Some versions of the story say it was the *chi-rho,* the first two letters of Christ in Greek. Constantine won the battle of the Milvian Bridge in 312 and issued the Edict of Milan the next year, which made most religions in the empire legal, including Christianity. What had been a large and influential movement—though also a persecuted one—was now positioned to reach new levels of power with the conversion of a Roman emperor.

Constantine himself was only nominally Christian. He continued to worship the sun, even as he allowed Christians to worship their own god. He delayed his baptism until he was on his deathbed, although this was a common practice among Roman officials, whose civic duties conflicted with their religious obligations. He made two major contributions to the development of Christianity, however, in addition to making the religion legal. First, he convened the Council of Nicea to resolve the many internal disputes that divided Christians around the Mediterranean. This council, and a subsequent one held toward the end of the fourth century, led to the adoption of the Nicene Creed, a document that clarified Christian teaching about Jesus and his relation to God. Second, Constantine established a capital city in the eastern empire, Constantinople (Byzantium), that would eventually rival the religious authority and power of Rome. Although administrative and cultural divisions between the eastern and western empire preceded Constantine, his sons eventually formalized a split into two empires. This east-west distinction further politicized already existing differences between eastern and western Christians who were separated by geography, language, and theology.

Christianity was as diverse in the first four centuries of its existence as it is today. Theological differences, as well as a variety of practices and church organizations, existed due to the diffusion of the faith throughout the Mediterranean, and beyond to Europe, Africa, and Asia. Isolated groups arose and maintained their own unique

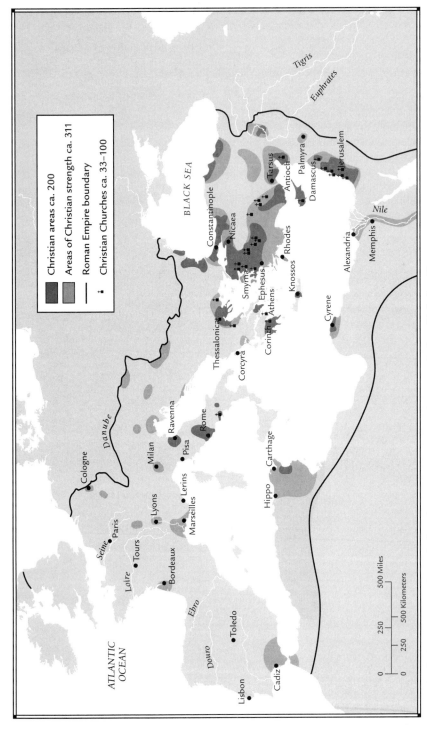

Growth of Christianity to the early fourth century.   By 311, Christianity had established itself
in regions throughout the Roman Empire, with particular strength in the East.

scriptures and beliefs about Jesus; many continued to be practicing Jews, observing the Sabbath on Saturday, and celebrating communion on the Lord's Day, Sunday. Others understood Christianity within the context of the mystery religions prevalent throughout the Roman Empire: it promised salvation and eternal life by initiating believers into sacred mysteries not readily available to outsiders. Thus, it may be

▨ The Mystery Religions

A number of different religious groups flourished throughout the Roman Empire in the earliest centuries of the Common Era. Because they shared the characteristic of initiating members into secret religious rites, they were called "mystery religions." Initiation gave individuals a new identity as part of the group, or cult—though we need to understand "cult" in terms of religious practices, and not in terms of "bad religion." The cult of the Egyptian goddess Isis, for example, was extremely popular. Isis was recognized as a goddess throughout the Hellenistic world, and her cult promised initiates eternal life. Novices were baptized into the mysteries after a ten-day fast. As part of the ritual, they took a symbolic journey to the lower and the upper worlds before being reborn. The cult of Dionysius—immortalized in Euripides' play *The Bacchae*—was an association of women who engaged in ecstatic, and sometimes orgiastic, activities. In the Eleusinian mystery cult, a priestess would pour water over an initiate as he or she reenacted the loss, grief, and return in the sacred myth of Demeter and her daughter Kore. The cult of Mithras appealed to men, especially sailors, who went through seven degrees of initiation. Mithras, like Isis, was a well-respected god in the Mediterranean, often depicted as sacrificing a bull in order to give his believers eternal life. A common theme in all of these groups is that the mysteries, or rites, provided the means to escape from one's fate in life, as well as from death.

In many ways, Christianity greatly resembled these cults. A virgin goddess named Mary (who became known as the Queen of Heaven, the same title used for Isis) had given birth to a divine son. He, in turn, had been killed, but then returned from the dead to give his followers life eternal. Believers were initiated through a rite called baptism, in order to receive this everlasting life. After a year of study, at midnight on Holy Saturday, the night before Easter, the initiates were stripped naked and dipped into water three times, reciting sacred vows. Only after this ceremony could they join the feast called the Lord's Supper, or Eucharist, in which they ate and drank the body and blood of their dying and rising god.

It was Christianity's ties to Judaism that helped keep it anchored within the traditions and teachings of the Old Testament, and prevented it from becoming just another mystery religion. By grounding Christians in what was believed to be the historical experience of their ancestors, the Israelites, scripture kept God as part of life in this world, as well as life in another world. The willingness of its adherents to die for their beliefs also set Christianity apart. Although many religions preached immortality of the soul, few initiates outside the church were willing to put the theory to the test.

helpful to think of early Christianity as a series of rivulets flowing from a single mountain, which over a period of several hundred years converged into larger and larger streams, and finally into not one, but three mighty rivers: Orthodoxy, Catholicism, and, much later, Protestantism.

Varieties of Early Christianity: Practices

Just as sedimentary rock reveals different time periods and events—floods, fires, volcanoes—so also do New Testament and early Christian writings reveal different strata of theological development. The sacraments provide an interesting example of these changes. Because Catholic, Orthodox, and Protestant Christians understand sacraments differently from one another, it is difficult to come up with a single, precise definition. In the Middle Ages, a sacrament was understood to be a symbol of something sacred—something physical or tangible that points to an invisible reality. For example, the water used in baptism represents the invisible reality of God's cleansing humans from sin (among other meanings). The bread and wine, or juice or water, used in communion symbolize the body and blood of Jesus for Protestant Christians; for Catholic Christians, however, they actually become the body and blood of Jesus. Christians today would also say that sacraments indicate, bear, or bestow the grace of God upon the recipient. By participating in these sacred rites, believers in Christ share in the holy mysteries of his life, death, and resurrection. Sacraments are central to the worship life of Catholic and Orthodox Christians; while important to Protestants, they are not quite as central, except in the Anglican and Lutheran traditions. Baptism, however, is a vital sacrament for all Christian denominations.

Baptism is an initiation rite marking the radical change in a believer from a life of sin to a new life of perfection in the Holy Spirit. It is marked by immersion into water or by pouring or sprinkling water over the initiate. It began as a Jewish rite of purification, although John the Baptist and the Essenes began to reinterpret it in a way that seemed to eliminate the need for any sort of ritual other than that of baptism. The New Testament gives several interpretations of what believers thought baptism would produce:

> For in the one Spirit we were all baptized into one body—Jews or Greeks, slaves or free—and we were all made to drink of one Spirit. (1 Corinthians 12:13)

> Therefore we have been buried with him by baptism into death, so that, just as Christ was raised from the dead by the glory of the Father, so we too might walk in newness of life. (Romans 6:4)

> John the baptizer appeared in the wilderness, proclaiming a baptism of repentance for the forgiveness of sins. (Mark 1:4)

> Peter said to them, "Repent, and be baptized every one of you in the name of Jesus Christ so that your sins may be forgiven; and you will receive the gift of the Holy Spirit." (Acts 2:38)

> Jesus answered, "Very truly, I tell you, no one can enter the kingdom of God without being born of water and Spirit. What is born of the flesh is flesh, and what is born of the Spirit is spirit." (John 3:5)

The New Testament indicates that members of the Jesus Movement practiced baptism in at least two different ways: in the name of Jesus (Acts 8:16, 10:48) and in the "threefold name," that is, in the name of the Father, the Son, and the Holy Spirit (Matthew 28:19). In addition, while most converts were baptized as adults, some infants may have been baptized as well. The book of Acts says that an entire household was baptized, and presumably this included children as well as slaves. The preference for infant baptism emerged over a period of centuries. For a time, however, both believer (adult) baptism and infant baptism co-existed.

Cyril, bishop of Jerusalem circa 349–386 C.E., delivered a number of sermons to catechumens that give us a good picture of what happened in a typical fourth-century adult baptism. Catechumens would study for at least a year and then be baptized at midnight of Easter Sunday. The first step in the baptismal process was an exorcism, which expelled sin from their hearts and minds. Cyril warns the catechumens to "tell nothing to a stranger; for we deliver to thee a mystery, even the hope of the life to come: keep the mystery for Him who pays thee. . . . See thou let out nothing; not that the things spoken do not deserve telling, but the ear that hears does not deserve receiving." In other words, the catechumens were being initiated into the mysteries of Christian faith. It is important to know that only baptized believers could participate in communion, or for that matter, even be present during that part of the service. The nonbaptized were sent out of church after the scripture readings or sermon. No wonder outsiders believed that the early Christians were cannibals who were eating bodies and drinking blood!

Baptism is not just one thing, according to Cyril:

> Great indeed is the Baptism which is offered you. It is a ransom to captives; the remission of offenses; the death of sin; the regeneration of the soul; the garment of light; the holy seal indissoluble; the chariot to heaven; the luxury of paradise; a procuring of the kingdom; the gift of adoption.

But later he also argues:

> Let no one then suppose that Baptism is merely the grace of remission of sins, or further, that of adoption; as John's baptism bestowed only the remission of sins. Nay we know full well, that as it purges our sins, and conveys to us the gift of the Holy Ghost, so also it is the counterpart of Christ's sufferings. (*Cyril of Jerusalem's Lectures*)

The first step in the baptismal service, according to Cyril, was the renouncing of Satan by the catechumens. "I renounce thee, Satan," they said, "and all thy works." The catechumens went separately—men with men, women with women—to be stripped, anointed with oil, "from the very hairs of your head to your feet." Then they were led to the "holy pool of Divine Baptism," where each descended three times into the water, imitating the three days Christ was buried.

The practice of communion also varied in the early church. The central rite of Christianity is that of observing the Lord's Supper, also known as communion, divine liturgy, the Mass, eucharist, and love-feast. The oldest evidence we have of a common meal being held in memory of Jesus comes from Paul in 1 Corinthians, where he called it the Lord's Supper:

> For I received from the Lord what I also handed on to you, that the Lord Jesus on the night when he was betrayed took a loaf of bread, and when he had given thanks, he broke it and said, "This is my body that is for you. Do this in remembrance of me." In the same way he took the cup also, after supper, saying, "This cup is the new covenant in my blood. Do this, as often as you drink it, in remembrance of me." For as often as you eat this bread and drink the cup, you proclaim the Lord's death until he comes. (1 Corinthians 11:23–26)

Paul indicates knowledge of what are called the "words of institution" by which Jesus instituted this sacrament, and he probably learned them from Peter. These words appear in the accounts of the Synoptic Gospels, but not in John's gospel. Note the differences and similarities in the three accounts.

> While they were eating, he took a loaf of bread, and after blessing it he broke it, gave it to them, and said, "Take; this is my body." Then he took a cup, and after giving thanks he gave it to them, and all of them drank from it. He said to them. "This is my blood of the [new]* covenant, which is poured out for many. Truly I tell you, I will never again drink of the fruit of the vine until that day when I drink it new in the kingdom of God." (Mark 14:22–25)

> While they were eating, Jesus took a loaf of bread, and after blessing it he broke it, gave it to the disciples, and said, "Take, eat; this is my body." Then he took a cup, and after giving thanks he gave it to them, saying, "Drink from it, all of you; for this is my blood of the [new]* covenant, which is poured out for many for the forgiveness of sins. I tell you, I will never again drink of this fruit of the vine until that day when I drink it new with you in my Father's kingdom." (Matthew 26:26–29)

> When the hour came, he took his place at the table, and the apostles with him. He said to them, "I have eagerly desired to eat this Passover with you before I suffer; for I tell you, I will not eat of it until it is fulfilled in the kingdom of God." Then he took a cup, and after giving thanks he said, "Take this and divide it among yourselves; for I tell you that from now on I will not drink of the fruit of the vine until the kingdom of God comes." Then he took a loaf of bread, and when he had given thanks, he broke it and gave it to them, saying, "This is my body, [which is given for you. Do this in remembrance of me." And he did the same with the cup after supper, saying, "This cup that is poured out for you is the new covenant in my blood."].* (Luke 22:14–20)

In John's gospel, there is no last supper; at least, Jesus does not say the special words that he says in the Synoptics. He does wash the feet of the disciples, however. But Jesus says something very interesting at the beginning of his ministry in John:

> Jesus said to them, "Very truly, I tell you, unless you eat the flesh of the Son of Man and drink his blood, you have no life in you. Those who eat my flesh and drink my blood have eternal life, and I will raise them up on the last day; for my flesh is true food and my blood is true drink. Those who eat my flesh and drink my blood abide in me, and I in them. Just as the living Father sent me, and I live because of the

---

* Material in brackets indicates that other ancient copies of the text lack the additional word(s).

Father, so whoever eats me will live because of me. This is the bread that came down from heaven, not like that which your ancestors ate, and they died. But the one who eats this bread will live forever." (John 6:53–58)

Was Jesus speaking literally or figuratively when he called the bread his body and the wine his blood? The church debated this question for many centuries. In 1215, the Fourth Lateran Council formally adopted the doctrine of transubstantiation—that is, that the bread and wine are transformed into the body and blood of Jesus once the priest consecrates them. This doctrine was challenged during the reformations of the sixteenth century, however, and debates about what exactly happens during communion were renewed (see Chapter Four). For now, let us look at the practices of the early church and how the understanding of the elements (the bread and the wine) changed over time.

First, we have the witness of the Synoptic Gospels and Paul, which seem to show that communion was some sort of memorial meal that Christians shared regularly. In fact, Paul is addressing the problem of people not sharing food when he writes about the Lord's Supper in 1 Corinthians. And yet, John's gospel seems especially graphic about flesh and blood. One thing is clear: early Christians shared a meal once a week; they sang hymns, they prayed, and they ate, generally some bread and fish, with water or wine. This might not sound too exciting but for the fact that people of different social classes were doing this—something unheard of in the ancient world.

The words of the Didache, a document known as *The Teaching of the Twelve Apostles,* probably compiled by the end of the first century, indicate how another Christian community was celebrating communion in a different fashion. Note the instructions given on fasting and prayer, as well as how the ritual and words for communion differ from those in the Synoptic Gospel accounts.

6.3 Now concerning food, observe the traditions as best you can. But be sure to refrain completely from meat which has been sanctified before idols, for it represents the worship of dead gods [see also Acts 15.29].

8.1 But do not let your fasts fall on the same days as "the hypocrites," who fast on Monday and Thursday. Rather, you should fast on Wednesday and Friday.

8.2 Nor should you pray as the "hypocrites" do, but pray as the Lord commanded in his gospel, thus:

Our Father who is in heaven, may your name be revered.
May your kingdom come, may your will be done on earth as it is done in heaven.
Let us partake today of our heavenly fare,
And forgive what we owe accordingly as we forgive those who are in debt to us.
And do not bring us into testing, but rescue us from evil.
For power and glory are yours forever.

8.3 Thrice daily you should pray in this manner.

9.1 Now concerning the giving of thanks. Give thanks in the following manner.

9.2 First, concerning the cup:

We thank you, our Father, for the holy vine of David your servant, which you have made known to us through Jesus your Servant.

Glory to you forever!

9.3 And concerning the broken loaf:

We thank you, our Father, for the life and knowledge, which you have made known to us through Jesus your Servant.

Glory to you forever!

9.4 Just as this loaf previously was scattered on the mountains and when it was gathered together it became a unity, so may your Church be gathered together from the ends of the earth into your kingdom. For glory and power are yours forever, through Jesus Christ!

9.5 But let no one eat or drink from your Eucharist except those who are baptized in the Lord's Name. For the Lord also has spoken concerning this: Do not give what is holy to dogs [Matt 7.6].

Justin Martyr (d. c. 165), a second-century Christian apologist (that is, a defender of Christianity), described communion in an effort to make the practice clear to outsiders:

> On finishing the prayers we greet each other with a kiss. Then bread and a cup of water and mixed wine are brought to the president [of the group] and he, taking them, sends up praise and glory to the Father of the universe through the name of the Son and of the Holy Spirit, and offers thanksgiving at some length that we have been deemed worthy to receive these things from [the Father]. When he has finished the prayers and the thanksgiving, the whole congregation assents, saying "Amen." . . . Those whom we call deacons give to each of those present a portion of the consecrated bread and wine and water, and they take it to the absent.

An early third-century document, the Apostolic Tradition, attributed to Hippolytus (c. 215), reveals other communion practices of the early church. The following excerpt comes from the service of ordination for a bishop. Again, note the differences and similarities it shares with communion services we have been reading about.

> And when he has been made bishop, all shall offer the kiss of peace, greeting him because he has been made worthy. Then the deacons shall present the offering to him; and he, laying his hands on it with all the presbytery, shall give thanks, saying:
>
> The Lord be with you;
> and all shall say:
>   And with your spirit.
> Up with your hearts.
>   We have them with the Lord.
> Let us give thanks to the Lord.
>   It is fitting and right.

After a number of prayers the bishop continues:

> And when he was betrayed to voluntary suffering that he might destroy death, and break the bonds of the devil, and tread down hell, and shine upon the righteous, and fix a term, and manifest the resurrection, he took bread and gave thanks to you, saying, "Take, eat; this is my body which shall be broken for you." Likewise, also the

cup, saying, "This is my blood, which is shed for you; when you do this, you make my remembrance."

Remembering therefore his death and resurrection, we offer to you the bread and the cup, giving you thanks because you have held us worthy to stand before you and minister to you . . .

By the fourth century, we begin to see a more literal and graphic understanding of body and blood, as in Cyril of Jerusalem's admonition "Contemplate therefore the Bread and Wine not as bare elements, for they are, according to the Lord's declaration, the Body and Blood of Christ; for though sense suggests this to thee, let faith establish thee. Judge not the matter from taste, but from faith be fully assured without misgiving, that thou hast been vouchsafed the Body and Blood of Christ." And we have this from a fourth-century liturgy from the Syrian church: "After this let the sacrifice take place, all the people standing and praying in silence: and when the oblation has been made, let every group by itself partake in order of the Lord's body and of the precious blood, and approach with reverence and godly fear, as to the body of a king." The seeds of a doctrine of transubstantiation already exist in the liturgy and beliefs of the early church.

Varieties of Early Christianity: Beliefs

Just as diverse practices existed in the early centuries of Christianity, so too did diverse beliefs. The beliefs that prevailed came to be accepted as orthodox, that is, as consistent with proper Christian teachings. The beliefs that did not prevail came to be viewed as heresy, that is, as inconsistent with accepted Christian teachings. It is important to remember, however, that the orthodoxy Christians accept today was not at all assumed or given in the earliest centuries of the church. Since history is written by the victors, the beliefs and teachings left behind have come to be called "heresies."

Heresies helped define what became mainstream Christian doctrine by forcing theologians and church leaders to defend what they believed was correct teaching—in other words, by making it clear what Christianity was *not*. For example, toward the end of the second century, a group of prophets in Phrygia (the Anatolian Highlands of Turkey) began revealing a new word from God. Montanus and two female prophets, Prisca and Maximilla, preached that the return of Jesus Christ was imminent. The Montanists, as some called them, lived a life of extreme asceticism. They claimed that the Spirit of God was speaking through them, and thus that a new revelation was occurring. But, said the traditionalists, God had spoken definitively through Jesus and the apostles, as well as through the prophets and pages of scripture. There could not be any new revelations. To ensure this, various church leaders began to compile a number of texts into an authoritative "New Testament" that could not be added to or subtracted from.

An earlier heretic, Marcion, also raised questions about what Christians should consider as authoritative scripture. Marcion (c. 84–160) believed that Jesus was not really human, but was divine; he merely appeared to be human—an idea known as Docetism, from the Greek word meaning "to appear" or "to seem." Marcion contrasted a perfectly divine Jesus with what he considered the evil creator god described in the Old Testament. These texts seemed to portray an entirely different god from that of Jesus Christ. This other god got angry, acted jealous, and went around smiting people, whereas the god Jesus described was forgiving, kind, and full of love. They could not possibly be the same deity. Marcion thought that Paul's letters supported this idea because Paul appeared to be criticizing the Jews. Marcion therefore attempted to "de-Judaize" all of scripture, that is, to remove all references to the creator God and to the Jewishness of Jesus. He put together a Bible that consisted only of Paul's letters and a heavily edited version of Luke's gospel.

Other early Christians shared Marcion's view that Jesus was never human. Many were part of a movement known as Gnosticism. Gnostics believed that Jesus was God's divine wisdom, descended from heaven to give humanity *gnosis,* or knowledge, of their true, heavenly nature. Many Gnostics, though not all, viewed the material world as evil, the product of an evil creator god who was jealous of humans. In fact, in the Gnostic interpretation of Genesis 2–3, Eve does the right thing by eating of the tree of knowledge and bringing its fruit *(gnosis)* to humanity. She and Adam are expelled by the evil creator god because he is jealous of their new awareness of their true spiritual nature. In Gnostic mythology, Sophia (Wisdom) comes from heaven to give people this original knowledge. (Sophia, by the way, is a feminine-gendered noun, and thus was personified as a female, much the way Justice and Liberty are depicted as female statues because Iustitia and Libertate are feminine-gendered in Latin.) Some Gnostics understood Jesus, though male, to be this feminine principle of God's wisdom, come down to return to us *gnosis* of our true identities. In this way, Jesus Sophia does not repair the damage that Eve and Adam caused—their introduction of sin into the world—but rather, restores the knowledge that they had gained but lost because of their expulsion from the garden by an angry god.

Various Christians found both Gnostic teachings and Marcion's version of scripture to be at odds with what they thought was acceptable Christian doctrine. Although church leaders in Rome excommunicated Marcion in 144—that is, kicked him out of the church by refusing to let him take communion—Gnostic Christianity remained a vibrant heresy throughout the Mediterranean, from the western edge of the empire in France, to North Africa, and east. Although the practices of the Gnostics varied, the belief that "Jesus saves" by bringing humanity saving knowledge of our original divinity seemed pervasive. Jesus revealed ourselves to ourselves: we all have a spark of divinity in us. Some Gnostics took this to mean that they should live a life of extreme renunciation, avoiding any indulgence of the flesh since we are spiritual, not physical, beings. Other Gnostics may have had an egalitarian leadership structure in which women participated. Some critics of Gnosticism, however, tended to accuse them of being licentious and of indulging in worldly pleasures.

Until the late twentieth century, most of our knowledge about Gnosticism came from Irenaeus of Lyon (c. 120/140–200/203), who wrote scathing critiques of Gnostics and their beliefs in a book called *Adversus Haereses (Against Heresies)*. Irenaeus, though critical, was extremely accurate in his representation of the Gnostics. We know this because in 1945, a number of Gnostic texts were found on the banks of the Nile River in Egypt. Called the Nag Hammadi Library, after the site where they were discovered, these texts provide a window onto the varieties of Gnosticism. There are genealogies of heavenly beings, retellings of the story of Adam and Eve (in which the two characters are heroes and victims, rather than weaklings and villains), and, most importantly, a number of gospels that present Jesus as a heavenly teacher of wisdom, such as the Gospel of Philip and the Gospel of Mary. These gospels depict Peter—Jesus' key disciple in the canonical Gospels of Matthew, Mark, Luke, and John, and a symbol for traditionalist, non-Gnostic Christianity—as a bad guy: petty, vindictive, and unwilling to listen to teachings imparted by Jesus' closest disciple, Mary Magdalene.

The Reading

One of the most interesting of the Gnostic texts is the Gospel of Thomas, which is not a narrative of Jesus' life or teachings, but rather a collection of Jesus' sayings. Many of these sayings appear in the canonical Gospels, but a number do not. The sayings present a rather cryptic teacher of wisdom who makes brief comments like "Be passersby" and "I am not your teacher." Scholars do not agree on the dating of Thomas. Some argue that it is one of the earliest collections of Jesus' sayings, dating it to the mid-first century. Others claim that it dates to a later period, especially because of its inclusion of canonical Jesus' sayings, and that it is a pastiche of authentic sayings and epigrams reflecting Gnostic ideas about Jesus.

The Gospel of Thomas is both easy and difficult to read. It's easy because it consists of short sayings; it's difficult because there are 114 of them, and they are not immediately accessible. If you have ever tried to read the book of Proverbs—a book of short epigrams that appears in the Hebrew Bible—at one sitting, you will recognize the difficulty in reading 114 little sound-bites. As an alternative to starting at the beginning and trying to read straight through to the end, try jumping around the text. Read different bits and pieces; read them out of sequence; let one lead you to the next. Read one or two dozen, set the book aside, and do something else. Then read another chunk, and later on, another until the Gospel of Thomas is completed. This gives your brain a chance to chew on what you have read and to think about the sayings as individual units rather than as a single mass.

Vocabulary note: *Didymos Judas Thomas* literally means "Judas Thomas the Twin." Is this the same Judas who wrote the letter of Jude in the New Testament, "a servant of Jesus Christ and brother of James?" Is this Judas claiming to be Jesus' twin brother? Is this the Thomas who appears in John's gospel as the disciple who doubted Jesus' resurrection? The likeliest explanation for the attribution of this gospel to Thomas is simply that of apostolic authority: a collection of writings about, or sayings of, Jesus had more legitimacy and credibility if it appeared to come from an authoritative source, such as an actual disciple.

Questions to Consider

1. What sayings seem incomprehensible to you? Note them, and attempt to paraphrase their meaning.

2. What sayings do you find meaningful? Why?

3. What in these sayings might threaten church order? Clearly, traditionalist Christianity found them distressing. Why?

4. What do these sayings imply about the location of the kingdom of God?

5. Think about these sayings within the context of Gnostic thought: if the body (flesh) is irrelevant to salvation, and if the spirit (soul) is everything, then what do these sayings mean? If the material world is bad, or evil, what should our ultimate goal be? How do these insights shed light on the many statements Jesus makes about life and death in this gospel?

6. Which sayings also appear in the Gospel of Mark? Which sayings seem familiar, and may have come from other Gospels?

7. Why do you think the Gospel of Thomas didn't make it into the canonical New Testament?

The Gospel of Thomas

These are the secret sayings that the living Jesus spoke and Didymos Judas Thomas recorded.

1 And he said, "Whoever discovers the interpretation of these sayings will not taste death."

2 Jesus said, "Those who seek should not stop seeking until they find. When they find, they will be disturbed. When they are disturbed, they will marvel, and will reign over all. [And after they have reigned they will rest.]"*

3 Jesus said, "If your leaders say to you, 'Look, the (Father's) kingdom is in the sky,' then the birds of the sky will precede you. If they say to you, 'It is in the sea,' then the fish will precede you. Rather, the kingdom is within you and it is outside you.

"When you know yourselves, then you will be known, and you will understand that you are children of the living Father. But if you do not know yourselves, then you live in poverty, and you are the poverty."

4 Jesus said, "The person old in days won't hesitate to ask a little child seven days old about the place of life, and that person will live.

---

* Material in brackets indicates scholars' attempts to clarify obscure texts.

"For many of the first will be last, and will become a single one."

5 Jesus said, "Know what is in front of your face, and what is hidden from you will be disclosed to you.

"For there is nothing hidden that will not be revealed. [And there is nothing buried that will not be raised.]"

6 His disciples asked him and said to him, "Do you want us to fast? How should we pray? Should we give to charity? What diet should we observe?"

Jesus said, "Don't lie, and don't do what you hate, because all things are disclosed before heaven. After all, there is nothing hidden that will not be revealed, and there is nothing covered up that will remain undisclosed."

7 Jesus said, "Lucky is the lion that the human will eat, so that the lion becomes human. And foul is the human that the lion will eat, and the lion still will become human."

8 And he said, "The person is like a wise fisherman who cast his net into the sea and drew it up from the sea full of little fish. Among them the wise fisherman discovered a fine large fish. He threw all the little fish back into the sea, and easily chose the large fish. Anyone here with two good ears had better listen!"

9 Jesus said, "Look, the sower went out, took a handful (of seeds), and scattered (them). Some fell on the road, and the birds came and gathered them. Others fell on rock, and they didn't take root in the soil and didn't produce heads of grain. Others fell on thorns, and they choked the seeds and worms ate them. And others fell on good soil, and it produced a good crop: it yielded sixty per measure and one hundred twenty per measure."

10 Jesus said, "I have cast fire upon the world, and look, I'm guarding it until it blazes."

11 Jesus said, "This heaven will pass away, and the one above it will pass away.

"The dead are not alive, and the living will not die. During the days when you ate what is dead, you made it come alive. When you are in the light, what will you do? On the day when you were one, you became two. But when you become two, what will you do?"

12 The disciples said to Jesus, "We know that you are going to leave us. Who will be our leader?"

Jesus said to them, "No matter where you are you are to go to James the Just, for whose sake heaven and earth came into being."

13 Jesus said to his disciples, "Compare me to something and tell me what I am like."

Simon Peter said to him, "You are like a just messenger."

Matthew said to him, "You are like a wise philosopher."

Thomas said to him, "Teacher, my mouth is utterly unable to say what you are like."

Jesus said, "I am not your teacher. Because you have drunk, you have become intoxicated from the bubbling spring that I have tended."

And he took him, and withdrew, and spoke three sayings to him. When Thomas came back to his friends they asked him, "What did Jesus say to you?"

Thomas said to them, "If I tell you one of the sayings he spoke to me, you will pick up rocks and stone me, and fire will come from the rocks and devour you."

14 Jesus said to them, "If you fast, you will bring sin upon yourselves, and if you pray, you will be condemned, and if you give to charity, you will harm your spirits.

"When you go into any region and walk about in the countryside, when people take you in, eat what they serve you and heal the sick among them.

"After all, what goes into your mouth will not defile you; rather, it's what comes out of your mouth that will defile you."

15 Jesus said, "When you see one who was not born of woman, fall on your faces and worship. That one is your Father."

16 Jesus said, "Perhaps people think that I have come to cast peace upon the world. They do not know that I have come to cast conflicts upon the earth: fire, sword, war.

"For there will be five in a house: there'll be three against two and two against three, father against son and son against father, and they will stand alone.

17 Jesus said, "I will give you what no eye has seen, what no ear has heard, what no hand has touched, what has not arisen in the human heart."

18 The disciples said to Jesus, "Tell us, how will our end come?"

Jesus said, "Have you found the beginning, then, that you are looking for the end? You see, the end will be where the beginning is.

"Congratulations to the one who stands at the beginning: that one will know the end and will not taste death."

19 Jesus said, "Congratulations to the one who came into being before coming into being.

"If you become my disciples and pay attention to my sayings, these stones will serve you.

"For there are five trees in Paradise for you; they do not change, summer or winter, and their leaves do not fall. Whoever knows them will not taste death."

20 The disciples said to Jesus, "Tell us what Heaven's kingdom is like."

He said to them, "It's like a mustard seed, the smallest of all seeds, but when it falls on prepared soil, it produces a large plant and becomes a shelter for birds of the sky."

21 Mary said to Jesus, "What are your disciples like?"

He said, "They are like little children living in a field that is not theirs. when the owners of the field come, they will say, 'Give us back our field.' They take off their clothes in front of them in order to give it back to them, and they return their field to them."

"For this reason I say, if the owners of a house know that a thief is coming, they will be on guard before the thief arrives and will not let the thief break into their house (their domain) and steal their possessions.

"As for you, then, be on guard against the world. Prepare yourselves with great strength, so the robbers can't find a way to get to you, for the trouble you expect will come.

"Let there be among you a person who understands.

"When the crop ripened, he came quickly carrying a sickle and harvested it. Anyone here with two good ears had better listen!"

22 Jesus saw some babies nursing. He said to his disciples, "These nursing babies are like those who enter the kingdom."

They said to him, "Then shall we enter the kingdom as babies?"

Jesus said to them, "When you make the two into one, and when you make the inner like the outer and the outer like the inner, and the upper like the lower, and when you make male and female into a single one, so that the male will not be male nor the female be female, when you make eyes in place of an eye, a hand in place of a hand, a foot in place of a foot, an image in place of an image, then you will enter [the kingdom]."

23 Jesus said, "I shall choose you, one from a thousand and two from ten thousand, and they will stand as a single one."

24 His disciples said, "Show us the place where you are, for we must seek it."

He said to them, "Anyone here with two ears had better listen! There is light within a person of light, and it shines on the whole world. If it does not shine, it is dark."

25 Jesus said, "Love your friends like your own soul, protect them like the pupil of your eye."

26 Jesus said, "You see the sliver in your friend's eye, but you don't see the timber in your own eye. When you take the timber out of your own eye, then you will see well enough to remove the sliver from your friend's eye."

27 "If you do not fast from the world, you will not find the kingdom. If you do not observe the sabbath as a sabbath you will not see the Father."

28 Jesus said, "I took my stand in the midst of the world, and in flesh I appeared to them. I found them all drunk, and I did not find any of them thirsty. My soul ached for the children of humanity, because they are blind in their hearts and do not see, for they came into the world empty, and they also seek to depart from the world empty.

"But meanwhile they are drunk. When they shake off their wine, then they will change their ways."

29 Jesus said, "If the flesh came into being because of spirit, that is a marvel, but if spirit came into being because of the body, that is a marvel of marvels.

"Yet I marvel at how this great wealth has come to dwell in this poverty."

30 Jesus said, "Where there are three deities, they are divine. Where there are two or one, I am with that one."

31 Jesus said, "No prophet is welcome on his home turf; doctors don't cure those who know them."

32 Jesus said, "A city built on a high hill and fortified cannot fall, nor can it be hidden."

33 Jesus said, "What you will hear in your ear, in the other ear proclaim from your rooftops.

"After all, no one lights a lamp and puts it under a basket, nor does one put it in a hidden place. Rather, one puts it on a lamp stand so that all who come and go will see its light."

34 Jesus said, "If a blind person leads a blind person, both of them will fall into a hole."

35 Jesus said, "One can't enter a strong person's house and take it by force without tying his hands. Then one can loot his house."

36 Jesus said, "Do not fret, from morning to evening and from evening to morning, [about your food—what you're going to eat, or about your clothing—] what you are going to wear. [You're much better than the lilies, which neither card nor spin.

"As for you, when you have no garment, what will you put on? Who might add to your stature? That very one will give you your garment.]"

37 His disciples said, "When will you appear to us, and when will we see you?"

Jesus said, "When you strip without being ashamed, and you take your clothes and put them under your feet like little children and trample then, then [you] will see the son of the living one and you will not be afraid."

38 Jesus said, "Often you have desired to hear these sayings that I am speaking to you, and you have no one else from whom to hear them. There will be days when you will seek me and you will not find me."

39 Jesus said, "The Pharisees and the scholars have taken the keys of knowledge and have hidden them. They have not entered nor have they allowed those who want to enter to do so.

"As for you, be as sly as snakes and as simple as doves."

40 Jesus said, "A grapevine has been planted apart from the Father. Since it is not strong, it will be pulled up by its root and will perish."

41 Jesus said, "Whoever has something in hand will be given more, and whoever has nothing will be deprived of even the little they have."

42 Jesus said, "Be passersby."

43 His disciples said to him, "Who are you to say these things to us?"

"You don't understand who I am from what I say to you.

"Rather, you have become like the Judeans, for they love the tree but hate its fruit, or they love the fruit but hate the tree."

44 Jesus said, "Whoever blasphemes against the Father will be forgiven, and whoever blasphemes against the son will be forgiven, but whoever blasphemes against the holy spirit will not be forgiven, either on earth or in heaven."

45 Jesus said, "Grapes are not harvested from thorn trees, nor are figs gathered from thistles, for they yield no fruit.

"Good persons produce good from what they've stored up; bad persons produce evil from the wickedness they've stored up in their hearts, and say evil things. For from the overflow of the heart they produce evil."

46 Jesus said, "From Adam to John the Baptist, among those born of women, no one is so much greater than John the Baptist that his eyes should not be averted.

"But I have said that whoever among you becomes a child will recognize the kingdom and will become greater than John."

47 Jesus said, "A person cannot mount two horses or bend two bows.

"And a slave cannot serve two masters, otherwise that slave will honor the one and offend the other.

"Nobody drinks aged wine and immediately wants to drink young wine. Young wine is not poured into old wineskins, or they might break, and aged wine is not poured into a new wineskin, or it might spoil.

"An old patch is not sewn onto a new garment, since it would create a tear."

48 Jesus said, "If two make peace with each other in a single house, they will say to the mountain, 'Move from here!' and it will move."

49 Jesus said, "Congratulations to those who are alone and chosen, for you will find the kingdom. For you have come from it, and you will return there again."

50 Jesus said, "If they say to you, 'Where have you come from?' say to them, 'We have come from the light, from the place where the light came into being by itself, established [itself], and appeared in their image.'

"If they say to you, 'Is it you?' say, 'We are its children, and we are the chosen of the living Father.'

"If they ask you, 'What is the evidence of your Father in you?' say to them, 'It is motion and rest.'"

51 His disciples said to him, "When will the rest for the dead take place, and when will the new world come?"

He said to them, "What you are looking forward to has come, but you don't know it."

52 His disciples said to him, "Twenty-four prophets have spoken in Israel, and they all spoke of you."

He said to them, "You have disregarded the living one who is in your presence, and have spoken of the dead."

53 His disciples said to him, "Is circumcision useful or not?"

He said to them, "If it were useful, their father would produce children already circumcised from their mother. Rather, the true circumcision in spirit has become profitable in every respect."

54 Jesus said, "Congratulations to the poor, for to you belongs Heaven's kingdom."

55 Jesus said, "Whoever does not hate father and mother cannot be my disciple, and whoever does not

hate brothers and sisters, and carry the cross as I do, will not be worthy of me."

56 Jesus said, "Whoever has come to know the world has discovered a carcass, and whoever has discovered a carcass, of that person the world is not worthy."

57 Jesus said, "The Father's kingdom is like a person who has [good] seed. His enemy came during the night and sowed weeds among the good seed. The person did not let the workers pull up the weeds, but said to them, 'No, otherwise you might go to pull up the weeds and pull up the wheat along with them.' For on the day of the harvest the weeds will be conspicuous, and will be pulled up and burned."

58 Jesus said, "Congratulations to the person who has toiled and has found life."

59 Jesus said, "Look to the living one as long as you live, otherwise you might die and then try to see the living one, and you will be unable to see."

60 He saw a Samaritan carrying a lamb and going to Judea. He said to his disciples, "That person . . . around the lamb." They said to him, "So that he may kill it and eat it." He said to them, "He will not eat it while it is alive, but only after he has killed it and it has become a carcass."

They said, "Otherwise he can't do it."

He said to them, "So also with you, seek for yourselves a place for rest, or you might become a carcass and be eaten."

61 Jesus said, "Two will recline on a couch; one will die, one will live."

Salome said, "Who are you mister? You have climbed onto my couch and eaten from my table as if you are from someone."

Jesus said to her, "I am the one who comes from what is whole. I was granted from the things of my Father."

"I am your disciple."

"For this reason I say, if one is whole, one will be filled with light, but if one is divided, one will be filled with darkness."

62 Jesus said, "I disclose my mysteries to those [who are worthy] of [my] mysteries. Do not let your left hand know what your right hand is doing."

63 Jesus said, "There was a rich person who had a great deal of money. He said, 'I shall invest my money so that I may sow, reap, plant, and fill my storehouses with produce, that I may lack nothing.' These were the things he was thinking in his heart, but that very night he died. Anyone here with two ears had better listen!"

64 Jesus said, "A person was receiving guests. When he had prepared the dinner, he sent his slave to invite the guests. The slave went to the first and said to that one, 'My master invites you.' That one said, 'Some merchants owe me money; they are coming to me tonight. I have to go and give them instructions. Please excuse me from dinner.' The slave went to another and said to that one, 'My master has invited you.' That one said to the slave, 'I have bought a house, and I have been called away for a day. I shall have no time.' The slave went to another and said to that one, 'My master invites you.' That one said to the slave, 'My friend is to be married, and I am to arrange the banquet. I shall not be able to come. Please excuse me from dinner.' The slave went to another and said to that one, 'My master invites you.' That one said to the slave, 'I have bought an estate, and I am going to collect the rent. I shall not be able to come. Please excuse me.' The slave returned and said to his master, 'Those whom you invited to dinner have asked to be excused.' The master said to his slave, 'Go out on the streets and bring back whomever you find to have dinner.'

"Buyers and merchants [will] not enter the places of my Father."

65 He said, "A [. . .] person owned a vineyard and rented it to some farmers, so they could work it and he could collect its crop from them. He sent his slave so the farmers would give him the vineyard's crop. They grabbed him, beat him, and almost killed him, and the slave returned and told his master. His master said, 'Perhaps he didn't know them.' He sent another slave, and the farmers beat that one as well. Then the master sent his son and said, 'Perhaps they'll show my son some respect.' Because the farmers knew that he was the heir to the vineyard, they grabbed him and killed him. Anyone here with two ears had better listen!"

66 Jesus said, "Show me the stone that the builders rejected: that is the keystone."

67 Jesus said, "Those who know all, but are lacking in themselves, are utterly lacking."

68 Jesus said, "Congratulations to you when you are hated and persecuted; and no place will be found, wherever you have been persecuted."

69 Jesus said, "Congratulations to those who have been persecuted in their hearts: they are the ones who have truly come to know the Father.

"Congratulations to those who go hungry, so the stomach of the one in want may be filled."

70 Jesus said, "If you bring forth what is within you, what you have will save you. If you do not have

that within you, what you do not have within you [will] kill you."

71 Jesus said, "I will destroy [this] house, and no one will be able to build it [. . .]."

72 A [person said] to him, "Tell my brothers to divide my father's possessions with me."

He said to the person, "Mister, who made me a divider?"

He turned to his disciples and said to them, "I'm not a divider, am I?"

73 Jesus said, "The crop is huge but the workers are few, so beg the harvest boss to dispatch workers to the fields."

74 He said, "Lord, there are many around the drinking trough, but there is nothing in the well."

75 Jesus said, "There are many standing at the door, but those who are alone will enter the bridal suite."

76 Jesus said, "The Father's kingdom is like a merchant who had a supply of merchandise and found a pearl. That merchant was prudent; he sold the merchandise and bought the single pearl for himself."

"So also with you, seek his treasure that is unfailing, that is enduring, where no moth comes to eat and no worm destroys."

77 Jesus said, "I am the light that is over all things. I am all: from me all came forth, and to me all attained.

"Split a piece of wood; I am there.

"Lift up the stone, and you will find me there."

78 Jesus said, "Why have you come out to the countryside? To see a reed shaken by the wind? And to see a person dressed in soft clothes, [like your] rulers and your powerful ones? They are dressed in soft clothes, and they cannot understand truth."

79 A woman in the crowd said to him, "Lucky are the womb that bore you and the breasts that fed you."

He said to [her], "Lucky are those who have heard the word of the Father and have truly kept it. For there will be days when you will say, 'Lucky are the womb that has not conceived and the breasts that have not given milk.'"

80 Jesus said, "Whoever has come to know the world has discovered the body, and whoever has discovered the body, of that one the world is not worthy."

81 Jesus said, "Let one who has become wealthy reign, and let one who has power renounce."

82 Jesus said, "Whoever is near me is near the fire, and whoever is far from me is far from the kingdom."

83 Jesus said, "Images are visible to people, but the light within them is hidden in the image of the Father's light. He will be disclosed, but his image is hidden by his light."

84 Jesus said, "When you see your likeness, you are happy. But when you see your images that came into being before you and that neither die nor become visible, how much you will have to bear!"

85 Jesus said, "Adam came from great power and great wealth, but he was not worthy of you. For had he been worthy, [he would] not [have tasted] death."

86 Jesus said, "[Foxes have] their dens and birds have their nests, but human beings have no place to lay down and rest."

87 Jesus said, "How miserable is the body that depends on a body, and how miserable is the soul that depends on these two."

88 Jesus said, "The messengers and the prophets will come to you and give you what belongs to you. You, in turn, give them what you have, and say to yourselves, 'When will they come and take what belongs to them?'"

89 Jesus said, "Why do you wash the outside of the cup? Don't you understand that the one who made the inside is also the one who made the outside?"

90 Jesus said, "Come to me, for my yoke is comfortable and my lordship is gentle, and you will find rest for yourselves."

91 They said to him, "Tell us who you are so that we may believe in you."

He said to them, "You examine the face of heaven and earth, but you have not come to know the one who is in your presence, and you do not know how to examine the present moment."

92 Jesus said, "Seek and you will find.

"In the past, however, I did not tell you the things about which you asked me then. Now I am willing to tell them, but you are not seeking them."

93 "Don't give what is holy to dogs, for they might throw them upon the manure pile. Don't throw pearls [to] pigs, or they might . . . it [. . .]."

94 Jesus [said], "One who seeks will find, and for [one who knocks] it will be opened."

95 [Jesus said], "If you have money, don't lend it at interest. Rather, give [it] to someone from whom you won't get it back."

96 Jesus [said], "The Father's kingdom is like [a] woman. She took a little leaven, [hid] it in dough, and made it into large loaves of bread. Anyone here with two ears had better listen!"

97 Jesus said, "The [Father's] kingdom is like a woman who was carrying a [jar] full of meal. While

she was walking along [a] distant road, the handle of the jar broke and the meal spilled behind her [along] the road. She didn't know it; she hadn't noticed a problem. When she reached her house, she put the jar down and discovered that it was empty."

98 Jesus said, "The Father's kingdom is like a person who wanted to kill someone powerful. While still at home he drew his sword and thrust it into the wall to find out whether his hand would go in. Then he killed the powerful one."

99 The disciples said to him, "Your brothers and your mother are standing outside."

He said to them, "Those here who do what my Father wants are my brothers and my mother. They are the ones who will enter my Father's kingdom."

100 They showed Jesus a gold coin and said to him, "The Roman emperor's people demand taxes from us."

He said to them, "Give the emperor what belongs to the emperor, give God what belongs to God, and give me what is mine."

101 "Whoever does not hate [father] and mother as I do cannot be my [disciple], and whoever does [not] love [father and] mother as I do cannot be my [disciple]. For my mother [. . .], but my true [mother] gave me life."

102 Jesus said, "Damn the Pharisees! They are like a dog sleeping in the cattle manger: the dog neither eats nor [lets] the cattle eat."

103 Jesus said, "Congratulations to those who know where the rebels are going to attack. [They] can get going, collect their imperial resources, and be prepared before the rebels arrive."

104 They said to Jesus, "Come, let us pray today, and let us fast."

Jesus said, "What sin have I committed, or how have I been undone? Rather, when the groom leaves the bridal suite, then let people fast and pray."

105 Jesus said, "Whoever knows the father and the mother will be called the child of a whore."

106 Jesus said, "When you make the two into one, you will become children of Adam, and when you say, 'Mountain, move from here!' it will move."

107 Jesus said, "The kingdom is like a shepherd who had a hundred sheep. One of them, the largest, went astray. He left the ninety-nine and looked for the one until he found it. After he had toiled, he said to the sheep, 'I love you more than the ninety-nine.'"

108 Jesus said, "Whoever drinks from my mouth will become like me; I myself shall become that person, and the hidden things will be revealed to him."

109 Jesus said, "The [Father's] kingdom is like a person who had a treasure hidden in his field but did not know it. And [when] he died he left it to his [son]. The son [did] not know about it either. He took over the field and sold it. The buyer went plowing, [discovered] the treasure, and began to lend money at interest to whomever he wished."

110 Jesus said, "Let one who has found the world, and has become wealthy, renounce the world."

111 Jesus said, "The heavens and the earth will roll up in your presence, and whoever is living from the living one will not see death."

Does not Jesus say, "Those who have found themselves, of them the world is not worthy"?

112 Jesus said, "Damn the flesh that depends on the soul. Damn the soul that depends on the flesh."

113 His disciples said to him, "When will the kingdom come?"

"It will not come by watching for it. It will not be said, 'Look, here!' or 'Look, there!' Rather, the Father's kingdom is spread out upon the earth, and people don't see it."

[Saying added to the original collection at a later date:] 114 Simon Peter said to them, "Make Mary leave us, for females don't deserve life." Jesus said, "Look, I will guide her to make her male, so that she too may become a living spirit resembling you males. For every female who makes herself male will enter the kingdom of Heaven."

If the Gnostics made Jesus other-worldly and divine, hardly human at all, other Christians wanted to make Jesus only too human. Some rejected the idea of Jesus' divinity outright, claiming that he remained human even after his exaltation by God at the resurrection. Others argued that Jesus was "adopted" as God's divine son by virtue of his willing obedience and moral perfection. Still others, like a group known as the Arians, believed that Jesus was the Son of God and the first-born of creation, but that he was not "coeternal" with God the Father. In other words, "there was a time when he was not," as the Arians liked to say. He was divine, but had not always been divine, and in some way remained subordinate to God the Father.

Was Jesus divine? And if so, was he equal to God the Father? Was Jesus really a human being, or did he merely appear to be one? Did he come to die a sacrificial death or to bring humanity special knowledge of their divine nature? In the early centuries of Christianity, these were burning questions. By the end of the fifth century, however, Christianity had developed a clear doctrine of the Trinity: the explanation

▨ The Influence of Hellenism

The Roman Empire, and Christianity, were greatly influenced by Hellenism—the thought-world of Greek culture and language. Introduced by Alexander the Great during his military campaigns of the fourth century B.C.E., Hellenism pervaded the territories of his conquest in the Mediterranean for centuries after his death. Hellenistic influences upon Judaic religions led, in part, to a conflict within Judea in the early second century B.C.E. At the same time, Hellenistic schools of philosophy—characterized by a teacher and his followers, who retained and recorded the teachings of the master—inspired Jewish schools of thought surrounding various sages, including the "school" of Jesus and his disciples.

Once Christianity became a Gentile movement outside of Judea, Hellenistic philosophy provided some of the language and concepts that eventually were used to describe God. Apologists—that is, interpreters of Christianity—tried to explain their beliefs in terms readily understandable to Gentile, rather than Jewish, audiences. They described a "logos" that educated people knew referred to the creative principle of "the One," the formless, unchangeable divine reality. (Both Greeks and some Hellenized Jews in the Diaspora thought of the logos as a lesser divinity that was involved in creating the world, since God was above all that.) Although we think of Greek and Roman culture as being polytheistic, it is important to differentiate between the gods of everyday citizens—which ordered specific realms such as sailing, hunting, and agriculture—and the god of the philosophers, which was the ultimate in One-ness. This Greek concept of the divine ultimately affected Christian discussions of the incarnation of the logos (divine) in the person of Jesus Christ (human), as well as deliberations concerning the relationship between these two aspects of Jesus' reality.

Christians interpreted their scriptural heritage and their understanding of Jesus using the philosophical concepts and language of Greek philosophy. Throughout history, Christians have tried to explain their beliefs in contemporary terms. In late antiquity, this meant utilizing the language of Hellenistic philosophy, including Neoplatonism, to describe the divine. In the Middle Ages, Christians used Aristotelian logic to comprehend the mysteries of faith. In the twentieth century, existentialism and Marxism influenced the vocabulary and culture of Christian theology. Thus, Christianity is always in dialogue with its surrounding culture.

that God is three divine persons—Father, Son, and Holy Spirit—in a single godhead. That is, God is three-in-one. Along the way to a unified doctrine, many other teachings about God and Jesus were debated, abandoned, or suppressed. The diverse forms of Christianity that existed throughout the Roman world—from the west to the east—would be supplanted and suppressed by a dominant orthodox teaching.

The Development of Creeds

The process of developing a clear and cogent statement of Christian belief about God and Jesus took several centuries. Although there are short proclamations in the New Testament (for example, "Jesus Christ is Lord"), there is no comprehensive statement of faith. There certainly is no trinitarian doctrine about the three-in-one nature of God in either the Hebrew Bible or the New Testament, but the Bible does give us a few early creeds about Jesus. A creed, or credo, is a confession of belief, not a statement of fact. Creeds may summarize core beliefs and cherished values, or they may be statements of faith, such as the Shema in Judaism and the Shahadah in Islam. In other words, creeds reflect theology rather than history.

Paul's statement in 1 Corinthians probably expresses the beliefs of the earliest Christians:

PAUL'S CREED

For I handed on to you as of first importance what I in turn had received: that Christ died for our sins in accordance with the scriptures, and that he was buried, and that he was raised on the third day in accordance with the scriptures, and that he appeared to Cephas [Peter], then to the twelve. Then he appeared to more than five hundred brothers and sisters at one time, most of whom are still alive, though some have fallen asleep. Then he appeared to James, then to all the apostles. Last of all, as to one untimely born, he appeared also to me. (1 Corinthians 15:3–8)

The second chapter of the New Testament book of Acts also presents an early Christian proclamation. Jesus' disciple Peter is preaching to a large group that has gathered and witnessed a miracle: tongues of fire descending on the heads of the disciples, who began speaking in "other languages." Jews from around the Mediterranean who were present were able to understand what these others were saying, kind of like having headset translations at the United Nations. Although some accused the disciples of being drunk, "all were amazed and perplexed." Peter explains to the crowd that they aren't drunk, but rather that they have witnessed the fulfillment of a prophecy. He goes on to give the following summary of the new movement's teachings:

PETER'S CREED

You that are Israelites, listen to what I have to say: Jesus of Nazareth, a man attested to you by God with deeds of power, wonders, and signs that God did through him among you, as you yourselves know—this man, handed over to you according to the definite plan and foreknowledge of God, you crucified and killed by the hands of those outside the law. But God raised him up, having freed him from death, because it was impossible for him to be held in its power. . . . This Jesus God raised up, and of that all of us are witnesses. Being therefore exalted at the right hand of God, and having received from the Father the promise of the Holy Spirit, he has poured out this that you both see and hear. . . . Therefore let the entire house of Israel know with certainty that God has made him both Lord and Messiah, this Jesus whom you crucified. (Acts 2:22–24, 32–34, 36)

Both Paul and Peter focus on the death and resurrection of Jesus. They don't say much about God, although Peter's proclamation implicitly indicates a distinction between God and Jesus: it is God who has raised Jesus and has made him "both Lord and Messiah." The Bible, in fact, is not much help in providing a clear trinitarian doctrine. Some Christians consider Genesis 1:26—where God says, "Let *us* create a human being"—a reference to the Trinity, even though a verse later Genesis says, "male and female *he* created them" (emphasis added). In addition, a late manuscript of 1 John, a New Testament letter dating to the late first or early second century, includes the phrase "There are three that testify in heaven, the Father, the Word, and the Holy Spirit, and these three are one" (1 John 5:7). The earliest manuscripts of the same text provide nontrinitarian language, however: "There are three that testify: the Spirit and the water and the blood, and these three agree."

There are really only two references to the three-fold name—Father, Son, Spirit—in the New Testament. First, Paul provides a benediction at the end of 2 Corinthians: "The grace of the Lord Jesus Christ and the love of God and the fellowship of the Holy Spirit be with you all" (2 Corinthians 13:13; some Bibles have 13:14). Matthew's gospel presents an early baptismal formula when it says, "Go therefore and make disciples of all nations, baptizing them in the name of the Father and of the Son and of the Holy Spirit" (Matthew 28:19). The word "trinity" does not appear in the Bible; it was coined at the end of the second century by a North African Christian named Tertullian (c. 160–220). A completely realized understanding of the relationship between the Father, the Son, and the Holy Spirit did not yet exist in the first century.

Matthew offers an early hint of the connection between saying the threefold name and baptism. Catechumens who were baptized in succeeding centuries would be asked, "Do you believe in the Father?" They would respond, "Yes, I believe in the Father," and then they would be immersed in the water of baptism. The process would be repeated by asking them if they believed in the Son and in the Spirit. They did not yet say, "God the Father," "God the Son," or "God the Holy Spirit"; that came later. One early statement of faith coming from the mid-second century (c. 150) was the Epistula Apostolorum, which probably was recited by catechumens when they officially became Christians.

EPISTULA APOSTOLORUM

[I believe] In the Father, the Ruler of the Universe,
And in Jesus Christ, our Redeemer,
In the Holy Spirit, the Paraclete,

In the Holy Church,
And in the Forgiveness of Sins.

A statement of faith more familiar to modern Christians is the Apostles' Creed. Although this creed contains elements of early traditions, it did not begin to appear until the late fourth century, and complete versions did not exist until the seventh or even eighth century. This is one of the oldest creeds that is still used in Christian churches today.

THE APOSTLES' CREED

I believe in God the Father almighty, creator of heaven and earth;

And in Jesus Christ, His only Son, our Lord, Who was conceived by the Holy Spirit, born of the Virgin Mary, suffered under Pontius Pilate, was crucified, dead and buried. He descended to hell, on the third day rose again from the dead, ascended to heaven, sits at the right hand of God the Father almighty, thence He will come to judge the living and the dead;

I believe in the Holy Spirit, the holy catholic Church, the communion of saints, the forgiveness of sins, the resurrection of the body, and the life everlasting. Amen.

We see the three-fold name in the Epistula Apostolorum and the Apostles' Creed, but it is not at all clear that the Son and the Spirit are divine, let alone equal to God the Father.

The Reading

As a result of disputes and dissension among Christians, especially over the divinity of Jesus and his connection to God, the emperor Constantine called a council of Christian bishops in 325 C.E. Over three hundred bishops formulated the Nicene Creed, which provided a clear statement of the relationship of the Son of God to God the Father. But the role that the Holy Spirit played, and the Spirit's equality with the Son and the Father, was unclear. So the bishops met again in 381 C.E. in Constantinople and revised the Nicene Creed to elaborate on the significance of the Spirit. As a result, the creed formalized a doctrine of the Trinity, although later ecumenical councils made further declarations. (An ecumenical council is a meeting of representatives from all churches; it was a very important step for the early church to take.) The revised Nicene Creed, which appears on page 90, is what Catholic, Lutheran, Episcopalian, and Orthodox Christians recite in churches today.

Questions to Consider

1. Can you identify any of the heresies the Nicene Creed seems to be addressing? What about the idea of there being two gods? What about the idea of Jesus not really being human? Is God the Son always divine?

2. What are some of the differences between the creed of 325 and that of 381? Why do you think changes or additions were made?

3. How do the creeds change over the centuries—from Paul and Peter, to second-century creeds, to Nicea and Constantinople?

4. There were an equal number of scriptural arguments for the subordination of the Son to the Father as there were for their equality. Why do you think the higher view prevailed?

5. Do you think some new creeds might be appropriate for Christians to adopt? Why or why not? (See the Nicene Creed on page 90.)

Nicea and Constantinople made it clear that Jesus, as the Son of God, was both fully human and fully divine. But how did that work in reality? Was he God on some days, and human on others? Was his mind divine, but his body human? Was he wearing a "space-suit" of human flesh, hiding a total divinity? And if Jesus was divine, did that make Mary the Mother of God? But how could God be born? These were all questions that the Nicene Creed did not address and that later church leaders pondered as they tried to understand how Jesus, the Son of God, could be human and divine all at the same time.

The problem was solved, or at least addressed, by the Council of Chalcedon in 451 C.E., when Jesus' divine and human natures were debated. The Definition of Chalcedon is exactly that: it is not a creed, but rather an explanation of the language to be used when talking about Jesus and his divine and human aspects. Moreover, it explicitly states that "Mary the virgin" is the "God-bearer" (*theotokos* in Greek), insofar as she gave birth to the human Jesus. Thus the definition exalts the status of Mary by saying she is the Mother of God.

THE DEFINITION OF CHALCEDON

Following, then, the holy fathers, we unite in teaching all men to confess the one and only Son, our Lord Jesus Christ. This selfsame one is perfect both in deity and also in human-ness; this selfsame one is also actually God and actually man, with a rational soul and a body. He is of the same reality as God as far as his deity is concerned and of the same reality as we are ourselves as far as his humanness is concerned; thus like us in all respects, sin only excepted. Before time began he was begotten of the Father, in respect of his deity, and now in these "last days," for us and on behalf of our salvation, this selfsame one was born of Mary the virgin, who is God-bearer in respect of his human-ness.

[We also teach] that we apprehend this one and only Christ—Son, Lord, only-begotten—in two natures; [and we do this] without confusing the two natures, without transmuting one nature into the other, without dividing them into two separate categories, without contrasting them according to area or function. The distinctiveness of each nature is not nullified by the union. Instead, the "properties" of each nature are conserved and both natures concur in one "person" and in one substance. They are not divided or cut into two persons, but are together the one and only and only-begotten Logos of God, the Lord Jesus Christ. Thus have the prophets of old testified; thus the Lord Jesus Christ himself taught us; thus the Symbol of the Fathers has handed down to us.

The Nicene Creed of 325 and 381: A Comparison

THE NICENE CREED OF 325

We believe in one God, the Father All Governing, creator of all things visible and invisible;

And in one Lord Jesus Christ, the Son of God, begotten of the Father as only begotten, that is, from the essence of the Father, God from God, Light from Light, true God from true God, begotten not created, of the same essence as the Father, through whom all things came into being, both in heaven and in earth;

Who for us men and for our salvation came down and was incarnate, becoming human. He suffered and the third day he rose, and ascended into the heavens. And he will come to judge both the living and the dead.

And [we believe] in the Holy Spirit.

But, those who say, Once he was not, or he was not before his generation, or he came to be out of nothing, or who assert that he, the Son of God, is of a different substance or essence, or that he is a creature, or changeable, or mutable, the Catholic and Apostolic Church anathematizes* them.

---

*Anathematize means to curse them; when you read the expression "let them be anathema," that means, "let them be damned." This curse is no longer said in churches today.

THE NICENE CREED OF 381
(WHAT IS SAID IN CHURCHES TODAY)

We believe in one God, the Father All Governing, creator of heaven and earth, of all things visible and invisible;

And in one Lord Jesus Christ, the only-begotten Son of God, begotten of the Father before all time, Light from Light, true God from true God, begotten not created, of the same essence as the Father, through Whom all things came into being, Who for us men and because of our salvation, came down from heaven, and was incarnate by the Holy Spirit and the Virgin Mary and became human. He was crucified for us under Pontius Pilate, and suffered and was buried, and rose on the third day, according to the Scriptures, and ascended to heaven and sits on the right hand of the Father, and will come again with glory to judge the living and the dead. His Kingdom shall have no end.

And in the Holy Spirit, the Lord and life-giver, Who proceeds from the Father,* Who is worshiped and glorified together with the Father and Son, Who spoke through the prophets; and in one, holy, catholic, and apostolic Church. We confess one baptism for the remission of sins. We look forward to the resurrection of the dead and the life of the world to come. Amen.

---

* Christian Churches of the west today say, "Who proceeds from the Father *and* the Son." These three little words, called the "filioque," were added to the creed in the sixth century by churches in the west that wanted to elevate the status of the Son of God. Since the change had not been agreed to by churches in the east, however, the filioque became a bone of contention between eastern and western Christianity, and remains an issue of dispute today. Some churches in the west are quietly dropping the filioque without debate.

Chalcedon was not the end of debates about what Christians believe. Creeds and creedal formulas have continued to be developed and adopted throughout the long history of Christianity. A number of new statements of faith, or confessions of faith, arose during the reformations, as Protestant Christians attempted to clarify what they believed over and against what Catholic Christians believed (see Chapter Four).

We find many creedal assertions in the hymns that Christians sing. Sometimes they take parts of the actual Nicene Creed and turn them into poetry; other times they take some of the concepts from the creeds and use them in the poems: incarnation, trinity, unity, Father, Son, and Holy Spirit. A hymn written by Charles Wesley in 1747 summarizes the Nicene Creed in poetic form:

> Maker, in whom we live, in whom we are and move,
> The glory, power, and praise receive for thy creating love.
> Let all the angel throng give thanks to God on high,
> While earth repeats the joyful song and echoes to the sky.
>
> Incarnate Deity, let all the ransomed race
> Render in thanks their lives to thee for thy redeeming grace.
> The grace to sinners showed ye heavenly choirs proclaim,
> And cry, "Salvation to our God, salvation to the Lamb!"
>
> Spirit of Holiness, let all thy saints adore
> Thy sacred energy, and bless thine heart-renewing power.
> Not angel tongues can tell thy love's ecstatic height,
> The glorious joy unspeakable, the beatific sight.
>
> Eternal Triune God, let all the hosts above,
> Let all on earth below record and dwell upon thy love.
> When heaven and earth are fled before thy glorious face,
> Sing all the saints thy love hath made thine everlasting praise.

Here's another verse from a Wesley hymn that should be familiar to Christians and non-Christians alike: "Hark! The Herald Angels Sing." It blends creedal assertions with passages from scripture.

> Christ, by highest heaven adored;
> Christ, the everlasting Lord;
> Late in time behold him come,
> Offspring of a virgin's womb.
> Veiled in flesh the Godhead see;
> Hail th'incarnate Deity,
> Pleased with us in flesh to dwell,
> Jesus, our Emmanuel.
> Hark! the herald angels sing,
> "Glory to the newborn King!"

On the Incarnation

The Gospel of John begins by saying: "In the beginning was the Word, and the Word was with God, and the Word was God. He was in the beginning with

God. . . . And the Word became flesh and lived among us, and we have seen his glory . . ." (John 1:1–2, 14). The "Word" is the Logos of God. In Greek, *logos* meant not only "word"—as in God's word spoken at creation—but also God's reason and rationality, God's wisdom and creative power. Both Greek and Jewish thinkers had adapted and adopted the concept of the Logos, seeing in it something of an intermediary figure between God and the world. John's gospel makes clear, however, that this being is actually God, not something different or apart from God. At the same time, the gospel also says that this Logos became human, that it took on human flesh.

The idea of incarnation—the "enfleshment" of God—which Christians now take for granted, was not easily accepted in the earliest centuries of Christianity. Jews found the concept abhorrent, for it made a man into God. But the idea horrified pagans as well, for the opposite reason: it was inconceivable that the transcendent and impassible One would enter the material world and take on human flesh. Pagan philosophers strongly believed that the material world was inferior to the spiritual world. The realm of ideas, or forms, vastly surpassed anything we might see, hear, taste, smell, or touch. Moreover, matter decayed; it changed, corrupted, died. How could the Eternal, which was unchanging, come into such a world? It was unthinkable.

Nevertheless, we clearly see an affirmation of the theology of incarnation stated in the Nicene Creed: "Who for us men and because of our salvation, came down from heaven, and was incarnate by the Holy Spirit and the Virgin Mary and became human." The New Testament letters of Timothy, Peter, and John all refer to the Son of God being revealed in the flesh. A short creed appears in the first letter to Timothy: "Who was revealed in flesh, vindicated in spirit, seen by angels, proclaimed among Gentiles, believed in throughout the world, taken up in glory" (1 Timothy 3:16). And the John letters warn against those who teach that the Son of God did *not* come in the flesh: "Many deceivers have gone out into the world, those who do not confess that Jesus Christ has come in the flesh; any such person is the deceiver and the antichrist!" (2 John 7). These New Testament texts are attacking Docetism, a belief especially prevalent among pagans who could not conceive of a divinity assuming flesh or materiality except as a temporary disguise.

The Reading

Athanasius of Alexandria wrote a defense of the idea of incarnation for Christians to understand *why* the Word of God had to become incarnate in Jesus. The son of wealthy parents, Athanasius (c. 298–373) was an Egyptian Christian who spent a lifetime combating the Arian heresy, even being excommunicated and losing his position as bishop of Alexandria for a time to Arian sympathizers. He wrote *On the Incarnation* in Greek when he was in his twenties, long before the Arian controversy even erupted. It is addressed to "Macarius," which might be a euphemism for any Christian, since *Macarius* means "blessed" in Greek.

On the Incarnation outlines the reasons why God became human. After presenting his argument, Athanasius then refutes specific criticisms made by Jews and pagans against the idea of incarnation. He clarifies why Jesus had to die, both in manner and timing. He provides a world history that sets the stage for asserting the need for incarnation as the only solution to the problems faced by a sinful and wretched humanity. This selection focuses on explaining the need for the divine to enter humanity.

Questions to Consider

1. Why does Athanasius feel there was a need for the incarnation? What was the human dilemma that required it? What does the incarnation accomplish for humanity?

2. How does Athanasius explain how God can be human and divine all at once?

3. What role does death play in this whole scheme of things? Why does Jesus have to die, according to Athanasius?

4. How does this reading relate to Genesis 1:26–27, in which humans are created in the "image and likeness" of God? How does this relate to Genesis 2–3?

5. What seem to be the questions that outsiders are asking about the incarnation? Deduce these concerns from Athanasius' analysis.

On the Incarnation: Chapter 3

ATHANASIUS OF ALEXANDRIA

(11) When God the Almighty was making mankind through His own Word, He perceived that they, owing to the limitation of their nature, could not of themselves have any knowledge of their Artificer, the Incorporeal and Uncreated. He took pity on them, therefore, and did not leave them destitute of the knowledge of Himself, lest their very existence should prove purposeless. For of what use is existence to the creature if it cannot know its Maker? How could men be reasonable beings if they had no knowledge of the Word and Reason of the Father, through Whom they had received their being? They would be no better than the beasts, had they no knowledge save of earthly things; and why should God have made them at all, if He had not intended them to know Him? But, in fact, the good God has given them a share in His own Image, that is, in our Lord Jesus Christ, and has made even themselves after the same Image and Likeness. Why? Simply in order that through this gift of Godlikeness in themselves they may be able to perceive the Image Absolute, that is the Word Himself, and through Him to apprehend the Father; which knowledge of their Maker is for men the only really happy and blessed life.

But, as we have already seen, men, foolish as they are, thought little of the grace they had received, and turned away from God. They defiled their own soul so completely that they not only lost their apprehension of God, but invented for themselves other gods of various kinds. They fashioned idols for themselves in place of the truth and reverenced things that are not, rather than God Who is, as St. Paul says, "worshipping the creature rather than the Creator" [Romans 1:25]. Moreover, and much worse, they transferred the honor which is due to God to material objects such as wood and stone, and also to man; and further even than that they went, as we said in our former book. Indeed, so impious were they that they worshipped evil spirits as gods in satisfaction of their lusts. They sacrificed brute beasts and immolated men, as the just due of these deities, thereby bringing themselves more and more under their insane control. Magic arts also were taught among them, oracles in sundry places led men astray, and the cause of everything in human life was traced to the stars as though nothing existed but that which could be seen. In a word, impiety and lawlessness were everywhere, and neither God nor His Word was known. Yet He had not hidden Himself from the sight of men nor given the knowledge of Himself in one way only; but rather He had unfolded it in many forms and by many ways.

(12) God knew the limitation of mankind, you see; and though the grace of being made in His Image was sufficient to give them knowledge of the Word and through Him of the Father, as a safeguard against their neglect of this grace, He provided the works of creation also as means by which the Maker might be known. Nor was this all. Man's neglect of the indwelling grace tends ever to increase; and against this further frailty also God made provision by giving them a law, and by sending prophets, men whom they knew. Thus, if they were tardy in looking up to heaven, they might still gain knowledge of their Maker from those close at hand; for men can learn directly about higher things from other men. Three ways thus lay open to them, by which they might obtain the knowledge of God. They could look up into the immensity of heaven, and by pondering the harmony of creation come to know its Ruler, the Word of the Father, Whose all-ruling providence makes known the Father to all. Or, if this was beyond them, they could converse with holy men, and through them learn to know God, the Artificer of all things, the Father of Christ, and to recognize the worship of idols as the negation of the truth and full of all impiety. Or else, in the third place, they could cease from lukewarmness and lead a good life merely by knowing the law. For the law was not given only for the Jews, nor was it solely for their sake that God sent the prophets, though it was to the Jews that they were sent and by the Jews that they were persecuted. The law and the prophets were a sacred school of the knowledge of God and the conduct of the spiritual life for the whole world.

So great, indeed, were the goodness and the love of God. Yet men, bowed down by the pleasures of the moment and by the frauds and illusions of the evil spirits, did not lift up their heads towards the truth. So burdened were they with their wickednesses that they seemed rather to be brute beasts than reasonable men, reflecting the very Likeness of the Word.

(13) What was God to do in face of this dehumanizing of mankind, this universal hiding of the knowledge of Himself by the wiles of evil spirits? Was He to keep silence before so great a wrong and let men go on being thus deceived and kept in ignorance of Himself? If so, what was the use of having made them in His own Image originally? It would surely have been better for them always to have been brutes, rather than to revert to that condition when once they had shared the nature of the Word. Again, things being as they were, what was the use of their ever having had the knowledge of God? Surely it would have been better for God never to have bestowed it, than that men should subsequently be found unworthy to receive it. Similarly, what possible profit could it be to God Himself, Who made men, if when made they did not worship Him, but regarded others as their makers? This would be tantamount to His having made them for others and not for Himself. Even an earthly king, though he is only a man, does not allow lands that he has colonized to pass into other hands or to desert to other rulers, but sends letters and friends and even visits them himself to recall them to their allegiance, rather than allow His work to be undone. How much more, then, will God be patient and painstaking with His creatures, that they be not led astray from Him to the service of those that are not, and that all the more because such error means for them sheer ruin, and because it is not right that those who had once shared His Image should be destroyed.

What, then, was God to do? What else could He possibly do, being God, but renew His Image in mankind, so that through it men might once more come to know Him? And how could this be done save by the coming of the very Image Himself, our Savior Jesus Christ? Men could not have done it, for they are only made after the Image; nor could angels have done it, for they are not the images of God. The Word of God came in His own Person, because it was He alone, the Image of the Father Who could recreate man made after the Image.

In order to effect this re-creation, however, He had first to do away with death and corruption. Therefore He assumed a human body, in order that in it death might once for all be destroyed, and that men might be renewed according to the Image. The Image of the Father only was sufficient for this need. Here is an illustration to prove it.

(14) You know what happens when a portrait that has been painted on a panel becomes obliterated through external stains. The artist does not throw away the panel, but the subject of the portrait has to come and sit for it again, and then the likeness is redrawn on the same material. Even so was it with the All-holy Son of God. He, the Image of the Father, came and dwelt in our midst, in order that He might renew mankind made after Himself, and seek out His lost sheep, even as He says in the Gospel: "I came to seek and to save that which was lost" [Luke 19:10]. This also explains His saying to the Jews: "Except a man be born anew . . ." [John 3:3]. He was not referring to a man's natural birth from his mother, as they thought, but to the re-birth and re-creation of the soul in the Image of God.

Nor was this the only thing which only the Word could do. When the madness of idolatry and irreligion filled the world and the knowledge of God was hidden, whose part was it to teach the world about the Father? Man's, would you say? But men cannot run everywhere over the world, nor would their words carry sufficient weight if they did, nor would they be, unaided, a match for the evil spirits. Moreover, since even the best of men were confused and blinded by evil, how could they convert the souls and minds of others? You cannot put straight in others what is warped in yourself. Perhaps you will say, then, that creation was enough to teach men about the Father. But if that had been so, such great evils would never have occurred. Creation was there all the time, but it did not prevent men from wallowing in error. Once more, then, it was the Word of God, Who sees all that is in man and moves all things in creation, Who alone could meet the needs of the situation. It was His part and His alone, Whose ordering of the universe reveals the Father, to renew the same teaching. But how was He to do it? By the same means as before, perhaps you will say, that is, through the works of creation. But this was proven insufficient. Men had neglected to consider the heavens before, and now they were looking in the opposite direction. Wherefore, in all naturalness and fitness, desiring to do good to men, as Man He dwells, taking to Himself a body like the rest; and through His actions done in that body, as it were on their own level, He teaches those who would not learn by other means to know Himself, the Word of God, and through Him the Father.

(15) He deals with them as a good teacher with his pupils, coming down to their level and using simple means. St. Paul says as much: "Because in the wisdom of God the world in its wisdom knew not God, God thought fit through the simplicity of the News proclaimed to save those who believe" [1 Corinthians 1:21].

Men had turned from the contemplation of God above, and were looking for Him in the opposite direction, down among created things and things of sense. The Savior of us all, the Word of God, in His great love took to Himself a body and moved as Man among men, meeting their senses, so to speak, half way. He became Himself an object for the senses, so that those who were seeking God in sensible things might apprehend the Father through the works which He, the Word of God, did in the body. Human and human minded as men were, therefore, to whichever side they looked in the sensible world they found themselves taught the truth. Were they awe-stricken by creation? They beheld it confessing Christ as Lord. Did their minds tend to regard men as Gods? The uniqueness of the Savior's works marked Him, alone of men, as Son of God. Were they drawn to evil spirits? They saw them driven out by the Lord and learned that the Word of God alone was God and that the evil spirits were not gods at all. Were they inclined to hero-worship and the cult of the dead? Then the fact that the Savior had risen from the dead showed them how false these other deities were, and that the Word of the Father is the one true Lord, the Lord even of death. For this reason was He both born and manifested as Man, for this He died and rose, in order that, eclipsing by His works all other human deeds, He might recall men from all the paths of error to know the Father. As He says Himself, "I came to seek and to save that which was lost" [Luke 19:10].

(16) When, then, the minds of men had fallen finally to the level of sensible things, the Word submitted to appear in a body, in order that He, as Man, might center their senses on Himself, and convince them through His human acts that He Himself is not man only but also God, the Word and Wisdom of the true God. This is what Paul wants to tell us when he says: "That ye, being rooted and grounded in love, may be strong to apprehend with all the saints what is the length and breadth and height and depth, and to know the love of God that surpasses knowledge, so that ye may be filled unto all the fullness of God" [Ephesians 3:17–19]. The Self-revealing of the Word

is in every dimension—above, in creation; below, in the Incarnation; in the depth, in Hades; in the breadth, throughout the world. All things have been filled with the knowledge of God.

For this reason He did not offer the sacrifice on behalf of all immediately He came, for if He had surrendered His body to death and then raised it again at once He would have ceased to be an object of our senses. Instead of that, He stayed in His body and let Himself be seen in it, doing acts and giving signs which showed Him to be not only man, but also God the Word. There were thus two things which the Savior did for us by becoming Man. He banished death from us and made us anew; and, invisible and imperceptible as in Himself He is, He became visible through His works and revealed Himself as the Word of the Father, the Ruler and King of the whole creation.

(17) There is a paradox in this last statement which we must now examine. The Word was not hedged in by His body, nor did His presence in the body prevent His being present elsewhere as well. When He moved His body He did not cease also to direct the universe by His Mind and might. No. The marvelous truth is, that being the Word, so far from being Himself contained by anything, He actually contained all things Himself. In creation He is present everywhere, yet is distinct in being from it; ordering, directing, giving life to all, containing all, yet is He Himself the Uncontained, existing solely in His Father. As with the whole, so also is it with the part. Existing in a human body, to which He Himself gives life, He is still Source of life to all the universe, present in every part of it, yet outside the whole; and He is revealed both through the works of His body and through His activity in the world. It is, indeed, the function of soul to behold things that are outside the body, but it cannot energize or move them. A man cannot transport things from one place to another, for instance, merely by thinking about them; nor can you or I move the sun and the stars just by sitting at home and looking at them. With the Word of God in His human nature, however, it was otherwise. His body was for Him not a limitation, but an instrument, so that He was both in it and in all things, and outside all things, resting in the Father alone. At one and the same time—this is the wonder—as Man He was living a human life, and as Word He was sustaining the life of the universe, and as Son He was in constant union with the Father. Not even His birth from a virgin, therefore, changed Him in any way, nor was He defiled by being in the body. Rather, He sanctified the body by being in it. For His

being in everything does not mean that He shares the nature of everything, only that He gives all things their being and sustains them in it. Just as the sun is not defiled by the contact of its rays with earthly objects, but rather enlightens and purifies them, so He Who made the sun is not defiled by being made known in a body, but rather the body is cleansed and quickened by His indwelling, "Who did no sin, neither was guile found in His mouth" [1 Peter 2:22].

(18) You must understand, therefore, that when writers on this sacred theme speak of Him as eating and drinking and being born, they mean that the body, as a body, was born and sustained with the food proper to its nature; while God the Word, Who was united with it, was at the same time ordering the universe and revealing Himself through His bodily acts as not man only but God. Those acts are rightly said to be His acts, because the body which did them did indeed belong to Him and none other; moreover, it was right that they should be thus attributed to Him as Man, in order to show that His body was a real one and not merely an appearance. From such ordinary acts as being born and taking food, He was recognized as being actually present in the body; but by the extraordinary acts which He did through the body He proved Himself to be the Son of God. That is the meaning of His words to the unbelieving Jews: "If I do not the works of My Father, believe Me not; but if I do, even if ye believe not Me, believe My works, that ye may know that the Father is in Me and I in the Father" [John 10:38].

Invisible in Himself, He is known from the works of creation; so also, when His Godhead is veiled in human nature, His bodily acts still declare Him to be not man only, but the Power and Word of God. To speak authoritatively to evil spirits, for instance, and to drive them out, is not human but divine; and who could see Him curing all the diseases to which mankind is prone, and still deem Him mere man and not also God? He cleansed lepers, He made the lame to walk, He opened the ears of the deaf and the eyes of the blind, there was no sickness or weakness that He did not drive away. Even the most casual observer can see that these were acts of God. The healing of the man born blind, for instance, who but the Father and Artificer of man, the Controller of his whole being, could thus have restored the faculty denied at birth? He Who did thus must surely be Himself the Lord of birth. This is proved also at the outset of His becoming Man. He formed His own body from the virgin; and that is no small proof of His Godhead, since He Who made that was the Maker of all else. And would not anyone infer from the fact of that body being begotten of a virgin only, without human father, that He Who appeared in it was also the Maker and Lord of all beside?

Again, consider the miracle at Cana. Would not anyone who saw the substance of water transmuted into wine understand that He Who did it was the Lord and Maker of the water that He changed? It was for the same reason that He walked on the sea as on dry land—to prove to the onlookers that He had mastery over all. And the feeding of the multitude, when He made little into much, so that from five loaves five thousand mouths were filled—did not that prove Him none other than the very Lord Whose Mind is over all?

Thus far, we have examined the Gnostic soteriology of the Gospel of Thomas and the incarnational soteriology of Athanasius. Soteriology is the doctrine of salvation. When Christians say, "Jesus saves," they have something particular in mind. The Gnostics believed that Jesus saved by bringing us knowledge of our true divinity. Early Christians rejected this view and instead upheld an incarnational soteriology in the creeds: that God saved by virtue of becoming incarnate in the person of Jesus and living among us as a human being. Christians today still accept this soteriology.

A third soteriology, however, has come to dominate western Christianity. This is the doctrine of the atonement: that Jesus Christ died for our sins. His sacrificial death on the cross wiped the slate clean between God and humanity, and allowed people to enter into a renewed relationship with the divine. Known as the substitutionary atonement, Jesus' death vicariously atoned for our sins so that we no longer had to pay the ultimate penalty for them. This is another way "Jesus saves." It is important to note that all three soteriologies appear in the New Testament, as do some others. Moreover, we see both incarnation and atonement in the Nicene Creed, for just as Jesus became human for our salvation, he was also crucified for us, the creed says.

All three soteriologies, even Gnosticism, continue to play a role in Christianity today, although eastern Orthodox Christians tend to emphasize the incarnation, while Western Christians, Catholic and Protestant, tend to emphasize the atonement. Atonement provides a legal solution that balances the problem of human sin against God's justice, while incarnation and Gnosticism provide alternate solutions. The theology of atonement saw its greatest development in the west, possibly as a result of the influence of Roman jurisprudence and later developments within canon law and medieval Christianity.

The Church of Empire

Constantine and Nicea changed the fortunes of the Christian Church. No longer outlawed or persecuted, the church emerged from catacombs and outposts as a transnational organization, with branches throughout the Roman Empire and even beyond. Nicea unified a heterodox (having many teachings) church by providing clear guidelines for what was, and was not, orthodox doctrine. The Nicene Creed was a boundary marker that differentiated between a strong, centralized church and everybody else. In the West, Rome was the capital city for the church, and for the growing centralization of power in the bishop of Rome, also known as the pope. Constantinople was the capital city for the eastern empire, but there a system of decentralized church patriarchs, or leaders, shared power and cooperated on decisions. While the bishop of Rome may have been first among equals, the western church emphasized his primacy, and the eastern church his equality.

This conflict was not initially a problem, though, as both East and West rejoiced in the new-found freedom and support that followed Constantine's decree. Eusebius, bishop of Caesarea (c. 313–339), delivered a long oration in praise of Constantine, seeing him as a "divinely favored emperor, receiving as it were, a transcript of the Divine sovereignty, [directing] in imitation of God himself, the administration of this world's affairs." Eusebius believed that the marriage between church and state effected by Constantine's conversion would benefit both parties and would result in universal salvation:

> The manifold forms of government, the tyrannies and republics, the siege of cities, and devastation of countries caused thereby, were now no more, and one God was proclaimed to all mankind. At the same time one universal power, the Roman empire, arose and flourished, while the enduring and implacable hatred of nation against nation was now removed: and as the knowledge of one God, and one way of religion and salvation, even the doctrine of Christ, was made known to all mankind; so at the self-same period, the entire dominion of the Roman empire being vested in a single sovereign, profound peace reigned throughout the world.

Eusebius' ode to Constantine sometimes seems to blur the line between the savior Jesus Christ and the savior Constantine.

Certainly in the decades and then centuries after Constantine's death, Eusebius' effusive praise seemed prophetic. Emperors gave church leaders more and more power in the form of financial support and tax exemptions. Large cathedrals (that is, churches over which the local bishop presided) were constructed. Missionaries spread northward up to the British Isles, westward across North Africa, and eastward into Asia.

The international, or global, nature of the church—with branches throughout the Mediterranean and beyond, and with members of power, prestige, and wealth—is what allowed it to survive the barbarian invasions of the fifth century. Indeed, it was the most powerful institution remaining after the sack of Rome in 410 and the fall of the western empire in 476. This explains why the church became the central institution in Europe during the Middle Ages: it was the *only* institution that remained.

In the fifth century, Augustine of Hippo (354–430) provided a cogent explanation for the fluctuating fortunes of both Christian and pagan empires. Like Athanasius, Augustine was a North African. He was born to a pagan father and a devout Christian mother. After a wild adolescence, followed by a more temperate young

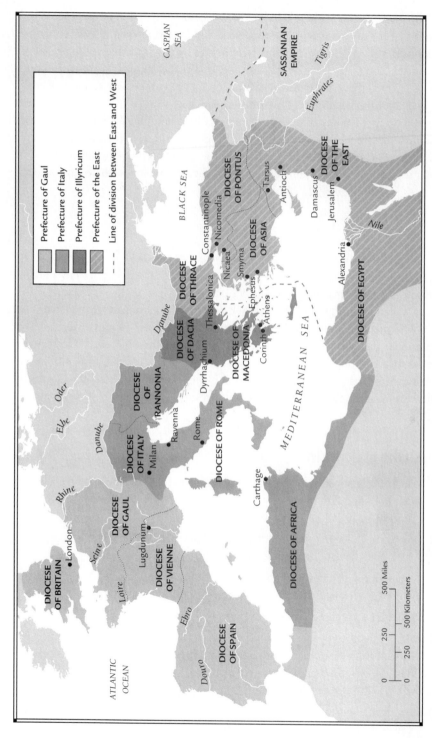

The Roman Empire in the fourth century.   *This map shows the administrative dioceses into which Diocletian divided the empire.*

adulthood, Augustine had a religious experience that turned him into an ascetic convinced that human sin was an inescapable fact of life. As a result of Adam and Eve's disobedience in the garden, all of us were bound by sin, incapable of doing or even willing the good. This explained why the world was in such a mess. Although pagans claimed that Christianity was the cause of the barbarian invasions, since the old gods had been neglected, Augustine catalogued a list of invasions and defeats that had occurred prior to the ascendancy of Christianity in the empire. Moreover, he added, these kinds of disasters would always occur in what he called the "earthly city." What else could you expect in a world run by humans who were controlled by sin? It was only in the heavenly city—that is, the city of God—where sin was overcome, that justice and peace would reign.

The Reading

Augustine compares and contrasts the characteristics of the earthly city and the heavenly city in his massive work *City of God*. He explains on the very first page that he has "taken upon [himself] the task of defending the glorious City of God against those who prefer their own gods to the Founder of that City." In other words, it is an impassioned defense of Christianity and its god. This defense is based on history and a recounting of Rome's past, as well as on theology, and an analysis of the central problem for Augustine: human sin. The following selection examines the origin and nature of sin, and how it has shaped the earthly city.

Questions to Consider

1. What is Augustine's view of human nature? What does he mean by the "flesh"? What does he mean by the "soul"? What do you think he means when he talks about the insubordination of the flesh?

2. Do humans have free will, according to Augustine? Be able to support your answer with specific examples.

3. What exactly is Augustine's argument in the following passage? Is there more than one? What evidence does he use to support his assertions?

4. Would a Christian find his claims persuasive? Would a non-Christian? Why or why not?

5. Why did Augustine's views prevail? Many Christians argued against his pessimistic views of human sin and reproduction. What was the appeal of Augustine's gloomy assessment?

6. How does Augustine use the stories from Genesis 1–3 in his argument? Who receives the most blame—Adam or Eve?

7. Compare and contrast the views of Augustine and those of Athanasius regarding the problem of human nature.

8. Does the idea of human sin help to rationalize the state of the world today? Does the idea of "two cities" help to account for the existence of wars, natural disasters, and other evils of earthly life? Explain why or why not.

City of God, Chapters from Book 14

AUGUSTINE OF HIPPO

IV. What it means to live according to man and what to live according to God.

Therefore, when man lives according to man and not according to God, he is like the devil, for even an angel should have lived, not according to an angel, but according to God if he was to adhere to the truth and speak the truth that came from God and not the falsehood that came from himself. For the Apostle says elsewhere concerning man too: "But if through my falsehood God's truthfulness has abounded" [Romans 3:7]. He speaks of falsehood as ours, but of truth as God's.

Consequently, when man lives according to truth, he does not live according to his own self but according to God. For it was God who said: "I am the truth" [John 14:6]. On the other hand, when he lives according to his own self, that is, according to man and not according to God, assuredly he lives according to falsehood. This does not mean that man himself is falsehood, since his author and creator is God, and God is certainly not the author and creator of falsehood. Rather it means that man was created right, in the sense that he was to live not according to his own self but according to his maker, that is, to do the latter's will instead of his own. Not to live after the fashion for which he was designed to live is falsehood.

Man has indeed a will to be happy even when he does not live in a way that makes it possible for him to be so, but what is falser than a will of that sort? Hence we may say without impropriety that every sin is a falsehood. For when a sin is committed, it is committed only because of the will that we have to fare well or not to fare ill. Consequently, the falsehood is this, that a sin is committed in order that we may fare well and the result is rather that we fare ill, or that a sin is committed in order that we may fare better and the result is rather that we fare worse. What is the reason for this except that a man's welfare comes from God, not from himself? But he forsakes God by sinning and sins by living according to his own self.

Consequently, my former statement, that the existence of two different and opposing cities is due to the fact that some people live according to the flesh and others according to the spirit, may also be put in this way that some people live according to man and others according to God. Paul told the Corinthians very plainly: "For while there is jealousy and strife among you, are you not of the flesh and behaving according to man?" [1 Corinthians 3:3]. Thus, whether we say that a man is of the flesh or that he behaves according to man, the sense is the same because the flesh, that is, a part of man, means man himself.

Those very same people, whom the Apostle here called carnal, were just previously referred to as animal when he said: "For what person knows a man's thoughts except the spirit of the man which is in him? So also no one knows the thoughts of God except the spirit of God. Now we have received not the spirit of this world, but the spirit which is from God, that we might understand the gifts bestowed on us by God. And we impart this in words not taught by human wisdom, but taught by the spirit, interpreting spiritual truths to those who possess the spirit. The animal man does not receive the gifts or the spirit of God, for they are folly to him" [1 Corinthians 2:11–14].

It is to such people then, that is to animal men, that he says a little later: "But I, brethren, could not address you as spiritual men, but as carnal men" [1 Corinthians

3:1]. Both terms, animal and carnal, illustrate the same figure of speech, that is, the use of a part for the whole. For both the soul (anima) and the flesh, which are parts of man, can serve to indicate the whole which is man. And thus the animal man is not something different from the carnal man, but both are one and the same, that is, man living according to man. Similarly, the allusion is merely to men not only where we read: "No flesh will be justified by works of the law," [Romans 3:20] but also in the scriptural passage: "Seventy-five souls went down with Jacob into Egypt" [Genesis 46:27]. For in the former quotation, we take "no flesh" to mean "no man," and in the latter, seventy-five souls to mean "seventy-five men."

Moreover, when the Apostle said: "In words not taught by human wisdom," he could equally well have used the phrase "carnal wisdom," just as when he said: "You behave according to man," he might have said: "According to the flesh." We see this more plainly in the words that he added: "For when one says, 'I belong to Paul,' and another, 'I belong to Apollos,' are you not merely men?" When he states here: "You are men," he shows more explicitly what he intended by the phrases "You are animal" and "You are carnal." What he means is this: "You live according to man, not according to God, for if you lived according to him, you would be gods."

XI. On the fall of the first man in whom a well-created natural state was impaired and can be restored only by its creator.

But God foreknew all things and must therefore also have been aware that man would sin. For this reason, we must base any doctrine of the holy city on his foreknowledge and dispensation and not on that which could not have come to our knowledge because it was not a part of God's dispensation. Man could not possibly upset the divine plan by his sin, as if he could have compelled God to change what he had decreed, for God through his foreknowledge had anticipated both the coming events, that is, both how bad the man whom he himself had created good would become and what good he himself would use him to effect even so.

God, it is true, is said to change his decrees, and hence we read in Scripture the statement in figurative speech even that God "repented" [Genesis 6:6; Exodus 32:14; 1 Samuel 15:11, 15:35; 2 Samuel 24:16]. But such a statement is based on man's expectation or on the prospect implicit in the orderly course of natural causes, not on the Almighty's foreknowledge of what he will do. Thus, as Scripture tells us, God made man upright [Ecclesiastes 7:29] and consequently of good will, for man would not have been upright without a good will. Good will then is the work of God, since man was created in possession of it by him.

On the other hand, the first evil act of will, preceding, as it did, all evil works in man, was rather a falling away from the work of God to the will's own works than any one work; and those works were evil because they followed the will's own pattern and not God's. Thus the will itself, or man himself in so far as he was possessed of an evil will, was the evil tree, as it were, that bore the evil fruit that those works represented. Further, although an evil will is not in accordance with nature but contrary to nature because it is a defect, nevertheless it belongs to the natural being of which it is a defect, for it can exist only in a natural substance. But it must exist in the natural substance that God created out of nothing, not in that which the Creator begot from himself, as he begot the Word through which all things were made. For, although God fashioned man from the dust of the earth, this very earth and all earthly matter are derived from nothing at all, and he gave to the body when man was created a soul that was made out of nothing.

But the good things prevail over the bad, so much so in fact that, although bad things are permitted to exist in order to show how the righteous Creator with his perfect foresight can make good use even of them, nevertheless good things can exist without bad, for example, the true and supreme God himself or again all visible and invisible creations in the heaven above our murky air. On the other hand, evil cannot exist without the good since the created things in which it is found are certainly good as created. Moreover, an evil is eliminated not by the removal of some substance, or any part of it, which had supervened, but by the healing and restoration of the substance that had become morbid and debased.

Accordingly, the decision of the will is truly free only when it is not a slave to faults and sins. It had that freedom when God first gave it, but, having lost such freedom by its own fault, it can regain it only from him in whose power it was to grant it originally. Truth says on this point: "If the Son sets you free, then you will be truly free" [John 8:36]. This is tantamount to saying: "If the Son saves you, then you will be truly saved." For the same act makes a savior a deliverer too.

Thus man lived according to God in a paradise that was both corporeal and spiritual. This paradise was not merely corporeal to supply the good things of the body without also being spiritual to supply the good things of the mind; nor was it merely spiritual for man to enjoy through his inner senses without also being corporeal for him to enjoy through his outer senses. It was clearly both for the good of both. Then, however, came that proud angel, whose very pride made him envious and also caused him to turn from God to follow himself. With the arrogance, as it were, of a tyrant he chose to rejoice over subjects rather than to be a subject himself; and consequently he fell from the spiritual paradise. I have discoursed as best I could in the eleventh and twelfth books of this work on the fall of this angel and of those leagued with him, the former angels of God who became his angels. After his fall he sought by corrupting guile to work his way into the heart of man, whose unfallen state surely he envied since he himself had fallen. For this purpose he chose as his mouthpiece a serpent in the corporeal paradise, where along with those two human beings, male and female, there dwelt also all the other terrestrial animals, who were tame and harmless. This slippery animal, of course, which moves in twisting coils, was a suitable tool for his work. By his stature as an angel and his superior being he made it subject to him in spiritual wickedness, and misusing it as his instrument he conversed deceitfully with the woman. In so doing he no doubt began with the lower member of that human couple in order to arrive gradually at the whole. Presumably he did not think that the man was readily gullible or that he could be snared by his own mistake, but only if he gave way to the mistake of another.

So was it with Aaron, for he did not agree with the mistaken multitude to construct an idol because he was persuaded, but he yielded to it because he was under pressure. Nor is it credible that Solomon mistakenly thought that he should serve idols; he was driven to such acts of irreligion by the blandishments of women. Similarly, when we consider the situation of that first man and his woman, two fellow human beings all alone and married to each other, we must suppose that he was not led astray to transgress the law of God because he believed that she spoke the truth, but because he was brought to obey her by the close bond of their alliance. For the Apostle was not speaking idly when he said: "And Adam was not de-ceived, but the woman was deceived." He must have meant that Eve had accepted what the serpent said to her as though it were true, while Adam refused to be separated from his sole companion even in a partner-ship of sin. Yet he was no less guilty if he sinned with knowledge and forethought. This also explains why the Apostle does not say: "He did not sin," but: "He was not deceived" [1 Timothy 2:14]. For he surely refers to him where he states: "Sin came into the world through one man;" and a little later when he says more explicitly: "Like the transgression of Adam" [Romans 5:12–14].

The Apostle meant us to understand the deceived as being those who do not think that what they do is sin. Adam, however, knew; otherwise, how can it be true to say: "Adam was not deceived"? But since he was not yet acquainted with the strict justice of God, he might have been mistaken in believing that his of-fence was pardonable. Hence, though he did not suf-fer the same deception as the woman, yet he was mistaken about the verdict that would inevitably be pronounced on this plea that he would make: "The woman whom thou gavest to be with me, she gave it to me, and I ate" [Genesis 3:12]. To put it briefly then, we may say that although they were not both deceived by believing, yet both were taken captive by sinning and ensnared in the devil's toils.

XII. On the character of the sin committed by the first human beings.

Someone may be moved to wonder why other sins do not change man's nature in the same way as the trans-gression of the first two human beings changed it. For as a result of that offence it was subjected to all the decay that we see and feel and consequently to death as well. Moreover, man became a prey to agita-tion and buffeting by many powerful and conflicting emotions and thus developed into something quite different from what he certainly was in paradise be-fore sin in spite of his animal body. Someone, as I said, may be moved to wonder at this, but if so, he must not regard that offence as slight or trivial on the ground that it involved only food, a food not bad or harmful except that it was forbidden. Indeed, God would not have created and planted anything bad in that place of immense happiness.

But in God's command obedience was enjoined, and this virtue is, in a sense, the mother and guardian of all virtues in a rational creature, inasmuch as man has been naturally so created that it is advantageous for him to be submissive but ruinous to follow his own will and not the will of his creator. This command, which forbade the eating of one kind of food where a great abundance of other kinds lay close at hand, was as easy to observe as it was brief to remember, especially since the will was not yet then opposed by desire. Such opposition arose later as punishment for the transgression. Consequently, the crime of violating the command was all the greater in proportion to the ease with which it could have been heeded and upheld.

XIII. That in Adam's transgression the evil act was preceded by an evil will.

When the first human beings began to be evil, they did so in secret, and this enabled them to fall into open disobedience. For the evil act could not have been arrived at if an evil will had not gone before. Further, what but pride can have been the start of an evil will? For "pride is the start of all sin" [Sirach 10:13]. Moreover, what is pride but a craving for perverse elevation? For it is perverse elevation to forsake the ground in which the mind ought to be rooted, and to become and be, in a sense, grounded in oneself. This happens when a man is too well pleased with himself, and such a one is thus pleased when he falls away from that unchangeable good with which he ought rather to have been pleased than with himself. Now this falling away is voluntary, for if the will had remained steadfast in love of the higher unchangeable good that provided it with light to see and kindled it with fire to love, it would not have been diverted from this love to follow its own pleasure. Nor would the will in consequence have grown so dark and cold as to allow either the first woman to believe that the serpent had spoken the truth or the first man to place his wife's will before God's injunction and to think that his transgression of the command could be pardoned if he did not forsake the partner of his life even when partnership in sin was involved.

Accordingly, the evil act, that is, the transgression that involved their eating of forbidden food, was committed only by those who were already evil. For only a bad tree could have produced that evil fruit. Moreover, the badness of the tree was an event contrary to nature, because, except for a defect of will, which is contrary to nature, it could surely not have come to pass. But only a thing created out of nothing could be corrupted by a defect. And consequently, while it owes its existence as a being to its creation by God, yet it owes its lapse from its true being to its creation out of nothing.

Yet man did not lapse so completely as to lose all being, but by turning to himself he ended by having less true being than he had when he was rooted in him who has the highest being. Therefore, to leave God and to have being in oneself, that is, to follow one's own pleasure, is not to be nothing already but to come nearer to being nothing. This is why in scriptural language the proud are also called self-pleasers. It is indeed a good thing to have an aspiring mind, yet aspiring not to oneself, which belongs to pride, but to God, which belongs to obedience, and obedience can belong only to the humble.

Accordingly, strange as it may seem, there is something in humility to uplift the mind, and there is something in exaltation to abase the mind. It does indeed appear somewhat of a paradox that exaltation abases and humility uplifts. But religious humility makes the mind submissive to what is superior; hence, since nothing is superior to God, humility elevates the mind in making it submissive to God. On the other hand, exaltation that is connected with a fault automatically scorns subordination and lapses from him who is supreme. This will bring it lower, and the words of Scripture come to pass: "Thou hast cast them down when they were being exalted" [Psalm 73:18]. Scripture does not say: "When they had been exalted," and thus imply that they were first exalted and afterwards cast down; but at the very moment that they were being exalted, then were they cast down. For the very act of being exalted is already an act of being cast down.

At this time, as we know, in the City of God and for the City of God during its pilgrimage in this world humility is most highly recommended and is also most emphasized in the case of Christ, its king. From the sacred Scriptures we learn also that the fault of exaltation, which is the antithesis of this virtue, reigns supreme in his adversary, the devil. This is surely the great difference that sets apart the two cities of which we are speaking, the one being a community of religious men, the other of irreligious men, each with the angels that belong to it. In one city love of God came first; in the other, love of self.

Accordingly, the devil would not have trapped man by the overt and manifest sin of doing what God had forbidden to be done if man had not already begun to be pleased with himself. This is why he was also delighted with the words: "You will be as gods" [Genesis 3:5]. But they could better have come to be such if they had through obedience adhered to their highest and true ground and not through pride set themselves up as their own ground. For created gods are gods not by any true being of their own but by participation in the true God. Striving for more diminishes a person, who by choosing to be sufficient unto himself suffers a deficiency in lapsing from the one who is truly sufficient for him.

The initial wrong therefore was that whereby, when man is pleased with himself, as if he were in himself a light, he is diverted from that light through which, if he would but choose it, he himself also becomes a light. This wrong, I repeat, came first in secret and prepared the way for the other wrong that was committed openly. For the words of Scripture are true: "Before a fall the mind is exalted but is humbled before honor" [Proverbs 18:12]. In short, the fall that takes place in secret precedes the fall that takes place in full view, but the former fall is not regarded as such. For who considers exaltation a fall, though there is already present in it the lapse whereby the Most High is deserted? On the other hand, who could fail to see that there is a fall when a manifest and unquestionable transgression of some command takes place?

This explains why God forbade that act which, when it was performed, could not be defended under any pretext of righteousness. I dare say too that it is useful for the proud to fall into some patent and obvious sin by which they may become displeased with themselves after they had already fallen by being pleased with themselves. Peter was in a healthier state when he was displeased with himself and wept than when he was pleased with himself and too confident. This idea is also expressed in a holy psalm: "Fill their faces with shame, and they will seek thy name, O Lord," that is: "Let those who had pleased themselves when they sought their own name be pleased with thee as they seek thine" [Psalm 83:16].

XIV. On the transgressor's pride, which was worse than the transgression itself.

But worse and more damnable is the pride that prompts a man to seek refuge in an excuse even when sins are clear to see. Thus, in the case of the first human beings, the woman said: "The serpent beguiled me, and I ate," and the man said: "The woman whom thou gavest to be with me, she gave me fruit of the tree, and I ate" [Genesis 3:12–13]. In these words nowhere do we hear of any entreaty for pardon, nowhere of any supplication for healing. For though they do not deny the offence that they committed, as did Cain, yet their pride still seeks to lay the blame

for its wrong act on another, the pride of the woman on the serpent, the pride of the man on the woman. But where the transgression of a divine command is manifest, such a pretext is really to accuse rather than to excuse oneself. For indeed this transgression was no less their act merely because the woman committed the offence on the advice of the serpent or because the man did it when the woman offered him the fruit, as if there were something that should take precedence of God when it is a question of reliance or compliance.

XV. On the justice of the retribution that was meted out to the first human beings for their disobedience.

Man, as we know, scorned the bidding of God who had created him, who had made him in his own image, who had placed him above the other animals, who had established him in paradise, who had provided him with an abundance of all things and of security, and who had not laden him with commands that were numerous or onerous or difficult but had propped him up for wholesome obedience with one very brief and easy command, whereby he sought to impress upon this creature, for whom free service was expedient, that he was the Lord. Therefore, as a consequence, just condemnation followed, and this condemnation was such that man, who would have been spiritual even in flesh if he had observed the order, became carnal in mind as well. Moreover, this man who had pleased himself in his pride was then granted to himself by God's justice; yet this was not done in such a way that he was completely in his own power, but that he disagreed with himself and so led, under the rule of the one with whom he agreed when he sinned, a life of cruel and wretched slavery in place of the freedom for which he had conceived a desire. He was willingly dead in spirit and unwillingly destined to die in body; a deserter of the eternal life, he was doomed also to eternal death, unless he were freed by grace. Whoever thinks that condemnation of this sort is either excessive or unjust surely does not know how to gauge the magnitude of wickedness in sinning when the opportunity for not sinning was so ample.

Just as Abraham's obedience is not undeservedly celebrated as great because he was ordered to do a very difficult thing, namely, to slay his son, so in paradise disobedience was all the greater because the command that was given would have involved no difficulty. And just as the obedience of the Second Man is the more laudable because "he became obedient unto death" [Philippians 2:8], so the disobedience of the first man is the more abominable because he became disobedient unto death. For where the proposed punishment for disobedience is great and the command of the Creator is easy to obey, who can adequately expound how grave an evil it is not to obey when an easy matter has been ordered by so mighty a power and is attended by the terror of such awful punishment?

To put it briefly then, in the punishment of that sin the requital for disobedience was no other than disobedience. For man's wretchedness consists only in his own disobedience to himself, wherefore, since he would not do what he then could, he now has a will to do what he cannot. In paradise, to be sure, man could not do everything whatsoever even before he sinned, yet, whatever he could not do, he did not have a will to do, and in that way he could do everything that he would. Now, however, as we recognize in his offspring and as holy Scripture attests, "Man has become like vanity" [Psalm 144:4]. For who can count up all the things that man has a will to do but cannot as long as he is disobedient to himself, that is, as long as his very mind and even his flesh, which is lower, are disobedient to his will? For even against his will his mind is very often agitated and his flesh feels pain, grows old, dies and suffers whatever else we suffer; but we should not suffer all this against our will if our being in every way and in every part gave obedience to our will.

Someone may perhaps protest that the flesh is unable to serve us because of what it suffers. But what difference does it make how this happens? It only matters that through the justice of God, who is our master and to whom we his subjects refused service, our flesh, which had been subject to us, is troublesome by its insubordination, though we by our insubordination to God have succeeded only in being troublesome to ourselves and not to him. For he does not need our service as we need that of the body; so that what we get is punishment for us, but what we did was none for him. Further, the so-called pains of the flesh are pains of the soul that exist in and proceed from the flesh. For what pain or desire does the flesh experience by itself apart from a soul?

When we say that the flesh feels desire or pain, we mean that it is either man himself, as I have argued, or some part of the soul affected by what the flesh experiences, whether it be harsh and painful or gentle and pleasant. Pain of the flesh is only a vexation of the soul arising from the flesh and a sort of disagreement with what is done to the flesh, just as the pain of the mind that we call grief is a disagreement with the things that have happened to us against our will. But grief is generally preceded by fear, which is also something in the soul and not in the flesh. Pain of the flesh, on the other hand, is not preceded by anything like fear on the part of the flesh that is felt in the flesh before the pain. Pleasure, however, is preceded by a certain craving that is felt in the flesh as its own desire, such as hunger, thirst and the desire that is mostly called lust when it affects the sex organs, though this is a general term applicable to any kind of desire.

Even anger itself, so the ancients defined it, is nothing but a lust for revenge, although at times a man vents his anger even upon inanimate objects, where no effect of vengeance can be felt, and in his rage smashes his style or breaks his reed pen when it writes badly. But even this lust, though rather irrational, is a sort of lust for revenge and something like a shadowy reflection, as it were, of the principle of retribution whereby they who do evil must suffer evil. There is then a lust for revenge, which is called anger; there is a lust for possessing money, which is termed greed; there is a lust for winning at any price, which is termed obstinacy; and there is a lust for bragging, which is termed vainglory. There are many different kinds of lust, of which some have special designations also while others have none. No one, for example, would find it easy to say what the lust to be overlord is called, though, as even civil wars attest, it exercises a very powerful influence in the minds of tyrants.

XXVIII. On the character of the two cities, the earthly and the heavenly.

The two cities then were created by two kinds of love: the earthly city by a love of self carried even to the point of contempt for God, the heavenly city by a love of God carried even to the point of contempt for self. Consequently, the earthly city glories in itself while the other glories in the Lord. For the former seeks glory from men, but the latter finds its greatest glory in God, the witness of our conscience. The earthly city lifts up its head in its own glory; the heavenly city says to its God: "My glory and the lifter of my head" [Psalm 3:3]. In the one, the lust for dominion has dominion over its princes as well as over the nations that it subdues; in the other, both those put in charge and those placed under them serve one another in love, the former by their counsel, the latter by their obedience. The earthly city loves its own strength as revealed in its men of power; the heavenly city says to its God: "I will love thee, O Lord, my strength" [Psalm 18:1].

Thus in the earthly city its wise men who live according to man have pursued the goods either of the body or of their own mind or of both together; or if any of them were able to know God, "they did not honor him as God or give thanks to him, but they became futile in their thinking and their senseless minds were darkened; claiming to be wise," that is, exalting themselves in their own wisdom under the dominion of pride, "they became fools, and ex-changed the glory of the immortal God for images resembling mortal man or birds or beasts or reptiles," for in the adoration of idols of this sort they were either leaders or followers of the populace, and worshipped and served the creature rather than the creator, who is blessed forever [Romans 1:21–23]. In the heavenly city, on the other hand, man's only wisdom is the religion that guides him rightly to worship the true God and awaits as its reward in the fellowship of saints, not only human but also angelic, this goal, that God may be "all in all" [1 Corinthians 15:28].

Conclusions

Augustine's assessment of the human condition was extremely pessimistic. He believed that we were in bondage to sin and that nothing less than the grace of God could correct the situation. There was nothing we could personally do because we had inherited the sin of Adam and Eve genetically, through the process of conception. (As Athansius had written, humans could not fix what was broken; only God acting through the incarnation could change us.) Other Christians protested that even if we had inherited this "original" sin, it was removed by Christian baptism. Quoting Paul the Apostle, theologians like Pelagius and Julian of Eclanum argued that in baptism we had died to sin, and therefore could live a new life in the spirit of God, freely choosing good over evil. The debate over sin and human freedom raged for several decades, and indeed continues even into our own day. Most Christians at the time agreed with Pelagius that baptism gave Christians the possibility of leading righteous lives with the help of the Holy Spirit. An optimistic spirit of possibility existed in the Middle Ages, which combined a belief in the inevitability of sin with the conviction that our sinful natures could be overcome. Augustine's pessimistic anthropology was renewed during the Reformation, however, and came to dominate Protestant theology.

Despite Augustine's clear division of the cosmos into two cities—one earthly and sinful, the other heavenly and perfect—the church began to contemplate the possibility of heaven on earth. This happened because in the western empire, the church was the only institution left standing after the invasions of the Goths and Visigoths. With wealth, organization, power, and control, it seemed that a new empire, that of Christendom, could exist in which a holy empire, with a holy Roman emperor, would give both temporal (worldly) and spiritual (heavenly) authority to a central Christian authority: the church.

Sources for Selections

The Didache [*The Teaching of the Lord to the Gentiles by the Twelve Apostles*]. Trans. R. A. Kraft. In *The Apostolic Fathers*. Ed. Jack N. Sparks. Nashville, Tenn.: Thomas Nelson, 1978.

Gospel of Thomas. In *The Complete Gospels: Annotated Scholars Versions*. Rev. and exp. ed. Trans. Robert J. Miller, ed. Marvin W. Meyer and Stephen J. Patterson. San Francisco: HarperSanFrancisco, 1994.

Leith, John, ed. *Creeds of the Churches: A Reader in Christian Doctrine, from the Bible to the Present,* 3rd ed. Atlanta: John Knox, 1982.

Saint Athanasius. *On the Incarnation: The Treatise* De Incarnatione Verbi Dei. C. S. Lewis, Introduction. Trans. and ed. Religious of C.S.M.V. Crestwood, N.Y.: St. Vladimir's Orthodox Theological Seminary, 1989.

Saint Augustine. *The City of God Against the Pagans*. Trans. Philip Levine. Cambridge, Mass.: Harvard University Press, 1966.

Shewring, W. H., trans. *The Passion of Saints Perpetua and Felicity*. London: 1931. From Internet Medieval Source Book. <http://www.fordham.edu/halsall/sbook.html>.

Additional Resources

Brown, Peter. *Augustine of Hippo: A Biography*. Rev. ed. Berkeley and Los Angeles: University of California Press, 2000.

Chadwick, Henry. *The Early Church*. New York: Pelican, 1967.

Cyril of Jerusalem. *St. Cyril of Jerusalem's Lectures on the Christian Sacraments: The Procatechesis and the Five Mystagogical Catecheses*. Ed. F. L. Cross. London: S.P.C.K., 1951.

Elliott, T. G. *The Christianity of Constantine the Great*. Scranton, Penn.: University of Scranton, 1996.

Eusebius of Caesarea. *Life of Constantine*. Trans. Averil Cameron and Stuart G. Hall. New York: Oxford University Press, 1999.

Kelly, Joseph F. *The World of the Early Christians*. Collegeville, Minn.: Liturgical Press, 1997.

Martyr, Justin. *The Writings of Justin Martyr and Athenagoras*. Trans. Marcus Dods, George Reith, and B. P. Pratten. Edinburgh: T&T Clark, 1867.

The Martyrdom of Polycarp, Bishop of Smyrna. In *Early Christian Fathers*. Trans. Cyril C. Richardson. New York: Macmillan, 1970.

Metzger, Marcel. *History of the Liturgy: The Major Stages*. Trans. Madeleine Beaumont. Collegeville, Minn.: Liturgical Press, 1997.

Norris, Richard A., Jr., trans. and ed. *The Christological Controversy*. Philadelphia: Fortress, 1980.

Stark, Rodney. *The Rise of Christianity*. San Francisco: HarperSanFrancisco, 1997.

Young, Frances. *The Making of the Creeds*. Philadelphia: Trinity Press International, 1991.

Films

Barabbas. Directed by Richard Fleischer, 1962.

Ben-Hur. Directed by William Wyler, 1959.

Gladiator. Directed by Ridley Scott, 2000.

Spartacus. Directed by Stanley Kubrick, 1960.

Part Two

PART TWO covers almost 1500 years of Christian history. Christianity became the central power and authority in Western Europe in the fifth century, and continued throughout the Middle Ages. By the end of the sixteenth century, however, the hegemony of the church was challenged by secular nobles and the rise of kings and nation-states. Later still, church authority was undermined by the turn to the authority of reason in assessing religious truths.

CHAPTER THREE describes the theological developments that occur during the Middle Ages, a period which runs from the fifth to the fifteenth centuries. It presents the variety of different ways of being Christian: from mysticism to monasticism, and from scholastism to festivals and pilgrimages. The chapter also considers events occurring within eastern Christianity, looking in particular at the iconoclastic controversy and the conflict over hesychasm. It shows how the church attempted to reform itself through the efforts of religious orders that repeatedly called the church back to its original mission.

CHAPTER FOUR describes the various reformations that occurred in the sixteenth century. These include the Lutheran, Reformed, English, Radical, and Catholic reformations. Each reformation contributed to the ongoing conversation within Christianity about the nature of humanity, salvation, and the sacraments. Texts from different factions illuminate the issues at stake for the reformers.

The reformations broke the power of the church centered in Rome, but they also shattered accepted sources of authority. CHAPTER FIVE examines these sources—scripture, tradition, experience, and reason—and looks at why different Christians trusted one source over another. Debates over authority contributed to the development of different denominations and set the stage for still more dramatic events to come in the modern era.

	410	Sack of Rome by Visigoths
Last western emperor deposed	476	
	c. 480	Birth of Benedict of Nursia
Death of Muhammad	632	
	787	Seventh Ecumenical Council
Missions of Saint Boniface to Germany	716–54	
	800	Charlemagne crowned by Pope Leo III
Cluniac Reform	909–c. 1109	
	1054	Mutual excommunication by Catholic and Orthodox church leaders
Gregorian reforms under Gregory VII	1074–85	
	c. 1084–98	New Religious Orders (Carthusians, Cistercians)
First Crusade	1096–99	
	c. 1170	Saint Dominic born (d. 1221)
Saint Francis born (d. 1226)	c. 1182	
	1204	Sack of Constantinople in Fourth Crusade
Mendicant Orders arise	c. 1210–15	
	1215	Fourth Lateran Council convened by Pope Innocent III
Avignon Papacy begins	1308	
	1311	Beguine Movement declared heretical
Great Famine	1315–22	
	1323	Spiritual Franciscans declared heretical
Black Death	1347–49	
	1378	Avignon Papacy ends
Great Western Schism	1378–1417	
	1415–18	Council of Constance; execution of Jan Hus (1415)
Council of Basel	1431–49	
	1453	Fall of Constantinople to Ottoman Turks

CHAPTER THREE

The Middle Ages
FOR THE LOVE OF GOD

The Middle Ages lasted a very long time—by some calculations, a millennium, from 500 to 1500 C.E. But who relegated these centuries to "the middle"? And the middle of what? It was the elite in the Renaissance, who characterized the period sandwiched between the glorious classical era of late antiquity and their own glorious era of neoclassicism as "middle." In other words, Middle Ages, like Dark Ages, is an arbitrary designation, a label of contempt. It certainly was not dark in the Orthodox world of the East, where Christians flourished in Byzantine culture and, later, under Islamic rule. Nor was it dark in Mesoamerica, where Mayan and Aztec civilizations had books, advanced science and mathematics, and highly developed cultures. And for that matter, it was not dark in Western Europe, either.

Nevertheless, when we think of the Middle Ages, many loaded words and negative images may come to mind: feudalism, crusades, serfs, inquisition, and excommunication, to list a few. Clearly, it was a chaotic time for secular authority. Europe was broken into tiny principalities, occasionally united under a distant king or emperor. But real power and authority existed at the local level: on the manor, ruled by the hereditary head of household—the lord—and operated by people who were legally bound to the land—the serfs. Though peasants faced an arduous life, there were certain expectations that the lord was required to fulfill on their behalf. They were guaranteed a living and had a right to occupy the land. The lord of the manor, though cruel and harsh at times, had a moral obligation to provide for his "family." The church, through the office of the bishop, could apply moral suasion and political coercion to help this system, known as feudalism, run smoothly.

In addition to the negative stereotypes that emerge, however, idealistic visions also come into view: knights, chivalry, courtly love, and the quest for the Holy Grail (supposedly the cup that caught Jesus' dying drops of blood; or, also, the cup used at the Last Supper). These images romanticize a brutal reality, however. Knights were simply soldiers on horseback. These horsemen were the younger sons of landed nobility: they had titles, but no property. These young men frequently created problems, feuding and fighting across the small principalities and duchies of Western Europe because they had little to lose. Pope Urban II channeled their energy by calling for a crusade to combat a common enemy: the Muslims who had taken over the Holy Land. The First Crusade, mounted between 1096 and 1099, was successful in pushing Muslims out of Jerusalem, but it also led to the massacre of Jews living in

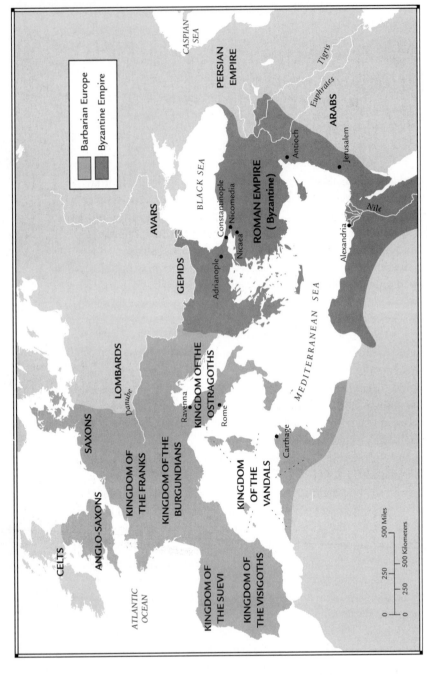

Europe and the Byzantine Empire c. 500.   *The decline of Roman rule in the West opened the way for Germanic tribes such as the Franks, Vandals, Visigoths, and Ostrogoths to establish their own kingdoms there.*

Europe as well as in the Holy Land. The crusades were actually fought to gain control of the Mediterranean, but religious reasons sounded far nobler. And so the wealthy sons joined military orders of knights and claimed a religious cause. The most famous were the Knights Templar, the source of many legends and quite a few contemporary novels.

I would like to depart from the usual stereotypes and introduce a different way by which to consider the Middle Ages: life and learning. By "life," I mean the desire of Christians to lead holy and pious lives, acting as God would want them to. By "learning," I mean the attempts of Christians to understand and explicate the faith they had inherited and been taught. The monasteries best exemplify the life and learning Christians attempted to follow. "Monastery" refers to both the community and the facilities of a group of men or women who commit themselves to a life of voluntary poverty, celibacy, and obedience, and live together communally in order to maintain those vows. The monasteries, with their focus on serving God in community, would act as a major force for theological development as well as church reform in the Middle Ages.

Monasticism

Since the time of Constantine, Christians had continually tried to recall the church to a state of holiness and purity. As early as the third century, the monk Anthony (250–356) left the cities and became a hermit in the Egyptian desert, renouncing his earlier life of modest wealth to get closer to God. After all, Christ had said that in order to follow him, a disciple must give up everything. Anthony was a model for hundreds, and probably thousands, of men and women in the early church, because of an inspirational biography Athanasius of Alexandria (c. 298–373) wrote about him. His model of self-renunciation became especially popular once Constantine legalized Christianity. Prior to the fourth century, the church could escape the world—and, indeed, had to in order to survive. Martyrdom was a real possibility. But with Christianity's change in fortunes, the world invaded the church, and as a result, its members had to purify themselves in order to purify the church. One route toward purification was asceticism.

Ascetics were essentially spiritual athletes, whose self-discipline brought them into union with God. Asceticism might take the form of poverty, celibacy, or obedience to church authorities, as well as physical austerities such as fasting, sleep deprivation, and more extreme forms of self-denial such as not bathing or sitting atop a tall pillar, as the stylites did in the eastern empire. These practices seem rather foreign today, but perhaps can best be understood in two ways: the love of God and the desire for freedom. If we love God, we might think about what we could do to show that love. Since God gave us everything—body and soul—the only thing we can give God in return is everything—body and soul. This is one reason the ascetics gave their entire selves to God in self-denial. Giving up something valuable—like having a family or living in comfort—became, in essence, a gift of oneself to God. The goal of fasting, for example, was not to lose weight for Jesus, but rather to keep one's mind directed toward divine rather than worldly things. This required the same kind of training that dedicated athletes practice.

But the ascetics also found freedom in the choice to abandon the world. This was especially true for women. In the early centuries of Christianity, wealthy women went on pilgrimages to the Holy Land. Several set up convents for virgins and widows. By entering a convent, a woman gained remarkable liberty. She did not have to assent to an arranged marriage. She did not have to bear children, and since death in childbirth was the leading cause of death among women, she might anticipate a long life. She could learn to read and write, and follow other unfeminine pursuits, such as administration and even preaching. And she could live in a community of women, generally outside the domination of men. Men found similar freedom in renouncing worldly cares and responsibilities. Many men who became monks came from wealthy families, the younger sons of the nobility who could not inherit the land, but who could, at times, continue to live a life of relative luxury, despite vows of poverty.

Monastic practices varied. A few ascetics acted as free agents, sponging off churches or wealthy patrons. We catch a glimpse of this in the New Testament letter of 1 Timothy, which suggests that "young widows" are draining the church financially (1 Timothy 5:11–15). Some monastics were hermits, who avoided human contact as much as possible, much like Hindu renunciates who sit by themselves on a mountain. Others lived in communities, observing a common life of prayer and contemplation. Many practiced extreme, even deadly, austerities. Thus, when Benedict of Nursia (c. 480–547) wrote a "rule" for living a religious life in community, he moderated the extremes by specifying what a community would tolerate. For example, he allowed a substantial ration of food and drink each day. He allowed sleep, as well as work and prayer. The monastery could not become a dumping ground for either rich parasites or casual laborers. A strict probationary period discouraged those with an idle interest. "Admission to the religious life should not be made easy for newcomers," the rule of Saint Benedict stated.

> Therefore, if he who comes perseveres in knocking, and is seen after four or five days to patiently endure the insults inflicted upon him, and the difficulty of ingress, and to persist in his demand: entrance shall be allowed him, and he shall remain for a few days in the cell of the guests. After this, moreover, he shall be in the cell of the novices, where he shall meditate and eat and sleep. (Chapter 58)

The rule of the community had to be read to newcomers every four months, "so he may know what he is getting into." After the individual makes his vows and promises to be part of the community, "if he owns anything, he must either give it to the poor beforehand, or deed it to the monastery, keeping nothing for himself, for he now owns nothing, not even his body."

▦ The Celtic Renaissance

Christian missionaries from Rome had established churches in what is now England by the fourth century. In the early fifth century, a Christian Briton named Patrick was ordained a bishop and sent as a missionary to Ireland. Patrick had been to Ireland before—enslaved for six years by Celtic tribesmen—but had nevertheless developed a love for the Celtic people. Although the story told to schoolchildren says that he drove the snakes from Ireland, what he did was actually much more miraculous: he and his missionary teams converted tens of thousands of pagan Celts, who had practiced human sacrifice and engaged in bloody warfare, to a religion that preached peace, cooperation, and a loving deity. While Patrick's teachings were completely orthodox, the forms Celtic Christianity took appeared somewhat unorthodox. The high places—that is, pagan holy sites on which stood a single column—became Christian holy sites, marked with a single column topped by a Celtic cross. The cross was inculturated into Celtic religious observance, as was the Trinity. Patrick's missionaries emphasized the threeness of God because of the rich Celtic pantheon, rather than the oneness of the deity, which the Roman church favored. The Celtic church celebrated Easter on a different date, and its priests were not tonsured; that is, they did not have the hair shaved from the tops of their heads. Finally, the form of religious life was familial rather than celibate. Many "monasteries" were villages of families committed to the Christian life, set apart from, and yet nearby to, their pagan neighbors. Monastic abbots, therefore, rather than bishops, were the church leaders in Celtic Christianity.

Christianity spread when missionaries from Ireland returned to Great Britain; proselytized the tribes of Scotland, England, and Wales; and then turned to continental Europe. Saint Columba established outposts in the western islands of Scotland, while Saint Columbanus founded monasteries in France and Italy. The Irish theologian John Scotus Eruigena (d. c. 877–879) moved from Ireland to France when the French king sought scholars to translate Greek and Hebrew texts in his court. English missionaries like Boniface (c. 675–754) and Leoba (d. c. 780) set up monasteries and convents in Germany in the eighth century. For two centuries, a great flowering of knowledge, culture, literature, and religious life spread outward from the British Isles.

The Celtic renaissance came to an abrupt halt with the Synod of Whitby in 664, which declared that the Celtic churches must observe Easter on the same date as the Roman church. Moreover, in 670, the Synod of Autun declared that all religious communities must follow the rule of Saint Benedict. Both councils targeted Celtic Christian practices—such as the lack of tonsure for monks—and attempted to "romanize" Christianity in the British Isles. The ideal church was the Roman church, and other churches had to follow Roman practices.

The abbot, or abbess for women, held complete control over the lives of community members. Monastics took a vow of obedience directed toward the abbot, who had to be followed implicitly and explicitly, for this superior "is believed to hold the place of Christ in the monastery." The abbot should treat all members fairly and equitably:

> He shall make no distinction of persons in the monastery. One shall not be more cherished than another, unless it be the one whom he finds excelling in good works or in obedience. A free-born man shall not be preferred to one coming from servitude, unless there be some other reasonable cause. But if, justice demanding that it should be thus, it seems good to the abbot, he shall do this no matter what the rank shall be. But otherwise they shall keep their own places; for whether we be bond [servant] or free we are all one in Christ; and, under one God, we perform an equal service of subjection; for God is no respecter of persons. Only in this way is a distinction made by Him concerning us: if we are found humble and surpassing others in good works. Therefore let him (the abbot) have equal charity for all: let the same discipline be administered in all cases according to merit. (Chapter 2)

Benedict's rule left nothing to chance, detailing when and where prayers were to be said, and discipline was to be administered; when to take bathroom breaks; and even how to sleep: one person per bed!

A final characteristic of the Benedictine rule was the equation of prayer and work: *ora est labora*. Prayer (*ora*) was work (*labora*)—a work of God. But work was also prayer, because a monk or nun had to be mindful of God in all tasks. In addition to the maintenance of the community itself by farming, cooking, cleaning, and so on, the work of the monasteries frequently involved copying manuscripts. Since there were no printing presses, all books were lettered by hand and individually assembled. These scribal tasks created an interest in reading and learning. Study of texts, in addition to prayer, then, was another type of "work." Work also included providing hospitality to travelers and pilgrims, running orphanages, educating children, and caring for the sick. The Knights Hospitalers, for example, were a crusading order dedicated to helping those wounded in battle. Eventually, the work would entail establishing universities and hospitals, teaching and preaching, and serving as missionaries around the world. Regardless of the task, all work was aimed at remaining attentive to the divine. The scheduling of the daily "office"—the set times throughout the day and night in which communal prayers were said—was both work and prayer, and was designed to keep God in the forefront of each community member's life. Benedict specified that the community should sing or chant all 150 Psalms in the course of a single week. Thus, the cycle of *ora-labora* structured the days, weeks, and years around God.

Many monks and nuns in Western Europe successfully followed Benedict's requirements. They were so successful, in fact, that Benedictine religious orders grew prosperous, acquiring much land and plenty of worldly goods donated by wealthy patrons or community members. Whenever it grew too comfortable and worldly, however, the church needed reformation, and so new movements arose again and again. While Benedict transformed monastic life, and the church as a result, subsequent Christians also renewed monastic life and created new religious orders, especially during the Middle Ages. The Cluniac Reform of Hugh of Sémur (1049–1109) focused on developing liturgies and establishing daughter monasteries throughout Europe. Robert of Molesme (d. 1111) founded the Cistercian order so that he and his community could follow Benedict's rule in a strict and demanding fashion. Bernard of Clairvaux (1090–1153), the most famous Cistercian of the Middle Ages, followed Robert's severe and rigorous model, requiring monks to work on the land as well as in the scriptoriums (writing halls). Norbert of Xanten (c. 1080–1134) founded the Premonstratensian order, named after the first abbey Saint Norbert established, in Prémontré, France. This group of ordained priests, known as "regular canons," provided clerical services to cathedrals. The "Norbertines," as they were later called, lived in community, celebrated communion in the churches, and performed other pastoral duties.

The Norbertines followed a rule that Saint Augustine had written for living in community. Its beauty was in its vagueness. Unlike Benedict, who had specified practices down to the smallest item, the rule of Saint Augustine merely outlined generalities, like praying together or eating together. The particulars were left to each community. Moreover, canons were not monks. Whereas monks and nuns tended to seclude themselves from the world, and generally lived in the country, canons—all male—lived in cities and towns, and involved themselves in worldly affairs. These worldly affairs frequently involved teaching, but they also included clerical duties or other requirements of running a church diocese, such as conducting divine worship, running hospices, or managing hospitals. The Augustinian canons emerged in the eleventh century and blossomed through the end of the Middle Ages. They flourished especially in England, where they were known as the Austin Canons, the largest single order of men.

In addition to the Norbertines, the Victorines were another well-known group of Augustinian canons. These canons lived at the Abbey of Saint Victor in Paris, where they lectured on the Bible and wrote commentaries on scripture. The Victorines gained a reputation for emphasizing the literal, or historical, sense of scripture. That is, rather than start with allegorical flights of fancy, the Victorines began with the historical meaning of the text before considering its spiritual meaning.

Perhaps the greatest reforms came from the mendicant orders—the Franciscans and the Dominicans—of the thirteenth century. These orders, committed to lives of poverty and charity, dramatically changed religious life. (This chapter returns to the mendicants later.)

In sum, monasticism worked a series of reforms that framed the means to live a holy life in the present, all for the love of God. By living a life of constant prayer and contemplation, nuns and monks followed an other-worldly path. At the same time, however, monasteries functioned as centers for charity, education, and hospitality, and so were deeply engaged in the world of peasants living on the surrounding land.

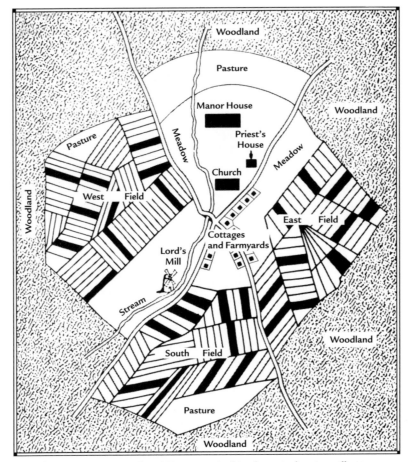

A rural community in Medieval Europe.   *In this schematic drawing, village, manor, and parish share the same boundaries. The dark strips in each field indicate how the holdings of one family—in this case, a fairly well-off family—were dispersed through the fields of the village. The extensive woodland shown here would have slowly shrunk over the Central Middle Ages, as peasants brought more land into arable or pastoral use.*

Mystical Theology

All religions, and not just Christianity, have an element of mysticism. Mysticism is an experiential form of knowing, in which an individual achieves union with God. According to William James, a nineteenth-century American philosopher and psychologist, mystical knowledge is sudden and unexpected: one cannot really summon it. It is also transient: it is fleeting. It brings some sort of revelation so that one no longer sees things in exactly same way. But, most importantly, it is experiential. It is something that happens *to* an individual. In the mystical encounter, the individual sense of self fades away, and some sort of cosmic consciousness takes its

▓ Popular Theology

While this chapter focuses on theological developments in the monasteries, schools, and universities, it is important to remember that for the vast majority of people in the Middle Ages, theology was what they encountered in itinerant holy men (and occasionally women), who were the earliest missionaries to European pagans, and, later on, in the parish church in the Mass, and in the festivals and feast days. Christianity was at once comforting and fearsome: comforting in the knowledge of a suffering Christ who knew what it was like to go hungry, and fearsome in the recognition of the fires of eternal torment that awaited those who sinned. The Mass was celebrated weekly, but few peasants had the opportunity to take advantage of services due to the necessities of agricultural labor. Thus, feast days became important occasions on which the lives of saints and martyrs were celebrated by taking time off from the endless round of work and by generally having more than enough to eat, thanks to the sponsorship of the local nobility.

The week between Palm Sunday and Easter—Holy Week—was a time of high festiveness, at once solemn and joyful. The mysteries and struggles of Christ's last days on earth, the Passion, were vividly depicted in music, drama, and liturgy. Passion plays emphasized the humanity of Christ and his sufferings, and also highlighted the villainy of his enemies, the Jews. As Christ became more human, his enemies became more inhuman, and Holy Week for Jews in the Middle Ages was always a time of great anxiety. Mel Gibson's movie *The Passion of the Christ* (2004) was a type of passion play, mixing gospel accounts with the visions of a nineteenth-century nun, in order to emphasize the agony of Jesus' death on the cross. Like their twenty-first century counterparts, medieval Christians wept openly as they watched the story of the Passion, and experienced anguish at the thought of their own wickedness.

Before worshipers could take communion, they had to confess their sins in order to receive the host (the bread) in a state of purity. It is easy to imagine a catalogue of medieval sin: stealing in general, and stealing food in particular (like poaching), as well as fornication, adultery, apostasy (returning to pagan ways), witchcraft, and sorcery. Although the custom of early Christians was to confess sins publicly in church, Irish missionaries to continental Europe introduced the practice of private confession in the sixth century. They relaxed the restrictions on "repeat offenses" and wrote penitentiary books for priests to use that assigned various forms of penance (restitution) for sinners to complete in order to be completely absolved of their sins.

It is important to remember that few people at this time were literate. Some in the nobility had small books of scripture readings or sermons for private devotions; few had a complete Bible, which usually was found only in a monastery or cathedral library. Parish churches had "epitomes," that is, digests of biblical texts to read at the Mass; they might have had a copy of the Gospels. Thus, peasants knew the scriptures and the teachings of Christianity only by hearing them in church.

(continued)

Nevertheless, sin and salvation were ever-present realities for the medieval peasant, who experienced the highest joy and the deepest sorrow by participating in parish festivals. Religion was never far away, and God was always close, both judging and accepting the weaknesses of humankind.

place. Some might argue that ecstatic events—like speaking in tongues for Christians, or dancing into a frenzy for Sufi Muslims—are mystical. They may well be. For the most part, however, the mysticism in the Middle Ages surfaced as an internal experience of the divine; in James' words, contact with the ineffable.

The relationship between the soul and Christ is a key element of Christian mysticism. Because *anima* in Latin is a feminine-gendered noun meaning "soul," all Christians—male and female alike—relate to Christ as female: Christ is the bridegroom, and the soul is the bride. Bernard of Clairvaux wrote passionately of this relationship in his sermons on the Song of Songs in the Bible. Both Christians and Jews allegorized that rather erotic poem, found in the Old Testament, as describing the intimate bond between God and the believer. For Jews, it was the marriage between God and Israel; for Christians, the marriage between God and the church. For the individual mystic, however, the marriage between the soul and Christ was consummated in an ecstatic experience that bore the overtones of a sexual encounter.

By virtue of their gender, female mystics could relate to Christ as their husband in fairly explicit terms, and in many respects naturally took to mysticism because they were excluded from society at large except in their role as child-bearers, and from religious society except as nuns or, more rarely, abbesses of convents. Convents provided one of the few acceptable ways women could contribute to Christian theology: through leadership, through charitable work, and through writing about mystical experiences. New orders of women—both cloistered (within convents) and worldly—emerged in the thirteenth and fourteenth centuries.

Many women mystics took the path of self-denial—their spiritual athleticism—to the limit. Caroline Walker Bynum, describing late medieval female mysticism in her book *Holy Feast and Holy Fast*, argues that it was the lust for food—rather than for sex or power—that dominated medieval religious concerns, given the climate of scarcity, hunger, and, at times, starvation. As a result, fasting, rather than chastity or obedience, became symbolic of true renunciation. Women mystics especially engaged in fasting, and some literally wasted away. They seemed to understand God as food, according to Bynum. Certainly, Julian of Norwich is a good example of a mystic who displayed this understanding.

Julian was an anchorite (1342–d. after 1416), that is, a person living in an anchorage as a recluse. Some anchorages were a mere cell attached to a church or monastery; others were a suite of rooms, and some a small house on some property. Since Julian had two female servants, it is likely that she lived in a house. Whereas a hermit was usually male and lived a solitary life of roaming, an anchorite was settled, like an anchor, in a single spot. People might make religious pilgrimages to be near an anchorite or to see one, hoping that the holiness these individuals possessed might rub off on them.

Not much is known about Julian, other than the fact that she probably lived as a recluse for twenty years. But she did leave a collection of revelations that she received from God at a time when she was ill: 8 May 1373, to be exact. She had asked God for three things: mindfulness of Christ's passion; physical illness in youth; and the gift of "God's wounds," namely, contrition, compassion, and yearning for

▨ Hildegard of Bingen

Perhaps the most famous medieval woman mystic was Hildegard of Bingen (1098–1179). The abbess of the convent of Disibodenburg in Germany, Hildegard was a woman of extraordinary vision, both in practical matters and in spiritual ones. She established her own convent in Rupertsberg near Bingen, against the wishes of her parent monastery, which wanted her community to remain attached so as to enjoy its wealth. She seemed to suffer from epilepsy or from migraine headaches. While in the throes of pain, however, she had remarkable visions that seemed to unite heaven and earth into a cosmic whole. Eco-theologians today who want to develop a theology that encompasses the environment as well as spiritual issues have turned to Hildegard's songs and visions for inspiration. Vision Four, Part 79 from her *Book of Divine Works*, illustrates her holistic view of life:

> The fertile Earth is symbolized by the sex organs, which display the power of generation as well as an indecent boldness. Just as unruly forces at times rise from these organs, the recurring fertility of the Earth brings about a luxuriant growth and an immense overabundance of fruits. Of course, everything we do under the sun and moon over the course of the months is achieved by our soul's power of wisdom, knowledge, and diligence. Through the soul, which is of a fiery and airy nature, we accomplish both good and evil like the moon, which waxes and wanes. Through this power in the soul, we are of a heavenly nature in our recognition of goodness. And thus we think about and achieve all our deeds. We distinguish the course of the Seasons as well as the elements of our actions through the decision-making power of the mind. We provide names for all the things we identify. And just as the power of correct procreation and infirmity, of happiness and misfortune, lies hidden within the sex organs, and just as the Earth causes both useful and useless things as well as everything needed for human existence to germinate through the sun, moon, and air, there exists a mighty power within the soul. By this capacity we are able to bring to fulfillment both good and evil, both useful and useless things.

Hildegard's songs, written for choirs of women, are available today on a number of different CDs and tapes, in different interpretations: classical and jazz.

God. She received these three requests during the month of May, so ill that she thought she would die, as did the parish priest who administered last rites to her. At this time, she received sixteen "showings," which revealed God's compassion and kindness, and which answered a number of questions she had about divine justice. For example, Julian had wondered how it was that God could punish people eternally if God were also merciful. In more than one revelation, she was told, "All will be well." She did not know how the problem of God's justice could be reconciled with God's mercy, but the words "all will be well" reassured her that somehow it would all come out okay.

The Reading

In the "showings" that follow, Julian equates Jesus Christ with a mother. She develops a Trinity of Father, Mother, and Lordship, giving specific qualities to each Person in the Trinity. Jesus as Mother would seem somewhat unusual, although the Bible had described God in maternal language. Mystical theology, however, allowed Christians, especially women, great freedom. Although Julian of Norwich questioned some church teachings, she never went so far as to be suppressed. Indeed, she remains rather traditional when she alludes to the seven sacraments of the medieval church: baptism and communion, confirmation, marriage, ordination, penance, and last rites. She interprets communion, which she calls the "Blessed Sacrament," in a rather novel way, however.

When we consider the writings of Christian mystics, male and female alike, it seems amazing that we still have their incredibly creative visions. Clearly, church authorities found something truthful and honest about the faith in Julian's writings. It is helpful, therefore, to think especially about the genre of this work, and about other texts like it. How would you list or identify the characteristics of mystical literature? How do we know when something is mystical? What makes it mystical?

Questions to Consider

1. In what way is Jesus "mother"? How does Julian develop this idea?

2. How orthodox, or appropriate, do you think Julian's description of the Trinity is? Obviously, her contemporaries saw nothing wrong in her description. Why did they accept what she said?

3. What are Julian's concerns?

4. Does the sample from Julian support or challenge Caroline Walker Bynum's assertion that food was a central concern for female mystics? What specific examples can you provide in support of your opinion?

5. How does Julian's view of human nature compare with that of Augustine's?

6. What do you think society's attitude toward anchorites and hermits would be today? What about the attitude toward men and women living in intentional religious communities? Explain your answer (in other words, give some examples or arguments in support of your point of view).

Revelations of Divine Love: The Fourteenth Revelation

JULIAN OF NORWICH

In essence we are complete; we fail in
our sensual nature; God heals it through
his mercy and grace; the higher part of our
nature is joined to God at our creation;
Jesus our God is united to the lower part
of our nature through his incarnation;
virtues arise from faith; Mary is our Mother

Chapter 57. With regard to our essential being, God made us so noble and rich that we always work in his will and for his honor. (I say "we," but, of course, I am thinking of "man-who-is-to-be-saved".) I saw, indeed, that it is we whom he loved, and who always do what he approves, without limit. We are able to do this through our soul's share of the wealth and great nobility given it when it was made one with our body. It is in this union that we have our sensuality.

As far as our essential nature goes we are complete. It is in the realm of our sensuality that we fail. This failing God will make good through the operation of mercy and grace which flows richly into us out of his own fundamental goodness. It is this goodness of his which makes mercy and grace work in us, and our natural goodness—given by God—enables us to accept it.

I saw that in God our nature is complete. There are different expressions of it, of which he is the source, all created to do his will. Their own nature preserves them, while mercy and grace restore and perfect them. None of these shall perish, for the higher part of our nature was united to God at our creation, and God united himself to our nature in its lower part when he became incarnate. In Christ therefore both parts are made one. For Christ means the Holy Trinity in whom our higher part is rooted and grounded; and he, the Second Person thereof, has taken our lower part, which had already been prepared for him. I saw clearly that all the works of God, past or future, were fully foreseen and known by him from before time was. For love he made mankind, and out of the same love he willed to become man.

The next "good" that we receive is our faith, from which all our blessings stem. It springs from the wealth that our essential nature contributes to our sensitive soul, and it is planted in us, and we in it, through God's essential goodness working by mercy and grace. And so come all those other good things by which we are guided and saved.

For instance, the commandments of God are one of these "goods." We ought to understand these in two ways: there are his orders, which we must love and keep; and there are also his prohibitions: we ought to know them so that we hate and refuse them. These two ways include all we do.

Or there are the seven sacraments, each following the other in God-appointed order. Or virtue of any sort. The very virtues which rise through the goodness of God out of our essential nature, are given by the Holy Spirit, working in mercy, restoring through grace. These virtues and gifts are our treasure in Jesus Christ. For when God united himself to our humanity in the Virgin's womb he took also our sensual soul. When he took it—having included us all in himself—he united it to our essential nature. In this uniting he was perfect man, for Christ who unites with himself every one who is to be saved is perfect man.

So our Lady is our Mother too and, in Christ, we are incorporated in her, and born of her. She who is the Mother of our Savior is Mother of all who are to be saved in our Savior. Indeed, our Savior himself is our Mother for we are for ever being born of him, and shall never be delivered!

All this was made abundantly and beautifully clear. It is referred to in the first revelation where it is said, "We are all enfolded in him and he in us." And the inclusion is mentioned in the sixteenth revelation where he is spoken of as "seated in our soul." It is his pleasure and bliss to reign in our intelligence and to sit at ease in our soul, dwelling there eternally, working us all into himself. In this task he wants us to help him, giving him our whole attention, learning his lessons, keeping his laws, wanting all that he does to be achieved, and really trusting him. I saw indeed that our essential being is in God!

> God is never displeased with the wife
> he has chosen; three attributes of the
> Trinity: fatherhood, motherhood, and
> lordship; our essence is in each Person, but
> our sensual nature in Christ alone

Chapter 58. God the blessed Trinity is everlasting Being. Just as he is eternal, without beginning, so has his purpose been eternal namely to make mankind. This fine nature was prepared in the first instance for his own Son, the Second Person. And when he so willed, with the concurrence of each Person of the Trinity, he made all of us at one and the same time. When he made us he joined and united us to himself. By such union we are kept as pure and noble as when we were first made. It is because of this most precious union that we can love our Maker, please him and praise him, thank him and rejoice in him for ever. And this is the plan continually at work in every soul to be saved—the divine will that I have already mentioned. So when he made us God almighty was our kindly Father, and God all-wise our kindly Mother, and the Holy Spirit their love and goodness; all one God, one Lord. In this uniting together he is our real, true husband, and we his loved wife and sweetheart. He is never displeased with his wife! "I love you and you love me," he says, "and our love will never be broken."

I saw the blessed Trinity working. I saw that there were these three attributes: fatherhood, motherhood, and lordship—all in one God. In the almighty Father we have been sustained and blessed with regard to our created natural being from before all time. By the skill and wisdom of the Second Person we are sustained, restored, and saved with regard to our sensual nature, for he is our Mother, Brother, and Savior. In our good Lord the Holy Spirit we have, after our life and hardship is over, that reward and rest which surpasses for ever any and everything we can possibly desire—such is his abounding grace and magnificent courtesy.

Our life too is threefold. In the first stage we have our being, in the second our growth, and in the third our perfection. The first is nature, the second mercy, and the third grace. For the first I realized that the great power of the Trinity is our Father, the deep wisdom our Mother, and the great love our Lord. All this we have by nature and in our created and essential being. Moreover I saw that the Second Person who is our Mother with regard to our essential nature, that same dear Person has become our Mother in the matter of our sensual nature. We are God's creation twice: essential being and sensual nature. Our being is that higher part which we have in our Father, God almighty, and the Second Person of the Trinity is Mother of this basic nature, providing the substance in which we are rooted and grounded. But he is our Mother also in mercy, since he has taken our sensual nature upon himself. Thus "our Mother" describes the different ways in which he works, ways which are separate to us, but held together in him. In our Mother, Christ, we grow and develop; in his mercy he reforms and restores us; through his passion, death, and resurrection he has united us to our being. So does our Mother work in mercy for all his children who respond to him and obey him.

Grace works with mercy too, and especially in two ways. The work is that of the Third Person, the Holy Spirit, who works by *rewarding* and *giving*. Rewarding is the generous gift of truth that the Lord makes to him who has suffered. Giving is a magnanimous gesture which he makes freely by his grace: perfect, and far beyond the deserts of any of his creatures.

Thus in our Father, God almighty, we have our being. In our merciful Mother we have reformation and renewal, and our separate parts are integrated into perfect man. In yielding to the gracious impulse of the Holy Spirit we are made perfect. Our essence is in our Father, God almighty, and in our Mother, God all-wise, and in our Lord the Holy Spirit, God all-good. Our essential nature is entire in each Person of the Trinity, who is one God. Our sensual nature is in the Second Person alone, Jesus Christ. In him is the Father too, and the Holy Spirit. In and by him have we been taken out of hell with a strong arm; and out of earth's wretchedness have been wonderfully raised to heaven, and united, most blessedly, to him who is our true being. And we have developed in spiritual wealth and character through all Christ's virtues, and by the gracious work of the Holy Spirit.

> In the elect, wickedness is transformed into blessedness by the work of mercy and grace; God's way is to set good against evil by Jesus, our Mother in grace; the most virtuous soul is the most humble; all virtues are grounded in God

Chapter 59. All this blessedness is ours through mercy and grace. We would never have had it or known it if goodness (that is, God) had not been opposed. It is because of this that we enjoy this bliss. Wickedness was allowed to rise up against goodness, and the goodness of mercy and grace rose up against wickedness and then turned it all into goodness and honor, at least as far as those who are to be saved are concerned. For it is the way of God to set good against evil. So Jesus Christ who sets good against evil is our real Mother. We owe our being to him—and this is the essence of motherhood!—and all the delightful, loving protection which ever follows. God is as really our Mother as he is our Father. He showed this throughout, and particularly when he said that sweet word, "It is I." In other words, "It is I who am the strength and goodness of Fatherhood; I who am the wisdom of Motherhood; I who am light and grace and blessed love; I who am Trinity; I who am Unity; I who am the sovereign goodness of every single thing; I who enable you to love; I who enable you to long. It is I, the eternal satisfaction of every genuine desire."

For the soul is at its best, its most noble and honorable, when it is most lowly, and humble, and gentle. Springing from this fundamental source and as part of our natural endowment, are all the virtues of our sensual nature, aided and abetted as they are by mercy and grace. Without such assistance we should be in a poor way!

Our great Father, God almighty, who is Being, knew and loved us from eternity. Through his knowledge, and in the marvelous depths of his charity, together with the foresight and wisdom of the whole blessed Trinity, he willed that the Second Person

should become our Mother, Brother, and Savior. Hence it follows that God is as truly our Mother as he is our Father. Our Father decides, our Mother works, our good Lord, the Holy Spirit, strengthens. So we ought to love our God in whom we have our own being, reverently thanking him, and praising him for creating us, earnestly beseeching our Mother for mercy and pity, and our Lord, the Spirit, for help and grace. For in these three is contained our life: nature, mercy, grace. From these we get our humility, gentleness, patience and pity. From them too we get our hatred of sin and wickedness—it is the function of virtue to hate these.

So we see that Jesus is the true Mother of our nature, for he made us. He is our Mother, too, by grace, because he took our created nature upon himself. All the lovely deeds and tender services that beloved motherhood implies are appropriate to the Second Person. In him the godly will is always safe and sound, both in nature and grace, because of his own fundamental goodness. I came to realize that there were three ways of looking at God's motherhood: the first is based on the fact that our nature is made; the second is found in the assumption of that nature—there begins the motherhood of grace; the third is the motherhood of work which flows out over all by that same grace—the length and breadth and height and depth of it is everlasting. And so is his love.

> We are brought back and fulfilled by the mercy and grace of our sweet, kind, and ever-loving Mother Jesus; the attributes of motherhood; Jesus, our true Mother, feeds us not with milk but with himself; opening his side to us, and calling out all our love

Chapter 60. But now I must say a little more about this "overflowing" as I understand its meaning: how we have been brought back again by the motherhood of mercy and grace to that natural condition which was ours originally when we were made through the motherhood of natural love—which love, indeed, has never left us.

Our Mother by nature and grace—for he would become our Mother in everything—laid the foundation of his work in the Virgin's womb with great and gentle condescension. (This was shown in the first revelation when I received a mental picture of the Virgin's genuine simplicity at the time she conceived.) In other words, it was in this lowly place that God most high, the supreme wisdom of all, adorned and arrayed himself with our poor flesh, ready to function and serve as Mother in all things.

A mother's is the most intimate, willing, and dependable of all services, because it is the truest of all. None has been able to fulfill it properly but Christ, and he alone can. We know that our own mother's bearing of us was a bearing to pain and death, but what does Jesus, our true Mother, do? Why, he, All-love, bears us to joy and eternal life! Blessings on him! Thus he carries us within himself in love. And he is in labor until the time has fully come for him to suffer the sharpest pangs and most appalling pain possible—and in the end he does. And not even when this is over, and we ourselves have been born to eternal bliss, is his marvelous love completely satisfied. This he shows in that overwhelming word of love, "If I could possibly have suffered more, indeed I would have done so."

He might die no more, but that does not stop him working, for he needs to feed us . . . [ellipses in original] it is an obligation of his dear, motherly, love. The human mother will suckle her child with her own milk, but our beloved Mother, Jesus, feeds us with himself, and, with the most tender courtesy, does it by means of the Blessed Sacrament, the precious food of all true life. And he keeps us going through his mercy and grace by all the sacraments. This is what he meant when he said, "It is I whom Holy Church preaches and teaches." In other words, "All the health and life of sacraments, all the virtue and grace of my word, all the goodness laid up for you in Holy Church—it is I." The human mother may put her child tenderly to her breast, but our tender Mother Jesus simply leads us into his blessed breast through his open side, and there gives us a glimpse of the Godhead and heavenly joy—the inner certainty of eternal bliss. The tenth revelation showed this, and said as much with that word, "See how I love you," as looking into his side he rejoiced.

This fine and lovely word *Mother* is so sweet and so much its own that it cannot properly be used of any but him, and of her who is his own true Mother—and ours. In essence *motherhood* means love and kindness, wisdom, knowledge, goodness. Though in comparison with our spiritual birth our physical birth is a small, unimportant, straightforward sort of thing, it still remains that it is only through his working that it can be done at all by his creatures. A kind, loving mother who understands and knows the needs of her child will look after it tenderly just because it is the nature of a mother to do so. As the child grows older she changes her methods—but not her love. Older still, she allows the child to be punished so that its faults are corrected and its virtues and graces developed. This way of doing things, with much else that is right and good, is our Lord at work in those who are doing them. Thus he is our Mother in nature, working by his grace in our lower part, for the sake of the higher. It is his will that we should know this, for he wants all our love to be fastened on himself. Like this I could see that our indebtedness, under God, to fatherhood and motherhood—whether it be human or divine—is fully met in truly loving God. And this blessed love Christ himself produces in us. This was shown in all the revelations and especially in those splendid words that he uttered, "It is I whom you love."

Monastic Theology

Mysticism was one way to know God; studying the Bible was another. The work of the monastic was, in part, to study the Bible. This was accomplished by copying the biblical texts; by listening to selections read out loud during meals; by hearing homilies and sermons that interpreted biblical passages; and by chanting Psalms and hearing scripture throughout the day and night during the office.

Those involved in religious communities lived, ate, and breathed holy scripture. This involvement reflected a deep interest in history. After all, in their eyes, the Bible was nothing but history, the history of the world up to the time of Christ. Many attempted to continue writing the history of what happened *after* Christ, both in the world and in Christ's kingdom, the church. Some in the monasteries wrote world histories. Although these accounts do not exactly resemble history as we think of it today (many begin with the creation account from the book of Genesis in the Bible), they did attempt to recount the deeds of the figures who played important roles in the past. These narratives emphasized the lives of holy men and women, as well as those of kings and noblemen, and tended to accentuate wars and battles.

Whereas mystical theology emphasized the individual's relationship with God, monastic theology emphasized the Bible and history. The Christian story was embedded in scripture, and it was clear to monastics that God worked in history and

The Carolingian Renaissance

Charlemagne (742–814) was a brilliant general who spent more than thirty years amassing territory in various wars fought to the north, south, and east of modern-day France. Pope Leo III (p. 795–816) crowned the King of the Franks "Emperor of the Romans" in 800. (Subsequent rulers in Europe, beginning with the coronation of Otto I in 962 and ending with the rule of Francis II in 1806, continued to use the title "emperor" and governed over what later historians called the Holy Roman Empire. The Habsburg dynasty controlled the empire for centuries, exercising both political and ecclesiastical authority in Germany, Austria, and, at times, Spain and the Netherlands.) While the installation of Charles the Great did not affect the churches of the eastern empire, which had their own empress at the time and a high degree of learning, it did reassure western Christians that church and state would once again be realigned under a sympathetic ruler.

Charlemagne revived education, learning, and culture in his court. He imported monks from Ireland—who still studied Greek and Hebrew imbibed from the earliest missionaries to the British Isles—to translate texts, to write, and to teach. (Indeed, during this period, Christian men and women came from the British Isles and missionized continental Europe, an irony of history given the fact that most Europeans considered the Celts, Angles, and Saxons to be savage, illiterate peoples.) He sought to standardize music sung in Frankish churches, and when he learned that papal delegates were not adequately instructing local clergy in proper liturgical music, he commissioned his own musicians to travel to Rome for further study. He instituted a program of cathedral schools to operate alongside monasteries to train future ecclesiastical leaders. His biographer, Einhard, wrote, "He thought that his children, both daughters and sons, should begin their education with the liberal arts, which he himself had studied."

In short, a "Carolingian Renaissance" of the ninth century established a system that for centuries prepared political as well as religious leaders, promoted culture and learning, and eventually led to the creation of universities.

The empire of the Franks under Charlemagne (c. 800).   *Charlemagne's many military campaigns vastly expanded Frankish territory and influence and resulted in thousands of conversions to Christianity.*

was continuing to be revealed in history, and not just in visions. If they studied history—that is, the Bible—they would know God. Monastics inherited a method of Bible study from earlier Christian theologians. All biblical interpretation could roughly be broken into two categories: literal and spiritual. The literal or historical sense of scripture depended on what the text actually said. If Moses parted the Red Sea in the book of Exodus, then this was the literal meaning: the sea was divided, and the Israelites walked through the parted waters (Exodus 14). The spiritual sense, however, was usually preferred to the literal, and thus the story about the Red Sea had little to do with Moses in later Christian interpretation. In the spiritual sense, Moses became a "type" or prefiguration of Jesus, and the waters of the Red Sea foreshadowed the sacrament of baptism.

The two main classifications were further refined, with the spiritual sense subdivided into at least two, and eventually three, further categories: the allegorical, the moral (or tropological), and the mystical (or anagogical). In the allegorical meaning, scripture is read in terms of symbols: one thing means something else. Allegorically, the waters of the Red Sea might mean the waters of baptism, and so crossing the sea might mean being baptized. The moral meaning focuses on what kind of ethical guidance the text provides. In the story of the crossing of the Red Sea, the moral meaning might be that one gains faith to do dangerous and risky things once one is baptized; or, one must have faith in order to go through the ritual of baptism; or, God will rescue those who have faith. Finally, the anagogical, or mystical, meaning of the text points to the mystery of God, and thus may not be immediately clear or apparent. Anagogically, the crossing of the Red Sea might indicate the spiritual transition from life on earth to life with God. One walks through the waters and "dies" in order to be reborn eternally on the other side. (Modern biblical scholars employ the historical-critical method of scriptural interpretation, although many Christians continue to employ the literal and the spiritual senses of scripture. See Chapters Five and Seven.)

The Reading

The following commentary on chapter 1 of the biblical book of Jonah was written by Haimo of Auxerre (d. c. 875), an important medieval exegete. Little is known about Haimo: he seems to have studied under the Irish grammarian Murethach, and he had two equally influential students—Heiric and Remigius—also of Auxerre in France. The three helped shape biblical commentary in the Carolingian Renaissance and continued to have an effect on later medieval biblical studies. For a long time, Haimo's commentaries were incorrectly attributed to Bishop Haimo of Halberstadt (d. 853). Scholars now believe that the Jonah commentary, as well as commentaries on Saint Paul, the book of Revelation, the Song of Songs, and the twelve minor prophets, were all written by the Benedictine monk Haimo, working at the Abbey of Saint-Germain in Auxerre.

Jonah was a popular book for Christian commentators. In part, this stemmed from New Testament references to the "sign of Jonah" (Matthew 16:4; Luke 11:29–32), and the parallel between Jonah's three days in the belly of a fish, and Jesus' three days before the resurrection (Matthew 12:40). The best way to see what Haimo is doing is to read the short book of Jonah: only four chapters. It is a somewhat humorous work in which God commissions a reluctant prophet named Jonah to preach repentance to the Ninevites. It is important to remember that Nineveh was the capital of Assyria, the great power that had invaded the northern kingdom of Israel in the eighth century B.C.E. Telling a Hebrew prophet to exhort the Ninevites would be similar to sending a religious person out to convert his or her worst enemy. Jonah doesn't want to deliver the message, and along the way, a great storm engulfs the boat he is on. When he tells the crew his god is angry at him, they promptly throw him overboard, where he has a chance to think about things inside the fish that swallows him. Ultimately, Jonah tells the Ninevites to repent, they do so instantly, and so God decides not to destroy them. Despite its brevity and humor, Jonah is a book with a message, although it may not be the message Haimo thinks. In Judaism, for example, the book of Jonah is read on Yom Kippur, the Day of Atonement, and the holiest day in the Jewish calendar. In other words, Jewish tradition understands this book to be about repentance. Haimo, however, reads Jonah as an allegory about Jesus, Jews, and Gentiles.

Biblical commentary is a particular genre of literature. Today called "exegesis" (for drawing the meaning out of the text), more generally, works of biblical interpretation are called commentaries. A commentary examines every verse in turn, carefully considering the meaning of each word, the speaker, and the author's intent. For this reason, a commentary takes more time to read than the actual text it is interpreting: there are many stops and starts as the author scrutinizes each element.

The Prologue and Haimo's commentary on chapter 1 follow.

Questions to Consider

1. Try to identify the various senses of scripture that Haimo uses to understand and explain the meaning of Jonah.

2. If you read the book of Jonah for yourself—or at least chapter 1—what do you think is the plain sense of the text? Would you interpret the character (that is, the personality) of Jonah the same way Haimo does? Why or why not?

3. Are there other allegories that might be used to interpret Jonah 1?

4. Do you think allegorical interpretation is the best way to understand scripture? What are the strengths of this type of reading? What are the weaknesses?

5. How does Haimo use the New Testament to interpret Hebrew scripture? What do you think of this type of interpretation? Could we use other texts to interpret the Old Testament?

6. What is Haimo's attitude toward Jews and Judaism? What is the relationship of Christianity to Judaism in his view?

7. How might a Jewish reader interpret the story of Jonah?

Commentary on the Book of Jonah: Prologue and Chapter 1

HAIMO OF AUXERRE

PROLOGUE

The Hebrews say that Jonah was the son of a widow in Zarephath; Elijah raised him from the dead, and when he had been returned to his mother, she gave thanks, and said, "Now by this I know that you are a man of the Lord, and the word of the Lord in your mouth is true" (1 Kings 17:24). For this reason, Jonah was called "son of Amittai." "Amittai" means "truth," and because Elijah spoke the truth, Jonah was called "the son of truth." They say Jonah's grave is in Geth, which is in Ophir. Others speak of his birth and burial in Lydda, that is, Diospolis. The book of Tobit mentions this prophet, when the father Tobit, about to die, said to his son, "The destruction of Nineveh is at hand, for it will not escape the word of the Lord" (Tobit 14:4). For, at first, in consequence of the preaching of Jonah, we understand that the converted Ninevites did penance and sought forgiveness from the Lord, but thereafter, having indeed relapsed into their former evil, as had been prophesied, they were destroyed by the Hebrews in the reign of Josiah and by the Medes in the reign of Astyages.

CHAPTER 1

And the word of the Lord came to Jonah, son of Amittai, saying, "Arise, and go to Nineveh, the great city, and preach in it, for the wickedness thereof is come up before me" (Jonah 1:1–2). It says that, "the wickedness thereof is come up before me," or, according to the Septuagint,* "the noise of its wickedness is manifest before me," because shamelessly and without any reverence or fear they sinned. So it is said concerning the Sodomites: "The cry of Sodom and Gomorrah . . . has come to me" (Genesis 18:20–21). Sin with the "voice" is sin hidden; sin with "shouting" is manifest and public. Mystically: Jonah, which means "dove," signifies the simple and gentle Christ, above whom the Holy Spirit appeared as a dove. Also, Jonah means "the grieving one," because He grieved for our sins and wept over the destruction of Jerusalem. Moreover, the Lord Himself attests in the Gospel that Jonah signifies Christ, saying, "For even as Jonah was in the belly of the fish three days and three nights, so will the Son of Man be three days and three nights in the heart of the earth" (Matthew 12:40). The Lord Himself is the *son of Amittai,* that is, of God, because God is truth. He is sent to Nineveh, which means "beautiful," which signifies the world, than which we see nothing more beautiful with earthly eyes. Whence also in Greek the world received its name from "an adornment," for it is called "cosmos." Therefore, because the Jews held in contempt the commandments of God, Jonah, that is, Christ, is sent to Nineveh, that is, to the Gentiles, in order that the whole world, believing in Him, might be saved. The wickedness of Nineveh, which comes up before the Lord, is the will always inclined toward evil, especially the worship of idols, which, when the Creator was abandoned, the world served with the greatest zeal.

And Jonah rose up to flee into Tharsis from the face of the Lord (Jonah 1:3). He did not flee because he envied the salvation of the Ninevites, but because he refused to destroy his own people, the Jews. For he knew that the penitence of the Gentiles would be the ruin of the Jews. Furthermore, he had seen other prophets sent to the lost sheep of the house of Israel, in order that they might rouse the people to penitence, and for that reason, he grieved his own selection, for he had been sent to the Assyrians, enemies of Israel. For he had learned by the spirit of prophecy that when the Gentiles would receive an understanding of God, Israel would be reproved. Therefore because he sometimes knew the future, he feared lest it be done in his own time; hence he wished to flee into

---

* The Septuagint was a Greek translation of the Hebrew Bible, made in the second century B.C.E. for Jews living outside the Land of Israel who knew only Greek. This translation was adopted by early Christians and formed what later became the Old Testament for Catholic and Orthodox Christians.

Tharsis, just as also Cain fled *from the face of the Lord.* Josephus* thinks that Tharsis was the city of Tarsus of Cilicia, from which came the apostle Paul, whence he is also called "of Tarsus." In Hebrew, however, they speak generally of the sea as "Tharsis." Therefore, the prophet did not wish to flee to any particular place, but he embarked upon a ship which could take him anywhere, so long as he could hurry, not caring where chance led him. For the fugitive may not choose the place to which he flees. And because it is read in the Psalm, "In Judea God is known; His name is great in Israel" (Psalm 76:1), he believed he would be able to flee from God, who was only known in Judea. Later, indeed, he recognized God through the tempest on the sea, for he confessed and said, *"I am a Hebrew, and I fear the Lord God of heaven, who made both the sea and the dry land"* (Jonah 1:9). Mystically: Our Jonah, that is, Christ, *fled into Tharsis,* because He left His fatherland, that is, heaven; and assuming the flesh, He came into the sea of this world. And so greatly did He love the people for whom He had assumed the flesh, that He did not refuse the Passion, and when Nineveh, that is, the Gentile people, was saved, He did not destroy the Synagogue. Whence He also said to the Father, "Father, if it is possible, let this cup pass away from me" (Matthew 26:39); and placed on the cross, on behalf of those who cried, "Crucify, crucify!" (Luke 23:21), He prayed, saying, "Father, forgive them, for they do not know what they are doing" (Luke 23:34).

And he went down to Joppa and found a ship going to Tharsis (Jonah 1:3). Joppa is a port in Judea, to which Hiram, king of Tyre, transported wood from Lebanon on barges, and from there the wood was brought by land to Jerusalem. Jonah, therefore, coming from the mountainous country of Judea to the sea coast and the plains, is rightly said to have *gone down. And he paid the fare to them, and went down into the ship, that he might go with them to Tharsis from the face of the Lord* (Jonah 1:3), that is, he paid the fees of transport. Moreover, he is said to have gone down into the ship, as it appears, because like a fugitive, he passes into the interior of the ship looking for a hiding place. "Tharsis" means "contemplation of joy"; "Joppa" means "beautiful." Mystically: Jonah, that is, Christ, leaving the mountains, *went down* into Joppa, because when they pursued Him in Judea, as we read in the

Gospel, He went across "into the districts of Tyre and Sidon" (Matthew 15:21), which are cities of the Gentiles. These cities are designated rightly by Joppa (that is, "the beautiful"), because they were set apart in the allotment of Israel. Therefore the Lord came to Tharsis, that is, the contemplation of joy, because He contemplated the salvation of the world, which was predestined before time. Moreover, the salvation of the world is His joy. And He descended into Joppa because, when the Passion was upon Him, He accomplished the salvation of the beautiful Gentile nations. But because He came for the lost sheep of the house of Israel, He did not wish to give "the children's bread" to dogs (Matthew 15:26). Therefore He pays the *fare,* that is, the pledge of expected salvation, to the sailors, whom we believe signify the Gentiles, so that at this time He might first save the Jews for whom He had come and then save the Gentiles, as it were, the neighbors of the sea. Whence He is also said to have *gone down into the inner part of the ship* and to have *fallen into a deep sleep* (Jonah 1:5) while the sea raged, as if ignoring the sailors, because He seemed to ignore the Gentiles, whose salvation He nevertheless accomplished by *sleeping* on the cross and *going down* into hell, as it were, into the hold of the ship.

But the Lord sent a great wind into the sea, and a great tempest was raised in the sea, and the ship was in danger of being broken (Jonah 1:4). Jonah thought he could advance himself by boarding the ship and fleeing; but on the contrary, both he and the ship were in danger and might be destroyed because of him. For those things which are considered fortunate, if God does not will it, instead become unfortunate, and nothing is secure with God opposing. Mystically: that tempest signifies the rage of the Jews who hoped for Him to die, crying "Crucify, crucify!" (Luke 23:21).

And the mariners were afraid, and the men cried to their god, and they cast forth the wares that were in the ship into the sea, to lighten it of them (Jonah 1:5). The *mariners,* not knowing the one and true God, invoked gods, knowing that nothing is done without the providence of God. From this we understand that He is feared and perceived by all men, although they may be seduced by false religions from the one and true God to many gods. They threw the *wares into the sea;* this is done in the greatest danger, in

---

* Josephus was a Jewish historian living in the first century C.E. who wrote in Greek about Jewish customs and culture for a Roman audience.

order that the ship, once *lightened,* may be borne up by the waves more easily. *And Jonah went down into the inner part of the ship and fell into a deep sleep* (Jonah 1:5). While the sailors, thrown into confusion, were invoking their own gods, Jonah remained secure with a quiet mind, so secure that he could sleep. In this, he showed the patience of a strong man, standing firm amidst prosperity and amidst adversity. It can be said that because he knew he was fleeing, he did not dare to look upon the waves avenging his flight. In another interpretation, he slept because he was overcome by weariness, just as we also read that the Apostles, overcome by sorrow, were pressed down by sleep in the Passion of the Lord (Mark 14:37–41).

And the shipmaster came to him and said to him, "Why are you fast asleep? Rise up, invoke your God, if it might be that God will think of us, that we may not perish" (Jonah 1:6). It is natural for anyone in danger to hope for more from another. Whence the *shipmaster,* who ought to comfort others, rouses the *sleeping* Jonah in order that he may *invoke God;* for those whose danger is common, their prayer should be common. Tropologically, this means that before Christ appeared, many gods were worshipped by the Gentiles, but after Christ died and the *tempest* of the world was calmed, now the one God is worshipped, and spiritual sacrifices are offered to Him.

And they said everyone to his fellow, "Come, and let us cast lots" (Jonah 1:7). Because they saw that the storm was greater than usual, they knew those things did not happen naturally; nor indeed could those who navigated at such a time neglect the causes of the winds and the waves, and therefore by means of the *cast lots* they sought the origin of the shipwreck. Where they said, *"that we may know why this evil is upon us,"* we ought to understand evil to mean affliction and calamity, concerning which it is said in the Gospel, "Sufficient to the day is the evil thereof" (Matthew 6:34). And through the prophet it is said, "Is there evil in a city which the Lord has not made?" (Amos 3:6). Elsewhere, evil is called "the contrary of virtue." *And they cast lots, and the lot fell upon Jonah. And they said to him, "Tell us for what cause this evil is upon us. What is your business? Of what country are you, and where do you go? Or of what people are you?"* (Jonah 1:7–8). They force him whom the lot revealed to make himself known in his own speech. They ask about his character, his homeland, his destination, and his city in order to discover the cause of the catastrophe.

And he said to them, "I am a Hebrew, and I fear the Lord God of heaven [who made the sea and the dry land]" (Jonah 1:9). *Hebrew* means "one who crosses over." He did not say "Judean," by which name they began to be called when the ten tribes were divided from the two, but he said, *"I am a Hebrew,"* a pilgrim and a stranger, according to the Psalmist, who says concerning these same people, *"They passed from nation to nation"* (Psalm 105:13). He said, *"I fear the Lord God of heaven,* not the gods whom you invoke, who cannot save you. He *made the sea,* on which I flee, *and the dry land,* from which I flee: that is, I fear Him who is maker of the universe." Moreover, Jonah feared God, from whom he wished to flee, with a slave's fear. This fear also can be taken as worship. He said, *"I fear the Lord God of heaven,"* that is, "I worship."

And the men were greatly afraid, and they said to him, "Why have you done this?" For the men knew that he fled from the face of the Lord, because Jonah had told them (Jonah 1:10). "If you fear God, why do you flee, when you know that you cannot escape His power?" They do not reprove him, but they question him, because they heard that he was a Hebrew and that he worshipped the God of heaven; and therefore they seek from him as from a holy man a remedy for this great evil.

And they said to him, "What shall we do to you, that the sea may be calm to us?" For the sea flowed and swelled (Jonah 1:11). "Because of you," they said, "the sea rises up against us, because we harbored a fugitive. What therefore shall we do with you? Should we kill you? But it is evil to strike down a worshipper of God. What therefore do you command us to do? Command what we are to do, by which we may appease God, whose anger we recognize through the tempest." *The sea,* it says, *flowed* to punishment, persecuting the fugitive prophet. It swelled, that is, it was stirred up in great waves, so as not to diffuse the vengeance of the Creator.

And he said to them, "Take me up, and cast me into the sea, and the sea shall be calm to you; for I know that for my sake this great tempest is upon you" (Jonah 1:12). "Against me," he says, "the tempest rises up; *cast me into the sea,* in order that by my death you may live." And the magnanimity of the fugitive is to be noted: he did not conceal or deny, but having confessed, he embraces punishment, lest others perish because of him. We refer all these things mystically to the Lord Christ, against whom the Judean tempest *swelled* in the Passion. The sailors who asked Him what they should do are the Apostles, who, deserting Him in the Passion, in a certain way *cast* Him into the waves. And it is as if the Lord says, "Because the world sees me sailing with you to Tharsis, that is, to the 'contemplation of joy,' such that I may lead you to the joy where I am, for that reason death rages and longs to devour me; death does not know that just as the fish is captured by the fish-hook, so death will die by my death. Therefore take me up, and *cast me into the sea.* You do the casting. For we ought not to bring on our own death, but to sustain it brought on by others."

And the men rowed to return to dry land, but they were not able, because the sea flowed and swelled upon them (Jonah 1:13). Even with the prophet commanding that they send him into the sea, they did not dare to lay hands on the worshipper of God. But also mystically: when the Jews, who had been the people of God, desired the death of Christ, the Gentiles did not want Him to die. For just as the sailors wanted to *row* to *dry land,* believing the world could be saved without the sacrament of the Passion, with the submersion of Jonah, that is, the Passion of Christ, the ship (that is, the world) might have been released.

And they cried to the Lord and said, "We beseech you, Lord, let us not perish for the life of this man, and lay not upon us innocent blood; because you, Lord, have done as it pleased you" (Jonah 1:14). It is as if they said, "We do not wish, Lord, to destroy your prophet, but *you, Lord, have done as it pleased you.* Your will is fulfilled through our hands. Therefore *lay not upon us innocent blood."* This speech of the sailors seems to be the confession of Pilate, who, taking the water, washed his hands and said, "'I am innocent of the blood of this man'" (Matthew 27:24). All these things were done by the will of the Father, just as in the Psalm it is said: "That I should do your will, my God, I have desired it" (Psalm 40:8).

And they took Jonah and released him into the sea (Jonah 1:15). It says *they took* him, that is, as if with a certain respect and honor carrying him, not casting him headlong, *they released him into the sea. And the sea ceased from raging* (Jonah 1:15). As if having found him whom it sought, just as when someone quickly pursuing a fugitive, when he has obtained him, he *ceases* and holds him whom he has seized. But also mystically: before the Passion of the Lord, the world ventured on the waves of diverse errors; but after His death, we see that everything is tranquil, and with secure unity of faith and the recognition of truth the whole world rejoices; and as if Jonah were sent into the sea, *the sea ceases from raging.*

And the men feared the Lord with a great fear, and they sacrificed victims to the Lord and made vows (Jonah 1:16). Before the Passion of the Lord, *the men cried to their god* (Jonah 1:5); after the Passion, they *feared the Lord,* and they worshipped not with little, but *with great fear,* according to what is commanded in the Law, that "with the whole heart and with the whole soul" He should be *feared* and "loved" (Deuteronomy 6:5). Moreover, *they sacrificed victims,* not animals, which, according to the literal level, they would not have had on the waves, but spiritual *victims,* that is, thanksgiving and praise. The Psalmist says, "Offer to God the sacrifice of praise" (Psalm 50:14), and the prophet says, "Take away all iniquity and receive the good, and we will render the calves of our lips" (Hosea 14:2).

Scholastic Theology

In addition to mystical theology and monastic theology, a third type of theology arose during the Middle Ages. Scholastic theology, as the name implies, developed in the schools that began in the twelfth century and flowered in the thirteenth and fourteenth centuries. It attempted to apply reason to theological questions, considering each issue logically and systematically. Rather than rely solely on biblical authority or on the opinions of respected church leaders to explain Christian doctrine, scholastic theologians used logic to rationally investigate the nature of truth.

This method commenced in the eleventh century with Anselm of Canterbury (1033–1109), who wrote several treatises in which he used reason in support of theology. He attempted to prove the existence of God in his *Proslogion* by arguing that God is "that being than which, nothing greater can be conceived." This is called the "ontological argument for God." What Anselm was saying is that the very concept of God, by definition, must include the existence of what the concept suggests. In other words, if we accept the concept of God—if we're willing to talk about God theoretically—then we are accepting the existence of what the concept implies, namely, God. In a short work titled "In Behalf of the Fool," a quick-thinking monk named Gaunilo points out that we can think of a lot of things that don't actually exist. We can imagine a fabulous island, for instance, but that doesn't mean it exists. Anselm replies to "the fool" by saying that if we can think about something, it must really exist; otherwise, we could not have that thought: "Therefore, if such a being can be conceived to exist, necessarily it does exist." In other words, we don't have thoughts about things that do not exist, because how could we even have these thoughts if we did not have some sort of conception based on reality?

This is where Anselm starts, with God, a being "than which, nothing greater can be conceived." Because he begins within a belief system, his "proof" works for those already within the system. He wasn't really attempting to speak to outsiders; rather, he was interested in insiders—especially students under his supervision—who wanted to understand their faith better. *"Fides quaerens intellectum,"* said Anselm: "faith seeking understanding." He had faith; he just wanted to understand that faith better by coming to a rational understanding of it.

Anselm also applied logic to the question of why God became human, just as Athanasius had eight centuries earlier. In *Why God Became Human* (in Latin, *Cur Deus Homo*), Anselm contends that humans had dishonored God with their failure to be subject to God's will. Much as a feudal lord would require "satisfaction" or restitution for the dishonor, God also required satisfaction. But how could humans, unequal to the divine, possibly make restitution? God's justice required satisfaction, but humans were incapable of producing it. Therefore, God had to become human in Jesus Christ in order to pay humanity's debt to God. God alone could pay what was owed to God; but since humans were the transgressors, God had to provide satisfaction as a human being. Anselm's explanation is called the "satisfaction theory of atonement." Jesus died an atoning sacrificial death in order to provide "satisfaction" to God. Many Christians today have adopted this soteriology, although they might not use Anselm's exact terminology.

Anselm carefully constructs his argument in the form of a dialogue between himself and a critic named Boso, "one of those persons who agitate this subject." Like the dialogues of Plato, in which Socrates asks questions but already has the answers, Anselm uses Boso as a foil for what he really wants to say. But note in the brief exchange below how he builds one logical premise upon another.

> *Anselm:* Observe this also. Everyone knows that justice to man is regulated by law, so that, according to the requirements of law, the measure of award is bestowed by God.

Boso: This is our belief.

Anselm: But if sin is neither paid for nor punished, it is subject to no law.

Boso: I cannot conceive it to be otherwise.

Anselm: Injustice, therefore, if it is cancelled by compassion alone, is more free
than justice, which seems very inconsistent. And to these is also added
a further incongruity, viz., that it makes injustice like God. For as God
is subject to no law, so neither is injustice.

Boso: I cannot withstand your reasoning . . . (*Cur Deus Homo,* Chapter 12)

Peter Abelard (1079–1142) offered an alternative view of atonement, one in
which Jesus dies on the cross to demonstrate the depth of God's love for humanity.
Called the "moral theory of atonement," this soteriology sees Jesus as being a moral
exemplar for Christians. His sacrificial death had nothing to do with debt or satisfaction, or God's honor, and everything to do with God's love. By demonstrating self-
sacrificing love, "laying down his life for his friends" (John 15:13), Jesus teaches us
to love God in return. Thus, Christians act out of love, rather than fear, freed from
bondage to sin due to God's forgiveness.

Abelard is undoubtedly the most famous of the twelfth-century teachers to
apply reason to theological questions. His brief autobiography, *Historia Calamitatum,*
details the story of the calamities that stemmed from his love affair with Heloise
(c. 1098–1164), the niece of his landlord in Paris, who also happened to be a canon
in the Cathedral of Paris. He impregnated Heloise and had to flee the city, although
not before being castrated by her uncle. They married in secret, and Heloise named
their son Astrolabe, after a medieval instrument used to determine the altitude of the
sun and stars. She founded a religious order for women, the Paraclete, and was an
effective administrator of the community, giving sermons, interpreting scripture, and
occasionally seeking Abelard's advice on theological questions. Meanwhile, Abelard
continued to teach those who wanted to bring a rational understanding to biblical
topics. Although he did not invent the method called "dialectic," he perfected this
type of argumentation, which looks at all sides of an issue in order to reach ultimate
truth. His book *Sic et Non (Yes and No)* examined a number of issues and discussed
the pros and cons of each.

Freelance teachers such as Abelard, approved by local bishops to teach in the
cathedral schools, would attract groups of students interested in their approach to
philosophy and theology. Organized universities arose from the informal freelance
teaching and learning structure. Just as the growth of cities had led to the development of lay corporations such as the guilds, they also led to the formalization of
teacher-student bodies, known as universities. The archbishop of Paris established
the University of Paris in 1231, and universities quickly opened in Bologna, Oxford,
and Salamanca. The university system granted licenses to graduates to teach theology, canon law, and medicine. Almost everything we find in colleges and universities
today comes from the Middle Ages: the graduation robes and funny hats; the titles of
degrees (bachelor's, master's, doctor's); the term *liberal arts* and what it suggests; and

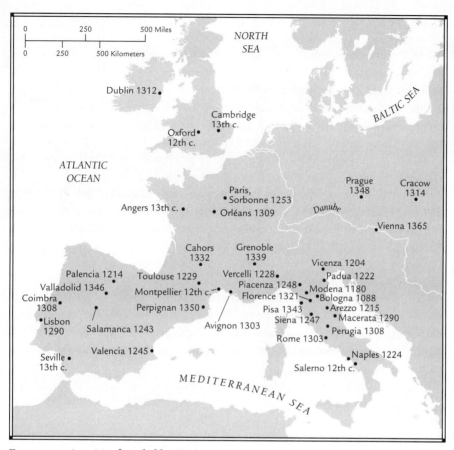

European universities founded by 1350.

the idea of disciplines and colleges, students, and faculties. We are reading this book because of the rise of universities during the Middle Ages!

Although teachers in these medieval universities belonged to religious orders—they continued to be monastics or canons—their approach to the subject matter, and indeed, the subject matter itself, differed radically from that of the mystics and the monastic theologians. The masters, or teachers, had traditionally taught the classical seven liberal arts: the trivium (grammar, rhetoric, and logic), and the quadrivium (arithmetic, geometry, music and astronomy). Beginning in the twelfth century, and expanding greatly in the thirteenth century, however, university masters emphasized the application of reason to questions of theology. The twelfth century saw an expanded reliance on reason with the writing of encyclopedias, textbooks, and summas (summaries) of Christian teachings. Arguing strictly from authority became passé: one had to use reason and logic to persuade twelfth-century students. What really pushed logic to the forefront, however, was the arrival of Greek philosophical works in Latin translation.

At the beginning of this chapter, I noted that the Dark Ages really referred to Western Europe. The rest of the world was brilliantly illuminated by works of classical philosophy, mathematics, and science. This was particularly true of the eastern empire, which was controlled by Muslims. To a certain extent, it was even true in Moorish Spain, where Muslims controlled culture, trade, and society until the 1400s. For example, the Middle Ages became known as the golden age of Hebrew poetry and philosophy as a result of Jewish life and learning in Muslim Spain. In the eastern Mediterranean, Muslims wrote commentaries on philosophy; and Jews translated the original works, as well as the commentaries, from Arabic into Latin. Although the west had had bits and pieces of Aristotle since the fifth century—most of it mediated through the writing of statesman and educator Boethius (c. 475–524)—the bulk of "the Philosopher's" writings arrived in translation in the mid-twelfth century, and eventually dominated Christian theological discussions from 1250 to 1350.

Following the groundwork laid by Anselm and Abelard, Christians in the thirteenth century continued to apply reason to discussions of faith and dogma. Aristotle, and other Greek, Muslim, and Jewish philosophers, offered the means to do this. They provided a systematic method by which to consider issues; they also provided convincing arguments. It was clear to Christians that if God created the world by the Word (Logos)—which they understood as God's reason, wisdom, and rationality—then they could apply reason to theological issues. They could argue logically and concisely, anticipating objections, refuting detractors, and advancing proofs anyone might accept—any Christian, that is, since they continued to work with Christian presuppositions.

The key figure of the scholastic period was Thomas Aquinas (c. 1225–1274), who continues to be extremely influential in contemporary Catholic theology. Thomas began his life, as did many monastics, as a rich young man. Although his parents sent him at an early age to a Benedictine abbey to be trained in ecclesiastical leadership, Thomas decided to join the Dominican order against their wishes. Thomas' brothers kidnapped him as he was en route to Paris and briefly imprisoned him in order to persuade him to give up his vocation, but he remained firm. Thomas eventually went to Cologne, Germany, where he studied under Albert the Great (c. 1200–1280). Albert was a Dominican priest, a scientist, a naturalist, an alchemist, and a Renaissance man well before the Renaissance. While his teacher pursued many different interests, Thomas seemed to focus on two: the interpretation of the Bible and, more importantly, the systematic exposition of Christian doctrine. Thomas' *Summa Theologiae* (*Summary of Theology*) is a massive, multivolume work that addresses a range of doctrinal questions in a series of short articles—from the existence of God to the morality of stealing.

The *Summa* follows a regular pattern of argumentation modeled after medieval debates in the schools. A teacher would pose a question in the morning, and students would spend the day debating the issue. In the late afternoon, the teacher would give a *sententia* (a sentence or opinion) on the question, critiquing various arguments and answering related questions. Aquinas uses this approach in the *Summa,* which effectively models how a good argument is made. A typical article would follow this format:

1. Statement of the question

2. Presentation of objections to the answer implied by the question (Aquinas usually phrased questions in a way that suggested "yes" answers, so initial objections usually argued for a "no" answer.)

3. Declaration of a contrary argument (usually based on scripture or some other source of authority)

4. Response by Aquinas in support of the answers implied by the question (usually based on logic, science, experience, or observation)

5. Conclusion, based on some source of authority (frequently, the Bible)

6. Reply by Aquinas to the initial objections

The Reading

The following selection from Aquinas' *Summa Theologiae* addresses the question of whether God exists. The scholastic anticipates the objections to his position. Unlike current talk show hosts who simply dismiss critics by calling them names, Aquinas takes the objections seriously and refutes them after he makes the case for his own position. Very important, however, is the fact that he outlines the objections to his position at the outset. Sometimes he may not be entirely fair or accurate in stating those objections, or he may miss the obvious. Certainly, his "science" is that of Aristotle and Albert the Great, and so he assumes things we would challenge today. Nevertheless, Aquinas furnishes a rigorous and systematic method for dealing with contentious issues.

When he refers to "the Philosopher," he means Aristotle; "the Apostle" is Paul; John of Damascus is a theologian of the eastern church. Be sure to think about Aquinas' quoting of various authorities. Is this a strong form of argumentation or a weak one? Be able to explain your opinion. Finally, do you think you might be able to write a paper—or answer an essay question on an exam—using this method? Think about its advantages and disadvantages.

Questions to Consider

1. Does Aquinas follow the outline given above? If not, how does he depart from it?

2. What are Aquinas' arguments in the sections where he advances his own arguments? What are they based on? (Are they based on logic? On practical experience? On someone else's authority?) What authorities (that is, people) does he

use? When does he use them? Why? What does he think of Anselm's ontological argument for the existence of God?

3. Note the progression of issues Aquinas addresses. What is his purpose or method in posing each question?

4. Aquinas was clearly a man of his time, providing arguments based on accepted logic and experience of his day and age. Do his arguments work now? Why or why not?

5. Are people using any of Aquinas' arguments today—for example, in the debate over creationism and "intelligent design" (that is, the world is too complex to have simply involved; therefore, an "intelligence" deliberately designed things to be the way they are)?

6. Construct an argument on a religious issue the class agrees to debate using Aquinas' method.

The Existence of God:
First Part, Question 2 of the Summa Theologiae

THOMAS AQUINAS

Article 1: Whether the existence of God is self-evident?

Objection 1: It seems that the existence of God is self-evident. Now those things are said to be self-evident to us the knowledge of which is naturally implanted in us, as we can see in regard to first principles. But as [John of Damascus] says, "the knowledge of God is naturally implanted in all." Therefore the existence of God is self-evident.

Objection 2: Further, those things are said to be self-evident which are known as soon as the terms are known, which the Philosopher says is true of the first principles of demonstration. Thus, when the nature of a whole and of a part is known, it is at once recognized that every whole is greater than its part. But as soon as the signification of the word "God" is understood, it is at once seen that God exists. For by this word is signified that thing than which nothing greater can be conceived. But that which exists actually and mentally is greater than that which exists only mentally. Therefore, since as soon as the word "God" is understood it exists mentally, it also follows that it exists actually. Therefore the proposition "God exists" is self-evident.

Objection 3: Further, the existence of truth is self-evident. For whoever denies the existence of truth grants that truth does not exist: and, if truth does not exist, then the proposition "Truth does not exist" is true: and if there is anything true, there must be truth. But God is truth itself: "I am the way, the truth, and the life" (John 14:6). Therefore "God exists" is self-evident.

On the contrary, No one can mentally admit the opposite of what is self-evident; as the Philosopher states concerning the first principles of demonstration. But the opposite of the proposition "God is" can be mentally admitted: "The fool said in his heart, There is no God" (Psalm 53:1). Therefore, that God exists is not self-evident.

I answer that, A thing can be self-evident in either of two ways: on the one hand, self-evident in itself, though not to us; on the other, self-evident in itself, and to us. A proposition is self-evident because the predicate is included in the essence of the subject, as "Man is an animal," for animal is contained in the essence of man. If, therefore the essence of the predicate and subject be known to all, the proposition will be self-evident to all; as is clear with regard to the first principles of demonstration, the terms of which are common things that no one is ignorant of, such as being and non-being, whole and part, and such like. If, however, there are some to whom the essence of the predicate and subject is unknown, the proposition will be self-evident in itself, but not to those who do not know the meaning of the predicate and subject of the proposition. Therefore, it happens, as Boethius says, "that there are some mental concepts self-evident only to the learned, as that incorporeal substances are not in space." Therefore I say that this proposition, "God exists," of itself is self-evident, for the predicate is the same as the subject, because God is His own existence as will be hereafter shown. [Aquinas addresses these issues elsewhere.] Now because we do not know the essence of God, the proposition is not self-evident to us; but needs to be demonstrated by things that are more known to us, though less known in their nature—namely, by effects.

Reply to Objection 1: To know that God exists in a general and confused way is implanted in us by nature, inasmuch as God is man's beatitude. For man naturally desires happiness, and what is naturally desired by man must be naturally known to him. This, however, is not to know absolutely that God exists; just as to know that someone is approaching is not the same as to know that Peter is approaching, even though it is Peter who is approaching; for many there are who imagine that man's perfect good which is happiness, consists in riches, and others in pleasures, and others in something else.

Reply to Objection 2: Perhaps not everyone who hears this word "God" understands it to signify something than which nothing greater can be thought, seeing that some have believed God to be a body. Yet, granted that everyone understands that by this word "God" is signified something than which nothing greater can be thought, nevertheless, it does not therefore follow that he understands that what the word signifies exists actually, but only that it exists mentally. Nor can it be argued that it actually exists, unless it be admitted that there actually exists something than which nothing greater can be thought; and this precisely is not admitted by those who hold that God does not exist.

Reply to Objection 3: The existence of truth in general is self-evident but the existence of a Primal Truth is not self-evident to us.

Article 2: *Whether it can be demonstrated that God exists?*

Objection 1: It seems that the existence of God cannot be demonstrated. For it is an article of faith that God exists. But what is of faith cannot be demonstrated, because a demonstration produces scientific knowledge; whereas faith is of the unseen (Hebrews 11:1). Therefore it cannot be demonstrated that God exists.

Objection 2: Further, the essence is the middle term of demonstration. But we cannot know in what God's essence consists, but solely in what it does not consist; as [John of Damascus] says. Therefore we cannot demonstrate that God exists.

Objection 3: Further, if the existence of God were demonstrated, this could only be from His effects. But His effects are not proportionate to Him, since He is infinite and His effects are finite; and between the finite and infinite there is no proportion. Therefore, since a cause cannot be demonstrated by an effect not proportionate to it, it seems that the existence of God cannot be demonstrated.

On the contrary, The Apostle says: "The invisible things of Him are clearly seen, being understood by the things that are made" (Romans 1:20). But this would not be unless the existence of God could be demonstrated through the things that are made; for the first thing we must know of anything is whether it exists.

I answer that, Demonstration can be made in two ways: One is through the cause, and is called "a priori," and this is to argue from what is prior absolutely. The other is through the effect, and is called a demonstration "a posteriori"; this is to argue from what is prior relatively only to us. When an effect is better known to us than its cause, from the effect we proceed to the knowledge of the cause. And from every effect the existence of its proper cause can be demonstrated, so long as its effects are better known to us; because since every effect depends upon its cause, if the effect exists, the cause must pre-exist. Hence the existence of God, in so far as it is not self-evident to us, can be demonstrated from those of His effects which are known to us.

Reply to Objection 1: The existence of God and other like truths about God, which can be known by natural reason, are not articles of faith, but are preambles to the articles; for faith presupposes natural knowledge, even as grace presupposes nature, and perfection supposes something that can be perfected. Nevertheless, there is nothing to prevent a man, who cannot grasp a proof, accepting, as a matter of faith, something which in itself is capable of being scientifically known and demonstrated.

Reply to Objection 2: When the existence of a cause is demonstrated from an effect, this effect takes the place of the definition of the cause in proof of the cause's existence. This is especially the case in regard to God, because, in order to prove the existence of anything, it is necessary to accept as a middle term the meaning of the word, and not its essence, for the question of its essence follows on the question of its existence. Now the names given to God are derived from His effects; consequently, in demonstrating the existence of God from His effects, we may take for the middle term the meaning of the word "God."

Reply to Objection 3: From effects not proportionate to the cause no perfect knowledge of that cause can be obtained. Yet from every effect the existence of the cause can be clearly demonstrated, and so we can demonstrate the existence of God from His effects; though from them we cannot perfectly know God as He is in His essence.

Article 3: Whether God exists?

Objection 1: It seems that God does not exist; because if one of two contraries be infinite, the other would be altogether destroyed. But the word "God" means that He is infinite goodness. If, therefore, God existed, there would be no evil discoverable; but there is evil in the world. Therefore God does not exist.

Objection 2: Further, it is superfluous to suppose that what can be accounted for by a few principles has been produced by many. But it seems that everything we see in the world can be accounted for by other principles, supposing God did not exist. For all natural things can be reduced to one principle which is nature; and all voluntary things can be reduced to one principle which is human reason, or will. Therefore there is no need to suppose God's existence.

On the contrary, It is said in the person of God: "I am Who am" (Exodus 3:14).

I answer that, The existence of God can be proved in five ways.

The first and more manifest way is the argument from motion. It is certain, and evident to our senses, that in the world some things are in motion. Now whatever is in motion is put in motion by another, for nothing can be in motion except it is in potentiality to that towards which it is in motion; whereas a thing moves inasmuch as it is in act. For motion is nothing else than the reduction of something from potentiality to actuality. But nothing can be reduced from potentiality to actuality, except by something in a state of actuality. Thus that which is actually hot, as fire, makes wood, which is potentially hot, to be actually hot, and thereby moves and changes it. Now it is not possible that the same thing should be at once in actuality and potentiality in the same respect, but only in different respects. For what is actually hot cannot simultaneously be potentially hot; but it is simultaneously potentially cold. It is therefore impossible that in the same respect and in the same way a thing should be both mover and moved, i.e. that it should move itself. Therefore, whatever is in motion must be put in motion by another. If that by which it is put in motion be itself put in motion, then this also must needs be put in motion by another, and that by another again. But this cannot go on to infinity, because then there would be no first mover, and, consequently, no other mover; seeing that subsequent movers move only inasmuch as they are put in motion by the first mover; as the staff moves only because it is put in motion by the hand. Therefore it is necessary to arrive at a first mover, put in motion by no other; and this everyone understands to be God.

The second way is from the nature of the efficient cause. In the world of sense we find there is an order of efficient causes. There is no case known (neither is it, indeed, possible) in which a thing is found to be the efficient cause of itself; for so it would be prior to itself, which is impossible. Now in efficient causes it is not possible to go on to infinity, because in all efficient causes following in order, the first is the cause of the intermediate cause, and the intermediate is the cause of the ultimate cause, whether the intermediate cause be several, or only one. Now to take away the cause is to take away the effect. Therefore, if there be no first cause among efficient causes, there will be no ultimate, nor any intermediate cause. But if in efficient causes it is possible to go on to infinity, there will be no first efficient cause, neither will there be an ultimate effect, nor any intermediate efficient causes; all of which is plainly false. Therefore it is necessary to admit a first efficient cause, to which everyone gives the name of God.

The third way is taken from possibility and necessity, and runs thus. We find in nature things that are possible to be and not to be, since they are found to be generated, and to corrupt, and consequently, they are possible to be and not to be. But it is impossible for these always to exist, for that which is possible not to be at some time is not. Therefore, if everything is possible not to be, then at one time there could have been nothing in existence. Now if this were true, even now there would be nothing in existence, because that which does not exist only begins to exist by something already existing. Therefore, if at one time nothing was in existence, it would have been impossible for anything to have begun to exist; and thus even now nothing would be in existence—which is absurd. Therefore, not all beings are merely possible, but there must exist something the existence of which is necessary. But every necessary thing either has its necessity caused by another, or not. Now it is impossible to go on to infinity in necessary things which have their necessity caused by another, as has been already proved in regard to efficient causes. Therefore we cannot but postulate the existence of some being having of itself its own necessity, and not receiving it from another, but rather causing in others their necessity. This all men speak of as God.

The fourth way is taken from the gradation to be found in things. Among beings there are some more and some less good, true, noble and the like. But "more" and "less" are predicated of different things, according as they resemble in their different ways something which is the maximum, as a thing is said to be hotter according as it more nearly resembles that which is hottest; so that there is something which is truest, something best, something noblest and, consequently, something which is uttermost being; for those things that are greatest in truth are greatest in being, as it is written in [Aristotle]. Now the maximum in any genus is the cause of all in that genus; as fire, which is the maximum heat, is the cause of all hot things. Therefore there must also be something which is to all beings the cause of their being, goodness, and every other perfection; and this we call God.

The fifth way is taken from the governance of the world. We see that things which lack intelligence, such as natural bodies, act for an end, and this is evident from their acting always, or nearly always, in the same way, so as to obtain the best result. Hence it is plain that not fortuitously, but designedly, do they achieve their end. Now whatever lacks intelligence cannot move towards an end, unless it be directed by some being endowed with knowledge and intelligence; as the arrow is shot to its mark by the archer. Therefore some intelligent being exists by whom all natural things are directed to their end; and this being we call God.

Reply to Objection 1: As Augustine says: "Since God is the highest good, He would not allow any evil to exist in His works, unless His omnipotence and goodness were such as to bring good even out of evil." This is part of the infinite goodness of God, that He should allow evil to exist, and out of it produce good.

Reply to Objection 2: Since nature works for a determinate end under the direction of a higher agent, whatever is done by nature must needs be traced back to God, as to its first cause. So also whatever is done voluntarily must also be traced back to some higher cause other than human reason or will, since these can change or fail; for all things that are changeable and capable of defect must be traced back to an immovable and self-necessary first principle, as was shown in the body of the Article.

Mendicant Theology

The "love of learning and the desire for God," in the words of a twentieth-century French Catholic historian, served as a powerful reforming force within medieval Christianity. Yearners for the divine sought God in prayer, in the Bible, and in reason. It manifested itself in the aspiration to lead a holy life, wholly devoted to God. Sometimes despite themselves, male and female religious transformed the church again and again ("religious" is used as a noun here, meaning a person who has accepted a vocation to live a life devoted to God). No group altered the status quo more radically than the mendicant orders. Unlike the Benedictine monastics or the Augustinian canons, the mendicants owned no property or land. Initially, they held no ecclesiastical offices. They survived by begging, that is, relying upon the charity of Christians wherever they went. They drew inspiration from Jesus' sending forth his own disciples with nothing:

> Take no gold, or silver, or copper in your belts, no bag for your journey, or two tunics, or sandals, or a staff; for laborers deserve their food. Whatever town or village you enter, find out who in it is worthy, and stay there until you leave. As you enter the house, greet it. If the house is worthy, let your peace come upon it; but if it is not worthy, let your peace return to you. If anyone will not welcome you or listen to your words, shake off the dust from your feet as you leave that house or town. (Matthew 10:9–14)

The mendicants, therefore, left the cloisters and cathedrals, and roamed the countryside, teaching and preaching to all who would listen. We know them by the familiar term *friar*. Friars, the male members of mendicant orders, lacked both individual and group property. What the order "owned" was actually held in trust by the pope. They had great mobility and were engaged in working with laypeople directly. Two groups stand out: the Franciscans and the Dominicans.

Saint Dominic of Spain (c. 1170–1221) left a distinguished ecclesiastical career to establish a group of friars who would root out heresy. Dominic had personally seen the results of the Albigensian heresy in southern France. The Albigensians were a group of ascetic Christians who, like the Docetists before them, did not believe in the humanity of Christ. Dominic was deeply concerned about people who were abandoning the church and Christian practice by falling into heresy. His religious community was an order of preachers—thus the initials O.P. to indicate the Dominican order—that traveled the countryside, preaching the true gospel and bringing the faithful back to proper doctrine. In addition to teaching and preaching correct dogma, however, the preaching friars instigated inquisitions, that is, aggressive searches for heresy. The Dominicans eventually gained a reputation for being heresy hunters, and became infamous for managing the brutal inquisitions in Spain and elsewhere in Europe. Dominicans also claim a tradition of education and letters, however, and in the Middle Ages could be found teaching in the newly established universities of Europe. Thomas Aquinas is the foremost examplar of the Dominican pursuit of truth and the "sanctification of human intelligence," but many other Dominicans contributed to Western thought and culture, including the scientist Albert the Great, the artist Fra Angelico, and the Italian philosopher Francisco de Vitoria. Domincans saw themselves as carrying on the traditions of the earliest apostles by engaging in teaching, missions, and social action.

Saint Francis of Assisi (1181/82–1226) founded the Franciscan order, another group of itinerant mendicants dedicated to preaching and serving the poor. A rich young man, Francis had a dream in which he heard a voice telling him to "rebuild my church." At first, the young man interpreted his dream literally and set about making church building repairs. But he soon came to believe that his dream meant he should reform the institution of the church itself. Thanks to gifts from wealthy patrons, the medieval church had grown large and complacent. Prosperous religious orders seemed to forget their lord and model, Jesus. Differences in wealth and privilege which existed outside the monasteries were perpetuated within. Francis, however, attempted to recall the church and its orders to the poverty and simplicity of Christ. He modeled his life after that of Christ, embracing what he called "Lady Poverty" and renouncing all comforts. He denounced books and reading, and supposedly mixed ashes with his food in order to reduce his enjoyment of it. The Order of the Friars Minor (OFM) reflected its founder's humility and intent: order of the little brothers. After hearing Saint Francis preach when she was eighteen years old, Saint Clare of Assisi (1193/94–1253) joined a convent and eventually founded a religious order for women, the Poor Clares, dedicated to helping the poor. Francis frequently consulted with Clare, and after his death, her order continued to promote his ideal of poverty.

Legend says that Francis preached to birds and animals, who listened intently, and today the Feast Day of Saint Francis is a time when Christians in liturgical traditions such as Catholicism and Anglicanism bring animals to church for a special blessing. The Cathedral of Saint John the Divine in New York City is the site of one such blessing, where elephants and giraffes, as well as cats and dogs, parade up the aisle for their blessing, sometimes to the music of the Paul Winter Consort playing an "Earth Mass/Missa Gaia." Christians today frequently sing Saint Francis' own "Canticle of the Sun" under the title "All Creatures of Our God and King" to a tune harmonized by the English religious composer Ralph Vaughan Williams. On the next page Francis' original poem runs side by side with the hymn sung now in churches.

It is one of the ironies of history that both of these mendicant orders, which began by stressing absolute poverty and itinerancy, eventually settled down into "conventual" (or monastic) houses and produced remarkable scholars, scientists, and leaders. Oxford University in particular was home to many brilliant Franciscans, while the University of Paris boasted Dominicans like Albert the Great and his still greater pupil Thomas Aquinas. The "taming" of the mendicants, however, did not occur without the suppression of one of the more radical outbursts of religious fervor: that of Joachim of Fiore, an Italian Cistercian who prophesied the imminent end of the world and the accession of the rule of monks in a heavenly kingdom on earth. Joachim (c. 1135–1202) identified a trinitarian succession of world epochs. The Age of the Father was that of ancient Israel, described in the Old Testament. The Age of the Son began with the New Testament and existed in the life of the church. But a new Age of the Spirit was dawning, in his view, and men and women religious best exemplified that spiritual age. While Joachim's new Age of the Spirit implicitly critiqued the worldly church, his successors the Joachites (who were Franciscans dedicated to poverty and itinerancy) explicitly attacked the church, which struck back. The poverty of the extreme mendicants— as well as their selfless work helping those who themselves were poor—exposed

Canticle of the Sun and *All Creatures of Our God and King*: A Comparative View

CANTICLE OF THE SUN

Most high, all powerful, all good Lord! All praise is yours, all glory, all honor, and all blessing. To you, alone, Most High, do they belong. No mortal lips are worthy to pronounce your name.

Be praised, my Lord, through all your creatures, especially through my lord Brother Sun, who brings the day; and you give light through him. And he is beautiful and radiant in all his splendor! Of you, Most High, he bears the likeness.

Be praised, my Lord, through Sister Moon and the stars; in the heavens you have made them, precious and beautiful.

Be praised, my Lord, through Brothers Wind and Air, and clouds and storms, and all the weather, through which you give your creatures sustenance.

Be praised, My Lord, through Sister Water; she is very useful, and humble, and precious, and pure.

Be praised, my Lord, through Brother Fire, through whom you brighten the night. He is beautiful and cheerful, and powerful and strong.

Be praised, my Lord, through our sister Mother Earth, who feeds us and rules us, and produces various fruits with colored flowers and herbs.

Be praised, my Lord, through those who forgive for love of you; through those who endure sickness and trial. Happy those who endure in peace, for by you, Most High, they will be crowned.

Be praised, my Lord, through our Sister Bodily Death, from whose embrace no living person can escape. Woe to those who die in mortal sin! Happy those she finds doing your most holy will. The second death can do no harm to them.

Praise and bless my Lord, and give thanks, and serve him with great humility.

ALL CREATURES OF OUR GOD AND KING

All creatures of our God and King, lift up your voice and with us sing
O praise ye, Alleluia!
O brother sun with golden beam, O sister moon with silver gleam!
O praise ye! O praise ye! Alleluia! Alleluia! Alleluia!

O brother wind, air, clouds, and rain, by which all creatures ye sustain,
O praise ye, Alleluia!
Thou rising morn, in praise rejoice, ye lights of evening, find a voice!
O praise ye! O praise ye! Alleluia! Alleluia! Alleluia!

O sister water, flowing clear, make music for thy Lord to hear,
Alleluia! Alleluia!
O brother fire who lights the night, providing warmth, enhancing sight,
O praise ye! O praise ye! Alleluia! Alleluia! Alleluia!

Dear mother earth, who day by day, unfoldest blessings on our way,
Alleluia! Alleluia!
The flowers and fruits that in thee grow, let them God's glory also show!
O praise ye! O praise ye! Alleluia! Alleluia! Alleluia!

All ye who are of tender heart, forgiving others, take your part,
O praise ye, Alleluia!
Ye who long pain and sorrow bear, praise God and on him cast your care!
O praise ye! O praise ye! Alleluia! Alleluia! Alleluia!

And thou, our sister, gentle death, waiting to hush our latest breath,
Alleluia! Alleluia!
Thou leadest home the child of God, and Christ our Lord the way has trod,
O praise ye! O praise ye! Alleluia! Alleluia! Alleluia!

Let all things their Creator bless, and worship him in humbleness,
O praise ye, Alleluia!
Praise, praise the Father, praise the Son, and praise the Spirit, Three in One!
O praise ye! O praise ye! Alleluia! Alleluia! Alleluia!

the religious hypocrisy of a well-fed clergy and its churches. The movement was ruthlessly suppressed.

Still other religious orders dedicated to helping the poor surfaced in the later Middle Ages. The Beguines were a group of single women, originating in the Rhineland and the low countries in the twelfth century, who lived in religious communities outside ecclesiastical control. The lay order addressed the problems presented by a surplus of unattached females living in urban areas. They took vows of voluntary poverty and chastity, and lived lives of prayer serving the poor, like their male counterparts, the much smaller lay order called the Beghards. Their service took the form of feeding the hungry, caring for the sick and elderly, or raising orphans—as most religious orders had done throughout the Middle Ages. The difference in these new orders, however, was that they were composed of laypeople who attempted to live a holy life outside the convent or monastery. In addition, one could voluntarily leave the order in order to marry.

Thus, one religious community after another called Christians back to the gospel message of feeding the poor, clothing the naked, caring for the sick, and visiting those in prison (Matthew 25:31–46). *Ecclesia semper reformanda:* "the church is always to be reformed," and monastic movements of men and women were at the forefront of reminding the church of Jesus' command to love neighbor as well as to love God.

Eastern Theology

The Theology of Icons

Thus far, we have focused on theological developments that occurred within the western church, concentrating on events and ideas arising in medieval Europe. But the eastern church also witnessed a creative burst of theological thinking at this same time. This Byzantine Empire retained its heritage of Greek culture, language, and learning. At the same time, Christians transformed their inheritance and tended to abandon the traditional simplicity of classical art and architecture. We get the word *byzantine*—colloquially meaning "convoluted, complicated, or ornate"—from the fabulous buildings of the time, structures that reveled in light and color, reflecting the glory of God. While Christianity in the West seemed at times dark and brooding, filled with images of the suffering Christ, Christianity in the East was bright and glistening, an integral part of the imperial power structure. Christ was king and sovereign of the universe: all-powerful, not all-suffering. Mosaics depicted him in his majesty and splendor.

Byzantium withstood external assaults until the rise of Islam in the seventh century. Even after the Muslim conquest, Christianity remained a strong institution in that part of the world. Islam provoked an intense debate in the eastern church, however, over the use of icons, or images, of Jesus. In this dispute, known as the Iconoclastic Controversy, some Christians started to think that it was wrong to depict the divine in artwork, and the emperor Leo the Isaurian (r. 717–741) banned

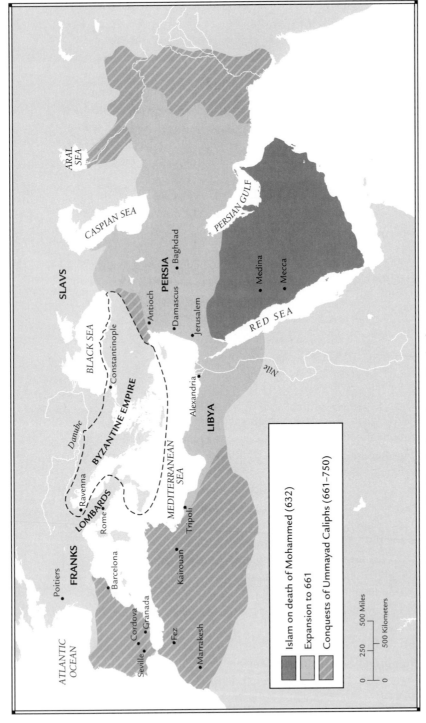

The expansion of Islam. *Beginning in Arabia, Islam had spread across North Africa, into Spain, and deep into Asia within a century after the Prophet's death in 632.*

all icons and encouraged icon-smashing (in Greek, *iconoclasm*). The iconoclasts believed that if the divine could not be represented in pictures—since it was a spiritual, rather than physical, reality—then neither could the Son of God be depicted. Others argued, however, that outlawing images of Jesus meant that Christians were denying the Son's humanity. The Byzantine emperors went back and forth on the question, and the church was in an uproar. The fight over icons was bloody, with hundreds of priests and monks who defended images being tortured, maimed, and executed. The western church opposed the iconoclasts, but some eastern Christians, undoubtedly influenced by Islamic charges of idol worship, saw these paintings and mosaics as theologically incorrect, and even dangerous to believers who worshiped the image rather than what the image stood for. Eventually, those arguing for icons, the iconodules, prevailed at the Seventh Ecumenical Council (787), which was also the second Council of Nicea. The invisible became visible when God became incarnate in Jesus Christ; therefore, the divine could, in fact, be represented in human form.

The Reading

John of Damascus (c. 675–749) was a Syrian theologian who defended the use of icons in three treatises written during the rule of Leo III. Far removed from the controversy, he lived as a recluse in the monastery of Saint Sabbas, near Jerusalem in Palestine, which at that time was under Muslim rule. He wrote a number of philosophical and theological treatises (the most famous of which—*The Orthodox Faith*—Thomas Aquinas used in his argument for the existence of God).

In this third treatise, John analyzes the nature of images—their origin and purpose. His discussion echoes Genesis 1–3, Athanasius' book *On the Incarnation,* and relies on several passages from the New Testament. He refers to Dionysius the Areopagite, a pagan convert to Christianity mentioned in the New Testament book of Acts (17:34). Another Dionysius was a Syrian monk whose mystical writings profoundly influenced eastern Christianity's ideas about the liturgy, about God, and about our relationship with God. John and his contemporaries believed that this Dionysius was the same one mentioned in Acts; scholars have since noted, however, that this was a different Dionysius who purported to be writing much earlier. For this reason, he is frequently called "Pseudo-Dionysius," that is, False Dionysius. I drop the "pseudo" because it suggests something false about his writings, and not just his name. We will return to Dionysius when we get to Gregory Palamas.

Questions to Consider

1. What is John's understanding of the relationship between scripture and subsequent theological ideas?

2. What arguments does he use to defend icons? How does he use scripture?

3. How does he define images? What kinds of different images are there?

4. How might icons present theology to illiterate Christians? What are the strengths and weaknesses of depicting religious ideas in this manner?

5. What similarities exist in the ideas of John of Damascus and Athanasius of Alexandria? Are there differences?

Third Apology Against Those Who Attack the Divine Images

JOHN OF DAMASCUS

10. . . . I have often seen lovers gazing at the garments of their beloved, embracing the garments with their eyes and their lips as if the garment were the beloved one. We must give every man his due, as the holy apostle Paul says: "honor to whom honor is due, whether it be to the emperor as supreme, or to governors sent by him" (Romans 13:7; 1 Peter 2:13), to each one, according to the measure of his dignity.

11. Where can you find in the Old Testament or in the Gospels explicit use of such terms as "Trinity" or "consubstantial" or "one nature of the Godhead," or "three persons," or anything about Christ being "one person with two natures"? But nevertheless, the meanings of all these things are found, expressed in other phrases which the Scriptures do contain, and the fathers have interpreted them for us. We accept them, and anathematize those who will not. I have proven to you that under the old covenant God commanded images to be made: first the tabernacle, and then everything in it. And in the Gospels the Lord Himself answered those who questioned and tested Him saying, "Is it lawful to pay taxes to Caesar?" He said to them, "Show me the money for the tax," and they brought Him a coin. And Jesus said to them, "Whose likeness and inscription is this?" They said, "Caesar's." Then He said to them, "Render therefore to Caesar the things that are Caesar's, and to God the things that are God's" (Matthew 22:17–21). Since the coin bears Caesar's likeness, it is united to Caesar's person and you must give it back to him. Likewise the icon of Christ is part of Him, and you must give it what is due.

12. The Lord called His disciples blessed, for He said, "Blessed are your eyes, for they see, and your ears, for they hear. Truly, I say to you, many prophets and kings longed to see what you see, and did not see it, and to hear what you hear, and did not hear it" (Matthew 13:16–17). The apostles saw Christ in the flesh; they witnessed His sufferings and His miracles, and heard His words. We too desire to see, and to hear, and so be filled with gladness. They saw Him face to face, since He was physically present. Since He is no longer physically present, we hear His words read from books and by hearing our souls are sanctified and filled with blessing, and so we worship, honoring the books from which we hear His words. So also, through the painting of images, we are able to contemplate the likeness of His bodily form, His miracles, and His passion, and thus are sanctified, blessed, and filled with joy. Reverently we honor and worship His bodily form, and by contemplating His bodily form, we form a notion, as far as is possible for us, of the glory of His divinity. Since we are fashioned of both soul and body, and our souls are not naked spirits, but are covered, as it were, with a fleshly veil, it is impossible for us to think without using physical images. Just as we physically listen to perceptible words in order to understand spiritual things, so also by using bodily sight we reach spiritual contemplation. For this reason Christ assumed both soul and body, since man is fashioned from both. Likewise baptism is both of water and of Spirit. It is the same with communion, prayer, psalmody, candles, or incense; they all have a double significance, physical and spiritual.

13. The devil has avoided all these things, saving his storm for icons alone. His great jealousy of icons may be learned by what the holy Sophronius, the patriarch of Jerusalem, records in his *Spiritual Garden*.

You see that those who prevent the veneration of images are the imitators and instruments of the devil, for instead of further tempting the old man, the demon of lust attempted to deprive our Lady's icon of honor, since he knew which would be the greater evil.

14. Since we are speaking of images and their veneration, let us bring forward and examine thoroughly every aspect concerning them. Let us consider these questions: 1) What is an image? 2) Why are images made? 3) How many kinds of images are there? 4) What may be depicted by an image, and what may not? 5) Who first made images?

First point—What is an image?

16. An image is a likeness, or a model, or a figure of something, showing in itself what it depicts. An image is not always like its prototype in every way. For the image is one thing, and the thing depicted is another; one can always notice differences between them, since one is not the other, and vice versa. I offer the following example: An image of a man, even if it is a likeness of his bodily form, cannot contain his mental powers. It has no life; it cannot think, or speak, or hear, or move. A son is the natural image of his father, yet is different from him, for he is a son, and not a father.

Second point—Why are images made?

17. All images reveal and make perceptible those things which are hidden. For example, man does not have immediate knowledge of invisible things, since the soul is veiled by the body. Nor can man have immediate knowledge of things which are distant from each other or separated by place, because he himself is circumscribed by place and time. Therefore the image was devised that he might advance in knowledge, and that secret things might be revealed and made perceptible. Therefore, images are a source of profit, help, and salvation for all, since they make things so obviously manifest, enabling us to perceive hidden things. Thus, we are encouraged to desire and imitate what is good and to shun and hate what is evil.

Third point—How many kinds of images are there?

18. There are different kinds of images. First there is the natural image. In every case it is necessary for a natural image to come first, and only later those images which are made by words or artistic representation. First we have a human being; only then can we have words or pictures. The Son of the Father is the first natural and precisely similar image of the invisible God, for He reveals the Father in His own person. "No one has ever seen God" (John 1:18), and again, ". . . not that any one has seen the Father" (John 6:46). The apostle says that the Son is the image of the Father: "He is the image of the invisible God" (Colossians 1:15), and to the Hebrews he says, ". . . who, being the brightness of His glory and the image of His substance" (Hebrews 1:3). In St. John's Gospel we see that He does manifest the Father in Himself, for when Philip says to Him, "Lord, show us the Father and it is enough for us," Jesus said to him, "Have I been so long a time with you, and you have not known Me? Philip, he who sees Me sees also the Father" (John 14:8–9). The Son is the natural image of the Father, precisely similar to the Father in every way, except that He is begotten by the Father, who is not begotten. For the Father begets, but Himself is unbegotten, while the Son is begotten, and is not the Father, and the Holy Spirit is the image of the Son for no one can say "Jesus is Lord," except by the Holy Spirit (1 Corinthians 12:3). Through the Holy Spirit we know Christ, who is God and the Son of God, and in the Son we see the Father. The Word is the messenger who makes the divine nature perceptible to us, and the Spirit is the interpreter of the Word. The Holy Spirit is the precisely similar image of the Son, differing only in His manner of procession, for the Son is begotten; He does not proceed. And the son of any father is his natural image. Therefore the first kind of image is the natural image.

19. The second kind of image is God's foreknowledge of things which have yet to happen, His changeless purpose from before all ages. The divine nature is immutable, and His purpose is without beginning. His plans are made before all ages, and they come to pass at the time which has been predetermined for them by Him. Images and figures of things He has yet to do, and the purpose of each of them, were called predeterminations by holy Dionysius. In God's providence, those things predetermined by Him were characterized, depicted, and unalterably fixed before they even came to pass.

20. The third kind of image is made by God as an imitation of Himself: namely, man. How can what is created share the nature of Him who is uncreated, except by imitation? Just as the Father, and the Son who is the Word, and the Holy Spirit, are one God, so also mind and spirit constitute one man, according to God's dominion and authority. For God says, "Let us make man according to our own image and likeness,"

and immediately He adds, "and let him have dominion over the fish of the sea, and over the birds of the air, and over all the earth" (Genesis 1:26).

21. The fourth kind of image consists of the shadows and forms and types of invisible and bodiless things which are described by the Scriptures in physical terms. These give us a faint apprehension of God and the angels where otherwise we would have none, because it is impossible for us to think immaterial things unless we can envision analogous shapes, as the great and holy Dionysius the Areopagite has said. Anyone would say that our inability immediately to direct our thoughts to contemplation of higher things makes it necessary that familiar everyday media be utilized to give suitable form to what is formless, and make visible what cannot be depicted, so that we are able to construct understandable analogies. If, therefore, the Word of God, in providing for our every need, always presents to us what is intangible by clothing it with form, does it not accomplish this by making an image using what is common to nature and so bringing within our reach that for which we long but are unable to see? The eloquent Gregory says that the mind which is determined to ignore corporeal things will find itself weakened and frustrated. Since the creation of the world the invisible things of God are clearly seen by means of images. We see images in the creation which, although they are only dim lights, still remind us of God. For instance, when we speak of the holy and eternal Trinity, we use the images of the sun, light, and burning rays; or a running fountain; or an overflowing river; or the mind, speech, and spirit within us; or a rose tree, a flower, and a sweet fragrance.

22. The fifth kind of image is said to prefigure what is yet to happen, such as the burning bush or the fleece wet with dew, which are foreshadowings of the Virgin Theotokos [God-bearer], as the rod of Aaron and the jar of manna. The brazen serpent typifies the cross and Him who healed the evil bite of the serpent by hanging on it. Baptismal grace is signified by the cloud and the waters of the sea.

23. The sixth kind of image is made for the remembrance of past events, such as miracles or good deeds, in order that glory, honor and eternal memory may be given to those who have struggled valiantly. They assist the increase of virtue, that evil men might be put to shame and overthrown, and they benefit generations to come, that by gazing upon such images we may be encouraged to flee evil and desire

good. These images are of two kinds: either they are words written in books, in which case the written word is the image, as when God had the law engraved on tablets (Deuteronomy 5:22) and desired the lives and deeds of holy men to be recorded (Exodus 17:14), or else they are material images, such as the jar of manna, or Aaron's staff, which were to be kept in the ark as an everlasting memorial (Exodus 16:33–34, Numbers 17:10), or the two onyx stones engraved with the names of the tribes which were set on the shoulder pieces of the ephod (Exodus 28:11–12) or the twelve stones which he commanded to be taken from the Jordan for a second memorial (Joshua 4:20–24) (such a mystery, truly the greatest ever to befall the faithful people!) of the carrying of the ark and the parting of the waters. Therefore we now set up images in remembrance of valiant men, that we may zealously desire to follow their example. Either remove these images altogether, and reject the authority of Him who commanded them to be made, or else accept them in the manner and with the esteem which they deserve.

Fourth point—What may be depicted by an image, and what may not, and how are images to be made?

24. Physical things which have shape, bodies which are circumscribed, and have color, are suitable subjects for image-making. Nevertheless, even if nothing physical or fleshly may be attributed to an angel, or a soul, or a demon, it is still possible to depict and circumscribe them according to their nature. For they are intellectual beings, and are believed to be invisibly present and to operate spiritually. It is possible to make bodily representations of them just as Moses depicted the cherubim. Those who were worthy saw these images, and beheld a bodiless and intellectual sight made manifest through physical means. The divine nature alone can never be circumscribed and is always without form, without shape, and can never be understood. If Holy Scripture clothes God with forms which appear to be physical, or even visible shape, these forms are still immaterial in an important sense, because they were not seen by everyone, nor could they be perceived with the unaided bodily eye, but they were seen through the spiritual sight of prophets or others to whom they were revealed. In a word, it may be said that we may make images of every form we see, and our apprehension of these forms is a kind of sight. If we sometimes understand forms by using our

minds, but other times from what we see, then it is through these two ways that we are brought to understanding. It is the same with the other senses: after we have smelled or tasted, or touched, we combine our experience with reason, and thus come to knowledge.

25. We know that it is impossible to look upon God, or a spirit, or a demon, as they are by nature. We would be able to see them, however, if they appeared in forms alien to their nature. Therefore God in His providence has clothed in forms and shapes things which are bodiless and without form, in order to lead us to more particular knowledge, lest we should be totally ignorant of God and of bodiless creatures. Only God by nature is utterly without a body, but an angel, or a soul, or a demon, when compared to God (who alone cannot be compared to anything) does have a body, but when these are compared to material bodies, they are bodiless. God wills that we should not be totally ignorant of bodiless creatures, and so He clothed them with forms and shapes, and used images comprehensible to our nature, material forms which could be seen by the spiritual vision of the mind. From these we make images and representations, for how else could the cherubim be shown as having form? But Scripture also has forms and images of God Himself.

Fifth point—Who first made images?

26. In the beginning He who is God begot His only Son, His Word, the living image of Himself, the natural and precisely similar likeness of His eternity. And He made man after His own image and likeness (Genesis 1:26). And Adam saw God, and heard the sound of His feet as He walked in Paradise in the cool of the evening, and hid himself (cf. Genesis 3:8). Jacob saw and struggled with God, for it is evident that God appeared to him as a man (Genesis 32:24ff). Moses saw, as it were, the back of a man (Exodus 33:17-23); Isaiah saw Him as a man sitting upon a throne (Isaiah 6:1). Daniel saw the likeness of a man, and one like a son of man coming before the Ancient of Days (Daniel 7:9, 13). No one saw the divine nature, but the image and figure of what was yet to come. For the invisible Son and Word of God was to become truly man, that He might be united to our nature, and be seen on earth. All who saw this image or figure of what was to come worshipped it, as Paul the apostle says in the Epistle to the Hebrews: "These all died in faith, not having received what was promised, but having seen it and greeted it from afar" (He-

brews 11:13). Shall I not make an image of Him who was seen in the nature of flesh for me? Shall I not worship and honor Him, through the honor and veneration of His image? Abraham did not see the divine nature, for no man has ever yet seen God, but he saw an image of God, and fell down and worshipped (Genesis 18:2). Joshua the son of Nun did not see the angel (Joshua 5:14) as he is by nature, but an image, for an angel by nature is not visible to bodily eyes, yet he fell down and worshipped, and Daniel did likewise. Yet an angel is a creature, a servant and minister of God, but not God. And they fell down in worship before the angels, not as God, but as God's ministering spirits. Shall I not make images of friends? Shall I not honor them, not as gods, but as the images of God's friends? Neither Joshua nor Daniel worshipped the angels they saw as gods. Neither do I worship an image as God, but through the images of Christ and of the holy Theotokos [God-bearer], and of the saints, I bring worship and honor to God, because of the reverence with which I honor His friends. God did not unite Himself with angelic nature, but with human nature. God did not become an angel; He became a man by nature and in truth. For surely it is not with angels that He is concerned, but with the seed of Abraham (Hebrews 2:16). The person of the Son of God did not assume angelic nature, but human nature. Angels do not share in this; they do not become partakers of the divine nature. But by the operation of grace, men do share in and become partakers of the divine nature, as many of them as receive the holy Body of Christ and drink His Blood, since His person is united with the Godhead, and the two natures of Christ's Body which we eat are inseparably joined in His person. We partake of both natures, of His Body physically, and of His divinity spiritually, or rather, of each in both. We do not become the same person as He is, for we also first exist as individual persons; only then can we be united by the commingling of His Body and Blood. Therefore, we are greater than the angels, provided that we guard this perfect union by faithfully observing the commandments. For our humble nature is far inferior to the angels, because of death, and the heaviness of the body, but because by God's good will it has been united to Him, human nature has become superior to the angels. The angels stand in fear and trembling before our own nature, for He has raised us up with Him and made us sit with Him in the heavenly places in Christ Jesus (Ephesians 2:6), and they will stand by in fear at the judgment. Nowhere does Scripture say that they will sit together with us, or become partakers of the divine nature. Are they not all ministering spirits sent forth to serve, for the sake of those who are to obtain salvation (Hebrews 1:14)? It is not their place to reign or be glorified together with those who shall sit at the Father's table; the saints, on the other hand, are sons of God, sons of the Kingdom, heirs of God, and fellow heirs of Christ (Romans 8:17), for they are servants by nature, friends by election, and sons and fellow-heirs by divine grace, as the Lord said to the Father (cf. John 17).

While the western church endorsed the use of images of Christ—indeed, medieval and Renaissance art celebrated the life of Jesus—the Protestant Reformation reintroduced iconoclasm into Christianity. Although we will discuss this in Chapter Four, it is important to note that even today, Protestant Christians frequently express skepticism about, and even disdain for, the use of images in Catholic and Orthodox Christianity. This seems to stem from a misunderstanding of the nature and purpose of icons. Are Christians worshiping the symbol or the reality? Both Catholic and Orthodox Christians are careful to describe what is occurring as "veneration" rather than "worship." This means that the believer deeply respects, or venerates, what the image stands for. Just as we may honor the American flag and what it symbolizes, we know we are not worshiping it. Exactly, say those who surround themselves with statues, pictures, and symbols of their faith. Orthodox Christians believe that icons are doorways that take the soul of the believer—through meditation and prayer—from this world into the next. They are the way to the divine, not the manifestation of the divine. Furthermore, in medieval societies, where literacy was rare and books were scarce, they were a way of telling the biblical story to the masses.

Eventually, western and eastern Christianity took different approaches to many other questions facing the church: political, theological, liturgical, and ecclesiastical (that is, in terms of church organization). In the West, the church reigned supreme in what historians call "Christendom," the dominance of Christian thought throughout medieval Europe. In the East, the church was subordinate to the emperor, or empress, yet maintained power and authority through its imperial association. Theologically, the western church tended to emphasize the soteriology of atonement, while the eastern church tended to emphasize the soteriology of incarnation. Liturgically, the eastern church claimed an ancient and venerable heritage that religious authorities traced back to the practices of the early church. The western church could not make quite the same claim since liturgies had changed in translation to Latin. Most significant, however, was the primacy of the bishop of Rome, who was the pope, whose authority over all Christians was not recognized by the autocephalous (literally, self-headed) churches of the East, which considered the pope one bishop among many.

A number of other issues divided eastern and western Christians in addition to the question of papal supremacy. We noted the problem of the filioque in Chapter Two, in which western Christians unilaterally changed the Nicene Creed to include the words "and the son" (*filioque*, in Latin), in an effort to bring in Visigothic converts. East and West disputed the dating of Easter and the type of bread to be served during communion. Language certainly divided the parties. Despite repeated attempts to bridge the gap, eastern and western Christians continued to misread each other, and historians provide several dates to mark significant conflict. The mutual excommunication of bishops by both eastern and western church authorities led to further alienation between East and West in 1054. There was the sack of Constantinople in 1204, in which western Christians attacked and killed eastern Christians during the Fourth Crusade. The Council of Constance (1415–1418) failed to resolve the hard feelings that existed on both sides. Finally, the fall of Constantinople to the Ottoman Turks in 1453 marked the last in a series of disasters that seemed to conspire to keep East and West divided.

Thus, there were many opportunities for reunion, and many occasions on which accord could have been achieved but was not. The result has been centuries of division and misinterpretation, coupled with repeated attempts to come together

▧ Missions and Authority in the Eastern Empire

Even when the empire split east and west, imperial peace generally prevailed in Byzantium. This allowed two Greek-speaking brothers—Saint Cyril (826/827–869) and Saint Methodius (d. 885)—to travel north into Crimea, Moravia (present-day Slovakia), Bulgaria, and Serbia. Cyril devised a Slavonic alphabet, called "Glagolitic," by which he and Methodius translated the Bible and Orthodox worship services into a unique Slavonic liturgy. The creation of an alphabet by which to depict Slavic letters and words obviously helped those in Slavic-speaking countries, believers and nonbelievers alike. In the midtenth century, Russia was missionized by Cyril and Methodius' successors, and eventually became an enormously influential outpost of Orthodoxy in the East.

Cyril and Methodius came into conflict with the pope. Local authorities, as well as local customs and traditions, were much nearer and dearer than the bishop of Rome, thousands of miles away. This was particularly true of Orthodox Christianity, which had, and continues to have, a tradition of autocephalous (self-headed) churches. This means that Orthodox Christians look to a national patriarch, such as the bishop of Serbia, or the metropolitan (bishop) of Moscow, or the Ecumenical Patriarch of Constantinople, spiritual leader of the sixteen autocephalous Orthodox churches. Estimates of the number of Orthodox Christians worldwide range from 214 to 300 million. Catholic Christians believe that the pope is the vicar of Christ (that is, the viceroy of Christ, or, more literally, "vicariously Christ"), but the autocephalous churches of eastern Orthodoxy, and the congregation- or denomination-based churches of western Protestantism, do not accept this. The Orthodox rejection of the bishop of Rome as the leader of all Christians has its roots in the Middle Ages, and even earlier.

in dialogue and love. Another consequence of the geographical and theological divisions, however, was the development of distinctive doctrines that seemed, at times, foreign to western Christians. If we use Paul's metaphor for the church as the "body of Christ" (1 Corinthians 12), then it seems clear that the Orthodox Church, as it came to be known, received a somewhat different set of gifts than the Latin, or Catholic, Church.

The Theology of Deification

The theology of Orthodoxy had always slightly differed from that of western Christianity in terms of emphasis and direction. The Greek East, for example, focused on the three-ness of the Trinity and the distinction of Persons, while the Latin West stressed the one-ness of God and God's unity. The East accentuated the incarnation, that is, the Word becoming flesh in the human being Jesus of Nazareth, as we saw in the reading from Athanasius in Chapter Two. The West highlighted sin and the atonement—Christ's sacrificial death for human sin—as we saw from the reading by Augustine in that same chapter and in the discussion of Anselm in this chapter.

One major distinction lay in the theology of deification. *Deification* in Latin literally means "to be made God;" the Greek term is *theosis*. Athanasius stated in his defense of the Nicene Creed, *De Decretis*, that "God became man so that man might become God." This idea came from his belief that God sent the Son, Jesus Christ, in order to restore or repair our lost divinity. After all, we had been created in the image and likeness of God in Genesis 1; although Adam and Eve lost their divine nature, God would not leave the problem unresolved. Thus, God's Son restored the image and likeness of God to humanity. At the same time, the Son defeated death and in essence returned us to the garden of original perfection. The concluding verses of Genesis 3 state that humans were expelled from Eden, "lest they become like us," that is, lest they become like gods. With our image and likeness restored, with death defeated, and with sin abolished—since sin came into the world through death, and not vice versa—we can indeed become divine, though Athanasius used stronger language: we can become God.*

Orthodox Christians—from the humble layperson, to the married priest, to the ascetical monastic—believed that heaven existed on earth in the worship life of the church and that God entered the heart of the believer to divinize it. These beliefs originated with the hermits living in the Palestinian and Egyptian deserts in the third and fourth centuries. They existed in the liturgy of the church, which the Syrian theologian Dionysius (b. c. 500) said mirrored the heavenly liturgy performed by the angels.

---

* Those in the Orthodox Church translate the original Greek in Romans 5:12 as follows: "As sin came into the world through one man and death through sin, so death spread to all men; and because of death, all men have sinned." This seems to be the proper sense of the text, which was mistranslated into Latin to read: "As sin came into the world through one man, and through sin, death, so death spread to all men because all men have sinned." John Meyendorff, *Byzantine Theology: Historical Trends and Doctrinal Themes* (New York: Fordham, 1974), 144.

Indeed, whenever and wherever the eucharist was performed on earth, angels in heaven performed it simultaneously, according to Dionysius. Through the liturgy, Christians participated in the divine life of angels, and of God. Before one could experience the divine, however, one had to suffer compunction—a feeling of contrition, of being pierced to the heart (or punctured), after reflecting on one's sins. Individuals experiencing compunction might be unable to control their crying, so great were the grief and sorrow they experienced over their sinfulness. The way to compunction, to participating in the divine liturgy, and to becoming God was through prayer.

Desert ascetics introduced the discipline of continuous prayer, which joins head and heart in perfect communication with the divine, perhaps as early as the second or third centuries, although it is not specifically mentioned until the fourth. This practice was called "hesychasm," after *hesychia,* meaning "stillness." Although some understood hesychasm in the philosophical sense of uniting the human mind with the mind of God, it is better understood as a way of concentrating one's entire being—head and heart—on God through the repetition of a prayer focused on Jesus. The complete text of the prayer says, "Lord Jesus Christ, Son of God, have mercy on me, a sinner," but one might recite abbreviated forms, such as "Lord Jesus Christ, Son of God, have mercy on me," or even "Lord Jesus Christ." By invoking the name of Jesus, one might eventually attach the prayer to one's breath so that one literally breathed the prayer. Even the beating of one's heart would be a form of prayer.

Some considered hesychasm a heresy, especially in western Christianity, because a few hesychasts had other, more unorthodox beliefs. The basic problem, however, seemed to be the hesychasts' explanation for what they thought was happening. Were they experiencing God Almighty when they said that God's grace infused their hearts and they could actually "see" God? But how could God—invisible and eternal—be seen at all? In some respects, the argument over hesychasm continued the iconoclastic controversy of the eighth century. Could God become "incarnated" in a believer's heart? Yes, said the hesychasts, because humans exist as body and soul, not as a disembodied Platonic mind. During prayer, the entire human being was transfigured by the light of God, just as Jesus had been transfigured into a being of light on Mount Tabor in the Gospels (Mark 9:2; Matthew 17:2). This was problematic for the critics of hesychasm, for some of the same reasons as in the critique of icons: How can God be incarnate in the believer, or in a painting? How could one receive a vision of something invisible?

The ingenious answer provided by Gregory Palamas (1296–1359) was to differentiate between God's energies and God's essence. Obviously, no human could know God in God's essence: that was beyond finite possibility. But one could experience God's energies, just as one could "see" the rays of the sun and feel their warmth while being incapable of looking directly into the sun.

Gregory Palamas became a monk at age twenty, and was ordained a priest at age thirty. He persuaded his mother, sisters, and brothers to accept monastic life as well. At one point, he lived in a hermitage with a few other monks and recited the Jesus Prayer continuously five days a week, before rejoining others on the weekends. Gregory was imprisoned for a while during a civil dispute, but eventually was elected archbishop of Thessalonica, though he was incarcerated again by Turks before being ransomed by Serbs and returned to his episcopate.

The Reading

Gregory wrote the *Triads* to defend the "Holy Hesychasts," in response to criticism. One of his chief critics was a Greek Italian philosopher named Barlaam the Calabrian, whom he mentions by name in the following selection. Gregory's intention, according to John Meyendorff, "is to formulate an objective theological foundation justifying his brothers, the hesychast monks, in their understanding of prayer and in the pursuit of their avowed goal: the deification or *theosis* of man in Christ."* One was not deified independently or apart from Christ; rather, Christ became incarnate in the heart of the hesychast.

This is an apologetic work, a defense, and so falls within the genre of *apologia*. These are explanations given to outsiders to help them understand Christian beliefs. Gregory relies on key authorities in the eastern church in support of his argument. He turns to Saint Basil the Great (c. 329–379) and Basil's brother Gregory of Nyssa (d. after 385/86), two of the three Cappadocian fathers who helped to foster general acceptance of the Nicene Creed. He also uses scripture to support his argument. Gregory sees himself working and writing within a long tradition of hesychasm that is fully orthodox.

This selection includes several unusual words that require definition. Gregory uses the word *thearchy* to indicate the "government" of God within the human soul, since *thearchy* means "rule by God." *Theurgic* means "magical," but when Gregory says that the "light which shone forth on Thabor [Mount Tabor] is called 'theurgic' light by the Fathers," he means that it is a supernatural light, one that comes from God. Mount Tabor is the place where Jesus appeared, bathed in dazzling white radiance, to his disciples (Mark 9:2–8). Christians call this the "Transfiguration" because Jesus is transfigured by light. The "Fathers" Gregory alludes to are his predecessors in the eastern tradition: Basil, Gregory of Nyssa, John Chrysostom, Macarius, Dionysius, Maximus the Confessor, and others. A final term he uses is *beatitude,* which simply means "blessedness"; this is the state of being completely "in Christ."

Gregory's treatise may be the most difficult text to read in this entire book. What makes it so hard? First, a number of new vocabulary words are introduced that describe complicated theological concepts. Also, Gregory's sentences are long, and because he is arguing against someone he quotes the opposition extensively: When is Gregory speaking, and when is he citing his opponent? Moreover, familiar words have multiple meanings and pronunciations—for example, read (reed) and read (red), and perfect (PER-fect) and perfect (per-FECT). A dictionary will help with

* John Meyendorff, "Introduction," in Gregory Palamas, *The Triads,* trans. Nicholas Gendle (New York: Paulist Press, 1983), 8.

some words (hypostatic, deify, and so on). Finally, some sentences have to be read twice. All of these factors make the text slow going. By "slow going," I mean that we must read more carefully in order to grasp the meaning. Reading out loud reduces our speed and frequently helps with comprehension. If you can rephrase Gregory's words in your own, then you have gotten his point.

Questions to Consider

1. Why do humans need deification? What is the basic problem for humanity?

2. How does Gregory of Palamas explain deification? What does he say happens?

3. What makes deification a distinctly Christian phenomenon, as opposed to some sort of generalized mystical experience?

4. Can you deduce the arguments of the opposition? What are they saying (based on Gregory's arguments against them)?

5. Does Gregory think it is possible to explain the state of deification to others who have not experienced it? Why or why not?

6. What does Gregory say we see when the hesychast sees God?

7. How does hesychasm compare with the other types of theology discussed in this chapter? What seems to be its closest sibling? Its most distant cousin?

The Triads: Excerpts from Book Three*

GREGORY PALAMAS

Chapter 31. . . . According to the Fathers, deification is an essential energy of God; but any essence of which the essential energies are created must itself necessarily be created! . . . Barlaam indeed does not blush to claim that all the powers and natural energies of God are created, even though our faith teaches us that every saint is a temple of God by reason of the grace that indwells him. How could the dwelling place of a creature be a temple of God? How could every saint become uncreated by grace, if this grace is created?

What is most astonishing to me is that he admits that the light which shone forth on Thabor is called "theurgic" light by the Fathers, but refuses to call it a deifying gift. Since the deifying gift of the Spirit is an energy of God, and since the divine names derive from the energies (for the Superessential is nameless), God could not be called "God," if deification consists only in virtue and wisdom! But He is called "God" on the basis of His deifying energy, while wisdom and virtue only manifest this energy. He could no longer be called "More-than-God" by reason of His transcendence in respect of this divinity; it would have to suffice to call Him "more-than-wise," "more-than-good," and so forth. So the grace and energy of deification are different from virtue and wisdom.

Chapter 32. . . . When you hear speak of the deifying energy of God and the theurgic grace of the

---

* With the exception of the beginning, all of the ellipses that appear in this selection occur in the original translation.

Spirit, do not busy yourself or seek to know why it is this or that and not something else; for without it you cannot be united to God, according to those Fathers who have spoken about it. Attend rather to those works which will allow you to attain to it, for thus you will know it according to your capacities; for, as Saint Basil tells us, he alone knows the energies of the Spirit who has learnt of them through experience. As for the man who seeks knowledge before works, if he trusts in those who have had the experience, he obtains a certain image of the truth. But if he tries to conceive of it by himself, he finds himself deprived even of the image of truth. He then puffs himself up with pride as if he had discovered it, and breathes forth his anger against the men of experience as if they were in error. Do not be overcurious, therefore, but follow the men of experience in your works, or at least in your words, remaining content with the exterior manifestations of grace.

Deification is in fact beyond every name. This is why we, who have written much about *hesychia* (sometimes at the urging of the fathers, sometimes in response to the questions of the brothers) have never dared hitherto to write about deification. But now, since there is a necessity to speak, we will speak words of piety (by the grace of the Lord), but words inadequate to describe it. For even when spoken about, deification remains ineffable, and (as the Fathers teach us) can be given a name only by those who have received it.

Chapter 33. The Principle of deification, divinity by nature, the imparticipable Origin whence the deified derive their deification, Beatitude itself, transcendent over all things and supremely thearchic, is itself inaccessible to all sense perception and to every mind, to every incorporeal or corporeal being. It is only when one or another of these beings goes out from itself and acquires a superior state that it is deified. For it is only when hypostatically united to a mind or body that we believe the divinity to have become visible, even though such union transcends the proper nature of mind and body. Only those beings united to It are deified "by the total presence of the Anointer"; they have received an energy identical to that of the deifying essence, and possessing it in absolute entirety, reveal it through themselves. For, as the Apostle says, "In Christ the fullness of the divinity dwells bodily" [Colossians 1:19].

This is why certain saints after the Incarnation have seen this light as a limitless sea, flowing forth in a paradoxical manner from the unique Sun, that is,

from the adorable Body of Christ, as in the case of the apostles on the Mountain. It is thus that the firstfruits of our human constitution are deified. But the deification of divinized angels and men is not the superessential essence of God, but the energy of this essence. This energy does not manifest itself in deified creatures, as art does in the work of art; for it is thus that the creative power manifests itself in the things created by it, becoming thereby universally visible and at the same time reflected in them. On the contrary, deification manifests itself in these creatures "as art in the man who has acquired it," according to Basil the Great.

This is why the saints are the instruments of the Holy Spirit, having received the same energy as He has. As certain proof of what I say, one might cite the charisms of healing, the working of miracles, foreknowledge, the irrefutable wisdom which the Lord called "the spirit of your Father," and also the sanctifying bestowal of the Spirit which those sanctified with these gifts receive from and through them. Thus God said to Moses, "I shall take the spirit which is on you and put it on them;" similarly, "when Paul laid his hands" on the twelve Ephesians, "the Holy Spirit came upon them" and at once "they spoke in tongues and prophesied."

Thus when we consider the proper dignity of the Spirit, we see it to be equal to that of the Father and the Son, but when we think of the grace that works in those who partake of the Spirit, we say that the Spirit is in us, "that it is poured out on us, but is not created, that it is given to us but is not made, it is granted but not produced." In the words of the great Basil, it is present in those still imperfect as a certain disposition, "because of the instability of their moral choice," but in those more perfect, as an acquired state, or in some of them, as a fixed state—indeed more than this, "the energy of the Spirit is present in the purified soul as the visual faculty in the healthy eye," as he puts it.

Chapter 34. The deifying gift of the Spirit thus cannot be equated with the superessential essence of God. It is the deifying energy of this divine essence, yet not the totality of this energy, even though it is indivisible in itself. Indeed, what created thing could receive the entire, infinitely potent power of the Spirit, except He who was carried in the womb of a Virgin, by the presence of the Holy Spirit and the overshadowing of the power of the Most High? He received "all the fullness of the Divinity."

As for us, "it is of *His* fullness that we have all received." The essence of God is everywhere, for, as it is said, "the Spirit fills all things," according to essence. Deification is likewise everywhere, ineffably present in the essence and inseparable from it, as its natural power. But just as one cannot see fire, if there is no matter to receive it, nor any sense organ capable of perceiving its luminous energy, in the same way one cannot contemplate deification if there is no matter to receive the divine manifestation. But if with every veil removed it lays hold of appropriate matter, that is of any purified rational nature, freed from the veil of manifold evil, then it becomes itself visible as a spiritual light, or rather it transforms these creatures into spiritual light. "The prize of virtue," it is said, "is to become God, to be illumined by the purest of lights, by becoming a son of that day which no darkness can dim. For it is another Sun which produces this day, a Sun which shines forth the true light. And once it has illumined us, it no longer hides itself in the West, but envelops all things with its powerful light. It grants an eternal and endless light to those worthy, and transforms those who participate in this light into other suns" [Basil the Great]. Then, indeed, "the just will shine like the sun." What sun? Surely that same one which appears even now to those worthy as it did then.

Chapter 35. Do you not see that they will acquire the same energy as the Sun of Righteousness? This is why various divine signs and the communication of the Holy Spirit are effected through them. Indeed, it is written: "Just as the air around the earth, driven upwards by the wind, becomes luminous because it is transformed by the purity of the ether, so it is with the human mind which quits this impure and grimy world: it becomes luminous by the power of the Spirit, and mingles with the true and sublime purity; it shines itself in this purity, becoming entirely radiant, transformed into light according to the promise of the Lord, who foretold that the just would shine like the sun" [Gregory of Nyssa].

We can observe the same phenomenon here below with a mirror or a sheet of water: Receiving the sun's ray, they produce another ray from themselves. And we too will become luminous if we lift ourselves up, abandoning earthly shadows, by drawing near to the true light of Christ. And if the true light which "shines in darkness" comes down to us, we will also be light, as the Lord told His disciples.

Thus the deifying gift of the Spirit is a mysterious light, and transforms into light those who receive its richness; He does not only fill them with eternal light, but grants them a knowledge and a life appro-

priate to God. Thus, as Maximus teaches, Paul lived no longer a created life, but "the eternal life of Him Who indwelt him." Similarly, the prophets contemplated the future as if it were the present.

So the man who has seen God by means not of an alien symbol but by a natural symbol, has truly seen Him in a spiritual way. I do not consider as a natural symbol of God what is only an ordinary symbol, visible or audible by the senses as such, and activated through the medium of the air. When, however, the seeing eye does not see as an ordinary eye, but as an eye opened by the power of the Spirit, it does not see God by the means of an alien symbol; and it is then we can speak of sense–perception transcending the senses.

Chapter 36. One recognizes this light when the soul ceases to give way to the evil pleasures and passions, when it acquires inner peace and the stilling of thoughts, spiritual repose and joy, contempt of human glory, humility allied with a hidden rejoicing, hatred of the world, love of heavenly things, or rather the love of the sole God of Heaven. Moreover, if one covers the eyes of him who sees, even if one gouges them out, he will still see the light no less clearly than before. How then could he be persuaded by someone who claims that this light is visible through the medium of air, and that it is in no way useful to the rational soul, as something belonging to the bodily senses?

But that contemplative, realizing full well that he does not see by the senses [as] senses, may think he sees by the mind. However, a careful examination will cause him to discover that the mind does not apprehend this light by virtue of its own power. Hence our expression, "mind surpassing mind," meaning thereby that a man possessing mind and sense perception sees in a way transcending both of these faculties.

And when you hear the great Denys [Dionysius] advising Timothy to "abandon the senses and intellectual activities" do not conclude from this that a man is neither to reason nor see. For he does not lose these faculties, except by amazement. But you should hold that intellectual activities are entirely bypassed by the light of union and by the action of this light. This is clearly shown by Peter, the leader of the apostles and foundation-stone of the Church: At the time of the holy Pentecost, when he was deemed worthy of the mysterious and divine union, he was nonetheless still able to see those who were being illumined and filled with light together with himself, and to hear what they were saying, and was aware what time of day it was ("It is the third hour," he said). For when energy of the Holy Spirit overshadows the human mind, those in whom He is working do not become disturbed in mind, for this would be contrary to the promise of the divine presence. He who receives God does not lose his senses. On the contrary, he becomes like one driven mad, so to speak, by the Spirit of wisdom; for this light is also the wisdom of God, present in the deified man, yet not separate from God. "Through it," we read, "all knowledge is revealed, and God truly makes Himself known to the soul He loves" [Macarius], as He makes known at the same time all justice, holiness and liberty.

As Saint Paul says, "Where there is the Spirit of God, there is liberty" [2 Corinthians 3:17]. And again, "He whom God has made wisdom, justice, sanctification and redemption for us" [1 Corinthians 1:30]. Hear what Saint Basil the Great teaches: "He who has been set in motion by the Spirit has become an eternal movement, a holy creature. For when the Spirit has come to dwell in him, a man receives the dignity of a prophet, of an apostle, of an angel of God, whereas hitherto he was only earth and dust." Hear also John Chrysostom: "The mouth by which God speaks is the mouth of God—for just as our mouth is the mouth of our soul, and the soul does not literally possess a mouth; so likewise the mouth of the prophets is the mouth of God." The Lord too set His seal on this truth, for after saying, "I will give you a mouth, and a wisdom which none of your enemies will be able to gainsay" [Luke 21:15]. He added "For it is not you who will speak, but the Spirit of your Father who speaks in you" [Matthew 10:20].

Political Theology

The attempt to live according to God's will and to order all life toward the divine had political as well as religious implications. Indeed, all theology has a political component, since beliefs affect peoples' behavior. Thus, the reforms that spread outward from medieval monasteries affected church and state alike. Political problems were bound to occur in the administration of a huge ecclesiastical apparatus that, though centered in Rome, extended from North Africa to Sweden. Conflicts had already arisen between secular authorities and church officials on a number of occasions, but the appointment of local bishops by the pope in Rome—a practice that arose in the Middle Ages—was particularly irksome. These appointments were important because they bequeathed large tracts of land, great wealth, and political power to the holder. Since the pope—the bishop of Rome and the western church's spiritual leader—appointed bishops, these positions fell to people whom the pope knew or who provided patronage to the pope and his family in Italy. Some Italian bishops, appointed by the pope, never once visited their bishoprics in Germany or France. Some were appointed bishop at age twelve, so that their families could manage the wealth that accompanied the appointment. When bishops did not live in the jurisdiction under their control, secular leaders would attempt to appoint local church leaders who were more pliable and willing to compromise on church policy.

Though it is a bit anachronistic to call it a church-state conflict—because the state as we know it today did not exist back them—disputes nevertheless arose between church leaders and secular authorities. Even the word *secular* is problematic, and it may be best to use the medieval terms *temporal* and *spiritual* to indicate these two powers. Pope Gregory VII (p. 1073–1085) wanted to free the papacy and the church from lay control. The chief bone of contention was lay investiture—who could "invest," or officially endorse, local religious authorities. The pope appointed

▦ The Medieval Papacy

With the fall of Rome and the dissolution of the western Roman Empire, centralized government collapsed. The church—an international body with bishops and priests throughout the former empire, and with its head remaining in Rome directing a well-organized institution with a clearly defined mission—filled the vacuum. The bishop of Rome (that is, the pope) assumed vast responsibilities and powers as a result. For ten centuries, the papacy—the office and authority of the pope—dominated the political landscape, in addition to supervising ecclesiastical affairs. Indeed, political and ecclesial (churchly) matters were intimately intertwined throughout this time.

Full independence from imperial control did not occur until Frankish (French) kings helped the papacy acquire territory in Italy in the eighth century, with the help of a forged document, the Donation of Constantine. (Purportedly, Emperor Constantine had actually given the papacy these lands much earlier; it wasn't until 1431 that the document was shown to be a forgery.) With Leo III's crowning of Charlemagne as emperor of Rome, the supremacy of church over state seemed assured, although stresses and strains emerged over the centuries.

The medieval popes had numerous other interests in addition to international politics. The earliest popes, beginning with Gregory I (p. 590–604), sent missionaries to the British Isles and continental Europe to spread the gospel to pagan tribes and villagers. As the importance of the papacy grew, the pope developed official advisory bodies, such as the college of cardinals. Papal legates, or representatives, were sent throughout Europe to ensure that the pope's instructions were carried out on the local level. Subsequent popes attempted to reform problems that existed within the church. In the eleventh century, for example, Gregory VII (p. 1073–1085) instituted what are now called the "Gregorian reforms." The pope tried to uproot the problem of simony (buying and selling church offices) and to enforce clerical celibacy through elimination of clerical marriage (married priests) and concubinage (semi-married priests). In 1095, Pope Urban II (p. 1088–1099) called for the first crusade to oust Muslims from the Holy Land. Such a move would protect pilgrims traveling to Jerusalem, as well as return control of Mediterranean and eastern trade routes to Christians.

The height of papal power came in the thirteenth century, with the accession of Innocent III (p. 1198–1216) to the papacy. Innocent III made kingdoms such as England and Portugal fiefs of the papacy (that is, the pope controlled them); he quashed heretical sects; he convened the Fourth Lateran Council (1215), which officially affirmed the doctrine of transubstantiation (see Chapter Four); he published the first official collection of canon (church) law. Later thirteenth-century popes oversaw the rise of the mendicant orders and the establishment of universities, but also the introduction of the inquisition as the means by which to eradicate heresy.

(continued)

Papal power declined as secular nobles flexed their muscles to challenge church claims to land, authority, and privilege. The height of this contest was the Avignon papacy: for seventy years, the popes resided in Avignon, France rather than in Rome due to the will and strength of French monarchs. The papacy had held the multifarious pieces of Europe together; eventually, however, these pieces sought—and found—the justification for challenging the popes in the rediscovery of political thought in the works of Aristotle and the rediscovery of Roman law. Various theologians, such as Marsilius of Padua (1280–c. 1343) and William of Ockham (see below), provided philosophical and even theological reasons for separating the realms of church and state—or, as they would have called it, the spiritual and the temporal realms. The Reformation of the 1500s would finalize the separation of powers, and Christendom as a political, rather than spiritual or cultural, entity would end.

bishops and clerics, but also wanted to "anoint" them officially, so to speak; but lay nobles wanted that power for themselves, given the fact that bishops would be operating within their jurisdictions. The problem came to a head in 1075, when Gregory issued the *Dictatus papae (Dictates of the Pope),* in which he claimed broad powers for the papacy, including the right to invest all ecclesiastical officers, the right to depose emperors, and the right (of the pope) to be judged by no one. When Henry IV, the Holy Roman Emperor, invested an archbishop on his own, Gregory threatened to unseat Henry. In retaliation, a German Diet (legislative body) declared Gregory no longer pope; in turn, Gregory excommunicated Henry and ousted him as emperor. The problem was temporarily resolved when Henry received absolution from the pope after waiting three days in the snow to see him, allegedly barefoot!

Time and again, the papacy made claims to worldly power while "temporal" leaders attempted to limit its role to spiritual affairs only. Pope Boniface VIII (p. 1295–1303) also asserted broad papal powers in the bull *Unam Sanctam,* in which he claimed that subjection to the Roman pontiff (the pope) was necessary for salvation. He also contended that there were "two swords" on earth, the temporal and the spiritual; while kings might wield the temporal sword, it was always subject to the spiritual sword, namely, the church. Finally, Boniface said that earthly power would be judged by the church (spiritual power), but if spiritual power erred, only God could be the judge.

France's King Philip IV, called Philip the Fair (r. 1285–1314), did not agree at all. In a tug of war between pope and king, neither side was willing to compromise. Philip launched a personal attack on the pope, charging that he was illegitimate and that he had engaged in sexual misconduct, blasphemy, simony, and heresy. Forces sympathetic to Philip kidnapped Boniface and planned to take him to France, but he was rescued by citizens of his hometown, though he died a few weeks after his rescue.

The solution for Philip was to arrange for the election of a French pope, Clement V (p. 1305–1314), who packed the Roman curia with French cardinals and then moved the papacy to Avignon, France, where it remained for seventy years.

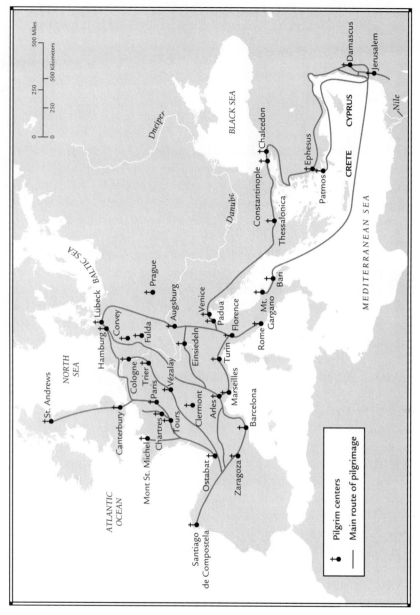

Medieval pilgrim routes. *Pilgrimage was one of the most visible features of popular piety in the Middle Ages. Some pilgrims undertook their journeys as acts of penance, others simply to express their devotion to God.*

Map labels:

500 Miles
500 Kilometers
250
250
250
250
0
0

Dnieper
BLACK SEA
Danube
BALTIC SEA
NORTH SEA
ATLANTIC OCEAN
MEDITERRANEAN SEA
Nile

Damascus
Jerusalem
Chalcedon
Constantinople
Ephesus
Patmos
CRETE
CYPRUS
Thessalonica
Prague
Augsburg
Venice
Padua
Bari
Lübeck
Hamburg
Corvey
Fulda
Einsiedeln
Florence
Rome
Mt. Gargano
Turin
Cologne
Trier
Vézalay
Paris
Marseilles
St. Andrews
Canterbury
Mont St. Michel
Chartres
Tours
Clermont
Arles
Barcelona
Ostabat
Zaragoza
Santiago de Compostela

Legend:
† ● Pilgrim centers
— Main route of pilgrimage

Even after the papacy returned to Rome (when an angry mob forced the election of an Italian pope who decided to remain in Rome), a second pope was elected in Avignon, and so two popes attempted to control ecclesiastical business at the same time. The Great Western Schism, which ran from 1378 to 1417, led to the election of a third pope in 1409 in Pisa, Italy. It was clear to everyone in church leadership that this deplorable situation needed amelioration.

Several attempts to restructure the church were made in the fifteenth century, well before *the* Reformation of the sixteenth century. A number of church councils were convened, comprising theologians, bishops, cardinals, and the pope from Pisa. The councils attempted to address the problems of heresy and schism, and the need for church reform in the area of clerical appointments. Nepotism, for example—selecting relatives for church offices—was an ongoing problem. A movement to restrict papal power, called "conciliarism" because it emphasized the authority of church councils over the papacy, arose, and served as the impetus to end the schism. The first item of business for the Council of Constance (1414–1417) was to return the papacy to Rome with the election of a new pope, and to remove the antipopes (unauthorized popes). Pope John XXIII, the second pope of Pisa, who convened the council, was promptly deposed by the bishops present.* Thus, the Council of Constance restored integrity, and power, to the papacy.

At the same time, however, the council dealt with the problem of heresy in a brutal way, as manifested in the treatment of a priest from Bohemia named Jan Hus (c. 1373–1415). Hus had adopted the views of John Wyclif (c. 1330–1384), a professor at Oxford University, who argued that the Bible should be translated into the vernacular, or common language, of the people so that they could understand the scripture that was read from the pulpit. Indeed, the Bible was more authoritative than papal pronouncements or church councils, said Wyclif. He also felt that clergy who were "unworthy," that is, corrupt, should be punished and removed, and that reprobate men could hold no authority over others. These were common complaints that popes and bishops alike had attempted to address over the centuries. Hus received a safe-conduct pass to attend the Council of Constance to present Wyclif's views, which the bishops quickly condemned as heretical. The council tried and sentenced Hus as a heretic, and he was burned at the stake on 6 July 1415.

Subsequent councils reflected a power struggle between the pope and his bishops over the issue of conciliarism. This came to a head at the Council of Basel (1431–1449), which ultimately elected its own pope and was discredited in the eyes of the rest of the church. Some of those participating in the Council of Basel left in

---

* Because Pope John XXIII was one of the antipopes, his name and number could be used again, since he was never officially a pope. It was not until the twentieth century, however, that Cardinal Angelo Roncalli adopted the name John XXIII and served in the papacy long enough (1958–1963) to convene a transformative church council, Vatican II. A sense of history as well as a sense of humor clearly marked Roncalli's adoption of this name.

the middle to attend the Council of Ferrara/Florence (1438–1439), convened by Pope Eugenius IV to effect a reconciliation with the eastern church. Although eastern and western Christians came to some agreements at this council, the fall of Constantinople to the Ottoman Turks in 1453 quickly halted the process. Conciliarism was formally rejected in 1460 by Pope Pius II (p. 1458–1464), who forbade appealing any papal decisions to future councils.

Throughout these centuries of conflict between church and state, and within Christianity itself, Christians had applied themselves to the issue of the proper balance of power and authority. Their analysis had its roots in the New Testament question put to Jesus: Should we pay taxes to Rome? Jesus answered by asking for a coin and inquiring whose image was on the coin. He then advised that we "render unto Caesar what is Caesar's, and unto God what is God's" (Mark 12:14–17). Eusebius of Caesarea envisioned a divine unity of church and state under the emperor Constantine, but Augustine of Hippo conceived of a radical break between the earthly city and the city of God. The rise of "Christendom" in the Middle Ages—that is, a *holy* Roman Empire that joined religion to political rule—created tensions between secular nobility and religious elites. Political philosophers argued that the political community had authority over the religious community and that the church must abide by temporal rules.

A number of scholastics wrote treatises on the subject of the proper relationship between temporal and spiritual power, and one in particular helped set the stage for the modern understanding of secular government. William of Ockham (c. 1285–1349), who died of the Black Death (a combination of three deadly plagues), was a Franciscan scholar who probably taught for a time at Oxford. He was part of a movement within scholasticism called "Nominalism," led by a group of radical Christian skeptics writing during the fourteenth century. The scholastics in the thirteenth century had great optimism about the ability of human reason to understand the divine mystery. After all, if God had created the world by the Word—that is, by rationality—then it was only logical—logos-like or god-like—to use reason to apprehend God. But the Nominalists were more pessimistic. They believed that humans could not ultimately understand the nature of God, and thus had no access to the divine essence and certainly could not prove anything about God. God could have created any number of worlds. William of Ockham argued that God simply, and rather arbitrarily, created this one.

Ockham also critiqued the medieval notion that universals existed—that is, that ideas about cats, or cat-ness, or about humans, or humanity, had a real existence, which the scholastics called "universals." Ockham and the Nominalists believed that general concepts such as love, humanity, and horse-ness were simply names or words for categories of things, hence the term *Nominalist*. Ockham may be best known for developing a test for evaluating the merit of an argument. Called "Ockham's Razor," it states that entities are not to be multiplied without necessity. Today, scientists and theoreticians who believe that the simplest explanation is usually the best one, to paraphrase, use Ockham's Razor to assess hypotheses and explanations.

It was his political writings, however, that had the most impact on subsequent Christian history, and particularly on the issue of the relationship between temporal or worldly power and spiritual or religious power. Ockham challenged the attempts of Pope John XXII to rewrite the rules of the Franciscan order. He supported the order's commitment to absolute poverty and the strict views of the Franciscan general (or head) Michael Cesena. Both were called to the papacy in Avignon for an investigation; and both fled before they could be arrested or condemned as heretics. They sought refuge with the Holy Roman Emperor, Ludwig of Bavaria, whose leadership of the empire was in dispute. The pope excommunicated Ludwig and, eventually, Ockham as well. It is understandable how William of Ockham might be somewhat critical of papal power as a result of these experiences.

The Reading

The following selection is taken from Ockham's attack on the power of the papacy. In it, he enumerates eight points that endeavor to show why the pope is subject to temporal authority, and not vice versa. The Nominalist uses a dialogue format in some of his treatises, in which a student questions the master, and they come up with the logical answers Ockham wants to present. This was a common form of logical argumentation in the Middle Ages, modeled on the philosophical dialogues of Plato. In this treatise, however, Ockham abandons the dialogue format, although he still retains a step-by-step approach to making his case, much as Thomas Aquinas did.

We are stepping into the middle of Ockham's argument in this selection from *Eight Questions on the Power of the Pope*. Question III asks "whether by Christ's institution it pertains to the pope and the Roman Church to entrust to the emperor and other secular rulers temporal jurisdictions, which otherwise they may not exercise." In Chapter 1, Ockham provides the arguments that support that view. In Chapter 2, where we begin, he presents opposing arguments and in Chapter 3, he responds to the arguments made in Chapter 1. In other words, he is attacking arguments that support the idea that Christ gave authority over secular powers to the pope.

William of Ockham uses the expression "by Christ's institution" to indicate an argument that has already been made, namely, that when Christ gave his disciple Peter "the keys of the kingdom of heaven," which will bind things on earth as well as in heaven (Matthew 16:18–19), he gave all subsequent bishops of Rome (that is, popes) the same power. In other words, papal authority over temporal government was instituted by Christ.

Questions to Consider

1. How does Ockham's method of argumentation compare with that of Aquinas?

2. What *is* his argument exactly? Who should have ultimate power? Why?

3. What kind of power is Ockham willing to grant to the pope? What kind of power does he allow to the secular rulers?

4. What does Ockham say that might be applied to contemporary politics? Where would he stand on the issue of separation of church and state? What about the question of separation of powers (e.g., legislative, executive, and judicial branches of government)?

Eight Questions on the Power of the Pope: Question III

WILLIAM OF OCKHAM

CHAPTER 2

Another opinion is that neither the pope nor the Roman Church has power by Christ's institution regularly to entrust temporal jurisdictions to the emperor and other secular rulers, and that they can exercise them without him. But there are various modes of asserting this.

One is that neither the pope nor the Roman Church has this from Christ, but it is by Christ's institution that the pope (as also the Roman Church) has absolutely no coercive power unless it is entrusted to him by the people or by the emperor or by someone else inferior to the emperor, and that in temporal matters the pope, if he commits any crime, secular or spiritual, is subject to the emperor or the people, to be regularly restrained by due penalty; and that the emperor and other secular rulers have power to exercise temporal jurisdictions without their being entrusted to them by the pope.

Another mode of assertion is that by Christ's institution the pope has power so that spiritual causes, both criminal and other, belong to him, and in them he has coercive power; but he does not have power to intervene either regularly or occasionally in temporal matters, unless it is entrusted to him by the people or the emperor or by some other secular.

A third mode of assertion is that the pope does not by Christ's institution have power regularly, but only occasionally, to entrust temporal jurisdictions to the emperor and other rulers, and that on occasion they should not otherwise exercise them.

These modes of assertion therefore agree in this, that neither the pope nor the Roman Church has by

Christ's institution power regularly to entrust temporal jurisdictions to the emperor and other secular rulers, and they can exercise them without his commission. For this it is possible to argue as follows. No one has power to entrust temporal jurisdiction to his lord. But the emperor is the lord of the highest pontiff, since the pope is the vassal of him—i.e. the emperor—to whom he owes tribute, "unless by the imperial kindness he has immunity." Pope Urban also seems to have confessed this, as we read. Speaking of giving tribute to Caesar for himself and the other clergy, he says, "What was appointed of old is to be paid from the external goods of the Church to the emperors, for the peace and quiet by which they should protect and defend us." From these words we gather that the pope should give the emperor tribute, which is "proof of subjection." Therefore the emperor is the lord of the highest pontiff; and thus the highest pontiffs have sometimes called the emperor their lord.

Further, property passes "with its burden"; therefore the pope, receiving cities and estates that owe tribute and service to the emperor, is by reason of such things subject to the emperor.

Again, the Christian religion frees no one from slavery, as was argued above. Therefore if the pope was subject to the emperor before he was made pope, he remains subject to the emperor and a slave, unless the emperor voluntarily grants him freedom and immunity.

But someone will say that a slave appointed to the papacy is set free from slavery, and also from all subjection, in favor of the Christian religion, just as a slave made priest is set free from slavery in favor of the

Church. To this it is said that nothing unjust should be enacted in favor of religion or of the Church, because impiety must not be done on the pretext of piety. Since, therefore, it is unjust and wicked that anyone should, without fault, be deprived of his right, the Church cannot enact that the emperor or another should be deprived of the right that he had in the person of the pope before he was appointed to the papal office, "lest," as the Apostle says, in 1 Timothy 6:1, "the Lord's name and teaching be blasphemed." Pope Gelasius seems to follow this teaching, as we read; he affirms that slaves should never evade their lords' rights on a pretext of religion, "lest it seem that by something established in the name of Christianity either the rights of others are invaded or public discipline is subverted." It seems, therefore, that if a slave becomes priest or highest pontiff, he is not delivered from slavery by either divine or natural law. Neither can he be delivered from slavery by canon law, because the canon laws can by no means abolish secular laws and rights of seculars that are not at all opposed to divine and natural law. Therefore, if a slave made pope or priest is delivered to freedom, it must be that his freedom is gained by the human law of the emperors.

CHAPTER 3

Having briefly reported these opinions, we must see how answer is made in accordance with them to the arguments brought against them. According to the opinion reported last, there are various ways of answering the argument brought forward above in Chapter 1 in favor of the first opinion.

In one way it is conceded that no community is best ordered unless it is subject to one supreme judge, and therefore it is conceded that, if all mortals should be governed by the best form of government, they should have one supreme judge, appointed by the choice of the totality of mortals or by the greater or sounder part. And this judge should not be the pope, but another who does not exercise the highest priesthood; and the pope and everyone else would be subject to him in all matters that belong to the office of supreme judge. So the pope, by Christ's institution, has no coercive jurisdiction or power, either regularly or occasionally, either in temporal or in spiritual matters—although he has from Christ the power to absolve from sin in the penitential forum, to administer the other Church sacraments, and to teach how we should live so as to acquire everlasting life.

This answer seems to be based on the divine Scriptures, for we read in them, it seems, that Christ pro-

hibited all coercive power to his apostles when he said, (Matthew 20:25–26), "You know that the rulers of the peoples lord it over them, and the great men exercise power over them; it will not be so among you." From these words we gather that the apostles should have exercised no power over others; this should be understood especially of coercive power; therefore neither does the pope, Peter's successor, have by Christ's institution any coercive power. This also seems provable from the fact that Christ, of whom the pope is only the vicar, never exercised any coercive power but wished to be judged by a secular judge; therefore neither does his vicar have any coercive power, but he is subject in all things to a secular judge.

In another way it is answered that in spiritual matters the pope has full and even coercive power, and another judge has power only in temporal matters; and yet the community of mortals, despite this, can be best ordered; and therefore the statement "A community is not best ordered unless it is subject to one supreme judge" is denied.

And in another way, according to the second opinion reported above, it is said that no community of persons able to have discords among themselves would be best ordered if it *were* subject regularly and in *every* case to one supreme judge: for in such a community the supreme judge could do wrong with impunity, to the destruction of the whole community, and this conflicts with the best ordering of any community. Again, it does not conflict with the best ordering of a community if other persons besides the supreme judge have, even regularly, a coercive power not prejudicial to the power of the supreme judge. Further, it does not conflict with the best ordering of a community if someone is regularly exempt from the coercive jurisdiction of the supreme judge, provided he is subject occasionally—namely, when the common good would otherwise be endangered. From these [propositions] it is inferred that it does not conflict with the best ordering of a community for the supreme judge, and others inferior to him, to be subject occasionally to someone other than the supreme judge, who would have coercive power over them.

Through this the above argument is answered as follows. No community of persons able to dissent is best ordered unless the whole of it is subject to one supreme judge *regularly or occasionally,* so that no one except the supreme judge is exempt from his power in such a way that in *no* case would it be permissible for the supreme judge to coerce him; but for someone to be exempt regularly from the power of the supreme judge but subject to him in case of necessity does not detract from the best ordering of any community, just as it does not detract from the best ordering of a community (general or particular) if the supreme member of that community is regularly exempt from the power of the whole community and is yet in case of necessity subject to that same community. And therefore the totality of mortals is not best ordered unless it is subject to one supreme judge in that way, although on occasion it may be beneficial to recede from that best arrangement at least for a time.

CHAPTER 4

However, because those statements do not seem clear at every point, but obscure, so that someone could doubt how they should be understood, to elucidate their meaning and thereby make it clearer whether they are true or false, we must say briefly, in accordance with that [second] opinion, which things are requisite to the best regime, prelacy, rectorship, or form of government, thus the pope and other clergy might have some coercive jurisdiction, they might regularly be exempt from the secular ruler's jurisdiction, and on occasion the secular ruler might be subject to their jurisdiction which things conflict with it, and which should be regarded as compatible with it.

It is said, therefore, that it is required for the best regime, first, that it should exist for the sake of the common good of the subjects, not for the ruler's own good. For by this the best regime—both general, in respect of all mortals, and particular, in respect of certain persons—differs, not only from a regime that is illicit, vitiated, and unjust, but also from a despotic regime, i.e., lordly rule for the ruler's own good, and from all other regimes, even licit ones, not directed to the common good.

But the papal and episcopal regime, insofar as it exists by Christ's ordinance, is of this kind. Christ seems to have suggested this when he appointed blessed Peter as pope, saying to him, "Feed my sheep," as if to say, "I appoint you ruler over my sheep, not to take from them wool and milk, except for your necessities" (in accordance with the text of the Apostle, 1 Corinthians 9:7, "Who feeds the flock, and does not eat of the milk of the flock?") "but to feed them." Christ also seems to have promised blessed Peter rulership of this kind when he said to him, as we read in Matthew 16:18–19, "You are Peter, and upon this rock I will build my Church, and the gates of hell will not prevail against it. And I will give you the keys of the kingdom of heaven": as if to say, "I

will promote you and put you over the rest only for the building up of my Church, not for dominating it" (as Peter himself suggests in his canonical epistle, 1 Peter 5:3, when he says, "Not as dominating your charge") "so that you may lead it into the kingdom of heaven." And therefore by the words of Christ that follow, "Whatever you bind upon earth will be bound also in the heavens, and whatever you loose upon earth will be loosed also in the heavens," it is meant that power was promised to Peter over his subjects, not over others, for their building up, not for their destruction. And the Apostle says, in 2 Corinthians, last chapter (13:10), that such a power over his subjects was given to him by the Lord.

Accordingly blessed Peter received no power from Christ except for the sake of his subjects' good in attaining the kingdom of heaven, so that he would not have been able to impose anything on them by commandment except what was necessary to them for reaching the kingdom of heaven. And therefore Christ's authority was of no avail to him against the rights and freedoms of the faithful granted to them by God and nature, because he received power from Christ for building up, not for destroying the rights and freedoms granted to the faithful by God and nature: lest he should have seemed to be not merely their shepherd and slave but their lord, contrary to his own teaching by which he guided other bishops when he said, "Feed God's flock which is in your charge, caring for them not by constraint but willingly according to God, not for the sake of shameful gain but voluntarily, not as dominating your charge, but being a wholehearted example to the flock" (1 Peter 5:2–3). Accordingly, if blessed Peter had ordered anything, either generally or in particular, contrary to the rights and freedoms of the faithful, outside of a situation of necessity and of a usefulness that could be equated with necessity, such an order would have obliged no one; and if he had pronounced any sentence against those not acquiescing, it would have been null by the law itself, as having been passed "by someone not his judge," according to the rule in [canon law]: "Things done by a judge which do not belong to his office have no force." For if what a prelate demands of his subject is contrary to a freedom granted to him by the pope, that subject is free to refuse [according to canon law]; and "a sentence contrary to a privilege of the pope is null, as being passed by one 'not his judge,'" in the gloss (and it seems to be taken explicitly from the text): *a fortiori* what Peter had demanded from his subject contrary to the freedom granted to him by God and nature that subject would have been free to refuse, and a sentence of Peter contrary to a privilege of God and nature would have been null, as being passed by one "not his judge," for in respect of the freedoms granted to the faithful by God and nature all were exempt from Peter's jurisdiction. Therefore, since the privileges and exemption that are granted by God and by nature should be more observed by everyone than those conferred by the pope or by blessed Peter, it seems to follow that, every sentence of Peter contrary to such freedoms would have been null by the law itself, as having been passed by one "not his judge."

Such rulership, which looks only to the good of the subjects and not to the ruler's own good except insofar as it is included in the good of others, Christ did not at all prohibit to the apostles, although he imposed on them, either by commandment or as advice, that they should abstain from all rulership existing for the sake of the ruler's own honor and advantage. He said to them, as we read in Matthew 20:25[-28]: "You know that the rulers of the peoples lord it over them, and the great men exercise power over them; it will not be so among you. But whoever wishes to be the greater among you, let him be your servant, and whoever wishes to be first among you shall be your servant, just as the Son of Man did not come to be served but to serve." By these words Christ did not prohibit to the apostles every rulership, but rather showed that some rulership was to be sought by them, when he said: "Whoever wishes to be the greater among you," and "Whoever wishes to be first among you," for greatness and being first are known to pertain to rulership; the Apostle, who was not ignorant of Christ's teaching, suggested this manifestly in 1 Timothy 3[:1] when he said, "If anyone desires the office of a bishop, he desires a good work." But what sort of rulership Christ wished the apostles to seek he makes clear when he says, "Just as the Son of Man did not come to be ministered to"—by commands, threats, or terrors demanding secular honors, gifts, tributes, and services (especially not compulsory services), such as worldly rulers who do not embrace the best mode of ruling demand and extort from their subjects, too often even violently—"but to minister"—not only physically, even by humbly washing the feet of his disciples, but also spiritually: out of very great love, teaching those who believed in him for their advantage, not his own, advising them and most salutarily directing them by commands and prohibitions, which are known to pertain to rulership, as the Gospel writer Matthew testifies. In chapter 10[:5ff] he says, "These twelve Jesus sent, commanding them, saying, 'Do not go on the road to the gentiles . . . Do not possess gold,'" etc. This is also found explicitly in a great many other places of the gospel teaching.

Therefore, although he said that he had come "not to be ministered to, but to minister," Christ by no means removed from himself all prelacy or rulership, but only rulership for the sake of his own advantage, glory, or honor, as he himself often testified. Therefore, since he wished the apostles to be imitators of him in caring for the advantage of the faithful, he in no way prohibited them from all rulership, but instructed them by commandment or advice that in ruling they should seek to be useful to the faithful: not to dominate, loving their own advantage, glory, and honor—things such as worldly rulers, as we know, always or often seek. And the apostles exercised the purest form of such rulership, for the good of others. (But according to some, the successors of the apostles are by no means bound by the necessity of salvation to the purity of such rulership, without any admixture of any other kind of rulership that the ruler assumes for the sake of his own good, glory and honor, unless there were some who renounced all such rulership by vow or oath; though an assertion some make affirms that those who succeed the apostles in rulership are obliged to the purity of such rulership.)

Conclusions

This chapter has focused on different theological responses to the question of how to live a life devoted to God. Mystics used prayer and meditation to commune with the divine. The monks, nuns, and canons in the West studied the Bible, divining God's plan in sacred and world history. The scholastics used reason and logic to explicate the mysteries of God, and to deduce God's will. They also discussed political theory to determine what limits, if any, existed in the practical ordering of God's world. The mendicants followed the Gospels as literally as they could, walking in the footsteps of Christ's suffering with the poor. The iconodules of Orthodox Christianity explained their theology of icons in terms of God's incarnation in Jesus Christ, while the hesychasts found God in ceaseless prayer and united themselves physically and spiritually with their Lord, Christ Jesus.

Some have called medieval religious practices two-tiered, with one form existing for laity in the churches and another for professional religious. The essence of Christianity as practiced by the simple folk centered on the sacraments and other tangible religious elements by which nonliterate people might understand and participate in Christianity. The sacred was embodied in the bread of communion (the consecrated host) and the wine. The holy could be accessed through the senses (sight, sound, taste, and smell), in the pilgrimages to shrines, in feast days and festivals, in the bones of saints, and in the central rite of Christianity, the Mass. The gothic cathedrals that were built at this time reached toward heaven, mirroring the outstretched hearts, minds, and hands of medieval Christians. Everything within these cathedrals pointed still higher toward the divine: stained glass windows, statues of saints and martyrs, icons, incense, altars, alcoves, and, of course, the soaring vaulted ceilings. An embodied spirituality imbued the material world with spirit and enraptured the believer's eyes, heart, and very being. We can anticipate the dangers inherent in an overly embodied spirituality: where the relic might be worshiped rather than God, and the pilgrimage lead to a completely human ecstasy rather than to a divine one.

Almost as a counterweight to the sensual elements of practical, on-the-street Christianity was the scholastic movement. If spiritual practices filled the heart, scholasticism filled the mind by applying reason to questions of faith. If God is a Trinity, for instance, what is the nature of this Trinity? How does it work? What is the relationship of the Persons in the Trinity to each other? Human reason was brought to bear on these and other questions. The scholastics used the philosophy of their own age to explicate matters of faith. They systematized, classified, and categorized theological as well as scientific knowledge. We can see the potential dangers in this approach as well, however: where the human mind might tame the divine mystery and put God in a small but rational box. Still, the scholastics began their investigations in a lived experience of faith, as did the mendicants and hesychasts, the mystics and visionaries.

These forms of religious commitment influenced lay religious practices. The mendicants were highly visible, known for their work with the poor and their rousing sermons calling the peasants to return to faithfulness. Even those who were cloistered had an impact, because peasants interacted with those running the monasteries in numerous ways: tending animals, cultivating land, selling or bartering or giving products, participating in festivals, and living in a mutually supportive community. Religion was not yet privatized or divorced from general society. Indeed, male and female monastics encountered conflict with both religious and secular authorities. Some believed that the practices or teachings were heretical; some justified the resistance to church authority raised by secular nobles; some criticized worldly kings for abandoning spiritual goals. The monastics continually exerted a reforming pull on the church because they questioned its very participation in temporal politics. At the same time, the world "outside" was pulling upon the church. By the end of the Middle Ages, tension between the church and the world was growing, as were tensions within the church itself.

The church in the Middle Ages exemplified Augustine's caution about the earthly city: nothing this side of heaven was without sin, and that included the church itself. It was obvious to those within the church, and to those outside, that it needed reform. Many priests were barely literate, despite repeated attempts to develop an educated clergy. Many others were married, or lived with the mother of their illegitimate offspring, despite the requirement of celibacy. Church offices and appointments were bought and sold. Even grace itself seemed to be for sale, through the purchase of an indulgence that reduced the amount of time one's relatives, or oneself, spent in purgatory. Although the church had seen numerous reforms during the Middle Ages, still bigger changes were yet to come.

Sources for Selections

Anselm of Canterbury. *St. Anselm: Basic Writings,* 2nd ed. Trans. S. N. Deane. La Salle, Ill.: Open Court, 1962.

Benedict of Nursia. *The Rule of St. Benedict.* Brooklyn, N.Y.: Internet Medieval Sourcebook, Fordham University Center for Medieval Studies. <http://www.fordham.edu/halsall/sbook.html>.

Francis of Assisi. *The Canticle of the Sun.* Trans. Bill Barrett. <http://www.thechaingang.co.uk/cycling-holidays/canticle-to-the-sun.php>.

———. "All Creatures of Our God and King." Trans. William H. Draper. In *The United Methodist Hymnal: Book of United Methodist Worship.* Nashville, Tenn.: United Methodist Publishing House, 1989.

Gregory Palamas. *The Triads.* Ed. John Meyendorff, trans. Nicholas Gendle. New York: Paulist Press, 1983.

Haimo of Auxerre. *Commentary on the Book of Jonah.* Trans. Deborah Everhart. Kalamazoo, Mich.: Medieval Institute Publications, for the Consortium for the Teaching of the Middle Ages, 1993.

John of Damascus. *On the Divine Images: Three Apologies Against Those Who Attack the Divine Images.* Trans. David Anderson. Crestwood, N.Y.: St. Vladimir's Seminary Press, 1980.

Julian of Norwich. *Revelations of Divine Love.* Trans. Clifton Wolters. New York: Penguin, 1966.

Thomas Aquinas. *Summa Theologiae.* Christian Classics Ethereal Library. <http://www.ccel.org/a/aquinas/summa/home.html>. (From *The "Summa Theologica" of St. Thomas Aquinas.* Trans. Fathers of the English Dominican Province. New York: Benziger, 1947.)

William of Ockham. *A Letter to the Friars Minor and Other Writings.* Ed. Arthur Stephen McGrade and John Kilcullen, trans. John Kilcullen. New York: Cambridge University Press, 1995.

Additional Resources

Anselm of Canterbury. *The Major Works.* Trans. Brian Davies and G. R. Evans. New York: Oxford University Press, 1998.

Bynum, Caroline Walker. *Holy Feast and Holy Fast: The Religious Significance of Food to Medieval Women.* Berkeley and Los Angeles: University of California Press, 1987.

Doyle, Leonard J., trans. *St. Benedict's Rule for Monasteries.* Collegeville, Minn.: Liturgical Press, 1948.

Elm, Susanna. *Virgins of God: The Making of Asceticism in Late Antiquity.* New York: Oxford University Press, 1994.

Hildegard of Bingen. *Hildegard of Bingen's* Book of Divine Works *with Letters and Songs.* Ed. Matthew Fox. Santa Fe, N.M.: Bear, 1987.

McMillan, Douglas J., and Kathryn Smith Fladenmuller. *Regular Life: Monastic, Canonical, and Mendicant* Rules. Kalamazoo, Mich.: Medieval Institute Publications, Western Michigan University, 1997.

Meyendorff, John. *Byzantine Theology: Historical Trends and Doctrinal Themes.* New York: Fordham, 1974.

Raitt, Jill, ed. *Christian Spirituality: High Middle Ages and Reformation.* New York: Crossroad, 1997.

Sherley-Price, L., trans. *The Little Flowers of Saint Francis, with Five Considerations on the Sacred Stigmata.* New York: Penguin Books, 1959.

Southern, R. S. *Western Society and the Church in the Middle Ages.* New York: Penguin Books, 1970.

Thomson, John A. F. *The Western Church in the Middle Ages.* New York: Arnold, 1998.

Tierney, Brian. *The Crisis of Church and State 1050–1300.* Englewood Cliffs, N.J.: Prentice-Hall, 1964.

Films

Becket. Directed by Peter Glenville, 1964.

Camelot. Directed by Joshua Logan, 1967.

Kingdom of Heaven. Directed by Ridley Scott, 2005.

The Name of the Rose. Directed by Jean-Jacques Annaud, 1986.

The Seventh Seal. Directed by Ingmar Bergman, 1956.

Sorceress. Directed by Suzanne Schiffman, 1988.

	c. 1455	Gutenberg Bible printed
Columbus' voyage to New World, Muslims expelled from Spain	**1492**	
	1517	Martin Luther posts 95 Theses
Ulrich Zwingli preaches in Zurich	**1519**	
	1525	Conrad Grebel performs believer baptism in Zurich
Peasants' Revolt	**1525**	
	1527	William Tyndale translates portions of Bible into English
Death of Zwingli	**1531**	
	1533–56	Thomas Cranmer, Archbishop of Canterbury
Act of Supremacy in England	**1534**	
	1534–35	"New Jerusalem" in Münster, Germany
Jacob Hutter executed for heresy	**1536**	
	1540	Society of Jesus (Jesuits) recognized by Pope Paul III
John Calvin begins (second) ministry in Geneva	**1541**	
	1545–63	Council of Trent meets
Death of Martin Luther	**1546**	
	1546–47	Schmalkald War
Act of Uniformity in England	**1549**	
	1555	Peace of Augsburg
Elizabethan settlement	**1559–1603**	
	1562	Establishment of Discalced (shoeless) Carmelite Order
Death of John Calvin	**1564**	
	1572	St. Bartholomew's Day Massacre
Edict of Nantes	**1598**	
	1618–48	Thirty Years' War
Peace of Westphalia	**1648**	
	1689	Act of Toleration by William and Mary (England)

The Reformation
A CLARIFICATION OF DOCTRINES

Reformation or Reformations?

Each age in the history of Christianity must address distinct theological issues somewhat unique to its time. Although some questions involve liturgy, practices, or ethics, the resolution of various debates always comes down to developing a theology that explains, justifies, or challenges existing practices. The early church, for example, had to determine the nature of the relationship of the Son of God to the Father and, further, to explicate why the Spirit fit into the existing sacramental practice of baptizing in the name of the Father, Son, and Holy Spirit. The explanation resulted in the doctrine of the Trinity, which stated that God is three Persons in one divine unity. Early Christian theologians also had to deal with christological issues, which meant determining the identity of Christianity's central figure, Jesus the Christ. Once these questions were resolved at church councils in the fourth and fifth centuries to the satisfaction of most, though rarely all, church leaders and practitioners, new questions came to the forefront.

If Christians must resolve different theological questions in each age, what were the issues facing Christians in the sixteenth century? They grew directly from the soil of medieval Christianity and included a number of concerns. First, what was the nature of humanity? Were humans basically good or basically bad? These were anthropological questions, that is, ones which focused on human nature. Second, what was the nature of salvation? How did humans obtain it? These were soteriological questions, that is, ones focused on salvation. Third, what role did the sacraments play in Christian salvation or practice? What were they actually doing or symbolizing? What exactly was happening? These questions encompassed sacramentology, that is, the nature and purpose of the sacraments. Fourth, who, or what, was the final authority for making theological decisions? Was it the church, embodied in the pope, that ought to be primary, since its role as a teaching authority allowed educated theologians to interpret theological issues and explicate them for the laity? Or was scripture the final authority, the last word, in any kind of theological debate? And could anyone reading the Bible decide what it meant without benefit of clergy? Who exactly was the church? These were ecclesiological questions, that is, ones pertaining to the role and function of the church.

These questions arose within the context of the humanist Renaissance, a movement that emphasized a return to classical sources in order to revitalize contemporary education and learning. Indeed, the church was very much a part of the Renaissance. Religious reformers, like their humanist counterparts, shared an interest in original languages, classic texts, and reevaluation of sources. They disliked translations, digests, and compilations of ancient writings that for centuries had been the primary sources for religious and political thinkers. They wanted to look at the originals, in the original languages. They knew that errors crept into translations and copies, and that digests and compilations said more about the digester and compiler than about the material compiled. This interest in ancient writings, including the Bible, did not occur in a vacuum, however. It resulted from the invention of the printing press in the 1450s.

The impact of the printing press in the fifteenth century was comparable to the impact of the Internet in the twenty-first. Suddenly, publications could reach a wide audience, almost instantly, in mass quantities. Any educated person living in Europe in the fifteenth and sixteenth centuries could read the latest pamphlets and books coming from Germany or the Netherlands because they were published in Latin, the universal language of scholarship at that time. With readier access to printed materials, more people discovered an interest in and a need to read. The printing press, like the Internet, was a democratizing technology: anyone could print a pamphlet, just as today anyone can electronically publish a manuscript. It is no exaggeration to say that the reformations of the sixteenth century would not have happened without the technology of printing.

The Renaissance generated an interest in ancient texts and classical languages, and for Christians this meant the Bible and the biblical languages of Hebrew and Greek. Because printing was now available, new translations of the Bible—based on its original languages—could be produced and made accessible to scholars and, eventually, to literate church-goers. Devotional literature had long been available, first to the wealthy and then to a rising middle class, but vernacular translations brought the Bible to all believers. This was revolutionary. Instead of hearing the Bible in Latin—a foreign language to all but the educated—Christians could now hear the Bible in their native languages: English, German, Dutch. Increased interest in the Bible—both in the study of its languages and in its theology—contributed to the development of answers to questions that Christians had inherited from the Middle Ages.

There is some debate among scholars as to whether we should call the changes of the sixteenth century *the* Reformation, in the singular, or reformations, plural. On the one hand, clearly there were a number of distinct movements within this century. A "mainline" Reformation comprised Lutheran, Calvinist or Reformed, and English reformations. A Radical Reformation, included Anabaptists, Spiritualists, and Rationalists. A Catholic Reformation, sometimes called the Counter-Reformation, wrought change within the Catholic Church itself. Catholic Christians were apt to be conservative reformers, preserving and clarifying much of the tradition practiced for 1500 years of Christianity. The mainline Protestants tended to be moderate, preserving some traditions and rejecting others, based on their interpretation of the Bible. Radicals did not believe that the moderates had gone far enough in their reform of prevailing beliefs and practices. They felt that the church needed fundamental changes, from top to bottom. Thus, there were indeed a plurality of reformations.

On the other hand, Reformation as a singular noun is also a useful term. By the end of the sixteenth century, Christians had resolved a number of theological questions. What were the sacraments, and what did they mean, or do? What role did human beings play in God's plan of salvation? How authoritative was the Bible? Although they split over the answers, different groups of Christians adopted confessional statements that made their positions clear. In addition, a number of abuses that had existed in the medieval church were eliminated: ecclesiastical appointments could no longer be bought; clergy had to be thoroughly trained and educated; and bishops had to live in the diocese to which they were appointed. Despite all the division and disagreement, then, there was indeed a thorough-going Reformation that did, in fact, transform western Christianity as a whole.

The biggest theological dispute at this time concerned the process of salvation. Christians proclaim that "Jesus saves," but what exactly does that mean? And *how* does Jesus save? What does one *do* to effect this salvation? The theological term for this is justification: being made right, or justified, in the eyes of God. Justification means that God sees individuals as righteous, or good, people. The question was: What do people have to do for God to see them as good?

Popular religious practices in the Middle Ages suggested that attending church, taking communion, participating in the sacraments, observing feast days, and trying to live by the Ten Commandments would lead to salvation. An optimistic anthropology recognized human sinfulness, but at the same time provided the means to overcome it. One way was to purchase an indulgence—that is, to make a contribution to the church and receive a "receipt." Indulgences existed, it was claimed, because Christ's bountiful grace was so overflowing that one could access it for a small donation. In return, one could ransom one's relatives and oneself out of Purgatory—the place where the souls of the righteous were refined and purged of their transgressions before going on to heaven.

Some reformers challenged these existing practices and beliefs, turning to the writings of Augustine to articulate a pessimistic anthropology that declared humans utterly sinful. This sinfulness made it impossible for humans to contribute anything to their salvation. Humans had inherited the sin of Adam and, according to Augustine, not only could not do good but were not able *not* to sin. Christians had long debated the nature of humanity: Can humans actually be good or do good? Are we basically inclined to the good, with an ability to do good? Or are we basically inclined to evil, with a predisposition to do evil? The answer most reformers gave was extremely gloomy: humans cannot be righteous or good, at least not without God's help.

It is only because God is gracious and generously sees humans as righteous that they are justified. The reason God is willing to do this, the reformers explained, relying on Paul's thought in the New Testament, is because Jesus Christ died a sacrificial death that wiped the slate clean. Jesus was the only one who could have effected this remarkable salvation, because he was God's divine Son. All that any individual could do was to believe that this was true, and God would "reckon them righteous," just as God had done for Abraham in the book of Genesis (Genesis 15 and 17).

These were some of the issues Martin Luther had in mind when he posted 95 Theses, or Propositions, on the door of Wittenberg's castle church in 1517 in preparation for a university debate. He had no intention of founding a movement. Instead, he was merely responding specifically to the sale of indulgences by Johann Tetzel, an emissary of the pope, who claimed that one could be redeemed for any offense—from committing adultery to raping the Virgin Mary—by purchasing an indulgence. Coincidentally, money from the sale of indulgences went to pay off the debts of Pope Leo X, who was in the process of outfitting the Sistine Chapel in Rome. Luther initially used the Bible to attack the practices of the papacy and eventually used scripture to attack the papacy itself. *Sola scriptura,* was his motto: "Scripture alone." By this he meant that all Christian beliefs and practices must be measured against biblical authority.

Luther's actions in Germany reflected what many across Europe were thinking: there seemed to be a disconnect between many church practices and what the Bible said. From indulgences, to sacraments, to priestly celibacy, almost everything considered normative in the Middle Ages was now questioned. Reforming priests used the Bible as their authority to attack tradition. Iconoclasts in Switzerland smashed stained glass windows and threw organs into the streets: the Bible said nothing about these things. Nuns were dragged out of convents by their families: there was nothing scriptural about convents. Priests in the evangelical churches, which is what the reformers called their churches, began to marry: it said they should right in the Bible. In short, reformers used the Bible to justify a range of reforms, changes, and even innovations.

The permanent split between Protestants and Catholics was not inevitable. Several within both camps, most notably Johannes Gropper and Gasparo Contarini on the Catholic side, and Philip Melanchthon and Martin Bucer on the Protestant side, attempted to engage in dialogue, arguing that misunderstanding rather than true differences existed between the parties. But many more within both camps refused what they saw as compromise with the truth. Adding to the momentum for schism were the ambitions of secular authorities, who saw in the reform movement the opportunity to break the power of the church. The most significant of these authorities was Henry VIII, king of England, who persuaded the English Parliament to pass the Act of Supremacy in 1534. The act stated that the king was the head of the church in England, which meant that church lands, revenues, and ecclesiastical appointments now devolved to the king rather than to the pope. No other noble in Europe had made such a sweeping claim or such a blatant grab for power. Still, many supported and harbored the reformers for political, rather than religious, reasons, although just as many secular rulers continued to be loyal to the Catholic Church and to the pope.

All secular officials, however, felt threatened by a new force: radical reformers who were not content with making doctrinal or practical changes, but who envisioned a complete renovation of church and society. Christians should live in apostolic communities, the radicals believed, following the model of the early church, in which possessions were held in common, wealth was redistributed, and leadership was drawn by lots (that is, through chance). The early church had no priests and no hierarchy, but rather a radical egalitarianism that created a new family in Christ. Furthermore, the wealth of the nobility rested upon the oppression of peasants, and the Bible seemed to clearly state that the rich must share their belongings with the poor. The radical reformers attacked both the church and the state for their failure to live according to biblical principles.

The turn toward the Bible as the sole authority, coupled with anticlerical sentiment (that is, anticlergy bias), led to a number of different movements, known collectively as the Radical Reformation. These were Christians who believed that moderate reformers, whom I have called "mainline" reformers simply to differentiate them from the more radical reformers, still supported the status quo and had failed to truly appreciate the revolutionary nature of Jesus' teachings about God's reign on earth. The radicals themselves did not compose a single entity or adopt a common set of beliefs. Some, like Andreas Bodenstein von Karlstadt and Menno Simons, focused on sacramental reform. Others, such as Jacob Hutter, focused on a return to the apostolic life described in the New Testament. Still others, like Thomas Müntzer, focused on political reform. There were also radicals who based their decisions upon inspiration or who emphasized reason and its application to understanding scripture. The one thing all radicals seemed to share was a disapproval of Catholics and mainline Protestants, who, in turn, viewed the radicals as disruptive, anarchic, and dangerous.

The moderates—those Protestants who retained many elements of Catholic Christian tradition while redefining or reappropriating what they believed to be biblical tradition—were not a single monolithic group either. Their leaders came from different parts of Europe and presented different theologies and strategies. Martin Luther, and the Lutheran Reformation, grew out of a Germany composed of many tiny states and principalities. Lutheranism spread through northern Germany and into Scandinavia, but only later took root in Poland and Russia. John Calvin, and the Reformed theology that he outlined in his *Institutes of the Christian Religion,* emerged from Switzerland, which had already seen its own reformation, led by Ulrich Zwingli. Although Calvin was French, and his first stay in Geneva ended abruptly, his final stay in Geneva helped to consolidate and clarify the theology of Calvinism or, more broadly, Reformed theology. Calvinism spread throughout the low countries of Europe, that is, Belgium and the Netherlands, and jumped the English Channel to Scotland, where it influenced John Knox and led to the establishment of the Presbyterian Church in that country. Reformed theology eventually moved to England, where it combined with Catholic tradition to form a unique type of Protestantism, known as Anglicanism, in the Church of England.

And what of the countries that remained solidly Catholic—Spain, France, and Italy? Although France and Italy had small movements of Protestantism within them, they did not take hold for very long, primarily for political reasons. Spain had already seen its own reformation in the fifteenth and early sixteenth centuries under the leadership of Cardinal Ximénez de Cisneros (1436–1517). Ximénez' reforming activities in Spain prefigured a number of the changes made by the Catholic Church at large later in the sixteenth century. Spain continued to produce major Catholic reformers in this era, as we shall see.

Leaders of the Catholic Church, now called the Roman Catholic Church by Protestants to differentiate it from the universal, or catholic, church, gathered in Trent, Italy, at a council that met off and on from 1545 to 1563. At the Council of Trent, Catholics clarified their position over and against that of Protestants on a number of key issues: justification, sacraments, human nature, church government, and the key question of authority. The council asserted that scripture and tradition were coequal sources of authorities, rejecting Luther's cry of "scripture alone." The council also rejected a number of other Protestant changes: it reaffirmed clerical celibacy, thereby prohibiting priests from marrying; it reaffirmed the authority of the Vulgate, a Latin translation of the Bible, thereby refusing to read scripture in the vernacular during the mass; and it reaffirmed the existence of seven sacraments, consisting of baptism, communion, confirmation, marriage, ordination, confession (now known as the sacrament of reconciliation), and anointing (formerly known as extreme unction, or last rites). And perhaps most importantly, the Council of Trent helped to raise the discipline, standards, and training of Catholic clergy.

(Vatican Council II, meeting from 1962 to 1965, reversed and amended many of the decisions made at Trent, so that Catholics who have grown up since then have little concept of the practice of Catholicism under Tridentine, or Trentish, guidance. Mass is said in the vernacular, rather than in Latin. Scripture is read in vernacular translation. The laity participate in communion, generally taking the cup in the United States; and until recently, some laypersons even gave the homily, or sermon, for the day. The priest faces the congregation rather than the altar. Thus, the Catholicism practiced today differs from that practiced in the centuries after Trent. See Chapter Seven for more details.)

While the Council of Trent serves as a convenient marker or dividing line to finalize the split between Catholics and Protestants, it merely formalized what had already been realized: the separation of western Christianity into two major groups. Catholics recognized the authority of the bishop of Rome over Christian life and practice; Protestants rejected this view, arguing that secular authority was located in the local princes while spiritual authority resided in the local bishops, or the local congregations, or even the individual. Catholics believed that God had instituted seven sacraments by which grace, salvation, and sanctification flowed to believers. (Sanctification is the process by which the Holy Spirit sanctifies, or purifies and makes holy, the heart of the believer.) Protestants believed that only two sacraments were clearly instituted—baptism and communion—and some thought that even those two were not absolutely essential for salvation. Catholics believed that scripture in conjunction with church teachings, or tradition, was the ultimate authority. Protestants believed that scripture alone served as the primary guide for faith. Other Protestants—namely, the radical reformers—subscribed to the authority of experience and personal revelation, or to reason.

The Reformation and reformations of the sixteenth century mark a critical turning point, not just for Christianity but for Western society as a whole. The hegemony of a single institution, that is, the church, was replaced by the competing claims of many nation-states. The power of corporate life and worship in which the church was understood to be the body of Christ in which all members participate sacramentally, was replaced with the power of individual life, and a priesthood of all believers who were free to interpret scripture for themselves. The nineteenth-century sociologist Max Weber argued that the Protestant Reformation was responsible for the rise of capitalism in Europe. While many scholars have critiqued Weber's view, the basic point remains: the Reformation permanently changed Western society in ways that were not even questioned until the end of the twentieth century.

The readings that follow obviously represent only a fraction of the issues and conflicts that emerged in the sixteenth century. They do, however, highlight the flavor of the debates, given the various styles and personalities involved. I have included a selection from each of the major reformations: Lutheran, Reformed, English, Radical, and Catholic. Because the Council of Trent occurred toward the end of the sixteenth century, after decades of momentous changes, many of its canons—that is, rules—were adopted in clear contrast to Protestant teachings. But many other canons developed out of earlier reforming movements and the conciliarism of the fifteenth century. It is important to see Trent not as a reaction—though it did react—but rather as a consolidation of numerous reforming movements that had existed in Catholicism for centuries. Nevertheless, I am placing selections from the Canons and Decrees from the Council of Trent after each Protestant selection, to better illuminate the contrasts and disputes of the period.

Martin Luther and the Lutheran Reformation

Martin Luther (1483–1546) would have stood out in any century. His pamphlets, sermons, commentaries, and letters, and most importantly for Germans, his translation of the Bible, laid the theoretical foundations for a radical re-visioning of Christian theology. Yet Luther argued then, and would argue today, that he was merely reading the Bible as it ought to be read. He took Paul, the apostle, at his word that God would overlook human sinfulness if humans would just believe in God's righteousness. Luther was irascible, dedicated, thoughtful, outrageous, opinionated, compassionate, vitriolic, faithful, ironic, and principled. He was not someone you would want as your enemy. He would just as soon accuse you of eating excrement (literally) as praise you if he thought you were corrupting the Word of God as written in the Bible.

Luther's father wanted him to become a lawyer, but Luther changed his mind during a particularly fearsome thunderstorm. He vowed to Saint Ann that he would become a monk if he survived, and when Saint Ann kept her part of the bargain, Luther kept his. He became an Augustinian friar, living according to a community rule that Saint Augustine had developed centuries earlier. At the age of twenty-two, he received a master's degree in liberal arts, and by age twenty-nine, he had a doctorate in theology. He began lecturing at the University of Wittenberg on the Psalms and the letters of Paul, and his close reading of these texts led him to conclude that God's grace alone—*sola gratia*—was what justified people, not anything they could do.

Luther presented his viewpoints in many ways and on a number of occasions: in debates and colloquies, in pamphlets and tracts, in sermons and letters, and perhaps most importantly, in biblical commentaries. His reading of scripture persuaded him that all men are liars and that God alone is true; for that reason, only God could justify the unrighteous. Even after justification, the sinner remained a sinner; it was merely that God chose not to see the sin. Thus, Luther's doctrine of *simul iustus et peccator*—"simultaneously justified and sinner"—reflected his understanding of both divine mercy and human nature.

The Readings

Luther wrote on many topics, ranging from polemics against Jews and peasants, to tracts against Sabbatarians (those Christians who kept the Sabbath on the seventh day of the week rather than the first day) and against the papacy. He translated the Bible into German, a translation that some say rivals the King James English translation of the Bible for beauty and poetry. There are almost sixty volumes of his writings in English translation, and so a logical question to ask would be which work by Luther is most representative or most indicative of his theology? Although several come to mind, such as his commentaries on Genesis and on the Psalms, one of Luther's clearest statements of his beliefs occurs in the "Preface" he wrote to his translation of Paul's letter to the Romans, which appears in the New Testament. Written in 1522, it presents Luther's summary of Christian doctrine, primarily because he believes that Romans is the New Testament's "purest Gospel," as he says in the first line of the "Preface."

What is a preface exactly? A preface generally acts as an introduction to a longer work and discusses the subject of that work. Frequently, it summarizes the contents of the longer work, highlighting key features and elements. In Luther's case, it does all of this and much more, providing his own interpretation of the letter itself. In fact, Luther's interpretation of the letter to the Romans has been so influential that it wasn't until the late twentieth century that biblical scholars tried to read the letter on its own terms, and on Paul's terms, without benefit of Luther's interpretive lenses.

Note: The translator of Luther's "Preface" notes that the German word *gerecht* can be translated as "just, justice, justify" and "righteous, righteousness, and make righteous." Similarly, the German word *Glaube* can mean both "faith" and "belief." So the English sentence "We are justified by faith" is just as accurate a translation as "We are made righteous by belief" for the same single German sentence. As we can see, however, those two sentences don't necessarily mean the exact same thing in English. The translator has made additional comments in brackets in the "Preface."

Questions to Consider

1. Why does Luther consider the letter to the Romans to be the fullest statement of Christian gospel, or good news?

2. What purpose does the law serve, in Luther's opinion?

3. What is faith, according to Luther?

4. How does Luther use the idea of Rome and Romans to make an argument against the Catholic Church? How does he use Paul's understanding of Jews and Jewish practices to attack the papacy? Is this a legitimate usage?

5. Luther mentions the names of Christian writers from the early church and from the Middle Ages. What is his opinion of these writers? How does his view compare with that of Augustine in the *City of God,* which we read in Chapter Two?

6. Would you say that Luther generally agrees with the Catholic view on justification, as outlined in the Canons on Justification from the Council of Trent, which follow the Luther reading? Why or why not? What are the strengths and weaknesses of both viewpoints?

7. Read the book of Romans in the New Testament to see if Luther's interpretation is fair or not.

Preface to the Letter of Saint Paul to the Romans

MARTIN LUTHER

This letter is truly the most important piece in the New Testament. It is purest Gospel. It is well worth a Christian's while not only to memorize it word for word but also to occupy himself with it daily, as though it were the daily bread of the soul. It is impossible to read or to meditate on this letter too much or too well. The more one deals with it, the more precious it becomes and the better it tastes. Therefore I want to carry out my service and, with this preface, provide an introduction to the letter, insofar as God gives me the ability, so that everyone can gain the fullest possible understanding of it. Up to now it has been darkened by glosses and by many a useless comment, but it is in itself a bright light, almost bright enough to illumine the entire Scripture.

To begin with, we have to become familiar with the vocabulary of the letter and know what Saint Paul means by the words law, sin, grace, faith, justice, flesh, spirit, etc. Otherwise there is no use in reading it.

You must not understand the word law here in human fashion, i.e., a regulation about what sort of works must be done or must not be done. That's the way it is with human laws: you satisfy the demands of the law with works, whether your heart is in it or not. God judges what is in the depths of the heart. Therefore his law also makes demands on the depths of the heart and doesn't let the heart rest content in works; rather it punishes as hypocrisy and lies all works done apart from the depths of the heart. All human beings are called liars [Psalm 116:11], since none of them keeps or can keep God's law from the depths of the heart. Everyone finds inside himself an aversion to good and a craving for evil. Where there is no free desire for good, there the heart has not set itself on God's law. There also sin is surely to be found and the deserved wrath of God, whether a lot of good works and an honorable life appear outwardly or not.

Therefore in chapter 2, Saint Paul adds that the Jews are all sinners and says that only the doers of the law are justified in the sight of God. What he is saying is that no one is a doer of the law by works. On the contrary, he says to them, "You teach that one should not commit adultery, and you commit adultery. You judge another in a certain matter and condemn yourselves in that same matter, because you do the very same thing that you judged in another." It is as if he were saying, "Outwardly you live quite properly in the works of the law and judge those who do not live the same way; you know how to teach everybody. You see the speck in another's eye but do not notice the beam in your own."

Outwardly you keep the law with works out of fear of punishment or love of gain. Likewise you do everything without free desire and love of the law; you act out of aversion and force. You'd rather act otherwise if the law didn't exist. It follows, then, that you, in the depths of your heart, are an enemy of the law. What do you mean, therefore, by teaching another not to steal, when you, in the depths of your heart, are a thief and would be one outwardly too, if you dared. (Of course, outward work doesn't last long with such hypocrites.) So then, you teach others but not yourself; you don't even know what you are teaching. You've never understood the law rightly. Furthermore, the law increases sin, as Saint Paul says in chapter 5. That is because a person becomes more and more an enemy of the law the more it demands of him what he can't possibly do.

In chapter 7, Saint Paul says, "The law is spiritual." What does that mean? If the law were physical, then it could be satisfied by works, but since it is spiritual, no one can satisfy it unless everything he does springs from the depths of the heart. But no one can give such a heart except the Spirit of God, who makes the person be like the law, so that he actually conceives a heartfelt longing for the law and henceforward does everything, not through fear or coercion, but from a free heart. Such a law is spiritual since it can only be loved and fulfilled by such a heart and such a spirit. If the Spirit is not in the heart, then there remain sin, aversion and enmity against the law, which in itself is good, just and holy.

You must get used to the idea that it is one thing to do the works of the law and quite another to fulfill it. The works of the law are everything that a person does or can do of his own free will and by his own powers to obey the law. But because in doing such works the heart abhors the law and yet is forced to obey it, the works are a total loss and are completely useless. That is what Saint Paul means in chapter 3 when he says, "No human being is justified before God through the works of the law." From this you can see that the schoolmasters [i.e., the scholastic theologians] and sophists are seducers when they teach that you can prepare yourself for grace by means of works. How can anybody prepare himself for good by means of works if he does no good work except with aversion and constraint in his heart? How can such a work please God, if it proceeds from an averse and unwilling heart?

But to fulfill the law means to do its work eagerly, lovingly and freely, without the constraint of the law; it means to live well and in a manner pleasing to God, as though there were no law or punishment. It is the Holy Spirit, however, who puts such eagerness of unconstrained love into the heart, as Paul says in chapter 5. But the Spirit is given only in, with, and through faith in Jesus Christ, as Paul says in his introduction. So, too, faith comes only through the word of God, the Gospel, that preaches Christ: how he is both Son of God and man, how he died and rose for our sake. Paul says all this in chapters 3, 4 and 10.

That is why faith alone makes someone just and fulfills the law; faith it is that brings the Holy Spirit through the merits of Christ. The Spirit, in turn, renders the heart glad and free, as the law demands. Then good works proceed from faith itself. That is what Paul means in chapter 3 when, after he has thrown out the works of the law, he sounds as though he wants to abolish the law by faith. No, he says, we uphold the law through faith, i.e. we fulfill it through faith.

Sin in the Scriptures means not only external works of the body but also all those movements within us which bestir themselves and move us to do the external works, namely, the depth of the heart with all its powers. Therefore the word "do" should refer to a person's completely falling into sin. No external work of sin happens, after all, unless a person commit himself to it completely, body and soul. In particular, the Scriptures see into the heart, to the root and main source of all sin: unbelief in the depth of the heart. Thus, even as faith alone makes just and brings the Spirit and the desire to do good external works, so it is only unbelief which sins and exalts the flesh and brings desire to do evil external works. That's what happened to Adam and Eve in Paradise [Genesis 3].

That is why only unbelief is called sin by Christ, as he says in John, chapter 16, "The Spirit will punish the world because of sin, because it does not believe in me." Furthermore, before good or bad works happen, which are the good or bad fruits of the heart, there has to be present in the heart either faith or unbelief, the root, sap and chief power of all sin. That is why, in the Scriptures, unbelief is called the head of the serpent and of the ancient dragon which the offspring of the woman, i.e. Christ, must crush, as was promised to Adam [Genesis 3:15]. *Grace* and *gift* differ in that grace actually denotes God's kindness or favor which he has toward us and by which he is disposed to pour Christ and the Spirit with his gifts into us, as becomes clear from chapter 5, where Paul says, "Grace and gift are in Christ, etc." The gifts and the Spirit increase daily in us, yet they are not complete, since evil desires and sins remain in us which war against the Spirit, as Paul says in chapter 7, and in Galatians, chapter 5. And Genesis, chapter 3, proclaims the enmity between the offspring of the woman and that of the serpent. But grace does do this much: that we are accounted completely just before God. God's grace is not divided into bits and pieces, as are the gifts, but grace takes us up completely into God's favor for the sake of Christ, our intercessor and mediator, so that the gifts may begin their work in us.

In this way, then, you should understand chapter 7, where Saint Paul portrays himself as still a sinner, while in chapter 8 he says that, because of the incomplete gifts and because of the Spirit, there is nothing damnable in those who are in Christ. Because our flesh has not been killed, we are still sinners, but because we believe in Christ and have the beginnings of the Spirit, God so shows us his favor and mercy, that he neither notices nor judges such sins. Rather he deals with us according to our belief in Christ until sin is killed.

Faith is not that human illusion and dream that some people think it is. When they hear and talk a lot about faith and yet see that no moral improvement and no good works result from it, they fall into error and say, "Faith is not enough. You must do works if you want to be virtuous and get to heaven." The result is that, when they hear the Gospel, they stumble and make for themselves with their own powers a concept in their hearts which says, "I believe." This concept they hold to be true faith. But since it is a human fabrication and thought and not an experience of the heart, it accomplishes nothing, and there follows no improvement.

Faith is a work of God in us, which changes us and brings us to birth anew from God [John 3:3]. It kills the old Adam, makes us completely different people in heart, mind, senses, and all our powers, and brings the Holy Spirit with it. What a living, creative, active powerful thing is faith! It is impossible that faith ever stop doing good. Faith doesn't ask whether good works are to be done, but, before it is asked, it has done them. It is always active. Whoever doesn't do such works is without faith; he gropes and searches about him for faith and good works but doesn't know what faith or good works are. Even so, he chatters on with a great many words about faith and good works.

Faith is a living, unshakeable confidence in God's grace; it is so certain, that someone would die a thousand times for it. This kind of trust in and knowledge of God's grace makes a person joyful, confident, and happy with regard to God and all creatures. This is what the Holy Spirit does by faith. Through faith, a person will do good to everyone without coercion, willingly and happily; he will serve everyone, suffer everything for the love and praise of God, who has shown him such grace. It is as impossible to separate works from faith as burning and shining from fire. Therefore be on guard against your own false ideas and against the chatterers who think they are clever enough to make judgments about faith and good works but who are in reality the biggest fools. Ask God to work faith in you; otherwise you will remain eternally without faith, no matter what you try to do or fabricate.

Now *justice* is just such a faith. It is called God's justice or that justice which is valid in God's sight, because it is God who gives it and reckons it as justice for the sake of Christ our Mediator. It influences a person to give to everyone what he owes him. Through faith a person becomes sinless and eager for God's commands. Thus he gives God the honor due him and pays him what he owes him. He serves people willingly with the means available to him. In this way he pays everyone his due. Neither nature nor free will nor our own powers can bring about such a justice, for even as no one can give himself faith, so too he cannot remove unbelief. How can he then take away even the smallest sin? Therefore everything which takes place outside faith or in unbelief is lie, hypocrisy and sin [Romans 14:23], no matter how smoothly it may seem to go.

You must not understand flesh here as denoting only unchastity or spirit as denoting only the inner heart. Here Saint Paul calls flesh (as does Christ in John 3) everything born of flesh, i.e. the whole human being with body and soul, reason and senses, since everything in him tends toward the flesh. That is why you should know enough to call that person "fleshly" who, without grace, fabricates, teaches and chatters about high spiritual matters. You can learn the same thing from Galatians, chapter 5, where Saint Paul calls heresy and hatred works of the flesh. And in Romans, chapter 8, he says that, through the flesh, the law is weakened. He says this, not of unchastity, but of all sins, most of all of unbelief, which is the most spiritual of vices.

On the other hand, you should know enough to call that person "spiritual" who is occupied with the most outward of works as was Christ, when he washed the feet of the disciples, and Peter, when he steered his boat and fished. So then, a person is "flesh" who, inwardly and outwardly, lives only to do those things which are of use to the flesh and to temporal existence. A person is "spirit" who, inwardly and outwardly, lives only to do those things which are of use to the spirit and to the life to come.

Unless you understand these words in this way, you will never understand either this letter of Saint Paul or any book of the Scriptures. Be on guard, therefore against any teacher who uses these words differently, no matter who he be, whether Jerome, Augustine, Ambrose, Origen or anyone else as great as or greater than they. Now let us turn to the letter itself.

The first duty of a preacher of the Gospel is, through his revealing of the law and of sin, to rebuke and to turn into sin everything in life that does not have the Spirit and faith in Christ as its base. [Here and elsewhere in Luther's preface, as indeed in Romans itself, it is not clear whether "spirit" has the meaning "Holy Spirit" or "spiritual person," as Luther has previously defined it.] Thereby he will lead people to a recognition of their miserable condition, and thus they will become humble and yearn for help. This is what St Paul does. He begins in chapter 1 by rebuking the gross sins and unbelief which are in plain view, as were (and still are) the sins of the pagans, who live without God's grace. He says that, through the gospel, God is revealing his wrath from heaven upon all mankind because of the godless and unjust lives they live. For, although they know and recognize day by day that there is a God, yet human nature in itself, without grace, is so evil that it neither thanks nor honors God. This nature blinds itself and continually falls into wickedness, even going so far as to commit idolatry and other horrible sins and vices. It is unashamed of itself and leaves such things unpunished in others.

In chapter 2, Saint Paul extends his rebuke to those who appear outwardly pious or who sin secretly. Such were the Jews, and such are all hypocrites still, who live virtuous lives but without eagerness and love; in their heart they are enemies of God's law and like to judge other people. That's the way with hypocrites: they think that they are pure but are actually full of greed, hate, pride and all sorts of filth [Matthew 23:27]. These are they who despise God's goodness and, by their hardness of heart, heap wrath upon themselves. Thus Paul explains the law rightly when he lets no one remain without sin but proclaims the wrath of God to all who want to live virtuously by nature or by free will. He makes them out to be no better than public sinners; he says they are hard of heart and unrepentant.

In chapter 3, Paul lumps both secret and public sinners together: the one, he says, is like the other; all are sinners in the sight of God. Besides, the Jews had God's word, even though many did not believe in it. But still God's truth and faith in him are not thereby rendered useless. Saint Paul introduces, as an aside, the saying from Psalm 51, that God remains true to his words. Then he returns to his topic and proves from Scripture that they are all sinners and that no one becomes just through the works of the law but that God gave the law only so that sin might be perceived.

Next Saint Paul teaches the right way to be virtuous and to be saved; he says that they are all sinners, unable to glory in God. They must, however, be justified through faith in Christ, who has merited this for us by his blood and has become for us a mercy seat [Exodus 25:17, Leviticus 16:14ff, and John 2:2] in the presence of God, who forgives us all our previous sins. In so doing, God proves that it is his justice alone, which he gives through faith, that helps us, the justice which was at the appointed time revealed through the Gospel and, previous to that, was witnessed to by the Law and the Prophets. Therefore the law is set up by faith, but the works of the law, along with the glory taken in them, are knocked down by faith. [As with the term "spirit," the word "law" seems to have for Luther, and for Saint Paul, two meanings. Sometimes it means "regulation about what must be done or not done," as in the third paragraph of this preface; sometimes it means "the Torah," as in the previous sentence. And sometimes it seems to have both meanings, as in what follows.]

In chapters 1 to 3, Saint Paul has revealed sin for what it is and has taught the way of faith which leads to justice. Now in chapter 4 he deals with some objections and criticisms. He takes up first the one that people raise who, on hearing that faith makes just without works, say, "What? Shouldn't we do any good works?" Here Saint Paul holds up Abraham as an example. He says, "What did Abraham accomplish with his good works? Were they all good for nothing and useless?" He concludes that Abraham was made righteous apart from all his works by faith alone. Even before the "work" of his circumcision, Scripture praises him as being just on account of faith alone [Genesis 15:6]. Now if the work of his circumcision did nothing to make him just, a work that God had commanded him to do and hence a work of obedience, then surely no other good work can do anything to make a person just. Even as Abraham's circumcision was an outward sign with which he proved his justice based on faith, so too all good works are only outward signs which flow from faith and are the fruits of faith; they prove that the person is already inwardly just in the sight of God.

Saint Paul verifies his teaching on faith in chapter 3 with a powerful example from Scripture. He calls as witness David, who says in Psalm 32 that a person becomes just without works but doesn't remain without works once he has become just. Then Paul extends this example and applies it against all other works of the law. He concludes that the Jews cannot

be Abraham's heirs just because of their blood relationship to him and still less because of the works of the law. Rather, they have to inherit Abraham's faith if they want to be his real heirs, since it was prior to the Law of Moses and the law of circumcision that Abraham became just through faith and was called a father of all believers. Saint Paul adds that the law brings about more wrath than grace, because no one obeys it with love and eagerness. More disgrace than grace come from the works of the law. Therefore faith alone can obtain the grace promised to Abraham. Examples like these are written for our sake, that we also should have faith.

In chapter 5, Saint Paul comes to the fruits and works of faith, namely: joy, peace, love for God and for all people; in addition: assurance, steadfastness, confidence, courage, and hope in sorrow and suffering. All of these follow where faith is genuine, because of the overflowing good will that God has shown in Christ: he had him die for us before we could ask him for it, yes, even while we were still his enemies. Thus we have established that faith, without any good works, makes just. It does not follow from that, however, that we should not do good works; rather it means that morally upright works do not remain lacking. About such works the "works-holy" people know nothing; they invent for themselves their own works in which are neither peace nor joy nor assurance nor love nor hope nor steadfastness nor any kind of genuine Christian works or faith.

Next Saint Paul makes a digression, a pleasant little side-trip, and relates where both sin and justice, death and life come from. He opposes these two: Adam and Christ. What he wants to say is that Christ, a second Adam, had to come in order to make us heirs of his justice through a new spiritual birth in faith, just as the old Adam made us heirs of sin through the old fleshly birth.

Saint Paul proves, by this reasoning, that a person cannot help himself by his works to get from sin to justice any more than he can prevent his own physical birth. Saint Paul also proves that the divine law, which should have been well-suited, if anything was, for helping people to obtain justice, not only was no help at all when it did come, but it even increased sin. Evil human nature, consequently, becomes more hostile to it; the more the law forbids it to indulge its own desires, the more it wants to. Thus the law makes Christ all the more necessary and demands more grace to help human nature.

In chapter 6, Saint Paul takes up the special work of faith, the struggle which the spirit wages against the flesh to kill off those sins and desires that remain after a person has been made just. He teaches us that faith doesn't so free us from sin that we can be idle, lazy and self-assured, as though there were no more sin in us. Sin is there, but, because of faith that struggles against it, God does not reckon sin as deserving damnation. Therefore we have in our own selves a lifetime of work cut out for us; we have to tame our body, kill its lusts, force its members to obey the spirit and not the lusts. We must do this so that we may conform to the death and resurrection of Christ and complete our Baptism, which signifies a death to sin and a new life of grace. Our aim is to be completely clean from sin and then to rise bodily with Christ and live forever.

Saint Paul says that we can accomplish all this because we are in grace and not in the law. He explains that to be "outside the law" is not the same as having no law and being able to do what you please. No, being "under the law" means living without grace, surrounded by the works of the law. Then surely sin reigns by means of the law, since no one is naturally well-disposed toward the law. That very condition, however, is the greatest sin. But grace makes the law lovable to us, so there is then no sin any more, and the law is no longer against us but one with us.

This is true freedom from sin and from the law; Saint Paul writes about this for the rest of the chapter. He says it is a freedom only to do good with eagerness and to live a good life without the coercion of the law. This freedom is, therefore, a spiritual freedom which does not suspend the law but which supplies what the law demands, namely eagerness and love. These silence the law so that it has no further cause to drive people on and make demands of them. It's as though you owed something to a moneylender and couldn't pay him. You could be rid of him in one of two ways: either he would take nothing from you and would tear up his account book, or a pious man would pay for you and give you what you needed to satisfy your debt. That's exactly how Christ freed us from the law. Therefore our freedom is not a wild, fleshly freedom that has no obligation to do anything. On the contrary, it is a freedom that does a great deal, indeed everything, yet is free of the law's demands and debts.

In chapter 7, Saint Paul confirms the foregoing by an analogy drawn from married life. When a man dies, the wife is free; the one is free and clear of the other. It is not the case that the woman may not or should not marry another man; rather she is now for the first time free to marry someone else. She could not do this before she was free of her first husband. In the same way, our conscience is bound to the law so long as our condition is that of the sinful old man. But when the old man is killed by the spirit, then the conscience is free, and conscience and law are quit of each other. Not that conscience should now do nothing; rather, it should now for the first time truly cling to its second husband, Christ, and bring forth the fruit of life.

Next Saint Paul sketches further the nature of sin and the law. It is the law that makes sin really active and powerful, because the old man gets more and more hostile to the law since he can't pay the debt demanded by the law. Sin is his very nature; of himself he can't do otherwise. And so the law is his death and torture. Now the law is not itself evil; it is our evil nature that cannot tolerate that the good law should demand good from it. It's like the case of a sick person, who cannot tolerate that you demand that he run and jump around and do other things that a healthy person does.

Saint Paul concludes here that, if we understand the law properly and comprehend it in the best possible way, then we will see that its sole function is to remind us of our sins, to kill us by our sins, and to make us deserving of eternal wrath. Conscience learns and experiences all this in detail when it comes face to face with the law. It follows, then, that we must have something else, over and above the law, which can make a person virtuous and cause him to be saved. Those, however, who do not understand the law rightly are blind; they go their way boldly and think they are satisfying the law with works. They don't know how much the law demands, namely, a free, willing, eager heart. That is the reason that they don't see Moses rightly before their eyes. [2 Corinthians 3:7–18.] For them he is covered and concealed by the veil.

Then Saint Paul shows how spirit and flesh struggle with each other in one person. He gives himself as an example, so that we may learn how to kill sin in ourselves. He gives both spirit and flesh the name "law," so that, just as it is in the nature of divine law to drive a person on and make demands of him, so too the flesh drives and demands and rages against the spirit and wants to have its own way. Likewise the spirit drives and demands against the flesh and wants to have its own way. This feud lasts in us for as long as we live, in one person more, in another less, depending on whether spirit or flesh is stronger. Yet the whole human being is both: spirit and flesh. The human being fights with himself until he becomes completely spiritual.

In chapter 8, Saint Paul comforts fighters such as these and tells them that this flesh will not bring them condemnation. He goes on to show what the nature of flesh and spirit are. Spirit, he says, comes from Christ, who has given us his Holy Spirit; the Holy Spirit makes us spiritual and restrains the flesh. The Holy Spirit assures us that we are God's children no matter how furiously sin may rage within us, so long as we follow the Spirit and struggle against sin in order to kill it. Because nothing is so effective in deadening the flesh as the cross and suffering, Paul comforts us in our suffering. He says that the Spirit, love and all creatures will stand by us; the Spirit in us groans and all creatures long with us that we be freed from the flesh and from sin. Thus we see that these three chapters, 6, 7 and 8, all deal with the one work of faith, which is to kill the old Adam and to constrain the flesh.

In chapters 9, 10 and 11, Saint Paul teaches us about the eternal providence of God. It is the original source which determines who would believe and who wouldn't, who can be set free from sin and who cannot. Such matters have been taken out of our hands and are put into God's hands so that we might become virtuous. It is absolutely necessary that it be so, for we are so weak and unsure of ourselves that, if it depended on us, no human being would be saved. The devil would overpower all of us. But God is steadfast; his providence will not fail, and no one can prevent its realization. Therefore we have hope against sin.

But here we must shut the mouths of those sacrilegious and arrogant spirits who, mere beginners that they are, bring their reason to bear on this matter and commence, from their exalted position, to probe the abyss of divine providence and uselessly trouble themselves about whether they are predestined or not. These people must surely plunge to their ruin, since they will either despair or abandon themselves to a life of chance.

You, however, follow the reasoning of this letter in the order in which it is presented. Fix your attention first of all on Christ and the Gospel, so that you may recognize your sin and his grace. Then struggle against sin, as chapters 1–8 have taught you to. Finally, when you have come, in chapter 8, under the shadow of the cross and suffering, they will teach you, in chapters 9–11, about providence and what a comfort it is. Apart from suffering the cross and the pangs of death, you cannot come to grips with providence without harm to yourself and secret anger against God. The old Adam must be quite dead before you can endure this matter and drink this strong wine. Therefore make sure you don't drink wine while you are still a babe at the breast. There is a proper measure, time and age for understanding every doctrine.

In chapter 12, Saint Paul teaches the true liturgy and makes all Christians priests, so that they may offer, not money or cattle, as priests do in the Law, but their own bodies, by putting their desires to death. Next he describes the outward conduct of Christians whose lives are governed by the Spirit; he tells how they teach, preach, rule, serve, give, suffer, love, live and act toward friend, foe and everyone. These are the works that a Christian does, for, as I have said, faith is not idle.

In chapter 13, Saint Paul teaches that one should honor and obey the secular authorities. He includes this, not because it makes people virtuous in the sight of God, but because it does insure that the virtuous have outward peace and protection and that the wicked cannot do evil without fear and in undisturbed peace. Therefore it is the duty of virtuous people to honor secular authority, even though they do not, strictly speaking, need it. Finally, Saint Paul sums up everything in love and gathers it all into the example of Christ: what he has done for us, we must also do and follow after him.

In chapter 14, Saint Paul teaches that one should carefully guide those with weak conscience and spare them. One shouldn't use Christian freedom to harm but rather to help the weak. Where that isn't done, there follow dissension and despising of the gospel, on which everything else depends. It is better to give way a little to the weak in faith until they become stronger than to have the teaching of the gospel perish completely. This work is a particularly necessary work of love especially now when people, by eating meat and by other freedoms, are brashly, boldly and unnecessarily shaking weak consciences which have not yet come to know the truth.

In chapter 15, Saint Paul cites Christ as an example to show that we must also have patience with the weak, even those who fail by sinning publicly or by their disgusting morals. We must not cast them aside but must bear with them until they become better. That is the way Christ treated us and still treats us every day; he puts up with our vices, our wicked morals and all our imperfection, and he helps us ceaselessly. Finally Paul prays for the Christians at Rome; he praises them and commends them to God. He points out his own office and the message that he preaches. He makes an unobtrusive plea for a contribution for the poor in Jerusalem. Unalloyed love is the basis of all he says and does.

The last chapter consists of greetings. But Paul also includes a salutary warning against human doctrines which are preached alongside the gospel and which do a great deal of harm. It's as though he had clearly seen that out of Rome and through the Romans would come the deceitful, harmful Canons and Decretals along with the entire brood and swarm of human laws and commands that is now drowning the whole world and has blotted out this letter and the whole of the Scriptures, along with the Spirit and faith. Nothing remains but the idol, Belly, and Saint Paul depicts those people here as its servants. God deliver us from them. Amen.

We find in this letter, then, the richest possible teaching about what a Christian should know: the meaning of law, gospel, sin, punishment, grace, faith, justice, Christ, God, good works, love, hope and the cross. We learn how we are to act toward everyone, toward the virtuous and sinful, toward the strong and the weak, friend and foe, and toward ourselves. Paul bases everything firmly on Scripture and proves his points with examples from his own experience and from the Prophets, so that nothing more could be desired. Therefore it seems that Saint Paul, in writing this letter, wanted to compose a summary of the whole of Christian and evangelical teaching which would also be an introduction to the whole Old Testament. Without doubt, whoever takes this letter to heart possesses the light and power of the Old Testament. Therefore each and every Christian should make this letter the habitual and constant object of his study. God grant us his grace to do so. Amen.

Justification and the Council of Trent

Church leaders meeting at the Council of Trent issued decrees on a number of topics. These decrees are essentially statements of faith, much like those drawn up by Protestant reformers to clarify their position on a number of topics, such as books of scripture, predestination, sacraments, and sin. As you read the following Decree Concerning Justification, think about what Martin Luther said about justification in his "Preface to Paul's Letter to the Romans." What are the points of agreement between these two texts? Where do they disagree? Why?

Decree Concerning Justification

COUNCIL OF TRENT, SIXTH SESSION, 13 JANUARY 1547

CHAPTER I. THE IMPOTENCY OF NATURE AND OF THE LAW TO JUSTIFY MAN.

The holy council declares first, that for a correct and clear understanding of the doctrine of justification, it is necessary that each one recognize and confess that since all men had lost innocence in the prevarication of Adam, having become unclean, and, as the Apostle says, by nature children of wrath, as has been set forth in the decree on original sin, they were so far the servants of sin and under the power of the devil and of death, that not only the Gentiles by the force of nature, but not even the Jews by the very letter of the law of Moses, were able to be liberated or to rise therefrom, though free will, weakened as it was in its powers and downward bent, was by no means extinguished in them.

CHAPTER II. THE DISPENSATION AND MYSTERY OF THE ADVENT OF CHRIST.

Whence it came to pass that the heavenly Father, the Father of mercies and the God of all comfort, when the blessed fulness of the time was come, sent to men Jesus Christ, His own Son, who had both before the law and during the time of the law been announced and promised to many of the holy fathers, that he might redeem the Jews who were under the law, and that the Gentiles who followed not after justice might attain to justice, and that all men might receive the adoption of sons. Him has God proposed as a propitiator through faith in his blood for our sins, and not for our sins only, but also for those of the whole world.

CHAPTER III. WHO ARE JUSTIFIED THROUGH CHRIST.

But though He died for all, yet all do not receive the benefit of His death, but those only to whom the merit of His passion is communicated; because as truly as men would not be born unjust, if they were not born through propagation of the seed of Adam, since by that propagation they contract through him, when they are conceived, injustice as their own, so if they were not born again in Christ, they would never be justified, since in that new birth there is bestowed upon them, through the merit of His passion, the grace by which they are made just. For this benefit the Apostle exhorts us always to give thanks to the Father, who hath made us worthy to be partakers of the lot of the saints in light, and hath delivered us from the power of darkness, and hath translated us into the kingdom of the Son of his love, in whom we have redemption and remission of sins.

CHAPTER IV. A BRIEF DESCRIPTION OF THE JUSTIFICATION OF THE SINNER AND ITS MODE IN THE STATE OF GRACE.

In which words is given a brief description of the justification of the sinner, as being a translation from that state in which man is born a child of the first Adam, to the state of grace and of the adoption of the sons of God through the second Adam, Jesus Christ, our Savior. This translation however cannot, since the promulgation of the gospel, be effected except through the laver of regeneration or its desire, as it is written: Unless a man be born again of water and the Holy Ghost, he cannot enter into the kingdom of God.

CHAPTER V. THE NECESSITY OF PREPARATION FOR JUSTIFICATION IN ADULTS, AND WHENCE IT PROCEEDS.

It is furthermore declared that in adults the beginning of that justification must proceed from the predispos-

ing grace of God through Jesus Christ, that is, from His vocation, whereby, without any merits on their part, they are called; that they who by sin had been cut off from God, may be disposed through His quickening and helping grace to convert themselves to their own justification by freely assenting to and co-operating with that grace; so that, while God touches the heart of man through the illumination of the Holy Ghost, man himself neither does absolutely nothing while receiving that inspiration, since be can also reject it, nor yet is he able by his own free will and without the grace of God to move himself to justice in His sight. Hence, when it is said in the sacred writings: Turn ye to me, and I will turn to you, we are reminded of our liberty; and when we reply: Convert us, O Lord, to thee, and we shall be converted, we confess that we need the grace of God.

CHAPTER VI. THE MANNER OF PREPARATION.

Now, they [the adults] are disposed to that justice when, aroused and aided by divine grace, receiving faith by hearing, they are moved freely toward God, believing to be true what has been divinely revealed and promised, especially that the sinner is justified by God by his grace, through the redemption that is in Christ Jesus; and when, understanding themselves to be sinners, they, by turning themselves from the fear of divine justice, by which they are salutarily aroused, to consider the mercy of God, are raised to hope, trusting that God will be propitious to them for Christ's sake; and they begin to love Him as the fountain of all justice, and on that account are moved against sin by a certain hatred and detestation, that is, by that repentance that must be performed before baptism; finally, when they resolve to receive baptism, to begin a new life and to keep the commandments of God. Of this disposition it is written: He that cometh to God, must believe that he is, and is a rewarder to them that seek him; and, Be of good faith, son, thy sins are forgiven thee; and The fear of the Lord driveth out sin; and, Do penance, and he baptized every one of you in the name of Jesus Christ, for the remission of your sins, and you shall receive the gift of the Holy Ghost, and, Going, therefore, teach ye all nations, baptizing them in the name of the Father, and of the Son, and of the Holy Ghost, teaching them to observe all things whatsoever I have commanded you; finally, Prepare your hearts unto the Lord.

CHAPTER VII. IN WHAT THE JUSTIFICATION OF THE SINNER CONSISTS, AND WHAT ARE ITS CAUSES.

This disposition or preparation is followed by justification itself, which is not only a remission of sins but also the sanctification and renewal of the inward man through the voluntary reception of the grace and gifts whereby an unjust man becomes just and from being an enemy becomes a friend, that he may be an heir according to hope of life everlasting. The causes of this justification are: the final cause is the glory of God and of Christ and life everlasting; the efficient cause is the merciful God who washes and sanctifies gratuitously, signing and anointing with the holy Spirit of promise, who is the pledge of our inheritance; the meritorious cause is His most beloved only begotten, our Lord Jesus Christ, who, when we were enemies, for the exceeding charity wherewith he loved us, merited for us justification by His most holy passion on the wood of the cross and made satisfaction for us to God the Father; the instrumental cause is the sacrament of baptism, which is the sacrament of faith, without which no man was ever justified; finally, the single formal cause is the justice of God, not that by which He Himself is just, but that by which He makes us just, that, namely, with which we being endowed by Him, are renewed in the spirit of our mind, and not only are we reputed but we are truly called and are just, receiving justice within us, each one according to his own measure, which the Holy Ghost distributes to everyone as He wills, and according to each one's disposition and co-operation. For though no one can be just except he to whom the merits of the passion of our Lord Jesus Christ are communicated, yet this takes place in the justification of the sinner, when by the merit of the most holy passion, the charity of God is poured forth by the Holy Ghost in the hearts of those who are justified and inheres in them; whence man through Jesus Christ, in whom he is ingrafted, receives in that justification, together with the remission of sins, all these infused at the same time, namely, faith, hope and charity. For faith, unless hope and charity be added to it, neither unites man perfectly with Christ nor makes him a living member of His body. For which reason it is most truly said that faith without works is dead and of no profit, and in Christ Jesus neither circumcision availeth nor uncircumcision, but faith that worketh by charity. This faith, conformably to Apostolic tradition, catechumens ask of the Church before the sacrament of baptism, when they ask for the faith that gives eternal life, which without hope and charity faith cannot give. Whence also they hear immediately the word of Christ: If thou wilt enter into life, keep the commandments. Wherefore, when receiving true and Christian justice, they are commanded, immediately on being born again, to preserve it pure and spotless, as the first robe given them through Christ Jesus in place of that which Adam by his disobedience lost for himself and for us, so that they may bear it before the tribunal of our Lord Jesus Christ and may have life eternal.

CHAPTER VIII. HOW THE GRATUITOUS JUSTIFICATION OF THE SINNER BY FAITH IS TO BE UNDERSTOOD.

But when the Apostle says that man is justified by faith and freely, these words are to be understood in that sense in which the uninterrupted unanimity of the Catholic Church has held and expressed them, namely, that we are therefore said to be justified by faith, because faith is the beginning of human salvation, the foundation and root of all justification, without which it is impossible to please God and to come to the fellowship of His sons; and we are therefore said to be justified gratuitously, because none of those things that precede justification, whether faith or works, merit the grace of justification. For, if by grace, it is not now by works, otherwise, as the Apostle says, grace is no more grace.

CHAPTER IX. AGAINST THE VAIN CONFIDENCE OF THE HERETICS.

But though it is necessary to believe that sins neither are remitted nor ever have been remitted except gratuitously by divine mercy for Christ's sake, yet it must not be said that sins are forgiven or have been forgiven to anyone who boasts of his confidence and certainty of the remission of his sins, resting on that alone, though among heretics and schismatics this vain and ungodly confidence may be and in our troubled times indeed is found and preached with untiring fury against the Catholic Church. Moreover, it must not be maintained, that they who are truly justified must needs, without any doubt whatever, convince themselves that they are justified, and that no one is absolved from sins and justified except he that believes with certainty that he is absolved and justified, and that absolution and justification are effected by this faith alone, as if he who does not believe this, doubts the promises of God and the efficacy of the death and resurrection of Christ. For as no pious person ought to doubt the mercy of God, the merit of Christ and the virtue and efficacy of the sacraments, so each one, when he considers himself and his own weakness and indisposition, may have fear and apprehension concerning his own grace, since no one can know with the certainty of faith, which cannot be subject to error, that he has obtained the grace of God.

CHAPTER X. THE INCREASE OF THE JUSTIFICATION RECEIVED.

Having, therefore, been thus justified and made the friends and domestics of God, advancing from virtue to virtue, they are renewed, as the Apostle says, day by day, that is, mortifying the members of their flesh, and presenting them as instruments of justice unto sanctification, they, through the observance of the commandments of God and of the Church, faith co-operating with good works, increase in that justice received through the grace of Christ and are further justified, as it is written: He that is just, let him be justified still; and, Be not afraid to be justified even to death; and again, Do you see that by works a man is justified, and not by faith only? This increase of justice holy Church asks for when she prays: "Give unto us, O Lord, an increase of faith, hope and charity."

John Calvin and Reformed Theology

While Luther's father had wanted his son to become a lawyer, John Calvin's father wanted his son to become a priest. Ironically, Calvin (1509–1564) obtained a degree in law in 1532. Around the same time, the twenty-two-year-old, who was interested in the humanist Renaissance occurring about him in Paris, converted to Protestantism. The lawyer became a minister after fleeing a largely Catholic France to the relative safety of Basel, Switzerland. However, his legal training remains evident in his major work, *The Institutes of the Christian Religion,* which he wrote and rewrote many times.

Whereas even Luther's critics admire his passion and warmth, Calvin's friends admit their hero's reserve and coldness. He has been described as censorious, petty, uncompromising, stern, and humorless. And whereas Luther was scattered and aimed his thoughts with a shotgun, Calvin was focused and shot with a laser. Luther's pessimism led him to conclude that two kingdoms existed: one a heavenly kingdom of peace and perfection, the other an earthly kingdom in which princes and magistrates maintained law and order, by force if necessary. Christians were members of both kingdoms, according to Luther. Although Calvin shared Luther's low opinion of the nature of humanity, he did believe that Christians could, and should, attempt to create a perfect society in which Christian values reigned supreme.

Though Calvin himself was far from reaching his goal of uniting religious and secular rule into a single entity, he came close in sharing religious authority with the magistrates in the city of Geneva. A type of church court, the consistory, monitored personal behavior—rather like a morals police—and criminalized personal and religious behavior under civil statute. Some anecdotes reveal Calvin's uncompromising attitudes, or pettiness if you will. He required a critic, for example, not just to apologize to him privately but to parade through the streets of Geneva in a shirt, asking for God's mercy. Calvin did not suffer fools or sin gladly.

Calvin's critical view of human nature rested on his belief in the sovereignty of God. God was absolute, and absolute mystery at that. Nothing that humans did could affect or change the unfathomable will of God. To claim, for example, that humans might play a role in their own salvation was blasphemy that denied God's awesome majesty and suggested that God's activity was contingent on human activity or will. Unthinkable! Thus, before God, all of us were sinners, inheriting the sin that Adam and Eve committed. God graciously selected some people for eternal life while condemning the rest to eternal death. This selection for salvation—called election or predestination—was much more than we deserved, considering our wretched state of sin.

Later Calvinists, such as John Knox (1513–1572), the founder of Presbyterianism, and others took Calvin's doctrine of election still further and began to look for signs of God's favor. We can never know for sure whom God has elected, but we might get a fair idea if we look at how people are living. If they appear moral, upright, and godly; if they prosper in their affairs, and have obedient children and a modest wife; then apparently they are among God's elect. Calvin himself, though, asserted that we simply cannot know our true state in this life.

Calvin outlines in great detail his understanding of the divine will in his *Institutes*. The four-volume work begins with "the knowledge of God the Creator" and moves to "the knowledge of God the Redeemer in Christ." It then discusses how humans receive Christ's grace and its benefits, and finally, how Christians are to live in the society of Christ. This last section deals primarily with ecclesiology, much of it an attack on the papacy and a call to return to the "ancient form of [church] government." Calvin states in his preface to the *Institutes* that "it has been my purpose in this labor to prepare and instruct candidates in sacred theology for the reading of the divine Word, in order that they may be able both to have easy access to it and to advance in it without stumbling." In other words, his purpose in composing the *Institutes* is to give readers the background for properly understanding the meaning of scripture.

The Readings

The reading by Calvin comes from the first chapter of Book 2 of the *Institutes:* "By the Fall and Revolt of Adam the Whole Human Race Was Delivered to the Curse, and Degenerated from Its Original Condition; the Doctrine of Original Sin." The title tells exactly what Calvin plans to discuss. First, we know that it will examine the story of Adam and Eve in Genesis 2–3. We also see that Adam's actions had consequences for the whole human race. Calvin notes that we fell or degenerated from a condition that was perfect, or as he points out in Book 1, in the image and likeness of God, citing Genesis 1:26–27. Finally, we see that Calvin will present the doctrine, or teaching, of Original Sin.

Note: Calvin affirms a teaching by Bernard in the following selection. He is referring to Bernard of Clairvaux, the Cistercian monastic we read about in Chapter Three.

Questions to Consider

1. What does it mean to "know thyself," as far as Calvin is concerned?

2. What is the doctrine of Original Sin, according to Calvin?

3. Think back to Chapter One and the readings from Genesis 1–3. What does Calvin appropriate from those readings? What does he neglect or ignore? How is this relevant to his argument?

4. How is original sin different from personal sin? How does Calvin view human nature?

5. What is Calvin's view about other Christian writers, whom he calls "fathers" of the church?

6. Calvin mentions a Christian from the fifth century named Pelagius, and one of Pelagius' followers, Caelestius. Can you deduce what Pelagius and Caelestius taught, based on what Calvin said about them?

7. What elements of Augustine's *City of God,* if any, do you find in Calvin?

8. How is the Reformed view of Original Sin different from the Catholic view, as expressed in the Canons of Trent that follow? How are the two views similar?

By the Fall and Revolt of Adam the Whole Human Race Was Delivered to the Curse, and Degenerated from Its Original Condition; the Doctrine of Original Sin

JOHN CALVIN

1. WRONG AND RIGHT KNOWLEDGE OF SELF

With good reason the ancient proverb strongly recommended knowledge of self to man. For if it is considered disgraceful for us not to know all that pertains to the business of human life, even more detestable is our ignorance of ourselves, by which, when making decisions in necessary matters, we miserably deceive and even blind ourselves!

But since this precept is so valuable, we ought more diligently to avoid applying it perversely. This, we observe, has happened to certain philosophers, who, while urging man to know himself, propose the goal of recognizing his own worth and excellence. And they would have him contemplate in himself nothing but what swells him with empty assurance and puffs him up with pride [Genesis 1:27].

But knowledge of ourselves lies first in considering what we were given at creation and how generously God continues his favor toward us, in order to know how great our natural excellence would be if only it had remained unblemished; yet at the same time to bear in mind that there is in us nothing of our own, but that we hold on sufferance whatever God has bestowed upon us. Hence we are ever dependent on him. Secondly, to call to mind our miserable condition after Adam's fall; the awareness of which, when all our boasting and self-assurance are laid low, should truly humble us and overwhelm us with shame. In the beginning God fashioned us after his image [Genesis 1:27] that he might arouse our minds both to zeal for virtue and to meditation upon eternal life. Thus, in order that the great nobility of our race (which distinguishes us from brute beasts) may not be buried beneath our own dullness of wit, it behooves us to recognize that we have been endowed with reason and understanding so that, by leading a holy and upright life, we may press on to the appointed goal of blessed immortality.

But that primal worthiness cannot come to mind without the sorry spectacle of our foulness and dishonor presenting itself by way of contrast, since in the person of the first man we have fallen from our original condition. From this source arise abhorrence and displeasure with ourselves, as well as true humility; and thence is kindled a new zeal to seek God, in whom each of us may recover those good things which we have utterly and completely lost.

2. MAN BY NATURE INCLINES TO DELUDED SELF-ADMIRATION

Here, then, is what God's truth requires us to seek in examining ourselves: it requires the kind of knowledge that will strip us of all confidence in our own ability, deprive us of all occasion for boasting, and lead us to submission. We ought to keep this rule if we wish to reach the true goal of both wisdom and action. I am quite aware how much more pleasing is that principle which invites us to weigh our good traits rather than to look upon our miserable want and dishonor, which ought to overwhelm us with shame. There is, indeed, nothing that man's nature seeks more eagerly than to be flattered. Accordingly, when his nature becomes aware that its gifts are highly esteemed, it tends to be unduly credulous about them. It is thus no wonder that the majority of men have erred so perniciously in this respect. For, since blind self-love is innate in all mortals, they are most freely persuaded that nothing inheres in themselves that deserves to be considered hateful. Thus even with no outside support the utterly vain opinion generally obtains credence that man is abundantly sufficient of himself to lead a good and blessed life. But if any take a more modest attitude and concede something to God, so as not to appear to claim everything for themselves, they so divide the credit that the chief basis for boasting and confidence remains in themselves.

Nothing pleases man more than the sort of alluring talk that tickles the pride that itches in his very marrow. Therefore, in nearly every age, when anyone publicly extolled human nature in most favorable terms, he was listened to with applause. But however great such commendation of human excellence is that teaches man to be satisfied with himself, it does nothing but delight in its own sweetness; indeed, it so deceives as to drive those who assent to it into utter ruin. For what do we accomplish when, relying upon every vain assurance, we consider, plan, try, and undertake what we think is fitting; then—while in our very first efforts we are actually forsaken by and destitute of sane understanding as well as true virtue—we nonetheless rashly press on until we hurtle to destruction? Yet for those confident they can do anything by their own power, things cannot happen otherwise. Whoever, then, heeds such teachers as hold us back with thought only of our good traits will not advance in self-knowledge, but will be plunged into the worst ignorance.

3. THE TWO CHIEF PROBLEMS OF SELF-KNOWLEDGE

God's truth, therefore, agrees with the common judgment of all mortals, that the second part of wisdom consists in the knowledge of ourselves; yet there is much disagreement as to how we acquire that knowledge. According to carnal judgment, man seems to know himself very well, when, confident in his understanding and uprightness, he becomes bold and urges himself to the duties of virtue and, declaring war on vices, endeavors to exert himself with all his ardor toward the excellent and the honorable. But he who scrutinizes and examines himself according to the standard of divine judgment finds nothing to lift his heart to self-confidence. And the more deeply he examines himself, the more dejected he becomes, until, utterly deprived of all such assurance, he leaves nothing to himself with which to direct his life aright.

Yet God would not have us forget our original nobility, which he had bestowed upon our father Adam, and which ought truly to arouse in us a zeal for righteousness and goodness. For we cannot think upon either our first condition or to what purpose we were formed without being prompted to meditate upon immortality, and to yearn after the Kingdom of God. That recognition, however, far from encouraging pride in us, discourages us and casts us into humility. For what is that origin? It is that from which we have fallen. What is that end of our creation? It is that from which we have been completely estranged, so that sick of our miserable lot we groan, and in groaning we sigh for that lost worthiness. But when we say that man ought to see nothing in himself to cause elation, we mean that he has nothing to rely on to make him proud.

Therefore, if it is agreeable, let us divide the knowledge that man ought to have of himself. First, he should consider for what purpose he was created and endowed with no mean gifts. By this knowledge he should arouse himself to meditation upon divine worship and the future life. Secondly, he should weigh his own abilities or rather, lack of abilities. When he perceives this lack, he should lie prostrate in extreme confusion, so to speak, reduced to nought. The first consideration tends to make him recognize the nature of his duty; the second, the extent of his ability to carry it out. We shall discuss each as the order of teaching demands.

4. THE HISTORY OF THE FALL SHOWS US WHAT SIN IS: UNFAITHFULNESS

Because what God so severely punished must have been no light sin but a detestable crime, we must consider what kind of sin there was in Adam's desertion that enkindled God's fearful vengeance against the whole of mankind. To regard Adam's sin as gluttonous intemperance (a common notion) is childish. As if the sum and head of all virtues lay in abstaining solely from one fruit, when all sorts of desirable delights abounded everywhere; and not only abundance but also magnificent variety was at hand in that blessed fruitfulness of earth!

We ought therefore to look more deeply. Adam was denied the tree of the knowledge of good and evil to test his obedience and prove that he was willingly under God's command. The very name of the tree shows the sole purpose of the precept was to keep him content with his lot and to prevent him from becoming puffed up with wicked lust. But the promise by which he was bidden to hope for eternal life so long as he ate from the tree of life, and, conversely, the terrible threat of death once he tasted of the tree of the knowledge of good and evil, served to prove and exercise his faith. Hence it is not hard to deduce by what means Adam provoked God's wrath upon himself. Indeed, Augustine speaks rightly when he declares that pride was the beginning of all evils. For if ambition had not raised man higher than was meet and right, he could have remained in his original state.

But we must take a fuller definition from the nature of the temptation which Moses describes. Since the woman through unfaithfulness was led away from God's Word by the serpent's deceit, it is already clear that disobedience was the beginning of the Fall. This Paul also confirms, teaching that all were lost through the disobedience of one man [Romans 5:19]. Yet it is at the same time to be noted that the first man revolted from God's authority, not only because he was seized by Satan's blandishments, but also because, contemptuous of truth, he turned aside to falsehood. And surely, once we hold God's Word in contempt, we shake off all reverence for him. For, unless we listen attentively to him, his majesty will not dwell among us, nor his worship remain perfect. Unfaithfulness, then, was the root of the Fall. But thereafter ambition and pride, together with ungratefulness, arose, because Adam by seeking more than was granted him shamefully spurned God's great bounty, which had been lavished upon him. To have been made in the likeness of God seemed a small matter to a son of earth unless he also attained equality with God—a monstrous wickedness! If apostasy, by which man withdraws from the authority of his Maker—indeed insolently shakes off his yoke is a foul and detestable offense, it is vain to extenuate Adam's sin. Yet it was not simple apostasy, but was joined with vile reproaches against God. These assented to Satan's slanders, which accused God of falsehood and envy and ill will. Lastly, faithlessness opened the door to ambition, and ambition was indeed the mother of obstinate disobedience; as a result, men, having cast off the fear of God, threw themselves wherever lust carried them. Hence Bernard rightly teaches that the door of salvation is opened to us when we receive the gospel today with our ears, even as death was then admitted by those same windows when they were opened to Satan [Jeremiah 9:21]. For Adam would never have dared oppose God's authority unless he had disbelieved in God's Word. Here, indeed, was the best bridle to control all passions: the thought that nothing is better than to practice righteousness by obeying God's commandments; then, that the ultimate goal of the happy life is to be loved by him. Therefore Adam, carried away by the devil's blasphemies, as far as he was able extinguished the whole glory of God.

5. THE FIRST SIN AS ORIGINAL SIN

As it was the spiritual life of Adam to remain united bound to his Maker, so estrangement from him was the death of his soul. Nor is it any wonder that he consigned his race to ruin by his rebellion when he perverted the whole order of nature in heaven and on earth. "All creatures," says Paul, "are groaning" [Romans 8:22], "subject to corruption, not of their own will" [8:20]. If the cause is sought, there is no doubt that they are bearing part of the punishment deserved by man, for whose use they were created. Since, therefore, the curse, which goes about through all the regions of the world, flowed hither and yon from Adam's guilt, it is not unreasonable if it is spread to all his offspring. Therefore, after the heavenly image was obliterated in him, he was not the only one to suffer this punishment—that, in place of wisdom, virtue, holiness, truth, and justice, with which adornments he had been clad, there came forth the most filthy plagues, blindness, impotence, impurity, vanity, and injustice—but he also entangled and immersed his offspring in the same miseries.

This is the inherited corruption, which the church fathers termed "original sin," meaning by the word "sin" the depravation of a nature previously good and pure. There was much contention over this matter, inasmuch as nothing is farther from the usual view than for all to be made guilty by the guilt of one, and thus for sin to be made common. This seems to be the reason why the most ancient doctors of the church touched upon this subject so obscurely. At least they explained it less clearly than was fitting. Yet this timidity could not prevent Pelagius from rising up with the profane fiction that Adam sinned only to his own loss without harming his posterity. Through this subtlety Satan attempted to cover up the disease and thus to render it incurable. But when it was shown by the clear testimony of Scripture that sin was transmitted from the first man to all his posterity [Romans 5:12], Pelagius quibbled that it was transmitted through imitation, not propagation. Therefore, good men (and Augustine above the rest) labored to show us that we are corrupted not by derived wickedness, but that we bear inborn defect from our mother's womb. To deny this was the height of shamelessness. But no man will wonder at the temerity of the Pelagians and Coelestians when he perceived from that holy man's warnings what shameless beasts they were in all other respects. Surely there is no doubt that David confesses himself to have been "begotten in iniquities, and conceived by his mother in sin" [Psalm 51:5]. There he does not reprove his father and mother for their sins; but, that he may better commend God's goodness toward himself, from his very conception he carries the confession of his

own perversity. Since it is clear that this was not peculiar to David, it follows that the common lot of mankind is exemplified in him.

Therefore all of us, who have descended from impure seed, are born infected with the contagion of sin. In fact, before we saw the light of this life we were soiled and spotted in God's sight. "For who can bring a clean thing from an unclean?) There is not one"—as The Book of Job says [Job 14:4, following the Vulgate].

6. ORIGINAL SIN DOES NOT REST UPON IMITATION

We hear that the uncleanness of the parents is so transmitted to the children that all without any exception are defiled at their begetting. But we will not find the beginning of this pollution unless we go back to the first parent of all as its source. We must surely hold that Adam was not only the progenitor but, as it were, the root of human nature; and that therefore in his corruption mankind deserved to be vitiated. This the apostle makes clear from a comparison of Adam with Christ. "As through one man sin came into the world and through sin death, which spread among all men when all sinned" [Romans 5: 12], thus through Christ's grace righteousness and life are restored to us [5:17]. What nonsense will the Pelagians chatter here? That Adam's sin was propagated by imitation? Then does Christ's righteousness benefit us only as an example set before us to imitate? Who can bear such sacrilege! But if it is beyond controversy that Christ's righteousness, and thereby life, are ours by communication, it immediately follows that both were lost in Adam, only to be recovered in Christ; and that sin and death crept in through Adam, only to be abolished through Christ. These are no obscure words: "Many are made righteous by Christ's obedience as by Adam's disobedience they had been made sinners" [Romans 5:19]. Here, then, is the relationship between the two: Adam, implicating us in his ruin, destroyed us with himself; but Christ restores us to salvation by his grace.

In such clear light of truth, I think that there is no need for longer or more laborious proof. In the first letter to the Corinthians, Paul wishes to strengthen the faith of the godly in the resurrection. Here he accordingly shows that the life lost in Adam is recovered in Christ [1 Corinthians 15:22]. Declaring that all of us died in Adam, Paul at the same time plainly testifies that we are infected with the disease of sin. For condemnation could not reach those untouched by the guilt of iniquity. The clearest explanation of his meaning lies in the other part of the statement, in which he declares that the hope of life is restored in Christ. But it is well known that this occurs in no other way than that wonderful communication whereby Christ transfuses into us the power of his righteousness. As it is written elsewhere, "The Spirit is life to us because of righteousness" [Romans 8:10]. There is consequently but one way for us to interpret the statement, "We have died in Adam": Adam, by sinning, not only took upon himself misfortune and ruin but also plunged our nature into like destruction. This was not due to the guilt of himself alone, which would not pertain to us at all, but was because he infected all his posterity with that corruption into which he had fallen.

Paul's statement that "by nature all are children of wrath" [Ephesians 2:3] could not stand, unless they had already been cursed in the womb itself. Obviously, Paul does not mean "nature" as it was established by God, but as it was vitiated in Adam. For it would be most unfitting for God to be made the author of death. Therefore, Adam so corrupted himself that infection spread from him to all his descendants. Christ himself, our heavenly judge, clearly enough proclaims that all men are born wicked and depraved when he says that "whatever is born of flesh is flesh" [John 3:6], and therefore the door of life is closed to all until they have been reborn [3:5].

7. THE TRANSMISSION OF SIN FROM ONE GENERATION TO ANOTHER

No anxious discussion is needed to understand this question, which troubled the fathers not a little—whether the son's soul proceeds by derivation from the father's soul—because the contagion chiefly lies in it. With this we ought to be content: that the Lord entrusted to Adam those gifts which he willed to be conferred upon human nature. Hence Adam, when he lost the gifts received, lost them not only for himself but for us all. Who should worry about the derivation of the soul when he hears that Adam had received for us no less than for himself those gifts which he lost, and that they had not been given to one man but had been assigned to the whole human race? There is nothing absurd, then, in supposing that, when Adam was despoiled, human nature was left naked and destitute, or that when he was infected with sin, contagion crept into human nature. Hence, rotten branches came forth from a rotten root, which transmitted their

rottenness to the other twigs sprouting from them. For thus were the children corrupted in the parent, so that they brought disease upon their children's children. That is, the beginning of corruption in Adam was such that it was conveyed in a perpetual stream from the ancestors into their descendants. For the contagion does not take its origin from the substance of the flesh or soul, but because it had been so ordained by God that the first man should at one and the same time have and lose, both for himself and for his descendants, the gifts that God had bestowed upon him.

But it is easy to refute the quibble of the Pelagians, who hold it unlikely that children should derive corruption from godly parents, inasmuch as the offspring ought rather to be sanctified by their parents' purity [1 Corinthians 7:14]. For they descend not from their parents' spiritual regeneration but from their carnal generation. Hence, as Augustine says, whether a man is a guilty unbeliever or an innocent believer, he begets not innocent but guilty children, for he begets them from a corrupted nature. Now, it is a special blessing of God's people that they partake in some degree of their parents' holiness. This does not gainsay the fact that the universal curse of the human race preceded. For guilt is of nature, but sanctification, of supernatural grace.

8. THE NATURE OF ORIGINAL SIN

So that these remarks may not be made concerning an uncertain and unknown matter, let us define original sin. It is not my intention to investigate the several definitions proposed by various writers, but simply to bring forward the one that appears to me most in accordance with truth. Original sin, therefore, seems to be a hereditary depravity and corruption of our nature, diffused into all parts of the soul, which first makes us liable to God's wrath, then also brings forth in us those works which Scripture calls "works of the flesh" [Galatians 5:19]. And that is properly what Paul often calls sin. The works that come forth from it—such as adulteries, fornications, thefts, hatreds, murders, carousings—he accordingly calls "fruits of sin" [5:19-21], although they are also commonly called "sins" in Scripture, and even by Paul himself.

We must, therefore, distinctly note these two things. First, we are so vitiated and perverted in every part of our nature that by this great corruption we stand justly condemned and convicted before God, to whom nothing is acceptable but righteousness, innocence, and purity. And this is not liability for another's transgression. For, since it is said that we became subject to God's judgment through Adam's sin, we are to understand it not as if we, guiltless and undeserving, bore the guilt of his offense but in the sense that, since we through his transgression have become entangled in the curse, he is said to have made us guilty. Yet not only has punishment fallen upon us from Adam, but a contagion imparted by him resides in us, which justly deserves punishment. For this reason, Augustine, though he often calls sin "another's" to show more clearly that it is distributed among us through propagation, nevertheless declares at the same time that it is peculiar to each. And the apostle himself most eloquently testifies that "death has spread to all because all have sinned" [Romans 5:12]. That is, they have been enveloped in original sin and defiled by its stains. For that reason, even infants themselves, while they carry their condemnation along with them from the mother's womb, are guilty not of another's fault but of their own. For, even though the fruits of their iniquity have not yet come forth, they have the seed enclosed within them. Indeed, their whole nature is a seed of sin; hence it can be only hateful and abhorrent to God. From this it follows that it is rightly considered sin in God's sight, for without guilt there would be no accusation.

Then comes the second consideration: that this perversity never ceases in us, but continually bears new fruits—the works of the flesh that we have already described—just as a burning furnace gives forth flame and sparks, or water ceaselessly bubbles up from a spring. Thus those who have defined original sin as "the lack of the original righteousness, which ought to reside in us," although they comprehend in this definition the whole meaning of the term, have still not expressed effectively enough its power and energy. For our nature is not only destitute and empty of good, but so fertile and fruitful of every evil that it cannot be idle. Those who have said that original sin is "concupiscence" have used an appropriate word, if only it be added—something that most will by no means concede—that whatever is in man, from the understanding to the will, from the soul even to the flesh, has been defiled and crammed with this concupiscence. Or, to put it more briefly, the whole man is of himself nothing but concupiscence.

9. SIN OVERTURNS THE WHOLE MAN

For this reason, I have said that all parts of the soul were possessed by sin after Adam deserted the fountain of righteousness. For not only did a lower appetite

seduce him, but unspeakable impiety occupied the very citadel of his mind, and pride penetrated to the depths of his heart. Thus it is pointless and foolish to restrict the corruption that arises thence only to what are called the impulses of the senses, or to call it the "kindling wood" that attracts, arouses, and drags into sin only that part which they term "sensuality." In this matter Peter Lombard has betrayed his complete ignorance. For, in seeking and searching out its seat, he says that it lies in the flesh, as Paul testifies; yet not intrinsically, but because it appears more in the flesh. As if Paul were indicating that only a part of the soul, and not its entire nature, is opposed to supernatural grace! Paul removes all doubt when he teaches that corruption subsists not in one part only, but that none of the soul remains pure or untouched by that mortal disease. For in his discussion of a corrupt nature Paul not only condemns the inordinate impulses of the appetites that are seen, but especially contends the mind is given over to blindness and the heart to depravity.

The whole third chapter of Romans is nothing but a description of original sin. From the "renewal" that fact appears more clearly. For the Spirit, who is opposed to the old man and to the flesh, not only marks the grace whereby the lower or sensual part of the soul is corrected, but embraces the full reformation of all the parts. Consequently, Paul not only enjoins that brute appetites be brought to nought but bids us "be renewed in the spirit of our mind" [Ephesians 4:23]; in another passage he similarly urges us to "be transformed in newness of mind" [Romans 12:2]. From this it follows that that part in which the excellence and nobility of the soul especially shine has not only been wounded, but so corrupted that it needs to be healed and to put on a new nature as well. We shall soon see to what extent sin occupies both mind and heart. Here I only want to suggest briefly that the whole man is overwhelmed—as by a deluge—from head to foot, so that no part is immune from sin and all that proceeds from him is to be imputed to sin. As Paul says, all turnings of the thoughts to the flesh are enmities against God [Romans 8:7], and are therefore death [8:6].

10. SIN IS NOT OUR NATURE, BUT ITS DERANGEMENT

Now away with those persons who dare write God's name upon their faults, because we declare that men are vicious by nature! They perversely search out God's handiwork in their own pollution, when they ought rather to have sought it in that unimpaired and uncorrupted nature of Adam. Our destruction, therefore, comes from the guilt of our flesh, not from God, inasmuch as we have perished solely because we have degenerated from our original condition.

Let no one grumble here that God could have provided better for our salvation if he had forestalled Adam's fall. Pious minds ought to loathe this objection, because it manifests inordinate curiosity. Furthermore, the matter has to do with the secret of predestination, which will be discussed later in its proper place. Let us accordingly remember to impute our ruin to depravity of nature, in order that we may not accuse God himself, the Author of nature. True, this deadly wound clings to nature, but it is a very important question whether the wound has been inflicted from outside or has been present from the beginning. Yet it is evident that the wound was inflicted through sin. We have, therefore, no reason to complain except against ourselves. Scripture has diligently noted this fact. For Ecclesiastes says: "This I know, that God made man upright, but they have sought out many devices." [7:29.] Obviously, man's ruin is to be ascribed to man alone; for he, having acquired righteousness by God's kindness, has by his own folly sunk into vanity.

11. "NATURAL" CORRUPTION OF THE "NATURE" CREATED BY GOD

Therefore we declare that man is corrupted through natural vitiation, but a vitiation that did not flow from nature. We deny that it has flowed from nature in order to indicate that it is an adventitious quality which comes upon man rather than a substantial property which has been implanted from the beginning. Yet we call it "natural" in order that no man may think that anyone obtains it through bad conduct, since it holds all men fast by hereditary right. Our usage of the term is not without authority. The apostle states: "We are all by nature children of wrath" [Ephesians. 2:3]. How could God, who is pleased by the least of his works, have been hostile to the noblest of all his creatures? But he is hostile toward the corruption of his work rather than toward the work itself. Therefore if it is right to declare that man, because of his vitiated nature, is naturally abominable to God, it is also proper to say that man is naturally depraved and faulty. Hence Augustine, in view of man's corrupted nature, is not afraid to call "natural" those sins which necessarily reign in our flesh wherever God's grace is absent. Thus vanishes the foolish trifling of the Manichees, who, when they imagined wickedness of substance in man, dared fashion another creator for him in order that they might not seem to assign the cause and beginning of evil to the righteous God.*

---

* The Manichees were followers of Mani, a third-century Mesopotamian mystic who taught that good and evil were two distinctly different substances. Thus, the Manichees were radical dualists who believed in a sharp distinction between the righteous and unrighteous.

Original Sin and the Council of Trent

What follows below is the Decree Concerning Original Sin adopted by the Council of Trent. How does the decree compare with Calvin on the issue of original sin? How does it compare with Augustine? Finally, what concerns are indicated by the document?

Vocabulary note: A certain phrase frequently appears at the end of each canon: "let him be anathema." We saw this expression in the Nicene Creed in Chapter Two. Remember, *anathema* means, "let him be damned" or, more colloquially, "he can go to hell."

Decree Concerning Original Sin

COUNCIL OF TRENT, FIFTH SESSION, 17 JUNE 1546

That our Catholic faith, *without which it is impossible to please God,* may, after the destruction of errors, remain integral and spotless in its purity, and that the Christian people may not be *carried about with every wind of doctrine,* since that old serpent, the everlasting enemy of the human race, has, among the many evils with which the Church of God is in our times disturbed, stirred up also not only new but also old dissensions concerning original sin and its remedy, the holy, ecumenical and general Council of Trent, lawfully assembled in the Holy Ghost, the same three legates of the Apostolic See presiding, wishing now to reclaim the erring and to strengthen the wavering, and following the testimonies of the Holy Scriptures, of the holy Fathers, of the most approved councils, as well as the judgment and unanimity of the Church herself, ordains, confesses and declares these things concerning original sin:

1. If anyone does not confess that the first man, Adam, when he transgressed the commandment of God in paradise, immediately lost the holiness and justice in which he had been constituted, and through the offense of that prevarication incurred the wrath and indignation of God, and thus death with which God had previously threatened him, and, together with death, captivity under his power who thenceforth *had the empire of death, that is to say, the devil,* and that the entire Adam through that offense of prevarication was changed in body and soul for the worse, let him be anathema.

2. If anyone asserts that the transgression of Adam injured him alone and not his posterity, and that the holiness and justice which he received from God, which he lost, he lost for himself alone and not for us also; or that he, being defiled by the sin of disobedience, has transfused only death and the pains of the body into the whole human race, but not sin also, which is the death of the soul, let him be anathema, since he contradicts the Apostle who says: *By one man sin entered into the world and by sin death; and so death passed upon all men, in whom all have sinned.*

3. If anyone asserts that this sin of Adam, which in its origin is one, and by propagation, not by imitation, transfused into all, which is in each one as something that is his own, is taken away either by the forces of human nature or by a remedy other than the merit of the one mediator, our Lord Jesus Christ, who has reconciled us to God in his blood, *made unto us justice, sanctification and redemption;* or if he denies that that merit of Jesus Christ is applied both to adults and to infants by the sacrament of baptism rightly administered in the form of the Church, let him be anathema; *for there is no other name under heaven given to men, whereby we must be saved.* Whence that declaration: *Behold the Lamb of God, behold him who taketh away the sins of the world,* and that other: *As many of you as have been baptized, have put on Christ.*

4. If anyone denies that infants, newly born from their mothers' wombs, are to be baptized, even though they be born of baptized parents, or says that they are indeed *baptized for the remission of sins,* but that they derive nothing of original sin from Adam which must be expiated by the laver of regeneration for the attainment of eternal life, whence it follows that in them the form of baptism for the remission of sins is to be understood not as true but as false, let him be anathema, for what the Apostle has said, *by one man sin entered into the world, and by sin death, and so death passed upon all men, in whom all have sinned,* is not to be understood otherwise than as the Catholic Church has everywhere and always understood it. For in virtue of this rule of faith handed down from the apostles, even infants who could not as yet commit any sin of themselves, are for this reason truly baptized for the remission of sins, in order that in them what they contracted by generation may be washed away by regeneration. For, *unless a man be born again of water and the Holy Ghost, he cannot enter into the kingdom of heaven.*

5. If anyone denies that by the grace of our Lord Jesus Christ which is conferred in baptism, the guilt of original sin is remitted, or says that the whole of that which belongs to the essence of sin is not taken away, but says that it is only canceled or not imputed, let him be anathema. For in those who are born again God hates nothing, because *there is no*

condemnation to those who are truly *buried together with Christ by baptism unto death, who walk not according to the flesh,* but putting off the old man and putting on the new one who is created according to God, are made innocent, immaculate, pure, guiltless and beloved of God, *heirs indeed of God, joint heirs with Christ;* so that there is nothing whatever to hinder their entrance into heaven. But this holy council perceives and confesses that in the one baptized there remains concupiscence or an inclination to sin, which, since it is left for us to wrestle with, cannot injure those who do not acquiesce but resist manfully by the grace of Jesus Christ; indeed, he who shall have *striven lawfully shall be crowned.* This concupiscence, which the Apostle sometimes calls sin, the holy council declares the Catholic Church has never understood to be called sin in the sense that it is truly and properly sin in those born again, but in the sense that it is of sin and inclines to sin. But if anyone is of the contrary opinion, let him be anathema.

This holy council declares, however, that it is not its intention to include in this decree, which deals with original sin, the blessed and immaculate Virgin Mary, the mother of God, but that the constitutions of Pope Sixtus IV, of happy memory, are to be observed under the penalties contained in those constitutions, which it renews.

The Anglican Reformation

Although the Lutheran and Calvinist reformations began as religious and theological protests against a misplaced trust in ecclesiastical, rather than scriptural, authority, they quickly gained government support in ethnic and regional politics. Princes and dukes, queens and countesses were generally Christians concerned about how to govern their subjects so that leader and subject alike would gain salvation. Luther's views appealed to German princes who chafed under papal claims and who eyed the tithes paid to the church as potential tax revenues. Calvin's reforms pleased some, though not all, of the cantons of Switzerland and spread to the low countries (the Netherlands), where the humanist Renaissance had already planted the idea of scriptural authority and individual responsibility.

The Anglican Reformation, in contrast, began as a political revolt against the papacy, and later developed a coherent theology, which blended Catholic practices and Reformed teachings into a unique form of Protestantism. Quite simply, King Henry VIII of England (1491–1547) sought a male heir to the throne. His first wife did not produce one, and he wanted a divorce. Pope Clement VII dithered and dallied so long that the king grew impatient, divorced Catherine of Aragon himself, and secretly married Anne Boleyn. Then, in 1534, Henry persuaded the English Parliament to pass the Act of Supremacy, which stated that the king, not the pope, was the head of the church in England. In all other respects, the English church was the same—and yet it was wildly different. Overnight, priests and prelates who were loyal to the supreme pontiff, head of the church, were asked to declare allegiance to the king as their head. Needless to say, many did not accede, and they were executed as disloyal and traitorous subjects. We can see today why the moral character of potential kings and queens of England is a topic of debate, if the monarch is also to become head of the church—even if that is only a nominal title.

English church history during this turbulent time most resembles a tennis match, with Christianity bouncing back and forth between Catholic and Anglican (that is, English Protestant) forms depending on the beliefs of the ruler. When the Catholic Queen Mary (1516–1558) was in charge, Protestants were imprisoned and executed. When her Protestant sister Queen Elizabeth (1533–1603) ascended the throne, the execution of Catholics outpaced the execution of Protestants. English anti-Catholicism grew, however, as can be seen in both the language and literature of the era. Nevertheless, the Elizabethan Settlement, as the religious policies of Elizabeth I are called, moderated the extremes of Catholic and Protestant partisans, politically as well as theologically. Although it took more than a century, Anglican Christianity eventually prevailed in England, with its supporters seeing it as a middle way—a *via media*—between Puritanism and Catholicism.

The English crown benefited greatly from the expropriation of formerly Catholic Church lands and properties, as well as from state control of religious politics. Obviously, the monarch could not oversee the daily operation of the churches in England, and so the archbishop of Canterbury became the chief architect of church policy and practices. Church reform had been discussed well before the Act of Supremacy, and some accounts show that heated discussions on justification by faith were held at the London taverns. The most influential person during this chaotic time was Thomas Cranmer (1489–1556), the archbishop of Canterbury from 1533 to 1556.

Cranmer began his career as a moderate, but under the reign of King Edward VI, the young and sickly son of Henry VIII, he instituted far-reaching reforms that permanently changed the Church of England. However, times change, as do rulers, and under the Catholic Mary Tudor (Bloody Mary) he was imprisoned and began to recant many of his reforms. When his Protestant colleagues were burned at the stake, however, and he saw no escape for himself, he recanted his own recantations. Legend says that on the day of his execution, he thrust his right hand into the flames to signify his rejection of the hand that penned his recantations.

Chief among Cranmer's accomplishments was compiling the *Book of Common Prayer,* a guide to worship, liturgy, prayer, and practice. Although the *Book of Common Prayer* (BCP) has gone through numerous revisions over the centuries, it remains the central component of every Anglican church service in the world—from the Episcopal churches of the United States to the Anglican Church of South Africa headed by Archbishop Desmond Tutu.* The BCP outlines services for marriage, baptism, funerals, and, of course, communion. It contains the complete Psalter, that is, the entire book of Psalms. It has prayers for every occasion. It guides priests, as Anglican ministers are called, through a worship service that looks remarkably Catholic or Lutheran, although the BCP reflects a distinctly Calvinist theology. It was this family resemblance to Catholicism in both worship and church structure

---

* Archbishop Tutu played a key role in mobilizing Anglican Christians and others around the world against the racist apartheid system in South Africa.

▨ Scorecard for the Anglican Reformation

It can be difficult to keep track of the changes that occurred during the Anglican Reformation. Monarchs change, their identifying numerals change (for example, James VI of Scotland becomes James I of England!), and their religious affiliations change. And where and how does Puritanism fit into the mix? I have found that it is easiest to keep track of English historical developments by creating a roster of players on the various teams. The following chart displays the instability of religious politics in sixteenth- and seventeenth-century England.

Henry VIII	r. 1509–47	Catholic; but has the English Parliament declare the king to be head of the Church of England
Edward VI, Henry's son	r. 1547–53	Protestant; dominated by Archbishop Cranmer's Reformed theology; *Book of Common Prayer* written
Mary I, Henry's daughter	r. 1553–58	Catholic; reinstitutes Catholic practices, burns 300 Protestant leaders (Bloody Mary)
Elizabeth I, Henry's daughter	r. 1558–1603	Protestant; new *Book of Common Prayer* compiled; persecutes Catholic opponents, especially Mary Stuart of Scotland
James I (James VI of Scotland), son of Mary Stuart	r. 1603–25	Protestant, of Presbyterian, rather than Anglican, background; authorizes new translation of Bible into English—the King James Version
Charles I, son of James I	r. 1625–49	Makes concessions to English Catholics, enrages English Puritans; dissolves Parliament and rules eleven years without it
The Long Parliament	r. 1640–60	Abolishes Anglicanism, attempts to establish Puritan authority based on Scottish Presbyterian model
Oliver Cromwell, "Lord Protector"	r. 1653–58	Has Charles I executed; runs Long Parliament and manages the military; religious toleration not extended to Catholics, Anglicans, or Quakers
Richard Cromwell, "Lord Protector"	r. 1658-60	Unable to maintain control his father did
Charles II, son of Charles I	r. 1660–85	Catholic, but restores Anglican Church; period known as the Restoration; persecutes dissenters such as Anabaptists and Puritans
James II	r. 1685–88	Catholic, attempts to return England to Catholicism
William of Orange and Mary, daughter of James II	r. 1689–94	Rule jointly as William III and Mary II; return England to Anglicanism; issue Act of Toleration (all but Catholics and Unitarians tolerated)

that fostered the rise of Puritanism, a movement that sought to "purify" the Church of England of its "popish" (read: Catholic) elements. While Puritans wanted to stay a part of a "purified" Anglicanism, another group, the Separatists, believed that reform was hopeless, and thus wanted to break completely from the Anglican Church. Puritans and Separatists eventually made their way to the shores of North America, where they founded two new types of Protestant churches: Congregational and Baptist.

Under the Act of Uniformity in 1549, the English Parliament specified that the BCP was the *only* book that could be used for church services. This meant that important doctrinal issues, such as the sacrament of communion, were resolved liturgically rather than confessionally. While all Christians observe the Lord's Supper, as it is also called, by taking either bread and wine, or bread and juice or water, their interpretation of what it signifies, and why it is important, varies. The New Testament shows Jesus at his last meal with the disciples, giving them bread and wine, and saying that the bread is his body, the wine his blood (Mark 14:22–25; Matthew 26:26–29; Luke 22:14–20). During the Middle Ages, a debate arose over whether Jesus meant these words literally or figuratively. At the Fourth Lateran Council in 1215, the western church adopted the doctrine of transubstantiation, which says that the substances of the bread and wine (though not the literal molecules) become the body and blood of Christ, thereby signifying Christ's "real" presence in the elements, or symbols, of communion.*

Reformers during the sixteenth century began to question this doctrine. Some, like Luther, argued that Christ was indeed really and truly present in the bread and the wine, but that the substances did not actually change into flesh and blood. Modern theologians call this view "consubstantiation," though Luther never used that term. According to consubstantiation, Christ is present in and with the bread, but neither the bread nor the wine is transformed. Others, however, like Ulrich Zwingli (1484–1531), claimed that Christ was only spiritually present, and that if the Son was at the right hand of God the Father, then he couldn't also be present at the altar at the same time.

Additional questions arose as well. Was communion a sacrifice, as the Mass had been called? The New Testament seemed to say that Christ was the final sacrifice, that there were to be no future sacrifices. Could believers take both the bread and the wine? Medieval practice had been to provide only the bread, and not the cup. Could a priest or minister who was unworthy effectively perform the sacrament? Church tradition had argued that sacraments were effective regardless of the personal morality of individual priests, surely a comfort to Christians who knew that their religious leaders were flawed human beings. And what was the point of com-

---

* It is important to note that the concept of a "substance" is an Aristotelian idea adopted by medieval theologians. A substance cannot be seen, although it truly exists. Thus, the substances of bread and wine do actually change into the body and the blood—metaphysically if not physically.

munion anyway? Did one receive grace by participating? Was it merely helpful rather than absolutely necessary? There were many points of view on these questions.

The Readings

The Anglican *Book of Common Prayer* seems to adopt a spiritual, rather than literal, interpretation of the communion elements, although there is some debate on this. While Cranmer may have believed in the real presence of Christ in the bread and the wine, the language he uses indicates a spiritual understanding. Certainly, later Anglicans interpreted communion spiritually. Because the eucharist is such an important sacrament for Christians, and because communion was hotly debated during the Reformation, the following selection provides a service of Holy Eucharist as it appeared in the 1552 edition of Cranmer's BCP.

Since this is a service of liturgy, it was intended to be read out loud, to be heard, and to be contemplated. Furthermore, it was always read in a congregational setting. In other words, it was not recited, or read, during private meditation, but rather as part of a corporate worship service. There is no easy way to read this material, but certainly reading it out loud will clarify the old English spelling. It will also provide a sense of the ebb and flow of the service. An interesting side note is that sometimes the word *the* appears spelled as "ye"; we often see this spelling in modern stores attempting to simulate an antique feeling—as in "Ye Olde Book Shoppe." The apparent *y* in "ye" is called a "thorn," because the character looks a bit like a thorn or tree branch, and was intended to signify "th." Thus, when you see the word "ye" it may in fact be "you," or it may be "the," depending on the context. In addition, English spelling was not entirely fixed at this time in history; we will see "moe" and "more" in the same text, "yf" for "if," and a final *e* on many words: "soone," "doe," "saye," and so on—or as it appears below, "&c." Sometimes, the *e* is dropped, as in "els" for "else." Sometimes, consonants are doubled in the plural: "God" becomes "Goddes." Reading aloud, or sounding out words, helps us recognize them despite their unfamiliar spelling.

Questions to Consider

1. If you were to chart out the components of the communion service, what parts would you identify? How are creeds and scripture incorporated into the service?

2. What indications of a spiritual, rather than literal, interpretation of body and blood do you see in this service?

3. What historical insights can we deduce about the special words given to those who are negligent in attending communion?

4. How does the view of the eucharist differ between Anglicans and Catholics, as expressed in the service in the BCP and in the Canons of Trent that follow?

The Order for the Administracion of the Lordes Supper, or Holye Communion (1552)

THOMAS CRANMER

SO many as entend to be partakers of the holye Communion, shall sygnifye theyr names to the Curate over nyghte, or els in the morning, afore the begynninge of mornynge prayer, or immediatly after.

And yf any of those be an open and notorious evyll lyver, so that the congregacion by hym is offended, or have done anye wronge to his neyghbours, by woord or deede: The Curate havynge knowledge thereof, shall call hym, and advertyse him, in anye wyse not to presume to the Lordes Table, untyll he have openly declared hymselfe to have truely repented, and amended hys former naughtye lyfe, that the congregacion maye thereby be satisfyed, why-che afore were offended: and that he have rec-ompensed the parties, whome he hathe done wronge unto, or at the least declare hym selfe to be in full purpose so to doe, as soone as he conveniently maye.

⁋ *The same ordre shall the Curate use with those, betwyxte whome he perceyveth malyce and hatred to rayne, not sufferinge them to be partakers of the LORDES table, untyll he know them to be reconcyled. And yf one of the parties so at variaunce be content to forgeve, from the bottome of hys hearte, all that the other hathe trespassed agaynst hym, and to make amendes for that he hym selfe hath oflended: and the other partie wyll not be per-suaded to a godly unitie, but remayne styll in hys frowardnesse and malyce: The Minister in that case, ought to admytte the penitent per-son to the holy Communion, and not hym that is obstinate.*

⁋ *The Table havyng at the Communion tyme a fayre white lynnen clothe upon it, shall stande in the body of the Churche, or in the chauncell, where Morning prayer and Evening prayer be appoynted to bee sayde. And the Priest standing at the north syde of the Table,* shall saye the Lordes prayer, with thys Collecte folowinge.

ALMIGHTIE God, unto whom all heartes be open, all desyres knowen, and from whom no secretes are hyd: clense the thoughtes of our heartes by the inspiracion of thy holy spirit, that we maye perfectlye love thee, and worthely magnify thy holy name: through Christ our Lorde. Amen.

⁋ *Then shal the Priest rehearse distinctly all the Ten Commaundments: and the people knelyng, shal after every Commaundment aske Gods mercy for theyr transgression of the same, after thys sorte.*

Ministre:　God spake these wordes, and sayd: I am the Lord thy God. Thou shalt have none other Goddes but me.

People:　Lord, have mercye upon us, and encline our heartes to kepe this lawe.

Ministre:　Thou shalt not make to thy selfe any graven ymage nor the likeness of any thyng that is in heaven above, or in the yearthe beneath, nor in the water under the yearth. Thou shalte not bowe downe to them, nor worshyppe them: for I the lord thy God am a gelous God, and visite the sinne of the fathers upon the children, unto the thyrde and fourth generacion of them that hate me, and shewe mercye unto thousandes in them that love me and kepe my commaundments.

People:　Lord, have mercye upon us, and encline our heartes to kepe thys lawe.

Ministre:　Thou shalte not take the name of the lord thy God in vayne: for the lord wil not holde him gilteles that taketh his name in vayne.

People:　Lord, have mercye upon us, and encline our. &c.

Ministre: Remembre that thou kepe holy the Sabboth day. Vi dayes shalt thou laboure and doe all that thou haste to doe, but the seventh day is the sabboth of the lorde thy god. In it thou shalte doe no maner of woork, thou and thy sonne and thy daughter, thy man servaunt, and thy maidservant, thy Catel, and the straunger that is within thy gates: for in vi days the lord made heaven and earth, the Sea, and al that in them is, and rested the seventh daye. Wherefore the Lorde blessed the seventh day, and halowed it.

People: Lorde, have mercye upon us, and encline our. &c.

Ministre: Honoure thy father and thy mother, that thy day may be long in the land which the lord thy god geveth thee.

People: Lorde, have mercye upon us, and encline our. &c.

Ministre: Thou shalt doe no murther.

People: Lorde, have mercye upon us, and encline our. &c.

Ministre: Thou shalt not commit adulterie.

People: Lorde, have mercye upon us, and encline our. &c.

Ministre: Thou shalt not steale.

People: Lorde, have mercye upon us, and encline our. &c.

Ministre: Thou shalt not beare false witnesse agaynste th neighboure.

People: Lorde, have mercye upon us, and encline our heart to kepe thys lawe.

Ministre: Thou shalt not covet thy neighbours house. Tho shalt not covet thy neighbours wife, nor his servaunt, nor maid, nor his oxe, nor his asse, nor any thing that is his.

People: Lorde, have mercye upon us, and write al these thy lawes in our heartes we beseche thee.

¶ Then shall folowe the Collecte of the daye with one of these two Collectes folowynge for the king: the Priest standing up and saying.

Let us praye.

ALMIGHTIE God, whose kingdome is everlasting, and power infinite: have mercye upon the whole congregacion, and so rule the heart of thy chosen servaunt Edwarde the sixth, our king and governoure, that he (knowing whose minister he is) may above al thynges seek thy honoure and glory: and that we his subjectes (duely considering whose aucthoritie he hath) may faythfully serve, honour, and humbly obey him, in thee, and for thee, accordyng to thy blessed worde and ordinaunce: Throughe Jesus Christ our lord, who with thee, and the holy ghost, liveth, and reigneth ever one god, world without end. Amen . . .

¶ Immediatly after the Collectes, the Priest shal reade the Epistle, begynnyng thus.

The Epistle written in the.   Chapter of.

And the Epistle ended, he shal saye the Gospel, beginning thus.

The Gospell wrytten in the.   Chapter of.

And the Epistle and Gospel beyng ended, shal be sayd the Crede.

I BELEVE in one God, the father almighty, maker of heaven and earth, and of al things visible, and invisible: And in one lorde Jesu Christ, the only begotten sonne of God, begotten of his father before al worldes: God of goddes, light of lyght, very God of very God: begotten, not made, beeyng of one substaunce with the father, by whom al thynges were made: who for us men and for our salvacion, came downe from heaven, and was incarnate by the holy gost, of the virgyn Mary, and was made man: and was crucified also for us, under Poncius Pilate. He suffred and was buried, and the thyrd day he rose againe accordyng to the scriptures: and ascended into heaven, and sytteth at the ryght hand of the father. And he shal come agayne with glory, to judge both the quicke and the dead: Whose kyngdome shal have none ende. And I beleve in the holy gost, the Lord and gever of lyfe, who procedeth from the father and the sonne, who with the father and the sonne together, is worshipped and glorifyed, who spake by the Prophetes. And I beleve in one Catholike and Apostolike churche. I acknowledge one Baptisme for the remission of synnes. And I loke for the resurreccion of the dead, and the life of the world to come. Amen.

*After the Crede, if there be no sermon, shal
follow one of the homelies already set forth, or
hereafter to be set forth by commune
aucthoritie.*

⁋ *After suche sermon, homelie, or
exhortacion, the Curate shal declare unto the
people whether there be any holye doyes or
fasting dayes the weke folowing: and
earnestly exhort them to remember the poore,
saying one or moe of these Sentences
folowing, as he thinketh most convenient by
his discrecion.*

LET your light so shine before men, that they may see
your good workes, and glorifie your father whiche is
in heaven. Math. v. . . .

⁋ *Then shal the Churche wardens, or some
other by them appointed, gather the devocion
of the people, and put the same into the
poremens boxe: and upon the offering daies
appointed, every man and woman shall paye to
the curate the due and accustomed offeringes:
after whiche done the priest shal saye.*

Let us pray for the whole state of Christes Church
militant here in earth.

ALMIGHTIE and everliving God, which by the holye
Apostle hast taught us to make prayers and supplica-
cions, and to geve thankes for all menne. We humbly
beseche thee most mercifullye to accepte our almose
[alms] and to receive these our prayers, which we
offer unto thy divine Majestie, beseching thee to inspire continually the universall churche with the
spirite of trueth, unitie, and concorde: And graunt
that all they that dooe confesse thy holye name, may
agree in the trueth of thy holy woord, and live in unitie and godlye love. We beseche thee also to save and
defende all Christian Kynges, Princes, and Gov-
ernoures, and speciallye thy servaunt, Edward our
Kyng, that under hym we maye bee godlye and quietly governed: and graunt unto hys whole counsayle,
and to all that bee putte in aucthoritie under hym,
that they may truely and indifferently minister justice, to the punishement of wickednes and vice, and
to the mayntenaunce of God's true religion and
vertue. Geve grace (O heavenly father) to all Bishops, Pastours, and Curates, that they maye bothe
by their lyfe and doctrine sette foorth thy true and
lyvely woord, and rightly and duely administer thy
holye Sacramentes: and to all thy people geve thy

heavenly grace, and especiallye to thys congregacion
here present, that with meke hearte and due reverence they may heare and receive thy holy woord, truely serving thee in holynesse and ryghteousnesse all
the dayes of theyr lyfe. And we most humbly beseche
thee of thy goodnesse (O Lord) to coumfort and suc-
cour all them, whiche in this transitory lyfe bee in
trouble, sorowe, nede, sickenes, or anye other adver-
sitie: Graunt this, O father, for Jesus Christes sake,
oure onely mediatour and advocate. Amen.

⁋ *Then shal folowe this exhortacion at
certaine tymes when the Curate shal see the
people negligent to come to the holy
Communion.*

WE be come together at this time, derely beloved
brethren, to fede at the Lord's supper, unto the
whiche in Goddes behalf I bydde you all that be here
present, and beseche you for the Lord Jesus Christes
sake, that ye will not refuse to come thereto, being so
lovingly called and bidden of god hymselfe. Ye
knowe how grevouse and unkynde a thing it is,
when a man hath prepared a riche feaste, decked his
table with al kinde of provision, so that there lacketh
nothing but the geastes to sit down: and yet they
which be called, without any cause most unthanke-
fully refuse to come. Which of you, in such a case,
would not be moved? Who would not thynke a great
injury and wrong done unto him? Wherfore, most
derely beloved in Christ, take ye good hede, lest ye
with drawyng yourselves from this holy supper, provoke god's indignacion against you. It is an easy matter for a man to saye, I wyll not communicate,
because I am otherwyse letted [=hindered] with
worldly busines: but suche excuses be not so easily
accepted and allowed beefore god. If any man saye, I
am a grevous sinner, and therefore am afraied to
come: wherefore then doe you not repent and
amend? When god calleth you, be you not ashamed
to saye you will not come? When you shoulde returne to god, wyll you excuse your selfe, and saye
that you be not ready? Consydre earnestly with
youreselves howe lytle such feyned excuses shall
avayl before God. They that refused the feaste in the
gospell, because they had boughte a farme, or would
trie theyr yokes of oxen, or because they were
maried, were not so excused, but counted unworthy
of the heavenly feast. I for my part am here present,
and according to mine office, I bidde you in the
name of God, I call you in Christ's behalf, I exhort

you, as you love your owne salvacion, that ye wilbe partakers of thys holy Communion. And as the sonne of God did vouchesafe to yelde up hys soule by death upon the Crosse for youre health: even so it is youre duetie to receyve the Communion together in the remembraunce of hys death, as he himself commaunded. Nowe if you wyll in nowyse thus doe, considre with youreselves howe greate injurye you do unto God, and howe sore punishmente hangeth over your heades for the same. And whereas ye offend god so sore in refusing this holy Banquet, I admonishe, exhort, and beseche you, that unto this unkindnes ye wyll not adde any more. Which thing ye shal doe, if ye stande by as gazers and lokers on them that doe communicate, and be no partakers of the same yourselves. For what thing can this be accoumpted els, then a further contempt and unkindness unto god. Truely it is a great unthankfuhnes to saye naye when ye be called: but the faulte is muche greater when men stand by, and yet wyll neither eate nor drynke this holy Communion with other. I pray you what can this be els, but even to have the mysteries of Christ in derision? It is said unto all: Take ye and eate. Take and drinke ye all of thys: doe this in remembraunce of me. With what face then, or with what countenaunce shal ye hear these words? What wil this be els but a neglecting, a despysing, and mocking of the Testament of Christ? Wherefore, rather then you should so doe, depart you hence and geve place to them that be godly disposed. But when you depart, I beseche you, pondre with yourselves from whom you depart: ye depart from the lordes table, ye depart from your brethren, and from the banquete of moste heavenly fode. These thynges if ye earnestly considre, ye shal by gods grace returne to a better mynd, for the obteyning whereof, we shal make our humble peticions while we shall receive the holy Communion.

> ¶ Yf there be none almosen [alms] geven unto
> the poore, then shal the wordes of acceptyng
> our almes be lefte out unsayde.

> ¶ And some tyme shal be sayd this also, at the
> discrecion of the Curate.

DERELY beloved, forasmuche as our duetie is to rendre to Almightie god our heavenly father most harty thankes, for that he hath geven his sonne our savioure Jesus Christ, not only to die for us, but also to be our spiritual fode and sustenaunce, as it is declared unto us, as wel by goddes word as by the holy Sacramentes of his blessed body and bloud, the whiche being so comfortable a thyng to them whiche receive it worthely, and so daungerous to them that wyl presume to receive it unworthely:

My duetie is to exhort you to consider the dignitie of the holy mistery, and the greate perel of the unworthy receiving thereof, and so to searche and examine your own consciences, as you should come holy and cleane to a moste Godly and heavenly feaste: so that in no wise you come but in the mariage garment, required of god in holy scripture; and so come and be received, as worthy partakers of suche a heavenly table. The way and meanes thereto is: First to examine your lives and conversacion by the rule of goddes commaundements, and whereinsoever ye shall perceive your selves to have offended, either by wil, word, or dede, there beewaile your owne sinful lives, confess your selfes to almightie god with ful purpose of amendment of life. And yf ye shal perceive your offences to be such, as be not only against god, but also againste your neighbours: then ye shal reconcile your selves unto them, ready to make restitucion and satisfaccion, accordyng to the uttermost of your powers, for all injuries and wronges done by you to any other: and likewise beeyng ready to forgeve other that have offended you; as you would have forgevenesse of your offences at gods hande: for otherwyse the receiving of the holy Communion doth nothyng els, but encrease your damnacion. And because it is requisite that no man shoulde come to the holy Communion but with a full truste in God's mercy, and with a quiet conscience: therefore if there be any of you which by the meanes afore said cannot quiet his own conscience, but requireth further comfort or counsel; then let him come to me, or some other discreet and learned minister of god's word, and open his griefe, that he may receive such gostlye [=spiritual] counsail, advise, and coumfort, as his conscience maye be relieved; and that by the ministery of god's word he may receive coumfort and the benefite of absolucion, to the quietting of his conscience, and avoiding of al Scruple and doubtfulnes.

> ¶ Then shal the Priest say thys exhortacion.

DERELY beloved in the Lord: ye that mynde to come to the holy Communion of the body and bloud of our saviour Christ, muste considre what St. Paul writeth to the Corinthians, how he exhorteth all persons diligently to trye and examine themselves, before they presume to eate of that bread, and drinke of that cup: for as the benefite is great, if with a truly penitent heart and lively fayth, we receive that holy Sacrament (for then we spirituallye eate the fleshe of Christ, and drynke hys bloud, then we dwel in Christ and Christ in us, we be one with Christ, and Christ with us;) so is the daunger great, if we receive the same unworthely. For then we be giltie of the bodye and bloud of Christ our saviour. We eate and drynke our own damnacion, not consideryng the Lordes body. We kindle Goddes wrath againste us, we provoke hym to plague us with divers diseases, and sundry kynds of death. Therfore, yf any of you be a blasphemer of God, an hynderer or slaunderer of his worde, an adulturer, or be in malice or envie, or in any other grevous cryme, bewayle your sinnes, and come not to thys holy Table; lest after the takyng of that holy Sacrament, the Devill entre into you, as he entred into Judas, and fyll you ful of al iniquities, and bryng you to destruccion, both of bodye and soule. Judge therefore your selves (brethren) that ye bee not judged of the Lorde. Repent you truely for your sinnes paste, have a lively and stedfaste fayth in Christe our savioure. Amende youre lyves, and be in perfecte charitie with al men, so shall ye be meete partakers of those holy misteries. And above all thynges, ye muste geve most humble and hartie thankes to God the father, the sonne, and the holy ghost, for the redempcyon of the worlde by the death and passyon of our Saviour Chryst, both God and man, who did humble hymself, even to the death upon the Crosse for us miserable synners, which laye in darkenesse and shadowe of death, that he myght make us the chyldren of God, and exalte us to everlastinge lyfe. And to thend that we shoulde alway remembre the exceding great love of our Maister, and onely Savioure Jesu Christ, thus dying for us, and the innumerable benefites, (whiche by his precyous bloud sheding) he hath obteined to us, he hath instituted and ordayned holy misteries, as pledges of his love, and continual remembraunce of hys death, to our great and endles comforte. To hym therefore, with the father and the holy ghost, let us geve (as we are most bounden) continuall thankes: submitting our selves wholy to hys holy wil and pleasure, and studying to serve him in true holyness and righteousnesse, all the dayes of oure lyfe. Amen.

¶ Then shal the Priest saye to them that come to receive the holy Communion.

You that doe truly and earnestly repente you of youre synnes, and bee in love and charitie with your neighbours, and entende to leade a newe lyfe, folowyng the commaundments of god, and walking from henceforth in his holy waies: Drawe nere and take this holy Sacramente to youre comfort: make your humble confession to almightie god, before this congregacion here gathered together in his holy name, mekely knelyng upon your knees.

¶ Then shal this general confession be made, in the name of al those that are mynded to receive the holy Communion, eyther by one of them, or els by one of the ministers, or by the Priest himself, al kneling humbly upon theyr knees.

ALMIGHTIE God, father of our Lorde Jesus Christe, maker of all thyngs, Judge of all men, we knowledge and bewayle oure manyfolde synnes and wyckednes, whiche we from tyme to tyme moste grevously have committed, by thoughte, woord and dede, agaynst thy devine Majestie: provokyng most justely thy wrath and indignacion agaynste us: we doe earnestlye repente, and be hartely sory for these our misdoynges: the remembraunce of them is grievouse unto us, the burthen of them is intollerable: have mercye upon us, have mercye upon us, moste mercifull father, for thy sonne oure Lorde Jesus Chrystes sake: forgeve us all that is past, and graunt that we maye ever here after serve and please thee, in newnesse of lyfe, to the honoure and glory of thy name: Through Jesus Christ our Lord.

¶ Then shal the Priest or the Bisshop (being present) stand up, and turning himselfe to the people, say thus,

ALMIGHTIE god, our heavenly father, who of his great mercy, hath promised forgeveness of synnes to all them, whiche with hartie repentaunce and true fayth turne unto hym: have mercye upon you, pardon and deliver you from all your synnes, confirme and strength you in all goodnesse and bring you to everlasting life: through Jesus Christe our Lorde. Amen.

¶ Then shal the Priest also saye,

Heare what comfortable woords our savioure Christe sayeth, to al that truly turne to hym.

Come unto me all that travaile, and be heavye laden, and I shal refreshe you. So god loved the world, that he gave his onely begotten sonne to thend that al that beleve in him, should not perishe, but have life everlasting.

Heare also what Sainct Paul sayeth.

This is a true saying, and worthy of all men to be received, that Jesus Christe came into the world to save synners.

Heare also what Sainct John sayeth.

If any man sinne, we have an advocate with the father, Jesus Christ the righteous, and he is the propiciacion for our synnes.

¶ *After the whiche the Priest shall procede, saying,*

Lyfte up your heartes.

Answer: We lyfte them up unto the Lorde.

Priest: Let us geve thankes unto our Lorde God.

Answer: It is mete and right so to doe.

Priest: It is very mete, ryght, and oure bounden duetie, that we should at al times, and in al places, geve thankes unto thee, O lord holy father, almightie everlastyng God . . .

¶ *After whiche preface, shal folowe immediatly,*

Therefore with Angelles and Archangelles, and with al the companye of heaven, we laude and magnifye thy glorious name, evermore praysing thee, and saying:

Holye, holye, holye, Lorde God of hostes: heaven and yearthe are full of thy glory: glory be to thee, O lord, most high.

¶ *Then shal the Priest, kneling down at Goddes borde, say in the name of all them that shal receive the Communion, this praier folowyng.*

WE doe not presume to come to this thy table (O mercyfull Lorde) trusting in our owne righteousnesse, but in thy manifolde and great mercies: we bee not worthye, so much as to gather up the crommes under thy table: but thou art the same Lorde whose propertie is alwayes to have mercye: graunt us therfore (gracious lord) so to eate the fleshe of thy dere sonne Jesus Christe, and to drinke his bloud, that our synfulle bodyes maye be made cleane by his body, and our soules wasched through his most precious bloud, and that we may evermore dwel in him, and he in us. Amen.

¶ *Then the Priest standing up shal saye, as foloweth.*

ALMIGHTY God oure heavenly father, whiche of thy tender mercye dyddest geve thine onely sonne Jesus Christ, to suffre death upon the crosse for our redempcion, who made there (by hys one oblacion of hymselfe once offered) a full, perfecte and sufficiente sacrifice, oblacion, and satisfaccion, for the synnes of the whole worlde, and dyd institute, and in hys holye Gospell commaund us to continue, a perpetuall memorye of that his precious death, untyll hys comynge agayne: Heare us O mercyfull father wee beeseche thee; and graunt that wee, receyving these thy creatures of bread and wyne, according to thy sonne our Savioure Jesus Christ's holy institucion, in remembraunce of his death and passion, maye be partakers of his most blessed body and bloud: who, in the same night that he was betrayed, tooke bread, and when he had geven thanks, he brake it, and gave it to his Disciples, sayinge: Take, eate, this is my bodye which is geven for you. Doe this in remembraunce of me. Lykewyse after supper he tooke the cup, and when he had geven thankes, he gave it to them, sayinge: Drink ye all of this, for this is my bloud of the new Testament, whiche is shed for you and for many, for remission of synnes: do this as oft as ye shal drinke it in remembraunce of me.

¶ *Then shal the minister first receyve the Communion in both kyndes hymselfe, and next deliver it to other ministers, yf any be there present (that they may help the chief minister,) and after to the people in their handes kneling.*

¶ *And when he delyvereth the bread, he shall saye.*

Take and eate this, in remembraunce that Christ dyed for thee, and feede on him in thy hearte by faythe, with thankesgeving.

¶ *And the Minister that delyvereth the cup, shal saye,*

Drinke this in remembraunce that Christ's bloude was shed for thee, and be thankefull.

¶ Then shall the Priest saye the Lordes prayer, the people repeating after him every peticion.

¶ After shalbe sayde as foloweth . . .

ALMIGHTIE and everliving God, we most hartely thank thee, for that thou dooest vouchsafe to fede us, whiche have duely receyved these holye misteries, with the spirituall foode of the most precious body and bloud of thy sonne our saviour Jesus Christ, and doest assure us thereby of thy favoure and goodnes towarde us, and that we bee verye membres incorporate in thy mistical body, which is the blessed companie of all faythfull people, and be also heyrs, through hope, of thy everlasting kingdom, by the merites of the most precious death and Passion of thy deare sonne. We now most humbly beseche thee, O heavenly father, so to assiste us with thy grace, that we may continue in that holy felowship, and do al such good workes, as thou hast prepared for us to walk in: through Jesus Christ our Lord, to whom, with thee and the holy ghost, be all honour and glorye, world without ende. Amen.

¶ Then shalbe sayd or song.

GLORYE bee to God on hyghe. And in yearth peace, good wyll towardes men. We prayse thee, we blesse thee, we worshippe thee, we glorifye thee, we geve thanks to thee for thy greate glorye, O Lorde God heavenly kyng, God the father almightie. O lord the onely begotten sonne Jesu Christ: O lord God, Lambe of god, sonne of the father, that takest away the sinnes of the worlde, have mercye upon us: Thou that takest away the sines of the world, have mercye upon us. Thou that takest awaye the sinnes of the world, receyve oure prayer. Thou that syttest at the ryght hande of God the father, have mercye upon us: For thou only art holy, Thou only arte the Lord. Thou only, (O Christ,) with the holy ghost, art most high in the glory of god the father. Amen.

¶ Then the Priest or the Bishop, if he be present, shal let them depart with thys blessyng:

THE peace of GOD which passeth al understanding kepe youre heartes and mynds in the knowledge and love of GOD, and of his sonne Jesus Christ our Lord: And the blessing of god almightye, the father, the sonne, and the holy ghost, be amongest you and remayne with you always. Amen . . .

Although no ordre can be so perfectlye devised, but it may be of some, eyther for theyr ignoraunce and infermitie, or els of malice and obstinacie, misconstrued, depraved, and interpreted in a wrong part: And yet because brotherly charitie willeth, that so much as conveniently may be, offences shoulde be taken awaye: therefore we willing to doe the same. Whereas it is ordeyned in the booke of common prayer, in the administracion of the Lord's Supper, that the Communicants knelyng shoulde receyve the holye Communion. whiche thynge beyng well mente, for a sygnificacion of the humble and gratefull acknowledgyng of the benefites of Chryst, geven unto the woorthye receyver, and to avoyde the prophanacion and dysordre, which about the holy Communion myght els ensue: Leste yet the same kneelyng myght be thought or taken otherwyse, we dooe declare that it is not ment thereby, that any adoracion is doone, or oughte to bee doone, eyther unto the Sacramentall bread or wyne there bodily receyved, or unto anye reall and essencial presence there beeyng of Christ's naturall fleshe and bloude. For as concernynge the Sacramentall bread and wyne, they remayne styll in theyr verye naturall substaunces, and therefore may not be adored, for that were Idolatrye to be abhorred of all faythfull christians. And as concernynge the naturall body and blood of our saviour Christ, they are in heaven and not here. For it is agaynst the trueth of Christes true natural bodye, to be in moe places then in one, at one tyme.

Sacraments and the Council of Trent

The selection from the Council of Trent includes a foreword, then canons on sacraments in general, and finally canons on the eucharist. A canon is a rule, or yardstick, by which to judge the orthodoxy of a particular doctrine. Canons can also refer to church law, but in this instance, the canons adopted by the Roman Catholic Church at Trent indicate what the bishops believed to be the correct understanding of doctrine. The canons that follow are not structured narratively, but rather appear as a list by which to judge and evaluate teachings about the sacraments. The foreword, which is exactly what it sounds like—the word, or words, before what is to come—provides the rationale for the decree on the sacraments. The canons themselves, pertaining both to the sacraments and to the eucharist, spell out exactly what Catholics are to believe. How are the Catholic and Anglican views of Communion similar? How do they differ? How important are the sacraments to Catholic and Anglican Christians? What Protestant views are the canons refuting?

Decree Concerning the Sacraments

COUNCIL OF TRENT, SEVENTH SESSION, 3 MARCH 1547

FOREWORD

For the completion of the salutary doctrine on justification, which was promulgated with the unanimous consent of the Fathers in the last session, it has seemed proper to deal with the most holy sacraments of the Church, through which all true justice either begins, or being begun is increased, or being lost is restored. Wherefore, in order to destroy the errors and extirpate the heresies that in our stormy times are directed against the most holy sacraments, some of which are a revival of heresies long ago condemned by our Fathers, while others are of recent origin, all of which are exceedingly detrimental to the purity of the Catholic Church and the salvation of souls, the holy, ecumenical and general Council of Trent, lawfully assembled in the Holy Ghost, the same legates of the Apostolic See presiding, adhering to the teaching of the Holy Scriptures, to the Apostolic traditions, and to the unanimous teaching of other councils and of the Fathers, has thought it proper to establish and enact these present canons; hoping, with the help of the Holy Spirit, to publish later those that are wanting for the completion of the work to begin.

CANONS ON THE SACRAMENTS IN GENERAL

Canon 1. If anyone says that the sacraments of the New Law were not all instituted by our Lord Jesus Christ, or that there are more or less than seven, namely, baptism, confirmation, Eucharist, penance, extreme unction, order and matrimony, or that any one of these seven is not truly and intrinsically a sacrament, let him be anathema.

Canon 2. If anyone says that these sacraments of the New Law do not differ from the sacraments of the Old Law, except that the ceremonies are different and the external rites are different, let him be anathema.

Canon 3. If anyone says that these seven sacraments are so equal to each other that one is not for any reason more excellent than the other, let him be anathema.

Canon 4. If anyone says that the sacraments of the New Law are not necessary for salvation but are superfluous, and that without them or without the desire of them men obtain from God through faith alone the grace of justification, though all are not necessary for each one, let him be anathema.

Canon 5. If anyone says that these sacraments have been instituted for the nourishment of faith alone, let him be anathema.

Canon 6. If anyone says that the sacraments of the New Law do not contain the grace which they signify, or that they do not confer that grace on those who place no obstacles in its way, as though they are only outward signs of grace of justice received through faith and certain marks of Christian profession, whereby among men believers are distinguished from unbelievers, let him be anathema.

Canon 7. If anyone says that grace, so far as God's part is concerned, is not imparted through the sacraments always and to all men even if they receive them rightly, but only sometimes and to some persons, let him be anathema.

Canon 8. If anyone says that by the sacraments of the New Law grace is not conferred *ex opere operato* [literally, from the work worked; figuratively, from the sacrament itself], but that faith alone in the divine promise is sufficient to obtain grace, let him be anathema.

Canon 9. If anyone says that in three sacraments, namely, baptism, confirmation and order, there is not imprinted on the soul a character, that is, a certain spiritual and indelible mark, by reason of which they cannot be repeated, let him be anathema.

Canon 10. If anyone says that all Christians have the power to administer the word and all the sacraments, let him be anathema.

Canon 11. If anyone says that in ministers, when they effect and confer the sacraments, there is not required at least the intention of doing what the Church does, let him be anathema.

Canon 12. If anyone says that a minister who is in mortal sin, though he observes all the essentials that pertain to the effecting or conferring of a sacrament, neither effects nor confers a sacrament, let him be anathema.

Canon 13. If anyone says that the received and approved rites of the Catholic Church, accustomed to be used in the administration of the sacraments, may be despised or omitted by the ministers without sin and at their pleasure, or may be changed by any pastor of the churches to other new ones, let him be anathema.

CANONS ON THE MOST HOLY SACRAMENT OF THE EUCHARIST

Canon 1. If anyone denies that in the sacrament of the most Holy Eucharist are contained truly, really and substantially the body and blood together with the soul and divinity of our Lord Jesus Christ, and consequently the whole Christ, but says that He is in it only as in a sign, or figure or force, let him be anathema.

Canon 2. If anyone says that in the sacred and holy sacrament of the Eucharist the substance of the bread and wine remains conjointly with the body and blood of our Lord Jesus Christ, and denies that wonderful and singular change of the whole substance of the bread into the body and the whole substance of the wine into the blood, the appearances only of bread and wine remaining, which change the Catholic Church most aptly calls transubstantiation, let him be anathema.

Canon 3. If anyone denies that in the venerable sacrament of the Eucharist the whole Christ is contained under each form and under every part of each form when separated, let him be anathema.

Canon 4. If anyone says that after the consecration is completed, the body and blood of our Lord Jesus Christ are not in the admirable sacrament of the Eucharist, but are there only *in usu,* while being taken and not before or after, and that in the hosts or consecrated particles which are reserved or which remain after communion, the true body of the Lord does not remain, let him be anathema.

Canon 5. If anyone says that the principal fruit of the most Holy Eucharist is the remission of sins, or that other effects do not result from it, let him be anathema.

Canon 6. If anyone says that in the holy sacrament of the Eucharist, Christ, the only begotten Son of God, is not to be adored with the worship of *latria* [due to God alone], also outwardly manifested, and is consequently neither to be venerated with a special festive solemnity, nor to be solemnly borne about in procession according to the laudable and universal rite and custom of holy Church, or is not to be set publicly before the people to be adored and that the adorers thereof are idolaters, let him be anathema.

Canon 7. If anyone says that it is not lawful that the Holy Eucharist be reserved in a sacred place, but immediately after consecration must necessarily be distributed among those present, or that it is not lawful that it be carried with honor to the sick, let him be anathema.

Canon 8. If anyone says that Christ received in the Eucharist is received spiritually only and not also sacramentally and really, let him be anathema.

Canon 9. If anyone denies that each and all of Christ's faithful of both sexes are bound, when they have reached the years of discretion, to communicate every year at least at Easter, in accordance with the precept of holy mother Church, let him be anathema.

Canon 10. If anyone says that it is not lawful for the priest celebrating to communicate himself, let him be anathema.

Canon 11. If anyone says that faith alone is a sufficient preparation for receiving the sacrament of the most Holy Eucharist, let him be anathema. And lest so great a sacrament be received unworthily and hence unto death and condemnation, this holy council ordains and declares that sacramental confession, when a confessor can be had, must necessarily be made beforehand by those whose conscience is burdened with mortal sin, however contrite they may consider themselves. Moreover, if anyone shall presume to teach, preach or obstinately assert, or in public disputation defend the contrary, he shall be *eo ipso* [by this very action] excommunicated.

The Radical Reformation

In 1525, Conrad Grebel baptized an ex-priest, who then proceeded to baptize several adults who had been part of a Bible study group in Zurich, Switzerland. A number of Swiss, German, and Moravian Protestants were coming to believe that their own baptisms as infants did not meet New Testament practice. Jesus was baptized as an adult, and the Acts of the Apostles give many examples of people being baptized once they accepted the new faith being preached. Of course, Acts also states that entire households were baptized, which may well have included children. Church practice—which initially had involved baptizing adults who had completed a year-long training program—increasingly turned to infant baptism. This occurred as more and more Christians grew up in Christian households, rather than converting to Christianity as adults. By the fourth century, Augustine had outlined a doctrine of Original Sin that seemed to necessitate infant baptism. Thus, both scripture and church tradition included infant baptism, although scripture also taught adult or believer baptism. Some of the radical reformers believed that a person must consciously make a choice or commitment to follow Jesus, and that required one to be of the age of reason. Consequently, they baptized—or rebaptized in the eyes of the church—adults wishing to make that choice. When they did so, they were arrested because anabaptism (rebaptism) was a capital offense. The punishment fit the crime, and those convicted of rebaptism were drowned—more than 5000 if estimates are correct.

Just as they had reconsidered the sacrament of communion, sixteenth-century reformers reevaluated baptism and its meaning. What actually occurred within the sacrament? Was it necessary or optional? And should infants be baptized? There was a range of opinions. The Canons of Trent reveal the various views that the Catholic Church rejected—but that other Christians accepted. The following four canons show Catholicism's rejection of the Anabaptist position, a position also rejected by all other Protestant churches at the time:

Canon 11. If anyone says that baptism, truly and rightly administered must be repeated in the one converted to repentance after having denied the faith of Christ among the infidels, let him be anathema.

Canon 12. If anyone says that no one is to be baptized except at that age at which Christ was baptized, or when on the point of death, let him be anathema.

Canon 13. If anyone says that children, because they have not the act of believing, are not after having received baptism to be numbered among the faithful, and for this reason are to be rebaptized when they have reached the years of discretion; or that it is better that the baptism of such be omitted than that, while not believing by their own act, they should be baptized in the faith of the Church alone, let him be anathema.

Canon 14. If anyone says that those who have been thus baptized when children, are, when they have grown up, to be questioned whether they will ratify what their sponsors promised in their name when they were baptized, and in case they answer in the negative, are to be left to their own will; neither are they to be compelled in the meantime to a Christian life by any penalty other than exclusion from the reception of the Eucharist and the other statements, until they repent, let him be anathema.

Behind the desire to be baptized as believers lay the conviction among radical reformers that the church was an entity called out of and apart from the world. The Bible had given clear instructions on how a Christian was to live: goods were to be shared in common; war was to be avoided; simplicity of dress, life, and thought were the norms. It was impossible to follow these norms when living in the world, however, and so these radicals—who believed in returning to the root, or radical, forms of Christian life—sought to live godly lives in their own communities. Of course, it was easier to live outside the norm when they had been exiled or forced to flee from their homes because of their opposition to state-sponsored religion. With the notable exception of the "New Jerusalem"—established in the city of Münster, Germany, in 1534—where biblical absolutism resulted in polygamy and in execution for moral infractions, most of the radical reformers were peaceful and peaceable. They just wanted to be left alone.

The Radical Reformation was not uniform, and Anabaptists, though playing a significant part, were not the only ones historians now categorize as radical. Like the Anabaptists, the Spiritualists emphasized personal piety and the necessity of living a moral life in accordance with biblical teachings. But their doctrine of inspiration by the Holy Spirit and ongoing revelation was a departure from even the Anabaptists. Mystics like Kaspar von Schwenckfeld (1489–1561) wanted to reinstitute the church of the apostles in the form of small, family-based groups. Sebastian Franck (c. 1499–1542) thought that the church comprised an invisible body of believers. The Spiritualists had an antimaterialist bias that emphasized individualism, and that turned to the authority of subjective inner experience. A third group, the Rationalists, took yet another tack. They emphasized the moral truths of the Bible, thought of worship as a human convention, and argued that there was no scriptural support for the doctrine of the Trinity. (As we recall, this doctrine took several centuries to develop in early Christianity, not reaching its clearest statement until 381 C.E.) Some Rationalists were called "Socinians," after Fausto (1539–1604) and Lelio Sozzini (1525–1562), whose teachings and writings led to the rise of Unitarianism in England (see Chapter Five).

What all these "radical" reformers had in common was the conviction that Christianity was a way of life in which piety and morality were key, and dogma and belief were secondary. The sacraments were indications of grace, but not necessarily the bearers of grace. What counted was a study of the Bible that would inform Christian life in practical ways: what kinds of occupations were worthy, how Christians should live together, and how they should treat outsiders. Although the Radical Reformation is frequently presented as a marginal part of the sixteenth-century reformations, its influence exceeds its numbers, especially in its emphasis on scripture. Luther claimed *sola scriptura;* the radicals lived it. Luther relied on scripture when it was useful, especially to attack the papacy or his opponents; but he retained so many elements of Catholic practice that the Lutheran Church looked much like the Catholic Church, especially in the practice of baptism and communion. The Anglican Church looked even more similar, although its outward appearance belied inner theological differences. Reformed Protestants made the most alterations, in the appearance of church buildings, the form of church services, and the articulation of church doctrine. But the radicals effected still more substantive changes: ecclesiastically, sacramentally, doctrinally, and interpretatively. Eventually, some of their views came to be adopted, and reinterpreted, by modern Christians. We see this most clearly in the practice of adult baptism, and rebaptism, within many nondenominational churches today.

Although baptism was the key sacramental issue for the radicals, and their chief distinguishing characteristic, what is perhaps most interesting about them was their commitment to Christian communism. What groups like the Mennonites and the Hutterites shared—like their predecessors in the early church and in the monasteries and convents—was the conviction that Christian life is to be lived in the community of other Christians. Frequently, these groups were persecuted for this belief, or for their refusal to take oaths or to serve in the military, since many were strict pacifists. Some moved further and further east, out of Western Europe and into Poland, Bohemia, Moravia, Silesia, and even Russia.

The Hutterites were one of the Anabaptist groups that practiced Christian communism. Although Jacob Hutter (1500?–1536) did not found the group, he did bring impressive organizational and spiritual talents to Anabaptist communalists living first in the Tirol of Austria and then in Moravia. Like his sister, who was executed in 1529, Hutter was executed for heresy in 1536, burned at the stake on the orders of Ferdinand, the Archduke of Austria. The Hutterites, along with the Swiss Brethren and the Mennonites, Dutch Anabaptists who settled in Pennsylvania, are among the few Anabaptist groups to survive as religious communalists to the present. They fled Europe and settled in Canada and the northern United States, where they continue to share their belongings and teach their children that true brotherly love means renouncing private property.

The Reading

Ulrich Stadler (d. 1540), a Moravian Hutterite who moved his community to Poland due to government persecution, wrote the following "Cherished Instructions" for his community. Stadler returned to Moravia, despite the torture and execution of Jacob Hutter there, because Moravians felt sympathetic toward the Hutterites.

The reading is another example of an apology, or explanation, of beliefs to help both insiders and outsiders understand important issues. In the first half of the instructions, Stadler clarifies the policy Hutterites hold on issues such as shunning (the practice of excluding dissidents), obedience, and sharing. This discussion seems directed at practitioners. The second half presents a series of counterarguments: this seems to be a manual for Hutterites to defend themselves and their practices against critics, undoubtedly unsympathetic family members, although the arguments may also be directed toward hostile governmental entities or unfriendly neighbors.

Note: I have started the selection with Stadler's discussion of the community of goods and excluded his explanation of the process of excommunication. This latter practice—also called shunning or "the ban"—is the primary way communal groups create and maintain a harmonious community. Without a police force, and without economic sanctions, the only way to control dissidents is to exclude or eject them from the group. Although this sounds harsh, it is preferable to other alternatives.

Questions to Consider

1. Who, or what, is the church, according to Stadler's document?

2. How is a Hutterite community organized?

3. What is the theological justification for sharing goods in common?

4. With whom do you think Stadler is arguing when he presents his responses to counterarguments against the Hutterite way of life?

5. Who makes the stronger argument in your opinion: Stadler or his fictional opponent?

6. Would you say that the Anabaptists have an optimistic or pessimistic anthropology? What are the reasons for thinking the way you do?

7. Do you think people can live as unselfishly as the way proposed by Stadler? Why or why not?

Cherished Instructions on Sin, Excommunication, and the Community of Goods

ULRICH STADLER

THE TRUE COMMUNITY OF THE SAINTS

There is one communion of all the faithful in Christ and one community of the holy children called of God. They have one Father in heaven, one Lord Christ; all are baptized and sealed in their hearts with one Spirit. They have one mind, opinion, heart, and soul as having all drunk from the same Fountain, and alike await one and the same struggle, cross, trial, and, at length, one and the same hope in glory. But it, that is, such a community must move about in this world, poor, miserable, small, and rejected of the world, of whom, however, the world is not worthy. Whoever strives for the lofty things [of this world] does not belong. Thus in this community everything must proceed equally, all things be one and communal, alike in the bodily gifts of their Father in heaven, which he daily gives to be used by his own according to his will. For how does it make sense that all who have here in this pilgrimage to look forward to an inheritance in the Kingdom of their Father should not be satisfied with their bodily goods and gifts? Judge, O ye saints of God, ye who are thus truly grafted into Christ, with him deadened to the world, to sin, and to yourselves, that you never hereafter live for the world or yourselves but rather for him who died for you and arose, namely, Christ. [They] have also yielded themselves and presented themselves to him intimately, patiently, of their own free will, naked and uncovered, to suffer and endure his will and, moreover, to fulfill it and thereafter also to devote themselves in obedience and service to all the children of God. Therefore, they also live with one another where the Lord assigns a place to them, peaceably, united, lovingly, amicably, and fraternally, as children of one Father. In their pilgrimage they should be satisfied with the bodily goods and gifts of their Father, since they should also be altogether as one body and members one toward another.

Now if, then, each member withholds assistance from the other, the whole thing must go to pieces. The eyes won't see, the hands won't take hold. Where, however, each member extends assistance equally to the whole body, it is built up and grows and there is peace and unity, yea, each member takes care for the other. In brief, equal care, sadness and joy, and peace [are] at hand. It is just the same in the spiritual body of Christ. If the deacon of the community will never serve, the teacher will not teach, the young brother will not be obedient, the strong will not work for the community but for himself and each one wishes to take care of himself and if once in a while someone withdraws without profit to himself, the whole body is divided. In brief, *one, common* builds the Lord's house and is pure; but *mine, thine, his, own* divides the Lord's house and is impure. Therefore, where there is ownership and one has it, and it is his, and one does not wish to be one with Christ and his own in living and dying, he is outside of Christ and his communion and has thus no Father in heaven. If he says so, he lies. That is the life of the pilgrims of the Lord, who has purchased them in Christ, namely, the elect, the called, the holy ones in this life. These are his fighters and heralds, to whom also he will give the crown of life on the Day of his righteousness.

Secondly, such a community of the children of God has ordinances here in their pilgrimage. These should constitute the polity for the whole world. But the wickedness of men has spoiled everything. For as the sun with its shining is common to all, so also the use of all creaturely things. Whoever appropriates them for himself and encloses them is a thief and steals what is not his. For everything has been created free in common. Of such thieves the whole world is full. May God guard his own from them. To be sure, according to human law, one says: That is mine, but not according to divine law. Here in this ordinance [in our community] it is to be heeded in such a way that unbearable burdens be not laid upon the children of the Lord, but rather ones which God, out of his grace, has put upon us, living according to which we may be pleasing to him. Thus only as circumstances dictate will the children of God have either many or few houses, institute faithful house managers and stewards, who will faithfully move among the children of God and conduct themselves in a mild and fatherly manner and pray to God for wisdom therein.

ORDINANCES OF THE SAINTS IN THEIR COMMUNITY AND LIFE HERE TOGETHER IN THE LORD WITH THE GOODS OF THEIR FATHER

In order to hold in common all the gifts and goods which God gives and dispenses to his own, there must be free, unhampered, patient, and full hearts in Christ, yea, hearts that truly believe and trust and in Christ are utterly devoted. Whoever is thus free, unhampered, and resigned in the Lord from everything, [ready] to give over all his goods and chattels, yea, to lay it up for distribution among the children of God—it is God's grace in Christ which prepares men for it. Being willing and ready—that makes one free and unhampered. But whoever is not thus at liberty to give over and lay up in Christ the Lord, as indicated, should nevertheless not hold back, nor conceal, nor disavow anything but instead be willing and ready to give even when there is nothing at hand, yea, even to let the deacons in to collect in order that [at least] they might have free access in the Lord to them and at all times to find a willing, open heart ready to share. The house managers who have devoted themselves to the Lord and his people with body and substance in the service of, and obedience to, the Lord in his community should not be changed where they are recognized as fitted for the work and found faithful nor the [management of] the necessities withdrawn from them in the Lord, as long as they deal faithfully. Where, however, avarice or selfishness is detected, it should not be permitted. They must also be more community-minded with all the wretched of the Lord.

[As] deacons of welfare, true men should be ordained who take care that everything proceeds equally in the whole house of the Lord, everywhere in all the households, lest one have and another want. They also should be fatherly with all the little children of God; and also do all the buying and selling for the community.

The children of God should group themselves and hold together here in misery after they have been driven out in the worst sort of way—if they can achieve this, for it is good and purposeful; however,

if it [can be managed] without hardship they should not make big concentrations but rather, as opportunity affords, they should have many or at least a few [separated] houses. In brief, it belongs to all the children of God to live, to serve, to work, to seek not their own benefit but that of another, since we are all of the Lord. [Such] is their behavior on their pilgrimage.

Again, the brethren ought not to do business with each other, buy and sell like the heathen, each being rather in the Lord the Lord's own. Finally, everything should be arranged for the good of the saints of God in the church of the Lord according to time, place, propriety, and opportunity, for one cannot set up a specific instruction for everything. The hearts which are free, willing, unhampered, patient, [ready] to serve all the children of God, to have everything in common with them, yea, to persevere loyally and constantly in their service, shall remain always in the Lord. Where such hearts of grace exist, everything is soon ordered in the Lord. But whoever goes about in the congregation and the community of the saints with cunning and deception, untruth or lies, the Lord will bring to ruin . . . however long postponed—[also him] who seeks himself or does not work faithfully as for the Lord himself or as with the goods of the Lord, and does not rightly go about in the fear of the Lord.

Now follow the counterarguments.

Someone says that it is better, because of bickering and complaining, to be separate from each other, and that if everyone takes care of and lives unto himself, it stays more peaceful.

Answer: The complainer and grumbler, of course, who have never mortified the flesh, who do not control their desires and lusts, who have indeed abandoned the patience and the true love of God (whoever has this love of God in his heart is longsuffering and patient along with the rest of the pious here in these troubled times lest he lose himself too far in the world), yea, because of these things it is difficult or even impossible [for them] to live along with and in the midst of the others—[for them] who seek themselves, [who seek] to maintain their own life here comfortably, and to cultivate their body, as they have since childhood learned and been accustomed to doing according to the perverse manner [of the world]. Indeed, for such unmortified, carnal, natural men without the Spirit, it certainly is a heavy, bitter, unbearable life. Such persons seek freedom only to dwell someplace unto themselves in order that they might live pleasantly according to the flesh and unto their corruption. Otherwise they would surely be captured by the snares of blessedness and love. Those who had not been constrained to love within their hearts would nevertheless endure it in order not to become obvious, but upon such as these, God's severity should be visited.

Secondly, it is said that the children of God cannot all dwell in the same place. They cannot all be even in one land; nor is this really necessary, for the whole earth is the Lord's and it makes no difference where one dwells, so long as it is in the fear of God.

Answer: This is indeed true, but as far as it can be had and achieved, it is very good and purposeful to be together as well as can be so that all is possessed as by sojourners who seek another habitation. For to wander in the world and to have much to do with it and still to keep from being unsullied is possible for only a few and very hazardous. But whoever likes danger very likely comes to disaster thereby, especially in these times, which are much more full of danger than ever before. In this time a place has been given to the bride of the Lamb in which to dwell amid the wasteland of this world, there to put on the beautiful bright linen garment and thus to await the Lord until he leads her after him here in tribulation and afterward receives her with eternal joy. The time is now. Whoever has ears to hear, let him hear.

But when some are with others in one place even in misery and nevertheless do not live communally as friends and brothers in the Lord (as even children driven out hold together), but rather seek excuses— the one on account of his stomach, the other because of his wife and child, the third with another excuse, as it has gone on now for some time—they [obviously] do not recognize the other in their heart as one of their own, for whom they have as much love as for self. Otherwise they would surely bear and suffer one another. And also the well and the strong would surely be considerate of him who is ill and has a weak stomach and distribute to each one what is necessary for him to maintain the poor, miserable body. There are, in fact, several gross members of the community without understanding, who think that everyone has a good stomach and can digest anything [but due care should be given the weak]. May the deacons of welfare have, in this [whole matter], faithful supervision, so that on neither side is too much done for anybody lest the body be coddled

with faithless eating and drinking! In brief, wherever things are as described and each one sets up his kitchen, there it can[not] be said in truth that there is the one heart, soul, and body which must, however, and always should be among the children of God. If that is not the case, it must be remedied in the house of the Lord.

Thirdly, it is alleged for the time of the apostles that the congregations of Christ were not so ordered and were not thereby thrown upon one another, having all in common, as their letters show, except for a brief period in Jerusalem up to the separation [from Judaism].

Answer: I say there is a great difference in the times. There, they [the primitive Christians] were left in their homes and not at once driven into misery, but now the children of God have no place in the whole Roman Empire. For the Babylonian whore who sits on the dragon with seven heads, I mean the Roman Church, a synagogue of the living devil, spews out all the children of God and only drives them into the wilderness, unto their place, as declared above. Nonetheless, truth is truth and must so stand. And, moreover, all the elect follow it. She [truth] says this: We are never for ourselves but of the Lord. We have in truth nothing of our own, but rather all the gifts of God in common, be they temporal or spiritual, except that they [the deacons] should adapt the ordinances to the circumstances of time, place, and situation for the good of the children of God and not rule [autocratically] over the children of God, but rather they should at all times be ordered and interpreted for the improvement of the people. So judge all ordinances according to propriety and opportunity for the good of the saints and take hold with strength and bring it to pass that property, that is, his, mine, thine, will not be disclosed in the house of the Lord, but rather equal love, equal care and distribution, and true community in all the goods of the Father according to his will.

I say also of our own times if there were so many faithful allowed to remain in their homes as with the communities of Paul, they should but be true, faithful house managers and dispensers, and all things would be nicely arranged, as Paul shows. But the free, unencumbered, community-minded and yielded hearts must still be and remain precisely those who have everything in common with the children of God, gladly distribute and dispense, and who also gladly endure and suffer with the pious.

Fourthly, it is said that not all are so free and re-signed that they are able to be one with the community of all the elect, and these should not be expelled.

Answer: Such a self-ful, unsurrendered heart must be hewn and circumcised; and only then will it be useful for the construction of the house of the Lord. He must be forthrightly shown his retarded behavior and insufficiency in order that it may be like-minded and of one color with all the other resigned, holy children of God.

Further, it is said that God wishes to have a joyful giver, indeed, unencumbered, [giving] out of love and desire, not out of pressure and coercion.

Answer: Wait until one finds such grace in the Lord in a person and take nothing that is proffered joylessly and despondently. It is proper, however, for the deacons of the Lord in such a case to instruct, guide, and admonish with all patience, neither coddling nor rejecting, like Paul in whom one has an ideal pattern. There is a lack of mortified, free, unencumbered, yielded hearts. In the beginning they were [present] in the Lord, but now that the pilgrimage is postponed, they nestle down again in the world; and therewith there are few who long to leave the world. Indeed, they really prefer to live than to die [in Christ]. The saying: Death is my reward, becomes rarer among them, among many of them.

In conclusion, it is very good for the children of God, while they make their pilgrimage in misery, to assemble and hold themselves together, as well as can be achieved in the Lord, and not to take counsel concerning this with the flesh, for the flesh would never recommend it but rather wants to be and have only its own and not suffer it out with the pious.

Again, it is contended that nowhere in holy Scripture can it be read that it is a command of the Lord to bring together all the goods and to place deacons and stewards over them.

Answer: It is true abandon to yield and dispose oneself with goods and chattels in the service of the saints. It is also the way of love. Moreover, true friends have all things in common; indeed, they are called two bodies with but one soul. Yea, we learn it in Christ to lose oneself in the service of the saints, to be and become poor and to suffer want, if only another may be served, and further, to put aside all goods and chattels, to throw them away in order that they may be distributed to the needy and the impoverished. That is the highest part and degree of divine abandon and voluntary surrender to the Lord and to his people through the Spirit of grace.

In brief, a brother should serve, live, and work for the other, none for himself; indeed, one house for another, one community for another in some other settlement in the land, wherever the Lord grants it that we gather together, one communion, as a body of the Lord and members one to another. This we see in all the writings of the holy apostles, namely, how one brother, one congregation, serves the other, extends assistance and supplies to the other in the Lord. Such is the life of the elect, holy children of God in their pilgrimage. Amen.

The Catholic Reformation

The first generation of Protestant reformers was Catholic. Initially, they had no desire to break away from the church, but they did want to see a number of changes made. As time passed, however, and as feelings hardened on both sides, it became more difficult to compromise. Within the Catholic communion, those who were loyal to the papacy but argued for church reform were accused of siding with Luther. Outside of Catholicism, those who wanted to retain elements of Catholic tradition were accused of being popish, or of "popery." A number of dialogues between reformers and papal representatives occurred, and at times it seemed as though accommodation could be achieved, but negotiations frequently broke down on the issue of the papacy itself.

Despite the inability of the pope to rein in dissidents, the Catholic Church itself did undergo enormous reform. In part, this came about through efforts of moderates within Catholicism who thought that a church council might be a final opportunity to mend the breach with the Protestants. The Council of Trent, however, meeting from 1545–1563, proved decisive for conservatives rather than moderates. Nevertheless, critical changes occurred, especially in the areas of clergy education, ecclesiastical abuses, and church organization. A better-educated and better-disciplined clergy would now maintain the church's presence throughout Europe, even while church power declined in secular society. Change also came in large part through the efforts of reforming religious orders that sought engagement with the world in hospitals, schools, orphanages, and general relief programs. Though several significant orders emerged during the sixteenth century, two seem particularly important: the Jesuits and the Carmelites.

Ignatius of Loyola (1491?–1556), a Spanish adventurer, founded the Society of Jesus, or the Jesuits. Severely wounded in battle, it took Ignatius three years to recover. During his long convalescence, he read devotional literature and the Bible, and reoriented his thinking, but it took several more years before the charismatic leader organized a group of men much like himself: willing to sacrifice and serve in complete obedience to the pope. Unlike other religious orders, which maintained close ties with local bishops, the Jesuits promised loyalty directly to the pope, vowing to go wherever and whenever the pope required. The order focused on what it called "faith in action," rather than in contemplation, and led the way in missionary activities—especially to Asia and North America—and in education. At the same time, however, the Jesuits engaged in a rigorous form of meditation that Ignatius developed. These spiritual exercises were designed to lead participants from a state of abject self-hatred for their sins, through a meditation on Christ's sufferings, and into a state of joy based on the realization that Christ's sacrifice brought release from the punishment due for those sins. Meditation on the resurrection ultimately directed participants into the world of service. For the Jesuits, mystical contemplation led to worldly activity, especially in the mission field.

A second religious order also achieved importance during the Catholic Reformation. Instead of being active in the world like the Jesuits, however, the Discalced (shoeless) Carmelites focused on contemplation and mysticism. The Carmelite order was founded in Palestine at the end of the twelfth and beginning of the thirteenth centuries. It began as an order of hermits who devoted themselves to prayer, fasting, and meditation. When it moved to Europe, however, the order lost some of its initial zeal, and some of its original principles—such as abstinence from meat and a six-month fast—were modified.

During the sixteenth century, the daughter of a family of Jewish *conversos* (forced converts to Christianity) attempted to return to the stark austerity of the original Carmelites. Teresa of Avila (1515–1582) joined the Carmelite order in 1535. Almost two decades later, she experienced a spiritual break-through that changed her life. She began having visions and dreams that gave her the courage to commit herself totally to her vocation, or calling. Those experiences prompted Teresa to found a Discalced Carmelite convent in August 1562. The Discalced Carmelite nuns wore sandals or went barefoot and followed a strict regimen of daily prayer, silence, and fasting. By the time Teresa died, she had founded fifteen monasteries for women, directed two additional houses, and inaugurated two houses for men. One of the most influential of all Christian mystics, Saint John of the Cross, sought refuge in Teresa's new order. The friar and the abbess contributed greatly to Christian mysticism, and their reforms—like those of Ignatius, another Spanish Catholic—brought a new sense of order and discipline to Catholicism.

John of the Cross (1542–1591) described the "dark night of the soul," when he was imprisoned by his own order, the regular Carmelites, on the charge of heresy. The dark night epitomizes the long periods of time in which the soul of a believer might experience absolutely nothing exceptional or ecstatic, and, indeed, might feel distant or alienated from God. Teresa herself was familiar with this dark night, having experienced what mystics call "aridity," or dryness, for almost twenty years. Despite her best efforts, she did not feel particularly religious or close to God until she had been a nun for a long while.

The Reading

Teresa was a tenacious leader, whom the Vatican declared a "doctor of the church"—that is, a recognized teacher—within the past decade. Clearly, she was an able administrator and a woman of high energy, despite her debilitating illnesses. She is best known, however, as a mystical theologian. She wrote four major books that describe her spiritual journey. They are remarkably frank and intimate, and at times even a bit embarrassing to read. Her autobiography details her naughtiness as a child, her disappointments as a nun, and her struggles to keep faith. It also describes her tremendous organizing efforts to advance her reforms of the Carmelite order. *The Interior Castle* describes the process of contemplation and reports a vision she had in 1577 of a castle with seven rooms.

A collection of *Spiritual Testimonies* (1560), which Teresa wrote before she completed her autobiography, comprises the thoughts she presented to her confessor; that is, to the priest who heard her confession. "Her Spiritual State and Manner of Prayer," from the *Spiritual Testimonies,* discusses her visions, her practices, and her observations. It is written almost in a stream-of-consciousness style, with one thought not necessarily following from the preceding, but rather with each thought tumbling over the other. It clearly belongs to the genre of confessional literature: that writing in which the author closely examines the self in painstaking, and painful, detail.

Questions to Consider

1. What is prayer?
2. To what does Teresa attribute her visions? In other words, what is the source of her visions? What purpose do her visions seem to have?

3. What is Teresa's opinion of herself?

4. Given the fact that this testimony is really a collection of thoughts rather than an essay with a clear beginning, middle, and end, is there nonetheless some sort of thematic unity to the piece? If so, what is it? If not, does the piece hang together in any way?

5. How does Teresa's view of grace compare with that of Luther or Calvin? In general, how does she differ from the Protestant writers you have read? How is she similar?

6. Do you ever conduct the same kind of intense self-examination that Teresa does?

7. How does this writing compare to Julian of Norwich's *Revelations of Divine Love,* which we read in Chapter Three? Does Teresa seem to fit the profile outlined by Caroline Walker Bynum?

8. Where does Teresa encounter the divine? In scripture? In service? In thoughts? Is her method of understanding God valid? Why or why not?

Her Spiritual State and Manner of Prayer

TERESA OF AVILA

My present procedure in prayer is as follows: I am seldom able while in prayer to use my intellect in a discursive way, for my soul immediately begins to grow recollected; and it remains in quiet or rapture to the extent that I cannot make any use of the senses. This recollection reaches such a point that if it were not for hearing—and this hearing does not include understanding—none of the senses would be of any avail.

2. It often happens to me that this recollection and elevation of the spirit comes upon me so suddenly I cannot resist; and in a moment I receive the effects and benefits that it carries in its wake. This recollection occurs without my desiring to reflect on the things of God and while I am dealing with other things and thinking that even if I tried to practice prayer I wouldn't be able to because of great dryness, intensified by bodily pains. It happens without my having a vision, or understanding anything, or knowing where I am. But while it seems to me that my soul is getting lost, I see what it gains, so that should I have desired to obtain these blessings myself in the course of a year I don't think it would have been possible to have acquired them.

3. At other times I receive a very intense, consuming impulse for God that I cannot resist. It seems my life is coming to an end, and so this impulse makes me cry out and call to God; and it comes with great frenzy. Sometimes I'm unable to remain seated because of the vomitings from which I suffer; and this pain comes upon me without my seeking it. It is of such a kind that the soul would never want to be relieved of it as long as it lives. I have longings not to live this apparent life any more. I cannot find any remedy for these longings, since the cure for the desire to see God is death; and I cannot take this cure. Along with this, it seems to my soul that everyone has the greatest consolation except itself and that all find a cure for their trials except itself. This causes such affliction that if the Lord didn't provide a remedy by means of a certain rapture, in which everything is made peaceful and the soul remains in deep quiet and satisfaction—now beholding something of what it desires, now understanding other things—it would be impossible to get free from that pain.

4. At other times, some desires to serve God come upon me with impulses so strong I don't know how to exaggerate them, and there is also pain in seeing of

what little use I am. It seems to me, then, that no trial, neither death, nor martyrdom, nor anything could be offered to me that I wouldn't easily undergo. This, too, occurs without reflection; but in an instant it changes me completely, and I don't know where I get so much strength. It seems to me I would want to cry out and make everyone understand what is gained by not being satisfied with a few things and how much good there is that God will give us if we dispose ourselves for it. I say these desires are of a kind that consume me, for I want what I am unable to procure. It seems to me this body and this state bind me, for they are no good at all for serving God. If I wasn't so bound, I would do very noble deeds insofar as my strength would allow. But I feel such pain in seeing I have no power to serve Him that I cannot exaggerate it. I end up with delight and recollection and consolations from God.

5. At other times, when these anxious longings to serve Him come upon me, I feel I want to do penance; but I am unable. Penance would bring me great relief, and it does bring me relief and joy, although the penances amount to almost nothing on account of the weakness of my body; yet were these desires to remain, I think I would do too much.

6. Sometimes it gives me great pain to have to have dealings with others; it afflicts me so much that it causes me to weep profusely, because all my longing is to be alone. And even though sometimes I do not pray or read, solitude consoles me. Conversation, especially with relatives, seems to me burdensome. I feel as though I am among strangers, except when I am with those whom I speak about prayer and the soul, for with these persons I am happy and consoled, although sometimes I have enough of them and do not want to see them but want to go where I can be alone; but this latter happens seldom, especially in the case of those to whom I manifest my conscience, for they are always a consolation to me.

7. At other times it gives me great pain to have to eat and sleep and to see that I more than anyone cannot give up these actions. I perform them to serve God, and so I offer them to Him. It seems to me that all time is short and that I don't have enough for prayer, for I never tire of being alone. I always want to have time to read because I have been very fond of reading. I read very little, for in picking up a book I become recollected in my contentment, and so the time for reading passes in prayer. This time amounts to little, for I have many duties; and though they are good, they do not provide me with the satisfaction reading does. So I go about always wanting time, and the

awareness that what I want and desire is not granted is that which, I think, makes everything insipid to me.

8. All these desires and those, too, for virtue were given me by our Lord after He gave me this quiet prayer with these raptures; and I found I was so improved that it seems to me I was previously a total loss. These raptures and visions leave in me the benefits I shall here describe. And I say that if I have anything good, it has come from these.

9. There has come upon me a very strong determination not to offend God, not even venially; for I would die a thousand deaths rather than offend Him knowingly. There is the determination not to omit anything I think is more perfect or will render greater service to our Lord when the one who has care for me and directs me says this is so; and even though I may perform such action reluctantly, I wouldn't for any treasure fail to do it. And if I should do the contrary, I don't think I would dare ask our Lord God for anything, or practice prayer, although in all these matters I commit many faults and imperfections. I obey my confessor, although imperfectly. Yet, once I have understood that he wants something or has given me a command and insofar as I know I wouldn't fail to carry it out; and were I to fail, I would think I was being very much mistaken.

I desire poverty, although imperfectly. Yet, I think that even were I to possess many treasures, I wouldn't keep any special income or any money for myself alone, nor would this matter to me. I would only want to have what's necessary. Still, I feel I'm very much lacking in this virtue. For although I don't desire any money for myself, I should like to have it so as to give it away, though I don't desire any income or anything for myself.

10. From almost all the visions I've experienced, I've received some benefit, except in those cases where there is deception from the devil. In this I submit to my confessors.

11. When I see something beautiful or rich, like water, fields, flowers, fragrances, music, and so on, it seems to me that I wouldn't want to see or hear these things, so great is the difference between them and what I am accustomed to seeing; thus all desire for such things is taken from me. And as a result I have come to care so little for them that, save for the first stirrings, they make no impression on me and seem like dung.

12. If I speak or have dealings with some secular persons because matters can't be otherwise, and even though the subject may concern prayer, I find that if

the conversation is prolonged, just a diversion and unnecessary, I am forcing myself to continue, because such conversation is a severe hardship for me. Amusements that I used to like and things of the world, all annoy me; and I cannot look at them.

13. These desires for loving and serving God and seeing Him, which I mentioned that I have, are not fostered by reflections as they were previously when it seemed to me I was very devout and when I shed many tears. But they come with so excessive an enkindling and fervor that I repeat that if God did not cure me by means of some rapture, in which it seems to me my soul is satisfied, I think my life would soon come to an end.

14. I greatly love those who I see are more advanced and who are determined, detached, and courageous; and they are the ones with whom I would want to converse; it seems they help me. Persons who I see are timid, who I think proceed with great circumspection so that things can be done here below in conformity with reason are oppressive to me and make me cry to God and to His saints, who undertook those things that now frighten us. I feel this, not because I think I am worth anything but because I think God helps those who set out to do much for Him and that He never fails anyone who trusts in Him alone. I should like to find someone who would help me believe this, and not have to worry about what I must eat and wear, but be able to abandon that to God. It shouldn't be thought that this abandonment to God in necessities means I don't try to procure them, but I mean I don't do so with a concern that makes me worry. Since He has given me this freedom, such abandonment does me good, and I strive to forget myself as much as I can. It doesn't seem a year has yet passed since our Lord has given me this freedom.

15. Insofar as I know, glory to God, there is no reason for me to experience vainglory. For I observe clearly in these things God grants that I don't do anything myself; rather, God gives me a feeling of my miseries. No matter how much thinking I might do, I would never be able to see all the truths I come to know in a moment.

16. For a few days now, it seems to me as if I am speaking of another person when I speak of these things. Before, I was ashamed sometimes that my experiences were known, but now I think I'm no better on account of so many favors but worse since I profit so little from them. Indeed, I think there hasn't been anyone worse than I in any part of the world. So it seems to me that the virtues of others have much

more merit, that I don't do anything but receive favors, and that God will give others all at once what He desires to give me here. I beseech Him not to want to pay me in this life, and so I believe that because I am weak and wretched the Lord has led me by this path.

17. While in prayer, and almost whenever I'm able to reflect a little, I'm unable to ask for rest or to desire it from God, even if I try. For I see that He didn't live but with trials; and I beg Him to give me these, granting me first the grace to suffer them.

18. All these kinds of things that have to do with very sublime perfection it seems are impressed upon me in prayer, so much so that I am amazed to see so many truths and so clearly, for the things of the world appear to me to be nonsense. So I need to be careful by reflecting on what my attitude was previously toward the things of the world, for it seems to me that to grieve over its deaths and trials is foolish, at least if the sorrow or the love of relatives, friends, and so on, lasts a long while. I say that I proceed carefully, reflecting on what I was and what I used to feel.

19. If in some persons I see things that clearly seem to be sins, I cannot come to the conclusion they have offended God. And if I stop somewhat to consider them—which happens hardly or not at all—I never reach that conclusion, although I may have seen the things clearly. It seems to me the care I have about serving God is had by all. In this matter He has granted me a great favor, for I never pause to consider anything evil; because when I afterward recall it, and if I recall it, I always see another virtue in that person. Thus these things never distress me, unless in the case of something that is common, or of heresies which often cause me affliction. And almost as often as I think about them it seems to me that this trial alone is the one that must be felt. I also grieve if I see some persons who used to practice prayer turn back. This grieves me, but not a lot, since I strive not to pause to think about it.

20. I also find improvement in regard to my former vanities, but it is not complete; for I'm not always mortified in this regard, although sometimes, yes.

21. All of this I have said is what ordinarily takes place in my soul insofar as I can understand. I very habitually keep my mind fixed on God; and when I am dealing with other things, without desire on my part—as I say—I am made attentive by I don't know who. I am not always made attentive but only when I'm dealing with some important matter; and this attentiveness to these matters lasts for only a short while and, glory to God, is not continuous.

22. It happens to me on some days—although not often, and the experience lasts about three, four, or five days—that it seems to me that all the good things, fervor, and visions have been taken away; and even taken from my memory, for I don't know, although I may want to, what good there has been in me. Everything seems to have been a dream, at least I'm not able to remember anything. All my bodily ills together afflict me. My intellect disturbs me because I cannot think anything about God, nor do I know what state I'm in. If I read, I don't understand. It seems to me I am full of faults, without any courage for virtue, and that that great courage I usually have dwindles to this: that I'd be unable to resist the least temptation or criticism from the world. It occurs to me then that I'm good for nothing, that no one could force me to do more than what is ordinary; I feel sad; I feel I've deceived all those who have given me some credit. I should like to hide some place where no one would see me; not solitude for virtue's sake, but out of pusillanimity. It seems to me I'd want to quarrel with everyone who contradicts me. I carry about with me this battle, except that God grants me the favor of not offending Him more than I usually do. Nor do I ask Him to take away this state, but that if it is His will it might remain always, that He keep me in His hands that I might not offend Him; and I conform myself to Him with all my heart. I believe it is an extraordinary favor He grants me that I am not always in this condition.

23. One thing amazes me, that, while I'm in this state, with one word alone of those I'm accustomed to hearing, or one vision, or a little recollection that lasts for the space of a Hail Mary, or in approaching to receive Communion, my soul and body will become very quiet, and my intellect very sound and clear, and I will feel all the fortitude and desires I usually have. I have experienced for more than a half year that at least when I am receiving Communion I noticeably and clearly feel bodily health. Sometimes I feel this by means of raptures, which occasionally last more than three hours. At other times I am greatly improved throughout the whole day. In my opinion this is not a matter of fancy, because I have observed and taken note of it. As a result, when I have this recollection I don't fear any illness. It is true that when I experience the prayer I did before, I do not feel this improvement.

24. All these things I mentioned make me believe these favors are from God. For since I know who I was, that I was walking on the road of perdition, it is certain that in a short while through these experiences my soul became amazed, not knowing where these virtues came from. I didn't know myself; I saw they were something given and not gained through toil. I understand in all clarity and truthfulness, and know I am not deceived, that this has been a means by which God not only brought me to His service but freed me from hell. All of this my confessors to whom I've made my general confessions know.

25. Also, when I meet any person who knows something about me, I want to explain my life to him. For I think it is an honor to me that our Lord be praised, and I don't care anything about the rest. He knows this well, or I am very blind; for there is no honor or life or glory or any good of body or soul that holds me back, nor would I want or desire my own gain, but only His glory. I cannot believe the devil sought out so many blessings to win my soul in order that he might afterward lead it astray, for I don't consider him to be that stupid. Nor can I believe, though on account of my sins I deserve to be deceived, that God would fail to hear so many prayers offered up over a period of two years by so many good people—for I don't do anything else but ask everyone for prayers—in order that He would either let me know if this is for His glory or lead me by another path. I don't believe His divine Majesty would permit these experiences always to continue if they were not from Him.

26. Since I am so wretched, these things and the teachings of so many saints give me assurance when I have these fears about whether or not my experiences are from God. But if when I'm in prayer or on the days in which I am quiet and my thoughts are on God, all the learned men and saints in the world were to join together and torture me with all the torments imaginable, and I wanted to believe them, I wouldn't be able to make myself believe that these things come from the devil; for I cannot. When they wanted to force me to believe that the devil was the cause, I feared, upon seeing who said this, and I thought they must be saying the truth and that I, being what I was, was being deceived. But at the first locution, or experience of recollection, or vision, all they had told me was blotted out; I couldn't do anything but believe God was the cause.

27. Although I can realize the devil could sometimes meddle—and this is so, as I have seen and said—the effects he causes are different. And whoever has experience will not be deceived, in my opinion. Still, I say that even were I to believe an experience is certainly from God, I wouldn't do anything for any reason if it didn't seem to the one who

has the charge over me that it would be for the service of our Lord. I have never thought but that I should obey and not be silent about anything, because this is good for me.

28. I am ordinarily reprimanded for my faults, and in such a way that it touches me to the very core. And when there is or can be some danger in what I am dealing with, I receive counsels which are very profitable to me. Often my past sins are brought to memory and cause me much grief.

29. I have gone on at great length, but it is certainly true that in regard to the blessings I see in myself when I come out of prayer I have been brief. Afterward I find that I have many imperfections and that I'm useless and very wretched. Perhaps I don't understand the good things, but am deceived; yet, the difference in my life is well-known and makes me reflect on what I have said. In all I've said, I've told what it seems to me I have truly experienced.

These are the perfect qualities I feel the Lord has wrought in me who am so wretched and imperfect. I submit everything to the judgment of your Reverence since you know my entire soul.

Conclusions

Many of the denominational differences we see in the twenty-first century have their roots in doctrinal debates from and decisions made in the sixteenth century. Church practices in the West—such as communion and baptism—underwent redefinition and clarification. Church teachings were further clarified, with theologians and apologists specifying what they believed led to justification and why humans seemed so prone to sinfulness. The very appearance of churches changed, as iconoclastic Christians eliminated the art and architecture they associated with Catholic Christianity and with idolatry.

In our present time of religious and cultural conflict, it may be easier for us to understand how religious disputes might lead to open war. That is, in fact, what happened in the sixteenth century, as Catholic and Protestant nobles and rulers clashed with Protestant and Catholic believers. All sides believed in the truth and righteousness of what they were doing, which was to defend the faith and to preserve fidelity to church teachings and to scripture. And on all sides many were executed for faithfulness to their creeds and confessions. Eventually, the Peace of Augsburg (1555) recognized what was, in fact, happening throughout Europe: the religion of the prince or ruler was to be accepted as the religion of the people. In Catholic countries, this meant that Catholicism was practiced; in Protestant countries or principalities, Protestantism was the norm.

The Reformation did not change only religion and politics. It also profoundly altered the way individuals looked at their relationship to authority, whether religious or secular. If some were challenging the power of the pope and the priests, then why not question the legitimacy of prince or monarch? Luther had addressed this issue with his advancement of a "two-kingdoms" doctrine, which attempted to protect worldly authority from religious challenges, and vice versa. The seeds of the demise of this doctrine, however, existed in another of Luther's ideas: that of the priesthood of all believers. If individual Christians no longer needed priests or

(*continued on page 237*)

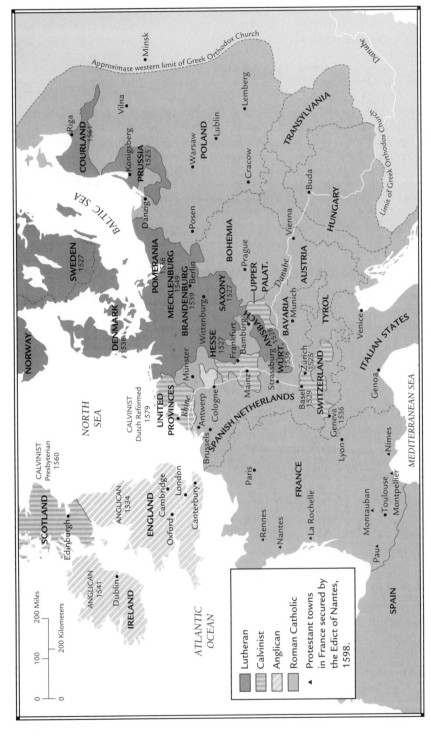

Distribution of religious groups in Europe, c. 1600.

▨ The Wars of Religion

Religious conflict led to bloodshed throughout the sixteenth and seventeenth centuries. Some of the violence came from Catholic mobs attacking Protestants, as in the Saint Bartholomew's Day massacre in Paris in 1572; some came from Protestant mobs attacking French armies in 1702. Some of the violence was state-sponsored persecution of religious minorities—whether Catholic, mainline, or radical—in which those accused of heresy were executed. And still other conflicts occurred between different nation-states that saw religious alliances, or differences, as a way to bolster territorial claims. In short, it was a time of wars and battles, both large and small.

Initial disputes between Catholics and Lutherans in Germany led to several edicts requiring religious toleration. These edicts were violated, however, and the Schmalkald War (1546–1547) ended in the defeat of the Protestant-organized Schmalkald League by Charles V (r. 1519–1556), the Holy Roman Emperor and nominal ruler of Germany. German Catholics rebelled against the Catholic emperor, however, because of his mistreatment of German Protestant princes. The Peace of Augsburg (1555) settled the dispute and granted religious toleration to Catholics and to signatories of the Augsburg Confession—which meant that only Lutheran Protestants were protected.

In Switzerland, Ulrich Zwingli sought the expulsion of all forms of Catholicism from the Swiss cantons. Swiss Catholics responded by attacking Zurich, and Zwingli died in battle. An agreement between Catholic and Protestant cantons emerged from this conflict, in which each canton would maintain its religious identity, as long as Catholic minorities were tolerated.

In France, the situation of French Huguenots (the French Protestants), who accounted for about ten percent of the French population, changed according to the wishes and whims of French kings and their advisors. When the Protestant king Henry of Navarre (r. 1589–1610) married a Catholic, Margaret of Valois, Huguenot leaders were murdered in their beds, thus sparking riots against Protestants throughout France. Henry converted to Catholicism upon becoming king, but issued the Edict of Nantes in 1598, proclaiming toleration for Protestants, except in Paris. The French period of toleration was short-lived, however, because Cardinal Richelieu (1585–1642)—the advisor to King Louis XIII—saw Protestant cities and forces as a threat to France. In 1627, the French army attacked La Rochelle, a Protestant stronghold, and Richelieu suspended the Edict of Nantes. The assault on La Rochelle mobilized Protestants around the country, who counterattacked. When they were defeated and subdued, Richlieu reinstituted the Edict of Nantes in 1629. While Richelieu sought to keep Protestants in check in France, he allied himself with Protestants abroad in order to protect French interests in war against the Catholic Habsburg dynasty. After Richelieu's death, French Protestants grew in number under Cardinal

Continued

Jules Mazarin (1602–1661). But with the ascension of Louis XIV (1638–1715) to the throne, Protestants again faced intimidation and oppression. Louis issued the Edict of Fontainbleu in 1685, invalidating the Edict of Nantes. This made it illegal to be a Protestant in France, and many fled to the Netherlands, to England, and to America.

During the Thirty Years' War (1618–1648), most political alliances fell along Catholic and Protestant lines, but there were some exceptions, as in the case of Cardinal Richelieu, noted above. Indeed, a number of Catholic princes outside of Germany sided with the Protestants, fearing the power of the Habsburgs. Catholic armies slaughtered Protestants, and Protestant forces wiped out Catholics. Denmark and Sweden, England and the Netherlands, France and Germany, and Bohemia—where the war began—all were drawn into the fight at one point or another. The war degenerated into a series of lootings, raids, and skirmishes. The Peace of Westphalia (1648) essentially restored the conditions set at the Peace of Augsburg, although Calvinists were now tolerated. The radical reformers, such as Anabaptists, remained excluded.

In addition to wars fought by nation-states, some of the radicals also engaged in holy wars to recover biblical principles. The Peasant Revolts of 1525 came about through Thomas Müntzer's (d. 1525) reading of the biblical proclamation of "good news" to the poor—and his apocalyptic vision of the great reversal of rich and poor—as well as from the desperate condition of poor farmers who had endured bad harvests. Thousands of peasants, armed only with farm implements, died at the hands of well-armed governmental forces. The "New Jerusalem," in the city of Münster, also saw a bloody reign of terror in which all Catholics and Lutherans were executed. Jan Matthys (d. 1534) abolished private property and created a communal economy. His follower, John of Leiden (1510–1536), made himself king and messiah, and ruled as a tyrant. The Catholic bishop of Münster had begun a siege against the city in 1534, and by June 1535, residents were starved out, and Catholicism restored.

The wars of religion were primarily fought for political and territorial reasons, with allegiances shifting due to expediency rather than religious conviction. They helped, in part, to set the stage for the eighteenth-century "Age of Reason" by undermining the spiritual authority of religious leaders. The wars revealed the worldly, rather than otherworldly, goals of prelates such as Cardinal Richelieu. Even when the goals were religious—such as those in "New Jerusalem" or in the Peasant Revolts—it was clear that Christianity could unleash powerful and destructive forces. A war-weary Europe would soon see a radical skepticism surface, with new battles to come.

(continued from page 233)

prelates, did they need princes and principalities? Although it was not the intent of any reformer, democratizing ideas flowed from their pens and within a few centuries would radically transform the world.

Sources for Selections

Calvin, John. "By the Fall and Revolt of Adam the Whole Human Race Was Delivered to the Curse, and Degenerated from Its Original Condition; the Doctrine of Original Sin." In *Institutes of the Christian Religion,* Book II, Chapter 1. Ed. John T. McNeill, trans. Ford Lewis Battles. Philadelphia: Westminster Press, 1960.

Cranmer, Thomas. *The Book of Common Prayer,* 1552 edition. Palo Alto, Calif.: Society of Archbishop Justus, n.d. <http://justus.anglican.org/resources/bcp/1552/Communion_1552.htm>.

Leith, John H., ed. *Creeds of the Churches: A Reader in Christian Doctrine from the Bible to the Present.* 3rd ed. Louisville, Ky.: John Knox Press, 1982.

Luther, Martin. *Preface to the Letter of St. Paul to the Romans.* Trans. Andrew Thornton, O.S.B. Ft. Wayne, Ind.: Concordia Theological Seminary, n.d. http://www.ccel.org/l/luther/romans/pref_romans.html.

Stadler, Ulrich. "Cherished Instructions on Sin, Excommunication, and the Community of Goods." In *Spiritual and Anabaptist Writers: Documents Illustrative of the Radical Reformation.* Ed. George Huntston Williams. Philadelphia: Westminster Press, 1957.

Teresa of Avila. "Her Spiritual State and Manner of Prayer." In *The Collected Works of St. Teresa of Avila,* Vol. One, *Spiritual Testimonies.* Trans. Kieran Kavanaugh and Otilio Rodriguez. Washington, D.C.: Institute of Carmelite Studies, 1976.

Additional Resources

Chadwick, Owen. *The Reformation.* New York: Penguin Books, 1990.

Hillerbrand, Hans J., ed. *The Oxford Encyclopedia of the Reformation.* New York: Oxford University Press, 1996.

Jedin, Hubert. *A History of the Council of Trent.* Trans. Ernest Graf. London: T. Nelson, 1957–61.

McGrath, Alister E. *Reformation Thought: An Introduction.* Oxford and New York: Blackwell, 1988.

Oberman, Heiko. *Luther: Man Between God and the Devil.* Trans. Eileen Walliser-Schwarzbart. New Haven: Yale University Press, 1989.

Ozment, Steven. *The Age of Reform (1250–1550): An Intellectual and Religious History of Late Medieval and Reformation Europe.* New Haven and London: Yale University Press, 1980.

Steinmetz, David. *Calvin in Context.* New York: Oxford University Press, 1995.

Williams, George Huntston. *The Radical Reformation.* Philadelphia: Westminster Press, 1962.

Films

Anne of the Thousand Days. Directed by Charles Jarrott, 1969.

Luther. Directed by Eric Till, 2003.

A Man for All Seasons. Directed by Fred Zinnemann, 1966.

The Six Wives of Henry VIII. Directed by Naomi Capon, 1972.

	c. 1624	Lord Herbert of Cherbury, De Veritate
Peace of Westphalia	1648	
	1649	Society of Friends founded by George Fox
Spinoza, Theologico-Political Treatise	1670	
	1675	Philipp Spener, Pia Desideria
John Locke, The Reasonableness of Christianity	1689	
	1722	Moravians found Herrnhut
First Great Awakening in U.S.	c. 1730–40	
	1775–83	American Revolution
Gotthold Lessing, Nathan the Wise	1779	
	1781	Immanuel Kant, Critique of Pure Reason
French Revolution	1787–99	
	1799	Friedrich Schleiermacher, On Religion: Speeches to its Cultured Despisers
Cane Ridge Revival: Second Great Awakening in U.S.	1801	
	1819	Joseph Marie de Maistre, De Pape (On the Pope)
?Sigmund Freud born (d. 1939)	1856	
	1859	Charles Darwin, On the Origin of Species
Syllabus of Errors	1864	
	1867	Karl Marx, Das Kapital
Vatican Council I	1869–70	
	1900	Adolf von Harnack, The Essence of Christianity
Alfred Loisy, The Gospel and the Church	1902	

CHAPTER FIVE

Rationalism and the Quest for Authority

While the reformations of the sixteenth century fractured the unity of Christendom, they also tended to consolidate secular power in nations under the rule of kings and queens. The religious wars of the sixteenth and seventeenth centuries had secular goals and purposes: securing borders, acquiring territory, and amassing wealth. Freeing communities from papal control and reclaiming land, and souls, for the pope balanced temporal benefits with spiritual ends.

Yet the combatants eventually tired of these wars. The Peace of Augsburg (1555) halted religious conflict in Germany for the most part, with inhabitants following the dictates of their local ruler—*cuius regio, eius religio* (the religion of the ruler is the religion of the people). This meant that large sections of what eventually became Germany remained Catholic, while equally large sections became Lutheran. The Elizabethan Settlement of 1559–1603 did not give Catholics equal rights in England, but it did allow them limited opportunity to practice their faith. The Edict of Nantes (1598) brought peace for a time to French Protestants, until its revocation in 1685 by Louis XIV. And the Peace of Westphalia concluded the Thirty Years' War between England and France in 1648, bringing a measure of stability, or perhaps exhaustion, to religious and political opponents.

Christians in the West take religious toleration for granted today, but in the tumultuous years following Luther, Calvin, Ignatius and others, toleration was not the norm, nor was it considered positive. Although scholars once viewed toleration as the triumph of reason over dogma, and of rationalism over superstition, today historians locate the rise of toleration within a religious context. Christians advocated tolerance and liberty of conscience in self-defense, frequently from the perspective of a persecuted minority. Thus, Catholics living in England, where they were denied many civil and legal rights, might support religious toleration, while Catholics living in France might deny those same rights to French Protestants. Sometimes religious toleration was imposed from the top down, such as that advocated by Frederick II of Prussia (1712–1786) or Joseph II of Austria (1741–1790). Occasionally, popular disgust with religious conflict or oppression fueled demands for toleration. An exception to popular toleration of difference was the violent persecution of women as witches, or "servants of Satan," in this period.

Challenges to religious authority, as well as war fatigue, seemed to accompany a fascination with science and scientific discovery. This convergence of factors in the eighteenth century is known as the Enlightenment. Although this era is credited with the concept of religious toleration, other factors were at work as well. There is no denying, however, the profound impact Enlightenment thinking had on western Christianity.

The Enlightenment

The Enlightenment describes the social, cultural, scientific, religious, and political milieu of eighteenth-century Europe. (Many of those developments resulted from European contact with other cultures, especially in Asia but also in Africa and the Americas; the next chapter addresses the impact of missionaries on international cultures, and their influence, in turn, on Christianity.) Eighteenth-century philosophers coined the expression "Enlightenment" to contrast their own thinking to that of previous generations, in much the same way that Renaissance thinkers called the Middle Ages "dark" and "middle" to differentiate their own rebirth of culture and civilization. Whatever we call it, great changes began to occur in the seventeenth century and continued into the nineteenth.

Scientific discoveries characterize these changes, beginning in the seventeenth century with Isaac Newton in physics and Robert Boyle in chemistry; continuing in the eighteenth century with Antoine Lavoisier, a French chemist and public servant, and Charles Linneaus, a Swedish botanist; and into the nineteenth, with the Swiss geologist Louis Agassiz and the English naturalist Charles Darwin. The new scientific method differed from the previous approach to science—once called natural philosophy—by inducing conclusions from empirical evidence, rather than deducing conclusions from propositions and axioms. The clearest example of this is Newton inducing the theory of gravity from observing an apple falling from a tree.

The rise in literacy among all segments of the populace in Europe, though especially in cities, also marks this epoch. The previous chapter noted the impact of the printing press on the dissemination of Reformation theology and arguments. Print grew as the major conveyor of ideas during the Enlightenment: through an active press, with many newspapers; through pamphlets; and through books written in the vernacular (the language that people spoke) or, if written in Latin, the international language of learning, then rapidly translated into local languages. John Locke's first *Letter on Toleration* is a good example of the rapid spread of ideas through print. First published in Latin in 1689, it was translated into English later that same year.

The growth of cities created new spaces and forums for public debate and expression. Coffeehouses and taverns, for example, served as locations for vigorous discussion of political and social issues. Drama was a growing field, with literally thousands of people attending popular productions in France and England by the end of the eighteenth century. We could say that theaters and bars served as the eighteenth-century chat rooms, where a broad variety of ideas were exchanged.

All of these developments influenced thinkers and writers in Europe. The *philosophes* of France, the Common Sense thinkers of Scotland, the philosophers of Germany—all shaped, and were shaped, by these currents of change. They articulated in striking terms an alternate source of religious authority: reason. Human reason, rather than supernatural revelation, was a more reliable source of authority. Accessible to all—or at least to all educated persons—reason and logic trumped dogma and doctrine because its truths were "self-evident." When Thomas Jefferson (1743–1826) wrote, "We hold these truths to be self-evident," he was saying that the U.S. Declaration of Independence was based on human reason and not on divine revelation—even though the self-evident, or obvious, truth was that God had created all people with equal and unalienable rights.

Indeed, an eighteenth-century Anglican preacher, John Wesley (1703–1791), articulated the key religious concern debated during the Reformation and in subsequent centuries: What is the primary source of authority for Christians? Another way of posing this same question is to ask: On what do Christians base their decisions? How do Christians know that what they claim to be true actually *is* true? Luther had argued *sola scriptura,* that is, "scripture alone": they turn to the Bible to confirm their beliefs and convictions. The Council of Trent gave equal weight to scripture and tradition. The Bible and the teachings of the church—what had been handed down by the apostles and preserved in Christian tradition—were equally authoritative. The Anglican Church added reason as a third "pillar" to the authority of scripture and tradition. Christians had to use reason in order to evaluate the authority claimed by scripture, tradition, and their interpreters.

Wesley came out of the Anglican tradition and its three pillars, but he was also influenced by another source of authority: the experience of the Holy Spirit in his life. This personal experience of holiness was the only thing that, for Wesley, made the scriptures come alive. He was influenced by a movement known as Pietism, which called for a religion of the heart, rather than of the head or of the will. His understanding of Christianity led to the formation of a new denomination, Methodism, that attempted to apply scripture and tradition methodically to daily life. As a result, Wesley developed what Methodists call the "Quadrilateral"—the four sources, or sides, of religious authority for Christians: scripture, tradition, experience, and reason. While the spiritual descendants of Wesley—United Methodists, Wesleyans, and Nazarenes—explicitly utilize the Quadrilateral in their religious decision making, all Christian denominations, as well as individual Christians, emphasize one or more of these sources. It may be Pentecostal Christians, who turn to the experience of the Holy Spirit (see Chapter Seven); Bible Baptists, who rely on scripture; Unitarians or Liberal Protestants, who include reason in their decision-making processes; or Catholic and Orthodox Christians, who value the traditions handed down through the centuries. All seem to be employing at least one element of Wesley's Quadrilateral.

The concept of the Quadrilateral is useful for understanding the developments within Christianity during the seventeenth, eighteenth, and nineteenth centuries.

Rather than limit the Enlightenment to the eighteenth century—beginning, perhaps, with John Locke's essay *The Reasonableness of Christianity* in 1695 and culminating in the French Revolution of 1789—it seems preferable to also consider the events occurring prior to and after this century to get a better understanding of the dynamic processes at work: the push and pull of movements, people, and ideas. Some have called this entire era the "Age of Reason," but that nomenclature is only partially true.

The nineteenth-century German philosopher Georg Hegel (1770–1831) saw history as a dialectical process of constant change, from thesis, to antithesis, to synthesis. In other words, we begin with a particular idea or worldview (thesis), which is challenged by other ideas and opinions (antithesis). A synthesis of these two elements occurs, and then the process begins all over again, with the synthesis serving as the new thesis. It is tempting to examine the seventeenth, eighteenth, and nineteenth centuries using this Hegelian analysis: religious wars led to reactions, which led to toleration; reason was countered with feelings, which led to romanticism; and so on. This oversimplifies, however, complex political, social, and religious issues. Nevertheless, Hegel's dialectical explanation for change, as well as Wesley's Quadrilateral, are concepts to keep in mind as we observe how Christians used a variety of methods to understand and explain Christian truths.

Although Wesley began with the authority of scripture and ended with that of reason, I have altered the order of his Quadrilateral by starting with reason and concluding with tradition. This rearrangement comes out of the argument I am trying to make, the natural flow of the readings, and a rough historical chronology. I commence with reason because most of the writers represented in this chapter had to deal with the impact of reason upon theology, and formulate a response, either positive or negative, to its demands upon faith.

The Authority of Reason

What is reason? It is the ability to think and to make judgments, the capacity to view facts or evidence and to come to conclusions. We usually associate reason with the head (where the brain is located) and feelings with the heart. While reason seems to be a universal human characteristic, facts—which we might assume to be unalterably true—actually seem to be variable over time. For example, the "fact" that the earth is flat or that the sun orbits the earth has been superseded by new "facts." And in our own lifetimes, we have seen scientists revise and revisit the known "facts" about the size of the universe, the components of the atom, and so on.

Reason had always played a role in the interpretation of Christian doctrine. We see it in the writings of early Christian apologists, who attempted to defend Christianity so that their contemporaries could understand it. We see it in the scholastic movement of the Middle Ages, when Christians tried to interpret doctrine according to logic. We see it to a lesser extent during the Reformation, when Christians argued from the Bible to advance and support their assertions. But reason becomes extremely important in the seventeenth and eighteenth centuries for one crucial reason: Christians could not, or would not, agree on doctrinal arguments advanced on scripture or tradition. Perhaps an appeal to reason would prove persuasive to skeptics and believers alike.

The critique of traditional metaphysics was a second motivation for using reason to examine theology. Metaphysics is the branch of philosophy that examines the nature of being, the origins of the world, and the foundations of our ability to know things. In other words, metaphysics shares the same concerns that Christian theology does, but starts from a different place, namely, in the mind and the world, rather than in the Bible and revelation. In the eighteenth century, the German philosopher Immanuel Kant (1724–1804) questioned our ability to reach truths merely by thinking about them. Kant criticized the speculative philosophy that "proved" self-evident truths through circular reasoning. We shouldn't assume what we are attempting to prove, he argued. In other words, our thoughts about God, or freedom, or immortality do not conform to the reality of these concepts; on the contrary, we create the reality with our thoughts. We can only truly know something if we can observe it empirically. Kant's philosophical approach challenged religious certainty as well as philosophical self-confidence. We can only prove the existence of God if we assume the existence of God, since there does not seem to be any solid empirical evidence about God's existence that all people can share.

Another philosopher, David Hume (1711–1776), was even more skeptical than Kant about our ability to know anything. The Scottish philosopher, historian, and economist restricted human knowledge solely to the experience of ideas and impressions. And even then, Hume doubted that we could form any certain conclusions. For example, he argued that causality is a habit of mind. What he meant was that we merely *think* one thing causes another when, in reality, they may be unrelated events that occur sequentially, but not necessarily consequentially. Hume claimed that there can be no knowledge of anything outside of human experience. This meant that revelation—the record of other human experiences of God—could not be authoritative for people living after the period of revelation.

Clearly, the philosophies of Kant and Hume greatly weakened the authority of scripture, and of Christian theology in general, since revelation and speculation generally existed outside the realm of direct human experience. Christians must rely on the testimonies of others, as recorded in the Bible, rather than on their own eyewitness knowledge of events. Accepting the Bible as a true and accurate source of information, therefore, requires an act of faith, since it is basically a historical account of people's experience of revelation. Just as we might question the accuracy of our history books today, we might question the accuracy of a "history" book such as the Bible. That is exactly what happened during the Enlightenment. (We will examine reactions to these challenges to biblical authority in Chapter Seven.)

Enlightment intellectuals also turned to the authority of reason because of a renewed interest in science. The new science was empirical; that is, it relied on experimentation and observation, rather than on dogma or axioms. If one could test an idea or hypothesis and verify the results empirically, the idea was deemed "true." Truth, therefore, was observable and provable from nature. At the same time, however, Newton and other scientists of this time were not a-religious, or antireligious; on the contrary, they saw the hand of God at work in various principles governing the operation of the universe. Only a supreme deity or First Cause could have so ordered the cosmos to function with such perfection.

This view profoundly affected Christianity by encouraging Christians to examine nature and use logic to explain their beliefs. Scientists at that time considered the natural world, or "Nature," as they called it, supreme evidence of the existence of God. It was not unreasonable to believe in God; on the contrary, it was eminently reasonable, or rational, to hold that a supreme being had created the world and all that was in it. We need not turn to the Bible or to revelation for evidence of God's existence or goodness, nor need we look to tradition. All, or almost all, we needed know about the divine and religion could be observed in Nature.

A distinctly American form of Christianity—Unitarianism—reflects the turn toward reason. Although the roots of Unitarianism can be found in Reformation Europe in the beliefs of the Socinians, who threw out the doctrine of the Trinity and upheld the absolute oneness of God, it was primarily in the United States that Unitarianism took hold. It grew out of the Deism of the founders and their optimistic assessment of the human capacity for virtue and common sense. While Unitarians denied the Trinity, they did not reject Christ, whom they viewed as God's divinely anointed Son, chosen because of his supremely moral nature. Christ was our exemplar, our model, and his faithfulness and obedience to God as a human being led to his being called the Son of God. The essence of Christianity, then, was faithfulness to God expressed in ethical behavior, rather than acceptance of a particular doctrine. Some Unitarians criticized the doctrine of the atonement in particular, arguing that the idea that God demanded a human sacrifice—of God's very own son—was undignified and unworthy of the deity they worshiped. Others saw in Jesus' death a mediation and reconciliation between God and humanity.

Christians then, as well as today, might question whether Unitarians could even be called Christians. Many, and perhaps most, Unitarians today might not call themselves Christians for the same reasons that their nineteenth-century forebears criticized certain Christian doctrines: they do not identify with some of the traditional teachings of Christianity, such as the idea of original sin or the divinity of Jesus. For this reason, the group has been excluded from the National Council of Churches, although Unitarians work closely with the NCC on a variety of social justice issues. Contemporary Unitarianism is extremely diverse, embracing a number of religious traditions, not just Christianity. Some Unitarians might more accurately be called humanists rather than Christians.*

---

* In 1961, the Unitarians united with the Universalists to form the Unitarian Universalist Association. The Universalists were a nineteenth-century group which believed that a loving God willed all people to be saved and did not condemn anyone to Hell.

▨ A Reasonable God

In the U.S. Declaration of Independence, Thomas Jefferson appeals to "the Laws of Nature and Nature's God." This language reflects the Enlightenment view that God was eminently reasonable and that God's rationality was evident in the ordering of nature. Religion was natural to humanity. Indeed, Lord Herbert of Cherbury (1583–1648) saw Christianity as just one more manifestation of a broader "natural religion" that existed at all times and in all places. In a book titled *De Veritate (On Truth)*, Cherbury identified five elements that make up natural religion. These included belief in the existence of a supreme being who ought to be worshiped by the practice of piety and virtue, the belief that vice and crime need expiation, and the belief that rewards and punishments exist in this life and the next.

John Locke's essay *The Reasonableness of Christianity*, published in 1695, took Cherbury one step further and argued for Christianity's basic rationality. Locke (1632–1704) was a key English philosopher, moralist, and empiricist of the late seventeenth century. He grew up in a liberal Puritan family, studied a number of subjects—including chemistry with Robert Boyle and medicine with Thomas Sydenham—and even considered becoming a minister. But political and social contacts guided him in the direction of political philosophy, and led to his exile in the Netherlands because he sided with opponents of the English monarchy. Locke wrote his first *Letter on Toleration* while in exile. He also composed an important *Essay Concerning Human Understanding* in which he argued that the human mind was essentially a blank slate upon which data could be inscribed during the process of education and formation. He profoundly influenced and inspired leaders in France, England, the United States, and Germany with his political writings; and he laid the groundwork for a clear turn to empiricism and experimentalism as ways of understanding reality. *The Reasonableness of Christianity* finds no conflict between biblical truth and logical truth, though today we might question Locke's presuppositions. Locke read the Bible and attempted to explicate it in rational, or "unbiased," terms. He used reason to understand and interpret the meaning of scripture.

These views of nature and reason led to the development of Deism in the eighteenth century. Deists believed in an impersonal creator God who was not providentially involved with the day-to-day operations of the world. The world appeared to be a majestic timepiece, a watch or clock, in which each cog worked with a divinely made precision. A hands-on, personal deity was simply unnecessary, except perhaps for the unenlightened. A number of the founders of the United States were essentially Deists, including Thomas Jefferson, George Washington, and Benjamin Franklin, and five U.S. presidents were Unitarians. Despite the prominence of a few Deists, Deism itself was a rather small movement; in fact, some historians deny that it was a movement at all, arguing instead that it merely describes the writings of a few individuals. Nevertheless, natural religion and Deism reflected a laissez-faire attitude toward doctrine. Virtue and piety, rather than sacrament and sermon, served as true worship. Any reasonable person could agree to these simple principles, and thus religious toleration was assured.

Unitarians in the nineteenth century, however, believed themselves to be well within Christian tradition and, in fact, considered themselves more enlightened than their "blood-thirsty" Protestant contemporaries. They were extremely active in the abolition movement in the United States, and once the Civil War was over, they engaged in progressive movements for women's voting rights (Susan B. Anthony), prison reform (Frances Willard), and the mitigation of suffering caused by war (Clara Barton, who founded the American Red Cross). Women could be ordained and preach in Unitarian churches. Unitarians attempted to create utopian communities, and they were involved in educational reform and a variety of other causes, all aimed at bringing God's reign to earth in the present.

One of the most prominent spokespersons for Unitarian Christianity was William Ellery Channing (1780–1842). Although he began his career as a Congregational minister, Channing's brand of liberal Congregationalism eventually coalesced into the American Unitarian Association in 1825. A minister at the Federal Street Church in Boston from 1803 until his death, he became a leading figure in the Transcendentalist movement in the United States. He also organized efforts to end slavery, drunkenness, poverty, and war.

The Reading

Channing wrote the lecture "Christianity a Rational Religion" as a follow-up to his lecture "Evidences of Christianity," in which he took Paul's statement "I am not ashamed of the gospel of Christ" as his point of departure. In his first sermon, or "lecture" as they are frequently called by Unitarians, he exhorted his listeners to claim the gospel for their own, and not let it be taken over by others who misunderstood, misinterpreted, or misused it. In this sermon, Channing asserts that he is proud to claim the gospel because it is rational and worthy of acceptance. Christianity does not require the suspension of critical faculties. On the contrary, it comports with reason because God created the world and everything in it, including our ability to think. We cannot receive revelation except via reason, and therefore revelation, and the gospel, must be rational, according to Channing.

Channing defines reason as the human ability to comprehend universal truths. A particular truth, he says, is the observation that a stone falls to the ground; a general truth is the understanding of gravity. He discusses universal truths as realities that are true here, everywhere, and always. Reason is also "the power which tends and is perpetually striving to reduce our various thoughts to unity or consistency." Our mind tries to bring scattered truths together into a single whole. Our reason is the image of the unity of God and the universe.

At one point in his lecture, Channing says that some would paint Christianity as extravagant and fanatical. He is undoubtedly referring to the great upsurge in religious affections that emerged during the revivals of the Second Great Awakening in the first part of the nineteenth century in the United States. Tent meetings, traveling evangelists, and a keen and vital religious fervor permeated the young nation, especially in the frontier states of Kentucky and Tennessee. Thus, we hear a bit of Channing's staid and respectable Bostonian Christianity coming through his discourse. His religion appears thoughtful, reasonable, and respectable, as opposed to the Christianity preached to frenzied masses in the camp meetings.

Questions to Consider

1. Channing offers several reasons why he thinks Christianity is reasonable. What are they? Do you agree with his argument?

2. Which traditional Christian doctrines does Channing oppose? What are the reasons he gives for opposition?

3. How does Channing's view of human nature (anthropology) compare with that of Athanasius and Augustine? With that of Luther and Calvin?

4. What exactly is the gospel that Channing refers to?

5. Induce (figure out) the arguments against Channing's viewpoint that he mentions. What is his defense against these arguments?

6. Were there other times in the history of Christianity when reason was used in service of the faith? If so, how do they compare with Channing's?

7. Do you think nature reveals a divine hand or divine plan? If so, is the Bible needed to reveal the existence of God?

8. Who do you think is Channing's audience? How would this sermon go over in the nineteenth century? What about in the twenty-first century?

Christianity a Rational Religion

WILLIAM ELLERY CHANNING

Romans 1:16: "I am not ashamed of the gospel of Christ."

Such was the language of Paul; and every man will respond to it who comprehends the character and has felt the influence of Christianity. In a former discourse, I proposed to state to you some reasons for adopting as our own the words of the Apostle, for joining in his open and resolute testimony to the gospel of Christ. I observed that I was not ashamed of the gospel, first, because it is true, and to this topic the discourse was devoted. I wish now to continue the subject, and to state another ground of undisguised and unshaken adherence to Christianity. I say, then, I am not ashamed of the gospel of Christ, because it is a *rational* religion. It agrees with reason; therefore I count it worthy of acceptation; therefore I do not blush to enroll myself among its friends and advocates. The object of the present discourse will be the illustration of this claim of Christianity. I wish to show you the harmony which subsists between the light of God's word and that primitive light of reason which He has kindled within us to be our perpetual guide. If, in treating this subject, I shall come into conflict with any class of Christians, I trust I shall not be considered as imputing to them any moral or intellectual defect. I judge men by their motives, dispositions, and lives, and not by their speculations or peculiar opinions;

and I esteem piety and virtue equally venerable whether found in friend or foe.

Christianity is a rational religion. Were it not so, I should be ashamed to profess it. I am aware that it is the fashion with some to decry reason, and to set up revelation as an opposite authority. This error, though countenanced by good men, and honestly maintained for the defense of the Christian cause, ought to be earnestly withstood; for it virtually surrenders our religion into the hands of the unbeliever. It saps the foundation to strengthen the building. It places our religion in hostility to human nature, and gives to its adversaries the credit of vindicating the rights and noblest powers of the mind.

We must never forget that our rational nature is the greatest gift of God. For this we owe him our chief gratitude. It is a greater gift than any outward aid or benefaction, and no doctrine which degrades it can come from its Author. The development of it is the end of our being. Revelation is but a means, and is designed to concur with nature, providence, and God's spirit, in carrying forward reason to its perfection. I glory in Christianity because it enlarges, invigorates, exalts my rational nature. If I could not be a Christian without ceasing to be rational, I should not hesitate as to my choice. I feel myself bound to sacrifice to Christianity property, reputation, life; but I ought not to sacrifice to any religion that reason which lifts me above the brute and constitutes me a man. I can conceive no sacrilege greater than to prostrate or renounce the highest faculty which we have derived from God. In so doing we should offer violence to the divinity within us. Christianity wages no war with reason, but is one with it, and is given to be its helper and friend.

I wish, in the present discourse, to illustrate and confirm the views now given. My remarks will be arranged under two heads. I propose, first, to show that Christianity is founded on and supposes the authority of reason, and cannot therefore oppose it without subverting itself. My object in this part of the discourse will be to expose the error of those who hope to serve revelation by disparaging reason. I shall then, in the second place, compare Christianity and the light of reason, to show their accordance; and shall prove, by descending to particulars, that Christianity is eminently a rational religion. My aim, under this head, will be to vindicate the gospel from the reproaches of the unbeliever, and to strengthen the faith and attachment of its friends. Before I begin, let me observe that this discussion, from the nature of the subject, must assume occasionally an abstract

form, and will demand serious attention. I am to speak of reason, the chief faculty of the mind; and no simplicity of language in treating such a topic can exempt the hearer from the necessity of patient effort of thought. . . . [Channing's definition of the term "reason" is omitted.]

I proceed to the discussion of the two leading principles to which this discourse is devoted.

First, I am to show that revelation is founded on the authority of reason, and cannot therefore oppose or disparage it without subverting itself. Let me state a few of the considerations which convince me of the truth of this position. The first is, that reason alone makes us capable of receiving a revelation. It must previously exist and operate, or we should be wholly unprepared for the communications of Christ. Revelation, then, is built on reason. You will see the truth of these remarks if you will consider to whom revelation is sent. Why is it given to men rather than to brutes? Why have not God's messengers gone to the fields to proclaim his glad tidings to bird and beast? The answer is obvious. These want reason; and wanting this, they have no capacity or preparation for revealed truth. And not only would revelation be lost on the brute; let it speak to the child, before his rational faculties have been awakened, and before some ideas of duty and his own nature have been developed, and it might as well speak to a stone. Reason is the preparation and ground of revelation.

This truth will be still more obvious if we consider not only to whom, but in what way, the Christian revelation is communicated. How is it conveyed? In words. Did it make these words? No. They were in use ages before its birth. Again I ask, Did it make the ideas or thoughts which these words express? No. If the hearers of Jesus had not previously attached ideas to the terms which he employed, they could not have received his meaning. He might as well have spoken to them in a foreign tongue. Thus the ideas which enter into Christianity subsisted before. They were ideas of reason; so that to this faculty revelation owes the materials of which it is composed.

Revelation, we must remember, is not our earliest teacher. Man is not born with the single power of reading God's word, and sent immediately to that guide. His eyes open first on another volume, that of the creation. Long before he can read the Bible he looks round on the earth and sky. He reads the countenances of his friends, and hears and understands their voices. He looks, too, by degrees, within himself, and acquires some ideas of his own soul. Thus his first school is that of nature and reason, and this is necessary to prepare him for a communication from heaven. Revelation does not find the mind a blank, a void, prepared to receive unresistingly whatever may be offered; but finds it in possession of various knowledge from nature and experience, and, still more, in possession of great principles, fundamental truths, moral ideas, which are derived from itself, and which are the germs of all its future improvement. This last view is peculiarly important. The mind does not receive everything from abroad. Its great ideas arise from itself, and by those native lights it reads and comprehends the volumes of nature and revelation. We speak, indeed, of nature and revelation as making known to us an intelligent First Cause; but the ideas of intelligence and causation we derive originally from our own nature. The elements of the idea of God we gather from ourselves. Power, wisdom, love, virtue, beauty, and happiness, words which contain all that is glorious in the universe and interesting in our existence, express attributes of the mind, and are understood by us only through consciousness. It is true, these ideas or principles of reason are often obscured by thick clouds and mingled with many and deplorable errors. Still, they are never lost. Christianity recognizes them, is built on them, and needs them as its interpreters. If an illustration of these views be required, I would point you to what may be called the most fundamental idea of religion, I mean the idea of right, of duty. Do we derive this originally and wholly from sacred books? Has not every human being, whether born within or beyond the bounds of revelation, a sense of the distinction between right and wrong? Is there not an earlier voice than revelation approving or rebuking men according to their deeds? In barbarous ages is not conscience heard? And does it not grow more articulate with the progress of society? Christianity does not create, but presupposes the idea of duty; and the same may be said of other great convictions. Revelation, then, does not stand alone, nor is it addressed to a blank and passive mind. It was meant to be a joint worker with other teachers, with nature, with Providence, with conscience, with our rational powers; and as these all are given us by God, they cannot differ from each other. God must agree with himself. He has but one voice. It is man who speaks with jarring tongues. Nothing but harmony can come from the Creator; and, accordingly, a religion claiming to be from God can give no surer proof of falsehood than by contradicting those previous truths which God is teaching

by our very nature. We have thus seen that reason prepares us for a divine communication, and that it furnishes the ideas or materials of which revelation consists. This is my first consideration.

I proceed to a second. I affirm, then, that revelation rests on the authority of reason, because to this faculty it submits the evidences of its truth, and nothing but the approving sentence of reason binds us to receive and obey it. This is a very weighty consideration. Christianity, in placing itself before the tribunal of reason, and in resting its claims on the sanction of this faculty, is one of the chief witnesses to the authority and dignity of our rational nature. That I have ascribed to this faculty its true and proper office may be easily made to appear. I take the New Testament in hand, and on what ground do I receive its truths as divine? I see nothing on its pages but the same letters in which other books are written. No miraculous voice from heaven assures me that it is God's word, nor does any mysterious voice within my soul command me to believe the supernatural works of Christ. How, then, shall I settle the question of the origin of this religion? I must examine it by the same rational faculties by which other subjects are tried. I must ask what are its evidences, and I must lay them before reason, the only power by which evidence can be weighed. I have not a distinct faculty given me for judging a revelation. I have not two understandings, one for inquiring into God's word and another into his works. As with the same bodily eye I now look on the earth, now on the heavens, so with the same power of reason I examine now nature, now revelation. Reason must collect and weigh the various proofs of Christianity. It must especially compare this system with those great moral convictions which are written by the finger of God on the heart, and which make man a law to himself. A religion subverting these it must not hesitate to reject, be its evidences what they may. A religion, for example, commanding us to hate and injure society, reason must instantly discard, without even waiting to examine its proofs. From these views we learn, not only that it is the province of reason to judge of the truth of Christianity, but, what is still more important, that the rules or tests by which it judges are of its own dictation. The laws which it applies in this case have their origin in itself. No one will pretend that revelation can prescribe the principles by which the question of its own truth should be settled; for, until proved to be true, it has no authority. Reason must prescribe the tests or standards to which a professed communication from

God should be referred; and among these none are more important than that moral law which belongs to the very essence and is the deepest conviction of the rational nature. Revelation, then, rests on reason, and in opposing it would act for its own destruction.

I have given two views. I have shown that revelation draws its ideas or materials from reason, and that it appeals to this power as the judge of its truth. I now assert, thirdly, that it rests on the authority of reason, because it needs and expects this faculty to be its interpreter, and without this aid would be worse than useless. How is the right of interpretation, the real meaning, of Scriptures to be ascertained? I answer, by reason. I know of no process by which the true sense of the New Testament is to pass from the page into my mind without the use of my rational faculties. It will not be pretended that this book is so exceedingly plain, its words so easy, its sentences so short, its meaning so exposed on the surface, that the whole truth may be received in a moment and without any intellectual effort. There is no such miraculous simplicity in the Scriptures. In truth, no book can be written so simply as to need no exercise of reason. Almost every word has more than one meaning, and judgment is required to select the particular sense intended by the writer. Of all books, perhaps the Scriptures need most the use of reason for their just interpretation; and this, not from any imperfection, but from the strength, boldness, and figurative character of their style, and from the distance of the time when they were written. I open the New Testament and my eye lights on this passage: "If thy right hand offend thee; cut it off and cast it from thee." Is this language to be interpreted in its plainest and most obvious sense? Then I must mutilate my body, and become a suicide. I look again, and I find Jesus using these words to the Jews: "Fill ye up the measure of your iniquities." Am I to interpret this according to the letter or the first ideas which it suggests? Then Jesus commanded his hearers to steep themselves in crime, and was himself a minister of sin. It is only by a deliberate use of reason that we can penetrate beneath the figurative, hyperbolical, and often obscure style of the New Testament, to the real meaning. Let me go to the Bible, dismissing my reason and taking the first impression which the words convey, and there is no absurdity, however gross, into which I shall not fall. I shall ascribe a limited body to God, and unbounded knowledge to man, for I read of God having limbs, and of man knowing all things. Nothing is plainer than that I must compare passage with passage, and limit one by another, and especially limit all by those plain and universal principles of reason which are called common-sense, or I shall make revelation the patron of every folly and vice. So essential is reason to the interpretation of the Christian records. Revelation rests upon its authority. Can it then oppose it, or teach us to hold it in light esteem?

I have now furnished the proofs of my first position, that revelation is founded on reason; and in discussing this, I have wished not only to support the main doctrine, but to teach you to reverence, more perhaps than you have done, your rational nature. This has been decried by theologians, until men have ceased to feel its sacredness and dignity. It ought to be regarded as God's greatest gift. It is his image within us. To renounce it would be to offer a cruel violence to ourselves, to take our place among the brutes. Better pluck out the eye, better quench the light of the body than the light within us. We all feel that the loss of reason, when produced by disease, is the most terrible calamity of life; and we look on a hospital for the insane as the receptacle for the most pitiable of our race. But, in one view, insanity is not so great an evil as the prostration of reason to a religious sect or a religious chief; for the first is a visitation of Providence, the last is a voluntary act, the work of our own hands.

I am aware that those who have spoken most contemptuously of human reason have acted from a good motive, their aim has been to exalt revelation. They have thought that by magnifying this as the only means of divine teaching, they were adding to its dignity. But truth gains nothing by exaggeration; and Christianity, as we have seen, is undermined by nothing more effectually than by the sophistry which would bring discredit on our rational powers. Revelation needs no such support. For myself, I do not find that to esteem Christianity, I must think it the only source of instruction to which I must repair. I need not make nature dumb to give power or attraction to the teaching of Christ. The last derives new interest and confirmation from its harmony with the first. Christianity would furnish a weapon against itself, not easily repelled, should it claim the distinction of being the only light vouchsafed by God to men; for, in that case, it would represent a vast majority of the human race as left by their Creator without guidance or hope. I believe, and rejoice to believe, that a ray from heaven descends on the path of every fellow-creature. The heathen, though in darkness when compared with the Christian, has still his light; and it comes from the same source as our own, just as the same sun dispenses, now the faint dawn, and now the perfect day. Let not nature's teaching be disparaged. It is from God as truly as his word. It is sacred, as truly as revelation. Both are manifestations of one infinite mind, and harmonious manifestations; and without this agreement the claims of Christianity could not be sustained.

In offering these remarks, I have not forgotten that they will expose me to the reproach of ministering to "the pride of reason"; and I may be told that there is no worse form of pride than this. The charge is so common as to deserve a moment's attention. It will appear at once to be groundless, if you consider that pride finds its chief nourishment and delight in the idea of our own superiority. It is built on something peculiar and distinctive, on something which separates us from others and raises us above them, and not on powers which we share with all around us. Now, in speaking as I have done of the worth and dignity of reason, I have constantly regarded and represented this faculty as the common property of all human beings. I have spoken of its most important truths as universal and unconfined, such as no individual can monopolize or make the grounds of personal distinction or elevation. I have given, then, no occasion and furnished no nutriment to pride. I know, indeed, that the pride of reason or of intellect exists; but how does it chiefly manifest itself? Not in revering that rational nature which all men have derived from God; but in exaggerating our particular acquisitions or powers, in magnifying our distinctive views, in looking contemptuously on other minds, in making ourselves standards for our brethren, in refusing new lights, and in attempting to establish dominion over the understandings of those who are placed within our influence. Such is the most common form of the pride of intellect. It is a vice confined to no sect, and perhaps will be found to prevail most where it is most disclaimed.

I doubt not that they who insist so continually on the duty of exalting Scripture above reason, consider themselves as particularly secured against the pride of reason. Yet none, I apprehend, are more open to the charge. Such persons are singularly prone to enforce their own interpretations of Scripture on others, and to see peril and crime in the adoption of different views from their own. Now, let me ask, by what power do these men interpret revelation? Is it not by their reason? Have they any faculties but the rational ones by which to compare Scripture with Scripture, to explain figurative language, to form conclusions as to the will of God? Do they not employ on God's

word the same intellect as on his works? And are not their interpretations of both equally results of reason? It follows, that in imposing on others their explications of the Scriptures, they as truly arrogate to themselves a superiority of reason as if they should require conformity to their explanations of nature. Nature and Scripture agree in this, that they cannot be understood at a glance. Both volumes demand patient investigation, and task all our powers of thought. Accordingly, it is well known that as much intellectual toil has been spent on theological systems as on the natural sciences; and unhappily it is not less known that as much intellectual pride has been manifested in framing and defending the first as the last. I fear, indeed, that this vice has clung with peculiar obstinacy to the students of revelation. Nowhere, I fear, have men manifested such infatuated trust in their own infallibility, such overweening fondness for their own conclusions, such positiveness, such impatience of contradiction, such arrogance towards the advocates of different opinions, as in the interpretation of the Scriptures; and yet these very men, who so idolize their own intellectual powers, profess to humble reason, and consider a criminal reliance on it as almost exclusively chargeable on others. The true defense against the pride of reason is, not to speak of it contemptuously, but to reverence it as God's inestimable gift to every human being, and as given to all for never-ceasing improvements, of which we see but the dawn in the present acquisitions of the noblest mind.

I have now completed my views of the first principle which I laid down in this discourse; namely, that the Christian revelation rests on the authority of reason. Of course, it cannot oppose reason without undermining and destroying itself. I maintain, however, that it does not oppose, that it perfectly accords with reason. It is a rational religion. . . . [The section in which Channing argues that Christianity fulfills universal truths and has the character of consistency, which corresponds with reasoned reflection is omitted.]

I do and must feel, my friends, that the claim of Christianity to the honor of being a rational religion is fully established. As such I commend it to you. As such it will more and more approve itself in proportion as you study and practice it. You will never find cause to complain that by adopting it you have enslaved or degraded your highest powers. Here, then, I might stop, and might consider my work as done. But I am aware that objections have been made to the rational character of our religion which may still linger in the minds of some of my hearers. A brief notice of these may aid the purpose, and will form a proper conclusion of this discourse.

I imagine that were some who are present to speak, they would tell me that if Christianity be judged by its fruits, it deserves any character but that of rational. I should be told that no religion has borne a more abundant harvest of extravagance and fanaticism. I should be told that reason is a calm, reflecting, sober principle, and I should be asked whether such is the character of the Christianity which has overspread the world. Perhaps some of you will remind me of the feverish, wild, passionate religion which is now systematically dispersed through our country, and I shall be asked whether a system under which such delusions prevail can be a rational one.

To these objections I answer, You say much that is true. I grant that reason is a calm and reflecting principle, and I see little calmness or reflection among many who take exclusively the name of Christ. But I say, you have no right to confound Christianity with its professors. This religion, as you know, has come down to us through many ages of darkness, during which it must have been corrupted and obscured. Common candor requires that you should judge of it as it came from its Founder. Go, then, to its original records; place yourselves near Jesus; and tell me if you ever found yourselves in the presence of so calm a teacher. We indeed discern in Jesus great earnestness, but joined with entire self-control. Sensibility breathes through his whole teaching and life, but always tempered with wisdom. Amidst his boldest thoughts and expressions, we discover no marks of ungoverned feeling or a diseased imagination. Take, as an example, his longest discourse, the Sermon on the Mount [Matthew 5–7]. How weighty the thoughts! How grave and dignified the style! You recollect that the multitude were astonished, not at the passionate vehemence, but at the authority, with which he spoke. Read next the last discourse of Jesus to his disciples in St. John's Gospel [John 13–17]. What a deep yet mild and subdued tenderness mingles with conscious greatness in that wonderful address! Take what is called the Lord's Prayer, which Jesus gave as the model of all prayer to God [Matthew 6:9–15; Luke 11:2–4]. Does that countenance fanatical fervor or violent appeals to our Creator? Let me further ask, Does Jesus anywhere place religion in tumultuous, ungoverned emotion? Does he not teach us, that obedience, not feeling, marks and constitutes true piety, and that the most acceptable offering to

God is to exercise mercy to our fellow-creatures? When I compare the clamorous preaching and passionate declamation too common in the Christian world, with the composed dignity, the deliberate wisdom, the freedom from all extravagance, which characterized Jesus, I can imagine no greater contrast; and I am sure that the fiery zealot is no representative of Christianity.

I have done with the first objection; but another class of objections is often urged against the reasonable character of our religion. It has been strenuously maintained that Christianity contains particular doctrines which are irrational, and which involve the whole religion to which they are essential in their own condemnation. To this class of objections I have a short reply. I insist that these offensive doctrines do not belong to Christianity, but are human additions, and therefore do not derogate from its reasonableness and truth. What is the doctrine most frequently adduced to fix the charge of irrationality on the gospel? It is the Trinity. This is pronounced by the unbeliever a gross offence to reason. It teaches that there is one God, and yet that there are three divine persons. According to the doctrine these three persons perform different offices, and sustain different relations to each other. One is Father, another his Son. One sends, another is sent. They love each other, converse with each other, and make a covenant with each other; and yet, with all these distinctions, they are, according to the doctrine, not different beings, but one being, one and the same God. Is this a rational doctrine? has often been the question of the objector to Christianity. I answer, No. I can as easily believe that the whole human race are one man, as that three infinite persons, performing such different offices, are one God. But I maintain that, because the Trinity is irrational, it does not follow that the same reproach belongs to Christianity; for this doctrine is no part of the Christian religion. I know there are passages which are continually quoted in its defense; but allow me to prove doctrines in the same way, that is, by detaching texts from their connection and interpreting them without reference to the general current of Scripture, and I can prove anything and everything from the Bible. I can prove that God has human passions. I can prove transubstantiation, which is taught much more explicitly than the Trinity. Detached texts prove nothing. Christ is called God; the same title is given to Moses and to rulers. Christ has said, "I and my Father are one;" so he prayed that all his disciples might be one, meaning not one and the same being, but one in affection and purpose. I ask you, before you judge on this point, to read the Scriptures as a whole, and to inquire into their general strain and teaching in regard to Christ. I find him uniformly distinguishing between himself and God, calling himself, not God the Son, but the Son of God, continually speaking of himself as sent by God, continually referring his power and miracles to God. I hear him saying that of himself he can do nothing, and praying to his Father under the character of the only true God.

Such I affirm to be the tenor, the current, the general strain of the New Testament; and the scattered passages on which a different doctrine is built should have no weight against this host of witnesses. Do not rest your faith on a few texts. Sometimes these favorite texts are no part of Scripture. For example, the famous passage on which the Trinity mainly rests, "There are three that bear record in heaven, the Father, the Word, and the Holy Ghost, and these three are one" [1 John 5:7–8].* This text, I say, though found at present in John's Epistle, and read in our churches, has been pronounced by the ablest critics a forgery; and a vast majority of the educated ministers of this country are satisfied that it is not a part of Scripture. Suffer no man, then, to select texts for you as decisive of religious controversies. Read the whole record for yourselves, and possess yourselves of its general import. I am very desirous to separate the doctrine in question from Christianity, because it fastens the charge of irrationality on the whole religion. It is one of the great obstacles to the propagation of the gospel. The Jews will not hear of a Trinity. I have seen in the countenance, and heard in the tones of the voice, the horror with which that people shrink from the doctrine that God died on the cross. Mahometans [Muslims], too, when they hear this opinion from Christian missionaries, repeat the first article of their faith, "There is one God"; and look with pity or scorn on the disciples of Jesus as deserters of the plainest and greatest truth of religion. Even the Indian of our wilderness, who worships the Great Spirit, has charged absurdity on the teacher who has gone to indoctrinate him in a Trinity. How many, too, in Christian countries, have suspected the whole religion for this one error. Believing, then, as I do, that it forms no part of Christianity, my allegiance to Jesus Christ calls me openly to withstand it. In so doing I would wound no man's feelings. I doubt not, that they who adopt this doctrine intend, equally with those who oppose it, to render homage to the truth and service to Christianity. They think that their peculiar faith gives new interest to the character and new authority to the teaching of Jesus. But they grievously err. The views by which they hope to build up love towards Christ detract from the perfection of his Father; and I fear that the kind of piety which prevails now in the Christian world bears witness to the sad influence of this obscuration of the true glory of God. We need not desert reason or corrupt Christianity to insure the purest, deepest love towards the only true God, or towards Jesus Christ, whom He has sent for our redemption.

I have named one doctrine which is often urged against Christianity as irrational. There is one more on which I would offer a few remarks. Christianity has often been reproached with teaching that God brings men into life totally depraved, and condemns immense multitudes to everlasting misery for sins to which their nature has irresistibly impelled them. This is said to be irrational, and consequently such must be the religion which teaches it. I certainly shall not attempt to vindicate this theological fiction. A more irrational doctrine could not, I think, be contrived; and it is something worse, it is as immoral in its tendency as it is unreasonable. It is suited to alienate men from God and from one another. Were it really believed (which it cannot be), men would look up with dread and detestation to the Author of their being, and look round with horror on their fellow-creatures. It would dissolve society. Were men to see in one another wholly corrupt beings, incarnate fiends, without one genuine virtue, society would become as repulsive as a den of lions or a nest of vipers. All confidence, esteem, love, would die; and without these the interest, charm, and worth of existence would expire. What a pang would shoot through a parent's heart, if he were to see in the smiling infant a moral being continually and wholly propensed to sin, in whose mind were thickly sown the seeds of hatred to God and goodness, and who had commenced his existence under the curse of his Creator! What good man could consent to be a parent, if his offspring were to be born to this infinitely wretched inheritance? I say, the doctrine is of immoral tendency; but

---

* Although the majority of Greek versions of 1 John say, "There are three that testify: the Spirit and the water and the blood, and these three agree," a few authorities present the quotation as Channing notes.

I do not say that they who profess it are immoral. The truth is, that none do or can hold it in its full and proper import. I have seen its advocates smile as benignantly on the child whom their creed has made a demon as if it were an angel; and I have seen them mingling with their fellow creatures as cordially and confidingly as if the doctrine of total depravity had never entered their ears. Perhaps the most mischievous effect of the doctrine is the dishonor which it has thrown on Christianity. This dishonor I would wipe away. Christianity teaches no such doctrine. Where do you find it in the New Testament? Did Jesus teach it, when he took little children in his arms and blessed them, and said, "Of such is the kingdom of God?" Did Paul teach it when he spoke of the Gentiles, who have not the law or a written revelation, but who do by nature the things contained in the law? Christianity indeed speaks strongly of human guilt, but always treats men as beings who have the power of doing right, and who have come into existence under the smile of their Creator.

I have now completed my vindication of the claim of the gospel to the character of a rational religion; and my aim has been, not to serve a party, but the cause of our common Christianity. At the present day, one of the most urgent duties of its friends is, to rescue it from the reproach of waging war with reason. The character of our age demands this. There have been times when Christianity, though loaded with unreasonable doctrines, retained its hold on men's faith; for men had not learned to think. They received their religion as children learned the catechism; they substituted the priest for their own understandings, and cared neither what nor why they believed. But that day is gone by, and the spirit of freedom which has succeeded it is subjecting Christianity to a scrutiny more and more severe; and if this religion cannot vindicate itself to the reflecting, the calm, the wise, as a reasonable service, it cannot stand. Fanatical sects may, for a time, spread an intolerant excitement through a community, and impose silence on the objections of the skeptical. But fanaticism is the epidemic of a season; it wastes itself by its own violence. Sooner or later the voice of reflection will be heard. Men will ask, What are the claims of Chris-

tianity? Does it bear the marks of truth? And if it be found to war with nature and reason, it will be, and it ought to be, abandoned. On this ground, I am anxious that Christianity should be cleared from all human additions and corruptions. If, indeed, irrational doctrines belong to it, then I have no desire to separate them from it. I have no desire, for the sake of upholding the gospel, to wrap up and conceal, much less to deny, any of its real principles. Did I think that it was burdened with one irrational doctrine, I would say so, and I would leave it, as I found it, with this mill-stone round its neck. But I know none such. I meet, indeed, some difficulties in the narrative part of the New Testament; and there are arguments in the Epistles which, however, suited to the Jews, to whom they were first addressed, are not apparently adapted to men at large; but I see not a principle of the religion which my reason, calmly and impartially exercised, pronounces inconsistent with any great truth. I have the strongest conviction that Christianity is reason in its most perfect form, and therefore I plead for its disengagement from the irrational additions with which it has been clogged for ages.

With these views of Christianity, I do and I must hold it fast. I cannot surrender it to the cavils or scoffs of infidelity. I do not blush to own it, for it is a rational religion. It satisfies the wants of the intellect as well as those of the heart. I know that men of strong minds have opposed it. But, as if Providence intended that their sophistry should carry a refutation on its own front, they have generally fallen into errors so gross and degrading as to prove them to be anything rather than the apostles of reason. When I go from the study of Christianity to their writings, I feel as if I were passing from the warm, bright sun into a chilling twilight which too often deepens into utter darkness. I am not, then, ashamed of the gospel. I see it glorified by the hostile systems which are reared for its destruction. I follow Jesus, because he is eminently "the Light"; and I doubt not that, to his true disciples, he will be a guide to that world where the obscurities of our present state will be dispersed, and where reason as well as virtue will be unfolded under the quickening influence and in the more manifest presence of God.

Although Unitarianism was a relatively small movement within world Christianity, it had an impact far beyond its numbers. Its leaders influenced American religious and cultural life and thought throughout the nineteenth century. They helped to shape the liberal Protestantism that emerged at the end of the nineteenth and the beginning of the twentieth centuries. And they contributed to the development of the Social Gospel movement, which we will examine in Chapter Seven. The Unitarian vision of an ethical, nondogmatic Christianity under the lordship of Jesus Christ continues to be seen today within Mainline (generally liberal) Protestantism.

The Authority of Scripture

William Ellery Channing embodied early nineteenth-century developments within American Christianity. Long before the rise of Unitarianism in the United States, however, the turn to reason had affected the study of the Bible. Seminarians and biblical theologians—that is, Christians studying within an academic setting—began to examine the Bible as they would any other ancient text. They began to ask: Who wrote it? When was it written? Why are there apparent contradictions and repetitions? Ironically, a Jewish philosopher in Amsterdam, Baruch Spinoza (1632–1677), helped to set the stage for this new approach to scripture. In his *Theological-Political Treatise* (1670), Spinoza maintained that the Bible could, and should, be understood on its own terms. It was not the province of a select group of interpreters (namely, the church); rather, any reader could access its truths (hence the political nature of Spinoza's theology). He believed that one could apply the methods of science to the study of scripture, by first identifying elements, then classifying them, and finally ordering them, all on their own terms, rather than on dogmatic or external terms. What this meant in practice was that the Bible could be used to interpret itself, just as other books—including the "book" of nature, that is, the natural world—could reveal itself by study and documentation. Dogmatic interpretations of the Bible essentially put the cart before the horse: scripture should dictate dogma, rather than dogma dictating the interpretation of scripture.

Christian theologians and historians followed Spinoza's advice in the seventeenth and succeeding centuries. Known as historical-critical study of the Bible (see Chapter Seven) this approach challenged traditional interpretations. For example, Christians and Jews had believed for centuries that Moses wrote the first five books of the Bible. But as Deuteronomy 34, which describes Moses' death, indicates, Moses could not have written *all* of these texts. And why didn't Genesis hang together very well? There were two creation accounts (Genesis 1:1–2:3 and Genesis 2:4–25); multiple stories of barren women (Sarah, Rebecca, Rachel); and the rather strange account of Joseph, who appears to be more Egyptian than Israelite. How could these facts and observations be explained?

While debate over the historical-critical method reached its height during the nineteenth century, and though the method continues to be used in the scholarly study of the Bible today, its origins in eighteenth-century writings began to shift the paradigm of 1700 years of Christian biblical interpretation. Gotthold Ephraim Lessing (1729–1781) was one leader in this shift to historical thinking about sacred writing. The son of an orthodox Lutheran pastor, Lessing studied theology, wrote plays, and collected books. Lessing's most famous work is the drama *Nathan the Wise*. A plea for religious toleration, the play features a dialogue between a Muslim, a Christian, and a Jew. Nathan, the Jew, appears to be the wisest of the three, cogently arguing for mutual toleration and respect.

It was Lessing's theological treatises, however, that profoundly helped to send biblical studies in a new, historical direction. Most of these were published after his death, due to their extremely controversial nature at the time.

The Reading

In the following essay, written in 1778 but not published until 1784, Lessing proposes a theory to explain the origins of the four Gospels in the New Testament. His essay reflects the consensus at the time—that Matthew was the first gospel written—although as Chapter One of this book indicated, contemporary scholarship now argues for the priority of Mark. Lessing considered this his best work in theology, and while it is quite systematic and organized with numbered points, his argument gets a bit technical when he argues about early heresies or ancient Christian writers and their opinions. He indicates with an asterisk the evidence he is providing, so that readers don't think he merely made up something.

Lessing is essentially arguing that the evangelists—that is, the writers of the four Gospels—were human beings and that, therefore, their writings may not be error-free. He analyzes discrepancies, coincidences, and differences, and notes what scholars since have called the "Synoptic problem": that Matthew, Mark, and Luke are remarkably similar, while John's gospel is quite different. His explanation for this difference reflects eighteenth-century scholarship, however, rather than twenty-first century scholarship, as do the majority of his conclusions. Nevertheless, this is an important work because it represents the infancy of modern critical biblical studies.

One of the ways that scholars read differently than nonscholars is that they examine *how* as well as *what* the author is saying. In other words, there is the question of content, the "what" of the reading; and there is the question of method, the "how" of the reading. How does the author construct the argument? What techniques, methods, and, yes, even tricks does the author use? Questions of method tell us a great deal about the author's approach to the material. Thus, we are reading on (at least) two levels: examining content and form. What is the argument, and how is the argument constructed? When we consider construction, we can begin to consider weaknesses or flaws.

Note: I have excised the Greek-language portions of this reading.

Questions to Consider

1. How does Lessing begin his essay? How does he set the stage before he jumps into his argument? What is his purpose or aim? Who is his audience?

2. What do we know just by reading the title and the first two sections of the essay?

3. How is Lessing reading scripture? What are his presuppositions and his assumptions? Why might this text be controversial in his own day, or in our day?

4. How does Lessing's approach differ from that of Christians today? Or does it?

5. What point or points is Lessing trying to make?

6. Why has he written this treatise? What problem is he trying to solve? Who is he arguing against?

7. Does Lessing's argument adequately explain differences that exist between the four Gospels? What do you think about his hypothetical Hebrew gospel that served as the template for the three Synoptics? Why was John written, in Lessing's opinion?

8. Lessing concludes his essay rather modestly in items 67 and 68. What is he saying in these two paragraphs?

New Hypothesis Concerning the Evangelists Regarded as Merely Human Historians

GOTTHOLD EPHRAIM LESSING

1. CONTENTS

First the hypothesis will be set forth in plain, straightforward prose. Then the critical proof of it will be given, and all that follows on from it.

After this will be shown the advantage which this hypothesis could have in making intelligible various difficulties and in providing a more exact explanation of disputed passages, and the conclusion will subject it to a closer scrutiny.

2. PREFACE

This is the first draft of a work on which I have been working for many years. My intention was admittedly not to lay it before the world until it was quite complete. But circumstances have intervened which compel me to give a foretaste of it.

For I have been dragged into explaining certain matters which are very closely bound up with the present hypothesis. I may be astray here and there or in more than one place. Yet it will be found that where I have gone astray it is not because I have failed to use a map; I have always used the same map, which is denounced as more erroneous than careful measurement would bear out.

To hit on the right road is often pure luck. To be anxious to find the right road is alone praiseworthy.

Since, moreover, I have only spoken of a hypothesis, and I neither dispute nor deny the higher worth of the evangelists, this higher worth may very well stand secure even on my hypothesis. Thus I hope not to cause more shock or scandal than I intend to give. It goes without saying that I acknowledge as my assessors and judges only those divines whose mind is as rich in cold critical learning as it is free from prejudices. I shall pay only little regard to the judgment of other members of this profession, however respectable they may seem to me on other grounds.

1. The first followers of Christ were pure Jews, and after Christ's example did not cease to live as Jews.* The other Jews gave them the name Nazarenes, for which I need merely refer to Acts 24:5.

2. Certainly the Jews may have given them this name out of scorn. But it was in profound accord with the mind of Christ's disciples that they did not reject a nickname which they had in common with their Master, but gladly accepted as an honorable title a name intended to discredit them.†

3. Therefore also there was nothing they could do to suppress this name again in a short time. Rather must we believe that even when the name "Christians" had been accepted in Antioch and for a long time been universal, the Palestinian Jewish Christians‡ would have preferred to keep their old name, Nazarenes, and would have been the more concerned to preserve it since it was convenient for distinguishing them from the uncircumcised Christians against whom they always had some slight hostility, many traces of which can be found in the New Testament.

4. Would it be safe to assume that those earliest Nazarenes, very early, very soon after the death of Christ, had a written collection of narratives concerning Christ's life and teaching, which arose out of orally transmitted stories of the apostles and all those people who had lived in association with Christ? Why not?¶

5. And how, speaking roughly, would this collection have appeared? Like a collection of narratives, the beginning of which is so small that the first originator can be forgotten without ingratitude; which by chance is enlarged by more than one and is copied by more than one with all the freedom that is usual with such works which are attributed to nobody just as any other such collection, I say, would always appear. Basically it is always the same. But with each copy it is in some places enlarged, in some places abbreviated, in some places altered, according as the copyist or the possessor of the copy might believe that he had included more or better narratives from the mouths of credible people who had lived with Christ.§

6. And when at last the process of increasing or altering the collection had to stop, because at length the contemporaries whose authentic narratives anyone believed he could include inevitably died out; how would this collection then be entitled? Either, I imagine, after the first authorities for the narratives therein contained, or after those for whose use the collection would chiefly have been made; or after this or that man who first gave the collection an improved form or put it into a more intelligible language.

7. If it had been called after the first authorities, how would it have been entitled? The first authorities were all people who lived with Christ, and had known him to a greater or less degree. Among them were indeed a number of women, whose little anecdotes about Christ ought the less to be despised the greater the degree of their familiarity with him. But it was chiefly his apostles from whose mouth without

---

*For if there were also some Jewish proselytes among them, yet they were not merely proselytes of the Torah but proselytes of righteousness, who with circumcision had accepted the entire Mosaic law.

†Epiphanius says this expressly. [Epiphanius was an early Christian heresy hunter.]

‡ At least in part. For how else could it have happened that many centuries later in just the same region under just the same name a kind of Christians should have survived which confessed the same doctrines and lived in complete separation from the universal church which consisted chiefly of Gentiles?

¶ What here I merely postulate, will be shown in the sequel really to have existed. One can have no conception of how curious the multitude is concerning every detail relating to a great man for whom they have once taken a fancy, if this postulate is to be disputed. And a multitude always swells to become a greater multitude: so it is natural that everything which can be learnt about the great man is passed from hand to hand; finally, when oral communication no longer suffices, it must be put into writing.

§ If we now, in modern times, have few or no examples of such historical narratives, like snowballs sometimes growing, sometimes melting away; the reason is that one or other of the first copies quickly receives its fixed form in writing by being printed. Anyone who has had frequent occasion to turn over the pages of ancient chronicles of great cities or distinguished families, will know to what extent every owner of a particular copy held himself to be permitted to exercise his right of possession, as often as he wished, even on the text, and would lengthen or abbreviate it.

doubt the most numerous and reliable narratives originated. Thus it would have been entitled, this collection (the word Gospel taken in the sense of a historical narrative of Christ's life and teaching)—*The Gospel of the Apostles.*

8. And if they were named after those for whose use they were particularly made: how would they have been entitled then? How else than *The Gospel of the Nazarenes*? Or among those who did not wish to use the word Nazarenes, *The Gospel of the Hebrews.* For this name quite properly belonged to the Nazarenes as Palestinian Jews.

9. Finally, if it had been named after this or that man who first gave it an improved form or translated it into a more intelligible language; how would it have been entitled then? How else than the Gospel of this man and that man, who had thus gained this credit?

10. Hitherto I shall seem to my readers to lose myself in pursuit of vain conjectures, whereas they expect something quite different from me. But only let them have patience. What seems to them so far to be vain conjectures is nothing else and nothing more than what I have abstracted from credible historical witnesses, which anyone else, who thought he could proceed less cautiously, might have used as an immediate proof of his assertion.

11. In fact we find that the Nazarenes of the fourth century not only desired to have, but actually had precisely such a collection of narratives concerning Christ and Christ's teaching. They had a Chaldaic-Syriac Gospel* of their own which among the Church Fathers is mentioned sometimes under the name of the Gospel of the Apostles, sometimes the Gospel of the Hebrews, sometimes the Gospel of Matthew. The first title was given for the first reason explained in §7; the second for the second reason in §8; and the last conjecturally for the third reason of §9.

12. I say conjecturally, and in my entire hypothesis this is the only conjecture that I allow myself and on which I build. It rests on so many grounds that no historical conjecture in the world could be found

which more deserved to be accepted as historical truth.

13. And yet from this correspondence of the actual Gospel of the later Nazarenes of the fourth century with a merely hypothetical Gospel such as the very first Nazarenes must have had, if they had one at all, I do not at once draw the conclusion that the one must necessarily have been identical with the other. For it may be said that the later Nazarenes were heretics and the very first Nazarenes were Jewish Christians of weak faith; thus the former could have put something together of which the latter knew nothing.

14. Let us therefore proceed as circumspectly as possible. Did any Church Father who mentioned the Gospel of the later Nazarenes ever express such a suspicion or even give any hint of it? Never. Not one.

15. Did not rather the most learned and acute Church Fathers always speak of it with a certain respect, not indeed as a Gospel inspired by the Holy Ghost but yet as an undoubtedly ancient work, written at or soon after the time of the apostles? Certainly.

16. Did not the same man, who was without doubt the only one of all the Church Fathers capable of using a Chaldaic-Syriac work, believe that on several occasions various passages from it could be used to explain the Greek text of the existing evangelists? Certainly. Jerome in fact.†

17. Did not this same Jerome even translate it and think it worth translating into two different languages? He says so himself.

18. Why then is there reason to deny that the Gospel of the later Nazarenes was written by the first and most ancient Nazarenes? Is it not, rather, perfectly credible that the Syriac-Chaldaic Gospel, which in Jerome's age was in the hands of the Nazarenes or Ebionites of that time,‡ may also have been in the hands of the Nazarenes at the time of the apostles, and that it may have been the written Gospel which the apostles themselves first used?

19. Admittedly the later Nazarenes were called heretics. But fundamentally they were no more

---

* [That is, an original in Aramaic, the vernacular of Palestinian Jews in Jesus' day.]

† [Saint Jerome (c. 345–419/420) translated Hebrew and Greek Jewish scriptures into Latin. His translations made up the Old Testament contained in the Vulgate Bible.]

‡ [The Nazarenes and Ebionites were considered heretical Christian groups in the fourth and fifth centuries because they continued to observe Jewish law, and some did not accept the divinity of Christ.]

heretics than the ancient Nazarenes to whom the name of heretics had not yet been given, as we may conclude from the silence of Irenaeus. For both the one and the other believed that the Mosaic ceremonial law must be maintained together with Christianity.

20. That the later Nazarenes had no connection whatever with the earlier Nazarenes is a fancy notion of [J. L.] Mosheim in his youth when he audaciously attacked one Church Father in order to hit at the others as well. This the old and more cautious Mosheim himself denied.*

21. The minor disagreements, however, which even now can be observed in the extant fragments of the Nazarene Gospel, some of which are concerned with the same question, from which some might prefer to force the conclusion that the Ebionite and Nazarene Gospels were quite different, are rather to be explained from the manner of origin such as I have assumed to be probable in §6. For since it could not occur to any ancient Nazarene to regard a work gradually compiled from various narratives as a divine book to which no subtraction or addition might be made, it was not surprising that the copies did not all agree.

22. If the Gospel of the Nazarenes was not an untimely birth substituted at a later date, it was even earlier than all our four gospels, the first of which was written at least thirty years after Christ's death.

23. Is it conceivable that in this thirty years there was no written record of Christ and his teaching? that the first person who decided to write one, after so long a time sat down to write it merely out of his or others' memories? that he had nothing before him by which he could justify himself in case he had to vindicate his statements in this or that detail? That is simply not credible even if he was inspired. For only he himself was aware of the inspiration, and probably even at that time people shrugged their shoulders over those who pretended to know historical facts by inspiration.

24. Thus there was a narrative of Christ written earlier than Matthew's. And during the thirty years it remained in that language in which alone its compilers could have written it. Or to put the matter less definitely and yet more accurately: it remained in the

Hebrew language or in the Syriac-Chaldean dialect of Hebrew as long as Christianity was for the most part still confined to Palestine and to the Jews in Palestine.

25. Only when Christianity was extended among the Gentiles, and so many who understood neither Hebrew nor a more modern dialect of it were curious to have better information about the person of Christ (which, however, may not have been during the first years of the Gentile mission, since all the first Gentile converts were content with the oral accounts which the apostles gave to each one), was it found necessary and useful to satisfy a pious curiosity by turning to that Nazarene source, and to make extracts or translations from it in a language which was the language of virtually the entire civilized world.

26. The first of these extracts, the first of these translations, was made, I think, by Matthew. And that, as I have said in §12, is the conjecture which may boldly be included among the historical truths, if we have any of these things at all. For all that we know both of the person of Matthew and of his Gospel, or that we can reasonably assume, not only agrees completely with this conjecture; but also a great deal which is a recurrent problem that has been insoluble to many scholars can only be explained by this conjecture.

27. For in the first place Matthew is to be held without contradiction to be the first and earliest of our evangelists. But this, as already observed, cannot possibly mean that he was absolutely the first of all who put anything into writing about Christ which was in the hands of the new converts. It can only mean that he was the first who wrote in Greek.

28. Secondly, it is very probable that Matthew was the only apostle who understood Greek, without needing to receive knowledge of this language directly through the Holy Ghost.

29. Thirdly, in favor of this view is the occasion on which Matthew must have composed his Gospel. For Eusebius writes (*Ecclesiastical History* iii. 24.13):† "Matthew for some years preached the Gospel to the Hebrews in Palestine; when he finally decided to go to others for this purpose, he left his Gospel in writing in his mother tongue, so that even in his absence

---

* [J. L. Mosheim was a historian writing during the time of Lessing.]

† [Eusebius of Caesarea (c. 260–339) was a Christian bishop and an important historian of the early church.]

he might remain their teacher."* Of this strictly speaking only half can be true. Only the occasion on which Matthew wrote his Gospel can be right. But this occasion was not that he had to write a Hebrew Gospel, but rather that he thought a Greek compilation to be required. That is: when he had preached for long enough to the Hebrews, he did not leave behind for the Hebrews his Gospel in Hebrew (among the Hebrews in Palestine there still remained many apostles whose oral instruction they could have at any moment), but for his future use, since he now intended to preach the Gospel to others who did not understand Hebrew, he made from the Hebrew Gospel of the Apostles a selection in the language understood by the majority.

30. Fourthly, the entire controversy concerning the original language of Matthew is settled in a way which can satisfy both parties: both those who, following the unanimous testimony of the Church Fathers, assert that the original language of Matthew's Gospel was Hebrew; and also the modern Protestant dogmatic theologians who have and must needs have their objections to this view.

31. Indeed, the original of Matthew was certainly Hebrew, but Matthew himself was not the actual author of this original. From him, as an apostle, many narratives in the Hebrew original may well derive. But he himself did not commit these narratives to writing. At his dictation others wrote them down in Hebrew and combined them with stories from the other apostles; and from this human collection he in his time made merely a connected selection in Greek. But because his selection, his translation, followed quickly on the original, because he himself could equally well have written in Hebrew, because in view of his personal circumstances it was more probable that he in fact wrote in Hebrew, it is not surprising that to some extent the original was confused with the translation.

32. And everyone will recognize how much may be gained from accepting this view by the modern divines who from the internal evidence of Matthew and for not inconsiderable dogmatic reasons think we must conclude that Matthew could not have written in any language other than that in which we now have him. Matthew wrote what he wrote in Greek; but he drew it from a Hebrew source.

33. If he made this selection in a better known language with all the diligence, with all the caution, of which such an enterprise is worthy, then indeed, to speak only humanly, a good spirit assisted him. And no one can object if one calls this good spirit the Holy Spirit. And in this way must Matthew have gone to work; such a good spirit must have guided and supported him. For his selection or his translation not only attained rapidly to canonical rank among the Christians generally, but even among the Nazarenes themselves the name of the Greek translator henceforth became attached to the Hebrew original, and this itself was given out to be a work of Matthew. The Gospel [according to the Apostles] came in time to be called by most people the Gospel [according to Matthew], as Jerome expressly says.

34. That I have not drawn a false conclusion here is shown by the long threads that do not snap, which I am in a position to unwind from a very tangled ball. That is: from this suggestion of mine I can explain twenty things which remain insoluble problems if one or other of the usual assertions about the original language of Matthew is maintained. I mention the most important, because in critical matters, as is well known, the new solutions which a fresh hypothesis provides, are equal to proofs of its truth.

35. When Epiphanius for example says that the Nazarenes possessed the Gospel of Matthew "quite complete in Hebrew," what can be said about this which avoids all objections? Was it Matthew himself who wrote this complete Hebrew text? Then our

---

* . . . And that Matthew really wrote for the Nazarenes, that is for Jewish Christians who wanted to associate Moses and Christ, is to be seen from chapter 5:17–20, where he attributes words to Jesus found in no other evangelist, and which no doubt must have made the Nazarenes obstinate. Especially verse 17, where it is ridiculous, instead of the Mosaic law in general, to understand the moral law alone. The exposition of the Babylonian Talmud is indisputably right. See the English Bible. We have now of course reason, indeed we can claim the right, to expound this passage differently. But should fault be found with the first Jewish Christians if they understood it in this way?

Similarly Mark and Luke have left out the command which according to Matthew 10:5–6, the Savior gave his disciples whom he sent out to heal and to do miracles.

Greek Matthew is not complete. If Matthew originally wrote in Greek, then in their version the Nazarenes added human additions to it, which they would not have done if it had stood in the canonical honor which it now possesses. And how could Origen* and Jerome treat these additions so indulgently? Only after my interpretation of this matter have Epiphanius' words their proper force. The Hebrew original of Matthew contained more than Matthew thought good to extract for his Greek selection. The overplus which was in the Hebrew Matthew was not interpolated by the later Nazarenes, but was omitted by Matthew.

36. Likewise, who can answer the following? If Matthew wrote originally in Greek, how does it come about that the Church Fathers unanimously assert that his Gospel was composed in Hebrew? And if he wrote his Gospel originally in Hebrew, how could his original Hebrew text be allowed to become lost? Who, I ask, can give so satisfactory an answer to this as I? The Church Fathers found a Hebrew Gospel which contained everything in Matthew and more. They thus believed it to be Matthew's own work. But this Hebrew text, supposed to be Matthew's, was in fact as regards its historical content the source of Matthew. But only the Greek selection was the actual work of the apostle, who wrote under higher oversight. Why then did it happen that the material he used was lost, after it had been used in the most authoritative way?

37. Nothing, however, more confirms my opinion that Matthew did not write in Hebrew but only translated and used a Hebrew original so faithfully and carefully that the original itself was given his name—nothing, I say, more confirms this opinion than the fact that it makes intelligible a sentence of Papias which has caused innumerable commentators so much ungrateful trouble.† Papias says, according to Eusebius, "Matthew wrote his Gospel in Hebrew; but each man translated it as well as he could."

38. The last words of this passage are admittedly so difficult that people have thought they must deny to the good Papias all credit in respect of the first. They have not been able to imagine that in these words Papias really intended to say what they so obviously do say. In particular it is very amusing to see

what trimming Clericus [a Protestant scholar, 1657–1736] gives him here, and how like a schoolmaster he corrected the Greek words for the Greek, without considering that he is schoolmastering not so much Papias as Eusebius, or at least Eusebius just as much as Papias (for every writer must also be responsible for the words he quotes from someone else, in so far as they appear to contain nonsense, if he passes them without a syllable of censure).

39. As I have said, of course one has reason to attack Papias and to ask him whether he knew what he was saying . . . Did he mean that our Greek Matthew was not such a good translation as any version could be? Or that in reality there existed several Greek translations of his Hebrew Matthew? If so, how does it come about that of these several translations there is nowhere the smallest trace? We cannot tell what Papias might answer to these questions.

40. But now assume with me that Papias had in mind not an original Hebrew Matthew, but the Hebrew original of Matthew, which, because Matthew had been the first to make it generally known and usable, thenceforward circulated under his name. What absurdity is there then when Papias says that nevertheless many still turned to the Hebrew original and produced new versions of it in Greek?

41. Have we not already seen that Matthew was not a mere translator of anything and everything which he found in the Gospel of the Nazarenes? He left much which was not familiar to him, though it had good authority. There were stories which originated from all eleven apostles; many of them were quite true but were not sufficiently useful for the later Christian world. There were stories which originated only from Christ's women associates, of which it was in part doubtful whether they had always understood correctly the wonder-man whom they so loved. There were stories which could only have come from his mother, from people who had known him in his childhood at the house of his parents; and however reliable they were, what help could they be to the world, which had enough to learn of what he did and said after entering upon his teaching office?

42. What was thus more natural? Since Matthew's translation could not be stamped with any unmistak-

---

* [Origen (184/185–253/254) was another early Christian exegete, whose work Jerome further developed.]

† [Papias of Hierapolis (c. 60 or 70–c. 130) was a bishop and early church historian. It is from Papias that the tradition of Mark's dependence on Peter comes from, as does the belief—challenged by Lessing—that Matthew wrote down Jesus' sayings in Hebrew. Papias also claimed he saw a Gospel according to the Hebrews.]

able sign of divinity, and since it only attained canonical status through examination and comparison, and so was confirmed by the Church and preserved—what was more natural than that several others who either did not know or did not entirely approve of Matthew's work, because they wished it contained this or that story, or because they would have preferred this or that story to be told differently, should undertake the same work, and should carry it out as each individual's powers enabled him?

43. And thus we stand here at the source from which flowed forth both the better Gospels that are still extant and the less good ones which on that account fell out of use and so were finally lost.*

It is, for example, not less than credible that Cerinthus made his own Gospel.† He had nothing more than his own translation of the Hebrew original of Matthew . . .

44. That there were many Gospels of this second kind, even if we did not know it from Church history, we should have to believe entirely on the evidence of Luke alone, who indeed could not have had in mind the entirely fictitious invented Gospels and apostolic writings of the heretics, but must necessarily have had in mind Gospels whose original matter was unexceptionable, but whose order, arrangement, and purpose was not entirely straightforward and clear,

when he says that through them he was encouraged and felt entitled also to write a history of the Lord. . . .

45. I might even be inclined to believe that in the passage of Luke now in question the Hebrew source is expressly mentioned, and by its title which may well have been (in Hebrew, of course) "Narrative of the things which have been fulfilled among us" were included in the title or were only added by Luke to give a much clearer designation of the authentic collection . . .

47. Indeed, although I only put forward this translation and explanation as a critical conjecture, which is far less bold and adventurous than critical conjectures usually are in these days, yet it seems to me that only this view can deal with all the difficulties which can be raised against Luke's words.‡

48. Yet be that as it may. It is enough that so much is certain, that Luke himself had before him the Hebrew document, the Gospel of the Nazarenes, and transferred, if not everything, at least most of the contents to his Gospel, only in a rather different order and in rather better language.

49. It is still more obvious that Mark, who is commonly held to be only an abbreviator of Matthew, appears to be so only because he drew upon the same Hebrew document, but probably had before him a less complete copy.¶

---

* It is a completely mistaken notion to suppose that the heretics forged false Gospels. On the contrary, because there were so many Gospels which all originated from the one Nazarene source, there were so many heretics, each one of whom has as much in his favor as any other.

† [Cerinthus (c. 100 C.E.) was a Gnostic teacher from Asia Minor who believed that the world was created by a subordinate power, not by God the Father; and that Jesus was human, who died upon the cross, but that Christ was a spirit, who did not die.]

‡ For if according to the usual translation he says: "Since many have ventured to draw up an account of the events which have happened among us, as it has been passed on to us by those who from the beginning have been eyewitnesses and ministers of the Word," have we not the right to interrupt Luke at once saying: "Have those many written nothing except in accord with the information of the eyewitnesses and first ministers of the Word? And if so, beloved Luke, what need is there of your work which all the labor you have bestowed upon it cannot make an improvement? Have you ascertained everything yourself from the beginning? Are you able to give a better testimony than the story 'as it has been passed on to us by those who from the beginning have been eyewitnesses and ministers of the Word'?" Only if these last words were either part of the title of the first Hebrew document or were added by Luke to designate it more closely and accurately, so that they refer to the Hebrew document itself and not to the ordering and translating undertaken by many, had Luke the right to undertake a similar work after he had ascertained everything from the beginning, i.e. after he had examined and confirmed everything which stood in the Hebrew document by comparison with the oral declarations of the apostles with whom he had had opportunity for conversation.

¶ That he in fact drew immediately upon the Hebrew document is shown by chapter 5:41, where he includes the actual Chaldaean words which Christ used when raising Jairus' daughter, which neither Matthew nor Luke have. Also 7:1, "Corban."

Mark must have been the interpreter and trusted disciple of Peter. This without doubt explains the fact that he omits what Matthew relates of Peter in 16:28–31. On the other hand, it is much more difficult to conceive why he also omitted what Matthew relates of Peter in 16:17, although he (Mark) preserves 8:33.

50. In short, Matthew, Mark, and Luke are simply different and not different translations of the so-called Hebrew document of Matthew which everyone interpreted as well as he could . . .

51. And John? It is quite certain that John knew and read that Hebrew document, and used it in his Gospel. Nevertheless his Gospel is not to be reckoned with the others, it does not belong to the Nazarene class. It belongs to a class all of its own.

52. The opinion that John intended to write a mere supplement to the other three Gospels is certainly unfounded. One need only read him to receive quite another impression.

53. That John did not know the other three Gospels at all is both unprovable and incredible.

54. Rather, just because he had read the other three and several other Gospels originating from the Nazarene document, and because he saw the effect of these Gospels, he found himself impelled to write his Gospel.

55. For we need only remind ourselves of the actual origins of the Gospel of the Nazarenes—from honest people who had had personal converse with Christ, and who thus must have been completely convinced of Christ as man, and apart from Christ's own words, which they had more faithfully impressed upon their memory than clearly grasped in their understanding, could not relate anything about him which could not have been true of a mere man, though doing miracles by an endowment of power from on high.

56. Is it therefore surprising that not only the Palestinian Jewish Christians to whom the name Nazarenes particularly applied, but all the Jews and Gentiles who had drawn their knowledge of Christ directly or indirectly from the Nazarene document, did not pay sufficient reverence to Christ in respect of his Godhead?

57. The former, even if our consideration goes back to their origins, could not possibly have intended to keep also the Mosaic law if they had regarded Christ as more than an extraordinary prophet. Indeed, even though they held him to be the true, promised Messiah, and as Messiah called him Son of God; yet it is beyond dispute that they did not mean by this title a Son of God who is of the same essence as God.

58. If anyone has doubts whether to concede this of the first Jewish Christians, he must at least grant that the Ebionites, that is, those Jewish Christians who before the destruction of Jerusalem escaped to Pella on the other side of Jordan, and even in the fourth century acknowledged no other Gospel than the Hebrew original of Matthew—that the Ebionites, I say, according to Origen's testimony, held a very poor opinion of Christ, even if it is not true that they received their name from the poverty of their way of thinking.

59. So also Cerinthus, who was certainly a Jew but hardly a Palestinian Jew because he was reckoned among the Gnostics, believed Christ to be simply the natural Son of Joseph and Mary born in the normal course of nature, because he accepted either the Hebrew original of Matthew or the Greek Matthew for the only Gospel (though he may have accepted it as such because he held this view).

60. The same is true of Carpocrates [an early Christian heretic] who similarly either could not hold any higher idea of Christ because he only accepted Matthew, or could only accept Matthew because he believed he should hold no higher idea of Christ.

61. In a word: Orthodox and Sectaries all had of the divine person of Christ either no idea at all or a quite wrong idea, as long as there existed no other Gospel but the Hebrew document of Matthew or the Greek Gospels which flowed from it.

62. If therefore Christianity was not to die down again and to disappear among the Jews as a mere Jewish sect, and if it was to endure among the Gentiles as a separate, independent religion, John must come forward and write his Gospel.

63. It was only his Gospel which gave the Christian religion its true consistency. We have only his Gospel to thank if the Christian religion, despite all attacks, continued in this consistency and will probably survive as long as there are men who think they need a mediator between themselves and the Deity; that is, forever.

64. That we accordingly have only two Gospels, Matthew and John, the Gospel of the flesh and the Gospel of the spirit, was long ago recognized by the early Church Fathers, and is actually denied by no modern orthodox theologian.

65. And now I would only have to explain how it came about that the Gospel of the flesh was proclaimed by three evangelists if I had not already explained it. For to speak more precisely, I would only have to explain why among many other Greek Gospels which originated from the Nazarene docu-

ment, the Church only preserved Mark and Luke in addition to Matthew; for the reason given by Augustine for this is scarcely satisfactory.

66. I will give my opinion briefly. Mark and Luke were preserved by the Church in addition to Matthew because in many respects they filled so to speak the gap between Matthew and John; and the one was a pupil of Peter and the other a pupil of Paul.

67. That, I say, is my opinion which provides an adequate reason why the four evangelists were put together in almost all ancient copies without variation. For it has not been shown that they must have been written in precise chronological order one after another.

68. But here I cannot produce the argument supporting this opinion because I must proceed by induction, and I have been unable to put enough examples together to give this induction the probability of demonstration.

Women in the Bible

As theologians and ministers began considering scripture in its historical context, others began to use the Bible in novel ways. Some argued that if scripture was to be normative and serve as the rule and guide for Christian life, then women ought to be able to speak at Christian gatherings. Those who denied women this opportunity appeared to be denying scripture as well. Although women continued to hold second-class status in Europe in terms of legal rights and economic prospects at this time, they nevertheless enjoyed increasing privileges as part of an overall rising tide. Many learned to read, and some even to write. Women in France in the eighteenth century organized salons, or high-level discussion groups, among the rich and privileged or those who worked on the margins of privilege, like artists and authors.

At the same time, however, institutional Christianity sought to extirpate any and all challenges to state religions, Catholic or Protestant, and this meant the eradication of folk religions and practices that women had dominated through the centuries. There had been persecutions and inquisitions during the Middle Ages, but none to match the ferocity and intensity of those conducted in the sixteenth and seventeenth centuries. Thousands, and some estimate millions, of women were tortured to death; many were single, or widowed, or old. Quite a few were herbalists who prescribed folk remedies in the countryside. Men were also tortured and executed, but not in the same numbers as women. Scholars provide different explanations for the outbreak of the witch hunts—from the Protestants' concern with evil inner impulses, to the desire of the urban elites to wipe out peasant culture, to the Catholics' wish to control all access to the supernatural—but none offer very clear reasons for why they began and why, just as suddenly, they ceased. When accusations and charges began to be leveled farther up the economic and social ladder, however, the trials abruptly stopped.

As we know from our readings in the Reformation, religious groups were also persecuted because of practices and beliefs at this time. One such group was the Religious Society of Friends, known as Quakers because of the ecstatic form of worship practiced in their early days. The Friends experienced great discrimination in England in the seventeenth century. A few early Quakers disrupted other religious meetings, which may account for some of the hostility they experienced. But opposition also arose because they refused to pay tithes to support the Church of England, or to take the Oath of Allegiance. They were pacifists who refused to fight in any army. They continued to hold religious meetings in private homes, despite a ban on such meetings. They were known for their plain dress and quiet ways, and perhaps most shocking, their use of the familiar form of "you"—"thee" and "thou"—with people of all classes, upper and lower. For those who have studied languages, it is the equivalent of saying "tu" instead of "Usted," or "tu" instead of "vous," or "du" instead of "Sie." Using the familiar "thou" reflected either a scandalous lack of respect or a total disdain for society's values and norms. In these practices, however, the Friends were guided by their experience of the Holy Spirit, which eliminated social distinctions.

This radical social equality seemed to extend to women. A debate existed in early Quakerism over whether women could preach in church. Most agreed that women could prophesy: they could speak spontaneously as they felt moved by the Holy Spirit. But a sermon was something else: it was planned and organized, and though perhaps inspired by the Holy Spirit in its composition, could not claim inspiration in its delivery. Margaret Fell, a prominent Quaker, argued from both the New Testament and the Old Testament for the right of women to address the church. Her defense of women's speaking "justified, proved and allowed by the scriptures" indicates that most Christians believed that gender equality was spiritual, or heavenly, rather than practical, or earthly.

Margaret Askew Fell Fox (1614–1702) bore nine children to Judge Thomas Fell. She and most of her family converted to Quakerism after a meeting in her home at which George Fox (1624–1691), the primary founder of Quakerism, spoke. After her husband died in 1658, Fell became more involved in Quakerism, and in 1660, she petitioned King Charles II on behalf of Fox, who was arrested at her house and put in prison. She herself was arrested and imprisoned in 1663 for continuing to allow Quaker meetings in her home; she was not released until mid-1668. She married George Fox the next year and accompanied him on travels throughout England, though she was arrested again in 1670.

The Society of Friends really belongs in the next section on the authority of experience because of the Friends' trust in the inner light of the Holy Spirit in each Christian's life. I have included Margaret Fell's defense of women here, however, because it shows just one of the many different ways scripture was used and interpreted, as well as how women's rights were defended on scriptural grounds.

The Reading

The first part of Margaret Fell's pamphlet begins with Adam and Eve, and uses God's curse of the serpent to express the idea that those who oppose women's speaking are on the side of the serpent rather than God. Fell focuses first on Old Testament prophecies and then on the life and teachings of Jesus, listing Jesus' women followers by name and noting the fact that women were the first to bring the message of Jesus' resurrection. She then deals with Paul and his positive and negative comments about women, arguing that Paul was misinterpreted by later readers who did not follow the logic, or rhetoric, of his argument. This first part was published in 1666, while Fell was in prison. A second edition came out in 1667 and included "A Further Addition," which appears here, and a Postscript, which does not. Thus, we are seeing only a fraction of Fell's argument, and one that seems to be a bit of an afterthought.

Note: I have retained most of the archaic spellings Fell used in her essay—for example, "busie-bodies" for "busy-bodies." If comprehension slows down, try reading the text out loud, especially since Fell has some very long sentences.

Questions to Consider

1. What examples from the Bible does Fell use in support of her argument? Are they effective?

2. What counterarguments can be made to her arguments? What arguments is she herself countering?

3. What is her strongest argument? Does she get in some "zingers"?

4. Plot or chart the lines of her logic throughout this little argument. Do you think your teacher would accept an essay written in this style? Why or why not?

5. Who is Fell arguing against? Catholics? Anglicans? Other Protestants? Quakers?

Women's Speaking Justified: A Further Addition

MARGARET FELL

A further Addition in Answer to the Objection concerning Women keeping silent in the Church. For it is not permitted for them to speak, but to be under obedience, as also saith the Law. If they will learn anything, let them ask their Husbands at home, for it is a shame for a Woman to speak in the Church. Now this, as Paul writeth in 1 Corinthians 14:34 is one with that of 1 Timothy 2:11, Let Women learn in silence, with all subjection.

To which I say, If you tie this to all outward Women, then there were many Women that were Widows which had no Husbands to learn of, and many were Virgins, which had no Husbands; and Philip had four Daughters that were Prophets; such would be despised, which the Apostle did not forbid. And if it were to all Women, that no Woman might speak, then Paul would have contradicted himself; but they were such Women that the Apostle mentions in Timothy. They grew wanton, and were busie-bodies, and tattlers, and kicked against Christ. For Christ in the Male and in the Female is one, and he is the Husband, and his Wife is the Church, and God hath said, that his Daughters should Prophesy as well as his Sons. And where he hath poured forth his

Spirit upon them, they must prophecy, though blind Priests say to the contrary, and will not permit holy Women to speak.

And whereas it is said, I permit not a Woman to speak, as saith the Law, but where Women are led by the Spirit of God, they are not under the Law, for Christ in the Male and in the Female is one; and where he is made manifest in Male and Female, he may speak, for he is the end of the Law for Righteousness to all them that believe. So here you ought to make a distinction what sort of Women are forbidden to speak, such as were under the Law, who were not come to Christ, nor to the Spirit of Prophecy. For Hulda, Miriam, and Hannah, were Prophets, who were not forbidden in the time of the Law, for they all prophesied in the time of the Law, as you may read, in 2 Kings 23 [2 Kings 22:15–20], what Hulda said unto the Priest, and to the Ambassadors that were sent to her from the King, "Go," saith she, "and tell the man that sent you to me, Thus saith the Lord God of Israel, Behold, I will bring evil upon this place, and on the inhabitants thereof, even all the words of the Book which the King of Judah hath read, because they have forsaken me, and have burnt Incense to others Gods, to anger me with all the works of their hands. Therefore my wrath shall be kindled against this place, and shall not be quenched. But to the King of Judah, that sent you to me to ask counsel of the Lord, so shall you say to him, Thus saith the Lord God of Israel, because [thine] heart did melt, and then humblest thyself before the Lord, when thou heardest what I spake against this place, and against the Inhabitants of the same, how they should be destroyed; Behold I will receive thee to thy Father, and thou shalt be put into thy Grave in peace, and thine eyes shall not see all the evil which I will bring upon this place." Now let us see if any of you blind Priests can speak after this manner, and see if it be not a better Sermon than any of you can make, who are against Women's speaking? And Isaiah, that went to the prophets, did not forbid her Speaking or Prophesying, Isaiah 8 [8:3]. And was it not prophesied in Joel 2 [2:28–29] that Handmaids should Prophesy? And are not Handmaids Women? Consider this, ye that are against Women's Speaking, how in the Acts [of the Apostles in the New Testament] the Spirit of the Lord was poured forth upon Daughters as well as Sons.

In the time of the Gospel, when Mary came to salute Elizabeth in the Hill Country in Judea, and when Elizabeth heard the Salutation of Mary, the Babe leaped in her Womb, and she was filled with the Holy Spirit; and Elizabeth spake with a loud voice, "Blessed art thou amongst Women, blessed is the fruit of thy Womb; whence this to me, that the Mother of my Lord should come to me? For lo, as soon as thy Salutation came to my ear, the Babe leaped in my Womb for joy, for blessed is she that believes, for there shall be a performance of those things which were told her from the Lord" [Luke 1:41–45]. And this was Elizabeth's Sermon concerning Christ, which at this day stands upon Record. And then Mary said, "My soul doth magnify the Lord, and my Spirit rejoiceth in God my savior, for he hath regarded the low estate of his Handmaid; for behold, from henceforth all Generations shall call me blessed; for he that is mighty, hath done to me great things, and holy is his Name; and his Mercy is on them that fear him, from Generation to Generation; he hath showed strength with his Arm; he hath scattered the proud in the imaginations of their own hearts; he hath put down the mighty from their Seats, and exalted them of low degree; he hath filled the hungry with good things, and the rich he hath sent empty away; He hath holpen [has helped] his servant Israel, in remembrance of his mercy, as he spake to his Father, to Abraham, and to his Seed forever" [Luke 1:46–55]. Are you not here beholding to the Woman for her Sermon, to use her words to put into your Common Prayer? And yet you forbid Women's Speaking. Now here you may see how these two women prophesied of Christ, and Preached better than all the blind Priests did in that Age, and better than this Age also, who are beholding to women to make use of their words.

And see in the Book of Ruth, how the women blessed her in the Gate of the City, of whose stock came Christ: "The Lord make the woman that is come into thy House like Rachel and Leah, which built the house of Israel; and that thou mayest do worthily in Ephrata, and be famous in Bethlehem, let thy house be like the house of Pharez, whom Tamar bare unto Judah, the Seed which the Lord shall give thee of this young woman. And blessed be the Lord, which hath not left thee this day without a Kinsman, and his Name shall be continued in Israel" [Ruth 4:11–14, paraphrased]. And also see in the first Chapter of Samuel, how Hannah prayed and spake in the Temple of the Lord, "Oh Lord of Hosts, if thou wilt look on the trouble of thy Handmaid, and remember me, and not forget thy Handmaid." And read in the second Chapter of Samuel, How she rejoiced in God, and said, "My heart rejoiceth in the Lord; My Horn is exalted in the Lord and my mouth is enlarged over my enemies because I rejoice in thy Salvation; there is none holy as the Lord, yea, there is none besides thee; and there is no God like our God. Speak no more presumptuously, let not arrogance come out of your mouth, for the Lord is a God of knowledge, and by him enterprises are established; the Bow, and the mighty Men are broken, and the weak hath girded to themselves strengths; they that were full, are hired forth for bread, and the hungry are no more hired; so that the barren hath born seven, and she that had many Children, is feeble; the Lord killeth, and maketh alive; bringeth down to the Grave, and raiseth up; the Lord maketh poor, and maketh rich, bringeth low and exalteth, he raiseth up the poor out of the dust, and lifteth up the Beggar from the dunghill to set them among Princes, to make them inherit the seat of Glory; for the Pillars of the earth are the Lord's; and he hath set the world upon them; he will keep the feet of his Saints, and the wicked shall keep silence in darkness, for in his own might shall no man be strong; the Lord's Adversaries shall be destroyed, and out of Heaven shall he thunder upon them; the Lord shall judge the ends of the World, and shall give power to his King, and exalt the Horn of his Anointed" [1 Samuel 2:1–10]. Thus you may see what a woman hath said, when old Ely the Priest thought she had been drunk, and see if any of you blind Priests that speak against Women's Speaking, can Preach after this manner? Who cannot make such a Sermon as this woman did, and yet will make a trade of this Woman and other women's words.

And did not the Queen of Sheba speak, that came to Solomon, and received the Law of God, and preached it in her own Kingdom, and blessed the Lord God that loved Solomon, and set him on the throne of Israel, because the Lord loved Israel forever; and made the King to do Equity and Righteousness? And this was the language of the Queen of Sheba. And see what glorious expressions Queen Hester [Esther] used to comfort the People of God, which was the Church of God, as you may read in the book of Hester, which caused joy and gladness of heart among all the Jews, who prayed and worshipped the Lord in all places, who jeoparded [jeopardized] her life contrary to the King's command, went and spoke to the King, in the wisdom and fear of the Lord, by

which means she saved the lives of the People of God; and righteous Mordecai did not forbid her speaking, but said, If she held her peace, [she] and her Father's house should be destroyed; and herein you blind Priests are contrary to Righteous Mordecai.

Likewise you may read how Judith spoke, and what noble acts she did, and how she spoke to the Elders of Israel, and said, "Dear Brethren, seeing you are the honorable and elders of the People of God, call to remembrance how our Fathers in time past were tempted, that they might be proved if they would worship God aright; they ought also to remember how our Father Abraham, being tried through manifold tribulations, was found a friend of God; so was Isaac, Jacob, and Moses, and all they pleased God, and were [unclear] in Faith through manifold troubles" [Judith 8, paraphrase]. And read also her prayer in the Book of Judith [chapter 16], and how the Elders commended her, and said, "All that she speaketh is true, and no man can reprove thy words, pray therefore for us, for thou art an holy Woman, and feareth God" [Judith 8:28–31]. So these elders of Israel did not forbid her speaking, as you blind Priests do; yet you will make a Trade of Women's words to get money by, and take Texts, and Preach Sermons upon Women's words; and still cry out, Women must not speak, Women must be silent; so you are far from the minds of the Elders of Israel, who praised God for a Woman's speaking. But the Jezebel, and the Woman, the false Church, the great Whore, and tattling women, and busie-bodies, which are forbidden to Preach, which have a long time spoke and tattled, which are forbidden to speak by the True Church, which Christ is the Head of; such Women as were in transgression under the Law, which are called a Woman in the Revelations [of John].

And see further how the wise Woman cried to Joab over the Wall, and saved the City of Abel, as you may read, 2 Samuel 20. How in her wisdom she spoke to Joab, saying, "I am one of them that are peaceable and faithful in Israel, and thou goest about to destroy a city and Mother in Israel; Why wilt thou destroy the Inheritance of the Lord?" [2 Samuel 20:19]. Then went the woman to the people in her wisdom, and smote off the head of Sheba, that rose up against David, the Lord's Anointed. Then Joab blew the Trumpet, and all the People departed in peace. And this deliverance was by the means of a Woman's speaking; but tattlers and busie-bodies, are forbidden to preach by the True woman, whom Christ is the Husband, to the Woman as well as the

Man, all being comprehended to be the Church; and so in this True Church, Sons and Daughters do Prophesy, Women labor in the Gospel; but the Apostle permits not tattlers, busie-bodies, and such as usurp authority over the Man would not have Christ Reign, nor speak neither in the Male nor Female; Such the Law permits not to speak, such must learn of their Husbands. But what husbands have widows to learn of, but Christ? And was not Christ the Husband of Philip's four Daughters? And may not they that learn of their Husbands speak then? But Jezebel, and Tattlers, and the Whore that denies Revelation and Prophecy, are not permitted, which will not learn of Christ; and they that be out of the Spirit and Power of Christ, that the Prophets were in, who are in the Transgression, are ignorant of the Scriptures; and such are against Women's Speaking, and Men's too, who Preach that which they have received of the Lord God; but that which they have preached, and do preach, will come over all your heads, yea, over the head of the false Church, the Pope. For the Pope is the Head of the False church, and the False Church is the Pope's Wife: and so he and they that be of him, and come from him, are against Women's Speaking in the True Church, when both he and the false Church are called Woman, in Revelation 17, and so are in the Transgression that would usurp authority over the Man Christ Jesus, and his Wife too, and would not have him to Reign; but the Judgment of the Great Whore is come. But Christ, who is the Head of the Church, the True Woman which is his Wife, in it do Daughters Prophesy, who are above the Pope and his wife and atop of them.

And here Christ is the Head of the Male and Female, who may speak; and the Church is called a Royal Priesthood; so the Woman must offer as well as the Man, Revelation 22:17. The Spirit saith, Come, and the Bride saith, Come; and so is not the Bride the Church? And doth the Church only consist of Men? You that deny Women's speaking, answer: Doth it not consist of Women as well as men? Is not the Bride compared to the whole Church? And doth not the Bride say, Come? Doth not the Woman speak then to the Husband Christ Jesus, the Amen, and doth not the false Church go about to stop the Bride's Mouth? But it is not possible for the Bridegroom is with his Bride, and he opens her Mouth. Christ Jesus, who goes on Conquering, and to Conquer, who kill[s] and flays with the Sword, which is the words of his Mouth; the Lamb and the Saints shall have the victory, the true Speakers of Men and Women over the false Speaker.

The Authority of Experience

Pietism: The Experience of the Holy Spirit

"Scripture alone" as the primary, and only, source of authority sounded good in theory, but didn't work in practice in the aftermath of the events of the sixteenth century. Most Protestant denominations, as well as the Catholic Church at the Council of Trent, adopted new statements of faith to clarify their positions on key issues: the books that belonged in the Bible; human involvement in justification; baptism, infant or adult; and so on. These various confessions supplemented the Nicene Creed and drew clear boundaries between different groups of Christians. The quest for doctrinal purity led to a new period of scholasticism, but this time on the Protestant, and especially Lutheran, side.

Protestantism had ignited a powerful urge within laypeople to live a Christian life, however, which scholasticism and confessionalism failed to satisfy. Lay movements to embody personal piety had arisen earlier in the Middle Ages, when groups of laypeople lived and worked together for the poor. Neither the emphasis on individual responsibility and accountability that seemed to accompany Protestant orthodoxy, nor the emphasis on corporate sin and salvation within Catholicism, seemed to fulfill some individuals' desire for an intimate relationship with the divine. The formality of the worship service distanced God and Jesus. Frequently, church leaders were allied with political leaders, and Christianity at times seemed a civic rather than religious duty. The Spiritualist wing of the Radical Reformation had already expressed dissatisfaction with these forms of Christianity in the sixteenth century.

As a result, a movement called Pietism emerged in the late seventeenth century and expanded and flourished in the eighteenth. In Germany, Philipp Jakob Spener (1635–1705) and August Hermann Franke (1663–1727) were among the first to outline a program of Pietism, which included group and individual Bible study, and regular meetings with other Christians in addition to church attendance and worship. Spener hoped to recapture the simplicity of the early apostles with his small groups, called *collegia pietatis*. He believed that Christianity consisted of practice—love in action—rather than knowledge or doctrine. For him and others, the content of the Bible, its substance, was what was vital, not its authority. In effect, the Bible was a devotional book, not a doctrinal thesis.

Pietists stressed the need for personal holiness, in addition to experiencing the divine through the Spirit of God. If justification was the watchword for sixteenth-century Christian reformers, sanctification was key for seventeenth- and eighteenth-century Pietists. They downplayed the need for sacraments, seeing them as symbols of grace rather than as means to grace, and disparaged formal leaders, preferring to meet in small groups, or conventicles, to pray and study. Service to Christ through acts of love and charity was more important than worship or academic study. The movement spread throughout Europe and North America. Although German Pietists generally remained within the Lutheran fold, in England, George Fox founded the Quakers, and John Wesley began the Methodists. George Whitefield and Jonathan Edwards ignited the colonists in a variegated revival movement in America. In France, the eighteenth-century followers of Cornelius Jansen sparked a revival within Catholicism known as Jansenism. Even within Judaism, a Pietist movement arose known as Hasidism—an ecstatic, spirit-filled faith that supplemented Talmud and Torah with song and dance.

Nicholaus Ludwig Count von Zinzendorf (1700–1760) entered Pietism somewhat obliquely by allowing a group of Moravians exiled from Austria to live on his property in Saxony (now part of Germany). Members of the Moravian Church, comprising descendants of Bohemian Brethren who emerged during the Reformation, accepted the essentials of Christian teachings, but believed in freedom of conscience when it came to what they felt were nonessentials. The group on Zinzendorf's estate was called *Herrnhut* (literally, "under the Lord's protection") and numbered three hundred residents by 1727. The *Herrnhut* Moravians followed monastic discipline and developed a communal economy in which the church owned property and businesses; but the "church" was the people, living in zealous piety.

Zinzendorf, the godson of Spener, was ordained a Lutheran minister in 1734, but was consecrated a Moravian bishop in 1737 thanks to his leadership and defense of the movement. He believed that small communities of brethren could survive within, rather than apart from, existing denominations, and thus he remained a

Lutheran all his life. He deliberately encouraged the development of many small communities and focused on missionizing Europe and Russia, though he also wanted to settle Moravians in the Pennsylvania colony in North America. His encounters and dialogues with John Wesley deeply influenced the Anglican minister and his brother Charles, a prolific writer of hymns. Wesley and Zinzendorf shared a number of views concerning personal holiness, the need for religious fellowship, and the internalization of truth—that is, an experience of assurance or love within the soul. While Zinzendorf traveled extensively, preaching and teaching, it was Wesley, through open-air sermons to thousands of poor and working-class people in England and Wales, who brought Pietism to the masses.

The Reading

Zinzendorf went to England in 1746 to clarify the position of the Moravian Church. He believed that one could be a member of the community of the Brethren and still remain an Anglican, or a Lutheran, or whatever affiliation one had. To this end, he lectured extensively and preached a number of sermons to enthusiastic audiences. He delivered the following sermon in the Brethren's Chapel in London, on 25 September 1746.

The count makes a big point of differentiating between being "in Christ" as opposed to being "a Christian." He does not see Christianity as a denomination, but rather as belonging to Christ or becoming a member of Christ's family. He then attempts to explain what it is that allows or creates membership in this family. Even though this is a sermon, Zinzendorf is still making an argument against one view of Christianity and in favor of an opposing view.

Note: Passages from scripture come from the Revised Standard Version of the Bible, but may appear as alternate readings.

Questions to Consider

1. What can you deduce about Zinzendorf's opinion of the current situation in European Christianity?

2. What does it mean to be called a Christian, in his opinion?

3. How does this sermon relate to what we have learned about Pietism?

4. How does this sermon relate to what we have learned about rational religion? Is it a continuation of the rationalist experience? Is it a refutation?

5. What does Zinzendorf mean when he says, "As soon as anyone appeals to the fact that he does not hold with another's logic, in that moment the other's right to censure him ceases"? Do you agree?

6. What is Zinzendorf's beef with rational religion? What would he say to William Ellery Channing?

7. How does Zinzendorf describe the conversion experience? What happens? How does it affect people?

8. What would he think about nondenominational Christianity today? What does he say about Christians criticizing Christians with whom they disagree?

On the Essential Character and Circumstances of the Life of a Christian

NICHOLAUS LUDWIG COUNT VON ZINZENDORF

John 21:16. "Do you love me?"

My purpose is to make clear from these words what constitutes the essential Christian.

These are common book titles and especially in England very much in style: *The Almost Christian; The Christian; The True Christian; The Christian's Journey to Eternity.* Thus almost nothing more stale and threadbare can be mentioned than such a subject, or rather such a wording of the subject, as when one says, "I will set forth the true, the essential Christian." But I will, nevertheless, say something rather new.

We want to look first at the essential character of a Christian, and secondly we will consider the circumstances of his life.

The genuine character of a Christian consists absolutely in this: when he speaks with the Savior, when he speaks with his brethren, when he has anything to straighten out with God the Father, when he needs the ministry of angels, when he shall present himself on the day of the Lord to join in judgment over the living and the dead—then he absolutely does not appeal to his religious denomination, but rather to his nature, to his descent. For the most serious objection on that day will be, "I do not know you nor where you come from" (Luke 13:25).

This is the *Crinomenon* [judgment] which decides on that day and in all similar circumstances and upon which it depends, that one is received and the other cast away. The Savior does or does not call a person to mind. "I will acknowledge him; I will say, 'I know you'" (Matthew 10:32).

Therefore, it is a rule belonging absolutely to the character of the true Christian that, properly speaking, he is neither Lutheran nor Calvinist, neither of this nor the other religious denomination, not even

Christian. What can be said more plainly and positively? What reformer, be it Hus or Luther or Wycliffe, or whatever his name might be, would be so presumptuous as to maintain that men are saved because they are his followers? For Paul excludes Christ Himself when he says, "Not of Paul, not of Cephas, not of Apollos, not of Christ" (1 Corinthians 1:12).

It is really a great misfortune that people read the scriptures but read them without the proper attention and that such main passages are not noticed. For seventeen hundred years men have written this for all the world to see, *Christianus sum* [Latin: "I am a Christian"], and for as many centuries have put this into the mouths of all the martyrs, *Christianus sum,* which is contrary to the plain words of the apostle Paul, who has expressly forbidden that any man call himself "of Christ" or Christian. Let our enemies call us that, let the Turks and pagans, let the Jews call us this in derision: *Vir bonus, sed malus, quia Christianus est* [Latin: "He is a good man, but bad because he is a Christian"], it is a pity that he is a Christian. But we must not speak this way. To be sure, the ancient fathers have themselves given occasion to this confusion: Prudentius says, *"Sectagenerosa Christi nobilitat viros,"* i.e., the noble, the excellent religion of Christ makes people even more noble than they were before.

Who directed the people to do this? Who directed them to make a religion out of the family of Christ, in direct contradiction to the Holy Scriptures? It does not matter that men have confessions of faith; it does not matter that they are divided into religious denominations; they may very well differentiate themselves according to their *tropo paedias* (form of doctrines). An upright Christian man can say, I side with Calvin; an upright Christian man may also say according to my judgment I rather side with Luther. But this gives neither the one nor the other the least warrant, the least right to salvation; this only distinguishes him according to his insight and as an honest man among the faithful; it entitles him not to be arbitrarily judged in his manner of acting, in his form, his method of treating souls, and in the outward appearance of his worship. Each thing has its peculiar external form, its external shape, and everything does not look alike. No man has the same point of view as another, and by this means he distinguishes himself innocently and inoffensively. For as soon as anyone appeals to the fact that he does not hold with another's logic, in that moment the other's right to censure him ceases. And it is a vulgar, mean disposition of mind when people of one religious denomination take pleasure in opposing people of another, or when on that account they show enmity toward each other. For as soon as someone says that he is of a persuasion different from mine, then he has taken away my spiritual right over him to censure him.

Now thus far it is good that we have many religious denominations; up to this point I am in agreement, so much so that I despise anyone who, without the deepest and most thoroughly examined reason, changes over from one denomination to another; so much so that nothing sounds more ridiculous to my ears than a proselyte [convert]. Only with the greatest difficulty can I make myself deal with such a person, when I become aware that he has left his former denomination, especially among the Protestants, who all take the Scriptures as the guiding principle of faith. Therefore, frivolity should not govern denominational matters. The differences in religious denominations are important and venerable concerns, and the distinction of religious denominations is a divine wisdom. No peculiarity should cause a disturbance. But all of these ideas still betray their human origin, of which it may be said that three hundred, five hundred, a thousand years ago things were not yet conceived in this way. There is only one of whom it may be said, "Yesterday, today, and forever He is ever still the same" (Hebrews 13:8):

> And His church stands as she has stood,
> Jehovah the Father is her God;
> She still retains her very first dress:
> Christ's own blood and righteousness.

Now then, I have said what a Christian is not, what a person must not presume to comprehend under the name of Christians, in what respect a person must not boast of Christ, what a Christian upon occasion must consider entirely as *skybala,* as refuse, as Paul calls it (Philippians 3:8), whenever it tends to interfere with the foundation, with the main point, even were it good and real in itself or could in a certain sense be valid.

Now, what then is the proper character of a Christian? Take notice, my dear friends, for here we must in advance set aside the common word as it is used in all languages, except the German, which has something special in its usage.

In all languages one says, a Christian, and in our German alone one says, *ein Christ,* and that is the right word. "All things are yours; and you are Christ's" (1 Corinthians 3:22b–23a); you belong to Christ, you are His heirs, you are His family. And in another place it is also put quite "germanly": "You are bone of his bone and flesh of his flesh," and this refers to Genesis 2:23. "She shall be called Woman [*Männin*], because she was taken out of Man [*Mann*]" (Genesis 2:23b). All the prophets make allusion to this when they say, "Those who are called according to my name" (Isaiah 43:7). In no way are we called by the name of Jesus or Christ in the sense of a religious denomination, as if Christ were our teacher, as if Christ were our prophet, our lawgiver, as if He were the founder, the author of our religion, as it is sometimes expressed by a pagan historian, as for example in Lucian: "The founder of this religion was crucified." In this sense we are not Christians. Rather, we are Christians in the same way that, in our European countries, a wife takes the name of her husband and afterwards is called not by her maiden name but by her husband's name. Thus every soul who has the right to call herself by this name, "because she was taken out of Man" (Genesis 2:23) belongs to Christ, is Christian. [And in the German, Zinzendorf uses the feminine form of "Christian."]

Now whoever will not grasp this and has no other support for himself than that he has read the teachings of Jesus and industriously given lectures on it, that he can recount this teaching, and that he is established in its principles according to his religious denomination; such a person can be considered nothing more than one of those Christianly-religious people. And even though he discharges all the duties according to his religious denomination, so that there can be no objection to him, yet he cannot on that basis lay claim to this: "O Lamb of God, you who take away the sin of the world (John 1:29), acknowledge me!" Rather, whoever wishes to claim this, he must be christened in his heart, as here in England it is said of one who is baptized, "He is christen'd"; he must be made a Christian; he must be of the bone and spirit of Christ; he must in truth take pride in this: "My Maker is my husband" (Isaiah 54:5); He has not only created me, and He is not only the potter of my clay, but "He is the husband of my soul, who has betrothed Himself to me for ever and has betrothed Himself to me in grace and mercy, yet, has betrothed Himself to me in faith" (Hosea 2:19, Luther's translation). I am certain who my Husband is; I know Him.

Thus far I have spoken about the character of a Christian, of a man who can call himself Christian without being a liar or a foolish, stupid person who does not know what he is saying.

Now I come to the other part of my discourse, to the chief circumstances which are found in the case of such a Christian.

The character of a Christian, the entrance into this state, and the entire progress in it as well are based on the text which I have read: "Do you love me?"

First of all, it is undeniable that if a person had no other certainty concerning the Savior than what the school teacher dictated to him about Him in his youth, he would certainly be in bad shape. For then this objection might be raised against him: "Who knows? If you had been born a Jew, then you would have believed what the rabbi had taught you; if you had been born a Turk, then you would have believed what the Mullah had taught you; if you had been born in a pagan religion, you would have believed what the bonze or the lama or some other pagan priest had taught you." And not much of a reply can be made to that.

Therefore there must necessarily be something which gives us more certainty than do all the achievements of our understanding, something which gives us a firm footing and enables a person to maintain in the face of everyone, "Yes, I still would have been a Christian even though I had been born a Jew. I still would not have remained a Turk or pagan, even though I had been born a Turk or a pagan."

But what is the special factor which so distinguishes us from all the religions, from all the persuasions and opinions, that every reasonable person must admit it? It is just that very thing which the Apostle Paul calls the folly of his preaching.

Here one would like for God's sake to beg all theologians, if they would only listen, not to take such pains constantly to represent our religion as agreeing with reason, as being common sense. If writings of this kind are assigned to pamphlets, by which people earn a living for themselves, then it may pass. But as soon as it is taken seriously, as soon as they want to demonstrate to atheists and common deists and people like that that our religion is a wisdom rooted in their heads, a discernment which they can take in their own way, then they are obviously threshing empty straw, according to all instruction of the Scripture.

This position is false from the very start, for Paul states positively that there is something foolish in our preaching, and none of the wise ones of this world can comprehend it. There is no ear that can hear our language; there is no eye that can see our concerns; there is no sight sharp enough, no natural understanding sufficient to penetrate our matters, and one must be prepared for this. As it is said in the Acts of the Apostles, *tetagmenoi*, "as many of them were ordained for eternal life" (Acts 13:48); there the work had been done, their head, their mind and their heart had been set straight, they could apprehend these things as wisdom, as wisdom in spite of everything. "Teach me wisdom in my secret heart," said David, "You purge me, you wash me, you make my bones rejoice, which before were broken, and you give me a ready spirit" (Psalm 51:6b–10); you give me ideas quite different from those I had before, and you do this, your wisdom in my secret heart does this. This is the wisdom in 1 Corinthians 1, which none of the wise people of this world were able to reach or obtain; and if a bet be made, says Paul, if there are contrasting opinions on how the Gospel shall be propagated, how the teaching of Jesus shall grasp the hearts, and an honorable man says, "Our wise, our understanding people will do this; the vulgar certainly will not comprehend it, but if it comes first to the learned, wise and devout people, they will understand it,"—then Paul tells them to their faces: now we do have Christianity, and we do have an example, a congregation of God; now, good friend, where are the wise, where are the intelligent, where are the nobles? Well? Show them to me.

This is the plain, true, and genuine meaning of all that Paul says in the place cited. This is to prove nothing else but that the ordinary means do not suffice, that the ordinary frame of mind is not enough, that the understanding of man, as man, is as insufficient for grasping our matters as is the understanding of a poor animal for comprehending our geometric or algebraic propositions. It is undeniable; it must first be given to us. I said in my last Sunday's sermon that He gives power (John 1:12); it must be given, and those to whom it has not yet been given ought by rights to say, "This is too profound a wisdom; we have not yet advanced so far." They ought to say what Aristotle said, when he threw himself into the Euripus: "O you being of all beings! *Eleeson* [have mercy]." They ought to say, "I am too stupid, too inept." Or as David, "I am a Behema [beast], a dumb animal before you; I cannot penetrate into the depths of things" (Psalm 73:22).

Instead of this the proud spirit of man, that presumptuous creature, which, however, is only a poor wretched human being, says in a quarrelsome way to its Creator, "It is foolishness, nonsense; it is enthusiasm; it is good for fanatics." This is quarreling and striving against the Creator; for the people who say this have our Bible as well as we do; they read it, they print it, and they circulate it among men as God's Word. What right do they have to call these same Biblical truths foolishness, just because they do not understand them? They have most certainly no right, but it is their pleasure. Every man loves to maintain his own assertion; every man is so disposed that if there is something he does not have, the other person shall not have it either, and what the other person does have is nothing at all, is not even worth the effort. Therefore I cannot help it: our theology, our mysteries, our Christianity I must let pass as foolishness for them, with the protestation that it is nevertheless wisdom for those who understand it; in this sense of it I will now mention what it is all about.

My friends, I will not dispute about how one enters into the state of being a Christian. Words are spoken, there is preaching; fine hymns and texts on glorious things contribute and are means to it, yes, may even be vehicles of it. But they are not the whole, not even the central concern. Then what is the central concern? My friends, it is this: whoever will answer Yes to the Savior's question, "Do you love me?" must have caught sight of the Savior when the Savior looked into his heart for the first time. This is the order: First the Savior looks at us, and we perceive him; at that moment we have the matter in hand, and the Christian is ready.

My friends, not even a quarter of an hour, not even a minute, not even as much time as it takes to stop to think must intervene between the point when the Savior looks at us and when we perceive Him. Afterward we again stop seeing; then we believe, and then it is the constant and unceasing act of the Savior to be looking at us: "His eyes remain open day and night toward us" (2 Chronicles 6:20). "I will counsel you with my eye upon you" (Psalm 32:8b).

I want to explain these two points a little more closely. When a person becomes a Christian [*ein Christ*], when the Savior receives him, when a person is admitted to the power to be a child of God, then it happens this way: for a moment the Savior becomes present to him in person. In an hour, in a moment (it may be in an indivisible point of time which cannot be compared with any measure of time that we have, including moments themselves), a person comes into the circumstances in which the apostles stood when they saw Him.

I do not pretend that we see a body with our corporeal eyes; I do not desire that the mind try to imagine a body or try to conceive a representation of it, or that the mind look into itself or turn its thoughts in toward itself until it sees a form standing before it. But I do ask for the essential in this, and that is that a person who has seen abstractly and purely must in the next moment realize that he has actually seen; that a person must know as certainly that his spirit has seen, that his heart has seen and felt, as when in ordinary human life one can be certain that he has seen or touched something. In the moment when this happens he does not need to have a sense-experience or see something visible (this cannot be excluded with any certainty, but neither is it essential); it is only necessary that afterward the essential effect remain, that one can say not only, "I have seen, I have heard"; but rather, "Thus have I seen it, and thus have I heard."

The Scripture says that our entire work of the gospel is to portray Jesus, to paint Him before the eyes, to take the spirit's stylus and etch—yes, engrave—the image of Jesus in the fleshly tablets of the heart, so that it can never be removed again.

Now the only question is, "In what kind of a form does one see the Savior?" In the Old Testament it was said, "You shall not make yourself a graven image or likeness" (Exodus 20:4), for this reason: in all your life you have never seen a likeness nor any original, and therefore you cannot make a copy. For I will not have my religion, my worship, profaned with masks and illusions; cherubim you may make, for you have seen some of them. But you shall make no god, for in your entire life you have never seen one.

In the New Testament this commandment is at an end: we have seen. Therefore the Lutherans are right in leaving this commandment out of the catechism, for it no longer has any relation on earth to us. This makes the particular distinction between us and the Reformed, for they combine the ninth and tenth commandments to make room for the commandment forbidding images, which we Lutherans, according to our understanding, leave out of the Decalogue.* We do not hold that a person should make himself no picture or image in the New Testament; a person may make an image, no, he should. It is a part of the Christian religion to form for oneself a picture of that God who took a body upon Himself. Augustine wishes to see *Jesum in carne,* Jesus in the flesh; and because I cannot do this, he said, He stands before my eyes as if I saw Him being crucified.

Some of the theologians have wanted to find the whole suffering form of the Savior in the Song of Songs, in the bride's description of her beloved, "This is my beloved" (Song 5:16), and think that there He is painted piece by piece, as His figure was on the cross. I do not want to enter into this discussion at present. But this is certain, that Christians can rightly, by divine right, sing:

> In that form appear to me
> As, for my great distress,
> Upon the Cross so tenderly
> You did bleed to death.

This they may claim; they have a right to speak this way, and all men, all souls have a right to say what Thomas said, "Unless I see in his hands the print of the nails, and place my finger in the mark of the nails, and place my hand in his side, I will not believe" (John 20:25).

And this is the advice which I give to all hearts. If anyone asks me about his salvation, I say to him, "Do not believe, if you do not want to be deceived, do not believe until you see the prints of the nails and place your finger in the prints of the nails and place your hand in His side: then believe."

But who must see? It is the heart which must see at least once. Afterward it goes on believing until it shall see Him again. I must freely concede that this advice does not at first sight seem to conform to the advice of the Savior, "Blessed are those who have not seen and yet believe" (John 20:29b). Now how shall I reconcile my advice with the words of the Savior? Nothing is easier: there is a seeing and a not seeing. The Scripture shows that this is possible: "They have eyes and do not see, they have ears and do not hear" (Jeremiah 5:21). Therefore a person may also not seem to see and yet be seeing; a person may not seem to hear and yet be hearing; a person may not seem to feel and yet be feeling. And so it is, "as dying, and behold we live" (2 Corinthians 6:9). According to the external senses and the human disposition we neither see, hear, nor feel the Savior. But why then does He so often say, "I will manifest myself" (John 14:21)? Why does He say, "He who has ears to hear, let him hear" (Mark 4:9)? And that He did not say this only to those people who were speaking with Him is made clear in that He repeated in the Revelation of John to those people who did not see Him, "He who has ears to hear, let him hear" (Revelation 3:22). Why does the apostle say, "You should seek Him until you feel Him" (Acts 17:27)? All His arrangement in the whole world was made for this purpose, that people may obtain a feeling of Him (Acts 17:27). And from where comes the testimony of the apostle, "When it pleased God to reveal His Son in me, I set out immediately" (Galatians 1:15–16)? And from where comes the constant witness of all the other apostles concerning the direct and immediate special relationship with Him?

Once one is involved in the Spirit, one comes into that extraordinary state concerning which John expresses himself thus, "I was in the Spirit on the Lord's day" (Revelation 1:10a). And this may happen with more or less sense experience, with more or less distinctness, with more or less visibility, and with as many kinds of modifications as the different human temperaments and natural constitutions can allow in one combination or another. One person attains to it more incontestably and powerfully, the other more gently and mildly; but in one moment both attain to this, that in reality and truth one has the Creator of all things, the fatherly Power, the God of the entire world, standing in His suffering form, in His penitential form, in the form of one atoning for the whole human race—this individual object stands before the

---

* Reformed churches tended to be iconoclastic; that is, they destroyed anything they felt could be considered an idol. As a result, church architecture was very plain and simple, lacking statuary, stained glass, or other artwork. Lutheran churches, by contrast, continued to be ornate.

vision of one's heart, before the eyes of one's spirit, before one's inward man. And this same inward man, who until now has been under the power of the kingdom of darkness, as soon as he catches sight of his Deliverer, this Deliverer reaches out His hand to him and plucks him immediately out of all corruption; He pulls him out of the dungeon of his prison and places him in the light before His face: "Take heart, my child, your sins are forgiven (Matthew 9:2); I will make a covenant with you, that you shall be mine (Jeremiah 31:33?); I will be your advocate in judgment, and you shall be allowed to appeal to me; but, will you have me?" That is the *Crinomenon,* the deciding factor. Do you want me? Do you receive me? Do I suit you? Am I acceptable to you? Do I please your heart? See, here I am! This is the way I look. For your sake I was made to be sin (2 Corinthians 5:21), and for your sake I was made a curse (Galatians 3:13); for the sake of your sins I was torn, beaten, and put to death. I have sweated the sweat of fear and anguish, the sweat of death, the sweat of the strife of penance; I have laid down my life for your sake. I have been laid into the dust of the grave for your sake. Does this suit you? Is this important to you? Are you satisfied with me? Do I in this way please you? Do I please you better in the idea of a mangled slave who is thrown to the wild beasts in the circus, or in the form of the emperor who sits high on the throne and takes pleasure in the destruction of the poor creature? How do I please you the best?

He who in this moment, in this instant, when the Savior appears to him and when He says to him, as to Peter, "Do you love me in this figure?"—he who can say, "You know all things; you know that I love you"; he who in this minute, in this instant, goes over to Him with his heart, passes into Him, and loses himself in His tormented form and suffering figure—he remains in Him eternally, without interruption, through all eons; he can no longer be estranged from Him. No possibility can be imagined, though the whole universe should join together, that anything could separate him from that friendship which is formed at the moment of His bloody appearing.

Now this is the entrance to this state, that one receives Him at that moment, looks at Him longingly, and falls in love with Him; that one says, "It is true; now I can do nothing more, now I want nothing more. Yes, God Creator, Holy Spirit! My eyes have seen your *soterion* [salvation] (Luke 2:30), they have seen your little Jesus; my heart wept for joy when His

nail prints, His wounds, His bloody side stood before my heart. You know this."

Then our perdition is at an end; then flesh and blood have lost. Satan, who had already lost his case in court, really lays no more claim on such a soul; and it is just as if a man, who had sold himself to Satan, gets back his promissory note, as if the slip of paper came flying into the meeting, torn to pieces. The signature, the note, says the apostle, is torn up and fastened to the cross, pounded through with nails, and forever cancelled; and this is registered at the same time, that is, we are set free; we are legally acquitted. When the books are opened, so it will be found.

What is called repentance in the world, what is called conversion, this David describes thus: "As the eyes of the servants look to the hand of their master, as the eyes of a maid to the hand of her mistress" (Psalm 123:2), so the eyes of the sinner look for Him until He appears before them. Then a person begins to look and to listen in the hope of finding the Savior as his Creator in His true, human suffering form, with His corpse wounded for us, before our eyes. When that has happened, then the person has seen Him and now believes continually, no more desiring to see and never again in his whole life losing the look of the tortured Savior; He remains engraved in one's heart. One has a copy of this deeply impressed there; one lives in it, is changed into the same image, and every year, I might say every day, is placed into a greater light streaming from the wounds: it looks more and more reddish around such a person, as the prophets express it (Isaiah 1:18); he appears more and more sinful; as we express it, he keeps to the point of His sufferings. Then one can no longer fluctuate. One knows of no other presence of the Creator than in the beauty of His sufferings.

But what kind of authority, what kind of eternal and incontestable effect on our heart does His perpetual look have afterward? This belongs to our progress. Here there is no need to tell people, do not steal, do not get drunk, do not lead a disorderly life, do not be so fond of the creature, do not set your heart on this and that, do not be hostile. Now there is no need to preach one point of morality after the other at a person, not even of the most refined and subtle. Even though a person were to be most adept in the matter and become an example to the whole country, still there would be no need for reasoning. For every loving look from the Savior indicates our morality to us throughout our whole life: one dissatisfied, one sorrowful, one painful look from the Savior embitters and makes loathsome to us everything that is immoral, unethical, and disorderly, all fleshly mindedness, as often as it is necessary.

I suppose that we remain men; it is a part of the state of sin not to think more highly of ourselves. But we shall succeed, if our Head but look now and then, at some interval, upon us.

We are not people who from the first moment of our spiritual life until into eternity itself remain unassaulted and unattacked. From a distance something comes at us; there is something in our own selves which we cannot name, to which we have as yet been unable to give the right name, until the proper position of the soul has been determined. This must be handled with great caution and watched over carefully; and even if it should stick in the deepest recesses of the mind, even if it is also lying imprisoned, so that it is actually not able to block our course in following Christ, yet it is still there, and no reading, no hearing, no moral doctrine guards against it. For the only remedy against all such alluring demands, gross or subtle, is the doubtful glance of the Savior, when the form of Jesus does not seem so pleasing, so joyful to our hearts, when He seems to us to be no longer so sweetly before our hearts as usual.

People who have murdered someone have said that the person and image of the murdered one always hovered before their eyes; they have neither been able to bear it nor escape from the sight of it. We also say of people who are very important to us, I see him as clearly as if he were here; I could paint him right now. This David applies to his Savior, "I have placed Him so directly before my eyes that I will never lose Him from my thoughts, from my point of view; I need only look up, and I have Him immediately there" (Psalm 139). Suppose, then, that one might fall into all sorts of questionable situations, if possible to go astray in something, to allow oneself to be implicated in something by one's thoughts, to wander from the Savior with one's senses. The Savior need only look at one, even though one does not look towards Him, and the glance of His eyes goes through one like a flame of fire: one is transparent, known throughout by Him; He knows the moment when He is to look at us, and He also knows how He is to look at us, for He has read our thoughts before they have formed themselves. When Judas came and betrayed Him, He preached him a sermon: "My friend, you give me a kiss and betray me." When Peter denied Him, He spoke no words but rather looked upon him. In the case of Judas the sermon availed nothing; the look had this effect on Peter: "He went out and wept bitterly" (Matthew 26:75); he bathed himself in tears. What kind of tears? Tears of love. He wept for love, for he had not owned, confessed, or affirmed his Master, for he had not risked his life for Him. And when the Savior said a few days later, "Do you love me?" the answer was, O dear Lord! I appeal to you; you have looked upon me: you have seen not only the faithful Nathanael under the fig tree, but you have also seen me, an unfaithful heart. You do know what your look has effected; you know indeed how your look operated upon my heart; my eyes were wet with tears; it went through body and soul. Yes, the Savior was obliged to say, it is true; you already have the right doctrine, and you are a good theologian; you know what you shall set forth to the church; you shall be a bishop. Point your diocese only toward my merits; point them only toward this method of coming to love me, toward this method which I have used, the method which you have experienced, which immediately brings a person out of all labyrinths into the right way. "Strengthen your brethren" (Luke 22:32) with the example of your conversion by the glance of my eyes.

It is this also, beloved in the Lord, which we have to wish each other at the end of this discourse, that we may be looked upon by the Savior so graciously, so powerfully, so essentially; and that at the same time we may be so blessed, so happy that we turn away our view and our eyes from everything which otherwise seemed to us proper or improper and turn them toward Him with no desire to look at or into anything else; that our eye may not be able to throw a glance anywhere else but to this point.

And when you have once caught sight of the beauty of His suffering, so that in all your life you will not be able to get rid of that sight, then He conducts you with His eyes wherever He will have you; then with His eyes He teaches you what good and evil is. Your knowledge of good and evil lies in His eyes, not in the tree from which Adam poisoned himself, from which Adam ate his curse. But rather in the eyes of the tortured Lamb, there lies your blessed, happy knowledge of good and evil. As far as this same image looks upon you, into the midst of your mortal bodies, so far shall you be changed, pervaded, captivated by the person of Jesus, so that your other brethren perceive you no longer as a man in your denomination, as a brother of the same persuasion only, but rather as a consort, as a playmate for the marriage-bed of the blessed Creator and eternal Husband of the human soul.

PRAYER

My dearest Savior! We beg of you this same blessed look, this same irresistible look, which You always know to fix upon the souls who like to look upon You, who like to receive You, who, when You come, are ready to pass over into Your heart and wounds, to whom the touching of Your corpse is important, for whom the first savour of Your corpse can banish all curse and guide them even to the sight of Your wounds. And to this look help, according to Your wisdom, all souls, high and low, rich and poor, in all the circumstances they are in, at the moment of their willingness. In the meantime let us witness so long and, as far as possible, propagate our testimony among mankind so long, until You have gradually accomplished the number of those who want to and will see Your saving Cross' image here in time, and until nothing more is remaining which pertains to election, so that Your witnesses, before they rest, may be able to bring You the answer: Lord, what You have commanded is done, and there is still room.

One chicken-and-egg question that remains unresolved is whether Pietism influenced the scientific method and helped to produce the Enlightenment state of mind, or whether the empiricism required by science evoked the emphasis on the personal experience of truth that existed in Pietism. Both science and Pietism relied on the authority of experience, rather than on tradition, to come to an understanding of truth. Like earlier Christians, Pietists used their experiences to test, interpret, and verify the truth of scripture. At the same time, however, danger seemed to accompany the effort to rely on an apparently subjective instrument—the self—to grasp religious truth. While experience had the security of being real, at least to the believer, it held the danger of bypassing traditional forms of authority, especially the clergy.

Romanticism: The Authority of Feeling

Another manifestation of the move toward the authority of experience was Romanticism, which blossomed in reaction to Enlightenment rationalism. In contrast to the mechanical order of creation prized by the Rationalists, the Romantics valued an organic universe that grew naturally into a unified totality. Everything was connected in a beautiful whole, much as a plant or an animal grows into its own unique entity. In place of the rational religion of the head, the Romantics emphasized feeling above all else—a religion of the heart.

Romanticism appeared in the United States in the form of Transcendentalism. Centered in New England from about 1836 to 1860, many Transcendentalists, coming out of a Unitarian background, rejected the strict Calvinism of American revivalism. Like their Romantic counterparts in Europe, the Transcendentalists prized Beauty, Nature, Friendship, and Truth—all in capital letters. God was to be found in the cathedrals of Nature, not in the stone mausoleums called churches. Truth existed in the human heart, not in books, and could be encountered in the companionship of like-minded souls. And Beauty led to Eternity.

Friedrich Schleiermacher (1768–1834) probably expressed the romantic religious sensibility best when he said that religion begins with feeling. The German theologian, preacher, and classical philologist is considered the founder of modern Protestant theology. His father was a Reformed (Calvinist) military chaplain, and his mother came from a family of clergymen. He attended school with members of Zinzendorf's *Herrnhut* and studied Kant in college. In 1804, he became university preacher and professor of theology at the University of Halle, the first Reformed thinker ever to teach theology at this Lutheran institution. He lectured on theology and philosophy, and preached almost every Sunday until he died. He was extremely influential until Protestants began to argue that his theological approach led away from the Gospels and toward the world, creating a kind of "cultural Christianity" that made too many accommodations to contemporary sensibilities.

The Reading

In 1799, Schleiermacher wrote a series of essays to justify the human need for religion, which he directed at some of his Romantic friends who had no use for what they saw as the dogmatism and formalism of Christianity. The following reading comes from Schleiermacher's apologetic work *On Religion: Speeches to Its Cultured Despisers*. In this excerpt from his second speech, Schleiermacher addresses two of his friends' concerns: metaphysics and morality. Even though metaphysics, broadly considered, encompasses philosophy, we can understand it by thinking about various Christian doctrines about the supernatural: the Trinity, the divinity of Jesus, miracles, the nature of heaven and earth, and so on. Morality is a bit more self-explanatory: it is the religion of the Rationalists that we saw exemplified in Deism, and in Unitarianism. The "cultured despisers" detest both forms of religion, as we can induce from Schleiermacher's essay. Schleiermacher therefore broaches a new way of approaching religion: from an intution, or feeling, of the divine.

Like most Romantics, Schleiermacher invoked the ancient Greeks, whether Simonides—a lyric poet (c. 556–468? B.C.E.) who wrote odes in honor of the Olympic games—in his opening lines, or Prometheus, the Greek deity who stole fire from the gods and gave it as a gift to humanity (and was thereafter eternally punished by having his liver eaten daily by an eagle or vulture). He also mentions Socrates. Think about why the Romantics might appeal to classical mythology and Greek philosophy for their ideology.

Vocabulary notes: First, you may remember from Chapter One that in the ancient world a proselyte was a convert to Judaism. But Schleiermacher is using the term to refer to converts in general. Second, he discusses "speculation" and "praxis," by which he means theory and practice: what is Christian doctrine (theory or speculation) about the nature of God and so on, and what is Christian practice (or praxis) in the real world. Finally, by "intuition" Schleiermacher means direct perception without rational thought; a good synonym for this is "experience."

Questions to Consider

1. What are the weaknesses of basing religion on metaphysics and morality, according to Schleiermacher?

2. What would be his view of Channing? Of Zinzendorf?

3. What would be the strengths of basing religion upon feeling or intuition? What would be the weaknesses?

4. How might Schleiermacher think about biblical revelation? In other words, what is his view of the authority of scripture?

5. Although Schleiermacher is directing his remarks to his friends who are fed up with religion as they understand it, what kind of Christianity is he actually critiquing? Do you agree with his criticisms?

6. Do you think that this approach to Christianity would lead to religious toleration? Why or why not?

7. Do you see any evidence of Kant in this work? What is Schleiermacher's view regarding the ability to prove religious truths?

Second Speech: On the Essence of Religion

FRIEDRICH SCHLEIERMACHER

You know how the aged Simonides, through repeated and prolonged hesitation, reduced to silence the person who had bothered him with the question, "What are the gods after all?" I should like to begin with a similar hesitation about the far greater and more comprehensive question, "What is religion?"

Naturally, this would not be with the intention of keeping silent and leaving you in embarrassment as he did, but that, kept waiting in impatient expectation, you might for a time steadily direct your gaze to the point we seek, while completely excluding all other thoughts. It is, after all, the first requirement of those who only conjure common spirits that onlookers, who want to see their manifestations and be initiated into their secrets, prepare themselves through abstinence from earthly things and through holy silence; then, without distracting themselves by the sight of other objects, they look with undivided attention at the place where the vision is to show itself. How much more will I be permitted to insist on a similar obedience, since I am to call forth a rare spirit that does not deign to appear in any oft-seen familiar

guise, a spirit you will have to observe attentively a long time in order to recognize it and understand its significant features. Only if you stand before the holy circles with the most unprejudiced sobriety of mind that clearly and properly comprehends every contour and, full of desire to understand the presented object on its own terms, is neither seduced by old memories nor corrupted by preconceived suspicions, can I hope that, even if you do not come to like my manifestation, you will at least agree with me concerning its form and recognize it as a heavenly being.

I wish I could present religion to you in some well-known form so that you might immediately remember its features, its movements, and its manners and exclaim that you have here or there seen it just this way in real life. But I would deceive you. For it is not found among human beings as undisguised as it appears to the conjurer, and for some time has not let itself be viewed in the form peculiar to it. The particular disposition of various cultivated peoples no longer shows itself so purely and distinctly in individual actions, since their commerce has become more many-sided and what they have in common has increased through all sorts of connections. Only the imagination can grasp the entire idea behind these qualities, which are encountered only singly as dispersed and mixed with much that is foreign. This is also the case with spiritual things, and among them with religion. It is well known to you how everything is now full of harmonious development; and precisely this has caused such a completed and extended sociability and friendliness within the human soul that none of the soul's powers in fact now acts among us distinctly, as much as we like to think of them as distinct. In every accomplishment each is immediately precipitated by polite love and beneficial support of the other and is somewhat deflected from its path. One looks around vainly in this cultured world for an action that could furnish a true expression of some capacity of spirit, be it sensibility or understanding, ethical life or religion.

Do not, therefore, be indignant and explain it as disdain for the present if, for the sake of clarity, I frequently lead you back to those more childlike times where, in a less perfected state, everything was still, distinct and individual. If I begin at once with that theme, and in some way or other meticulously come back to it, this is to warn you emphatically about the confusion of religion with things that sometimes look similar to it and with which you will everywhere find it mixed.

If you put yourselves on the highest standpoint of metaphysics and morals, you will find that both have the same object as religion, namely, the universe and the relationship of humanity to it. This similarity has long since been a basis of manifold aberrations; metaphysics and morals have therefore invaded religion on many occasions, and much that belongs to religion has concealed itself in metaphysics or morals under an unseemly form. But shall you, for this reason, believe that it is identical with the one or the other? I know that your instinct tells you the contrary, and it also follows from your opinions; for you never admit that religion walks with the firm step of which metaphysics is capable, and you do not forget to observe diligently that there are quite a few ugly immoral blemishes on its history. If religion is thus to be differentiated, then it must be set off from those in some manner, regardless of the common subject matter. Religion must treat this subject matter completely differently, express or work out another relationship of humanity to it, have another mode of procedure or another goal; for only in this way can that which is similar in its subject matter to something else achieve

a determinate nature and a unique existence. I ask you, therefore, What does your metaphysics do—or, if you want to have nothing to do with the outmoded name that is too historical for you, your transcendental philosophy. It classifies the universe and divides it into this being and that, seeks out the reasons for what exists, and deduces the necessity of what is real while spinning the reality of the world and its laws out of itself. Into this realm, therefore, religion must not venture too far. It must not have the tendency to posit essences and to determine natures, to lose itself in an infinity of reasons and deductions, to seek out final causes, and to proclaim eternal truths.

And what does your morality do? It develops a system of duties out of human nature and our relationship to the universe; it commands and forbids actions with unlimited authority. Yet religion must not even presume to do that; it must not use the universe in order to derive duties and is not permitted to contain a code of laws. "And yet what one calls religion seems to consist only of fragments of these various fields." This is indeed the common concept. I have just imparted to you doubts about that; now it is time to annihilate it altogether. The theorists in religion, who aim at knowledge of the nature of the universe and a highest being whose work it is, are metaphysicians, but also discreet enough not to disdain some morality. The practical people, to whom the will of God is the primary thing, are moralists, but a little in the style of metaphysics. You take the idea of the good and carry it into metaphysics as the natural law of an unlimited and plenteous being, and you take the idea of a primal being from metaphysics and carry it into morality so that this great work should not remain anonymous, but so that the picture of the lawgiver might be engraved at the front of so splendid a code. But mix and stir as you will, these never go together; you play an empty game with materials that are not suited to each other. You always retain only metaphysics and morals. This mixture of opinions about the highest being or the world and of precepts for a human life (or even for two) you call religion! And the instinct, which seeks those opinions, together with the dim presentiments that are the actual final sanction of these precepts, you call religiousness! But how then do you come to regard a mere compilation, an anthology for beginners, as an integral work, as an individual with its own origin and power? How do you come to mention it, even if only to refute it? Why have you not long since analyzed it into its parts and discovered the shameful plagiarism?

I would take pleasure in alarming you with some Socratic questions and bringing you to confess that, even in the most common things, you know the principles according to which like must be related to like and the particular subordinated to the universal, and that you only wish not to apply these principles here in order to be able to make fun of a serious subject in a worldly manner. Where, then, is the unity in this whole? Where does the unifying principle lie for this dissimilar material? If it is an attractive force of its own, then you must confess that religion is the highest in philosophy and that metaphysics and morals are only subordinate divisions of it; for that in which two varied but opposed concepts are one can only be the higher under which the other two belong. If this binding principle lies in metaphysics, you have recognized, for reasons that are related to metaphysics, a highest being as the moral lawgiver. Therefore annihilate practical philosophy, and admit that it, and with it religion, is only a small chapter of the theoretical. If you want to assert the converse, then metaphysics and religion must be swallowed up by morality, for which indeed, nothing may any longer be impossible after it has learned to believe and in its old age has acquiesced in preparing a quiet spot in its innermost sanctuary for the secret embraces of two self-loving worlds.

Or do you want to say that the metaphysical in religion does not depend on the moral, nor the latter on the former? Or that there is a remarkable parallelism between the theoretical and the practical, and that to perceive and represent this is religion? To be sure, the solution to this parallelism can lie neither in practical philosophy, which is not concerned about it, nor in theoretical philosophy, which, as part of its function, strives most zealously to pursue and annihilate the parallelism as far as possible. But I think that you, driven by this need, have already been seeking for some time a highest philosophy in which these two categories unite and are always on the verge of finding it; and religion would lie so close to this! Would philosophy really have to flee to religion as the opponents of philosophy like to maintain? Pay close heed to what you say there. With all this either you receive a religion that stands far above philosophy as it exists at present, or you must be honest enough to restore to both parts of philosophy what belongs to them and admit that you are still ignorant of what concerns religion. I do not wish to hold you to the former, for I want to take no position that I could not maintain, but you will very likely agree to the latter.

Let us deal honestly with one another. You do not like religion; we started from that assumption. But in conducting an honest battle against it, which is not completely without effort, you do not want to have fought against a shadow like the one with which we have struggled. Religion must indeed be something integral that could have arisen in the human heart, something thinkable from which a concept can be formulated about which one can speak and argue. I find it very unjust if you yourselves stitch together something untenable out of such disparate things, call it religion, and then make so much needless ado about it. You will deny that you have begun deceitfully. You will call upon me to roll out all of the ancient sources of religion—since I have, after all, already rejected systems, commentaries, and apologies—from the beautiful compositions of the Greeks to the holy writings of the Christians, and to state whether I would not find the nature of the gods and their will everywhere, and everywhere praise persons as holy and blessed, who acknowledge the former and fulfill the latter.

But that is precisely what I have said to you. Religion never appears in a pure state. All these are only the extraneous parts that cling to it, and it should be our business to free it from them. After all, the corporeal world provides you with no primal element as nature's pure product—you would then, as happens to you in the intellectual world, have to regard very rough things as simple—but rather it is only the ceaseless aim of analytic skill to be able to depict such a primal element. In spiritual things the original cannot be brought forth for you, except when you beget it through an original creation in yourselves, and even then only in the moment when you beget it. I beg you, understand yourselves on this point, for you shall be ceaselessly reminded of it. But as far as the sources and original documents of religion are concerned, this interference of metaphysics and morals with them is not merely an unavoidable fate; it is rather an artificial plan and a lofty intention. What is presented as the first and last is not always the truest and highest. If you only knew how to read between the lines! All holy writings are like the modest books that were in use some time ago in our modest fatherland, which treated important matters under a sketchy title. To be sure, they only give notice of metaphysics and morals, and in the end are happy to return to that which they have announced, but you are encouraged to crack open this shell. Thus even the diamond lies wholly enclosed in a base substance, yet surely not in order to remain hidden but rather to be found all the more certainly. To make proselytes out of unbelievers is deeply engrained in the character of religion; those who impart their own religion can have no other purpose. Thus it is in fact hardly a pious deception but an appropriate method to begin with and appear concerned about a matter for which the sensibility already exists, so that something may occasionally and unnoticeably slip in for which the sensibility must first be aroused. Since all communication of religion cannot be other than rhetorical, it is a clever engagement of an audience to introduce them into such good company. Yet this device has not only reached but overstepped its goal, since even for you religion's essence has remained hidden under this mask. Therefore it is time to take up the subject from the other end and to start with the sharp opposition in which religion is found over against morals and metaphysics. That was what I wanted. You distracted me with our ordinary concept; I hope it is now settled and you will interrupt me no more.

In order to take possession of its own domain, religion renounces herewith all claims to whatever belongs to those others and gives back everything that has been forced upon it. It does not wish to determine and explain the universe according to its nature as does metaphysics; it does not desire to continue the universe's development and perfect it by the power of freedom and the divine free choice of a human being as does morals. Religion's essence is neither thinking nor acting, but intuition and feeling. It wishes to intuit the universe, wishes devoutly to overhear the universe's own manifestations and actions, longs to be grasped and filled by the universe's immediate influences in childlike passivity. Thus, religion is opposed to these two in everything that makes up its essence and in everything that characterizes its effects. Metaphysics and morals see in the whole universe only humanity as the center of all relatedness, as the condition of all being and the cause of all becoming; religion wishes to see the infinite, its imprint and its manifestation, in humanity no less than in all other individual and finite forms. Metaphysics proceeds from finite human nature and wants to define consciously, from its simplest concept, the extent of its powers, and its receptivity, what the universe can be for us and how we necessarily must view it. Religion also lives its whole life in nature, but in the infinite nature of totality, the one and all; what holds in nature for everything individual also holds for the human being; and wherever everything, in-

cluding man, may press on or tarry within this eternal ferment of individual forms and beings, religion wishes to intuit and to divine this in detail in quiet submissiveness. Morality proceeds from the consciousness of freedom; it wishes to extend freedom's realm to infinity and to make everything subservient to it. Religion breathes there where freedom itself has once more become nature; it apprehends man beyond the play of his particular powers and his personality, and views him from the vantage point where he must be what he is, whether he likes it or not.

Thus religion maintains its own sphere and its own character only by completely removing itself from the sphere and character of speculation as well as from that of praxis. Only when it places itself next to both of them is the common ground perfectly filled out and human nature completed from this dimension. Religion shows itself to you as the necessary and indispensable third next to those two, as their natural counterpart, not slighter in worth and splendor than what you wish of them. To want to have speculation and praxis without religion is rash arrogance. It is insolent enmity against the gods; it is the unholy sense of Prometheus, who cowardly stole what in calm certainty he would have been able to ask for and to expect. Man has merely stolen the feeling of his infinity and godlikeness, and as an unjust possession it cannot thrive for him if he is not also conscious of his limitedness, the contingency of his whole form, the silent disappearance of his whole existence in the immeasurable. The gods have also punished this crime from the very beginning. Praxis is an art, speculation is a science, religion is the sensibility and taste for the infinite. Without religion, how can praxis rise above the common circle of adventurous and customary forms? How can speculation become anything better than a stiff and barren skeleton? Or why, in all its action directed outwardly and toward the universe, does your praxis actually always forget to cultivate humanity itself? It is because you place humanity in opposition to the universe and do not receive it from the hand of religion as a part of the universe and as something holy. How does praxis arrive at an impoverished uniformity that knows only a single ideal and lays this as the basis everywhere? It is because you lack the basic feeling for the infinite, whose symbol is multiplicity and individuality. Everything finite exists only through the determination of its limits, which must, as it were, "be cut out of" the infinite. Only thus can a thing be infinite and yet be self-formed within these limits; otherwise you lose everything in the uniformity of a universal concept. Why, for so long, did speculation give you deceptions instead of a system, and words instead of real thoughts? Why was it nothing but an empty game with formulas that always reappeared changed and to which nothing would ever correspond? Because it lacked religion, because the feeling for the infinite did not animate it, and because longing for it and reverence for it did not compel its fine, airy thoughts to assume more rigorous consistency in order to preserve. itself against this powerful pressure. Everything must proceed from intuition, and those who lack the desire to intuit the infinite have no touchstone and indeed need none in order to know whether they have given any respectable thought to the matter.

And how will the triumph of speculation, the completed and rounded idealism, fare if religion does not counterbalance it and allow it to glimpse a higher realism than that which it subordinates to itself so boldly and for such good reason? Idealism will destroy the universe by appearing to fashion it; it will degrade it to a mere allegory, to an empty silhouette of our own limitedness. Respectfully offer up with me a lock of hair to the manes of the holy rejected Spinoza! The high world spirit permeated him, the infinite was his beginning and end, the universe his only and eternal love; in holy innocence and deep humility he was reflected in the eternal world and saw how he too was its most lovable mirror; he was full of religion and full of holy spirit; for this reason, he also stands there alone and unequaled, master in his art but elevated above the profane guild, without disciples and without rights of citizenship.

I entreat you to become familiar with this concept: intuition of the universe. It is the hinge of my whole speech; it is the highest and most universal formula of religion on the basis of which you should be able to find every place in religion, from which you may determine its essence and its limits. All intuition proceeds from an influence of the intuited on the one who intuits, from an original and independent action of the former, which is then grasped, apprehended, and conceived by the latter according to one's own nature. If the emanations of light—which happen completely without your efforts—did not affect your sense, if the smallest parts of the body, the tips of your fingers, were not mechanically or chemically affected, if the pressure of weight did not reveal to you an opposition and a limit to your power, you would

intuit nothing and perceive nothing, and what you thus intuit and perceive is not the nature of things, but their action upon you. What you know or believe about the nature of things lies far beyond the realm of intuition.

The same is true of religion. The universe exists in uninterrupted activity and reveals itself to us every moment. Every form that it brings forth, every being to which it gives a separate existence according to the fullness of life, every occurrence that spills forth from its rich, ever-fruitful womb, is an action of the same upon us. Thus to accept everything individual as a part of the whole and everything limited as a representation of the infinite is religion. But whatever would go beyond that and penetrate deeper into the nature and substance of the whole is no longer religion, and will, if it still wants to be regarded as such, inevitably sink back into empty mythology.

Thus it was religion when the ancients, annihilating the limitations of time and space, regarded every unique type of life throughout the whole world as the work and reign of an omnipresent being. They had intuited a unique mode of acting of the universe in its unity, and designated this intuition accordingly. It was religion when, for every helpful event whereby the eternal laws of the world were illuminatingly revealed through contingency, they gave the god to whom it belonged its own name and built its own temple to it; they had comprehended an act of the universe and thus denoted its individuality and its character. It was religion when they rose above the brittle iron age of the world, full of fissures and unevenness, and again sought the golden age on Olympus among the happy life of the gods; thus they intuited the ever-active, ever-living, and serene activity of the world and its spirit, beyond all change and all the apparent evil that only stems from the conflict of finite forms. But when they keep a wondrous chronicle of the descent of these gods or when a later faith trotted out for us a long series of emanations and procreations, that is empty mythology. To present all events in the world as the actions of a god is religion; it expresses its connection to an infinite totality; but while brooding over the existence of this god before the world and outside the world may be good and necessary in metaphysics, in religion even that becomes only empty mythology, a further development of that which is only the means of portrayal as if it were the essential itself, a complete departure from its characteristic ground.

Intuition is and always remains something individual, set apart, the immediate perception, nothing more. To bind it and to incorporate it into a whole is once more the business not of sense but of abstract thought. The same is true of religion; it stops with the immediate experiences of the existence and action of the universe, with the individual intuitions and feelings; each of these is a self-contained work without connection with others or dependence upon them; it knows nothing about derivation and connection, for among all things religion can encounter, that is what its nature most opposes. Not only an individual fact or deed that one could call original or first, but everything in religion is immediate and true for itself.

A system of intuitions? Can you imagine anything stranger? Do views, and especially views of the infinite, allow themselves to be brought into a system? Can you say that one must look at a thing a certain way just because one had to look at something else in such a manner? Others may stand right behind you, right alongside you, and everything can appear differently to them. Or do by chance the possible standpoints on which a mind can stand in order to observe the universe progress in measured intervals so that you can exhaust, enumerate, and precisely determine the characteristic of each? Are there not infinitely many of these, and is not every entity only a continual transition between two others? I speak your language in these matters, for it would be an infinite business, and you are not accustomed to connect the concept of something infinite with the term "system," but rather the concept of something that is limited and completed in its limitation. Elevate yourselves for once—after all, it is still an elevation for most of you—to that infinite dimension of sensible intuition, to the wondrous and celebrated starry sky. The astronomical theories, which orient a thousand suns with their world systems around a common point, and seek for each common point again a higher world system that could be its center, and so on into infinity, outwardly and inwardly—surely you would not want to call this a system of intuitions as such? The only thing to which you could attribute this name would be the age-old work of those childlike minds that have gathered the infinite mass of these phenomena into definite, but scanty and unseemly, pictures. But you know that there is no semblance of a system in that, that still other stars are discovered between these pictures, that even within their limits everything is undetermined and endless, and that the pictures themselves remain something purely arbitrary and highly changeable. When you have persuaded another person to join you in drawing the image of the Big Dipper onto the blue background of the worlds, does he not nevertheless remain free to conceive the adjacent worlds in contours that are completely different from yours? This infinite chaos, where of course every point represents a world, is as such actually the most suitable and highest symbol of religion. In religion, as in this chaos, only the particular is true and necessary; nothing can or may be proved anything else. Everything universal under which the particular is supposed to be treated, each collection and combination of this sort, either exists in a different territory, if it is to be referred to the inner and essential realm, or is only the work of playful imagination and freest caprice. If thousands of you could have the same religious intuitions, each of you as an individual would certainly draw other outlines in order to portray how you viewed them alongside or in succession to one another; that would depend not on each mind but, rather, on an accidental condition, on a triviality. Individual persons may have their own arrangement and their own rubrics; the particular can thereby neither win nor lose. Those who truly know about their religion and its essence will utterly subordinate to the particular every apparent connection and will not sacrifice the smallest part of the particular to it. The realm of intuition is so infinite precisely because of this independent particularity.

If you place yourself at the most distant point of the material world, you will not only see from there the same objects in another order; and if you wish to cling to your former arbitrary images that you do not find there again, you will be completely in error. Instead you will even discover wholly new objects in new regions. You cannot say that your horizon, even the broadest, comprehends everything and that nothing more is to be intuited beyond it, or that nothing within this horizon escapes your eye, even the best aided. You find limits nowhere and are not able to think of any. This is true of religion in an even far higher sense; from an opposite point you would receive new intuitions not only in new regions; but also in old, well-known places the first elements would unite in different forms and everything would be different. Religion is infinite not only because acting and being acted upon ceaselessly alternate between the same limited matter and the mind—you know that such thinking is the sole infinity of speculation—not only because it is, like morality, internally incapable of completion; it is infinite in all respects, an infinity of matter and form, of being, of vision, and of knowledge about it. This feeling must accompany everyone who really has religion. Each person must be conscious that his religion is only a part of the whole, that regarding the same objects that affect him religiously there are views just as pious and, nevertheless, completely different from his own, and that from other elements of religion intuitions and feelings flow, the sense for which he may be completely lacking.

You see how immediately this lovely modesty, this friendly inviting tolerance springs from the concept of religion and how intimately tolerance nestles up to it. How wrongly, therefore, do you turn on religion with your reproaches that it is bent on persecution and spitefulness, that it wrecks society and makes blood flow like water. Indict those who corrupt religion, who want to inundate it with philosophy and fetter it to a system. What is it in religion over which men have argued, taken sides, and ignited wars? Sometimes over morals and always over metaphysics, and neither of these belongs to it. Philosophy indeed strives to accommodate those who wish to know under one common knowledge, as you can daily see; but religion does not strive to bring those who believe and feel under a single belief and a single feeling. It strives, to be sure, to open the eyes of those who are not yet capable of intuiting the universe, for everyone who sees is a new priest, a new mediator, a new mouthpiece; but for just this reason it avoids with aversion the barren uniformity that would again destroy this divine abundance.

The mania for system does indeed reject what is foreign, even if it is quite conceivable and true, because it could spoil one's own well-formed ranks and disturb the beautiful connections by claiming its place. In this mania lies the seat of contradiction; it must quarrel and persecute; for to the extent that the particular is again related to something individual and finite, the one can indeed destroy the other through its existence. But in the infinite everything finite stands undisturbed alongside one another; all is one, and all is true. Moreover, only the systematizers have caused all this. Modern Rome, godless but consistent, hurls anathemas and excommunicates heretics; ancient Rome, truly pious and religious in a lofty style, was hospitable to every god and so it became full of gods. The adherents of the dead letter that religion casts out have filled the world with criers and tumult; the true contemplators of the eternal have ever been

quiet souls, either alone with themselves and the infinite or, if they glanced around themselves, happily granting his own way to everyone who only understood the mighty word. But with this broad view and this feeling of the infinite, religion also looks at what lies outside its own realm and contains in itself the capacity for unlimited multiplicity in judgment and in contemplation that, in fact, cannot be found elsewhere. No matter what inspires a person—I exclude neither ethical life nor philosophy but rely instead, as far as they are concerned, on your experience—his thinking and striving, to whatever object they may be directed, draw a narrow circle around him in which his highest lies enclosed and outside of which everything appears to him to be common and unworthy. Whoever only thinks systematically and acts from principle and design and wants to accomplish this or that in the world inevitably circumscribes himself and constantly sets himself in opposition to what as an object of aversion does not further his actions. Only the drive to intuit, if it is oriented to the infinite, places the mind in unlimited freedom; only religion saves it from the most ignominious fetters of opinion and desire. Everything that exists is necessary for religion, and everything that can be is for it a true indispensable image of the infinite; it is just a question of finding the point from which one's relationship to the infinite can be discovered. However reprehensible something may be in another connection or in itself, in this respect it is always worthy of existence and of being preserved and contemplated. To a pious mind religion makes everything holy and valuable, even unholiness and commonness itself, everything it comprehends and does not comprehend, that does or does not lie within the system of its own thoughts and is or is not in agreement with its peculiar manner of action; religion is the only sworn enemy of all pedantry and all one-sidedness.

Finally, to complete the general picture of religion, recall that every intuition is, by its very nature, connected with a feeling. Your senses mediate the connection between the object and yourselves; the same influence of the object, which reveals its existence to you, must stimulate them in various ways and produce a change in your inner consciousness. This feeling, of which you are frequently scarcely aware, can in other cases grow to such intensity that you forget both the object and yourselves because of it; your whole nervous system can be so permeated by it that for a long time that sensation alone dominates and resounds and resists the effect of other impressions. But that an action is brought forth in you, that the internally generated activity of your spirit is set in motion, surely you will not ascribe this to the influence of external objects? You will, of course, admit that this lies far beyond the power of even the strongest feelings and must have a completely different source in you. The same is true for religion. The same actions of the universe through which it reveals itself to you in the finite also bring it into a new relationship to your mind and your condition; in the act of intuiting it, you must necessarily be seized by various feelings. In religion, however, a different and stronger relationship between intuition and feeling takes place, and intuition never predominates so much that feeling is almost extinguished.

On the contrary, is it really a miracle if the eternal world affects the senses of our spirit as the sun affects our eyes? Is it a miracle when the sun so blinds us that everything else disappears, not only at that moment, but even long afterward all objects we observe are imprinted with its image and bathed in its brilliance? Just as the particular manner in which the universe presents itself to you in your intuitions and determines the uniqueness of your individual religion, so the strength of these feelings determines the degree of religiousness. The sounder the sense, the more sharply and definitely will it apprehend every impression. The more ardent the thirst and the more persistent the drive to grasp the infinite, the more manifoldly will the mind itself be seized by it everywhere and uninterruptedly, the more perfectly will these impressions penetrate it, and the more easily will they awaken again and again and retain the upper hand over everything else. That is how far the realm of religion concerns us in this respect; its feelings are supposed to possess us, and we should express, maintain, and portray them.

But should you wish to go beyond that dimension with these feelings, should they cause actual actions and incite you to deeds, then you find yourselves in an alien realm. If you still hold this to be religion, however rational and praiseworthy your action may appear, you are absorbed in an unholy superstition. All actual action should be moral, and it can be too, but religious feelings should accompany every human deed like a holy music; we should do everything with religion, nothing because of religion. If you do not understand that all action is supposed to be moral, then I add that this also applies to everything else. People should act calmly and whatever they may undertake should be done with presence of mind. Ask the moral, the political, and the artistic

person, and all will say that this is their first precept; but calm and thoughtfulness are lost when a person permits himself to be driven to action by the powerful and disturbing feelings of religion. It is also unnatural that this should happen, for by their very nature religious feelings inhibit the strength of our action and invite us to calm and dedicated enjoyment; that is why the most religious people, for whom other impulses to action were lacking and who were nothing but religious, forsook the world and yielded themselves wholly to leisurely contemplation. Man must first master himself and his pious feelings before they press actions out of him; and, if I may refer directly to you, it is a part of your accusation that so many senseless and unnatural things have come to pass in this way. You see, I concede not only this point to you but also the most excellent and most praiseworthy ones. Whether meaningless rites are manipulated or good works performed, whether humans are slaughtered on bloody altars or whether they are made happy by a charitable hand, whether life is spent in dead inactivity or in dull, tasteless order or in frivolous and sumptuous sensual desire, these are certainly things that differ widely from one another if we wish to talk about morality or life and worldly affairs; but if they are supposed to pertain to religion and to have arisen from it, then they are all the same as one another, only slavish superstition, each one like the others.

You reproach the person who lets his behavior toward another person be determined by the impression the other makes upon him. You desire that even the most accurate feeling about the impact of a human being should not lead us to action for which we have no better grounds; thus that person is also to be reproached whose actions, which should always be oriented toward the whole, are solely determined by the feelings that precisely this whole awakens in him. He is singled out as someone who sacrifices his honor, not only from the standpoint of morality, because he gives way to extraneous motives, but also from that of religion, because he ceases to be what, in its eyes, alone gives him unique worth, a free part of the whole, active through his own power. This entire misunderstanding that religion is supposed to act can, at the same time, be nothing other than a dreadful misuse, and to whichever side the activity should turn, it ends in mischief and ruin. But to have the soul full of religion while performing a calm action that must proceed from its own source, that is the goal of the pious. Only evil spirits, not good ones, possess a person and drive him, and the legions of angels with which the heavenly Father had equipped his Son were not in him but around him; they also did not help him in his actions, nor were they supposed to, but they instilled serenity and rest into a soul wearied by deed and thought. Occasionally he lost sight of them in the moments when his whole power was roused to action, but then they hovered around him again in joyous throng and served him.

But before I lead you into the particulars of these intuitions and feelings, which must certainly be my next business with you, permit me first for a moment to mourn the fact that I cannot speak of both other than separately. The finest spirit of religion is thereby lost for my speech, and I can disclose its innermost secret only unsteadily and uncertainly. But reflection necessarily separates both; and who can speak about something that belongs to consciousness without first going through this medium? Not only when we communicate an inner action of the mind, but even when we merely turn it into material for contemplation within ourselves and wish to raise it to lucid consciousness, this unavoidable separation immediately occurs. This state of affairs intermingles with the original consciousness of our dual activity, what predominates and functions outward and what is merely sketching and reproducing, which seems rather to serve things. Immediately upon this contact the simplest matter separates itself into two opposing elements, the one group combining into an image of an object, the other penetrating to the center of our being, there to effervesce with our original drives and to develop a transient feeling. We cannot escape this fate even with the innermost creation of the religious sense; we cannot call up its products to the surface again and communicate them except in this separate form. Only do not think—for this is one of the most dangerous errors—that in the first stirring of the mind religious intuitions and feelings may originally be as divided as we must unfortunately consider them here. Intu-

ition without feeling is nothing and can have neither the proper origin nor the proper force; feeling without intuition is also nothing; both are therefore something only when and because they are originally one and unseparated.

That first mysterious moment that occurs in every sensory perception, before intuition and feeling have separated, where sense and its objects have, as it were, flowed into one another and become one, before both turn back to their original position—I know how indescribable it is and how quickly it passes away. But I wish that you were able to hold on to it and also to recognize it again in the higher and divine religious activity of the mind. Would that I could and might express it, at least indicate it, without having to desecrate it! It is as fleeting and transparent as the first scent with which the dew gently caresses the waking flowers, as modest and delicate as a maiden's kiss, as holy and fruitful as a nuptial embrace; indeed, not *like* these, but it is *itself* all of these. A manifestation, an event develops quickly and magically into an image of the universe. Even as the beloved and ever-sought for form fashions itself, my soul flees toward it; I embrace it, not as a shadow, but as the holy essence itself. I lie on the bosom of the infinite world. At this moment I am its soul, for I feel all its powers and its inifinite life as my own; at this moment it is my body, for I penetrate its muscles and its limbs as my own, and its innermost nerves move according to my sense and my presentiment as my own. With the slightest trembling the holy embrace is dispersed, and now for the first time the intuition stands before me as a separate form; I survey it, and it mirrors itself in my open soul like the image of the vanishing beloved in the awakened eye of a youth; now for the first time the feeling works its way up from inside and diffuses itself like the blush of shame and desire on his cheek. This moment is the highest flowering of religion. If I could create it in you, I would be a god. . . .

Mysticism: The Truth of Experience
Even though Schleiermacher is describing a religion based on intuition and feeling, he still seems to approach religion intellectually. Religion may begin with the sensibility he describes, but as soon as we reflect upon our emotions, the experience changes. What starts out as a mystical event is quickly rationalized. We may even lose the memory of the feelings that initially brought us to the divine.

Orthodox Christian mysticism takes a different approach to the experience of God, as we saw in Chapter Three and the discussion of hesychasm. Rather than commencing with emotion, hesychasm starts with prayer and moves into transcendent experience. Whereas Schleiermacher's experience of God is transformed by reflection upon the experience, hesychasm begins with a practice—the repetition of the Jesus Prayer—which is then transformed into the pure experience of God. This experience of Christ within the mystic has an authority that transcends all other Christian claims to legitimacy, for it synchronizes the life of the believer to the divine.

The teachings in *The Philokalia* served as the basis for a strange little book that emerged in nineteenth-century Russia titled *The Way of a Pilgrim.* Anyone who has read J. D. Salinger's *Frannie and Zooey* has already encountered this text. In Salinger's novel, Frannie has a nervous breakdown as she tries to implement the discipline of "praying without ceasing" that *The Way of a Pilgrim* describes. In the second part of Salinger's story, Zooey goes on to analyze the meaning of spirituality, mysticism, and asceticism. When adolescents and college students first read *Frannie and Zooey* in the 1960s, they also turned to *The Philokalia,* wanting to learn more about mysticism and to experience it themselves.

The Reading

The narrator of *The Way of a Pilgrim* wants to know how he can implement Saint Paul's admonition to "pray without ceasing." He travels around until he meets a *starets,* that is, a holy man or, in modern terms, a guru. The *starets* tells him what to pray, and how, and gives him an assignment: repeat the prayer 3000 times, then 6000 times, and then 12,000 times, and then, always. The pilgrim does so and comes up with startling results.

The Russian title of *The Way of a Pilgrim* is *Candid Narratives of a Pilgrim to His Spiritual Father.* It was probably written before the freeing of the serfs in Russia in 1861, while a reference to the Crimean War suggests that it was written after 1853. The volume has an interesting printing history. Somehow, a copy turned up in the Greek monastery of Mount Athos; a Russian monk copied the manuscript, and it was printed in Russian in 1884. It was extremely difficult to obtain copies of the 1884 edition, the only version that existed until 1930. But today, and as witnessed by *Frannie and Zooey,* it is widely available and acts as a popular and accessible introduction to both the Jesus Prayer and Orthodox Christian mysticism.

The narrative is written as a first-person account—kind of a journey of discovery—in which the pilgrim describes his travels, adventures, and experiments with repeating the prayer "Lord Jesus Christ, have mercy on me." The pilgrim criticizes traditional forms of piety and practice. He wants to know how to pray without ceasing, and even when he learns the secret, he continues to travel from place to place. The first chapter appears here in its entirety, and may entice readers to finish the book and its sequel, *The Pilgrim Continues His Way.*

▨ *The Philokalia*

Although Orthodox Christianity relies strongly on tradition and its legitimate claim to an antiquity that surpasses both Catholicism and Protestantism, it has an equally venerable heritage of valuing the authority of experience. This is apparent in an important spiritual text called *The Philokalia* (*The Love of the Beautiful*). Compiled over a millennium, *The Philokalia* contains mystical and ascetical writings by Orthodox theologians from the fourth to the fifteenth centuries, with a focus on hesychasm and the Jesus Prayer. *The Philokalia* was first published in Venice in 1782 but was quickly translated into Slavonic— the religious language of Russia and Eastern Europe—in 1793, and then into Russian between 1876 and 1890.

The Philokalia presents a variety of texts on the ascetical path to God. Saint Neilos the Ascetic (d. c. 430) writes about spiritual struggles that are "far harder than any gymnastic contest. When an athlete's body is thrown to the ground, he can easily get up; but in the spiritual warfare it is men's souls that fall, and then it is very difficult for them to rise once more." Other aphorisms include the following:

> What seems reasonable and convincing to the inexperienced is not necessarily correct. The skilled craftsman judges things quite differently from the unskilled man, for the first is guided by precise knowledge, the second by what seems to him probable.

> Let no one imagine that to be a spiritual guide is an excuse for ease and self-indulgence, for nothing is so demanding as the charge of souls. Those who have charge of horses and other animals keep them under control, and so they generally achieve their purpose. But to govern men is harder, because of the variety of their characters and their deliberate cunning.

Saint Hesychios the Priest (after the sixth or seventh century) has this to say:

> When the heart has acquired stillness it will perceive the heights and depths of knowledge; and the ear of the still intellect will be made to hear marvellous things from God.

> When combined with watchfulness and deep understanding, the Jesus Prayer will erase from our heart even those thoughts rooted there against our will.

> Just as it is impossible to cross the sea without a boat, so it is impossible to repulse the provocation of an evil thought without invoking Jesus Christ.

The texts in *The Philokalia* reveal hard-won knowledge of practices that were collected in order to provide guidance to spiritual athletes. As Saint Hesychios observed, just as a traveler will put up signs and guideposts along the way in order to make the return trip easier, "the watchful man, foreseeing this same thing, will use sacred texts to guide him." *The Philokalia* is just such a text.

Questions to Consider

1. How would you contrast the pilgrim's approach to Christianity with that of the traditional forms he encounters?

2. How does the pilgrim's experience shape his beliefs and actions?

3. What do you think about the discussion of the Bible and *The Philokalia*? Is the *starets* correct that sometimes Christians need help in understanding the truths of the Bible?

4. What is your opinion concerning the religious commitment of the pilgrim? Has he gone too far? Is he making a mountain out of a molehill?

5. The Jesus Prayer seems to function as a mantra, a series of words designed to focus and concentrate the mind as they do in Hinduism. Do you think this is an accurate comparison? Why or why not?

6. What would this approach to religious experience have in common with that described by Schleiermacher? How does it differ?

7. Does this approach to religious practice have any appeal for you? Why or why not?

The Way of a Pilgrim

CHAPTER 1

By the grace of God I am a Christian man, by my actions a great sinner, and by calling a homeless wanderer of the humblest birth who roams from place to place. My worldly goods are a knapsack with some dried bread in it on my back, and in my breast pocket a Bible. And that is all.

On the twenty-fourth Sunday after Pentecost I went to church to say my prayers there during the liturgy. The first Epistle of St. Paul to the Thessalonians was being read, and among other words I heard these—"Pray without ceasing." It was this text, more than any other, which forced itself upon my mind, and I began to think how it was possible to pray without ceasing, since a man has to concern himself with other things also in order to make a living. I looked at my Bible and with my own eyes read the words which I had heard, that is, that we ought always, at all times and in all places, to pray with uplifted hands. I thought and thought, but knew not what to make of it. "What ought I to do?" I thought. "Where shall I find someone to explain it to me? I will

go to the churches where famous preachers are to be heard; perhaps there I shall hear something that will throw light on it for me." I did so. I heard a number of very fine sermons on prayer—what prayer is, how much we need it, and what its fruits are—but no one said how one could succeed in prayer. I heard a sermon on spiritual prayer, and unceasing prayer, but how it was to be done was not pointed out.

Thus listening to sermons failed to give me what I wanted, and having had my fill of them without gaining understanding, I gave up going to hear public sermons. I settled on another plan—by God's help to look for some experienced and skilled person who would give me in conversation that teaching about unceasing prayer which drew me so urgently.

For a long time I wandered through many places. I read my Bible always, and everywhere I asked whether there was not in the neighborhood a spiritual teacher, a devout and experienced guide, to be found. One day I was told that in a certain village a gentleman had long been living and seeking the salvation of his soul. He had a chapel in his house. He never left his estate, and he spent his time in prayer and reading devotional books. Hearing this, I ran rather than walked to the village named. I got there and found him.

"What do you want of me?" he asked.

"I have heard that you are a devout and clever person," said I. "In God's name please explain to me the meaning of the Apostle's words, 'Pray without ceasing.' How is it possible to pray without ceasing? I want to know so much, but I cannot understand it at all."

He was silent for a while and looked at me closely. Then he said, "Ceaseless interior prayer is a continual yearning of the human spirit toward God. To succeed in this consoling exercise we must pray more often to God to teach us to pray without ceasing. Pray more, and pray more fervently. It is prayer itself which will reveal to you how it can be achieved unceasingly; but it will take some time."

So saying, he had food brought to me, gave me money for my journey, and let me go. He did not explain the matter.

Again I set off. I thought and thought, I read and read, I dwelt over and over again upon what this man had said to me, but I could not get to the bottom of it. Yet so greatly did I wish to understand that I could not sleep at night.

I walked at least 125 miles, and then I came to a large town, a provincial capital, where I saw a monastery. At the inn where I stopped I heard it said that the abbot was a man of great kindness, devout and hospitable. I went to see him. He met me in a very friendly manner, asked me to sit down, and offered me refreshment.

"I do not need refreshment, holy Father," I said, "but I beg you to give me some spiritual teaching. How can I save my soul?"

"What? Save your soul? Well, live according to the commandments, say your prayers, and you will be saved."

"But I hear it said that we should pray without ceasing, and I don't know how to pray without ceasing. I cannot even understand what unceasing prayer means. I beg you, Father, explain this to me."

"I don't know how to explain further, dear brother. But, stop a moment, I have a little book, and it is explained there." And he handed me St. Dmitri's book, on *The Spiritual Education of the Inner Man,* saying, "Look, read this page."

I began to read as follows: "The words of the Apostle, 'Pray without ceasing,' should be understood as referring to the creative prayer of the understand-

ing. The understanding can always be reaching out toward God and praying to Him unceasingly."

"But," I asked, "what is the method by which the understanding can always be turned toward God, never be disturbed, and pray without ceasing?"

"It is very difficult, even for one to whom God Himself gives such a gift," replied the abbot.

He did not give me the explanation.

I spent the night at his house, and in the morning, thanking him for his kindly hospitality, I went on my way—where to, I did not know myself. My failure to understand made me sad, and by way of comforting myself I read my Bible. In this way I followed the main road for five days.

At last toward evening I was overtaken by an old man who looked like a cleric of some sort. In answer to my question he told me that he was a monk belonging to a monastery some six miles off the main road. He asked me to go there with him. "We take in pilgrims," said he, "and give them rest and food with devout persons in the guesthouse." I did not feel like going. So in reply I said that my peace of mind in no way depended upon my finding a resting place, but upon finding spiritual teaching. Neither was I running after food, for I had plenty of dried bread in my knapsack.

"What sort of spiritual teaching are you wanting to get?" he asked me. "What is it puzzling you? Come now! Do come to our house, dear brother. We have *startsi* [plural of *starets*] of ripe experience well able to give guidance to your soul and to set it upon the true path, in the light of the Word of God and the writings of the holy Fathers."

"Well, it's like this, Father," said I. "About a year ago, while I was at the liturgy, I heard a passage from the Epistles which bade men to pray without ceasing. Failing to understand, I began to read my Bible, and there also in many places I found the divine command that we ought to pray at all times, in all places; not only while about our business, not only while awake, but even during sleep—'I sleep, but my heart waketh.' This surprised me very much, and I was at a loss to understand how it could be carried out and in what way it was to be done. A burning desire and thirst for knowledge awoke in me. Day and night the matter was never out of my mind. So I began to go to churches and to listen to sermons. But however many I heard, from not one of them did I get any teaching about how to pray without ceasing. They always talked about getting ready for prayer, or about its fruits and the like, without teaching one how to pray without ceasing, or what such prayer means. I have often read the Bible and there made sure of what I have heard. But meanwhile I have not reached the understanding that I long for, and so to this hour I am still uneasy and in doubt."

Then the old man crossed himself and spoke. "Thank God, my dear brother, for having revealed to you this unappeasable desire for unceasing interior prayer. Recognize in it the call of God, and calm yourself. Rest assured that what has hitherto been accomplished in you is the testing of the harmony of your own will with the voice of God. It has been granted to you to understand that the heavenly light of unceasing interior prayer is attained neither by the wisdom of this world, nor by the mere outward desire for knowledge, but that on the contrary it is found in poverty of spirit and in active experience in simplicity of heart. That is why it is not surprising that you have been unable to hear anything about the essential work of prayer, and to acquire the knowledge by which ceaseless activity in it is attained. Doubtless a great deal has been preached about prayer, and there is much about it in the teaching of various writers. But since for the most part all their reasonings are based upon speculation and the working of natural wisdom, and not upon active experience, they sermonize about the qualities of prayer rather than about the nature of the thing itself. One argues beautifully about the necessity of prayer, another about its power and the blessings which attend it, a third again about the things which lead to perfection in prayer, that is, about the absolute necessity of zeal, an attentive mind, warmth of heart, purity of thought, reconciliation with one's enemies, humility, contrition, and so on. But what is prayer? And how does one learn to pray? Upon these questions, primary and essential as they are, one very rarely gets any precise enlightenment from present-day preachers. For these questions are more difficult to understand than all their arguments that I have just spoken of, and they require mystical knowledge, not simply the learning of the schools. And the most deplorable thing of all is that the vain wisdom of the world compels them to apply the human standard to the divine. Many people reason quite the wrong way round about prayer, thinking that good actions and all sorts of preliminary measures render us capable of prayer. But quite the reverse is the case; it is prayer which bears fruit in good works and all the virtues. Those who reason so take, incorrectly, the fruits and the results of prayer for the means of attaining it, and this is to depreciate the power of prayer. And it is quite contrary to Holy Scripture, for the Apostle Paul says, 'I exhort therefore that first of all supplications be made' (1 Timothy 2:1). The first thing laid down in the Apostle's words about prayer is that the work of prayer comes before everything else: 'I exhort therefore that first of all . . .' The Christian is bound to perform many good works, but before all else what he ought to do is to pray, for without prayer no other good work whatever can be accomplished. Without prayer he cannot find the way to the Lord, he cannot understand the truth, he cannot crucify the flesh with its passions and lusts, his heart cannot be enlightened with the light of Christ, he cannot be savingly united to God. None of those things can be effected unless they are preceded by constant prayer. I say 'constant,' for the perfection of prayer does not lie within our power; as the Apostle Paul says, 'For we know not what we should pray for as we ought' (Romans 8:26). Consequently it is just to pray often, to pray always, which falls within our power as the means of attaining purity of prayer, which is the mother of all spiritual blessings. 'Capture the mother, and she will bring you the children,' said St. Isaac the Syrian. Learn first to acquire the power of prayer and you will easily practice all the other virtues. But those who know little of this from practical experience and the profoundest teaching of the holy Fathers have no clear knowledge of it and speak of it but little."

During this talk, we had almost reached the monastery. And so as not to lose touch with this wise old man, and to get what I wanted more quickly, I hastened to say, "Be so kind, reverend Father, as to show me what prayer without ceasing means and how it is learnt. I see you know all about these things."

He took my request kindly and asked me into his cell. "Come in," said he. "I will give you a volume of the holy Fathers from which with God's help you can learn about prayer clearly and in detail."

We went into his cell and he began to speak as follows. "The continuous interior prayer of Jesus is a constant uninterrupted calling upon the divine name of Jesus with the lips, in the spirit, in the heart, while forming a mental picture of His constant presence, and imploring His grace, during every occupation, at all times, in all places, even during sleep. The appeal is couched in these terms, 'Lord Jesus Christ, have mercy on me.' One who accustoms himself to this appeal experiences as a result so deep a consolation and so great a need to offer the prayer always that he can no longer live without it, and it will continue to voice itself within him of its own accord. Now do you understand what prayer without ceasing is?"

"Yes indeed, Father, and in God's name teach me how to gain the habit of it," I cried, filled with joy.

"Read this book," he said. "It is called *The Philokalia,* and it contains the full and detailed science of constant interior prayer, set forth by twenty-five holy Fathers. The book is marked by a lofty wisdom and is so profitable to use that it is considered the foremost and best manual of the contemplative spiritual life. As the revered Nicephorus said, 'It leads one to salvation without labor and sweat.'"

"Is it then more sublime and holy than the Bible?" I asked.

"No, it is not that. But it contains clear explanations of what the Bible holds in secret and which cannot be easily grasped by our shortsighted understanding. I will give you an illustration. The sun is the greatest, the most resplendent, and the most wonderful of heavenly luminaries, but you cannot contemplate and examine it simply with unprotected eyes. You have to use a piece of artificial glass that is many millions of times smaller and darker than the sun. But through this little piece of glass you can examine the magnificent monarch of stars, delight in it, and endure its fiery rays. Holy Scripture also is a dazzling sun, and this book, *The Philokalia,* is the piece of glass which we use to enable us to contemplate the sun in its imperial splendor. Listen now: I am going to read you the sort of instruction it gives on unceasing interior prayer."

He opened the book, found the instruction by Saint Simeon the new theologian, and read: "'Sit down alone and in silence. Lower your head, shut your eyes, breathe out gently, and imagine yourself looking into your own heart. Carry your mind, that is, your thoughts, from your head to your heart. As you breathe out, say "Lord Jesus Christ, have mercy on me." Say it moving your lips gently, or simply say it in your mind. Try to put all other thoughts aside. Be calm, be patient, and repeat the process very frequently.'"

The old man explained all this to me and illustrated its meaning. We went on reading from *The Philokalia* passages of St. Gregory of Sinai, St. Callistus, and St. Ignatius, and what we read from the book the *starets* explained in his own words. I listened closely and with great delight, fixed it in my memory, and tried as far as possible to remember every detail. In this way we spent the whole night together and went to matins [morning prayer] without having slept at all.

The *starets* sent me away with his blessing and told me that while learning the prayer I must always come back to him and tell him everything, making a very frank confession and report; for the inward process could not go on properly and successfully without the guidance of a teacher.

In church I felt a glowing eagerness to take all the pains I could to learn unceasing interior prayer, and I prayed to God to come to my help. Then I began to wonder how I should manage to see my *starets* again for counsel or confession, since leave was not given to remain for more than three days in the monastery guesthouse, and there were no houses near.

However, I learned that there was a village between two and three miles from the monastery. I went there to look for a place to live, and to my great happiness God showed me the thing I needed. A peasant hired me for the whole summer to look after his kitchen garden, and what is more gave me the use of a little thatched hut in it where I could live alone. God be praised! I had found a quiet place. And in this manner I took up my abode and began to learn interior prayer in the way I had been shown, and to go to see my *starets* from time to time.

For a week, alone in my garden, I steadily set myself to learn to pray without ceasing exactly as the *starets* had explained. At first things seemed to go very well. But then it tired me very much. I felt lazy and bored and overwhelmingly sleepy, and a cloud of all sorts of other thoughts closed round me. I went in distress to my *starets* and told him the state I was in.

He greeted me in a friendly way and said, "My dear brother, it is the attack of the world of darkness upon you. To that world, nothing is worse than heartfelt prayer on our part. And it is trying by every means to hinder you and to turn you aside from learning the prayer. But all the same the enemy does only what God sees fit to allow, and no more than is necessary for us. It would appear that you need a further testing of your humility, and that it is too soon, therefore, for your unmeasured zeal to approach the loftiest entrance to the heart. You might fall into spiritual covetousness. I will read you a little instruction from *The Philokalia* upon such cases."

He turned to the teaching of Nicephorus and read, "'If after a few attempts you do not succeed in reaching the realm of your heart in the way you have been taught, do what I am about to say, and by God's help you will find what you seek. The faculty of pronouncing words lies in the throat. Reject all other thoughts (you can do this if you will) and allow that faculty to repeat only the following words constantly, "Lord Jesus Christ, have mercy on me." Compel yourself to do it always. If you succeed for a time, then without a doubt your heart also will open to prayer. We know it from experience.'

"There you have the teaching of the holy Fathers on such cases," said my *starets,* "and therefore you ought from today onward to carry out my directions with confidence, and repeat the prayer of Jesus as often as possible. Here is a rosary. Take it, and to start with say the prayer three thousand times a day. Whether you are standing or sitting, walking or lying down, continually repeat 'Lord Jesus Christ, have mercy on me.' Say it quietly and without hurry, but without fail exactly three thousand times a day without deliberately increasing or diminishing the number. God will help you and by this means you will reach also the unceasing activity of the heart."

I gladly accepted this guidance and went home and began to carry out faithfully and exactly what my *starets* had bidden. For two days I found it rather difficult, but after that it became so easy and likeable, that as soon as I stopped, I felt a sort of need to go on saying the prayer of Jesus, and I did it freely and willingly, not forcing myself to it as before.

I reported to my *starets,* and he bade me say the prayer six thousand times a day, saying, "Be calm, just try as faithfully as possible to carry out the set number of prayers. God will vouchsafe you His grace."

In my lonely hut I said the prayer of Jesus six thousand times a day for a whole week. I felt no anxiety. Taking no notice of any other thoughts however much they assailed me, I had but one object, to carry out my *starets*' bidding exactly. And what happened? I grew so used to my prayer that when I stopped for a single moment I felt, so to speak, as though something were missing, as though I had lost something. The very moment I started the prayer again, it went on easily and joyously. If I met anyone I had no wish to talk to him. All I wanted was to be alone and to say my prayer, so used to it had I become in a week.

My *starets* had not seen me for ten days. On the eleventh day he came to see me himself, and I told him how things were going. He listened and said, "Now you have got used to the prayer. See that you preserve the habit and strengthen it. Waste no time, therefore, but make up your mind by God's help from today to say the prayer of Jesus twelve thousand times a day. Remain in your solitude, get up early, go to bed late, and come and ask advice of me every fortnight."

I did as he bade me. The first day I scarcely succeeded in finishing my task of saying twelve thousand prayers by late evening. The second day I did it easily and contentedly. To begin with, this ceaseless

saying of the prayer brought a certain amount of weariness, my tongue felt numbed, I had a stiff sort of feeling in my jaws, I had a feeling at first pleasant but afterward slightly painful in the roof of my mouth. The thumb of my left hand, with which I counted my beads, hurt a little. I felt a slight inflammation in the whole of that wrist, and even up to the elbow, which was not unpleasant. Moreover, all this aroused me, as it were, and urged me on to frequent saying of the prayer. For five days I did my set number of twelve thousand prayers, and as I formed the habit I found at the same time pleasure and satisfaction in it.

Early one morning the prayer woke me up as it were. I started to say my usual morning prayers, but my tongue refused to say them easily or exactly. My whole desire was fixed upon one thing only—to say the prayer of Jesus, and as soon as I went on with it I was filled with joy and relief. It was as though my lips and my tongue pronounced the words entirely of themselves without any urging from me. I spent the whole day in a state of the greatest contentment. I felt as though I was cut off from everything else. I lived as though in another world, and I easily finished my twelve thousand prayers by the early evening. I felt very much like still going on with them, but I did not dare to go beyond the number my *starets* had set me. Every day following I went on in the same way with my calling on the name of Jesus Christ, and that with great readiness and liking. Then I went to see my *starets* and told him everything frankly and in detail.

He heard me out and then said, "Be thankful to God that this desire for the prayer and this facility in it have been manifested in you. It is a natural consequence which follows constant effort and spiritual achievement. So a machine to the principal wheel of which one gives a drive works for a long while afterward by itself; but if it is to go on working still longer, one must oil it and give it another drive. Now you see with what admirable gifts God in His love for mankind has endowed even the bodily nature of man. You see what feelings can be produced even outside a state of grace in a soul which is sinful and with passions unsubdued, as you yourself have experienced. But how wonderful, how delightful, and how consoling a thing it is when God is pleased to grant the gift of self-acting spiritual prayer, and to cleanse the soul from all sensuality! It is a condition which is impossible to describe, and the discovery of this mystery of prayer is a foretaste on earth of the bliss of heaven. Such happiness is reserved for those who seek after God in the simplicity of a loving heart.

Now I give you my permission to say your prayer as often as you wish and as often as you can. Try to devote every moment you are awake to the prayer, call on the name of Jesus Christ without counting the number of times, and submit yourself humbly to the will of God, looking to Him for help. I am sure He will not forsake you and that He will lead you into the right path."

Under this guidance I spent the whole summer in ceaseless oral prayer to Jesus Christ, and I felt absolute peace in my soul. During sleep I often dreamed that I was saying the prayer. And during the day if I happened to meet anyone, all men without exception were as dear to me as if they had been my nearest relations. But I did not concern myself with them much. All my ideas were quite calmed of their own accord. I thought of nothing whatever but my prayer. My mind tended to listen to it, and my heart began of itself to feel at times a certain warmth and pleasure. If I happened to go to church, the lengthy service of the monastery seemed short to me and no longer wearied me as it had in time past. My lonely hut seemed like a splendid palace, and I knew not how to thank God for having sent to me, a lost sinner, so wholesome a guide and master.

But I was not long to enjoy the teaching of my dear *starets,* who was so full of divine wisdom. He died at the end of the summer. Weeping freely I bade him farewell and thanked him for the fatherly teaching he had given my wretched self, and as a blessing and a keepsake I begged for the rosary with which he said his prayers.

And so I was left alone. Summer came to an end and the kitchen garden was cleared. I had no longer anywhere to live. My peasant sent me away, giving me by way of wages two rubles, and filling up my bag with dried bread for my journey. Again I started off on my wanderings. But now I did not walk along as before, filled with care. The calling upon the name of Jesus Christ gladdened my way. Everybody was kind to me; it was as though everyone loved me.

Then it occurred to me to wonder what I was to do with the money I had earned by my care of the kitchen garden. What good was it to me? Yet stay! I no longer had a *starets;* there was no one to go on teaching me. Why not buy *The Philokalia* and continue to learn from it more about interior prayer?

I crossed myself and set off with my prayer. I came to a large town, where I asked for the book in all the shops. In the end I found it, but they asked me three rubles for it, and I had only two. I bargained for a long time, but the shopkeeper would not budge an inch. Finally he said, "Go to this church nearby, and speak to the churchwarden. He has a book like that, but it's a very old copy. Perhaps he will let you have it for two rubles." I went, and sure enough I found and bought for my two rubles a worn and old copy of *The Philokalia.* I was delighted with it. I mended my book as much as I could, I made a cover for it with a piece of cloth, and put it into my breast pocket with my Bible.

And that is how I go about now, and ceaselessly repeat the prayer of Jesus, which is more precious and sweet to me than anything in the world. At times I do as much as forty-three or four miles a day and do not feel that I am walking at all. I am aware only of the fact that I am saying my prayer. When the bitter cold pierces me, I begin to say my prayer more earnestly, and I quickly get warm all over. When hunger begins to overcome me, I call more often on the name of Jesus, and I forget my wish for food. When I fall ill and get rheumatism in my back and legs, I fix my thoughts on the prayer and do not notice the pain. If anyone harms me I have only to think, "How sweet is the prayer of Jesus!" and the injury and the anger alike pass away and I forget it all. I have become a sort of half-conscious person. I have no cares and no interests. The fussy business of the world I would not give a glance to. The one thing I wish for is to be alone, and all by myself to pray, to pray without ceasing; and doing this, I am idled with joy. God knows what is happening to me! Of course, all this is sensuous, or as my departed *starets* said, an artificial state that follows naturally upon routine. But because of my unworthiness and stupidity I dare not venture yet to go on further and learn and make my own spiritual prayer within the depths of my heart. I await God's time. And in the meanwhile I rest my hope on the prayers of my departed *starets.* Thus, although I have not yet reached that ceaseless spiritual prayer which is self-acting in the heart, yet I thank God I do now understand the meaning of those words I heard in the Epistle—"Pray without ceasing."

The Authority of Tradition

Romanticism led Christians in the direction of tradition and dogma as well as experience and feeling. This is not hard to understand if we see the return to tradition as an indication of the belief in an organic, unified Christianity that existed in the ancient institution of the church. Experience was too variable, too ephemeral, too subjective to count on. Scripture, dissected under the microscope of critical studies, could be twisted and turned, used and abused to support all sorts of ideas. Rationalism had undermined the authority of revelation and led to the horrors of the French Revolution. Moreover, the Bible's human origins rendered it susceptible to criticism. The teachings of the church, however, handed down from the earliest apostles in an unbroken chain, were reliable, guaranteed because they had remained in the hands of a single institution dedicated to preserving them. Wholeness and beauty, truth and eternity, existed within the Roman Catholic Church.

In England, this interest in tradition was visible in the Tractarian movement. A group of Anglican theologians and priests wrote pamphlets, or tracts, extolling the virtues of a return to tradition. This meant retaining a high church liturgy in the Church of England. ("High church" means a formal service, with music, liturgy, and worship conducted with great ceremony and splendor; "low church" refers to a more informal church style.) Church services in the Anglican Church at that time began to look more and more Roman Catholic. Advocates of this move were called Anglo-Catholics, and some—like John Henry Newman (1801–1890) and Henry Edward Manning (1808–1892)—converted to Catholicism and rapidly rose in the hierarchy of English Catholicism, eventually becoming cardinals. In the United States, Isaac Thomas Hecker (1819–1888) felt a religious calling that initially led him to visit the Transcendentalists. But Transcendentalism left him unmoved, and he converted to Catholicism in 1844. He founded the Society of Missionary Priests of Saint Paul the Apostle, a religious community also known as the Paulists, in order to interpret Catholicism to non-Catholics and to demonstrate that the Catholic Church was not the enemy, but rather the guardian, of liberty. Paulist Press, which he founded as the Catholic Publication Society, still exists today and publishes a wide variety of books on many different religions.

Other efforts to revive tradition celebrated Christian history and the past but still retained their Protestant identity. In the United States, John Williamson Nevin (1803–1886) and Phillip Schaff (1819–1893) developed a movement known as Mercersberg theology that decried American Protestantism's lack of unity and lack of historical consciousness regarding Christianity. They encouraged the reading of early Christian theologians, and toward that end, Schaff wrote a comprehensive multivolume encyclopedia of Christianity that detailed major figures and developments in church history. Many college and university libraries still have the Schaff-Herzog Encyclopedia on their shelves. At the end of the nineteenth century, a group of scholars in England translated the works of early Christian theologians from Greek and Latin into English. This patristic literature—the writings of the "fathers" of

Christianity—brought early Christianity to local clergy for the first time. They could read, as we are doing in this volume, primary-source literature in translation. It was a recovery of tradition in its most basic sense.

Nineteenth-century Catholics tried to regain the authority of tradition in several ways. In 1864, Pope Pius IX (p. 1846–1878) issued a *Syllabus of Errors* that listed eighty theological errors of Catholics and others, including beliefs in pantheism, naturalism, "absolute" rationalism, and modern liberalism. It also condemned socialism, communism, secret societies, Bible societies, and liberal clerical groups. These errors needed to be eradicated from Catholic schools, churches, and seminaries. While the *Syllabus* may seem a bit extreme, it needs to be understood in the historical context of a church that felt itself under attack by excessive rationalism. The French Revolution of 1787–1799 resulted in the execution of priests, nuns, and monks, and the elimination of all religion, at least for a time, in France. The revolutionaries even erected a temple to the Goddess of Reason, and although that "temple" had come crashing down, elements of secularism still permeated European society. The rise of industrialization led to broad social movements—socialism and communism, as well as trade unionism—that tried to improve the living conditions of working people. Indeed, Marxism promised a rosy future in which all would have enough to eat and would live in peace, harmony, and justice, without God or government. These social movements appeared to destabilize society, though unfettered capitalism and industrialization seemed just as destabilizing at the time. Pius IX was attempting to defend a way of life that was probably beyond recovery.

Another movement within Catholicism aimed at bolstering tradition—this time by promoting the primacy of the papacy—was known as Ultramontanism. Because Rome was on the other side of the Alps from English, French, and German Catholics, those who looked to the Vatican (the center of Catholic power and the home of the pope) for guidance, looked "over the mountain." Ultramontanism challenged the nascent nationalism of European countries, as well as the desire among some Catholics to localize hierarchical decisions regarding prelates and policies. Many "Ultramontanes" lived in France, where the French national church tended to follow its own customs and practices. Joseph Marie de Maistre (1754–1821) wrote what became the "Bible" for Ultramontanism, a book titled *Du Pape* (1819), which laid out a clear doctrine of papal supremacy. Another Frenchman, Louis François Veuillot (1813–1883), vigorously defended Ultramontanism in his news publication *L'Univers*. The Ultramontanists wanted to centralize power within the papacy, a necessary move in many Catholics' eyes, given the heretical environment of the nineteenth century. As the bastion of truth and guidance, the church had to be protected and strengthened at all costs. While many Catholic leaders certainly did not favor Ultramontanism—most notably, American bishops—the emergence of the Ultramontanist faction indicates the extent to which tradition became a rallying cry for Catholics.

The Ultramontanists eventually succeed in strengthening the power of the papacy with the adoption of the doctrine of papal infallibility, at Vatican Council I (1869–1870), a meeting of all Catholic Church leaders called by Pope Pius IX.

> We teach and define . . . that the Roman Pontiff, when he speaks *ex cathedra*, that is, when in the exercise of his office as pastor and teacher of all Christians, he defines, by virtue of his supreme apostolic authority, a doctrine of faith or morals to be held by the whole church—is, by reason of the divine assistance promised to him in blessed Peter, possessed of that infallibility with which the Divine Redeemer wished his church to be endowed in defining doctrines of faith and morals; and consequently that such definitions of the Roman Pontiff are irreformable of their own nature, and not by reason of the church's consent. (*Pastor Aeternus,* 1870)

In other words, the doctrine of infallibility states that when the pope makes a pronouncement *ex cathedra*—that is, in his official capacity as pope—that statement is unquestionably and unmistakably true. The pope does not infallibly predict the

▨ Episcopal Infallibility

In the 125 years since papal infallibility became official Catholic doctrine it has been appealed to only once. In 1950, Pope Pius XII (p. 1939–1958) infallibly declared that Mary, the mother of Jesus, went straight to heaven, body and soul, bypassing Purgatory. Thus, Mary lives now in heaven with God the Father and God the Son. (In 1854, Pius IX had already declared that Mary had been "immaculately conceived"—that is, conceived without original sin, which explained why God chose her to be the mother of Jesus. The immaculate conception is a statement about Mary's worthiness, while the virginal conception is a statement about Jesus' miraculous incarnation by the Holy Spirit. This dogma is considered infallible, although it was made before the official declaration of infallibility in 1870.)

At Vatican Council II (see Chapter Seven), Catholic bishops extended the doctrine of infallibility to include the body of bishops meeting at an ecumenical council.

> Just as, by God's will, Saint Peter and the other apostles constituted one apostolic college, so in a similar way the Roman Pontiff as the successor of Peter and the bishops as the successors of the episcopal order are joined together. The collegial nature and meaning of the episcopal order found expression in the very ancient practice by which bishops . . . were lined with one another and with the bishop of Rome . . . also, in the conciliar assembles which made common judgments about more profound matters in decisions reflecting the views of many. The ecumenical councils held through the centuries clearly attest to this collegial aspect. (*Dogmatic Constitution on the Church,* 1964)

If the bishops maintain their unity, or meet in a united setting, they too, like the pope, can make infallible statements, just as church councils in previous centuries have made binding doctrinal rulings. We can hear echoes of the conciliar movement of the fifteenth century—when bishops engaged in a power struggle with popes and antipopes—in the statement from Vatican II. Such a conflict is unlikely within the Roman Catholic Church today, however.

weather or current affairs; only when clearly making an important statement is the doctrine invoked. Most American bishops had left the council before the vote on infallibility was taken. It was a decisive victory for the Ultramontanists, who now had a clear statement of papal authority.

Most nineteenth-century Protestants continued to minimize the authority of tradition, with the exceptions noted previously. Theologians, priests, and lay Protestants believed that Catholics had adulterated the purity of early Christianity and distorted the teachings of Christ. Anti-Catholic prejudice existed at many levels of society, from the prohibition of Catholics from holding public office in Protestant countries to the widespread belief that priests and nuns had illicit sex behind cloister doors. Perhaps the most sophisticated defense of Protestantism—and attack on Catholicism—came from Adolf von Harnack (1851–1930), a German biblical scholar. His book *The Essence of Christianity* (1900) attempted to strip Christianity of the centuries of accretions of tradition. Harnack disliked what he considered the Hellenization of Christianity by Greek philosophy and the Judaization of Christianity by Catholics. How could Catholics Judaize, or make Christianity Jewish? Harnack claimed that the emphasis on rites and rituals departed from the basic teachings of Jesus. As a biblical scholar, Harnack attempted to deduce the basic teachings of Jesus from the New Testament and to pull back the layers of Catholic teaching that had obscured its purity.

Alfred Loisy (1857–1940), a French Catholic biblical scholar, responded to Harnack two years later with his own book, *The Gospel and the Church.* Loisy was a priest who had been excommunicated in 1886 for holding heretical views, and five of his books, including *The Gospel and the Church,* appeared on the Catholic Church's *Index* of forbidden books. Initially, the church's problem with the historian and biblicist concerned his challenge to biblical inerrancy. As tension between Loisy and the church grew, the priest rejected Christian dogma in its traditional sense and even turned to atheism, although he was a practicing priest at the time of his "deconversion." In 1908, he publicly renounced Catholicism and all Christianity, and adopted a "religion of humanism."

Loisy was part of a movement within Catholicism known as Modernism. Like its Protestant counterpart Liberalism (see Chapter Seven), Modernism attempted to reconcile contemporary science, such as Darwinism, and contemporary biblical scholarship, such as the historical-critical method, with a modern and up-to-date faith. Faith need not oppose reason, said the Liberals and the Modernists: they could peacefully coexist. Indeed, it was only through an act of will that one could abandon reason and discard modern scientific findings. Loisy and other Catholic Modernists were criticized by the church, however, and their books were banned. The church considered Modernism or Liberalism—the two were frequently lumped together—a heresy that had its own dogma, or antidogma, that questioned and subverted the infallible teachings of the Catholic Church. In a secular culture awash in change, with established religious authority such as the Bible challenged by Rationalism and Romanticism, tradition seemed an infallible bulwark.

The Reading

It is ironic that *The Gospel and the Church* is such a good defense of the authority of tradition. It uses rational arguments to attack the subjectivism of liberal Protestantism. Loisy questions Harnack's views in his book's Introduction by asking whether Christian doctrine is a kernel that is never once altered or transformed by time and interpretation. Loisy wonders if perhaps Christianity is more like a mustard seed that grows and develops into something different from where it started: from a seed to a plant that is large and widely sheltering.

Loisy claims that we can never understand doctrine outside of tradition. Even at the earliest levels of scripture, we are still reading the traditions that the first disciples maintained and passed along. It was his historical criticism of the biblical text that got Loisy in trouble with church authorities. But because he adopts an evolutionary view of Christian tradition, looking at the history of theological developments and changes, the Catholic Church has since appropriated many of his arguments for understanding the development of doctrine, and thus defending the authority of tradition.

Note: Loisy, or his translator, uses archaic language to describe Islam, calling Muslims "Mussulmans," and Islam "Mahometanism." This reflects the nineteenth-century misconception that Islam worshiped its founder as Christianity does. Loisy also notes, and criticizes, one of the key criteria Protestants used to determine the authenticity of Jesus' sayings: that they were *different* from Judaism. Loisy argues that because Jesus was a Jew, many of his teachings would reflect the Judaism from which he emerged.

Questions to Consider

1. Can you deduce what Harnack's arguments were from what Loisy says about them? (We would have to read Harnack himself to judge the accuracy of Loisy's representation.)

2. What is Loisy's main point? What is his view of history?

3. What do you think Loisy is defending?

4. Which view makes more sense: Harnack's or Loisy's? Why?

5. If even the Bible is only a record of traditions (stories and accounts handed down by inspired writers or disciples), then how can Christians be sure of anything?

6. Many Protestants today criticize Catholicism for its reliance on tradition rather than, or in addition to, scripture. Loisy claims that "We know Christ only by the tradition, across the tradition, and in the tradition" and that no one can know Jesus apart from the tradition. How well does Loisy make the case for this claim? Do you agree?

The Gospel and the Church: Introduction

ALFRED LOISY

The lectures of Herr A. Harnack on the essence of Christianity have made considerable stir in the Protestant world, particularly in Germany. Embodying the profession of a personal faith in the form of a historical review, they answered without doubt to the needs of many minds, and summarized a whole group of ideas in such a way as to make a satisfactory meeting-ground for several forms of belief. But the votes of the theologians have been divided. Some have formulated reservations, others have criticized sharply a definition of Christianity which eliminates from its essence almost everything that is regarded ordinarily as Christian belief.

No doubt this work would have attracted more attention in France and even among Catholics, had it not followed the "Esquisse d'une philosophie de la religion" ["Outlines of a Philosophy of Religion," 1897] of M[onsiuer] A. Sabatier,* a book strongly resembling it in point of view and in conclusions. However, a French translation has recently been published, and already some of the Catholic reviews have drawn the attention of their readers to it, giving analyses of its contents while insisting on the need of certain amendments. The originality of such a theologico-historical synthesis strikes the intelligence, at a time when science is becoming erudite and distrustful of generalizing theories, when religious problems are discussed from a point of view that may be called purely phenomenal, when many think theology a vain thing, whilst others, on the contrary, regard it still as too divine to be concerned with all that rash investigators relate of its past. It may possibly be of some use to examine this work attentively, not so much with the object of refuting it, as of determining its exact historical position.

The aim of the work, as a matter of fact, is just to catch the point of view of history. In no sense is it an attempt to write an apologia for Catholicism or traditional dogma. Had it been so intended, it must have been regarded as very defective and incomplete, especially as far as concerns the divinity of Christ, and the authority of the Church. It is not designed to demonstrate the truth either of the gospel or of Catholic Christianity, but simply to analyze and define the bonds that unite the two in history. He who reads in good faith will not be misled.

Since the learned professor announces his work as historical, it shall be discussed solely according to the data of history. M. Sabatier sets down psychology, side by side with history, as the source of his religious philosophy. Herr Harnack appeals, above all, to facts; he sets forth less a religious philosophy, than a religion, or rather *the* religion, in the sole and unchangeable principle he deems to constitute it; this principle he extracts from the gospel, and uses as a touchstone to test the whole Christian development, which is held of worth only in so far as this precious essence has been preserved in it. The whole doctrine of the book is based on this fundamental point; that the essence of the gospel consists solely in faith in God the Father, as revealed by Jesus Christ. On the validity or insufficiency of this principle depends the value of the judgments delivered on the Evolution of the Church, of Her dogmas, and of Her worship, from the beginning, and in all the different forms of creed that are founded on the gospel and the name of Jesus. It is not surprising therefore, that from the first a certain anxiety should be felt, to see a movement as far reaching as Christianity, based on a single idea or a solitary sentiment. Is this really the definition of a historical reality, or merely a systematic method of consideration? Can a religion that has filled such a place in history, and renewed, so to speak, the conscience of humanity, take its origin and derive its whole value from a single thought? Can this great force be made up of one element? Can such a fact be other than complex? Is the definition of Christianity, put forward by Herr Harnack, that of a historian or merely that of

---

* Louis Auguste Sabatier (1839–1901) was a French Protestant theologian with liberal ideas who, like Schleiermacher, found the origin of religion in feeling, though in a feeling of anxiety or unworthiness.

a theologian who takes from history as much as suits his theology? The theory set forth in the lectures on the essence of Christianity, is the same theory that dominates the author's learned history of dogma. But is the theory actually deduced from history? Is not history rather interpreted by the light of the theory?

It will be remembered that Renan,* with some lack of reverence, compared the liberal theologian to a bird whose wings have been clipped; as long as it remains at rest, its attitude is natural, but when it attempts to fly, its movements are hampered. This comparison of the author of "Origines du Christianisme," was directed not against Catholic theologians, who, like orthodox Protestants, resemble caged birds, but against certain rationalist professors, who unite the most absolute and daring theories to a criticism so minute, that one would expect their general conclusions to be founded on experience. The remark of Renan is not an axiom beyond discussion. There is no fundamental incompatibility between the professions of theologian and historian. Possibly, there have already existed theologians who could be also historians, that is, could deal with facts as they appear from evidence intelligently investigated, without introducing their own conceptions into the texts they explored, and able to take account of the change that the ideas of past times inevitably undergo when adapted to modern thought. But it must be admitted that there have been, and always will be, a far greater number, who, starting from a general system, furnished by tradition, or elaborated by themselves under the influence of tradition, unconsciously, or perhaps sometimes consciously, bend the texts and the facts to the needs of their doctrine, though often honestly believing they avoid the danger. It must be added that the adversaries of the theologians have often brought to the discussion of these matters of religious history, prejudices acquired before the examination of the facts, prejudices that can interfere with calm and just investigation, fully as much as any theological bias.

At bottom, M. Sabatier and Herr Harnack have wished to reconcile Christian faith with the claims of science and of the scientific spirit of our time. The claims must indeed have become great, or be believed to be great, for the faith has become very small and modest. What would Luther have thought of his doctrine of salvation by faith, had it been presented to him with the amendment, "independently of creeds," or with this other—"Faith in a merciful Father, for faith in the Son is no part of the gospel of Jesus"? Religion is thus reconciled with science, because it no longer encounters it. This trust in the goodness of God either exists in a man or it does not; but it seems impossible for a sentiment to contradict any conclusion of biblical or philosophical criticism.

However, this negative reconciliation is perhaps less solid than it seems. Every absolute assertion that defies the control of the intelligence can become, at one moment or another, an obstacle to the free and legitimate course of thought. Although this minimum of faith, extracted from the Bible, seems to authorize a complete and unlimited liberty in biblical criticism, it would nevertheless prove an obstacle to the exercise of that liberty, and an obstacle the more serious just where the exercise is most indispensable, namely, in regard to the gospel, if by chance this minimum were not to be found in the gospel, or not in the sense in which the gospel is understood. Those who would compel themselves to see it there, would be forced no longer to take the gospel as it stands. It has been said for a long time, and with reason, that the dogma of biblical inspiration, in so far as it presented the Bible as a book whose truth knew no limit, nor imperfection, nor shades of meaning, and as a book full of the absolute science of God, prevented the perception of the real and historical sense of the Scriptures; but as much might be said of the conviction, arrived at before examination of the facts, or from motives other than historical, that a certain religious system, that is believed to be true, must have been the gospel of Christ. The gospel has an existence independent of us; let us try to understand it in itself, before we interpret it in the light of our preferences and our needs.

In seeking to determine historically the essence of the gospel, the rules of a healthy criticism forbid the resolution to regard as non-essential all that today must be judged uncertain or unacceptable. That which has been essential in the gospel of Jesus, is all that holds the first and most considerable place in His authentic teaching, the ideas for which He strove and for which He died, not only such part of them as is

---

* Joseph Ernst Renan (1823–1892) was a biblical scholar and a philosopher. Though he studied for the priesthood, he ended up becoming an expert in Semitic languages, best known for his popular *Life of Jesus* (1863), in which Jesus was presented as merely human.

held to be vital today. In the same way, to define the essence of primitive Christianity, we must seek the dominant preoccupation of the early Christians, and all that their religion lived by. After applying the same analytical procedure to all epochs successively, and comparing the results, we can determine if Christianity has remained faithful to the law of its origin; if the basis of Catholicism today is that which supported the Church of the Middle Ages, or the early centuries, and if that basis is substantially identical with the gospel of Jesus; or if, on the other hand, the clear light of the gospel was soon obscured, to be freed from the darkness in the sixteenth century, or only in our own time. If any common features have been preserved or developed in the Church from its origin till today, these features constitute the essence of Christianity. At least, the historian can take account of no others; he has no right to apply to Christianity a method that he would not apply to any other religion whatsoever. To decide the essence of Mahometanism, we should take from the teaching of Mahomet and the Mussulman tradition not what we judge to be true and fruitful, but all that seemed most important to the prophet and his followers in matters of faith, morality, and worship. Otherwise, with a little good will, the essence of the Koran could readily be discovered to be identical with the essence of the gospel—faith in a benign and merciful God.

Further, there would be little logic in taking for the whole essence of one religion the points that differentiate it from another. The monotheistic faith is common to Judaism, Christianity, and Mahometanism; but we are not therefore to conclude that the essential features of these three religions must be sought apart from the monotheistic conception. No Jew, no Christian, no Mussulman will admit that his faith in one God is other than the first and principal article of his belief. Each will criticize the particular form that the idea receives in the creed of his neighbor, but none will deny that monotheism is an element of his own religion on the ground that it belongs also to the religion of others. The essential distinction between religions lies in their differences, but it is not solely of their differences that they are constituted.

It is, therefore, in the highest degree arbitrary to decide that Christianity in its essence must be all that the gospel has not borrowed of Judaism, as if all that the gospel has retained of the Jewish tradition must be necessarily of secondary value. Herr Harnack finds

it quite natural to place the essence of Christianity in the faith in God the Father, because he supposes, somewhat hastily by the way, that this element of the gospel is foreign to the Old Testament. Even if the hypothesis were well founded the conclusion drawn from it would not be legitimate. It might present itself to the mind of a Protestant theologian, for whom the word "tradition" is synonymous with "Catholicism" and "error," and who rejoices to think that the gospel was the Protestantism of the law. But the historian can see in it only an assertion, whose proof is still to seek. Jesus has claimed not to destroy the law, but to fulfill. We should, therefore, expect to find in Judaism and in Christianity elements common to both, equally essential to both, the difference between the two religions lying in that "fulfillment" which is the special feature of the gospel, and should form with the common elements the whole essence of Christianity. The importance of these elements depends neither on their antiquity nor on their novelty, but on the place they fill in the teaching of Jesus, and on the value Jesus himself attached to them.

The essence of the gospel can only be determined by a critical discussion of the gospel texts, the most sure and most clearly expressed texts, and not those whose authenticity or whose meaning may be doubtful. To build a general theory of Christianity on a small number of texts of moderate authority, neglecting the mass of incontestable texts of clear significance, would be to sin against the most elementary principles of criticism. Following such a method, a more or less specious doctrinal synthesis might be offered to the public, but not the essence of Christianity according to the gospel. Herr Harnack has not avoided this danger, for his definition of the essence of Christianity is not based on the totality of authentic texts, but rests, when analyzed, on a very small number of texts, practically indeed on two passages—"No man knoweth the Son, but the Father: neither knoweth any man the Father, save the Son" (Matthew 11:27), and "The kingdom of God is within you" (Luke 17:21), both of them passages that might well have been influenced, if not produced, by the theology of the early times. This critical prepossession might thus have exposed the author to the misfortune, supreme for a Protestant theologian, of having founded the essence of Christianity upon data supplied by Christian tradition.

No great harm would be done, from the point of view of history, if it were not that these texts are isolated by having preference given to them over the others. It must be admitted that it is often difficult to distinguish between the personal religion of Jesus and the way in which His disciples have understood it, between the thought of the Master and the interpretations of apostolic tradition. If Christ had Himself drawn up a statement of His doctrine, and a summary of His prophecy, a detailed treatise on His work, His mission, His hopes, the historian would submit it to a most attentive examination, and would determine the essence of the gospel, according to irrefutable testimony. But no such treatise has ever existed, and nothing can take its place. In the Gospels there remains but an echo, necessarily weakened and a little confused, of the words of Jesus, the general impression He produced upon hearers well disposed towards Him, with some of the more striking of His sentences, as they were understood and interpreted; and finally there remains the movement which He initiated.

Whatever we think, theologically, of tradition, whether we trust it or regard it with suspicion, we know Christ only by the tradition, across the tradition, and in the tradition of the primitive Christians. This is as much as to say that Christ is inseparable from His work, and that the attempt to define the essence of Christianity according to the pure gospel of Jesus, apart from tradition, cannot succeed, for the mere idea of the gospel without tradition is in flagrant contradiction with the facts submitted to criticism. This state of affairs, being natural in the highest degree, has nothing in it disconcerting for the historian: for the essence of Christianity must be in the work of Jesus, or nowhere, and would be vainly sought in scattered fragments of His discourse. If a faith, a hope, a feeling, an impulse of will, dominates the gospel and is perpetuated in the Church of the earliest times, there will be the essence of Christianity, subject to such reservations as must be made on the literal authenticity of certain words, and on such more or less notable modifications that the thought of Jesus must of necessity have endured in transmission from generation to generation.

"The essences of things are unchangeable," said the ancient philosophy, when considering the eternal types of contingent realities. To determine such an essence in Christianity, it must be transformed into a metaphysical entity, into a logical quintessence, into something resembling the scholastic notion of species, that certain theologians still fear to corrupt by admitting the idea of evolution. Herr Harnack

seems also to fear that his essence of Christianity might be spoiled if he introduced into it any idea of life, of movement and development. On the other hand, he distrusts abstract essences, and has taken care not to give any theoretical definition of religion, which should be at the same time a definition of Christianity, although he maintains the Hegelian proposition that Christianity is the one absolute religion. He finds the essence of Christianity in a sentiment—filial confidence in God, the merciful Father. Therein is to lie all religion and all Christianity. The identity of this sentiment in Jesus and in all Christians, is to constitute the continuity of the religion and the unchangeableness of its essence.

But is this essence, even in these reduced proportions, actually unchangeable, and why should it be? Has the Divine mercy been understood in absolutely the same way by the apostles and by Herr Harnack? The apostles had a conception of the world, and even of God the merciful, somewhat different from the idea that is suggested in the peroration of "The Essence of Christianity." Now, sentiment is not independent of thought; if the idea change, the form of the sentiment will also change, though the sentiment retains its first direction, because of the spirit that sustains it; and if on this point (the Divine merciful Fatherhood) the attitude of Christianity is held to be unchanged, because it retains the direction and the impulse of Christ, why should not its attitude towards other points be held unchanged for the same reason? What, for instance, of the hope of an eternal kingdom, constantly preached by Christ, and never allowed to perish by the Christian Church? What of the mission of the apostles charged to propagate this hope? What of Christ Himself, Whose place as Messiah belongs to the Primitive Church, and has never ceased to occupy the thought of the Church from the beginning? What of all the different themes of evangelical teaching, of which not one has been regarded during the Christian centuries as accessory? All these elements of Christianity, in all the forms in which they have been preserved, why should they not be the essence of Christianity? Why not find the essence of Christianity in the fullness and totality of its life, which shows movement and variety just because it is life, but inasmuch as it is life proceeding from an obviously powerful principle, has grown in accordance with a law which affirms at every step the initial force that may be called its physical essence revealed in all its manifestations? Why should the essence of a tree be held to be but a particle of the seed from which it has sprung, and why should it not be recognized as truly and fully in the complete tree as in the germ? Are the processes of assimilation by which it grows to be regarded as an alteration of the essence present potentially in the seed, and are they not rather the indispensable conditions of its being, its preservation, its progress in a life always the same and incessantly renewed?

The historian cannot but refuse to regard as the essence of living Christianity a germ that multiplies without growing. Rather he should return to the parable of the mustard seed, comparing the new-born Christianity to a little grain. The grain was small, for the new religion was without the prestige of antiquity enjoyed by the ancient religions, still surviving, of Egypt and Chaldea; it was less, in external power, than Greco-Roman paganism: it was even less, apparently, than Judaism, of which it must have seemed a variety, with no future, since Judaism rejected it. This grain, nevertheless, enclosed the germ of the tree that we now see; charity was its sap: its life impulse was in the hope of its triumph; its expanding force was in its apostleship, its pledge of success in sacrifice: for its general form this budding religion had its faith in the unity and absolute Sovereignty of God, and for its particular and distinctive feature that faith in the Divine mission of Jesus, which earned it its name of Christianity. All this was in the little seed, and all this was the real essence of the Christian religion, needing only space to grow to reach its present point, still living after all its growth.

To understand the essence of Christianity we must look to those vital manifestations which contain its reality, its permanent quintessence, recognizable in them, as the principal features of primitive Christianity are recognizable throughout their development. The particular and varied forms of the development, in so far as they are varied, are not of the essence of Christianity, but they follow one another, as it were, in a framework whose general proportions, though not absolutely constant, never cease to be balanced, so that if the figure change, its type does not vary, nor the law that governs its evolution. The essence of Christianity is constituted by the general features of this figure, the elements of this life and their characteristic properties; and this essence is unchangeable, like that of a living being, which remains the same while it lives, and to the extent to which it lives. The historian will find that the essence of Christianity has been more or less preserved in the different Christian communions: he will not believe it to be compromised by the development of institutions, of creeds, and of worship, so long as this development has been ruled by the principles verified in the first commencement. He will not expect this essence to have been absolutely and definitely realized at any point of past centuries; he will believe that it has been realized more or less perfectly from the beginning, and that it will continue to be realized thus more and more, so long as Christianity shall endure.

Herr Harnack does not conceive Christianity as a seed, at first a plant in potentiality, then a real plant, identical from the beginning of its evolution to the final limit and from the root to the summit of the stem, but as a fruit, ripe, or rather overripe, that must be peeled, to reach the incorruptible kernel; and Herr Harnack peels his fruit with such perseverance, that the question arises if anything will remain at the end. This method of dismembering a subject does not belong to history, which is a science of observation of the living, not of dissection of the dead. Historical analysis notices and distinguishes, it does not destroy what it touches, nor think all movement digression, and all growth deformity. It is not by stripping Christianity leaf by leaf that the law of its life will be found. Such a dissection leads of necessity to a special theory, of philosophical value doubtless, but of little account from the positive standpoint of history. It is not for the theologian (unless in quite a personal exercise of his intelligence), and still less is it for the critic, to seize religion on the wing, dismember it, extract a something and declare it unique, by saying, "This is the essence of Christianity." Let us regard the Christian religion in its life, observing by what means it has lived from the beginning and is still sustained; let us note the principal features of this venerable existence, convinced that they lose nothing in reality or importance, because today they are presented to us under colors that are not those of a former time.

To reduce Christianity to a single point, a solitary truth that the conscience of Jesus has perceived and revealed, is to protect religion against all attacks far less than might be expected, because it is thus almost put out of touch with reality, and deprived of historical support, and of every defense against the reasoning faculty. Christ is presented as a man who had but one true thought among many false ones, and those that are now held erroneous and valueless are not those that occupied His attention the least. If the sole truth that He revealed fails to make its appeal, there is nothing else to look for from Him; and to feel this incomparable truth, to find it more true than the rest of His conceptions, the only truth in fact among them, to see in it absolute religion, it is not enough merely to contemplate it, but a kind of intellectual and moral enthusiasm is also demanded, prepared to see only this and be content.

It might be said that the God of Herr Harnack, driven from the domain of Nature, driven also from history, in so far as history is made of facts and play of thoughts, has taken refuge on the heights of human conscience, and is now only to be seen there by those who have keen perception. Is it so certain that He cannot be seen elsewhere, or that if not seen elsewhere, He will be infallibly found there? Is it not possible, if no effort is made to keep Him, that He will be driven also from this last retreat, and identified as one of "the category of the Ideal," or as "Imperfect activity aspiring to Perfection," phantoms of divinity with which the reason plays when wandering to find the explanation of itself, phantoms of no account for religion? Can the conscience keep for long a God that science ignores, and will science respect forever a God that it does not know? Can God be goodness if He is not first—Life and Truth? Is it not as easy and as necessary to conceive Him as the Source of Life and Truth as of indulgent goodness? Shall we have need of Him to reassure the conscience, if we have no need of Him to strengthen the intelligence? Is it not with all his soul and all his might, that man should search after God to find him? Must not God live in Nature and in man, and must not the integral formula of true religious philosophy be "God everywhere," as the integral formula of Christianity is "Christ in the Church, and God in Christ."

But this is not the place to examine Herr Harnack's theology. Our aim is only to determine if his "Essence of Christianity," instead of being absolute religion, absolute Christianity, entities that have little chance of taking a place in history, does not rather mark a stage in Protestant development, or form merely a basic formula of Protestantism.

The questions that Loisy poses remain relevant today, as Protestants challenge the Catholic appeal to tradition, and Catholics question the Protestant reliance on scripture. He seems to be asking if scripture itself *is* tradition, and certainly the remainder of *The Gospel and the Church* attempts to make this case. If Loisy is correct, then the divide between Protestants and Catholics may not be as large as both groups seem to think.

Conclusions

Christianity in the period of Rationalism and Romanticism was extremely diverse: from Deism and Pietism, to Romanticism, Ultramontanism, Modernism, and all sorts of other -isms. What these developments had in common was the quest for a sure authority. Could it be found in the Bible? But the Bible seemed to have been written by humans who erred, or at least who were not divine. Did authority rest in the head or in the heart? Neither relied upon God alone, and Rationalism had led to the excesses of the French Revolution, while Romanticism privileged nature and feeling. What about tradition, the teachings handed down through the centuries? Ancient and venerable, but perhaps distorted for human, rather than divine, ends?

The unity of Christianity had splintered in the sixteenth century, and all the priests, prelates, popes, and pastors could not put it back together again. We see in the centuries after the Reformation different arguments for understanding Christianity, religion, theology, and the Bible. Persuasive claims to different authorities were made on all sides; God alone knew the truth.

At the very same time that Christianity was wracked with strife and division, Christians were taking their religion outside the confines of Europe and the Americas to new lands and new peoples. Missionaries brought what they believed were the saving words of Jesus to people who had never heard them before, and a few who had. In the process, the world would be transformed, and so would Christianity.

Sources For Selections

Channing, William Ellery. "Christianity a Rational Religion." In *The Works of William E. Channing, D.D.* Boston: American Unitarian Association, 1897.

Fell, Margaret. *Women's Speaking Justified.* Introduction by David J. Latt. Los Angeles: William Andrews Clark Memorial Library, University of California, 1979.

Fiedler, Maureen, and Linda Rabben, eds. *Rome Has Spoken: A Guide to Forgotten Papal Statement and How They Have Changed Through the Centuries.* New York: Crossroad, 1998.

French, R. M., trans. *The Way of a Pilgrim* and *The Pilgrim Continues His Way.* San Francisco: HarperSanFrancisco, 1965.

Lessing, Gotthold. *Lessing's Theological Writings.* Introduced by Henry Chadwick. Stanford, Calif.: Stanford University Press, 1956.

Loisy, Alfred. *The Gospel and the Church.* Trans. Christopher Home. New York: Charles Scribner, 1912.

The Philokalia. Trans. and ed. C. E. H. Palmer, Philip Sherrard, and Kallistos Ware. 4 vols. London: Faber & Faber, 1979.

Schleiermacher, Friedrich. "Second Speech: On the Essence of Religion." In *On Religion: Speeches to Its Cultured Despisers.* Trans. Richard Crouter. New York: Cambridge University Press, 1988.

Zinzendorf, Count Nicholaus Ludwig von. *Nine Public Lectures on Important Subjects in Religion.* Ed. and trans. George W. Forell. Iowa City: University of Iowa Press, 1973.

Additional Resources

Barnett, S. J. *The Enlightenment and Religion: The Myths of Modernity.* Manchester and New York: Manchester University Press, 2003.

Bradley, James E., and Dale K. Van Kley, eds. *Religion and Politics in Enlightenment Europe.* Notre Dame, Ind.: University of Notre Dame Press, 2001.

Grell, Ole Peter, and Roy Porter, eds. *Toleration in Enlightenment Europe.* Cambridge, U.K.: Cambridge University Press, 2000.

Harnack, Adolf von. *What Is Christianity?* Trans. Thomas Bailey Saunders. New York: Harper Torchbooks, 1957.

Levine, Alan, ed. *Early Modern Skepticism and the Origins of Toleration.* Lanham, Md.: Lexington Books, 1999.

Locke, John. *A Letter Concerning Toleration.* Ed. John Horton and Susan Mendus. London and New York: Routledge, 1991.

Munck, Thomas. *The Enlightenment: A Comparative Social History 1721–1794.* London: Arnold, 2000.

Outram, Dorinda. *The Enlightenment.* Cambridge, U.K.: Cambridge University Press, 1995.

Welch, Claude. *Protestant Thought in the Nineteenth Century.* Vol. I, 1799–1870; Vol. II, 1870–1914. New Haven and London: Yale University Press, 1972.

Films

The Cardinal. Directed by Otto Preminger, 1963.

The Crucible. Directed by Nicholas Hytner, 1996.

Monsignor. Directed by Frank Perry, 1982.

Shoes of the Fisherman. Directed by Michael Anderson, 1968.

INVITATION TO
Part Three

PART THREE brings us into the modern world and considers the variety of ways Christianity is expressed and experienced around the globe.

CHAPTER SIX examines the concepts of missions and inculturation diachronically, that is, from two time periods. It looks at the historical reality of Christian missions beginning in the sixteenth century and at the ways in which indigenous peoples have inculturated—that is, adopted and adapted—Christianity into their own lifeways. The mission experience was mixed for both missionaries and converts, with missions frequently serving as the vehicle for the imposition of European values upon others. Christian theology thus developed within a framework of an imbalance of power in which two types of Christianity—colonial and indigenous—existed side by side. Hearing the voices of contemporary Asians, Africans, and Americans puts the mission experience in perspective.

CHAPTER SEVEN wraps up by discussing key twentieth-century figures and movements. It considers the question posed by Dietrich Bonhoeffer from a Nazi prison cell: How do we speak about God in a world come of age? Different theologians wrestle with different issues through the century: from the relationship between Christianity and non-Christian religions, to problems of racism, sexism, and oppression. Christians addressed these problems in a variety of ways, relying on the Bible, on evangelization, and on philosophy to analyze problems and present solutions.

The twentieth century posed unique challenges to humanity, confronting us with the potential destruction of all life on the planet. While the writers in Part Three admit mistakes on the part of Christians in the past, they also bring a message of hope for the future of Christianity in an increasingly pluralistic global community.

	1492 — Columbus' voyage to "New World"
Pope Alexander VI issues Bull of Demarcation, dividing up "New World" —	**1493** — Expulsion of Muslims from Spain
	1498 — Vasco da Gama sails around Africa to Indian Ocean
Vision of Virgin of Guadalupe —	**1531**
	1537 — Pope Paul III excommunicates those who enslave Native Americans in "New World"
Bartolomé de las Casas' account of treatment of Indians —	**1540–42**
	1544 — African slaves imported to Chiapas, Mexico
Expulsion of Christians from Japan —	**1614**
	1639 — Pope Urban III outlaws enslavement of Indians
Pope Alexander VII allows Jesuits in China to use Chinese language and rites in Mass —	**1656**
	1698 — Society for Promoting Christian Knowledge founded in England
Society for Propagation of Gospel in Foreign Parts established in England —	**1701**
	1754 — Pope Benedict XIV recognizes Virgin of Guadalupe as Mary, the mother of God
French National Assembly outlaws slavery and slave trade in French colonies —	**1794**
	1808 — England bans African slave trade
Native American "Trail of Tears" in United States —	**1830**
	1839 — Pope Gregory XVI denounces slavery and slave trade
Universities' Mission to Central Africa founded in England —	**1857**
	1863 — Emancipation Proclamation in United States
Founding of Maryknoll Mission Society in United States —	**1911**

CHAPTER SIX

Missions and Inculturation
SINGING THE LORD'S SONG IN A NEW KEY

In the Gospel of Matthew, Jesus appears to his disciples after the resurrection and says: "All authority in heaven and on earth has been given to me. Go therefore and make disciples of all nations, baptizing them in the name of the Father and of the Son and of the Holy Spirit, and teaching them to obey everything that I have commanded you" (Matthew 28:19–20). Subsequent Christians have interpreted these words—called the Great Commission—as a mandate to spread the good news they had received, and experienced, in Jesus. Much of the language and purpose of Christianity emphasizes this mandate: missions, apostles, evangelization. Literally, a *mission* is a job or task that someone is assigned or sent to do. We see this usage today when diplomats go on "peace missions" or when health care workers go on "medical missions." *Apostle* refers to one who is sent out to broadcast the message. The apostles belonged to the first and second generations of Jesus' followers, who attempted to teach and preach about Jesus in Jewish synagogues and pagan temples. *Evangelization* has its root in the Greek word *evangelium,* or "good news." (We can see the word *angel* in evangelize, since angel in Greek means "messenger.") Thus, we get evangelist, evangelize, evangelization, and evangelical from the Greek word for good news, which in English is sometimes translated "gospel."

The New Testament shows that Jesus' followers had serious discussions about missions. We see in the letter to the Galatians that Peter and Paul divided the mission field, with Peter preaching to Jews and Paul preaching to Gentiles. The book of Acts contains a discussion about requirements that the early church thought it should impose on Gentile converts. Other New Testament texts show the diversity of converts, revealing their past lives as pagans or Jews and their efforts to conform to a different way of life, a new way of thinking at odds with their cultural heritage. Still other texts from the first centuries of the early church reveal the spread of Christianity throughout the Mediterranean, especially to Africa.

Some of the most ancient forms of Christianity are practiced even today in Egypt and Ethiopia. Saint Anthony's example of asceticism in the Egyptian desert in the second century served as a model for thousands to follow in succeeding centuries. By the third century, the city of Alexandria was one of the five patriarchates—that is, centers—of early Christian leadership: Alexandria, Jerusalem, Antioch, Constantinople, and Rome. Coptic Christians continue to worship in Egypt today.

Missionaries to Ethiopia in the fourth century established churches that retained certain Ethiopian customs from Judaism, such as worshiping on the Sabbath. In fact, North Africa served as fertile ground for early Christianity, with many prominent theologians emerging from the region, including Tertullian, Cyprian, Augustine, Clement, and Origen.

In other parts of the world, however, Christianity is a relative newcomer. It wasn't until the age of exploration—the great ocean voyages carried out by Spanish and Portuguese, French and English seamen beginning in the sixteenth century—that Christians began to appreciate the immensity of the globe and the diversity of its peoples. There were souls to save, according to Christians, and hundreds of men and women took great risks to share what they believed was God's salvation for all. The story of missions—which frequently is also part of the story of conquest—varies from Central and South America, to North America, to Africa, and to Asia. At the same time, however, indigenous resistance to forces of foreign domination is a common theme, as is the process of inculturating Christianity into local languages, customs, and traditions to help it cohere with preexisting thought worlds.

While Christianity has changed the world, it has also been changed by it through the process of missions and inculturation. Some of us may have heard missionaries speak about the dramatic conversions that occur in individuals' lives when they hear of God's love; or we may have read about how communities are revived when churches, schools, hospitals, or houses are constructed. Less frequently, however, do we hear about inculturation: the process by which Christianity is digested, appropriated, and transformed into an authentic expression of local faith. The process of inculturation started at the very beginning, when Jesus' teachings were interpreted by Jewish followers to pagan audiences. It continues today and helps explain why so many people identify with Christianity: it has been inculturated into a multitude of forms and appearances.

Underlying the process of inculturation is the theological concept of incarnation: God's Word, or Logos, become flesh. When God became human in the person of Jesus, God took on all aspects of human, material reality. Although Christians believe this occurred more than 2000 years ago, most would also argue that Jesus Christ is alive for them today. That is why Jesus is depicted in the cultural idioms of his followers. In Iran, Jesus looks Persian; in Korea, he is Korean. African representations of the Madonna and child make Mary and Jesus real for African Christians. Depictions of the incarnation in the West show Jesus looking European, and missionaries exported the image of Jesus as a blond, blue-eyed, fair-skinned man of above-average height. Anthropological reconstructions of first-century skulls found in Israel indicate that it is much more likely that Jesus was rather short, dark-haired, and dark-skinned. Neither representation matters, however. Christians believe that for Jesus to be truly incarnate, he must be inculturated, and encountered in the face of one's neighbor. This is why Jesus and Christianity look somewhat different wherever they have been planted.

It was not until the sixteenth century and the age of exploration that missionary activity extended outside the area bounded by the Atlantic Ocean, the North Sea, the Ural Mountains, and the Mediterranean Sea. The age of exploration became the age of Christian expansion. This chapter looks at that age, and the global diffusion of Christianity, diachronically, that is, from two different time periods. It demonstrates the ways in which the original inhabitants of the Americas, Asia, and Africa have struggled to maintain their cultural identity while forging a new Christian identity. By juxtaposing texts from periods of intense missionary activity—from the 1500s to the 1900s—with texts from the twentieth century, we can observe the process of inculturation and see how different peoples have adopted and adapted Christianity in new idioms.

Christianity in the New World

Spanish and Portuguese exploration began before the dawn of the sixteenth century and the upheavals of the Protestant Reformation. Imperial and commercial trading benefited from the religious chaos, however, under a weakened papacy and a Europe in transition from feudalism to modern capitalism. Although Christopher Columbus provided a religious justification for his voyages in *El Libro de las Profecías,* the motivation of his financiers was economic and geopolitical: land,

▨ "Christian" Holidays?

Christianity has long appropriated pagan customs and holidays, "baptizing" them by giving them new meaning. For example, 25 December—the traditional birthday celebration for the Roman deity Mithras—became the date for commemorating Christ's birth. The practice of having a nativity scene was introduced by Saint Francis in the thirteenth century. Samhain (pronounced SOW-in) was a pagan holiday observed on 31 October, which marked the end of summer and the time of year when the border between heaven and earth was at its thinnest. Samhain became All Saints' Eve in the Christian calendar, that is, Halloween.

Most of the symbols for Christmas are reappropriations of druidic or pagan symbols: the evergreen tree, the Yule log, holly, wreaths, and so on. It is safe to assume that most, though not all, Christian symbols that feature natural objects such as eggs, butterflies, trees, and animals reflect the reinterpretation of pagan symbols, frequently relating to fertility or to pagan holidays. (One exception might be Easter eggs, which may come from the Jewish celebration of Passover.) These are all examples of inculturation—embedding Christianity within the cultural forms and symbolic world of its practitioners—but ones so much a part of European Christianity that they are taken for granted.

resources, wealth. If souls could be saved for God, all the better. Enormous mission-ary fervor emerged from the Catholic Reformation, with the new order of Jesuits and revitalized orders of Carmelites, Franciscans, Dominicans, and Augustinians, lead-ing the way toward missions, and martyrdom. Protestants eventually established a strong missionary presence outside of Europe, which coincided with the rise of the Dutch and the English as rivals to Spanish, Portuguese, French—and therefore Catholic—maritime power. But the sixteenth and seventeenth centuries belonged to Catholic missionaries.

Not all mission fields, or missionaries, were created equal, however. Missionar-ies going to the "New World" of North and South America came across vastly differ-ent peoples and cultures than did the missionaries who sailed east to the well-established civilizations of Asia: India, China, Japan. The story of missions depended on which continent and which missionaries.

While most of Europe struggled with the challenges created by the Protestant Reformation, Spain and Portugal looked abroad. By the end of the sixteenth cen-tury, these two countries controlled Central and South America and large areas of North America and operated trading centers in India and Japan, and on the African coastline. Even by contemporary standards, it was an impressive accumulation of territory.

The promise of wealth, of fame and fortune, lured the sons of Iberian nobility—frequently strapped for cash—abroad. Part of the push undoubtedly came from the final expulsion of Muslims from Spain in 1492, the year of Columbus' first voyage. Freed from political and military intrigue on the home front, Spanish energy flowed outward to follow, and stalk, Muslim economic power. Spain and Portugal rivaled each other on the high seas—so much so that Pope Alexander VI (p. 1492–1503) drew a longitudinal line in the Atlantic Ocean ceding territory west of it to Spain and east of it to Portugal. In 1494, the two nations renegotiated territorial rights bilater-ally: Portugal claimed Brazil, while Spain claimed the Philippines.

There was a tremendous human cost, however. Colonization of the Americas was brutal, despite the efforts of missionary friars and Jesuits to prevent the worst atrocities. Beginning with Hernán Cortés' (1485–1547) betrayal of the Aztecs in Mexico, the story of conquest is one of depravity and dehumanization. Those Indi-ans—so-called because Columbus believed he had reached India—who were not killed were forced to work in mines, in the fields, or in other extractive industries, although technically slavery was prohibited. In return for Indian labor, the colonists were expected to instruct Indians in Catholic Christianity and pay them a modest wage. In reality, neither occurred.

The civilizations of the Aztecs, the Incas and the late Missippian cultures of North America were destroyed. While Europe had been foundering in the Dark Ages, the peoples of the Americas had established cultures with highly developed astronomy, mathematics, literature, and cosmology. Their books, their science, their cities and temples—all were destroyed in the effort to extirpate all forms of idolatry, as well as to subdue resistance by eliminating symbols of national pride and culture.

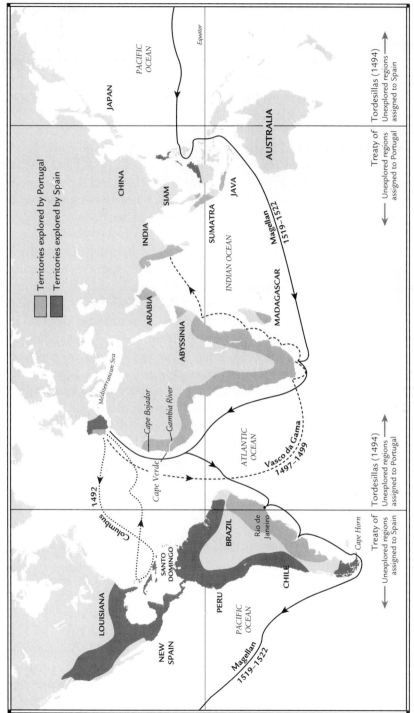

The age of exploration. *Spanish and Portuguese exploration of the Americas, Africa, and Asia led to colonization of new territories and the conversion of their populations to Catholic Christianity.*

Hundreds of missionaries accompanied the conquistadores. Some proposed creating settlements of indigenous peoples centered around mission churches. This was the system that eventually developed in California in the eighteenth century, one that led to its own share of exploitation of native peoples. An alternate economic system of *encomiendas*—privately owned ranches and farms supplied with forced native labor—arose in the Caribbean. Improbably, one *encomiendero* (ranch owner) became a leading voice for the exploited.

Bartolomé de las Casas (1474/1484–1566) was an unlikely advocate for the Indians. At various times in his life, he was a warrior, a merchant, and a priest. His father had accompanied Columbus on his second voyage, and in 1502, de las Casas traveled with his father to the island of Hispaniola (modern-day Haiti and the Dominican Republic). Although de las Casas received an *encomienda* and had financial interests in Jamaica, Puerto Rico, Cuba, and Santo Domingo (and owned the African slaves working on his ranches and plantations), he was ordained a priest in 1510. He was granted land on the Venezuelan coast to establish a utopian community of free Indians; after it failed, he entered a Dominican monastery, and in 1522, he joined the Dominicans. Shortly thereafter, de las Casas began writing his three-volume *History of the Indies,* which detailed the atrocities perpetrated against the original inhabitants of the land.

De las Casas was not the first to protest the abusive treatment of the Indians. Antonio de Montesinos (d. c. 1545), another Dominican, had advocated ending the *encomienda* system and abolishing forced labor. But de las Casas was the most persistent, the most vocal, and the most effective advocate. In 1537, Pope Paul III (p. 1534–1549) issued a papal bull which stated that because the Indians were rational human beings, they could not be enslaved (though the pope added that they were in dire need of self-improvement). The colonists still needed labor in their new world, and, unfortunately, in 1544, de las Casas asked for papal permission to import African slaves to Chiapas, Mexico, where he had been named bishop. Although he later repudiated African slavery, in his effort to defend those whom he called "the scourged christs of the Indies," de las Casas had helped to open the door to the chattel slavery system that would endure for centuries.

The Reading

The following excerpt comes from de las Casas' *Account, Much Abbreviated, of the Destruction of the Indies,* in which he describes in horrifying detail events he witnessed or heard about from other missionaries or Indians. He spent two years in Spain (1540–1542) writing a treatise for the Spanish emperor Charles V. It is essentially a catalogue of abuses perpetrated by the Spanish throughout the Americas. In other words, it is a work of propaganda, intended to shock the emperor into changing the policies of the Spanish government regarding *encomiendas* and forced labor. In that regard, the work was successful: Charles attempted to bring peace to the Spanish who were warring in the New World.

Questions to Consider

1. What was the attitude of the Spanish entrepreneurs toward the Indians they encountered?

2. How would you have handled the natives if you were a Christian missionary? How would you have handled the Spanish colonists?

3. How effective is this type of writing? Is it persuasive? What does it persuade you to do or feel?

4. How do you explain the double standard regarding the enslavement of Indians as opposed to the enslavement of Africans in the "New World"? Or is there much of a difference?

5. What would you say is the legacy of missions in the New World, at least according to this account? Do systems or structures of exploitation continue to exist in Central and South America? And more specifically, what is currently happening in the region of Chiapas, located on the Yucatan Peninsula?

On the Kingdom of the Yucatan

BARTOLOMÉ DE LAS CASAS

In the year 1526, another wretched man* was made governor of the kingdom of Yucatan and sent there, thanks to the lies and falsehoods he told and offerings he made to the king, as the other tyrants have also done until now, so that they might be given offices and positions from which they might rob and steal. This kingdom of Yucatan was filled with infinite numbers of people, for it is land in great measure healthful and abundant with food and fruits (even more than the land of Mexico) and particularly abounding in honey and wax above any other part of the Indies that has so far been seen. It has nearly three hundred leagues of the tree they call *boja*† around about it. The people of said kingdom were notable among all those of the Indies, both in prudence and policy and in their lack of vices and sins more than others, and very fit and worthy to be brought to the knowledge of the Spaniards' God, and their land a fit place where there could be made great

cities of Spaniards and they might live in them as though in an earthly paradise, were they worthy of it—but they were not, because of their great covetousness and greed and insensibility and great sins, as they have been unworthy of the many other parts that God had shown them in those Indies.

And this tyrant began with three hundred men that he brought with him to wage cruel wars on those good, innocent people, who were in their houses without offence to any, where he slew and destroyed infinite people. And because the land has no gold—because if it did have, to take it from the ground he would have killed them all—yet in order to make gold of the bodies and souls of those for whom Jesus Christ did die, he brought together all those he had not slain and made them slaves, and in the many ships that came to the smell and fame of the slaves, he sent them off filled with people, and they were sold for wine and oil and vinegar, and for bacon, and

---

* The reference is to Francisco de Montejo (1479–1553), who took part in the conquest of Cuba, founded Vera Cruz in 1519, and began the long conquest of Yucatan in 1526 that was continued by his son.

† Probably sagebrush or a similar large flowering shrub.

for shirts and other clothing, and for horses, and for what he and they had need of, according to his judgment and as he saw fit. He would offer up between fifty and a hundred maidens, one of more lovely appearance than the next, that each man might choose one in exchange for an arroba of wine or oil or vinegar, or for a ham, and the same with a well-disposed boy, between a hundred and two hundred to be chosen, for another such sum. And it fell out that he gave a boy who appeared to be the son of a king, for a cheese, and an hundred persons for a horse. And he continued in this wise from the year 1526 until the year 1533, which were seven years, laying waste and depopulating those lands and slaying those people without mercy, until there came the news of the wealth and riches of Peru, and at that, the Spanish people that were there with him went straightway to Peru, and that hell that had existed in Yucatan, it ceased for some days. But then his ministers returned to do great mischief and thefts and captivities and great offences in the eyes of God, and still today they cease not to do them, and so they have all those three hundred leagues which were (as I have said) so full and populous, almost wiped clean of people.

It would be hard to persuade a person to believe, and harder still to tell, the particular cases of cruelty that have been committed there; I shall tell but two or three that come to my mind. When the sorry Spaniards were journeying about with savage dogs, seeking out the Indians and setting those dogs on them, women and men both, one Indian woman who was ill, seeing that she would not be able to flee the dogs, to escape them tearing her to pieces as they did to some others, took up a rope and tied it to the foot of a child she had, of one year old, and she hanged him from a beam, but she did not do it before the dogs came, and they tore the child apart, although before he had died completely he was baptized by a friar.

When the Spaniards were leaving out of that kingdom, one of them told the son of a lord of a certain village or province that the son was to come with him; the boy said that he did not want to leave his land. To that, the Spaniard replied: "Come with me, or I shall cut off thine ears." And still the boy said no. And as the boy was saying that he did not wish to leave his land, the Spaniard cut off his nose, laughing as though it were no more than pulling his hair.

This iniquitous man boasted and made much of himself in the presence of a venerable man of the cloth, most shamelessly saying that he worked as hard as ever he was able, to get many Indian women with child so that selling them into slavery pregnant, he might receive that much greater price for them.

In this kingdom, or in a province of the New Spain, a certain Spaniard was going along one day with his dogs to hunt for deer or rabbits, and not finding game, he bethought himself that his dogs were hungry, and he took a little boy from its mother and taking a knife he hacked off its arms and legs, giving each dog its part, and after those pieces had been eaten, he threw the little body onto the ground in among the pack. See, then, how great is the inhumanity and unfeelingness of the Spaniards in those lands, and how God has brought them in *reprobus sensus* ["Of reprobate sense or mind," from Romans 1:28], and in what esteem they hold those poor people, born and raised up in the image of God and redeemed by His blood. But worse things yet, shall we see below.

Leaving the infinite and never before heard-of cruelties that were done in this kingdom by those who call themselves Christians, and which there is not sufficient mind or reason to think about them, I wish to conclude with only this. Once all the hellish tyrants of this kingdom had left, filled as they were with such eagerness and avidity for the gold and riches of Peru that it fair blinded them, the padre Friar Jacobo set off with four other men of the cloth of his order of Saint Francis to go to that kingdom to pacify and preach and take Jesus Christ to the leavings that remained of that hellish harvest and those tyrannical slaughters that the Spaniards had for seven years perpetrated. I believe that those religious fathers went in the year 1534, sending ahead certain Indians of the province of Mexico as messengers, to ask the peoples they encountered if they would allow said religious fathers to enter into their lands to take them news of our one God, who was the true God and Lord of all the world. And so they entered into council and held many meetings, taking first a great deal of information, what men these were who called themselves friars and priests and what it was that they sought and desired, and in what particulars they differed from the Christians from whom they had received so many offences and so much violence and injustice. Finally they agreed to receive them, so long as they only, and no Spaniards, should enter there. The holy fathers made that promise to them, for thus they had been promised in turn by the viceroy of New Spain, who had vowed to them that they might promise that no more Spaniards would enter there, but only men of the cloth, nor that any violence or offence would be done the Indians there by any Christians. They preached to them the evangel [good news] of Christ, as is their wont, and the holy intention of the king and queen of Spain toward them. And how much love and savor did the Indians take with the doctrine and example of the friars, and how much pleasure from the news of the king and queen of Castile (of whom in all the seven years past the Spaniards had never spoken, never saying that there was another ruler besides that one who was tyrannizing over them and destroying)! And at the end of forty days since the friars had entered those lands and begun preaching, the lords of the land brought them and delivered up to them their idols, that they should be burned, and after this they delivered up their sons that they should be taught, whom they love more greatly than the light of their eyes, and they made churches and temples for the friars, and houses, and they were invited by other provinces, to go and preach to them and give them news of God and of him who they said was the great king of Castile. And persuaded by the friars, the Indians did a thing that never before in the Indies had been done before, or to this day has been done again, and all those things that are bruited by some of the tyrants who have destroyed those kingdoms and great lands are falsehoods and lies. Twelve or fifteen lords, possessors of many vassals and lands, each one gathering together his peoples and taking their vows and consent, subjected themselves of their own will to the rule of the monarchs of Castile, taking the emperor, as the king of Spain, for their supreme and universal lord, and they made certain signs to affix as though it were their name, which I have in my power as witness of said friars.

And while the friars were yet rejoicing in this progress of the faith, and with the greatest joy and hope of bringing to Jesus Christ all those peoples of that kingdom who from the deaths and unjust wars of the past still remained alive, for there were not a few, eighteen tyrannical Spanish cavalrymen, with twelve foot, which were thirty altogether, came into a certain place there, and they brought with them a great load of idols taken from other provinces of the Indians, and the captain of those thirty Spaniards called a lord of this land into which they had entered and told him to take that load of idols and distribute it throughout his land, selling each idol for a male or female Indian to be a slave, and threatening him that

if he did not do this, there would be war. This lord, obliged by fear to do what he had been required, distributed the idols throughout his land, and he ordered his vassals to take them and worship them, and to give him male and female Indians to give to the Spaniards to make slaves of them. The Indians, in fear, whoever had two children would give one, and who had three gave two, and in this wise did perform that vile sacrilegious commerce, and the lord or cacique [chief] contented the Spaniards, who called themselves Christians.

One of these impious infernal thieves, called Juan Garcia, being taken sick and near to death, had two baskets of idols underneath his bed, and he ordered an Indian woman who served him to see to it that those idols not be given in exchange for chickens or such goods, because they were very good ones, but rather each one for a slave. And finally, with this will and testament, and his mind taken up with this care, the wretch died, and who can doubt that his resting place is now among the fires of hell?

Look now here and consider what the progress and religion and examples of Christianity is of those Spaniards who go to the Indies, what honor they bring to God and procure for Him, in what wise they work so that He may be known and adored by those peoples, what care they take that in those souls there be sown and doth grow and prosper the Holy Faith, and judge whether this sin be less than that of Jeroboam, *qui peccare fecit Israel* ["Who made Israel sin," 2 Kings 17:21] by making the two golden calves that the people should worship, or be equal to that of Judas, or more scandal has caused. These, then, are the works of the Spaniards who go to the Indies, which in sooth many, yea infinite times, owing to the greed and covetousness which they have for gold, have sold and still today do sell and deny Jesus Christ, time and time again.

The Indians having seen that it had not been true what the friars had promised them, that no Spaniards should enter, and seeing furthermore that the Spaniards themselves had brought idols from other lands to sell, when they themselves had delivered over to the friars all their own gods so that they might be burned and one God alone worshipped, the entire land thereabout rose up in indignation against the friars, and they went to them and said: "Why have you lied to us and deceived us, telling us that no Christians would enter into these lands? And why have you burned our idols, for your Christians bring other gods from other lands, to sell here? Were not our gods better than those of other nations?" The friars appeased them as best they could, though having naught in truth to reply, and they went to seek out the thirty Spaniards, to tell them the harm they had done. They ordered them to go, but they would not, instead giving the Indians to understand that the friars it was who had bade them come to that place, which was a most consummate piece of malice. At last, the Indians resolved to slay the friars; the friars, having been told of the plan by several Indians, did flee one night, and after they had fled, the Indians came to understand the innocence and virtue of the friars and the evil of the Spaniards and they sent messengers for fifty leagues after them, praying that they should turn back and begging their forgiveness for the distress they had caused them. The friars, like the good servants of God that they were, and mindful of those souls, and believing them, returned to that land and were received like angels, the Indians doing them a thousand services, and they remained there for four or five months more. And because those other evil Christians never wanted to depart those lands, nor could the viceroy, despite all his efforts, remove them, for it is far from New Spain (although he caused them to be denounced as traitors), and because they did not cease from working their accustomed insults and outrages upon the Indians, it seemed to the friars that sooner or later, against such evil deeds the Indians would become resentful and perhaps fall upon them. And they thought this especially since they could not preach to the Indians with good conscience about what they would, and without constant alarms owing to the Spaniards' evil works, and so they resolved to forsake that kingdom, and so it was left without the light and sustenance of doctrine, and those souls condemned to that same darkness of ignorance and spiritual poverty in which they then were, for they had been deprived at the most seasonable time of the remedy and watering of the news and knowledge of God, which they had begun to take with the most fervid pleasure, as though we had taken from plants sowed within but a few days, the water of their sustenance. And all this because of the inexplicable sinfulness and consummate evil of those Spaniards.

The Virgin of Guadalupe

The same process of inculturation that transformed paganism in the Mediterranean world of late antiquity and the pagan cultures of medieval Europe occurred in the New World. A major event was the appearance of the Virgin Mary to a poor Indian, Juan Diego, in 1531. When challenged by the Spanish bishop to prove his claim, Juan Diego unfurled his cloak. According to Christian legend, the rose petals he had gathered in honor of the virgin had disappeared, replaced by a mysterious portrait of Mary. The Virgin of Guadalupe inspired the construction of a cathedral in Mexico City, on the site where the Aztec goddess Tonantzin had been worshiped. But more significantly, the Virgin was clearly an Indian maiden. She was someone who heard the sighs of the poor and the oppressed, not just in Mexico but throughout the Americas. Under the pontificate of John Paul II, she became the patron saint of the Western Hemisphere, and Juan Diego was canonized, that is, made a saint.

Other elements of Christianity were inculturated in the lands colonized by the Spanish and Portuguese. In an effort to eliminate the practice of human sacrifice, the Spanish introduced a novel crucifix: it featured only Jesus' head at the center of the cross beams, and his hands on the cross bar. There was no body. Instead, Jesus' hands opened to welcome his children. The actual experience of Indians at the hands of Europeans, however, was one of brutal sacrifice, and today a more frequently seen crucifix features a battered and bloody Jesus. This savior was intimately familiar with the sufferings of the Indians. The festival of the Day of the Dead—a celebration memorializing loved ones who have died—was incorporated into All Saints' Day and All Souls' Day, 1 and 2 November. The practice of cemetery visits and all-night parties persists, and though it is not officially a Christian celebration, most Catholic Christians in Central America see it as both Christian and indigenous.

The Reading

Virgilio Elizondo is a Catholic priest and theologian from San Antonio, Texas, where he grew up in the Mexican barrio. His childhood was rich in love, family, and religion, although poor by economic standards. Ordained to the priesthood in 1963, he learned that he was in a privileged minority among a disprivileged marginalized group. His experiences working with the Mexican American community of San Antonio radicalized him and led him to become a voice for the poor in the struggle for freedom and equality. The experience of marginality helped him to develop what he called *mestizaje*, which he sees as a blend of Mexican and American culture and theology. *Mestizaje* "is the most common phenomenon in the evolution of the human species," namely, the mixture of different races. More broadly, however, it is the celebration of the combination of skin color, language, food, music, religion—everything that goes into a culture. Thus, Elizondo concludes that "the future is mestizo," that is, mixed.

In the essay "Our Lady of Guadalupe as a Cultural Symbol," written in 1977, Elizondo describes the historical and theological significance of the apparition of the Virgin of Guadalupe for Mexican Christianity. He shows how the vision inculturated indigenous traditions into Spanish Catholicism, giving new meaning and significance to the gospel message.

Questions to Consider

1. Why is it possible to reinterpret, rather than reject, pagan symbols, according to Elizondo?

2. What was the historical context of Juan Diego's vision? What is the significance of that context?

3. How did the apparition change Mexican Christianity?

4. Elizondo argues that a new Christianity emerged with the appearance of the Virgin of Guadalupe, "a new cultural expression of Christianity in the Americas." Do you think this includes Protestant Christianity? Why or why not?

5. Why is the Virgin Mary important to Catholic and Orthodox Christians? Why is she less important for Protestant Christians?

6. Think about the contrast between the writings of de las Casas and those of Elizondo. How do you account for the differences? Would you agree with Elizondo on the transformative power of the Virgin of Guadalupe? Why or why not?

Our Lady of Guadalupe as a Cultural Symbol

VIRGILIO ELIZONDO

Nowadays we realize that religious symbols which the theologian has labeled as "popular" religion and has looked upon as a species of pagan practice do not have to be rejected, but reinterpreted. In past decades the tendency of rational theology was to consider symbols as fantasies, to underline their ambiguity, and therefore to speak of them only in negative terms. This leads to an opposition between the religion of the people, which is not looked upon as true faith, and faith in Christ, which appears as the religion of the intellectual elite. A closer view of reality leads to a different understanding.[1] Even to the theologian, popular devotion appears ambiguous; nevertheless, it is the way the people relate to the God of Jesus. Therefore, from the pastoral as well as from the theological point of view, we have to try to answer the following question: What is the meaning of popular symbols and how do they function in relation to the Gospel? In this article I will try to clarify the problem by considering one of the most important living symbols of the Catholicism of the Americas: Our Lady of Guadalupe.

If Our Lady of Guadalupe had not appeared, the collective struggles of the Mexican people to find meaning in their chaotic existence would have created her. The cultural clash[2] of sixteenth-century Spain and Mexico was reconciled in the brown Lady of Tepeyac[3] in a way no other symbol can rival. In her the new *mestizo*[4] race, born of the violent encounter between Europe and indigenous America, finds its meaning, uniqueness, and unity. Guadalupe is the key to understanding the Christianity of the New World[5] and the Christian consciousness of the Mexicans and the Mexican Americans of the United States.

HISTORICAL CONTEXT OF THE APPARITION

To appreciate the profound meaning of Guadalupe it is important to know the historical setting at the time of the apparition. Suddenly an exterior force, the white men of Europe, intruded on the closely knit and well-developed system of time-space relationships of the pre-Columbian civilizations.[6] Neither had ever heard of the other, nor had any suspicion that the other group existed. Western historiographers have studied the conquest from the justifying viewpoint of the European colonizers, but there is another perspective, that of the conquered. With the conquest, the world of the indigenous peoples of Mexico had, in effect, come to an end. The final battles in 1521 were not just a victory in warfare, but the end of a civilization. At first, some tribes welcomed the Spaniards and joined them in the hope of being liberated from Aztec domination. Only after the conquest did they discover that the defeat of the Aztecs was in effect the defeat of all the natives of their land.[7] This painful Calvary of the Mexican people began when Cortez landed on Good Friday, April 22, 1519. It ended with the final battle on August 13, 1521. It was a military as well as a theological overthrow, for their capital had been conquered, their women violated, their temples destroyed, and their gods defeated.

We cannot allow the cruelty of the conquest to keep us from appreciating the heroic efforts of the early missioners. Their writings indicated that it was their intention to found a new Christianity more in conformity with the Gospel, not simply a continuation of that in Europe. They had been carefully prepared by the universities of Spain. Immediate efforts were made to evangelize the native Mexicans. The lifestyle of the missioners, austere poverty and simplicity, was in stark contrast to that of the conquistadors. Attempts were made to become one with the people and to preach the Gospel in their own language and through their customs and traditions. Yet the missioners were limited by the socio-religious circumstances of their time. Dialogue was severely limited, since neither side understood the other. The Spaniards judged the Mexican world from within the categories of their own Spanish world vision. Iberian communication was based on philosophical and theological abstractions and direct, precise speech. The missioners were convinced that truth in itself was sufficient to bring rational persons to conversion. They were not aware of the totally different way of communicating truth, especially divine truth, which the native Mexicans believed could only be adequately communicated through flower and song.[8] Even the best of the missioners could not penetrate the living temple of the Mexican consciousness.

This was also the time of the first *audiencia* of Guzmán which was noted for its corruption and abuses of the Indians. During this period the church was in constant conflict with the civil authorities because of these authorities' excessive avarice, corruption, and cruel treatment of the natives. The friars were good men who gradually won the love and respect of the common people. However, the religious convictions of generations would not give way easily, especially those of a people who firmly believed that the traditions of their ancestors were the way of the gods. As the friars tried to convert the wise men of the Indians by well-prepared theological exposition, the Indians discovered that the friars were in effect trying to eliminate the religion of their ancestors. The shock of human sacrifices led many of the missioners to see everything else in the native religion as diabolical, whereas the shock of the Spaniards' disregard for life by killing in war kept the Indians from seeing anything good or authentic in the conquerors' religion. This mutual scandal made communication difficult.[9] Furthermore, the painful memory of the conquest and new hardships imposed upon the Indians made listening to a "religion of love" difficult. Efforts to communicate remained at the level of words, but never seemed to penetrate to the level of the symbols of the people, which contained the inner meanings of their world vision. For the Indians these attempts at conversion by total rupture with the ways of their ancestors were a deeper form of violence than the physical conquest itself. Christianity had in some fashion been brought over, but it had not yet been implanted. The Indians and missioners heard each other's words but interpretation was at a standstill. Many heroic efforts were made, but little fruit had been produced. The missioners continued in prayer and self-sacrifice to ask for the ability to communicate the Gospel.

THE APPARITIONS AND THEIR MEANING

In 1531, ten years after the conquest, an event happened whose origins are clouded in mystery, yet its effects have been monumental and continuous. Early documentation about what happened does not exist, yet the massive effect which the appearance of Our Lady of Guadalupe had and continues to have on the Mexican people cannot be denied. The meaning of the happening has been recorded throughout the years in the collective memory of the people. Whatever happened in 1531 is not past history but continues to live, to grow in meaning, and to influence the lives of millions today.

According to the legend, as Juan Diego, a Christianized Indian of common status, was going from his home in the *barriada* near Tepeyac, he heard beautiful music. As he approached the source of the music, a lady appeared to him. Speaking in Nahuatl, the language of the conquered, she commanded Juan Diego to go to the palace of the bishop of Mexico at Tlateloco and to tell him that the Virgin Mary, "Mother of the true God through whom one lives," wanted a temple to be built at Tepeyac so that in it she "can show and give forth all my love, compassion, help, and defense to all the inhabitants of this land . . . to hear their lamentations and remedy their miseries, pain, and sufferings." After two unsuccessful attempts to convince the bishop of the Lady's authenticity, the Virgin wrought a miracle. She sent Juan Diego to pick roses in a place where only desert plants existed. Then she arranged the roses in his cloak and sent him to the bishop with the sign he had demanded. As Juan Diego unfolded his cloak in the presence of the bishop, the roses fell to the ground and the image of the Virgin appeared on his cloak.

The Mexican people came to life again because of Guadalupe. Their response was a spontaneous explosion of pilgrimages, festivals, and conversions to the religion of the Virgin. Out of the meaningless and chaotic existence of the postconquest years, a new meaning erupted. The immediate response of the church ranged from silence to condemnation. Early sources indicated that the missioners, at least those who were writing, were convinced that it was an invention of the Indians and an attempt to re-establish their previous religion. Yet gradually the church accepted the apparition of Guadalupe as the Virgin Mary, Mother of God. In 1754 Pope Benedict XIV officially recognized the Guadalupe tradition by bringing it into the official liturgy of the church.[10]

To understand the response of Juan Diego and the Mexican people it is necessary to view the event not through western categories of thought but through the system of communication of the Nahuatls of that time. What for the Spanish was an aberration for the conquered and dying Mexican nation was the rebirth of a new civilization. The details of the image conveyed a profound meaning to the Indian peoples. In reading the legend, the first striking detail is that Juan Diego heard beautiful music, which alone was enough to establish the heavenly origin of the Lady. For the Indians, music was the medium of divine communication. The Lady appeared on the sacred hill of Tepeyac, one of the four principal sacrificial sites in Mesoamerica. It was the sanctuary of Tonantzin, the Indian virgin mother of the gods. The dress was a pale red, the color of the spilled blood of sacrifices and the color of Huitzilopochtli, the god who gave and preserved life. Indian blood had been spilled on Mexican soil and fertilized mother earth and now something new came forth. Red was also the color for the East, the direction from which the sun arose victorious after it had died for the night. The predominant color of the portrait is the blue-green of the mantle, which was the royal color of the Indian gods. It was also the color of Ometeotl, the origin of all natural forces. In the color psychology of the native world, blue-green stood at the center of the cross of opposing forces and signified the force unifying the opposing tensions at work in the world. One of the prophetic omens which the native wise men interpreted as a sign of the end of their civilization was the appearance, ten years before the conquest, of a large body of stars in the sky. The stars had been one of the signs of the end, and now the stars on her mantle announced the beginning of a new era. Being supported by heavenly creatures could have meant two, not necessarily contradictory, things. First, she came on her own and, therefore, was not brought over by the Spaniards. Second, the Indians saw each period of time as supported by a god. This was recorded by a symbol representing the era being carried by a lesser creature. The Lady carried by heavenly creatures marked the appearance of a new era. She wore the black band of maternity around her waist, the sign that she was with child. This child was her offering to the New World. The Lady was greater than the greatest in the native pantheon because she hid the sun but did not extinguish it. Thus she was more powerful than the sun god, their principal deity. The Lady was also greater than their moon god, for she stood upon the moon, yet did not crush it. However, great as this Lady was, she was not a goddess. She wore no mask as the Indian gods did, and her vibrant, compassionate face in itself told anyone who looked upon it that she was the compassionate mother.

The fullness of the apparition developed with the Lady's request for a temple. In the Indian hieroglyphic recordings of the conquest, a burning, destroyed temple was the sign of the end of their civilization and way of life. Therefore, the request for the temple was not just for a building where her image could be venerated, but for a new way of life. It would express continuity with their past and yet radically transcend that past. One civilization had indeed ended, but now another one was erupting out of their own mother soil.

Not only did the Lady leave a powerful message in the image, but the credentials she chose to present herself to the New World were equally startling. For the bishop, the roses from the desert were a startling phenomenon; for the Indians, they were the sign of a new life. Flowers and music to them were the supreme way of communication through which the presence of the invisible, all-powerful God could be expressed. As the apparition had begun with music, giving it an atmosphere of the divine, it reached its peak with flowers, the sign of life beyond life, the sign that beyond human suffering and death there was something greater-than-life in the dwelling place of the wonderful giver of life.[11]

The narration as it exists today does not appear to be historical, at least in the western scientific understanding of the word. It is not based on objective, verifiable, written documentation. However, it is a historical narrative to the people who have recorded their past through this specific literary genre.[12] Furthermore, popular religion has often been too easily labeled by outsiders, especially sociologists and theologians of the dominant groups, as alienating and superstitious. Popular piety is not necessarily and of itself alienating; in fact, for a defeated, conquered, and colonized people, it serves as a final resistance against the way of the powerful. Popular religion becomes alienating when agents of religion use it to legitimize and maintain the status quo. However, it becomes liberating when used as a source of unity and strength in the struggle for dignity and subsequent change against the powerful of society. It is the collective voice of the dominated people crying out: "We will not be eliminated; we will live on! We have been conquered, but we will not be destroyed." In the first stages, it gives meaning to an otherwise meaningless existence and thus a reason for living. As the triumphant group has its way of recording history, so those who have been silenced by subjugation have their interpretation of the past. Their accounts exist in an even deeper way. For the defeated and powerless, history is recorded and lived in the collective memory of the people: their songs, dances, poetry, art, legends, and popular religion. For the powerful, history is only a written record, whereas for the defeated, history is life, for it is the memory that keeps telling them that things are not as they ought to be. This memory cannot be destroyed or opposed by the powerful because they do not understand it. Accordingly it is not surprising that in the history of Mexico there is no place for the Tepeyac tradition. Guadalupe, the most persistent influence in Mexico, is found only in the folklore and popular religious practices of the masses.

At the time of the apparition, the Spanish were building churches over the ruins of the Aztec temples. The past grandeur and power of Tenochtitlan-Tlatelolco (the original name of present-day Mexico City) was being transformed into the glory of New Spain. Juan Diego dared to go to the center of power and with supernatural authority (as the Lady commanded) demanded that the powerful should change their plans and build a temple—a symbol of a new way of life—not within the grandeur of the city, in accordance with the plans of Spain, but within the *barriada* of Tepeyac in accordance with the desires of the people. The hero of the story is a simple conquered Indian from the *barriada* who is a symbol of the poor and oppressed refusing to be destroyed by the dominant group. This story's purpose was to convert the bishop, the symbol of the new Spanish power group, and to turn the attention of the conquering group from amassing wealth and power to the periphery of society where the people continued to live in poverty and misery.

The narration is only a wrapping for the continuing struggle of the masses for survival and liberation from the imposition of the ways of the powerful, a struggle which has been going on for nearly five hundred years. Through unceasing struggle, a dynamic tradition has emerged from the primitive story. This tradition has come to stand for the dignity, identity, unity, personal and collective emancipation, and the liberation movements of the Mexican people. Miguel Hidalgo fought for Mexican independence under the banner of Our Lady of Guadalupe. Emiliano Zapata led his agrarian reform under her protection. Cesar Chavez battled against one of the most powerful economic blocks in the United States under the banner of Our Lady of Guadalupe and succeeded in his struggle for justice against all human odds. This tradition was relegated to the area of fable or legend not because it was lacking in historical veracity, but precisely because its living historical veracity cannot be

fully accepted by the powerful political, economic, educational, sociological, or religious elite of any moment of history. The full truth of Tepeyac is the obvious disturbing truth of the millions of poor, powerless, peripheral oppressed of our society. Guadalupe's significance is the voice of the masses calling upon the elite to leave their economic, social, political, and religious thrones of pseudo-security and work with them—within the *movimientos de la base*—in transforming society into a more human place for everyone.

It was through the presence of Our Lady of Guadalupe that the possibility of cultural dialogue began. The missioners' activity had won a basis of authentic understanding, bringing to a climax their work of pre-evangelization. As at Bethlehem when the Son of God became man in Jesus and began the overthrow of the power of the Roman Empire, at Tepeyac Christ entered the soil of the Americas and began to reverse the European domination of the people in those lands. Tepeyac marks the beginning of the reconquest and the birth of Mexican Christianity.

It is from within the poor that the process of conversion is begun. The poor become the heralds of a new humanity. This critical challenge of our compassionate and liberating mother to the powerful of any moment and place in the Americas continues today; it is the dynamic voice and power of the poor and oppressed of the Americas groaning and travailing for a more human existence. Her presence is not a pacifier but an energizer which gives meaning, dignity, and hope to the peripheral and suffering people of today's societies. Her presence is the new power of the powerless to triumph over the violence of the powerful. In her, differences are assumed and the cathartic process of the cultural-religious encounter of Europe-America begins, but it has a long way to go. Nevertheless, it has begun and is in process. This is the continuing miracle of Guadalupe—the mother—queen of the Americas. Now, the dream of the early missionaries, a new church and a New World, has definitely begun. The new people of the land would now be the *mestizo* people—*la raza*—and the new Christianity would be neither the cultural expression of Iberian Catholicism nor the mere continuation of the pre-Cortez religions of indigenous America, but a new cultural expression of Christianity in the Americas.

Today, theologians cannot afford to ignore the function and meaning of popular religion for the popular masses.[13] A theologian's task is not the canonization or rejection of the religious symbols of the people, but a continuous reinterpretation of them in relation to the whole Gospel. In this way popular religion will not be alienating but will help to lead people to a deeper knowledge of the saving God. It will not be alienating or enslaving, but salvific and liberating. Popular religion which is regenerated (not eliminated) by the Gospel becomes the invincible and efficacious power of the powerless in their struggle for liberation.[14]

For millions of Mexicans and Mexican Americans of the United States, Our Lady of Guadalupe is the temple in whom and through whom Christ's saving presence is continually incarnated in the soil of the Americas and it is through her mediation that:

> He shows strength with his arm.
> He scatters the proud in the imagination of
>   their hearts.
> He puts down the mighty from their thrones,
> and exalts the oppressed.
> He fills the hungry with good things,
> and the rich he sends away empty handed.
>   (Luke 1:51–52)

Notes

1. For an excellent exposition of this point in relation to the popular religion of Mexico see Jean Meyer, *La Cristiada* (Mexico: Siglo Veintiuno Editores, 1974), 316-323.
2. "Culture" is used here as all those solutions that a group finds in order to survive its natural and social situation. It is the complete world vision—norms, values, and rituals—of a group. Spain and Mexico had very highly developed cultures at the time of the clash.
3. *Tepeyac* is the hill north of Mexico City where the sanctuary of Tonantzin (which means our Mother)—the female aspect of the deity—was located. It was one of the most sacred pilgrimage sites of the Americas. Bernardino de Sahagún, *Historia general de las cosas de Nueva Espana* (Mexico, written in mid-1500s) 3:352.
4. *Mestizo* is the Spanish word for a person who is born from parents of different races. In contemporary Latin America it is acquiring a positive meaning and the arrival of Columbus is celebrated as the day of *la raza* (the race), meaning the new race formed of Europe and Native America. There is no English translation of this concept as the English word "half-breed" (a social rather than a biological term) is very derogatory and would have a completely different meaning.
5. For the first twelve missioners who came to Mexico, "New World" was a theological term indicating the place where the new Christianity was now to emerge. It would not be simply a continuation of the Christianity of Europe, but a new, evangelical Christianity. Silvio Arturo Zavala, *Recuerdo de Vasco de Quiroga* (Mexico: Editorial Porrua, 1965); Jacques Lafaye, *Quetzalcoatl et Guadalupe* (Paris: Gallimard, 1974) 52–67.
6. Some of the Native American cultures were very well developed and in many ways superior to those of the Europe of the sixteenth century. For a good description of this, see: Miguel LeonPortilla, *Aztec Thought and Culture* (Norman, Okla.: University of Oklahoma Press, 1963) esp. 134–76.
7. Octavio Paz, *The Labyrinth of Solitude* (New York: Penguin, 1961) 93-96.
8. Leon-Portilla, *Aztec Thought and Culture,* 74–79.
9. Jacques Soustelle, *La Vie quotidienne des Azteques a la veille de la conquete espagnole* (Paris: Hachette 1955).
10. For a good description of the development of the Guadalupe tradition, see Lafaye, *Quetzalcoatl et Guadalupe,* 281–396.
11. Leon-Portilla, *Aztec Thought and Culture,* 102.
12. For a good example of a scholar who has been able to penetrate the historical consciousness alive in the folklore of the people, see: Nathan Wachtel, *La Vision des vaincus* (Paris: Gallimard, 1971); Rodolfo Acuna, *Occupied America* (New York: Harper & Row, 1981).
13. Pope Paul VI, *Evangelii Nuntiandi* (8 December 1975), sections 48 (on popular piety) and 63 (on adaptation and fidelity in expression). See also Meyer, *La Cristiada,* 307, which brings out the false way that North American and European missioners have judged Mexican Catholicism.
14. *La Cristiada,* 275–323.

Christianity in North America

The treatment of the indigenous peoples in the New World varied with the location, religious group, and time period. The Spanish and Portuguese—among the first Europeans to arrive—pursued a policy of aggressive exploitation, mitigated somewhat by the efforts of missionaries. The colonists used, and abused, the Indians, although they also intermarried with Indians so that a new people, the *mestizo,* came to populate vast territories in a subservient role to the white colonialists. With South and Central America virtually closed, the French settled primarily in North America, traveling along the Mississippi and the Missouri, and north into Canada. Jesuit missionaries, called "black robes," accompanied the trappers, loners who pursued an independent, nomadic existence not terribly different from that of the indigenous peoples. The black robes were often brutally tortured as they attempted to enter hostile Indian territory. But they also succeeded in catechizing many natives, who retained their customs, culture, and language.

Unlike the French, the Spanish, and the Portuguese—who attempted to bring the indigenous peoples to Christianity—the English colonists, primarily Protestant, tended to avoid those whom they called "savages." The English skirmished with Indians over land and territory, but otherwise, with a few exceptions, had little to do with the Indians. It was only as English settlements in North America increased that competition for land arose—a tragic story of broken treaties, betrayals, and massacres. As more Europeans crossed the Atlantic, population pressures squeezed Indians further west, onto smaller tracts of land. The Indian Removal Act of 1830 forced the evacuation of thousands of Indians from east of the Mississippi River, to the Indian Territory in Oklahoma west of the river. Thousands died on the "Trail of Tears," though 100,000 survived.

Nineteenth-century U.S. history was characterized by the clash of competing economic systems: agriculture versus hunting-gathering. By destroying buffalo by the millions, Europeans ruined the Indians' commissary, as one U.S. army officer called the buffalo. Enclosure on reservations only barely prevented mass starvation and the complete extermination of Native Americans. Both Protestant and Catholic missionaries instituted a boarding school system for Indians in which children were separated from their parents, punished for speaking their native languages, and taught to be "Americans." Clearly, Christians believed that European civilization was concomitant to Christianity: the two were inextricable in their minds. It is only with the rise in environmental awareness in recent decades that interest in Indian religions and lifeways has emerged. That, coupled with a resurgence of Native American consciousness of identity, has generated interest in preserving native cultures, not merely as artifacts of bygone life but as models for human survival.

At the close of the twentieth century, Native Americans began to reclaim their heritage by calling things by their traditional names. Christian missionaries had identified all things native as heathen or, worse, devilish and diabolical. Sacred native sites, in Christian eyes, belonged to Satan: Devil's Tower, Devil's Lake, Devil's

Post Pile. Native Americans returned to names that reflected the specialness or sacredness of their holy places: Spirit Lake, for example, replaced Devil's Lake; and Paha Sapa replaced the Black Hills, from which the Lakota tribe had originated, according to its own sacred stories. Native Christianity in North America began to look more indigenous. Traditional Indian decorative arts, such as quilting or beading, became incorporated into altar cloths and chasubles. Eagle feathers and sage smoke replaced censers and incense. A star quilt might adorn the wall behind the altar, and a native dance might express praise of God. Church didn't have to look "European"; it could look "Indian."

The Reading

It has been a long journey for Native American Christians who wish to claim both their traditional heritage and their new identity as Christians. These Christians are now interpreting Christianity in nonoppressive, inclusive ways that celebrate and uphold traditional values, yet clearly place Jesus Christ at the center of life and worship. In the reading that follows, Steve Charleston argues for an "Old Testament" of Native America that recognizes the fact that Indians had a covenant with a creator God—just as the Israelites of the Bible had—prior to their encounter with Christ. Denying one's native heritage makes it harder, rather than easier, to be a Native American Christian. Charleston's essay appears in a book on liberation theology (see Chapter Seven) titled *Lift Every Voice: Constructing Christian Theologies from the Underside* (1990), and so he takes both an educational or informational approach and an advocacy position in the piece.

Questions to Consider

1. Compare and contrast Charleston's approach with that of the traditional missionary. How are they similar? How are they different?

2. How far can inculturation go before Christianity departs from its origins? Can outward forms vary if the interior message remains the same? What is nonnegotiable?

3. Think back to the previous chapter and the debate between Alfred Loisy and Adolf von Harnack. Who best describes the model of inculturation? Who would resist this model?

4. What do you think about the idea of an "Old Testament" of Native America? Is Charleston's comparison of the Israelite story with the Native American story compelling? Logical? Why or why not? Can you envision "Old Testaments" from other cultures inculturating Christianity into specific ethnic forms?

5. Can Christianity survive if inculturation is resisted? In other words, is there only a single form or practice of Christianity? Should Native American Christianity be identical to European Christianity? Why or why not?

The Old Testament of Native America

STEVE CHARLESTON

I come from Oklahoma. I was born in the southern part of the state in a small town called Duncan. My grandfather and great-grandfather were Presbyterian ministers. Like most people in our tribe, the Choctaw Nation, they were Presbyterians who preached and sang in Choctaw. My own family was tied up with the oil fields. We moved out of Duncan and went up to Oklahoma City as the jobs changed. That means that I experienced a number of different churches. I was baptized a Southern Baptist, but I've known everything from Roman Catholic to Unitarian to the Baha'i faith. I think that's partly because Oklahoma Indian life can be so eclectic. There are dozens of tribes to go along with dozens of churches. Things are very mixed in Oklahoma. It's a cultural patchwork quilt laid down over ranch land, red dirt, and eastern timberland. I've inherited some of that mixture and it's followed me around wherever I've gone.

I am an Indian. I am a Christian. Being both wasn't always easy. Like many other Native People, I've known my share of confusion, frustration, anger, and struggle. But I've also known a lot of hope, joy, and visions. So the two balance each other out. Today I feel comfortable talking about Christianity as a faith that emerges from Native America. I came to that feeling after many years of travel through different Native communities. I would credit a great many Native men, women, and children (Traditional, Christian, and a little of both) as being my real teachers. They helped me to grow up and find the sense of spiritual balance that I think is central to life. Of course, keeping the balance takes a lifetime, but at least I have a place to stand.

The place I stand is in the original covenant God gave to Native America. I believe with all my heart that God's revelation to Native People is second to none. God spoke to generations of Native People over centuries of our spiritual development. We need to pay attention to that voice, to be respectful of the covenant, and to be unafraid to lift up the new covenant as the fulfillment of the ancient promise made to the Native People of North America. That means seeing Jesus not as a white plastic messiah taken off the dashboard of a car and dipped in brown to make things look more Indian, but a living Christ that arises from the Native covenant and speaks with the authority and authenticity of Native America.

I have been talking about what I call a Native People's Christian theology for over fifteen years. I started out when I was one of only four Native People in seminary and I am still doing it today. So I feel a deep commitment to this new theology. I want to do all that I can to help bring Native People together. That means healing the false divisions brought into our tribes by Western colonialism. It means helping Native People who think of themselves as being either Traditional or Christian find common ground, a common center. In time, it will mean carrying the voice of Native America around the world to join with millions of other Christians in a second reformation. I may not be around for that time, but I want to help make it happen by proclaiming the indigenous theology of this continent.

And that brings me full circle, because I also believe that theology is autobiography. If we are really honest about all of this, about all of the millions of words we produce each year on theology, we have to admit that when we start out trying to talk about God, we usually wind up talking about ourselves. At least, between the lines. So, I think you can read Oklahoma in what I have to say: and Presbyterian preachers baptizing Native People in the river, and Choctaw camp meetings, and some struggle to be made whole. I also hope that you can hear commitment, energy, and strength, and that you recognize the power of God to help and to heal and a messiah who is changing the world.

Imagine a supermarket: not one of the small local convenience stores, but a really big supermarket, the kind of place with aisle after aisle of things from which to choose. The shelves are loaded. There are hundreds of different brands. There are different departments or sections. The merchandise is carefully organized to make shopping easier. This is a real American store, a place that testifies to our abundance and our right to choose for ourselves.

Now imagine that instead of groceries, this supermarket sells theologies. As you roll your cart along the aisles, what do you see? Dozens of different brands: a theology for every taste. There is a department for basic Western theologies, the old standbys. There are sections reserved for feminist theology, for Black theology, for liberation theology. There are shelves for African theology and Asian theology. There is even a gourmet section for New Age theologies. At first glance, it seems that this supermarket has a Christian theology from every culture and community. Almost. But not quite. Something is missing. As strange as it may seem, the Great American Religious Supermarket is incomplete. It has some shelves that are standing empty. Go down the aisles and try to find the section for a Native People's Christian theology. It isn't there. Look for a department called Native American or American Indian Christian theology. Still not there. The fact is: in all of the abundance of Christian theologies flooding the religious marketplace in contemporary America, one is conspicuous by its absence. There is no strong presence of Native American Christians in the theological marketplace.

Why? That's the simple but profound question that needs to be answered. Why have Native People not entered visibly into the Christian debate? Why is there no quickly recognizable Christian theology from Native America? Why not several brands for Native Americans to choose from? Why not a whole shelf of theologies from Native Christian theologians? Is it because they are content to let others do the talking for them? Or are there other reasons that need to be examined, understood, proclaimed?

"Conspicuous by their absence." That's the phrase I used and I wonder if you caught it? There is an irony in using those words, because I doubt if Native People have really been conspicuous by their absence. I doubt it, because I have rarely heard the question "Why?" asked before. Not too many Christians seem troubled by the absence of a Native People's Christian theology. I think if we are honest with one another, we will admit that most religious shoppers have gone down the aisles and never noticed that Native People were missing. They assumed that the supermarket was complete: new products arrive daily, old products are repackaged—new and improved theologies, special sales on hot items. In all of the abundance, in all of the excitement, I don't believe many people have noticed a few empty shelves. This fact alone raises another question. Why have so very few people questioned the absence of Native

Americans? Given the proliferation of theologies from many racial, cultural, ethnic, and economic communities, given the rise of theologies from the feminist community, given the increased awareness on the part of consumers of theology why has the absence of Native People's theology gone unnoticed?

If we tackle that question first, we may find that we are starting to surface some clues to the more fundamental reasons for Native America's silence in the Christian debate. Here is a place to begin: many people may have overlooked the absence of a Native People's Christian theology because they assumed it was covered by the supermarket sections reserved for spirituality. I think that's a fair guess. After all, there are many shelves these days loaded with works on Native American spirituality. Some are historical, others are anthropological or biographical; some are journalistic accounts by white authors who went to live with the Indians and returned to share the exotic secrets they discovered. In fact, there has been something of a minor gold rush in Native American "spirituality," with lots of people writing about it. What is described as Native American spirituality crops up in all kinds of places, especially in the gourmet section of the theological supermarket. In a style not too far removed from the 1960s and early 1970s, it's become chic to be Indian again, or, at least, to know an Indian, particularly if that Indian is a medicine person. It's romantic, earthy, "creation centered."

The Native spirituality craze, therefore, may account for the neglect of a Native People's Christian theology. Well-intentioned shoppers may have simply thought that this talk about spirituality was the voice of Native America in the religious dialogue. And up to a point, they're right. Traditional Native spirituality does represent a major and crucial voice for Native People. It is a voice that has frequently been misquoted, distorted, or co-opted, but it's a voice nonetheless. I am certainly not prepared to argue against a legitimate role for that spirituality. In fact, I am going to argue that this spirituality is something extremely central to Native America, and to the Christ, and faith. Still, the spirituality section alone does not complete the supermarket. It is still not an expression of a Native Christian viewpoint. As good (or bad) as these works may be at articulating Native tradition, they do not offer a clear voice for Native American Christianity. They are not a Native People's Christian theology. Instead they are the source for materials for that theology—they are reference points, or commentaries.

So far, we've said that the answer to why most people have ignored the absence of a Native People's Christian theology is because they thought they were getting it through Native "spirituality." But that still doesn't explain why the theology itself is missing. Now, we have a clue to follow. What would happen if instead of speaking about Native American spirituality we began speaking of an Old Testament of Native America? What would that do for us?

Well, first of all, it would give us a new vocabulary in dealing with what we've been describing as Native spirituality. For example, a great many of those books in the supermarket would become Old Testament commentaries. They would be books about the source material of Native America's Old Testament. Books about the traditions of Old Testament times, about the culture of Old Testament times, about the personalities of Old Testament times, and the theology of Old Testament times. We might start treating them more seriously and critically, since they would be describing the foundational theology for a contemporary Christian theology. They would have to be weighed and judged on a much finer scale than we have been accustomed to. The authors of these books would begin to seem like Old Testament scholars, not hack writers. Their standard of scholarship would be open to public inspection and criticism. Tossing off a book about "living with an Indian medicine woman" might not qualify as research so easily anymore. We would want to know how accurate the work was. How genuine. How consistent with any tradition. If Ralph Nader were a theologian, he would be proud of us for our new sense of comparison shopping.

What about the Old Testament scholars themselves? Who would they be? My own guess is that the gold rush would be over. Instead of Western writers hacking away at Native spirituality, we would begin to see the emergence of more theologians from within the Native community itself. That might not be as romantic, exotic, or exciting as what we've been used to, but I expect it would be a great deal more valuable. Native American women and men could finally speak for themselves, not as gurus for Western theological science fiction, but as reputable scholars for an Old Testament tradition. Their voices would be clear and distinct. They would be listened to seriously. These speakers would not necessarily be Christian, but they would be treated with respect by the Christian community, just as Jewish scholars are respected. Their contribution to the larger interfaith dialogue would be profound. It would change us. It would

open us up to a whole new dimension in theological exploration.

As a result, attitudes toward Native People and their Tradition would alter. Naming that Tradition an "Old Testament" is a powerful statement of recognition for Native America. It says that Native People are not just historical curiosities, footnotes for Western colonial expansion, but the living members of a world-class religious heritage. Since the first Western missionary or anthropologist walked into a Native community, the Tradition of Native America has been called everything but an Old Testament. It has been named by others. It has been named by the West, not the People themselves. It has been called "superstition," "tribal religion," "nature worship," "animism," "shamanism," "primitive," "Stone Age," "savage," "spirituality," anything and everything, but never an Old Testament. The namers themselves have had mixed motives, some innocent, some racist, some just ignorant. But the results have been the same: the names attached to the Old Testament of Native America have consigned that Tradition to the backwaters of serious Christian scholarship. Native American spiritual tradition has been considered the proper study of historians, ethnologists, anthropologists, or even the gourmet writers of the New Age, but not for most Christian theologians. There is a big difference for Western theologians between a "spirituality" and a "theology," just as there is between a "tradition" and the "Old Testament." By claiming the right to name the Tradition an Old Testament, Native America would be walking into the private club of Christian theology, even if that means coming in uninvited.

Finally, shifting our vocabulary to Old Testament language gives us an answer to that original question: Why hasn't there been a Native People's Christian theology? The whole purpose of such a theology would be to talk about the New Testament. It would be the Native perspective on Jesus and the gospels, on Paul, eschatology, redemption, salvation, sin, resurrection, community, grace, love, and God. To truly be a "Christian" theology, it would have to cover the whole range of ideas that form the Christian understanding of the New Testament. It would also have to be directly related to what we have always called the "Old Testament," i.e., the Old Testament of Israel. You can't have one without the other.

And there's the problem: you can't have a "new" testament if you don't have an "old" testament. Christians have invented those adjectives to distinguish between the original covenant relationship between

God and the people and the "new" relationship established through the person of Jesus as the Christ. For Western People those distinctions work. For Native People they don't work.

Why? Because Native People also have an "old" testament. They have their own original covenant relationship with the Creator and their own original understanding of God prior to the birth of a Christ. It is a Tradition that has evolved over centuries. It tells of the active, living, revealing presence of God in relation to Native People through generations of Native life and experience. It asserts that God was not an absentee landlord for North America. God was here, on this continent among this people, in covenant, in relation, in life. Like Israel itself, Native America proclaims that God is a God of all times and of all places and of all peoples. Consequently, the "old" testament of Native America becomes tremendously important. It is the living memory, the living tradition of a people's special encounter with the Creator of Life.

So what are Native People supposed to do with that memory when they pick up the New Testament? Forget it? Pretend it doesn't matter? Assume that millions of their ancestors were just ignorant savages who didn't have any ideas about the reality of God in their lives? Was God just kidding around? Was the Creator passing off disinformation onto Native America? Was it just a joke?

It should be painfully obvious that Native People have only one choice to make. To erase the collective memory of Native America would not only be a crime against humanity, but a macabre theological position that would so limit the nature of God as to cease to be Christian. Or Jewish. God is the God of all time, of all space, of all people. Moreover, God relates to humanity through love, not through disinformation. When God spoke to Native America, it wasn't a joke. It wasn't primitive. It wasn't Stone Age. It wasn't nature worship. It wasn't superstition. It was the call of God to all people to draw near, to listen, to believe, and to love. Did Native America hear this call? Yes. Did Native America encounter God? Yes. Did Native America remember that encounter and try to explain it to their children? Yes. Did they always get it right? No. Like any human community, Native America is finite and fallible. Its "old" testament is full of mistakes, false starts, guesses, hopes, dreams, wishes, just like any other Old Testament. And yet it is also full of truth, prophecy, and promise. It reveals something genuine and precious. It tells us a little more about the Creator we call God.

When Native People were denied access to that religious legacy, when they were told that their Old Testament was nothing more than a grab bag of primitive superstitions, when they were forbidden to share the memory with their own children, when they were commanded to undergo spiritual amnesia, to lose their memories, to go blank, to forget their own story and let others do the naming for them, it was exactly at this moment that any "New" Testament was jerked away from them. We need to press this point again: you cannot have a "new" testament if you do not have an "old" testament. You cannot fulfill what you do not have. The shelves are empty of a Native People's Christian theology because the theologians who would fill them have been brainwashed. They have been told to be content with another People's story, and to forget their own. They have been reduced to silence. It is the silence of any man or woman who cannot remember their own name. Who cannot remember where they came from. Who cannot remember having a family. Who cannot remember having a home. It is a silence of terror and of dread. An insane silence. A silence of isolation. The silence of a People who have been exiled from the love of their God.

The reason for proclaiming an Old Testament of Native America is to break the silence. It is my intention to be a Christian theologian. To be a Native Christian theologian. But I cannot do that if I am not allowed to name myself. To name my tradition, and to use it. I cannot write about Jesus of the gospels or the letters of Paul if I don't interpret them through the truth as I try to understand it. That means the truth of the original covenant that God maintained with Israel, the truth of the witness to Jesus as the Christ as it is upheld in the "new" covenant, and the truth of the covenant between God and the Native People as it is revealed in the ancient testimony of Native America. Like any theologian from any community that retains its memory of God through tradition, I have to work with at least three primary sources: the Old Testament of Israel, the New Testament of the Christian scriptures, and the Old Testament of my own People. The three are integral. They cannot be separated.

In saying this I am very aware of the negative reaction it can produce among Christians, among Jews, and among Native People themselves. The words "old" and "new" testaments account for part of that reaction. The words certainly are not accurate, nor do they promote interfaith understanding. The term Old Testament is too pejorative; it leaves the impression that it is something we can dismiss, something that has been replaced, something secondary. I know that within the Jewish community there is a strong reaction when Christians describe the Bible in this way. And yet, I feel bound by the words, as they have become a shorthand for signifying distinctions. At least for now. At least until people begin to accept the Native Old Testament for what it is. Then in a few years' time, we can bypass the words "Old Testament of Native America" and begin to speak of the Native Covenant.

Until that time, I want to push for recognition of a Native American Old Testament, even if it evokes a strong reaction from all directions. To be honest, *because* it evokes a strong reaction. The kind of silence I have described is not going to be broken by whispers, but by shouts. Therefore, I announce the Old Testament of Native America and invite others to do the same. Even if the language is imprecise, it is familiar language. It telegraphs a clear message across a wide spectrum. It makes Christians uncomfortable. It makes Jews uncomfortable. It makes Native People uncomfortable.

The discomfort arises because all of us have been conditioned to think of the Old Testament. Good, bad, or indifferent: we all know what we mean. We say the Old Testament and we know that we are referring to the first 39 books of the Bible. That's the Christian position, of course, but it is understood by both Native People and the Jewish community when Christians use the term in conversation or discourse. We all assume that there is only one Old Testament, just as Christians assert that there is only one New Testament. Challenging that assumption makes people nervous. To use the term *Old Testament* conventionally seems to question the validity of the traditional canon.

It also opens a closetful of theological and doctrinal issues. Can there be more than one "Old Testament"? If so, then what is the relationship between them? What is their relationship to the "New Testament"? Does one supplant the other? Where is the final claim on truth? Can the Christ be said to fulfill other Old Testaments? Wouldn't that be heresy at best and syncretism at worst? I doubt that I will be able to answer all of these questions here, anymore than I may be able to reassure all concerned that the Old Testament of Native America is a valid idea. Still, I think there are some basic points that may be covered and that may prove to be helpful.

First, my own awareness of a Native American Old Testament began to grow while I was sitting in an introductory Old Testament class during my first year of seminary. The professor described what was unique about the religious worldview of ancient Israel. He said that Israel, unlike its neighbors, had a special understanding of the relationship between God and humanity. This was the covenant between a single God and a particular People. It involved the promise of a homeland. It was sustained by the personal involvement of God in history. It was communicated through the prophets and the Law. It made Israel a nation. It brought them together as a People.

It was the most simple, important understanding of the Old Testament that we share as Christians. And yet, during that lecture, I couldn't help but make a list of comparisons in my mind. Each time the professor mentioned some aspect of the Old Testament story that was "unique" to early Israel, I was reminded of my own Tradition and People. To help you understand what I mean, I will repeat that list in abbreviated form:

1. God is one.
2. God created all that exists.
3. God is a God of human history.
4. God is a God of all time and space.
5. God is a God of all People.
6. God establishes a covenant relationship with the People.
7. God gives the People a "promised land."
8. The People are stewards of this land for God.
9. God gives the People a Law or way of life.
10. The People worship God in sacred spaces.
11. God raises up prophets and charismatic leaders.
12. God speaks through dreams and visions.
13. The People maintain a seasonal cycle of worship.
14. The People believe God will deliver them from their suffering.
15. God can become incarnate on earth.

These fifteen items for comparison each merit more discussion, but the point I wish to make is simply that the religious worldviews of ancient Israel and ancient Native America have much in common. This is not to say that their understandings were identical. There are many variations on the theme not only between the two communities, but within them as well. What is striking, however, is that for many key concepts the two traditions run parallel. Like Israel, Native America believed in the oneness of God; it saw God as the Creator of all existence; it knew that God was active and alive in the history of humanity; it remembered that the land had been given to the people in trust from God. Native People accepted the revelation from God as it was given to them through prophets and charismatic leaders; they recognized sacred ground and holy places in their worship; they maintained a seasonal liturgical calendar; they had a highly developed belief in the incarnational presence of God and expected that presence to be revealed in times of strife or disaster. Is it strange, therefore, that Native Americans would consider themselves to be in a covenant relationship to their Creator or that they would think of themselves as a People "chosen" by God? Take the names which the People used for themselves in their own languages and you get a clear sense of this: in the tribal languages, the many nations of Native America announced their identity as "The People" or "The Human Beings." Moreover, they tied this identity to the land given to them by God. It was this land-based covenant that gave them their identity as "The People," as the community special to a loving God.

Comparisons, of course, and especially sketchy ones, don't "prove" any claim to an Old Testament for Native America. I don't intend for them to. Their function is only to illustrate the depth of the Native Tradition itself. Talking about an Old Testament which emerges from the genius of Native America is not a wild leap into the unknown. There are sound theological reasons for taking the Native heritage seriously. It embodies the collective memory of an encounter with God that should cause any theologian to stop and think. As with Israel, this memory was transmitted through all of those channels that make up any Old Testament: through stories, histories, poetry, music, sacraments, liturgies, prophecies, proverbs, visions, and laws. The mighty acts of God in North America were witnessed and remembered. They were interpreted and passed on. Taken all together, they constitute an original, unique, and profound covenant between God and humanity.

If this is true then we are confronted with a problem. Suppose that we do allow Native People to claim an "Old Testament" status for their Tradition. Then what do we do with "the" Old Testament? What is the relationship between the two? What is the relationship to the "New" Testament?

An immediate answer is that we will have to be more concise when we speak of the original covenant with ancient Israel. We won't be able to use that word in quite the same way. As Christians, we're going to have to make some elbow room at the table for other "old testaments." Not only from Native America, but from Africa, Asia, and Latin America as well. That's another door that is opening up in Christianity, and I doubt that anyone is going to be able to close it again. The fact is, Christians must permit the same right for other peoples that they have claimed for themselves. God was as present among the tribes of Africa as God was present among the tribes of America, as God was present among the tribes of Israel. Consequently, we must be cautious about saying that God was "unique" to any one people; God was in a special relationship to different tribes or in a particular relationship with them, but never in an exclusive relationship that shut out the rest of humanity.

This understanding broadens our dialogue about the connections between old testaments. It allows us to say that while there was nothing "unique" about God's relationship to either Native America or ancient Israel, there are elements to both that were special or particular. Obviously, for Christians, the concern focuses on christology. As a theologian of Native America, I can feel comfortable (not to mention orthodox) in saying that it was into the Old Testament People of Israel that God chose to become incarnate. Consequently, the story of this community becomes of primary importance to me. I need to honor, as well as understand, the Old Testament of Israel as the traditional culture into which God came as a person. In this way, the Old Testament of the Hebrew People remains central to my faith as a Christian and vital to my reading of the Christian scriptures.

At the same time, I can stand on my own Old Testament Tradition and let it speak to me just as clearly about the person, nature, and purpose of the Christ. I maintain that this Christ fulfills both Old Testaments. In the Pauline sense, I can assert that while as a man Jesus was a Jew, as the risen Christ, he is a Navajo. Or a Kiowa. Or a Choctaw. Or any other tribe. The Christ does not violate my own Old Testament. The coming of the Christ does not erase the memory banks of Native America or force me to throw away centuries of God's revealing acts among my People. But let me be careful about this: I am not glossing over the Old Testament of Native America with the Western whitewash of a theology that gives out a few quick platitudes about the "Christ of all cultures." When I speak of a fulfillment of Native America's Old Testament, I mean just that: a Christ that emerges from within the Native Tradition itself; that speaks of, by, and for that Tradition; that participates in that Tradition; that lives in that Tradition. Grounded in the Old Testament of Native America, it is the right of

Native People to claim fulfillment of Christ in their own way and in their own language. I am not looking simply to paint the statues brown and keep the Western cultural prejudices intact. I am announcing the privilege of my own People to interpret the Christian canon in the light of Israel's experience, but also in the light of their own experience. Whether this interpretation is compatible with Western opinions is open for discussion.

The Old Testament of Native America, therefore, does not replace the Old Testament of Israel. It stands beside it. The Native People's claim to truth is not a competition with other traditions. The answer to the question about the relationship between the two Old Testaments is this: they do not cancel one another out (any more than they are cancelled out by the New Testament); rather, they complement each other. I firmly believe that if the Christian faith is ever to take root in the soil of Native America, both testaments will be needed. Native People can read through the New Testament from both perspectives and see the gospel far more clearly for themselves. In turn, the gospel can speak to the Tradition with far more clarity. And here's a critical point: when we talk about the "fulfillment" of the Old Testament by Christ, we are describing the dual role of Christ in both confirming and correcting a People's memory. There was much in the memory of Israel that Jesus confirmed; there was also a great deal that he sought to correct. The same applies to the Old Testament memory of Native America. There is much that the Christ confirms and much that stands corrected. No Old Testament has a monopoly on perfection. The two traditions stand side-by-side under the fulfillment of Christ. As Native People begin to actively use their own Old Testament in reading the Christian scriptures they will find strengths that were missing from the experience of Israel, just as they will find weaknesses that need to be changed.

In the end, the naming of an Old Testament of Native America should not be a cause for alarm among any group or People. It is not a threat, but a hope. Our knowledge of God will not be diminished by this act of a People to regain their memory, but enhanced. The testimony of Israel will remain central to all Christians, Western and Native alike. The Tradition of Native People will be as changed by the gospel of Christ as it changes our understanding of that gospel. Native People will discover that they can read and understand both the Old and New Testaments of the Bible with a much clearer vision. Suddenly, they will

start to make sense. Not the sense of the West perhaps, the imported versions of truth handed down from a community that fears it has lost its own Old Testament, but the common sense of any People that remembers, that recounts, that reasons, that reveals, and that responds. The "old" and the "new" will merge. They will enter deeply into the Kivas and Lodges of Native America and come back out stronger than we ever dreamed possible.

In the next century, the Christian church is going to experience a second major reformation. It will be far more powerful than the one we knew in sixteenth-century Europe. For one thing, it will be international, not just regional. It will cross over not only denominational lines, but also over lines of color, class, gender, and age. It will be more important than the last reformation because it will change the way people think and feel about themselves. While the West will participate in this reformation, it will not play a dominant role. The leaders of the coming reformation will be women. They will be from Africa, Asia, Latin America, and Native America. They are being born right now.

One of the guiding theologies of the second reformation will be the Christian theology of Native America. The emergence of that theology is already taking place. Not that too many people have noticed yet. In the centers of Western religious power, the revolution occurring in Native America is far too distant and obscure to be disturbing. It only shows up occasionally, for example, at meetings to discuss "Indian ministries," at conferences on racism or spirituality, and in books like this one.

The Native People's Christian theology is being overlooked, because it is being born in silence. That silence is so strong, so pervasive, so smothering that even the shout of a human voice cannot escape it. Not alone. But with each day that passes, more and more voices are beginning to take up the cry. In little backwater reservation chapels. In urban slums. In Arizona and Alaska and Minnesota and California and Manitoba. In sweat lodges and camp meetings. In Christian homes and Traditional homes. In Cheyenne homes and Mohawk homes. In Tribes all across Native America.

Native People are shouting into the silence of Western colonialism. They are shouting their names. They are saying that they are still the Tribe of the Human Beings. The Memory is coming back and with it the voice of a whole nation. Against that kind of power, no silence will long endure.

The midwife to the Native Reformation is the Old Testament of Native America. It is going to give birth to a cry of freedom. Old divisions between the People will be healed. The Traditional and the Christian People will once again become whole. The spiritual center of the Tribe will be regained and the People will unite as a family once more. With their combined strength they will begin to reclaim their rightful Tradition. It will not be "old." It will not be "new." It will be alive—right here and right now.

In the next century, the Old Testament of Native America is going to be fulfilled.

Old World Missions

The Portuguese found ancient and well-established Christian communities on the coast of India when their ships arrived in 1498. These Christians were not Romanized, however; that is, they were not Catholic Christians, and Latin was not the language of their churches. Their liturgical language was Syriac; their priests married; they prohibited images (what they considered idols in a land of many deities); they continued to observe Indian customs such as vegetarianism; and, like other Christians in the East, they believed that Mary was the mother of Christ, but not the mother of God. The Catholic Christian missionaries therefore came into conflict with the so-called Thomas Christians of India, as did their Catholic converts. Mass baptisms of fishing peoples, the Paravas, coupled with the cultivation of elite Hindu Brahmins, created a new type of Indian Christian, one who was loyal to Rome and its practices.

Although many missionaries worked with the poor and those despised in the caste system of India, Jesuit missionaries to India, and later to China, also directed their efforts toward the educated upper classes. Roberto de Nobili (1577–1656) in India and Matteo Ricci (1552–1610) in China adopted the customs of their host countries and attempted to interpret Christianity in the idioms of Hinduism and Confucianism, respectively. These ancient civilizations had more in common with the new arrivals than had many of the cultures of the New World: international trade and commerce; ancient literature, especially written scriptures such as the Vedas and the Analects; and governments structured somewhat along the lines of European principalities and duchies, with strong centralizing leaders emerging in various dynasties over the centuries. The missionaries felt that by translating Christianity into local ways of thinking and conceptualizing religion, the upper classes would be converted, and the lower classes would then fall in line.

The problem with this strategy was that Christianity was seen by many leaders as aligned with a foreign power, with its priests acting as agents of alien governments. This was especially true in India, which had its own indigenous priests in the Thomas churches but also had Portuguese priests in the Catholic churches. When Protestant missionaries later accompanied British colonialists to India in the nineteenth century, they, too, were seen as the enemy. The twentieth-century nationalist movement for independence in India was thus a Hindu movement, although Indian Christians also supported independence. Ironically, many nationalists were educated in schools and universities established by Christians.

▦ South Asian Christianity and the Acts of Thomas

One of the oldest forms of Christianity still practiced today can be found on the west coast of India. Indian Christianity traces its origins to Thomas the disciple, who is said to have traveled east on two occasions, although the earliest documented presence of Christianity dates to 550 C.E. Legends of Thomas' miracles persuaded wealthy rajas to accept his message long after encounters with his holiness had convinced the poor, and Indian Christians believe he was martyred near Madras. Christianity in India was planted by missionaries from east Syria. The Indian-Syriac church was administered by bishops operating out of the patriarchate of the Church of the East, located in Baghdad, but is now affiliated with the Syrian Orthodox Church. The church uses a Syriac rite, and is evidence of some of the earliest missionary activity in Asia.

The Acts of Thomas, which describe Thomas' adventures in India, are part of the New Testament Apocrypha—books that did not make it into the official canon of the New Testament. The Acts indicate that Thomas reluctantly went to India, but while there, performed a number of miracles, including raising the brother of a king from the dead. A brief excerpt from the second act concerns Thomas' coming to the king Gundaphorus. The king gave the disciple money to build a palace and was somewhat upset when he learned how Thomas had spent it:

> And from time to time he [Gundaphorus] sent money and provision, and victual for him and the rest of the workmen. But Thomas receiving it all dispensed it, going about the cities and the villages round about, distributing and giving alms to the poor and afflicted, and relieving them, saying: The king knoweth how to obtain recompense fit for kings, but at this time it is needful that the poor should have refreshment. . . .
>
> Now when the king came to the city he inquired of his friends concerning the palace which Judas that is called Thomas was building for him. And they told him: Neither hath he built a palace nor done aught else of that he promised to perform, but he goeth about the cities and countries, and whatsoever he hath he giveth unto the poor, and teacheth of a new God, and healeth the sick, and driveth out devils, and doeth many other wonderful things; and we think him to be a sorcerer. Yet his compassions and his cures which are done of him freely, and moreover the simplicity and kindness of him and his faith, do declare that he is a righteous man or an apostle of the new God whom he preacheth; for he fasteth continually and prayeth, and eateth bread only, with salt, and his drink is water, and he weareth but one garment alike in fair weather and in winter, and receiveth nought of any man, and that he hath he giveth unto others. And when the king heard that, he rubbed his face with his hands, and shook his head for a long space.
>
> And he sent for the merchant which had brought him, and for the apostle, and said unto him: Hast thou built me the palace? And he said: Yea. And the king said: When, then, shall we go and see it? but he answered him and said: Thou canst not see it now, but when thou departest this life, then thou shalt see it. And the king was exceeding wroth, and commanded both the merchant and Judas which is called Thomas to be put in bonds and cast into prison until he should inquire and learn unto whom the king's money had been given, and so destroy both him and the merchant.

One of the earliest examples of Christianity being perceived as an alien force involved the expulsion of Christians from Japan by Shogun Ieyasu Tokugawa in 1614. The Jesuit Francis Xavier (1506–1552), a close colleague of Ignatius of Loyola, had brought the first missionaries to Japan in the early sixteenth century. When the Italian missioner Alessandro Valignano (1539–1606) arrived in Japan in 1579, there were already 150,000 Japanese Christians. Valignano founded seminaries, colleges, and novitiates in order to create an indigenous Japanese church. Dutch and English Protestant merchants in the late sixteenth and early seventeenth centuries, however, persuaded Japanese leaders that Catholic Christianity disguised Portuguese imperialistic aims toward Japan. While probably true, the Dutch and the English had imperialistic goals as well, as subsequent historical events demonstrated. But Catholicism was well entrenched in Japan, with more than 300,000 Christians in a population of 20 million. Even Buddhist priests considered it a threat. When Christianity was outlawed, 5000–6000 Japanese Christians were executed, as were Portuguese Jesuit missionaries. Christianity went underground in Japan for several centuries until the opening of Japan—at the point of gunships—in the nineteenth century.

The time of persecution looms large in the history of Japanese Christianity, for it was an era of martyrdom that paralleled western Christianity's earliest days. Many Japanese Christians were crucified on the edge of the sea, where they died of exposure after several agonizing days. Others were hung upside-down in a pit—small incisions in their head and neck allowed blood to drip out slowly—until they apostatized, that is, renounced their faith. While many died, many more apostatized by stepping on a bronze relief of either Jesus or Mary. This small stepping-stone, called a *fumie*, became the symbol of turning one's back on God.

A contemporary Japanese Catholic, Shusaku Endo (1923–1996), writes about the experiences of Christians in Japan. In the 1930s, his mother converted to Catholicism, and to please her, he converted as well. The number of Christians prior to World War II was less than 1 percent of the total population of Japan, a ratio that continues today. Throughout his life, Endo had something of a love-hate relationship with his faith. It wasn't until he visited Palestine that he truly understood the life and message of Jesus, whom he began to understand as a person defined by rejection. He saw a continual culture clash between Christianity and Japan, and believed that Christianity had to change in order to be effective in his native land. Despite their Christian orientation and message, Endo's books are immensely popular in Japan.

The Reading

In a novel called *Silence* (1969), two Portuguese missionaries, Father Garrpe and Father Rodriguez, sneak into Japan to learn why their Jesuit mentor, Father Ferriera, has publicly apostatized. They cannot believe he has abandoned the faith he once taught them. They discover many underground Christians, but they also discover the horror of betrayal and torture. Garrpe refuses to renounce Christianity, even to save the lives of some Japanese Christians. Although he does not apostatize, he does jump into the ocean to save one of the victims. They both perish.

In the following excerpt, Rodriguez is in a cell, awaiting his own torture and death. He hears someone snoring and cannot believe that anyone can sleep at a time like this. His Japanese captors want him to apostatize, and they bring him Ferreira (called "Sawano" by the Japanese). This is the man Rodriguez has been seeking throughout the novel.

It is important to remember that this is a chapter in a novel. We are jumping into the story at its climax: everything has been leading to this moment. Will Rodriguez apostatize or not? Why did Ferreira apostatize? The events that the book

▨ Christian Fiction

The Left Behind series by Tim LaHaye and Jerry B. Jenkins—which presents a fictional account of events mentioned in the New Testament book of Revelation—carries on a long tradition of Christian fiction, that is, books depicting biblical stories or Christian-themed topics in novel form. Christian bookstores as well as mass market chains in the United States are doing a booming business selling novels to Christians and non-Christians alike. Christian fiction is nothing new, however.

One of the earliest Christian novels (1678) was John Bunyan's *Pilgrim's Progress (from this World to That Which is to Come),* which depicted the troubles a Christian must undergo in this life. *Pilgrim's Progress,* like other books, was designed to inspire and encourage Christian readers. The twentieth century saw a tremendous number of novels, especially by secular writers, that addressed a variety of biblical and theological themes: from Lew Wallace's *Ben Hur (A Tale of the Christ)* in 1880, to Nikos Kazantzakis' *The Last Temptation of Christ* in 1960. Thornton Wilder's novel about the Christian meaning of love and death, *The Bridge of San Luis Rey,* won the author a Pulitzer Prize (1927). The British novelist Graham Greene wrote many books from a Catholic perspective, while another British author, C. S. Lewis, wrote an allegory about outer space and a new Eden, the Perelandra Trilogy. Lewis is probably best known for his series of children's books, the Chronicles of Narnia, which begins with *The Lion, the Witch, and the Wardrobe,* and which also allegorizes Christian themes.

What is significant about Christian fiction is that both Christians and non-Christians absorb a great deal of history and theology from these books. The Left Behind series, for example, has profoundly shaped Christian thinking about the end of days. Millions find Christian-themed novels inspirational as well as instructional. They also find them entertaining and enjoyable, if market sales are any indication.

describes actually happened, although individual characters are fictional. We don't know what has happened to Rodriguez before we meet him in this reading, and we don't know what will happen to him afterwards. But what we do know is that he is at a moment of profound crisis.

We should also remember that we are looking backwards: this is historical fiction, quite faithful to history, but not in the same category as a first-person account from the same period or as a work of theology. Yet, in its own way, it does present a theology for present-day Japanese Christians.

Note: Ellipses are in the original except where noted.

Questions to Consider

1. What is the moral issue presented by the reading?

2. Do you think Father Rodriguez does the right thing or the wrong thing? Explain.

3. What do you the think the author intended to indicate with Rodriguez' confusion about the snoring man?

4. We have read of martyrdom on several occasions. Does this seem to be an essential component of Christianity? Is it a requirement?

5. We have seen, in the cases of Bartolomé de las Casas and this reading, that Christian missionaries traveled to places where they were detested (though detested for different reasons). Why should Christian missionaries persist?

6. Is there an inherent message of superiority in the idea of Christian missions? Or of any missions, for that matter? Why or why not?

7. In the first chapter of this textbook, we read the Gospel of Mark. Are there any allusions to the Passion Narrative in this current excerpt? If so, what are they?

Silence: Chapter 8

SHUSAKU ENDO

Bending down, the priest made his way into the room in the thick darkness. Suddenly he was halted by a foul stench. It was the smell of urine. The floor was completely covered with it; and for a moment he stood still, trying to keep himself from vomiting. After some time, through the darkness he was at last able to distinguish the walls from the floor; and with his fingers against the wall groping his way around the room, he suddenly hit against another wall. Stretching out his arms he realized that the tips of his fingers could touch both walls at the same time. This gave him some idea of the size of the room he was in.

He strained his ears, but could hear no voice. It was impossible to know what part of the magistrate's building he was in. But the deathly silence assured him that there was no one anywhere near. The walls were made of wood, and as he touched the upper part his fingers discovered a large, deep crack. At first he thought that this was one of the cracks between the boards, but somehow he also had the feeling that it could not be so. As he kept on feeling it with his hands, he gradually realized that it was the letter "L." The next letter was "A." Like a blind man his fingers felt their way around the ensuing letters and found "Laudate Eum" [Praise Him]. Beyond this his fingers felt nothing more. Probably some missionary, cast into this prison, had cut out these words in Latin for the benefit of the next person who might be here. While in this place, this missionary had not apostatized; he had been burning with faith. And here, all alone in the dark, the priest was filled with emotion to the point of tears at the thought of what had happened. He felt that to the end he himself was being protected in some way.

He did not know what time of night it was. In the long journey through the streets to the magistrate's office, the interpreter and the officials whom he did not know had kept repeating the same questions. Where had he come from; what society did he belong to; how many missionaries were in Macao. But they had not urged him to renounce his faith. Even the interpreter seemed to change his tune completely; for with expressionless face he had simply performed his duty of translating the words of the officials. When this absurd examination was finished, they had brought him back to his cell.

"Laudate Eum." Leaning his head against the wall, the priest followed his usual custom of thinking about that man whom he loved. Just as a young man might envisage the face of his intimate friend who is far away, the priest from long ago had the habit of imagining the face of Christ in his moments of solitude. And yet since he had been captured—especially during the nights of imprisonment in that copse when he had listened to the rustling of the leaves—a different sensation filled his breast when the face of that man rose behind his closed eyelids. Now in the darkness, that face seemed close beside him. At first it was silent, but pierced him with a glance that was filled with sorrow. And then it seemed to speak to him: "When you suffer, I suffer with you. To the end I am close to you."

While thinking of this face, the priest thought also of Garrpe. Soon he would be with Garrpe again. In his dreams at night he had sometimes seen that black head chasing after the boat and sinking in the sea; and then he was intolerably ashamed to think about himself who had abandoned the Christians. So intolerable was the thought that sometimes he would try not to think about Garrpe at all.

Far in the distance he heard a voice. It was like that of a couple of dogs yelping and fighting. He strained his ears, but the sound had already ceased and then for a long time it continued. Unconsciously the priest laughed to himself in a low voice. He had realized that it was the sound of someone snoring. One of the guards was sound asleep, drunk with sake [pronounced sah-kee; rice wine].

For some time the snoring continued intermittently. Now it was high, now low like the sound of a badly played flute. Here he was in this dark cell overwhelmed with the emotion of a man who faces death, while another man snored in this carefree way—the thought struck him as utterly ludicrous. Why is human life so full of grotesque irony, he muttered quietly to himself.

The interpreter had confidently asserted that tonight he would apostatize. (If only he knew my true feelings . . .) As these thoughts crossed his mind, the priest withdrew his head from against the wall and laughed gently. Before his eyes there floated the untroubled face of that guard snoring in his deep sleep. If he's snoring like that, he doesn't fear that I'll try to escape, he reflected. Yet he no longer had the slightest intention of trying to escape; but just to give himself some distraction he pushed the door with both hands; but the bolt was shot from outside and he could not move it.

Theoretically, he knew that death was near; but, strangely enough, emotion did not seem to keep pace with reason.

Yes, death was drawing near. When the snoring ceased, the tremendous stillness of the night surrounded the priest. It was not that the stillness of the night was completely without sound. Just as the darkness floats over the trees, the awfulness of death suddenly descended upon him, filling him with terror. Wringing his hands he yelled in a loud voice. And then the terror receded like the tide. But once again, like the tide, it came surging on. He tried earnestly to pray to Our Lord; and intermittently there came into his mind the words: "his sweat became like drops of blood." As he saw the emaciated face of that man, there was no consolation in the thought that he, too, had tasted this same terror in the face of death. Wiping his brow with his hand, the priest got up and began to walk around his narrow cell to give himself some distraction. He could not stay still; he had to move . . . [portion omitted].

Ah! That snoring again! It was like the sound of a windmill turned around in the breeze. The priest sat down on the floor soaked with urine, and like an idiot he laughed. What a queer thing man was! Here was the stupid groaning snore, now high, now low, of some ignorant fellow who felt no fear of death. There, fast asleep like a pig, opening his big mouth he could snore just like that. He felt that he could see the guard's face with his own eyes. It was a fat face, heavy with sake and bloated, health itself—but for the victims the face was terribly cruel. Moreover this guard did not possess any aristocratic cruelty; rather was it the cruelty of a low-class fellow toward beasts and animals weaker than himself. He had seen such fellows in the countryside in Portugal, and he knew them well. This fellow had not the slightest idea of the suffering that would be inflicted on others because of his conduct. It was this kind of fellow who had killed that man whose face was the best and the most beautiful that ever one could dream of.

Yes, and that on this, the most important night of his whole life, he should be disturbed by such a vile and discordant noise—this realization suddenly filled him with rage. He felt that his life was simply being trifled with; and when the groaning ceased for a moment, he began to beat on the wall. But the guards, like those disciples who in Gethsemane slept in utter indifference to the torment of that man, did not get up. Again he began to beat wildly on the wall. Then there came the noise of the door being opened, and from the distance the sound of feet hastening rapidly toward the place where he was.

"Father, what is wrong? What is wrong?" It was the interpreter who spoke; and his voice was that of the cat playing with its prey. "It's terrible, terrible! Isn't it better for you not to be so stubborn? If you simply say, 'I apostatize,' all will be well. Then you will be able to let your strained mind relax and be at ease."

"It's only that snoring," answered the priest through the darkness.

Suddenly the interpreter became silent as if in astonishment. "You think that is snoring . . . that is . . . Sawano, did you hear what he said? He thought that sound was snoring!"

The priest had not known that Ferreira was standing beside the interpreter. "Sawano, tell him what it is!"

The priest heard the voice of Ferreira, that voice he had heard every day long ago—it was low and pitiful. "That's not snoring. That is the moaning of Christians hanging in the pit."

Ferreira stood there motionless, his head hanging down like an old animal. The interpreter, true to type, put his head down to the barely opened door and for a long time peered in at the scene. Waiting and waiting, he heard no sound, and uneasily whispered in a hoarse voice: "I suppose you're not dead. Oh no! no! It's not lawful for a Christian to put an end to that life given him by God. Sawano! The rest is up to you." With these words he turned around and disappeared from sight, his footsteps echoing in the darkness.

When the footsteps had completely died out, Ferreira silent, his head hanging down, made no movement. His body seemed to be floating in air like a ghost; it looked thin like a piece of paper, small like that of a child. One would think that it was impossible even to clasp his hand.

"Eh!" he said putting his face in at the door. "Eh! Can you hear me?"

There was no answer and Ferreira repeated the same words. "Somewhere on that wall," he went on, "you should be able to find the lettering that I engraved there. 'Laudate Eum.' Unless they have been cut away, the letters are on the right-hand wall . . . Yes in the middle . . . Won't you touch them with your fingers?"

But from inside the cell there came not the faintest sound. Only the pitch darkness where the priest lay huddled up in the cell through which it seemed impossible to penetrate.

"I was here just like you." Ferreira uttered the words distinctly, separating the syllables one from another. "I was imprisoned here and that night was darker and colder than any night in my life."

The priest leaned his head heavily against the wooden wall and listened vaguely to the old man's words. Even without the old man's saying so, he knew that that night had been blacker than any before. Indeed, he knew it only too well. The problem was not this; the problem was that he must not be defeated by Ferreira's temptings—the tempting of a Ferreira who had been shut up in the darkness just like himself and was now enticing him to follow the same path.

"I, too, heard those voices: I heard the groaning of men hanging in the pit." And even as Ferreira finished speaking, the voices like snoring, now high, now low, were carried to their ears. But now the priest was aware of the truth. It was not snoring. It was the gasping and groaning of helpless men hanging in the pit.

While he had been squatting here in the darkness, someone had been groaning, as the blood dripped from his nose and mouth. He had not even adverted to this; he had uttered no prayer; he had laughed. The very thought bewildered him completely. He had thought the sound of that voice ludicrous, and he had laughed aloud. He had believed in his pride that he alone in this night was sharing in the suffering of that man. But here just beside him were people who were sharing in that suffering much more than he. Why this craziness, murmured a voice that was not his own. And you call yourself a priest! A priest who takes upon himself the sufferings of others! "Lord, until this moment have you been mocking me?" he cried aloud.

"Laudate Eum! I engraved those letters on the wall," Ferreira repeated. "Can't you find them? Look again!"

"I know!" The priest, carried away by anger, shouted louder than ever before. "Keep quiet!" he said. "You have no right to speak like this."

"I have no right? That is certain. I have no right. Listening to those groans all night I was no longer able to give praise to the Lord. I did not apostatize because I was suspended in the pit. For three days, I who stand before you was hung in a pit of foul excrement, but I did not say a single word that might betray my God." Ferreira raised a voice that was like a growl as he shouted: "The reason I apostatized . . . are you ready? Listen! I was put in here and heard the voices of those people for whom God did nothing. God did not do a single thing. I prayed with all my strength; but God did nothing."

"Be quiet!"

"Alright. Pray! But those Christians are partaking of a terrible suffering such as you cannot even understand. From yesterday—in the future—now at this very moment. Why must they suffer like this? And while this goes on, you do nothing for them. And God—he does nothing either."

The priest shook his head wildly, putting both fingers into his ears. But the voice of Ferreira together with the groaning of the Christians broke mercilessly in. Stop! Stop! Lord, it is now that you should break the silence. You must not remain silent. Prove that you are justice, that you are goodness, that you are love. You must say something to show the world that you are the august one.

A great shadow passed over his soul like that of the wings of a bird flying over the mast of a ship. The wings of the bird now brought to his mind the memory of the various ways in which the Christians had died. At that time, too, God had been silent. When the misty rain floated over the sea, he was silent. When the one-eyed man had been killed beneath the blazing rays of the sun, he had said nothing. But at that time, the priest had been able to stand it; or, rather than stand it, he had been able to thrust the terrible doubt far from the threshold of his mind. But now it was different. Why is God continually silent while those groaning voices go on?

"Now they are in that courtyard." (It was the sorrowful voice of Ferreira that whispered to him.) "Three unfortunate Christians are hanging. They have been hanging there since you came here."

The old man was telling no lie. As he strained his ears the groaning that had seemed to be that of a single voice suddenly revealed itself as a double one— one groaning was high (it never became low): the high voice and the low voice were mingled with one another, coming from different persons.

"When I spent that night here five people were suspended in the pit. Five voices were carried to my ears on the wind. The official said: 'If you apostatize, those people will immediately be taken out of the pit, their bonds will be loosed, and we will put medicine on their wounds.' I answered: 'Why do these people not apostatize?' And the official laughed as he answered me: 'They have already apostatized many times. But as long as you don't apostatize these peasants cannot be saved.'"

"And you . . ." The priest spoke through his tears. "You should have prayed. . . ."

"I did pray. I kept on praying. But prayer did nothing to alleviate their suffering. Behind their ears a small incision has been made; the blood drips slowly through this incision and through the nose and mouth. I know it well, because I have experienced that same suffering in my own body. Prayer does nothing to alleviate suffering."

The priest remembered how at Saishoji when first he met Ferreira he had noticed a scar like a burn on his temples. He even remembered the brown color of the wound, and now the whole scene rose up behind his eyelids. To chase away the imagination he kept banging his head against the wall. "In return for these earthly sufferings, those people will receive a reward of eternal joy," he said.

"Don't deceive yourself!" said Ferreira. "Don't disguise your own weakness with those beautiful words."

"My weakness?" The priest shook his head; yet he had no self-confidence. "What do you mean? It's because I believe in the salvation of these people . . ."

"You make yourself more important than them. You are preoccupied with your own salvation. If you say that you will apostatize, those people will be taken out of the pit. They will be saved from suffering. And you refuse to do so. It's because you dread to betray the Church. You dread to be the dregs of the Church, like me." Until now Ferreira's words had burst out as a single breath of anger, but now his voice gradually weakened as he said: "Yet I was the same as you. On that cold, black night I, too, was as you are now. And yet is your way of acting love? A priest ought to live in imitation of Christ. If Christ were here . . ."

For a moment Ferreira remained silent; then he suddenly broke out in a strong voice: "Certainly Christ would have apostatized for them."

Night gradually gave place to dawn. The cell that until now had been no more than a lump of black darkness began to glimmer in a tiny flicker of whitish light.

"Christ would certainly have apostatized to help men."

"No, no!" said the priest, covering his face with his hands and wrenching his voice through his fingers. "No, no!"

"For love Christ would have apostatized. Even if it meant giving up everything he had."

"Stop tormenting me! Go away, away!" shouted the priest wildly. But now the bolt was shot and the door opened—and the white light of the morning flooded into the room.

"You are now going to perform the most painful act of love that has ever been performed," said Ferreira, taking the priest gently by the shoulder.

Swaying as he walked, the priest dragged his feet along the corridor. Step by step he made his way forward, as if his legs were bound by heavy leaden chains—and Ferreira guided him along. In the gentle light of the morning, the corridor seemed endless; but there at the end stood the interpreter and two guards, looking just like three black dolls.

"Sawano, is it over? Shall we get out the *fumie*?" As he spoke the interpreter put on the ground the box he was carrying and, opening it, he took out a large wooden plaque.

"Now you are going to perform the most painful act of love that has ever been performed." Ferreira repeated his former words gently. "Your brethren in the Church will judge you as they have judged me. But there is something more important than the Church, more important than missionary work: what you are now about to do."

The *fumie* is now at his feet.

A simple copper medal is fixed on to a grey plank of dirty wood on which the grains run like little waves. Before him is the ugly face of Christ, crowned with thorns and the thin, outstretched arms. Eyes dimmed and confused the priest silently looks down at the face which he now meets for the first time since coming to this country.

"Ah," says Ferreira. "Courage!"

"Lord, since long, long ago, innumerable times I have thought of your face. Especially since coming to this country have I done tens of times. When I was in hiding in the mountains of Tomogi; when I crossed over in the little ship; when I wandered in the mountains; when I lay in prison at night . . . Whenever I prayed your face appeared before me; when I was alone I thought of your face imparting a blessing; when I was captured your face as it appeared when you carried your cross gave me life. This face is deeply ingrained in my soul—the most beautiful, the most precious thing in the world has been living in my heart. And now with this foot I am going to trample on it."

The first rays of the dawn appear. The light shines on his long neck stretched out like a chicken and upon the bony shoulders. The priest grasps the *fumie* with both hands bringing it close to his eyes. He would like to press to his own face that face trampled on by so many feet. With saddened glance he stares intently at the man in the center of the *fumie*, worn down and hollow with the constant trampling. A tear is about to fall from his eye. "Ah," he says trembling, "the pain!"

"It is only a formality. What do formalities matter?" The interpreter urges him on excitedly. "Only go through with the exterior form of trampling."

The priest raises his foot. In it he feels a dull, heavy pain. This is no mere formality. He will now trample on what he has considered the most beautiful thing in his life, on what he has believed most pure, on what is filled with the ideals and the dreams of man. How his foot aches! And then the Christ in bronze speaks to the priest: "Trample! Trample! I more than anyone know of the pain in your foot. Trample! It was to be trampled on by men that I was born into this world. It was to share men's pain that I carried my cross."

The priest placed his foot on the *fumie*. Dawn broke. And far in the distance the cock crew.

Wherever the imperial nation went, the conqueror introduced Christianity to subject peoples. When England, the Netherlands, and other nations supplanted Spain and Portugal on the high seas, the religion of empire changed from Catholic to Protestant. Or, more precisely, where the English sailed, there went Anglicanism; where the Germans went, so went Lutheranism; the French took Catholicism; the Dutch, Reformed Protestantism; while eventually Americans took Methodist, Baptist, and Presbyterian teachings. Missions to the Old World turned solidly Protestant in the nineteenth century. Unlike Catholic missionaries, who generally were single men and women, priests and nuns, Protestants frequently sent missionary couples. Women could gain access to home and hearth much more easily than men, and thereby influence women. Just as early Christianity had spread by the marriage of Christian women to pagan men, so Christianity in India, Indonesia, and Africa spread via the family through female interpersonal contacts. Frequently, Christian women taught their pagan counterparts how to read and write, and trained them for professions such as teaching and nursing, sometimes against the wishes of the men in the culture.

While Protestantism took hold in India, Catholics missionized China and the Indo-Chinese peninsula. A new missionary order founded in America, the Maryknoll Missioners, aggressively proselytized in Asia. Maryknoll's earliest missionaries went to China in the 1920s, and the stories of priests and sisters abound with courage, humor, and heroism. But the popular missionary society made a fateful error in the 1930s. Because they were afraid of the growing power of Chinese communists, they supported Japan's invasion of Manchuria in 1931–1933. Instantly, the Chinese perceived the missionaries as traitors, betraying their commitment to the Chinese people. A similar anticommunist commitment led to Catholic support of a corrupt, but Catholic, regime in Vietnam in the 1960s. Ngo Dinh Diem served as the first president of South Vietnam (1955–1963). Diem murdered enemies and oppressed the Vietnamese people, but because he opposed Communism, and because of the strength of Vietnamese Catholicism, American Catholics supported the Vietnam War for many years. (A notable exception was Dorothy Day and the Catholic Worker Movement in the United States.)

Japanese Christianity reemerged in the nineteenth century after three centuries of repression. About 30,000 crypto-Christians known as the Kakure, came out of hiding. They weren't quite Catholic, but they definitely weren't Protestant; they practiced a Christianity that featured scrambled Latin and seventeenth-century garb.

Both Catholic and Protestant missionaries could now enter Japan, but they met with only modest success. One of the most important Japanese Protestant Christians was Toyohiko Kagawa (1888–1960), who was raised in a traditionalist family but who converted to Christianity when he was a teenager. From 1910 to 1924, he lived in a six-foot square shed (except for two years spent studying at Princeton University), serving the poor of Kobe. He unionized first shipyard workers, in 1912, and then factory and farm workers in 1918. He worked hard to gain voting rights for the poor, and in 1925, the government granted universal male suffrage. He founded the Anti-war League in Japan, and in 1941 was arrested for publicly apologizing to China for Japan's invasion. Clearly, Kagawa's understanding of Christianity led him to become a social reformer and advocate for democracy. "I am a socialist because I am a Christian," he asserted.

The Reading

Kagawa wrote the following essay as one chapter in the book *Christ and Japan,* in which he analyzes both the Japanese and their character, and Christianity and its appeal. He was writing during the 1930s, a time of growing nationalist sentiment in Japan, during which Shinto, the national religion of Japan, dominated Japanese political and religious life. Shinto combined elements of nationalism, emperor worship, Japanese folk traditions, and respect for ancestors. In the 1930s, the Japanese had a sense of "manifest destiny" to expand and spread Japanese culture throughout Asia. The belief that Christianity represented a foreign power and an alien cultural intrusion fueled the turn to Shinto.

In addition to Shinto, the Japanese also practiced Buddhism, folk traditions, and even Confucianism, a Chinese ethical philosophy. Buddhism tended to concentrate on the afterlife, and people relied on Buddhist priests in times of illness or death. Folk traditions included placating angry or vengeful spirits and paying proper respect to departed relatives. It is incorrect to call the practice "ancestor worship." It is more accurate to identify the honoring of dead relatives in terms of the Japanese (and other Asians') belief in the ongoing power and relevance of those who went before. We are part of an unbroken chain of remembrance, and duty requires us to honor those who gave us life, according to Japanese tradition.

We can call Kagawa's chapter, "Japan Needs Christ," apologetic, in that it attempts to explain a way of life. Apologetics is a genre in which one defends something to skeptical outsiders. Although we think of an apology as expressing sorrow or regret for something we did, in the original Greek, the word means "from logic." In other words, a writer makes a case based on reason rather than revelation, on logical arguments rather than on claims to authority. This is exactly what Kagawa does in *Christ and Japan.*

We should also consider the chapter in the historical context in which it was written: the 1930s. Kagawa refers to the Great Depression being experienced in

Europe and North America, though he does not directly address Japanese political issues. But Kagawa is implicitly criticizing Shinto and Japanese imperialism by presenting Christianity as an alternative worldview.

Questions to Consider

1. What does Christianity offer that traditional Asian religions do not, according to Kagawa?

2. What are the positive aspects Kagawa finds in Shinto, Buddhism, and Confucianism?

3. How has Christianity shaped the Occident (that is, the Western world)?

4. What does Kagawa mean by "redemptive love"?

5. Would you say that Kagawa is appealing to logic? Are his arguments based on experience, tradition, scripture, or reason?

6. What objections can you come up with to Kagawa's arguments?

7. How does Kagawa echo Endo?

Japan Needs Christ

TOYOHIKO KAGAWA

Shinto teaches reverence. Buddhism teaches transcendentalism. Confucianism teaches the golden mean and the harmonies of life. In the presence of these faiths, does Japan need Christ?

My father abandoned Buddhism and became a Shintoist. When he died the family returned to the Buddhist fold. The Buddhist faith of my home, however, was entirely of a traditional, formal type. In it there was not the least trace of an experience which transcends this earth-born existence. At the age of ten I went regularly to the Buddhist temple and studied the teachings of Confucius. No, it was not Confucianism I was studying. It was Chinese calligraphy that actually captured my boyish enthusiasm. Yet I did accept Confucianism as a legalistic code of conduct, for, as a system, it is more legalistic even than the Mosaic law.

It is not strange that Shinto became the causative factor behind the Meiji Restoration. For, after all, the religion most readily understood by the Japanese is neither Chinese Confucianism nor Indian Buddhism. It is rather the centuries-old, intuitive spirit of religious devotion which is native to the soil and soul of Japan. As a child I was thrilled by the Shinto teaching that when men die they become miniature gods. But what a long period of waiting. No possibility of becoming a son of God until after death! And, when I contemplated the tragic world that these men-become-god had left behind them, my soul was filled with unutterable sadness. To my childish mind there was no hope of becoming a sage as Confucius promised; nor could I make real the elusive transcendentalism of the Buddhistic teaching. I wept unceasingly over the moral corruption of my home and the iniquity of the world.

My father was devout, according to the Japanese conception of devoutness, but morally he was impossible. In Japanese religions and religious devotion, piety and personal morals are wholly unrelated. Unfortunately Buddhism, with its otherworldliness, gave no promise of furnishing any fundamental solution for the contradictions of this chaotic, earthly life.

Notwithstanding the profundity of the Buddhistic system, I failed to find in the Buddhism of thirty years ago a single priest who commanded my respect. Modern Buddhism is increasingly producing priests who inspire esteem, but at that time, possibly because of the hold-over of the anti-Buddhistic sentiment of the Meiji Restoration period, I learned to scoff at the Buddhistic faith. Even today the Buddhism of my native town of Awa is concerned only with ceremonials connected with death and utterly fails to renew and enrich man's present life.

Ah! When will the Japanese find in Buddhism fundamental truths that will produce a revival of life? It promises a transcendental religious experience, but where is the Japanese who really understands its doctrine of transcendentalism? After all, Buddhism forever remains merely a system of academic doctrines divorced from actual life, and it tends to be relegated to the scholar's mind. Is it not a fact that the Buddhism of the masses is simply the intuitive religious devotion of the Japanese people expressed in Buddhistic terms and forms? There is no relation whatever between its piety and fundamental religious truth. Therefore, the Buddhism of the masses, while it has a sense of piety, like Shinto, lacks the driving power which integrates the total personality.

Its goal is not the building of the kingdom on this earth. It is dominated by the exceedingly selfish motive of satisfaction with one's own salvation and that of the nation. Regardless of its philosophy, this is the actual result. I was driven to despair. Moreover, because of mental perplexities and the corruption of my home life, I spent the days of my youth in sorrow and bitter tears.

Just at that time an urge to study English led me to join a missionary's Bible class. In this study I came upon Luke 12:27, "Consider the lilies, how they grow: they toil not, neither do they spin; but I say unto you, even Solomon in all his glory was not arrayed like one of these." Through this verse of scripture I made the momentous discovery that the love of God enfolds this universe. I was beside myself with joy. Not only so, I awoke to the tremendous truth that, instead of becoming a little god after death, I was here and now a son of God, the creator and ruler of this vast universe. I fairly leaped with joy. I was completely captured by the Christ who gave his life

that he might reveal the love of this Father-God to all mankind. With high and holy resolve I dedicated myself to translating that cross-revealed love into present-day life.

Does the love of God stir no responsive chord in the Japanese heart? God forbid! The spirit of reverence of Shinto, the other-worldliness of Buddhism and the golden mean of Confucianism are all milestones for pilgrims out in search of the love of God. I am grateful for Shinto, for Buddhism, and for Confucianism. I owe much to these faiths. The fact that I was born with a spirit of reverence, that I have an insatiable craving for values which transcend this earthly life, and that I strive to walk the way of the golden mean, I owe entirely to the influence of these ethnic faiths.

Yet these three faiths utterly failed to minister to my heart's deepest needs. I was a pilgrim journeying upon a long, long road that had no turning. I was weary. I was foot-sore. I wandered through a dark and dismal world where tragedies were thick. Tears were my meat day and night. Until I discovered that God, the creator and ruler of the universe and man's maker, is my Father; that he is the God of love who wipes away my tears and saves me from sorrow and from the sin hidden in my soul; until I discovered all this, I knew nothing—absolutely nothing—about the joy of life. The fact that Christ revealed this love of God not merely by teaching, but exemplified it in his life, caused me to understand that religion is life—a life completely absorbed in God.

It is a cause for profound gratitude that the missionaries who came to Japan some thirty years ago had not forgotten the spirit of the great Lincoln. They abounded in the spirit which emancipated the slaves, and they incarnated democracy. This spirit of emancipation which wiped out slavery was wanting in our land.

Japan had no slaves, but it had a system as vicious as slavery. The public prostitutes and geisha girls who were bartered for gold and robbed of their freedom were in stark reality slaves. My own mother was a servile geisha girl. Her lot and life led me to dedicate myself to the work of emancipating these pitiful women and the lower classes which produce them. My father was secretary of the Senate of Elder Statesmen. My mother was his concubine. My father's wife, being childless, I was registered as her child. In this home, enmeshed in the tragedy of triangular love, I spent my days in the midst of plenty but in tears.

Aside from Christianity, where is the religion that assures the realization of a life of purity and peace, and nourishes a piety that penetrates and motivates man's total life? The peoples of the Occident have lived under the aegis of the Christian faith for nineteen hundred years. Consequently they utterly fail to comprehend their deep indebtedness to Christ.

Blot out Christ for a season! Efface every trace of his presence and power! In the resultant Christless world, no matter how scientific or philosophical or naturalistic it may become, it will soon be discovered to what extent the family life will break down, what a gap will develop between science and morals, the extent that politics will be divorced from the laborer and his needs, and the way that factional, feudalistic conditions will plague both society and the nation.

Are not the economic chaos and the unemployment crisis which today have plunged the nations of the West into unspeakable agony, directly due to the fact that the peoples of these lands have wandered away from Christ's way of life? If men everywhere gave Christ the right of way, toiled as he toiled, loved purity as he loved it, devoted themselves to a service motivated by love and had his passion for peace, would the present problem of unemployment and this economic distress have come upon the world? The love-divorced reverence of Shinto, the love-divorced other-worldliness of Buddhism and the love-divorced Confucian way of the golden mean doomed me to pass my boyhood in tears. Today the nations of the West are weeping. Why these tears? The cause is clear. Devotion to doctrine stifles love. Scientific civilization crowds love out of life. The economics of capitalism makes love an alien.

After all, how much difference is there between a doctrinal devotion which fails to revolutionize life and ritualistic Shinto? How far is an atheistic, scientific civilization separated from a Buddhism which advocates an atheistic and impersonal transcendentalism? Moreover, Confucianism with its earth-born realism will readily countenance the self-centered success of capitalism. A nominal Christianity which does not strive to realize, in actual living, the Christ who revealed the love of God and was impelled by redemptive love to give himself on the Cross—this Christianity contains all that Shinto, Buddhism and Confucianism possess, and still is not real Christianity. Unless we dedicate our machines, our capital, our social order to God we shall seek in vain for peace.

And there is only one way by which to bring our capital, our social order and our world to God. That is the way of the Cross.

This must be remembered: Shinto, Buddhism and Confucianism all teach love to a certain degree. There is a vast difference, however, between the instinctive love of animals, the ethical love of human beings and the redemptive love which God revealed through Christ. Animal love is purely instinctive, and is not subject to the correction and control of reason. Human love, though more than instinctive, attempts to become rationalized only within the bounds of human relations. Confucius called this *jin,* the way of benevolence. But the *jin* of Confucius is not rooted in God, who embraces the whole universe. Therefore it is a love that makes concession to seeming necessity and permits the killing of an enemy and leaves sinners in the lurch. In Christ alone, and for the first time, was made known to mankind the love of the Cross which forgives enemies and saves sinners.

Buddhism teaches great compassion. This goes deeper and further than the *jin* of Confucius. Buddha was a man of virtue. A blacksmith gave him putrid pork to eat, which caused his fatal illness. Yet, on his death-bed Buddha preached the way of forgiveness and love to this man. But since the beginning of time, who has declared, "this is my blood of the covenant, which is poured out for many unto remission of sins"?

Over-individualized twentieth-century man knows nothing about the inner consciousness of this redemptive love. It is not merely sacrifice. Only a God-consciousness could give expression to those wonderful words. Christ, the God-conscious Savior, taught sinners the love of God. Nay, he did not stop with teaching. He shed his blood. He gave his life. He gave it on the Cross. Only a sinner weeping over his sins can comprehend the marvel of this love.

The church has dealt with this simply as doctrine. It has not endeavored to make the consciousness of redemptive love part and parcel of the life of every man. Here lies the difference between doctrinal Christianity and a Christianity that lives in the whole of life. To me, born a child of sin, this redemptive love fills and thrills every fiber of my being. It stirs within me a poignant sense of gratitude.

Is redemptive love merely a doctrinal matter? Did Christ die for the sake of doctrine? No, he did not die for theological dogma. He gave his life for love. If

God reveals himself in ways which transcend human logic, he will do so through redemptive love. This love it is that moves me. To a life actually incarnating this love I dedicate all my days and all my ways. Christ, who died for sinners, summons us to become the concrete expression of this redeeming love to the so-called scum of society, of the nation and of the world. In Colossians 1:24 Paul calls us to carry redemptive love on to its God-given goal: "Now I rejoice in my sufferings for your sake, and fill up on my part that which is lacking of the afflictions of Christ in my flesh for his body's sake, which is the church."

I am profoundly convinced that, aside from the practice of redeeming love, there is no way to dedicate our capital, our machines and our social order to God. This love alone can build an unexploiting economic order. The consciousness of this love alone can create a cooperative community and a national and international life where there shall be no sense of color. Therefore, even though the nations of the West turn their backs on Christ, I stake my all on the adventure to realize Christ's redemptive love in the total life of my land.

At the time of the Meiji Restoration neither Confucianism nor Buddhism proved a renewing, renovating force. It was the conception of a god-destined nation that produced the Meiji Restoration. Unfortunately that conception was too abstract. Hence it failed to build a nation grounded in the love of God. For this reason Japan has been compelled to advance along a path of pain.

I am not endeavoring to introduce a foreign Christ to my fellow nationals. I am striving to introduce the life that, in its totality, is conscious of this redemptive love. This was incarnate in Christ—the supreme manifestation of eternal love—the unique revealer of the love of God. Neither Confucius nor Buddha gave any assurance regarding this love. Buddha was a noble character, but the love which he taught was of a philosophical type. It was not a love that risks its all and sheds its life-blood. His universe was not a universe of reality. It was an illusion. Mahayana Buddhism teaches the mercy of Amida, but that is a pious device. Its universe is an empty nothingness. In such a universe of naught, how can you seriously consider redemptive love?

Since the beginning of time Christ, with his crystal-clear consciousness of a cosmic personal God and his manifestation of a love related to reality in behalf of sinful men, he and he alone has clearly taught the forgiveness of sin. In him only can the foundation stone of the world's redemptive love be laid.

If the West rejects this redeeming love and contents itself with divisive class strife, capitalistic plunder and racial selfishness, we, here in Japan, will preserve this religion of love. The Japanese military clique may trample it under its feet. We once hid this faith, that redeems through love, in the recesses of our island Empire during persecutions which lasted through three hundred unhurried years. We can do it again.

Unfortunately mankind is still living on the animal plane. We awaken in the morning. We fall asleep at night. In the same way civilization influenced by human change, sleeps and wakes. The present is an age of unbroken sleep. In ancient times when Europe slept, the brothers of Christian love preserved this religion of the Cross in the desert, in mountains, in secluded valleys, in monasteries and through fraternal orders.

When the Holy Spirit moves in the hearts of men, making them conscious of the will of God, this redemptive love will leap forth from the desert, the monastery, the hidden mountain retreats and the secluded valleys, into the streets, the factories, the shops and all the varied haunts of men. This movement will take the form of Christian cooperatives, Red Cross activity, prison reform, movements for befriending sinners and for realizing world peace.

Alas! the Cross is again trampled to the ground! The weeping Christ once more retreats to Gethsemane! Yet, should he there again suffer arrest and be slain, he would know the way of the Resurrection. Redemptive love is itself the Resurrection way. There can be no life without blood. As long as Japan—as long as Shinto, Buddhism, Confucianism, Mohammedanism and the world are content with a life only half-conscious, a life based on the natural instincts, they may be satisfied with the present status of their religious experience. But when they awaken and yearn for a life that is fully conscious, a life under the guidance of the divine spirit, they will make the momentous discovery that this religion of the Cross, the religion of redeeming love, is the unique way of life.

Slave Christianity

The slave trade of the seventeenth and eighteenth centuries took Christian and Muslim adventurers deep into West Africa to capture millions upon millions of Africans to work in the New World. Some slaves were actually practicing Muslims, sold into slavery by rival tribes. When the Dutch and the English surpassed the Spanish and the Portuguese on the high seas, Protestants took over for the Catholic slavers who transported human cargo in the brutal transatlantic voyage known as the "Middle Passage." Slavery existed throughout North, Central, and South America, and the Caribbean to support large plantations of sugar cane, coffee, and cotton. But slavery differed from place to place.

The enslavement of the indigenous peoples of Central and South America led to repeated papal injunctions against the practice, since Spain and Portugal were the primary colonial powers there, and subject to papal threats, if not control. Ultimately, Pope Urban III (p. 1623–1644) abolished Indian enslavement in 1639. Although colonists in North America also attempted to enslave Indians to work on plantations in the southern colonies in the eighteenth century, the Indians tended to run away. In the nineteenth century, Indians were confined to reservations, where some were able to preserve their traditional ways; those living off the reservations tended to become assimilated and to lose their native identity. Attempting to enslave Native Americans was not nearly as effective as bringing in Africans.

Thus, it was the importation of slaves from Africa that fueled the economy of the American colonies in the eighteenth century and the United States in the nineteenth. "By 1820 nearly 8.7 million slaves had departed for the New World from Africa, as opposed to the 2.6 million whites who had emigrated from Europe," according to David Brion Davis, thereby making up 77 percent of the immigrant population. Millions died in captivity, though, which accounts for the fact that in 1825, despite the large numbers of immigrants, only 18.6 percent of those living in the New World were of African descent. Slaves in North America performed the most strenuous, back-breaking labor: the result was the creation of the United States as a major world economy.

The French National Assembly banned slavery and slave trading in French colonies in 1794, and Great Britain outlawed the slave trade in 1808. Pope Gregory XVI (p. 1831–1846) denounced slavery and the slave trade in 1839. Meanwhile, slavery remained legal in the United States throughout the South, as well as in New York until 1827, in Connecticut until 1848, and in New Jersey until 1865. The Missouri Compromise of 1820 forbade the introduction of slavery into northern, federally controlled territories, but did not prohibit it in the states. President Abraham Lincoln's Emancipation Proclamation, declared in 1863 during the Civil War, freed only those slaves in states at war against the Union. It wasn't until passage of the Thirteenth Amendment to the U.S. Constitution in 1865 that slavery was no longer allowed in the United States.

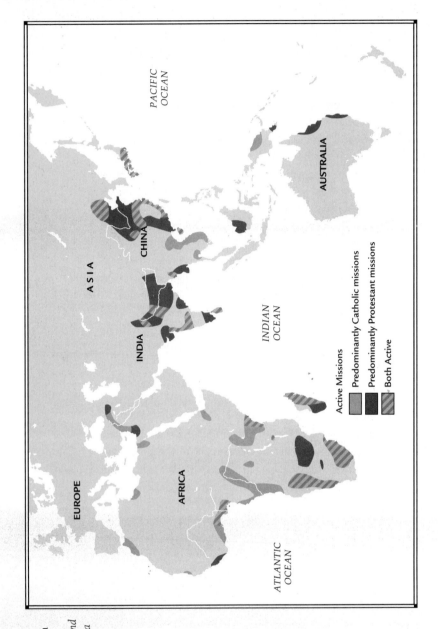

Christian missionary activity in the nineteenth century. This included highly successful Catholic and Protestant missions in Africa and Asia.

Despite the misgivings some slaveholders had about bringing the gospel to slaves, Christianity was taught to many, although only in controlled conditions. Slaves could meet and worship with the supervision of the slave owner; but under no circumstances were slaves to meet on their own or learn to read the Bible. In the American South, teaching a slave to read was a crime, and no wonder. Slaves saw the deliverance of the Israelites from slavery in the Exodus account (Exodus 14); they saw the love of Jesus for the poor and the outcast; and they saw the great reversal of the status quo promised by the New Testament. Slave owners reading the same Bible, however, saw slavery justified by the curse of Cain and Ham (Genesis 4 and 9), and read repeated admonitions for slaves to obey their masters (Ephesians 6:5; Colossians 3:22).

Notwithstanding the suppression of indigenous African religions, languages, and customs, black slaves maintained a culture of resistance about which their owners knew nothing. Slaves met secretly, apart from whites, to worship in the "hush harbors" of forests. Echoes of their native religions—which were forbidden—could be heard in ecstatic services, which included singing and dancing. A biblical message of redemption and freedom given by a preacher who could "talk the gospel" gave them strength and hope to "keep on keepin' on."

Africa for Christ

It is somewhat ironic that nineteenth-century Protestant missionary societies saw the salvation of African souls as a higher priority than the salvation of slaves. Despite an active abolition movement in the northern United States, foreign missions took priority. Missionary societies financed great numbers of Protestants to bring Christianity, and what they viewed as civilization, to Africa. The missionaries who traveled to Africa included former slaves, or the descendants of slaves, who endured the hardships of African missions in order to help their black brothers and sisters. Alice Walker's novel *The Color Purple* describes the missionary activities of the main character's sister in the 1920s. Free blacks from the North traveled to Africa in the nineteenth century, and the accounts of ex-slaves are perhaps the most fascinating. Thomas Lewis Johnson (b. 1836?) was one such missionary to Africa.

Johnson was a slave freed by the Emancipation Proclamation in 1863. He and his wife married when they were slaves, and after manumission, they felt called to gain "Africa for Christ." Like most missionaries, then and now, part of Johnson's task was to raise funds for his work, so he traveled to England on speaking engagements. His missionary work took him to Cameroon, which he calls Cameroons. While in Africa from February to November 1879, he reports that he did not go for two weeks in succession without being ill. His wife, whom he calls Mrs. Johnson, fell ill when they were in the interior of Cameroon and died within a few months of their arrival. The Johnsons were accompanied by another Black couple, Mrs. Johnson's sister

(continued on page 359)

▨ Go, Tell It On the Mountain!

Negro spirituals, the Christian hymns developed out the African American slave experience, interpreted biblical literature in a way that made sense to oppressed people. The songs told stories of bondage and freedom, of sorrow and joy, and of hope for the promised tomorrow. Bible stories, especially ones from the Christian Old Testament, were understood as describing the current, as well as past, status of God's people.

I

Ezek'el saw de wheel
'Way up in the middle o' de air
Ezek'el saw de wheel
'Way up in the middle o' de air
De big wheel run by faith,
De little wheel run by de Grace o' God
A wheel in a wheel
'Way up in the middle o' de air

II

Little David, play on your harp,
Hallelu! Hallelu!
Little David, play on your harp,
Hallelu!

Little David was a shepherd boy,
He killed Goliath and shouted for joy.

(refrain)

Joshua was the son of Nun,
He never would quit till the work was done.

(refrain)

Done told you once, done told you twice,
There're sinners in hell for shooting dice.

III

Didn't my Lord deliver Daniel
D'liver Daniel, d'liver Daniel?
Didn't my Lord d'liver Daniel,
And why not every man?

He deliver'd Daniel from the lion's den,
Jonah from the belly of the whale,
And the Hebrew children from the fiery furnace,
And why not every man?

IV

When Israel was in Egypt's land:
Let my people go;
Oppressed so hard they could not stand,
Let my people go;
Go down, Moses,
Way down in Egypt land,
Tell ole Pharaoh,
Let my people go.

[and the eighteenth verse, rarely heard]

We need not always weep and moan,
Let my people go;
And wear these slavery chains forlorn
Let my people go . . .

While songs referring to the stories of the Old Testament frequently spoke of freedom, the spirituals about Jesus tended to identify with his suffering and with his promise of deliverance. They also expressed the joy that slaves felt about their new life in Christ and their hopeful expectation of release in both this life and the next.

V

They crucified my Lord,
An' He nevuh said a mumbalin' word.
They crucified my Lord,
An' He nevuh said a mumbalin' word,
Not a word, not a word, not a word . . .

VI

Were you there when they crucified my Lord?
Were you there when they crucified my Lord?
Oh! Sometimes it causes me to tremble, tremble, tremble.
Were you there when they crucified my Lord?

VII

Oh, my Good Lord's done been here!
Blessed my soul and gone away,
My Good Lord's done been here,
Blessed my soul and gone.

When I get up in heaven
And my work is done,
Goin' to sit down by Sister Mary,
And chatter with the darlin' Son.

(refrain)

Continues

Hold up the Baptist finger,
Hold up the Baptist hand,
When I get in the Heavens,
Going a-join the Baptist Band.

VIII

Great day! Great day, the righteous marching.
Great day, God's going to build up Zion's walls.
This is the day of jubilee,
The Lord has set his people free,
God's going to build up Zion's walls!

In addition to the traditional gospels that came out of the experience of slavery, African American composers and lyricists contributed to a body of hymnody that is used by Christians today around the world. James Weldon Johnson (1871–1938), the first African American president of the National Association for the Advancement of Colored People, wrote "Lift Every Voice and Sing," which has become what some call the Negro National Anthem. He wrote the third verse in 1900 to commemorate the birthday of Abraham Lincoln.

Lift ev'ry voice and sing, till earth and heaven ring,
Ring with the harmonies of liberty;
Let our rejoicing rise, high as the list'ning skies,
Let it resound loud as the rolling sea.
Sing a song full of the faith that the darkness has taught us,
Sing a song full of the hope that the present has brought us;
Facing the rising sun of our new day begun,
Let us march on till victory is won.

Stony the road we trod, bitter the chast'ning rod,
Felt in the days when hope unborn had died;
Yet with a steady beat, have not our weary feet,
Come to the place for which our fathers sighed?
We have come over a way that with tears has been watered,
We have come, treading our path through the blood of the slaughtered,
Out from the gloomy past, till now we stand at last
Where the white gleam of our bright star is cast.

God of our weary years, God of our silent tears,
Thou who has brought us thus far on the way;
Thou who hast by thy might, led us into the light,
Keep us forever in the path, we pray.
Lest our feet stray from the places, our God, where we met Thee,
Lest our hearts, drunk with the wine of the world, we forget Thee;
Shadowed beneath Thy hand, may we forever stand,
True to our God, true to our native land.

Johnson's stirring words, and other spirituals of the slave community, show how African Americans inculturated Christianity into their experience of oppression to develop a unique and creative form of resistance—one that was at once deeply religious and deeply political. The spirituals have made it into numerous hymnals and songbooks, and are widely sung in congregations both black and white. Indeed, such gospel tunes as "This Little Light of Mine," "Go, Tell It on the Mountain," and "He's Got the Whole World in His Hands" have become familiar to a broad American audience, many of whom are unaware of their origins in the history of African American resistance to slavery.

(continued from page 355)

(Mrs. Richardson) and her husband, who also died in the interior. Johnson returned to Liverpool in 1880 and then to the United States, spending his remaining years as an evangelist in both England and the states.

The Reading

Johnson's autobiography—*Twenty-Eight Years a Slave, or the Story of My Life in Three Continents*—was published in 1909. It belongs to an interesting genre of literature that portrays the lives of slaves and former slaves in the United States. The narratives of ex-slaves, such as those by Sojourner Truth and Frederick Douglass, helped to arouse the abolition movement. After the Civil War, other autobiographical accounts served as inspirational messages for ex-slaves, such as Booker T. Washington's story of the creation of Tuskegee Institute, and the adventures of Thomas Johnson, which we will read here. Undoubtedly, Johnson's book not only inspired others but also helped raise money by being sold at speaking engagements.

Questions to Consider

1. In what ways did Johnson's experience as a slave shape his missionary outlook?

2. What did he see his role to be?

3. Would you say that Johnson saw himself as a Christian first? As an American? As a descendant of Africans?

4. What was Johnson's view of Africa and Africans?

5. Why do the Africans call the black missionaries ("colored," in their language) "white people"?

6. What was Johnson's view of African religions?

7. How does his approach to missions differ from that described by de las Casas?

8. Do you think this tract would work as a fund-raising item? Why or why not?

Twenty-Eight Years a Slave

THOMAS LEWIS JOHNSON

After stopping a short time at the island of Fernando Po, where we were entertained by the wife of the British Consul, we arrived at Victoria, Cameroons, on the afternoon of Saturday, December 14th, 1878. This was our destination.

Victoria was a beautiful little place with a population of 500 inhabitants, fronting Ambas Bay, with a commanding view of bay and sea. On the North, South, and East are high hills. In the distance can be seen the Cameroon Mountains, 13,000 feet above the level of the sea. The place was beautifully laid out with broad streets. Each house had a large garden, in many of which were to be seen the palm, lime, cocoa-nuts, bread fruit, custard fruit, orange, banana, and plantain trees. The cottages were neat and clean, and built after the style of European cottages. These were occupied by the English-speaking people who were native Christians, and many of them had for long years been earnest workers for our blessed Jesus.

The day after our arrival being the Sabbath, the late Rev. Q. W. Thomson, Missionary-in-charge, invited me to take the morning service. A few minutes before seven o'clock in the morning the bell rang, and we were soon at the church, a fine stone building capable of seating 350 to 400 people. In a short time quite a number of well-dressed intelligent looking people had assembled. I gave out a hymn, and they sang as well as many congregations I have preached to in America and England. When I began to read, nearly all of them opened their Bibles to follow me in the lesson. Here I had the opportunity for the first time to preach in Africa about Jesus.

I took for my text, "Believe on the Lord Jesus Christ, and thou shalt be saved" (Acts 16:31). I cannot remember ever preaching to a more attentive audience.

At ten o'clock we all went to the sabbath school. Rev. C. H. Richardson and myself were invited to take classes; my class was of young men. All of them could read the Bible. At the close of the school I requested the children to sing, "Come to the Savior." They sang it beautifully. The school was well attended and perfect order was observed during the service.

For years Victoria was a city of refuge. The late Reverend Alfred Saker, who labored in Africa about thirty years, established this station in the year 1858. He purchased from the natives for the Baptist Missionary Society of Great Britain a tract of land extending ten miles along the coast and five miles inland—Victoria about center. Here no one was allowed to hold slaves or to sell his daughters for wives, and no one was to be punished for witchcraft. It was the custom for each man to have as many wives as he was able to purchase among the natives. On returning to the coast from the interior I stopped with a chief who had forty wives. At Victoria no man was permitted to have more than one. It often happened among the natives that when a child died one wife accused another of having bewitched it. The accused was then arrested and made to drink the juice of a wood called cass-wood, which often killed at once. Men also were accused of witchcraft, and were made to drink this juice. If they died they were considered guilty; but if they recovered, as some did, a payment was enforced. If the people who were accused made their escape to Victoria they were safe.

The Missionaries and Christians have for years rescued many of these people who were on the very verge of death. In one month the late Rev. Q. W. Thomson rescued eight who had been condemned to death. In 1880 there were over 400 of these refugees in Victoria, where they were under the influence of the Gospel, and their children were taught in the day school. Many of them became Christians.

This barbarous superstition still exists in many places. The following appeared in the *Daily Chronicle*, August 18th, 1897:

> West Coast of Africa.—A strange superstition.—The British and African Company's royal mail steamer *Roquelle* arrived at Liverpool yesterday morning from the west coast of Africa. The *Roquelle* left Bereby on the Kroo coast, on the 21st July, when a re-

markable circumstance was reported. Some time ago a steamer was lost and a number of Kroo boys from Bereby were drowned. Several other Kroo boys from the same place were saved, and returned home. The relatives of the deceased boys became imbued with the idea that the surviving Kroomen had caused the accident to the ship which resulted in the death of their relatives. They thereupon resorted to the native superstitious method of making them drink cass water. This cass water is a poisonous liquid, but if the native drinks and survives it is taken as a proof that he is innocent. Should he, however, die he is regarded as guilty. It is seldom that any who drink the real cass water recover. In the present case it was reported that the natives were not content with dealing with the survivors they could lay their hands upon, but also made some of their relatives pass through the terrible ordeal. It was said that in all about twenty natives perished in this way.

We had been in Victoria three days only when I was taken with the fever. On January 20th, Rev. C. H. Richardson and Rev Q. W. Thomson left for the interior, to select a new station; I, being ill, could not go. On the 4th of February, Mr. Thomson returned. Mr. Richardson having suffered with fever, had been left at Bakundu, eighty miles in the interior, with two native Christians. Bakundu had been selected as the new mission station, and he would remain there until joined by his wife and by Mrs. Johnson and myself. The only roads through this country were narrow footpaths from town to town, sometimes in the tracks of the elephant. All provisions or luggage had to be carried on men's heads. The account we had of the route was anything but attractive to Mrs. Johnson and Mrs. Richardson— high rugged hills to climb and strong swift flowing streams to cross. Although we knew that the traders along the river objected to interior mission work we concluded that we should go by water on account of my wife and her sister. The late Rev. George Grenfell, at that time a merchant at Victoria, kindly offered to go with us.

On Thursday, the 6th of February, before daybreak, and after a season of prayer with the Rev. Mr. Thomson and the native brethren, we left Victoria in an open boat rowed by Kroomen, followed by a large canoe with our provisions and eight men, and before night we came to Mungo Creek. Here our one interpreter and guide lost his way. We had intended to get by Mungo and Mbungo, the two principal towns, in the night. We passed Mungo, but at daybreak we found ourselves between the two towns. At about eight o'clock we got under the bank of the river, took out our things, and prepared breakfast under the palm trees. Being discovered by the natives we left in the afternoon. As we passed Mbungo there were a few people on the bank, to whom we spoke, and passed unmolested. On Friday night, a man passed us in a canoe, and commenced to beat his drum as he went up the river.

These people can talk to each other on their drums almost as well as we can send a message in this country by telegraph. They have schools in which to teach their children this drum-beating telegraphy. On this occasion this man said on his drum, "White man come into our country." The natives with us, twelve in number, did not tell me of this till the next day.

On Saturday morning at nine o'clock, as we were taking our breakfast on the river bank, several canoes passed us, with fifteen to twenty men in each. Seeing they were well armed with guns and cutlasses, we began to feel suspicious. About ten o'clock we came up with them. They had all stopped on the bank, put on their war caps, and stood in a line along the river.

We were ordered to come ashore. We told them we would not; if they had anything to say to us they must come out in their canoes. They tried to make us leave our boat and go on the beach, but we resolved to stay in our boat. I do not know of any time in my life when I realized the precious promise of my blessed Jesus more than in this hour, "Lo, I am with you always." I said to my wife and her sister, Mrs. Richardson, "We lean upon the Lord."

At one time we were surrounded by nearly one hundred men, armed with cutlasses, ready to cut into us as soon as the young prince gave the word of command. We soon found that it was impossible for us to proceed.

We had to return as prisoners to Mungo. We were within six hours of Bakundu beach. Late in the night we arrived at Mungo. Here they wanted us to leave our boat, and go into the town and see the King. We knew how superstitious they were about our English boat, so we resolved, if we had to die, to die in the boat.

There were many of the traders in Mungo who could talk broken English, and who knew how the English protected the Missionaries. Mr. Grenfell, who had been several years in Africa, and knew something of the people, threatened them with English authority. After the King and his men had held a consultation, the King said to me, "You must pay for passing through my country." To this we agreed. I gave him a large overcoat, a bag of rice, a box of sugar, a blanket, and a barrel of hard biscuits. While he was admiring the coat which he soon put on, we pushed off. I have never seen that King since.

Great was the anxiety of that night; the continual looking back to see if we were being pursued, and a constant outlook also on either side of the narrow river against wild beasts; but God, who had said, "Go," was with us.

Our disappointment at having to return so far was very great indeed, but not so great as our anxiety about Mr. Richardson, alone, ill, eighty miles up country, with hostile tribes between him and us. A report, circulated by the natives, reached us that Mr. Richardson had died. Something had to be done. A consultation was held, and the late Rev. James R. Newby, who was present, volunteered to go at once to Bon Junga, seven miles up the mountain, and at that time the only station on that line to the interior, in the direction of Bakundu. This journey had to be made at night, for it was after dark when the brethren met. It had also to be made on foot, on a narrow path, through the thick wood and bush, where there were many wild beasts and great serpents. A young man offered to go with Mr. Newby. They put their trust in God, and set out with guns and lanterns in their hands, and were soon out of sight. Thank God they reached the Mission Station in safety. Rev. Mr. Wilson, a native missionary, and one of the native Christians, joined them for Bakundu the next morning. The following Saturday night they returned with the good tidings that Mr. Richardson was much better and at work, preparing to receive us.

Nine days after our return to Victoria we commenced our journey, this time going overland. Mrs. Johnson and Mrs. Richardson were carried in hammocks when they did not prefer walking. Our provisions and luggage were carried on men's heads.

I have already mentioned that the best roads in this part of Africa are mere footpaths through the forest, from town to town, on which the natives walk in single file, a few yards from each other, each man with his load on his head, and his cutlass in his hand or at his side, to defend himself against any beast or serpent that might be in the path. This was the way we started out of Victoria for our long journey through the wilderness.

The first day's journey we made seven miles only, as we were advised by our chief, Mr. Thomson, to stop the first night at the Mission Station, Bon Junga. On Tuesday we traveled about seventeen miles, as far as we could judge, and we spent the night at the house of a chief, who made us welcome, and who begged to have a missionary left with him. On the Wednesday we made an early start, but did not make much progress. I became very ill. Then began our experiences of the native carriers in the overland travel in Africa. Several of the men refused to go any further. Some were away ahead in the path, and some a long way behind. After a short "palaver" or talk with the men, we persuaded them to go on, Mrs. Johnson and Mrs. Richardson helping to carry some of the loads. We had hoped to get more native help at the next town, but the tribe was at war, so we could not get any men to come with us. Our next difficulty was the crossing of a deep river; the natives plunged in and swam across. We had to cut down trees and make a raft; on this we put a large tub, into which first Mrs. Johnson got and the raft was then pushed out into the current. Some of the natives swam by the sides of the raft, keeping it up and directing its course. Mrs. Johnson was not sorry when the other side was reached. Then the men brought back the raft and tub and her sister crossed in the same way; and last of all I came with the provisions.

As we advanced into the interior we found the people along the route in a better condition than we had expected. They had fixed dwellings, many of them built neatly of bamboo, and well thatched with mats made from the palm fronds. They had their gardens and farms, their laws and customs, so that wherever we stopped at night we and our goods were safe.

There are some eight or ten towns between Victoria and Bakundu. We left Victoria on Monday morning. On the following Saturday afternoon we arrived at Bakundu, where we found Mr. Richardson well. We had a company of thirty men with us when we arrived and our arrival gave rise to much excitement.

The first thing that struck me as singular was the joy of the old King. For years he had desired to have a

Missionary in his town, to teach the people, as he had heard that the natives were taught on the coast. Not only the King, but his sons and all his head men seemed delighted to see us. On Sunday we held a meeting in an old unoccupied house. We found the people slaves to superstition and witchcraft, but not so bad as the other tribes around them.

The custom of giving cass-wood juice prevailed here as among the Bakwalli people, of whom I have made mention. The first case we heard of was a young man in the town who was accused of witching his sister's child. He was made very ill from the effects of the juice, but finally recovered. As soon as we heard of it, Mr. Richardson, who was always fearless and ready on all occasions to admonish the people, went at once to the King and told him how wrong it was to allow such a practice. The King promised to put a stop to it. He kept his word, and during the nine months I was in the interior I did not hear of another case.

When we first arrived at Bakundu we could hardly sleep at night for the yells of the people in their dance and the beating of the drums. This was kept up day and night. They knew nothing of a Sabbath; hence they continued their drum-beating all the week round. Mr. Richardson went to the King to have a law passed that no work or drum-beating or dancing be done on the Sabbath. The old King at once consented. The people then wanted to know how they were to distinguish the Sabbath. Mr. Richardson promised to walk up and down the street every Friday night blowing a trumpet, to tell the people that the next day was Saturday, and that they must bring enough provisions from their farms to last them over the Sabbath. This plan is worth adoption in civilized countries where there is an increase of the heathen rioting, though it appears a little more intelligent.

The people had great faith in what the Bible said. On one occasion, while Mr. Richardson was away with men at Victoria, the women came to me to get me to ask the Bible if their husbands were safe, and I read the promises of protection to them that believed.

Not long after we came to Bakundu we all began to pray that God would convert the King, who was about ninety years of age. One day we heard that he was very ill, and soon afterwards he sent for us and we attended him, gave him some medicine which seemed to do him good; but we soon found that his sickness was unto death. One day he sent for me, and

I noticed that he was very ill indeed. He had a wooden bowl by his bed, in which was a liquid thick and black, and this he was taking occasionally as I talked with him. I asked him what it was. He said, "Witch make me sick, tell me not to take white man's medicine, and I take this medicine get my stomach full, old witch come in my mouth, go in my stomach, then get blind and come out." I tried to persuade him that all power was in the hands of God; that by believing Him and trusting in Him all these fears would leave him. He had always listened attentively to what we had to tell him about the great plan of salvation.

We continued to visit him, and day after day he would send for medicine. One Sabbath afternoon my wife and I both lay ill in bed. Mr. and Mrs. Richardson went into the town to hold a service; they found the King very ill. The excitement was such that he could not hold a meeting, so he returned home. Then we were sent for; I was hardly able to get out of bed and crawl into the King's house. Women were not allowed to see the King, not even his wives, but the house was full of men, and one man sat at his back to hold him up, and two men were on either side, three of these men being his sons. The old man was very weak, and it seemed he would soon pass from time into eternity. He looked first at Mr. Richardson and then at me. His youngest son, "Ngatee," about ten years old, was called to his side. He took one hand of the lad and put it into Mr. Richardson's hand, the other into mine, and said, "I give this boy to you. Take him and bring him up as your own child; dress him like white man; teach him to talk English and to read and write. His brothers will get a wife for him." He requested that we should also take the girl whom the brothers selected and keep her in the family and educate her. He then said: "Don't fear; I am going now. The town belongs to me and I now give it to you. My son Etau will succeed me. Take care of him, be a father to him and the people." This son Etau was about thirty years old. He then charged Mr. Richardson to take the names of the boys and commence school at once. Some sixty names were taken the next day. Mr. Richardson then told him again the story of God's great love, and that if he would believe and rest in what the Word of God said they would meet each other in heaven. I then said, "Ta Ta Nambulee" (for that was his name), "you say that you are going now; are you prepared to meet God?" "Ah!" said the old man, "I have been ill these ten days, and He has taken care of me; I can still trust

Him." We then wanted to pray with him, but his sons preferred that we should let him rest, as he was so weak; so we went away, leaving our interpreter, who told us that after we had gone the King said to his son who was to succeed him: "Etau, whatever these men tell you, believe it, for I have found them to be true men."

Oh, how we all rejoiced to hear this; so often had we prayed for the conversion of this man. One evening we sent our cook up to the King to tell his experience and to pray with him. He was a native convert. The old King enjoyed it very much, and said, "Tell white man to pray to God and ask Him, if it is His will please spare me a little longer; but if not, please prepare me to meet Him."

For years this King had heard of the work of the Missionaries on the coast, eighty miles away. A year before we settled at Bakundu, Rev. Q. W. Thomson had visited him and promised to send a Missionary to labor among his people. After we had settled among them he was anxious to see how we succeeded. He sent for the women, who do nearly all the work on the farms, and charged them not to work on the Sabbath, as it was God's day; that they must attend Divine Service instead.

This old King, with whom we had to speak through an interpreter, and who usually referred to us as the "white people," was eventually taken to his farm, where he died in two or three days. We arrived in Bakundu in February 22nd, 1879. The King died in the latter part of June in the same year.

Oh what gratitude we ought to feel for that we have been favored with the Gospel which opens the heart of man and the country he inhabits.

I believe there are today in West Africa thousands like Ta Ta Nambulee, who have heard through traders and travelers something about the great mission work and the one true God, and who are anxious to hear more; who are not satisfied with their condition, and who want to know more but who have no way to learn; their souls craving something upon which to rest, something stronger, better and firmer than idols of wood and stone. In this condition they move about from year to year like the beast in the cage, ever walking up and down, trying to escape, but never able to succeed. But how can they hear without a preacher?

"Come over and help us," is their cry,
"Come now, oh, do not pass us by;
"We are seeking truth, we are seeking light,
"We seek deliverance from dark night.

"Can you, who have the Gospel, fail
"To hear our cry, our doleful wail?"

God is now preparing the hearts of the people to receive the truth. Let us send it to them.

The attention which the people gave to the preaching of the Word every Sabbath was very encouraging. The men and boys always attended in the morning, the women in the afternoon. One Sabbath afternoon it was found that some of the women had gone to their farms to work. The young King at once left the meeting, called his brothers and the head men together and passed a law that "if any man or woman did work on the Sabbath they should pay a cow. If they had no cow, their house should be pulled down over their heads."

In Bakundu, as in all the towns along the route in 1879, all the children were naked. Men and women had a cloth around their waists. The men generally dressed more than the women. As soon as they became better acquainted with us they wanted us to give them clothing. Tobacco and cloth are the currency in trade in the interior. Some of the people on the Mungo river raise corn and sweet potatoes, and when baked, fried or roasted, it is a very good substitute for bread. The yam and cocoa are plentiful; the former is very like potatoes when cooked. These they raise on their farms. They have fowls, goats, sheep, and cattle all through the country. The sheep have hair like goats. The Bakundu people are not a savage people, nor cruel like their neighbors and other tribes. One never hears of any murdering among them as among other tribes. They are very kindhearted, and in every way differ much from the surrounding and coast tribes. Many of the West African tribes are continually at war.

You hear of their drinking the blood and eating the heart of their enemies; of walls covered with human skulls; of a pavement made of human skulls on which to walk. Truly the dark places of the earth are full of the habitations of cruelty.

Some tribes pay homage to lakes, rivers, and mountains, believing that their gods live there. In some places you hear houses are kept for serpents, and these repulsive reptiles are worshipped. At Dix Cove, on the west coast, it is said they once had a crocodile which they worshipped. At Duke Town, on the Old Calabar River, in 1859, human flesh was sold in the markets; but I saw nothing of this at Bakundu.

These people have queer superstitions, and one must be among them to realize what slaves they are to them. When it rains they beat their drums to make it stop. There is a bird which makes a noise at night something like an owl. This is called a witch bird. When it is heard the children are afraid to go out, and guns are fired to frighten it away. In passing their farms you often see a stick set in the ground, split at the top, with a piece of cloth or wool put crosswise in it. I was told that this was to keep off thieves. One night a man came to get medicine for his child, and soon after he left the house he cried out in the most pitiful manner—"Witch come to take my child." How sad and helpless are those who are without a knowledge of God.

During the rainy season food generally becomes scarce; the elephants destroy their plantain farms, and the continual heavy rains prevent hunting. One day I heard the natives shouting and singing near our house while it was raining very fast. I looked out and saw a crowd of men at the gate putting up palm branches over it, and burying something under the gateway. I was told that the palm branches were to keep away famine, and that what was buried was to draw game near the town. It was indeed remarkable to see the earnestness and the excitement of these people while they were going through this performance, for they appeared so confident of success.

It was very amusing one day to see their excitement at the lighting of a match. The news soon spread through the country that I could carry fire in my pockets, and take it out and make it burn when I wanted it. One day some ten or twelve men and boys came to see us light a match. When I took the box out of my pocket, they ran as though I had taken a pistol to shoot them. "That's it, that's it," cried the knowing ones, and their consternation seemed to have no bounds.

These people have their Ju Ju houses, or Fetish Temples, like the rest of the tribes; there were three in Bakundu. Here they have their secret meetings. What they do and how they do it I could never find out; but this I do know, that the preaching of the Gospel and the untiring zeal of Mr. Richardson, fighting against error, have been the means of many of the young men losing faith in Ju Ju. Before I left Bakundu, Mr. Richardson had been to hold services in the Ju Ju temples.

They believe that there is a Supreme Being who has great power, but they do not in any way connect Him with themselves. In this they are not much worse than some professed Christians. They do not expect anything from Him; neither do they attribute to Him any qualities good or bad. Their gods are many. The name of their general profession is "Ekodde"; when they are performing any religious ceremony they will tell you that they are "doing Ekodde." Certain medicines have certain names and powers attributed to them. They will take a medicine and use it, and then ask the Ekodde god or other god governing that medicine to give power. Here is instruction for those worshipping the true God. They have a wooden man in their Ju Ju temples called "Mosango," upon which they take oath, believing that a lie told by any person who puts his hand on the head of this image will be exposed.

I was told by a native Christian that men often hold out till they get to the Ju Ju house, but so great is their fear of "Mosango" that they will confess before putting their hand on his head. They used to think that after death they would roam about in some unseen form, often troubling those who had come in for property they had left behind.

Rev. Mr. Wilson told me that the lives of many of the Bakwilli people were miserable all the time; nothing but one continual dread of the witch and what this spirit can do and may do at any time. I believe it to be the same to a great extent among the Bakundu people.

But thank God the everlasting Gospel has made a great change in the people, in a short time.

I was greatly impressed with the intense desire of the people to be taught. Their great wish seemed to be to have their children taught how to read and write, and to talk English. Mr. Richardson had not begun school more than two or three days before he had over a hundred boys. The children learned remarkably quickly, and were very intelligent. Their interest was soon awakened, and they were bright and eager learners.

I was much moved one Sabbath morning. While Mr. Richardson was telling about the love of Jesus, a man asked if the children would be able to tell them the same story out of the Bible after Mr. Richardson had taught them to read and talk English. Here was a joy in store for them.

The young king and several of his head men requested me to form a class of men and to teach them, while Mr. Richardson taught the children. One Sabbath evening after the service about twenty came to the Mission to be more fully informed about the plan of salvation.

Here is a little report of the work as recorded in *The Sword and the Trowel,* August, 1879:

Messrs. Johnson and Richardson in Africa.—We have news from our colored friends down to the middle of May. When they wrote they had been for some time settled in their new station, Bakundu, Victoria, Cameroons, where they had commenced work under the auspices of the chief of the village, which contains about 1,000 people. This worthy was very ill in April, and thinking he was going to die, made his will. In one of the clauses he commended his youngest son to the care of the Missionaries, and in another commanded his subjects to obey and protect the Missionaries and their wives. He seems to have been still living when our friends wrote, and through his influence all the boys in the village had been sent to the Mission School. On Sundays services are held in the hut which serves as a temporary schoolroom, and by this time Messrs. Johnson and Richardson are probably able to preach to the people in their own language, although at first they need an interpreter. The people appear to be very favorably inclined toward the Missionaries, and ask them many questions about the Gospel they bring.

The rainy season had commenced when the last letter was written, and Mrs. Johnson and Mrs. Richardson were still suffering from the fever from which their husbands had recovered. They send very kind messages for all Tabernacle and other friends, and ask our prayers that they may be sustained and blessed in their work. If any friends wish to help them they need not send money, as that is of no use where they are, but they require clothes for the naked population, cloth, prints, buttons, cottons, thread, medicines, etc., for barter and use, and books, slates, pencils, etc., for their school of one hundred and six boys.

Modern African Christianity

Christianity took root in Africa thanks to the efforts of missionaries. Part of the success stemmed from affinities African religions had with Christianity: belief in a high god; a commitment to prophecy and divination; an emphasis on healing and on seeing Jesus as the great physician, or healer, of physical as well as spiritual disease, and, today, the inculturation of African aesthetics such as music, dance, art, and expression into Christian worship. Another reason Christianity grew was because the historical mission churches—Catholic, Anglican, Lutheran, Methodist, and others—developed a core of indigenous leadership: African preachers, teachers, bishops, and scholars. The most famous of these is probably Archbishop Desmond Tutu, the leader of the Anglican Church in South Africa and a vigorous opponent of the apartheid system that existed in that nation until 1994.

The historical mission churches, however, still turned to Europe theologically and culturally. In reaction to this European, or American, orientation, new denominations arose in Africa. Called AICs—for African independent churches, or African indigenous churches—these denominations were established by Africans, for Africans. They take many forms and tend to blend African cultural practices with traditional forms of Christianity. Some of these churches emphasize what is known as Prosperity Christianity, a form of Christianity that emphasizes material wealth and well-being. One becomes a Christian because Christianity offers a way out of poverty and the means to happiness and success. On a continent devastated by AIDS, however, the religious emphasis may shift to health from wealth.

As the next chapter shows, Christianity is growing rapidly in the Southern Hemisphere, especially in Africa. African Christians, for example, are sending missionaries to Europe and the United States to spread the gospel to what they feel are secular societies radically in need of hearing gospel truths. Conservative African denominations and bishops are welcoming American Christians who are unhappy with their denominations' position on social issues such as same-sex marriage and biblical inerrancy, that is, infallibility. The World Council of Churches, an international ecumenical body, has been adding African denominational members at a rapid pace. The next pope may well come from Africa.

Though I have been talking about Africa as a single place, I should emphasize that Africa is huge, more vast than either North or South America. There is great tribal and national diversity, and as a result, great religious diversity, with many differences among Christians there. The following essay notes some of those differences, yet emphasizes similarities as well.

The Reading

Mercy Amba Oduyoye is a Methodist lay preacher who comes from the Akan people, a tribe originating in Ghana in West Africa. The foremost feminist theologian in Africa, she has served as an official with the World Council of Churches. She is the director of the Institute of Women in Religion and Culture in Ghana, and continues to write extensively on African Christianity in general and on liberation theology in particular.

The following essay, first published in 1997 in the Jesuit journal *The Way,* examines a number of theological issues. It attempts to explain African Christianity to outsiders, and in that sense is apologetic. But it also appears directed toward other African Christians in its critique of power relationships within African churches, and in that sense is prophetic—that is, a work that challenges the current situation and calls for a change in behavior and attitudes. Thus, the essay is directed to both insiders and outsiders.

Note: *Theophorous,* literally means "god-bearing"; thus, a theophorous name is one that includes the word "god" in it. The ellipses appear in the original work.

Questions to Consider

1. Why does Oduyoye identify herself as an Akan woman? What is the significance of her identification?

2. In what ways were Africans predisposed to accept Christianity?

3. What problems does Oduyoye see in contemporary African Christianity?

4. How does Oduyoye's idea of God's absence compare with Endo's discussion of God's silence?

5. What are some of the different images of God that Africans have?

6. What is the role of the divine in the struggle for justice in Africa?

7. How does Oduyoye's description of inculturation in Africa compare with Elizondo's analysis of Mexican Christianity? With Charleston's? With Kagawa's?

The African Experience of God Through the Eyes of an Akan Woman

MERCY AMBA ODUYOYE

> Africans experience God—Nana—as the good parent, the grandparent. Some say he is father; others say she is mother. But the sentiment is the same: Nana is the source of loving-kindness and protection.

Writing about Africa is a hazardous enterprise. One needs to draw up many parameters and make explicit the extent of the study. This becomes even more difficult considering the subject in hand. Whose experience of God are we dealing with? What is the extent of the Africa we are talking about? From the Mediterranean to the Cape of Good Hope there have been primal religious experiences of God issuing, for instance, in the building of the pyramids and continuing to undergird the annual festivals celebrated by West Africans. There are Muslims from Cape Verde to the Red Sea and down to Dar and throughout the continent, some of them having roots going to the beginnings of Islam while others are recent converts. The same goes for Christians. Africa also hosts Hindus and Sikhs and Buddhists and many others. We, therefore, want to talk about the experience of God in a multi-religious context.

To create a handle for the subject we shall limit ourselves to the Primal Religion (designated African Religion, AR) as it has been documented by recent studies, and the new Christianity that Africa is living in our days. Geographically we shall limit ourselves to Africa south of the Sahara. The scope of the content will be guided by the experiences of God I have gathered through reading and participation in events that have afforded me the possibility of hearing Africans talk about God. I have in mind the traditional notions as captured by the early African theologians from the AR, the experience of God in South Africa in the days of the struggle against racism, and the emerging profile of God being sketched by African women through creative literature and theological reflection. But first we need to establish the nature of the reality of God in African cosmology and culture.

"The fool says in his heart 'There is no God.'" In traditional Africa there are no such "fools." In his inaugural lecture delivered at Ibadan in 1974, Professor Bolaji Idowu discussed "the reality and unreality of God" under the title "Obituary: God's or man's?," bringing to that university the "God is dead" debate of the 1960s. Idowu believes that "man's estimate of himself and his destiny, his interpretation of the phenomena of the universe and his philosophy of history depend upon this one central point: belief in God, because He is; or unbelief . . ." Elsewhere Idowu asserts that "God is universal and so is revelation." Here he agrees with the Tanzanian who said that as people everywhere see the one sun, so they all have the one God.[1] On the other hand, Betty Goviden, in her article "In search of our own wells," quotes Malusi Mpumlwanas, a South African poet, who asks "What do I mean when I say I believe in God? . . . Is God of the 'Die Stem' and 'Nkosi Sikelela' one and the same God?"[2]

In traditional Africa, that is, Africa when people are being themselves, discounting Christianity, Islam, and Western norms, God is experienced as an all-pervading reality. God is a constant participant in the affairs of human beings, judging by the everyday language of West Africans of my experience. A Muslim never projects into the future nor talks about the past without the qualifying phrase *insha Allah,* "by the will of Allah." Yoruba Christians will say "DV" ("God willing"), though few can tell you its Latin equivalent, and the Akan will convince you that all is "by the grace of God." Nothing and no situation is without God. The Akan of Ghana say *Nsem nyina ne Onyame* ("all things/affairs pertain to God"). That Africans maintain an integrated view of the world has been expressed by many. In his autobiography, Nelson Mandela writes:

> My father was an unofficial priest and presided over ritual . . . and local rites, . . . he did not need to be ordained, for traditional religion of the Xhosa is characterized by a cosmic wholeness so that there is little distinction between the sacred and the secular, between the natural and the supernatural.[3]

The Yoruba respond to prayer with Ase, the divine and highly potent power with which Olodumare (God) created the universe and maintains its physical laws.[4] The belief in the all-pervading power and presence of God endows the universe with a sacramental nature.[5] The African view of the world is nourished by a cosmology that is founded on a Source Being, the Supreme God, and other divine beings that are associated with God. As God is the foundation of life, so nothing happens without God. God lives, God does not die, and so indeed humans do not die. Even when we do not occupy a touchable body, we still live on.

The way we experience God is portrayed in the language we use about God, especially the names by which God is known. Early researchers into AR like G. Parrinder, E. B. Idowu, and J. S. Mbiti have recorded for us several African names of God with copious annotations, which it is not necessary to rehearse at this stage.[6] What needs to be said is that these names are still current and that more names descriptive of people's experience of God are available in proverbs, songs, and prayers. These names, says Idowu, are not mere labels: "They are descriptive of character and depict people's experience of God."

When words fail, symbols take over. For the Akan of Ghana the Adinkra symbols, the minuscule figures for gold weights and those on royal maces, include many that are theophorous. The star in Adinkra is a symbol that says "Like the star, I depend on God and not on myself." The symbol of hope says, "God, there is something in the heavens, let it reach my hands." The dependence of the existence of the human spirit on the spirit of God is expressed in another symbol; and the more well-known *Gye Nyame* is the Akan expression of the belief that without God nothing holds together, and is variously interpreted as "except God" or "unless God"—God is experienced as the very foundation of existence.[7] All these examples demonstrate the difficulty of translation and the inadequacy of words to express our experience of God.

People believe that all the good and well-being they enjoy come from God, and that if one is not yet enjoying well-being it is because one's time has not yet come. "AR holds that the world and nature are good gifts that God entrusted to human beings: they provide nourishment for life, security and home for our bodies" (Lutheran World Federation [LWF] document on AR). The experience of God as beneficent is not only Muslim or Christian, but a living faith of Africans that has been reinforced by these "missionary" religions.

The current interest in the nature of Christian missions has sparked off studies in the theology of religions, interreligious relations, multi-religious communities, gospel and cultures, and has therefore renewed interest in the religion of "the other." It is in this context that the LWF established a working group on AR which is described as "an indigenous system of beliefs and practices integrated into the culture and world views of African peoples." This original religion of Africans expresses the African experiences of God and pervades all cultural norms. All human relations are affected by the belief that we all belong together in God. *Onyame nti* (because of God, or for the sake of God), we act or refrain from acting. God is experienced as the sole creator and sustainer of all things, who expects human beings to be to God as children and to each other as siblings, and to respect the earth and other natural phenomena.

The belief in the unity of God goes with the unity of the cosmos. God's sustenance and beneficence are seen in the rain as in the sunshine. Indeed when the dark clouds begin to gather, some say the rain is angry, while others say God is angry. But even as we say *muna,* which in the human face is a sign of anger and displeasure, the *muna* of God issues forth in the blessing of the rain. If there is too much rain or flood, we do not attribute them to God but to the anger of the divinities that are associated with nature or the ancestors whom we may have wronged by some unethical behavior or lack of reverence for what pertains to the spirit world. God always gives what is sufficient. The experience of God as good and the experience of evil becomes a challenge to Africans. In the tradition, some would say both come from God but that "when God gives you disease, God also gives you the cure."[8]

We experience the total dependence on God in AR in the prayers.[9] God is the ultimate receiver of all prayers, so all libations begin with calling upon God. This God has been with Africans from the beginning and features in prayers and greetings, blessings and curses: "God will pay you back" is feared as a most potent curse. People are discouraged from using it as it may rebound on them when they deserve what they have received at the hands of those they curse. In AR it is not God who suffers from the evil we do to each other. God does not suffer at the hands of the exploiter and the oppressor, it is the individual who suffers. However, when individuals suffer through evil not of their doing, God who is the Creator of all humans demonstrates concern. Behind the unpronounceable curse is the expectation that God judges impartially, that God sees when we cheat and exploit the weak. Most important is the experience that God guards the weak. Often, when children and others deemed weak in society escape calamity, all agree that it is God's doing.

The immediacy of God in African affairs is also demonstrated through the God-related names we bear. Theophorous names like Nyamekye (gift of God) and Dardom (depend on God) are examples from Akan names. Yoruba names beginning with Olu or Oluwa speak of human experience of God. In names we encounter the African ontology that is centered on God who is the source of life and cohesion, whose sovereignty over all cannot be questioned. We experience blessings when ideals like unity, community, caring, faithfulness, excellence, steadfastness, etc., abound among human beings, for in these we experience God.

God is experienced as the good parent, the grandparent Nana, a source of loving-kindness and protection. Some say Nana is father while others say Nana is

mother, but the sentiment is the same: human beings experience a closeness to God which they describe in terms of motherhood and fatherhood. There was never any need to debate the existence of God. The challenge was always to discern God at work. Does God take sides? If so, whose side is God on, and why? The African experience of God is that ultimately God is on the side of the weak and the side of justice. No one can explain God. *Nsa baako ntumi nkata Onyame ani* (no single hand can cover the eye of God), and so Africans grant a plurality of approaches to God and experiences of God. Experiences of God vary according to the circumstances surrounding people's daily life. To illustrate this we will review some contemporary scenes that indicate shifts in the language about God that correspond to changed situations.

The South African case is illustrative of how traditional Christian language about God is modified to cope with the people's experience of God at work. Alan Boesak, writing on "Coming in out of the wilderness" in *Emergent Gospel,* tells of Isaiah Shembe (1870–1935), the founder of an AIC (African independent church), and records this statement made by people in his church:

> You my people, were once told of a God
> who had neither arms nor legs, who
> cannot see, who has neither love nor pity.
> But Isaiah Shembe showed you God who
> walks on feet and who heals with his
> hands, and who can be known by men.[10]

In this church the African meets a God who loves and has compassion. Like Betty Goviden, Isaiah Shembe underlines the South African dilemma of a God who seems to decree injustice so as to favor some and oppress others. In this, as in other contexts, the experience of God as a healer and companion on life's journey is very important for Africans, and the "exodus" from white-led churches into AICs, says Boesak, is a theological statement. Further theological statements issuing out of the South African experience of God have been collected in *Black Theology: The South African Voice*[11] edited by Basil Moore. In South Africa, God was experienced by the Africans as active and operating with a whole lot of envoys when missionaries arrived to declare the whole system of AR idolatrous and without God. It has taken the AICs to reestablish African language about God in the vocabulary of African Christians. The South African experience of racism included a Christian God who was boss (the South African secret police) and partial to the dominant group. Black theology had to debunk the underlying theory that God is partial and favored the white race and subjected the black race to servitude under them. A fresh profile of God was needed to heighten the experience of God as compassionate and just. Revelation is through experience, and South Africans, black and white, were experiencing afresh the presence and essence of God in that situation. In this collection of essays we find a testimony to people's experience of God in South Africa.

In the context of apartheid, where white people set themselves up as gods who determined how the humanity of others was to develop, it was a real challenge to talk about the Source Being in meaningful terms. God in the apartheid system was depicted in patriarchal and hierarchical terms, lending support to the oppressive regime. Traditional Christian theological terms like omniscience and omnipotence fueled the oppressive authoritarianism and were no use to a people who understood God as abhorring slavery. The Africans found white authority incongruent to their traditional philosophy in which authority derives from serving the unity and well-being of the whole people. Authority is not power over. Besides, their traditional experience of being human is in life-giving relationships. This results in images of God that are freeing and that depict unity and wholeness.

God has to be experienced as the source of humanizing relationships of love, truth and justice, of mercy and kindness. New language developed and South Africans, both those of African descent and those of European and Asian descent who were awakened to the evil of apartheid, began to experience God as freedom. God as freedom became a theological symbol. They began to discard the anthropomorphic language which fuels sexism and to create relational expressions. In the contribution of Sabelo Ntwana and Basil Moore titled "The Concept of God in Black theology," they state that "God is love" means that God is a person who loves me, but "God is freedom" means that God is the freedom made known in our history, calling us from oppression into wholeness of life. God is this wholeness which exists in the spaces between people when their dignity and worth is mutually affirmed in love, truth, honesty, justice, and caring warmth. God cannot be represented in any created object.[12]

Mokgethi Motlhabi in his essay declares that the Church had become an oppressive human organization. "Only God is freedom." By definition, therefore, our freedom is reflected in the image of God.[13] From Motlhabi's experience in the South African context, God was to be imaged as "both creator and liberator to all people in their entire situation, not only religious but also social, political and economic."[14] Here is a call to the holistic cosmology of AR that is also biblical. In South Africa, God has been experienced as freedom and truth, as comrade and friend in the struggle for freedom.

The South African reimaging of God revolved around ridding themselves of the patriarchal model that supports the hierarchy, domination, and sexism of their experience under apartheid. On this, the editors of *Black Theology: The South African Voice* wrote: "The symbol 'person' for God attracts both gender and color and has strong overtones of authority." "God is male" has had repercussions in Christianity that one cannot continue to uphold; therefore, "Black theology of liberation that is relevant to South Africa cannot afford to perpetuate any form of domination, not even male domination; if its liberation is not human enough to include the liberation of women, it will not be liberation."[15] The constitution of the new South Africa has been true to this vision, a vision shared by many African women and articulated by women who have constituted themselves into a Circle of Concerned African Women Theologians.[16]

Since in the Church in Africa men and the clergy presume to speak for God, and to demand the obedience of women, it is not easy to experience God as empowering and liberating when one is in the Church's ambit. Women experience God as the one who orders their subordination, who requires them to serve and never be served. God is the one who made them women, with a body deemed to be the locus of sin and impurity. God is experienced as source of women's oppression and Jesus as the author of the exclusion of women from sacramental roles in the Church. This is the God the Christian tradition wants women to love and obey.

For many women, however, this is a clear substitution of the will of God for the will of the male of the human species. Many women experience God differently and cannot allow themselves to be subjected to cultural codes that mask the image of God in women. They experience God as empowering them with a spirituality of resistance to dehumanization. The androcentric Bible and Church have not been able to warp women's direct experience of God as a loving liberator.

The experience of God is articulated by these women in terms of a theology of creation and the implications of the Christian affirmation that "God was in Christ." The Christology of African women is centered on Jesus, friend and liberator who upholds the dignity of the humanity of women. They experience God in Christ as affirming the goodness of the sexuality of women, a factor that has been a pretext in both AR and Christianity for the diminution of women, discrimination against them and their marginalization from centers of power and the ministration of sacraments. Writings of women theologians from Africa are replete with these experiences.[17]

In *The Will to Arise* Teresia Hinga describes an experience of God in Christ that is very real to African women. Women often describe Jesus as the friend and companion who helps them bear life's burdens.[18] There is also the prophetic Jesus who challenges oppressors and hypocrites but forgives sinners. In Jesus, women experience the God who is love. These experiences of God are affirmed by women in terms of "nevertheless." Women describe themselves as being in the image of God even if sexism denies their dignity.

In the women theologians' circle, studies of God's hospitality, African hospitality, and women in the household of God reveal women's experience of God as the Great Householder who empowers all and recognizes all as children in a parent's home and around the one table. They give expression to experiences of the God who sustains in times of dire need and who brings victory where it is least expected. They have constantly attributed all recognition and inclusiveness to the power of God which transforms human beings and human conditions. They express their experience of God in affirming cultural beliefs and practices, while they feel called by God to denounce and to deconstruct oppressive ones.

Despite sexism's making it difficult for women to experience God in the Church, women have nevertheless witnessed to their experience of God in Christ, the one who brings salvation. While critical of certain aspects of biblical culture, they have nevertheless testified to their experience of the liberating God of the Bible in events in their own lives. Rereading Scripture, and especially the stories of women in the Bible, has brought God closer and enhanced the Presence around us.[19] Women experience God as groaning with them as they participate in straining toward the birth of a new Africa free from sexism and racism, from poverty, exploitation, and violence.

All experiences of "love beyond self," all that is just and life-giving, are understood to be expressions of the presence of God.[20] All that enhances the dignity and worth of women is attributed to the presence of God. Women who take the image of God in human beings seriously see it in the faces of the starving children around them and in all those who suffer needlessly in Africa. When women live by caring, they are expressing the caring God in whose image they are created. Hopefully those who experience love and justice and compassion will realize that God is present.

How do these experiences of God in Africa relate to the building up of the Body of Christ in Africa? How do the churches respond to peoples' experiences of God? There is a revival of traditional African images of God, in the AICs and, to a lesser extent, in the "Prosperity Christianity" that has taken Africa by storm for nearly two decades. The AICs have a profile of being prophetic-healing-praying churches. Africans move to these churches to hear God through prophets, as they used to do through the divination of AR. They seek and experience healing of body and soul and the efficacy of communing with God in prayer. Religion comes alive, it ceases to be a formal gathering with an ambience that is devoid of African culture. However, to a significant extent the charismatic-pentecostal-prosperity churches have returned Africans to the anti-African culture of the Western missionaries. They maintain that to succeed you must move away from African beliefs related to ancestors, African practices and ritual, and seek "deliverance" from evil and poverty through the Church, your new family. The music, song and dance, tithing, and exuberant demonstration of spirituality may be similar in both types of church, but there is a marked difference in their attitudes to things African. Those who flock to join these churches presumably do so because they experience the presence of God they yearn for. These churches are building up the Body of Christ by seeking to meet the felt needs of people.

The South African experience of God as liberator has encouraged churches in other parts of Africa to confront governments with their lack of care for the populace. Contemporary experiences of atrocities committed in Africa by Africans on Africans lead people to ask "Where is God in all this?" "On whose side is God?" some have asked. Some have surmised that

God is apparently not interested in what happens to humanity in Africa.[21] In other words, Africa experiences the absence of God when evil triumphs. This is the case with adherents of AR as with Christians. Mandela quotes the ending of a speech given during his initiation into manhood:

> I know that Qameta (God) is all-seeing and never sleeps, but I have a suspicion that Qameta may in fact be dozing. If this is the case, the sooner I die the better, because then I can meet him and shake him awake and tell him that the children of Ngubengcuku, the flower of the Xhosa nation, are dying.[22]

When apartheid was formally dismantled, all Africa, indeed the whole of the justice-loving world, rejoiced and the religious gave glory to God. The presence of God has been demonstrated.

To build up Christ's body we need to demonstrate the liberating presence of God. When we are able to empower Zaire and Rwanda, Sudan and Nigeria to learn to live creatively and justly with difference, we shall be helping to unveil God. African myths of separation attribute the felt absence of God to human acts of greed and callousness. To build up the Body of Christ everywhere requires building up human relations, seeing humanity as one family under God who is the source of the life of the human family. We cannot continue the rhetoric of loving, caring words about God if people are not experiencing loving, caring acts from one another.

We cannot tell people that creation is a "pure gift from God, unsolicited" when some enjoy more of these gifts than others and the Church does little to alleviate poverty. African affirmations about God and creation have to come alive in the projects, program and attitudes of the Church. What does it mean when we say "Nothing is too difficult for God," when we affirm it is "God who gives the cow to the Masai" or that "When God gives no one can snatch"? All of this is empty rhetoric if people cannot testify that "What God says God does." And how is this to be demonstrated if the Church proclaims a "God in Christ" who has arms too short to reach the hurt of people? We seek the presence of God who saves now, in the being and doing of the Church. For many it is the absence of God, the alienation from God the source of life, that is the immediate experience.[23]

Faith in a God of love lives on in Africa in spite of the apparent absence. For Africans like the Masai for whom there is no life after death, and even for the Akan who are gathered to God and to the ancestors when they die, it is important to see the goodness of God here in the land of the living, for that is what establishes the presence of God among human beings. Many of the women I know are like Buchie Emecheta: they know that God has more important things to do than to punish them for having "ambitions" of fulfilling their potential. Like her they pray for miracles. God is a miracle-working God. Emecheta says, "When I saw a miracle flying by I would grab it." Winning a scholarship for secondary school education was for her one such miracle. African women expect God to "deliver." In lyrics, traditional and modern, they sing about the God who says and does and they invite all to come and see what God has actually done. They declare that words are not up to the task of expressing thanks to God.[24] When Africans can testify to sight for the blind, that becomes evidence that God is being experienced. To respond to these expectations and experiences of God in Africa is to build up the Body of Christ, not only in Africa, but worldwide. For God cannot treat Africa and Africans differently from other places and people and still remain the sole source of human being. The Church will build up the Body of Christ if it acts to heal, strengthen, nourish, and treat with dignity all of its members, and that means acting as God-in-Christ expects of the Church.

Notes

1. Joseph Healey and Donald Sybert, eds., *Towards an African Narrative Theology* (Pauline Publishers Africa, 1995), 295.
2. Betty Goviden Devarakshanam, "In Search of Our Own Wells" in Musimbi R. A. Kanyoro and Nyambura J. Njoroge, eds., *Groaning in Faith: African Women in the Household of God* (Nairobi: Acton Publishers, 1996), 112–135.
3. Nelson Mandela, *Long Walk to Freedom* (Abacus, 1994), 15.
4. Wande Abimbola, *Ifa Divination Poetry* (Paris: UNESCO, 1975), n. 115.
5. Osalador Imasogie, 84.
6. Healey and Sybert, *Towards an African Narrative Theology,* 80–82, record names collected between 1992 and 1995.
7. For other examples of the use of symbolic language in narrative theology in Africa, see Mercy Amba Oduyoye, *Daughters of Anowa: African*

Women and Patriarchy (Maryknoll, N.Y.: Orbis Books, 1995).

8. Kwesi A. Dickson, *African Theology,* 60.

9. J. S. Mbiti, *Prayers of an African Religion.*

10. Allan Boesak, "Coming Out of the Wilderness," in Sergio Torres and Virginia Fabella, eds., *The Emergent Gospel* (London: Geoffrey Chapman, 1976), 76.

11. Basil Moore, ed., *Black Theology: The South African Voice* (London: Hurst, 1973).

12. Ibid., 25.

13. Mokgethi Motlhabi, "Black Theology: A Personal View" in ibid., 74–75.

14. Ibid., 77.

15. Ibid., 25.

16. The Circle of Concerned African Women Theologians came into being on the initiative of Mercy Amba Oduyoye to enable African women to contribute to the theological literature that is being developed by Africans. Since its inauguration in October of 1989 two pan-African books and three regional ones have been published.

Papers from the August pan-African conference are being processed for publication.

17. See Part 1 of Kanyoro and Njoroge, *Groaning in Faith,* for examples.

18. Teresia Hinga in Mercy Amba Oduyoye and Musimbi Kanyoro, *The Will to Arise* (Maryknoll, N.Y.: Orbis Books, 1995), 190–191.

19. Christine Landman, "A Land Flowing With Milk and Honey," in Musimbi R. A. Kanyoro and Nyambura J. Njoroge, *Groaning in Faith,* 99–111.

20. Grace Ndyabahika, "Women's Place in Creation," in Kanyoro and Njoroge, *Groaning in Faith,* 256.

21. Kwesi A. Dickson, *African Theology,* 91.

22. Nelson Mandela, *Long Walk to Freedom,* 35.

23. Healey and Sybert, *Towards an African Narrative Theology,* 29.

24. Buchie Emecheta's *Head Above Water: An Autobiography* and several Fante lyrics, including the one below, testify to this experience of God.
Nyame a ose a oye ho. Waaye o!
wommesen 'nkohwe. Efurafo weenya enyiwa.

Conclusions

The missionary experience brought a mixture of good and bad: schools, hospitals, literacy, education, and even women's rights; but also disease, destruction, and decimation of peoples and their cultures. Missionaries often mixed the Christian proclamation with a message of cultural superiority, confusing Christianity with (European or American) civilization. Thus, civilizing and Christianizing went hand in hand, often at the expense of life and hope for converts. At the same time, Christianity contributed to the liberation of its converts by providing both the tools and the seeds of freedom in its message of redemption. For example, Bible translators have created alphabets for indigenous peoples who had no written language. These translations have led to increased literacy, an interest in indigenous language and culture, and the development of vernacular literature in a variety of places around the world.

Part of the impetus for missionizing came from the belief that Christianity was the sole pathway to God. Many Christians today quote John 14:6 in support of this conviction: "I am the way, the truth, and the life," said Jesus, and "No one can come to the Father but through me." Although Jesus' words should be understood within the apologetic context of John's gospel, and though other Gospels contradict Jesus' statement in John (for example, Matthew 7:21–23), nevertheless Christians have argued that theirs is the only true faith.

In the 1960s, D. T. Niles identified five different attitudes Christians have had regarding other world religions. First, Christianity is destined to surpass and supplant all other religions—a "polemical view." A second view is that Christianity is the fulfillment of other religions, especially Judaism. Other religions manifest a yearning for God that is completed only in Christianity. A third attitude is that all religions contain the possibility of relationship between God and humanity, but only in Christianity is this relationship a free gift to all. A fourth position states that all religions eventually will be judged by Jesus; Christianity and Christians will be judged as well as non-Christians. The final view is that Christians ought to present Jesus to non-Christians, not with the idea of creating converts, but in the hope that the encounter with Christ will help others to reconceptualize their own faith. Ultimately, a new religion will emerge, one that includes Christianity as well as all others.

Christian missions have changed since Niles wrote about them, however. A somewhat different sensibility exists, at least among some. Paul F. Knitter, a former missionary and current university professor, describes three main approaches to world religions, and thus to missions. The first, which he calls the evangelical approach, sees other religions as evil and false, a product of the devil. For these missionaries, all existing religious and cultural practices must be eradicated, because they are satanic. This view is apparent among many conservative Christians, who consider Islam satanic and idolatrous. The second approach, which Knitter terms mainline, does not consider other religions evil or satanic; rather, people may be ignorant of the superior truths of Christianity, but they are neither wicked nor deceived. Mainline Protestants have focused on building schools and hospitals, and establishing other programs, rather than preaching the Bible alone. The third approach, which is that of contemporary Catholicism, tries to preserve what is "good and holy" in all religions. This is a continuation of the Jesuit approach to missions, which involved learning the language of the people, appropriating indigenous objects and symbols into worship, and "translating" Christianity into familiar religious idioms. In fact, Mother Teresa—the Albanian holy woman who devoted her life to serving the poor in Calcutta, India—is reported to have said that her role was not to turn Hindus into Christians, but to make Hindus better Hindus.

Just as the Son's relationship to the Father had to be determined in the early centuries of Christianity, and the meaning of justification and the importance of biblical authority clarified in the sixteenth century, so today a major theological issue facing Christians is that of their relation to non-Christians. Is there only one way? Are there many paths to God? Are there many paths that ultimately will be judged by Christ? For two millennia, Christians encountered non-Christians with a sense of superiority and mission—we could even say empire—that allowed them to face severe hardships in order to do what they believed was God's will for the world. Both Christianity and the world changed as a result. Today, Christians meet non-Christians on a religiously and culturally plural planet, less sure of their superiority when they find pious Buddhists, faithful Muslims, and devout Hindus doing the will of the divine. A new Christian theology of world religions and missions may emerge in this different environment. Indeed, it already has among missionaries who see their first task as being that of walking with the poor and oppressed as Jesus once did. For them, Christ has become incarnate in the hungry, the sick, the thirsty, and the incarcerated (Matthew 25:31–40). They see inculturation as nothing less than making the Christian message real in the lives of those they encounter.

Sources for Selections

Casas, Bartolomé de las. *An Account, Much Abbreviated, of the Destruction of the Indies.* Ed. Franklin W. Knight, trans. Andrew Hurley. Indianapolis, Ind.: Hackett, 2003.

Charleston, Steve. "The Old Testament of Native America." In *Lift Every Voice: Constructing Christian Theologies from the Underside.* Rev. and exp. ed. Ed. Susan Brooks Thistlethwaite and Mary Potter Engel. Maryknoll, N.Y.: Orbis Books, 2000.

Elizondo, Virgilio. "Our Lady of Guadalupe as a Cultural Symbol." In *Beyond Borders: Writings of Virgilio Elizondo and Friends.* Ed. Timothy Matovina. Maryknoll, N.Y.: Orbis Books, 2000.

Endo, Shusaku. *Silence.* Trans. William Johnson. New York: Taplinger, 1980.

Johnson, James Weldon. "Lift Every Voice and Sing." In *Songs of Zion.* Nashville, Tenn., Abingdon Press, 1981.

Johnson, Thomas Lewis. *Twenty-Eight Years a Slave, or the Story of My Life in Three Continents.* <http://docsouth.unc.edu/johnson/johnson.html>.

Kagawa, Toyohiko. *Christ and Japan.* Trans. William Axling. New York: Friendship Press, 1934.

Oduyoye, Mercy Amba. "African Christianity Through the Eyes of an Akan Woman." <http://www.aril.org/african.htm>.

Additional Resources

Davis, David Brion. *Challenging the Boundaries of Slavery.* Cambridge, Mass.: Harvard University Press, 2003.

Dickson, Kwesi A. *Uncompleted Mission: Christianity and Exclusivism.* Maryknoll, N.Y.: Orbis Books, 1991.

Elizondo, Virgilio. *The Future Is Mestizo: Life Where Cultures Meet.* New York: Crossroad, 1992.

Griffiths, Paul J., ed. *Christianity Through Non-Christian Eyes.* Maryknoll, N.Y.: Orbis Books, 1990.

Hill, Brennan R., Paul Knitter, and William Madges. *Faith, Religion, and Theology: A Contemporary Introduction.* Mystic, Conn.: Twenty-Third Publications, 1997.

Knitter, Paul F. *No Other Name? A Critical Survey of Christian Attitudes Toward the World Religions.* Maryknoll, N.Y.: Orbis Books, 1985.

Niles, D. T. *Upon the Earth: The Mission of God and the Missionary Enterprise of the Churches.* New York: McGraw-Hill, 1962.

Roof, Wade Clark, ed. *World Order and Religion.* Albany: State University of New York, 1991.

Williams, Juan and Quinton Dixie. *This Far by Faith: Stories from the African American Religious Experience.* New York: HarperCollins, 2003.

Films

Black Narcissus. Directed by Michael Powell, 1947.
Black Robe. Directed by Bruce Beresford, 1991.
1492: The Conquest of Paradise. Directed by Ridley Scott, 1992.
The Mission. Directed by Roland Joffe, 1986.

	1906	Azusa Street Revival in Los Angeles sparks Pentecostal movement
World War I	1914–18	
	1915	Armenian Genocide
Russian Revolution	1917	
Walter Rauschenbusch publishes A Theology for the Social Gospel	1925	United States refuses to join League of Nations
Stock Market crash in United States; banks fail	1929	
	1931	Japan invades Manchuria
"Crystal Night," wave of destruction against Berlin Jews	1939	
	1939–45	World War II
Atomic bombs dropped on Hiroshima and Nagasaki, Japan; United Nations charter drafted	1945	
	1948	World Council of Churches established
Chinese Communist Revolution	1949	
	1950–53	Korean War
Cuban Revolution	1959	
	1960	National independence of Nigeria and Democratic Republic of Congo
Vatican Council II	1962–65	
	1968	Assassination of Martin Luther King Jr.
Lunar landing	1969	
	1970	First Earth Day celebrated
Fall of Saigon to North Vietnam	1975	
	1978	Election of Pope John Paul II to papacy
Radiation released by Chernobyl nuclear reactor, U.S.S.R.	1986	
	1989	Fall of Berlin Wall
Genocide in Bosnia (Serbian "ethnic cleansing")	1992	
	1994	Genocide in Rwanda; end of apartheid in South Africa
Attacks on World Trade Center, Pentagon in United States	2001	
	2005	Tsunami in Indian Ocean kills 250,000

CHAPTER SEVEN

Voices for the Future

My parents' generation grew up without television, without jet planes, and without interstate highways. My own generation saw the introduction of television—though initially it was black-and-white—computers, and microwave ovens. We are all witnesses to changes both profound and trivial. We have seen hairstyles go from crew cuts, to mop tops and afros, to ponytails, to shaved heads. And we have seen the world shrink in size thanks to globalization, transportation, and mass media. It is no surprise, then, that Christians in the twentieth century had to reflect upon how these phenomena affected their faith. What within Christianity could remain fixed and eternal? What needed to change, or be updated, according to the signs of the times?

The events of the twentieth century shook the Western world's self-confidence and its faith in a benevolent supreme being. Wars, diseases, famine, holocaust, and terror—all seemed to reveal the absence of God. How could a kind and loving God allow such atrocities, such innocent suffering, to occur? At the same time, world travel, immigration, and globalization made Christians cognizant of other world religions, of the diversity of beliefs and believers. Actually meeting Muslims and Jews, and talking with Buddhists and Hindus, challenged the traditional Christian conviction of exclusivity—that is, that Christianity provided the only path to ultimate salvation. Scientific advances seemed to push God to the periphery, as discoveries in physics, chemistry, and biology led to previously unthinkable possibilities in human endeavor. There was also a growing concern about the welfare of the entire planet. Nuclear war, chemical herbicides and pesticides, global warming, deforestation, the daily loss of dozens of plant and animal species—all seemed to indicate that humans had embarked upon a suicidal path that not even God could halt.

Even though Christians in previous centuries had faced trials and tribulations, had suffered martyrdom and exile, these agonies paled in comparison to the persecution that Christians suffered at the hands of totalitarian regimes in the twentieth. The U.S. State Department estimates that hundreds of thousands of Christians around the world were killed in the previous century simply because they were Christians or because their witness to faith brought them into conflict with government authorities. One of the most famous examples of this was the rape and murder of three U.S. Catholic nuns and a lay sister in El Salvador in 1980 during the civil war there. The four women—Jean Donovan and Sisters Ita Ford, Maura Clarke, and Dorothy Kazel—were working with the poor and were executed by a death squad for their opposition to government policies. More recently, Christian missionaries in India were murdered by Hindu nationalists who feared that their work might create an anti-Indian Christian subculture. The list of twentieth-century martyrs is long.

It is no wonder that Christians in this period were tormented by incredible human suffering: the execution of Christians and the repression of Christianity in communist countries; the Nazi Holocaust in which millions of Jews, Slavs, gays, gypsies, the mentally and physically disabled, and political dissidents were systematically murdered; the oppression of people living under dictatorships in Uganda, South Africa, El Salvador, China, Iraq, and elsewhere; the fratricidal civil wars in Bosnia and Serbia, in Rwanda and Burundi, and in Nigeria, in which women were repeatedly raped, children were drafted into military service, and in some instances organized squads deliberately maimed civilians by cutting off hands, arms, and legs.

"How can we speak of God in a world come of age," asked Dietrich Bonhoeffer from a German prison cell during World War II. This was indeed the question that Christians had to address throughout the twentieth century. Despite the horrors associated with technological advances, political oppression, and moral weaknesses, Christians continued to speak and write of God's gracious revelation in Jesus Christ—but with a difference. Gone was some of the arrogance and self-confidence; gone were some of the foundational assumptions about the social order and one's place in it, whether black or white, male or female, rich or poor. Christians debated other Christians about key theological and social issues with a new eye to outsiders and their views. The awareness that Christianity was a minority religion within the broader global community was evident in many of the themes and subjects that Christians addressed in the twentieth century.

Christianity began the century on a high note. One hundred years of aggressive missionizing to the peoples of the European colonial empires had brought hundreds of thousands, and perhaps millions, into the Christian fold. Africa seemed particularly fertile missionary territory, given the fact that Central and South America were largely Catholic, and Asia had religious traditions like Hinduism and Buddhism, which seemed relatively impervious to proselytizing. Christians remained optimistic about the further spread of the gospel as colonial expansion opened new markets and new mission fields.

In addition, the Social Gospel movement was in full swing. Products of nineteenth-century liberal theology, ministers of the Social Gospel believed that by enacting social and political reforms they could Christianize the social order and bring about the "brotherhood of man under the fatherhood of God." An outgrowth of the abolition, temperance, and suffrage movements in the United States and Great Britain, the Social Gospel movement attempted to bring about collective redemption in the form of labor laws, welfare programs, prison reform, and political change. One of the Protestant leaders of the movement in the United States, Walter Rauschenbusch (1861–1918), a Baptist minister and theologian, said that because sin is collective as well as individual, salvation must also be collective. On the Catholic side, Father John A. Ryan (1869–1945), who became known as the Right Reverend New Dealer, outlined a package of welfare benefits that eventually became public policy in the United States during the Great Depression. Christians of all denominations attempted to alleviate the poverty and misery of millions of immigrants who were crowding into the cities of the East Coast looking for work and freedom. In Great Britain, some Christians became part of a program of Christian socialism, which saw in biblical Christianity a type of primitive socialism.

Liberalism, Fundamentalism, and Neo-Orthodoxy

All of these Social Gospel programs grew out of the optimism of nineteenth-century liberal theology, which tried to reconcile Christianity with advances in the modern world. Liberals believed that people were basically good and could improve themselves if given the right incentives and proper environment. This view mirrors an Enlightenment rationalism that asserted the ultimate perfectibility of the human race. Charles Darwin's theory of evolution seemed to confirm the liberal belief that the human species was making progress, and would continue to do so in future. Liberal Christians (both liberal Protestants and Catholic Modernists) felt at home in the world of rationalism. They applied contemporary methods of historical research and textual criticism to the study of the Bible. This new approach, sometimes called "higher criticism," discussed authorship and dating of the Bible. It looked at differences between various accounts, at the words used, and at the very manuscripts from which translations were made. Critical biblical studies helped Christians consider the Bible in a new way. Biblical criticism allowed believers to consider familiar stories and texts as theological truths—the products of revelations, dreams, visions and prophecies—rather than as historical or scientific facts. Liberal Christians could accept conflicts, contradictions, and figures of speech (metaphors, similes) as constitutive of sacred texts written by people living in a preindustrial, prescientific world. This made the challenges posed by zoological, biological, and geological discoveries—such as estimations of the age of the earth and theories about natural selection and evolution—less threatening.

Other Christians resisted these changes, however, and beginning at the end of the nineteenth century, a movement arose within the United States that eventually came to be known as fundamentalism. The label came from a periodical titled *The Fundamentals,* published in the early twentieth century, that sought to outline what conservative Protestant Christians believed to be the essence of Christianity. That essence could be boiled down to five or six key beliefs: the inerrancy of scripture, the virgin birth, the literal resurrection, the substitionary atonement, and (either) miracles or Jesus' second coming. Fundamentalists claimed that those who do not believe in these fundamentals cannot call themselves Christian. Thus, liberals who did not think the virgin birth of Jesus was particularly important to their faith, or thought they could explain miracles or the resurrection naturalistically, rather than super-naturalistically, were not Christians, according to fundamentalists.

The conflict within Protestantism between liberal and fundamentalist Christians hinges on understanding the word *inerrancy*. Some Christians believe that the Bible is inerrant, that is, without error, with regard to moral or spiritual truths, but is not inerrant with regard to historical or scientific truths. They would interpret many stories metaphorically, that is, nonliterally or nonhistorically. Therefore, the account of God creating the world in six days in Genesis 1 might indicate six ages or epochs of creation; or it might speak of a theological truth that God is involved in the creation of the world and everything in it. The strictest fundamentalists, however, are biblical literalists, who believe that Adam and Eve were the first man and the first woman in history, that they spoke to a big snake, and that all sorts of evil resulted from that conversation. For these Christians, the stories in the Bible are historical—they actually happened, exactly as written.

Like liberal Protestantism, fundamentalist Protestantism represents a response to Enlightenment rationalism. Biblical criticism threatened to undermine the authority of scripture, while rationalism questioned all texts, even sacred ones. Just as the Protestant Reformation challenged the authority of tradition, as expressed through church teachings, and claimed that the Bible was the sole authority, the Enlightenment weakened the authority of the Bible by claiming that reason was the ultimate arbiter of truth. Fundamentalists attempted to bolster biblical authority by asserting that God is the author of scripture and that the Bible is historically accurate. The irony of the liberal and fundamentalist positions is that both sides want certainty. Liberal Christians find the Bible too unreliable a source to grant it absolute authority, while fundamentalists give it unqualified and unconditional power in their lives. Both liberal and fundamentalist Christians have succumbed to Enlightenment claims about the nature and source of truth.

Although fundamentalism began as a minority movement within Christianity, and at its narrowest, still remains marginal, many of its tenets have been adopted by the wider evangelical community. Evangelical Christianity is the dominant form of Protestantism in the United States today: it is theologically conservative, at times verging on fundamentalist, but may be either socially conservative or progressive. We see this in the proliferation of Bible-based or nondenominational churches in the United States. Millennialist Protestantism is another type of conservative Christianity. Christians have always believed that Jesus Christ would return to rule in God's kingdom on earth. Millennial Christians such as Seventh-day Adventists, members of the Church of Jesus Christ, Latter-day Saints (that is, Mormons), and Jehovah's Witnesses, believe Christ's return is imminent and that we should be prepared. These denominations provide definite answers in an age of uncertainty.

Yet another response to liberal theology arose in the seminaries and universities. Karl Barth (1886–1968), a Swiss theologian, gave birth to a movement known as neo-orthodoxy in the early twentieth century. Unlike fundamentalism, neo-orthodoxy did not always take the Bible literally; but it did take the Bible and Christian doctrine seriously. Barth argued that God was utterly transcendent and radically "other" from human beings. God sent Jesus, the Word, to bridge the gap between the divine and the human. We know this only by the revelation contained in the Bible, however, and so we must believe in the revelation. Barth differed from the fundamentalists in that he was concerned with biblical revelation rather than literal biblical truth. But he differed from the liberals, who seemed to have reduced the revelation to moral teachings. Moreover, Barth had a traditional Augustinian anthropology, viewing humans as basically sinful and in need of redemption. Neo-orthodoxy clearly rejected the optimism of liberal rationalism.

Martin Luther King Jr. (1929–1968), drew one of the clearest contrasts between liberalism and neo-orthodoxy in an account of his "Pilgrimage to Nonviolence." In an article written for the *Christian Century* in 1960, King outlined his own objections to both approaches to Christianity. An excerpt from that article is included here in order to clarify the differences between liberal theology, neo-orthodoxy, and the Social Gospel, according to King.

Ten years ago I was just entering my senior year in theological seminary. Like most theological students I was engaged in the exciting job of studying various theological theories. Having been raised in a rather strict fundamentalistic tradition, I was occasionally shocked as my intellectual journey carried me through new and sometimes complex doctrinal lands. But despite the shock the pilgrimage was always stimulating, and it gave me a new appreciation for objective appraisal and critical analysis. My early theological training did the same for me as the reading of Hume did for Kant: it knocked me out of my dogmatic slumber.

At this stage of my development I was a thoroughgoing liberal. Liberalism provided me with an intellectual satisfaction that I could never find in fundamentalism. I became so enamored of the insights of liberalism that I almost fell into the trap of accepting uncritically everything that came under its name. I was absolutely convinced of the natural goodness of man and the natural power of human reason.

The basic change in my thinking came when I began to question some of the theories that had been associated with so-called liberal theology. Of course there is one phase of liberalism that I hope to cherish always: its devotion to the search for truth, its insistence on an open and analytical mind, its refusal to abandon the best light of reason. Liberalism's contribution to the philological-historical criticism of biblical literature has been of immeasurable value and should be defended with religious and scientific passion.

It was mainly the liberal doctrine of man that I began to question. The more I observed the tragedies of history and man's shameful inclination to choose the low road, the more I came to see the depths and strength of sin. My reading of the works of Reinhold Niebuhr made me aware of the complexity of human motives and the reality of sin on every level of man's existence. Moreover, I came to recognize the complexity of man's social involvement and the glaring reality of collective evil. I came to feel that liberalism had been all too sentimental concerning human nature and that it leaned toward a false idealism.

I also came to see that liberalism's superficial optimism concerning human nature caused it to overlook the fact that reason is darkened by sin. The more I thought about human nature the more I saw how our tragic inclination for sin causes us to use our minds to rationalize our actions. Liberalism failed to see that reason by itself is little more than an instrument to justify man's defensive ways of thinking. Reason, devoid of purifying power of faith, can never free itself from distortions and rationalizations.

In spite of the fact that I had to reject some aspects of liberalism, I never came to an all-out acceptance of neo-orthodoxy. While I saw neo-orthodoxy as a helpful corrective for a liberalism that had become all too sentimental, I never felt that it provided an adequate answer to the basic questions. If liberalism was too optimistic concerning human nature, neo-orthodoxy was too pessimistic. Not only on the question of man but also on other vital issues neo-orthodoxy went too far in its revolt. In its attempt to preserve the transcendence of God, which had been neglected by liberalism's overstress of his immanence, neo-orthodoxy went to the extreme of stressing a God who was hidden, unknown and "wholly other." In its revolt against liberalism's overemphasis on the power of reason, neo-orthodoxy fell into a mood of antirationalism and semifundamentalism, stressing a narrow, uncritical biblicism. This approach, I felt, was inadequate both for the church and for personal life.

So although liberalism left me unsatisfied on the question of the nature of man, I found no refuge in neo-orthodoxy. I am now convinced that the truth about man is found neither in liberalism nor in neo-orthodoxy. Each represents a partial truth. A large segment of Protestant liberalism defined man only in terms of his essential nature, his capacity for good. Neo-orthodoxy tended to define man only in terms of his existential nature, his capacity for evil. An adequate understanding of man is found neither in the thesis of liberalism nor in the antithesis of neo-orthodoxy, but in a synthesis which reconciles the truths of both.

During the past decade I also gained a new appreciation for the philosophy of existentialism. My first contact with this philosophy came through my reading of Kierkegaard and Nietzsche. Later I turned to a study of Jaspers, Heidegger and Sartre. All of these thinkers stimulated my thinking; while finding things to question in each, I nevertheless learned a great deal from study of them. When I finally turned to a serious study of the works of Paul Tillich I became convinced that existentialism, in spite of the fact that it had become all too fashionable, had grasped certain basic truths about man and his condition that could not be permanently overlooked.

Its understanding of the "finite freedom" of man is one of existentialism's most lasting contributions, and its perception of the anxiety and conflict produced in man's personal and social life as a result of the perilous and ambiguous structure of existence is especially meaningful for our time. The common point in all existentialism, whether it is atheistic or theistic, is that man's existential situation is a state of estrangement from his essential nature. In their revolt against Hegel's essentialism, all existentialists contend that the world is fragmented. History is a series of unreconciled conflicts and man's existence is filled with anxiety and threatened with meaninglessness. While the ultimate Christian answer is not found in any of these existential assertions, there is much here that the theologian can use to describe the true state of man's existence. . . .

Not until I entered theological seminary, however, did I begin a serious intellectual quest for a method to eliminate social evil. I was immediately influenced by the social gospel. In the early fifties I read Rauschenbusch's *Christianity and the Social Crisis,* a book which left an indelible imprint on my thinking. Of course there were points at which I differed with Rauschenbusch. I felt that he had fallen victim to the nineteenth century "cult of inevitable progress," which led him to an unwarranted optimism concerning human nature. Moreover, he came perilously close to identifying the kingdom of God with a particular social and economic system—a temptation which the church should never give in to. But in spite of these shortcomings Rauschenbusch gave to American Protestantism a sense of social responsibility that it should never lose. The gospel at its best deals with the whole man, not only his soul but his body, not only his spiritual well-being, but his material well-being. Any religion that professes to be concerned about the souls of men and is not concerned about the slums that damn them, the economic conditions that strangle them and the social conditions that cripple them is a spiritually moribund religion awaiting burial.

Shaking the Foundations

The events of the twentieth century generated diverse viewpoints within the Christian communion. Neo-orthodoxy and fundamentalism coincided with the disillusionment and despair that resulted from World War I and its failure to "make the world safe for democracy." Existentialism, and a movement in the 1960s called "death of God," followed the Holocaust and atomic blasts of World War II. Although a number of different theologians espoused the radical death-of-God theology, Thomas J. J. Altizer (b. 1927) is perhaps the best known. Altizer claimed that "Christian atheism" grows out of the biblical witness to the death of God in Christ's crucifixion. God's act of total self-negation—allowing the deity itself to be put to

▓ Christian Existentialism

Existentialism can claim Christian parentage in the writings of Søren Kierkegaard (1813–1855), a Danish philosopher. Kierkegaard bitterly criticized the "cultural Christianity" of his time—that is, the normative faith that people espoused but did not really practice in their daily lives. He hated hypocrisy and pretension, and, like the sixteenth-century Martin Luther, felt unworthy. Unlike Luther, however, Kierkegaard did not particularly accept the Bible as ultimate truth. Instead, he believed that one must *choose* to believe in God and God's goodness. This leap of faith—Kierkegaard coined the term—resembled the existentialist rejection of all truth claims and its privileging of existence, or one's actions, over essence, or one's being.

Thus, the Christian existentialist, and there were a few in the 1950s, believed in God, despite evidence to the contrary, and tried to act in accord with God's will. The utter assurance of conviction that existed in liberal theology, fundamentalism, and neo-orthodoxy had vanished. Yet one can see hints in Kierkegaard's philosophy of the possible danger of fideism—literally, "faith-ism." Since reason cannot prove the truths of religion, one must decide to believe, regardless of any rational justification or argument. One might summarize fideism in the bumper sticker slogan "God said it, I believe it, that settles it." The existentialist would qualify this by adding, "That settles it *for me.*" But the fideist adopts a position of faith that appears unquestioning, and the expression "blind faith" might well be applied to this type of commitment.

death—subverts the idea of Christendom and all notions of religiosity. The death of God meant loyalty to the gospel, which preached the immanence of the divine in Jesus Christ.

Still other movements in theology and biblical studies shook the foundations of traditional notions of Christianity. New Testament scholar Rudolf Bultmann (1884–1976) argued for "demythologizing" the gospel accounts of Jesus' life. Bultmann felt that the New Testament presented profound truths in mythological form, as a primitive way of expressing transcendent concepts. Modern biblical interpreters, however, needed to radically reinterpret the gospel stories. Once reinterpretation was completed—generally by hearing the gospel message proclaimed—the believer could make an existential choice to either accept or reject God. Bultmann rejected any notion of "presuppositionless" interpretation; that is, all interpreters bring prior worldviews and opinions to the texts they read and interpret. To understand something, especially scripture, is to establish a relationship between reader and text.

Historical Jesus studies also challenged traditional ways of thinking about Jesus (see Chapter One). They raised questions about the historicity—or factualness—of the gospel accounts of Jesus' life, death, and resurrection. A group of New Testament scholars, known as the Jesus Seminar, met throughout the 1990s and voted on which biblical sayings and actions of Jesus they believed were authentic and historical. Rather than seeking to "demythologize" Jesus, they sought to historicize him by identifying the distinction between the historical Jesus of Nazareth and the post-Easter Christ of early Christian belief.

Demythologizing and the quest for the historical Jesus were just two ways Christian theologians responded to Immanuel Kant's challenge to the authority of knowledge gained by the revelation in scripture. Yet another way came from Catholic theologians, who sought to integrate the insights of Thomas Aquinas with the reality of post-Kantian science and philosophy. Called "transcendental Thomism," this theological movement examined the subjective conditions of possible knowledge in order to preserve the truths of revelation. Like Thomas Aquinas in the Middle Ages, these new Thomists enlisted reason in the service of faith. "This effort was powerful and effective because it neither jettisoned the past out of fascination with the modern nor rejected the modern out of nostalgia for the past."* Founded by Joseph Maréchal (1878–1944), a Belgian Jesuit, transcendental Thomism attracted a number of towering figures in twentieth-century Catholic theology, including Karl Rahner, a German, and Bernard Lonergan, a Canadian. Both men were Jesuits, and both shared the same years of birth and death: 1904–1984.

These new Thomists were "transcendental" in a number of ways. Scholastic writers in the Middle Ages used "transcendental" to mean whatever could be applied to all being. Goodness, for example, pertained to everything, while quantity could

---

* I am indebted to Francis Schüssler Fiorenza's analysis for my discussion of transcendental Thomism.

pertain only to material items. Kant used "transcendental" to indicate what could be known by analyzing human reason. The transcendental Thomists essentially combined these two views to allow for the possibility of revelation (and so included Kant's analysis of human cognition); but they also used "transcendental" in the scholastic sense to encompass all that humans could know. Like their Protestant counterparts in movements such as neo-orthodoxy and biblical criticism, Catholic theologians were attempting to reconcile, or at least recognize, that the modern world presented new challenges and opportunities for long-held traditions.

While deep theological debates raged in the universities and seminaries, Christians in large, industrialized cities and in small, remote villages continued to attend church, read their Bibles, and pursue Christlike lives. World events conspired to make it more and more difficult to follow this practice, however. Though practicing Christianity had never been easy—after all, Jesus admonished his disciples to take up their crosses if they were to follow him—it seemed even more difficult in the twentieth century. The fact that humanity could exterminate vast numbers of people, wipe out entire plant and animal species, and threaten the future of all life on earth made the day and age radically different from the past.

A World Come of Age

Although writing in mid-century, Dietrich Bonhoeffer (1906–1945) could have been describing the fundamental questions that Christianity faced at any point in the last hundred years—from the destruction of World War I; to the Great Depression, and worldwide poverty and hunger; to the rise of fascism, Nazism, and Soviet-style communism; to problems that emerged after Bonhoeffer's execution by Nazi Germany. Though he died shortly before the atomic bombs fell at Nagasaki and Hiroshima, and long before the Korean and Vietnam wars, the Cold War, the civil wars of national liberation around the globe, and the rise of terrorism, Bonhoeffer prophetically asked how Christians could address the basic human problem of survival, given the apparent lack of a *need* for god or God as the answer to pressing questions.

Bonhoeffer, a pastor and theologian in Germany's Confessing Church, which was a type of evangelical Christianity opposed to Nazism, had the chance to escape his fate. He was invited to lecture at Union Theological Seminary in New York City at the height of the Nazis' power in Germany in 1939. He could have stayed in the United States, and was urged by friends to do so. But, Bonhoeffer asked, how could he participate in a postwar Germany, and how would he have any moral credibility as a theologian in his homeland, if he spent its most critical years abroad. Bonhoeffer returned, and what he saw prompted him to make a fateful decision: he joined a small group opposed to Hitler and Nazism. He worked as an unpaid double agent in German military intelligence and served as a courier for a German resistance group. Its plan to smuggle Jews out of the country brought the group to the attention of the Gestapo, and Bonhoeffer and some of his colleagues were arrested in 1943. Although Bonhoeffer was in prison at the time, a plot to assassinate Hitler went forward; the plan was foiled shortly before it could be implemented. Bonhoeffer spent two years in a German military prison before he was moved to a death camp. He was hanged just three weeks before the war in Europe ended.

The Reading

Bonhoeffer, as much as any other Christian in the twentieth century, raised the crucial question of the day: What, if anything, does Christianity have to say to those who are suffering, to those who are at war, to those who have nothing? He lived, and died, his beliefs. Some of the books he authored were pulled together posthumously, from student lecture notes or letters he sent from prison. Others he wrote intentionally as books. His *Letters and Papers from Prison* was compiled by his student and relative, Eberhard Bethge. The letters range from the picayune to the profound: send me more cigarettes; the bombs are falling, I have to stop now; Barth was wrong; no one sent me a letter today. Included in the collection are notes and observations he wrote for future books. The first year he was in the prison, the letters indicated his belief that he would be released quite soon. The second year, however, there was less talk of his release and more reflection on his situation in prison, or rather, on life in general. It is from these later writings, in 1944, that the selections are drawn.

Letters are a peculiar genre of literature. They are brief, bound by time—which is to say, by current events—and usually quite personal. In an age of e-mail and cell phones, it is difficult to imagine the age of letter writing. Yet during times of war, letters always serve as the main vehicle of communication. The letters included here were sent by Bonhoeffer from prison to Bethge, who was serving in the German army in Italy and elsewhere in Europe. Both men were in life-and-death situations; both had experienced separation from loved ones; both had known the terror of falling bombs. Bonhoeffer wrote in the context of a Christian who resisted evil, but also as one who knew that most of the other Christians in Germany did not resist Hitler. In the midst of death—we might say, "in the valley of the shadow of death" (Psalm 23)—Bonhoeffer calmly discussed theological questions that seemed to him as important as the need to comfort those in prison who were scared by the blasts.

Vocabulary Note: Bonhoeffer uses two terms that may be unfamiliar. First, he says that "Christian preaching and theology rest on the 'religious *a priori*' of mankind." By this he means that throughout history we have been assuming that people are basically religious. But what if this isn't the case, he asks. He uses the second term, "positivist doctrine," when he discusses Karl Barth. This relates to Kierkegaard's fideism: the assertion of faith without leaving any room for questions or even for a range of opinions. In Bonhoeffer's own words, this is a "like it or lump it" approach to Christianity.

Questions to Consider

1. What do you understand Bonhoeffer to mean when he says we are moving to a "religionless" time?

2. Can you relate Bonhoeffer's interior sense of God's presence (beyond words!) with Gregory Palamas' discussion of God's energies?

3. Bonhoeffer claims that God is not here to solve our personal problems. Why does he say this? Is this a belief others would share? How does this view compare with the depiction of God (rather than Jesus) in the Gospel of Mark?

4. What do you think about Bonhoeffer's part in the plot to assassinate Hitler? Do you think this can be justified on religious grounds? Why or why not?

5. Would you describe Bonhoeffer's faith as this-worldly or otherworldly? What do you understand these terms to mean?

6. Are there any weaknesses in his assertions? What are his presuppositions? Are these reasonable? Do his conclusions follow?

7. Bonhoeffer seems to respect the Bible and what he calls "biblical faith" more than traditional Christianity or its teachings. What evidence exists in support of this view? What is the difference between the two?

Letters and Papers from Prison
DIETRICH BONHOEFFER

30 April 1944

Dear Eberhard,

Another month gone. Does time fly as fast with you as it does with me here? I'm often surprised at it myself—and when will the month come when you and Renate, I and Maria, and we two can meet again? I have such a strong feeling that great events are moving the world every day and could change all our personal relationships, that I should like to write to you much oftener, partly because I don't know how much longer I shall be able to, and even more because we want to share everything with each other as often and as long as we can. I'm firmly convinced that, by the time you get this letter, great decisions will already be setting things moving on all fronts. During the coming weeks we shall have to keep a stout heart, and that is what I wish you. We shall have to keep all our wits about us, so as to let nothing scare us. In view of what is coming, I'm almost inclined to quote the biblical [Greek] and I feel that I "long to look," like the angels in 1 Peter 1:12, to see how God is going to solve the apparently insoluble. I think God is about to accomplish something that, even if we take part in it either outwardly or inwardly, we can only receive with the greatest wonder and awe. Somehow it will be clear—for those who have eyes to see—that Psalm 58:11b and Psalm 9:19f are true; and we shall have to repeat Jeremiah 45:5 to ourselves every day. It's harder for you to go through this separated from Renate and your boy than it is for me, so I will think of you especially, as I am already doing now.

How good it would seem to me, for both of us, if we could go through this time together, helping each other. But it's probably "better" for it not to be so, but for each of us to have to go through it alone. I find it hard not to be able to help you in anything—except by thinking of you every morning and evening when I read the Bible, and often during the day as well. You've no need to worry about me at all, as I'm getting on uncommonly well—you would be surprised, if you came to see me. People here keep on telling me (as you can see, I feel very flattered by it) that I'm "radiating so much peace around me," and that I'm "always so cheerful"—so that the feelings that I sometimes have to the contrary must, I suppose, rest on an illusion (not that I really believe that at all!). You would be surprised, and perhaps even worried, by my theological thoughts and the conclusions that they lead to; and this is where I miss you most of all, because I don't know anyone else with whom I could so well discuss them to have my thinking clarified. What is bothering me incessantly is the question what Christianity really is, or indeed who Christ really is, for us today. The time when people could be told everything by means of words, whether theological or pious, is over, and so is the time of inwardness and conscience—and that means the time of religion in general. We are moving towards a completely religionless time; people as they are now simply cannot be religious any more. Even those who honestly describe themselves as "religious" do not in the least act up to it, and so they presumably mean something quite different by "religious."

Our whole nineteen-hundred-year-old Christian preaching and theology rest on the "religious a priori" of mankind. "Christianity" has always been a form—perhaps the true form—of "religion." But if one day it becomes clear that this a priori does not exist at all, but was a historically conditioned and transient form of human self-expression, and if therefore man becomes radically religionless—and I think that that is already more or less the case (else how is it, for example, that this war, in contrast to all previous ones, is not calling forth any "religious" reaction?)—what does that mean for "Christianity"? It means that the foundation is taken away from the whole of what has up to now been our "Christianity," and that there remain only a few "last survivors of the age of chivalry," or a few intellectually dishonest people, on whom we can descend as "religious." Are they to be the chosen few? Is it on this dubious group of people that we are to pounce in fervor, pique, or indignation, in order to sell them our goods? Are we to fall upon a few unfortunate people in their hour of need and exercise a sort of religious compulsion on them? If we don't want to do all that, if our final judgment must be that

the western form of Christianity, too, was only a preliminary stage to a complete absence of religion, what kind of situation emerges for us, for the church? How can Christ become the Lord of the religionless as well? Are there religionless Christians? If religion is only a garment of Christianity—and even this garment has looked very different at different times—then what is a religionless Christianity?

Barth, who is the only one to have started along this line of thought, did not carry it to completion, but arrived at a positivism of revelation, which in the last analysis is essentially a restoration. For the religionless working man (or any other man) nothing decisive is gained here. The questions to be answered would surely be: What do a church, a community, a sermon, a liturgy, a Christian life mean in a religionless world? How do we speak of God—without religion, i.e. without the temporally conditioned presuppositions of metaphysics, inwardness, and so on? How do we speak (or perhaps we cannot now even "speak" as we used to) in a "secular" way about "God"? In what way are we "religionless-secular" Christians, in what way are we the [ek-klesia, the "called out"], those who are called forth, not regarding ourselves from a religious point of view as specially favored, but rather as belonging wholly to the world? In that case Christ is no longer an object of religion, but something quite different, really the Lord of the world. But what does that mean? What is the place of worship and prayer in a religionless situation? Does the secret discipline, or alternatively the difference (which I have suggested to you before) between penultimate and ultimate, take on a new importance here?

I must break off for today, so that the letter can go straight away. I'll write to you again about it in two days' time. I hope you see more or less what I mean, and that it doesn't bore you. Good bye for the present. It's not easy always to write without an echo, and you must excuse me if that makes it something of a monologue.

I'm thinking of you very much.   Your Dietrich

I'm not really reproaching you for not writing. You have too much else to do.

I find, after all, that I can write a little more.—The Pauline question whether [circumcision] is a condition of justification seems to me in present-day terms to be whether religion is a condition of salvation. Freedom from [circumcision] is also freedom from religion. I often ask myself why a "Christian instinct" often draws me more to the religionless people than to the religious, by which I don't in the least mean with any evangelizing intention, but, I might almost say, "in brotherhood." While I'm often reluctant to mention God by name to religious people—because that name somehow seems to me here not to ring true, and I feel myself to be slightly dishonest (it's particularly bad when others start to talk in religious jargon; I then dry up almost completely and feel awkward and uncomfortable)—to people with no religion I can on occasion mention him by name quite calmly and as a matter of course. Religious people speak of God when human knowledge (perhaps simply because they are too lazy to think) has come to an end, or when human resources fail—in fact it is always the *deus ex machina* that they bring on to the scene, either for the apparent solution of insoluble problems, or as strength in human failure—always, that is to say, exploiting human weakness or human boundaries. Of necessity, that can go on only till people can by their own strength push these boundaries somewhat further out, so that God becomes superfluous as a *deus ex machina.* I've come to be doubtful of talking about any human boundaries (is even death, which people now hardly fear, and is sin, which they now hardly understand, still a genuine boundary today?). It always seems to me that we are trying anxiously in this way to reserve some space for God; I should like to speak of God not on the boundaries but at the center, not in weaknesses but in strength; and therefore not in death and guilt but in man's life and goodness. As to the boundaries, it seems to me better to be silent and leave the insoluble unsolved. Belief in the resurrection is *not* the "solution" of the problem of death. God's "beyond" is not the beyond of our cognitive faculties. The transcendence of epistemological theory has nothing to do with the transcendence of God. God is beyond in the midst of our life. The church stands, not at the boundaries where human powers give out, but in the middle of the village. That is how it is in the Old Testament, and in this sense we still read the New Testament far too little in the light of the Old. How this religionless Christianity looks, what form it takes, is something that I'm thinking about a great deal, and I shall be writing to you again about it soon. It may be that on us in particular, midway between East and West, there will fall a heavy responsibility.

Now I really must stop. It would be fine to have a word from you about all this; it would mean a great deal to me—probably more than you can imagine. Some time, just read Proverbs 22:11, 12; there is

something that will bar the way to any escapism disguised as piety.

All the very best.   Your Dietrich

5 May 1944

Dear Eberhard,

I keep hoping that you will already be on leave—you must be about due for it by now so that you can see your son—and that my letter will be sent on to you (and so be out of date). However, everything is so uncertain nowadays—and long experience suggests that everything is more likely to remain as it is than to change soon—that I'll write to you all the same. I learnt from Christel, who visited me yesterday, that things are going relatively well with you, and that you can at least delight Renate with a letter. It's really worth a great deal that Renate can be in Sakrow all the time and that you are at least spared worry for her with the alerts here. I would very much like to talk to Renate myself one day, but it doesn't seem possible to arrange that at the moment. I'm only glad that at least we were able to see each other in December. That was a good piece of work by your father-in-law . . . [ellipses in original]. I so much wish that you could come soon, though it will be sad that presumably we shall still not be able to see each other. I'm getting along quite well and so is the case, but the question of the date is still quite open. But all good things come over night, and I'm waiting and hoping confidently. In my earlier letter there was an address that you can use if you want; but it isn't necessary; I simply wanted to let you know.

A few more words about "religionlessness." I expect you remember Bultmann's essay on the "demythologizing" of the New Testament? My view of it today would be, not that he went "too far," as most people thought, but that he didn't go far enough. It's not only the "mythological" concepts, such as miracle, ascension, and so on (which are not in principle separable from the concepts of God, faith, etc.), but "religious" concepts generally, which are problematic. You can't, as Bultmann supposes, separate God and miracle, but you must be able to interpret and proclaim *both* in a "non-religious" sense. Bultmann's approach is fundamentally still a liberal one (i.e. abridging the gospel), whereas I'm trying to think theologically.

What does it mean to "interpret in a religious sense"? I think it means to speak on the one hand metaphysically, and on the other hand individualistically. Neither of these is relevant to the biblical message or to the man of today. Hasn't the individualistic question about personal salvation almost completely left us all? Aren't we really under the impression that there are more important things than that question (perhaps not more important than the matter itself, but more important than the question!)? I know it sounds pretty monstrous to say that. But, fundamentally, isn't this in fact biblical? Does the question about saving one's soul appear in the Old Testament at all? Aren't righteousness and the Kingdom of God on earth the focus of everything, and isn't it true that Romans 3:14ff is not an individualistic doctrine of salvation, but the culmination of the view that God alone is righteous? It is not with the beyond that we are concerned, but with this world as created and preserved, subjected to laws, reconciled, and restored. What is above this world is, in the gospel, intended to exist *for* this world; I mean that, not in the anthropocentric sense of liberal, mystic pietistic, ethical theology, but in the biblical sense of the creation and of the incarnation, crucifixion, and resurrection of Jesus Christ.

Barth was the first theologian to begin the criticism of religion, and that remains his really great merit; but he put in its place a positivist doctrine of revelation which says, in effect, "Like it or lump it": virgin birth, Trinity, or anything else; each is an equally significant and necessary part of the whole, which must simply be swallowed as a whole or not at all. That isn't biblical. There are degrees of knowledge and degrees of significance; that means that a secret discipline must be restored whereby the mysteries of the Christian faith are protected against profanation. The positivism of revelation makes it too easy for itself, by setting up, as it does in the last analysis, a law of faith, and so mutilates what is—by Christ's incarnation!—a gift for us. In the place of religion there now stands the church—that is in itself biblical—but the world is in some degree made to depend on itself and left to its own devices, and that's the mistake.

I'm thinking about how we can reinterpret in a "worldly" sense—in the sense of the Old Testament and of John 1:14—the concepts of repentance, faith, justification, rebirth, and sanctification. I shall be writing to you about it again.

Forgive me for writing all this in German script; normally I do this only when my writing is for my own use—and perhaps what I've written was more to clear my own mind than to edify you. I really don't want to trouble you with problems, for you may well have no time to come to grips with them, and they may only bother you; but I can't help sharing my thoughts with you, simply because that is the best way to make them clear to myself. If that doesn't suit you at present, please say so.—Tomorrow is Cantate, and I shall be thinking of you and enjoying very pleasant memories.

My parents were here recently and said how nice and healthy the little boy is . . .

Good bye. Be patient, as we are, and keep well.

With all my heart—you're daily in my thoughts.

Your Dietrich

21 July [1944]

Dear Eberhard,

All I want to do today is to send you a short greeting. I expect you are often with us here in your thoughts and are always glad of any sign of life, even if the theological discussion stops for a moment. These theological thoughts are, in fact, always occupying my mind; but there are times when I am just content to live the life of faith without worrying about its problems. At those times I simply take pleasure in the days' readings—in particular those of yesterday and today; and I'm always glad to go back to Paul Gerhardt's beautiful hymns.

During the last year or so I've come to know and understand more and more the profound this-worldliness of Christianity. The Christian is not a *homo religiosus,* but simply a man, as Jesus was a man—in contrast, shall we say, to John the Baptist. I don't mean the shallow and banal this-worldliness of the enlightened, the busy, the comfortable, or the lascivious, but the profound this-worldliness, characterized by discipline and the constant knowledge of death and resurrection. I think Luther lived a this-worldly life in this sense.

I remember a conversation that I had in America thirteen years ago with a young French pastor. We were asking ourselves quite simply what we wanted to do with our lives. He said he would like to become a saint (and I think it's quite likely that he did become one). At the time I was very impressed, but I disagreed with him, and said, in effect, that I should like to learn to have faith. For a long time I didn't realize the depth of the contrast. I thought I could acquire faith by trying to live a holy life, or something like it. I suppose I wrote *The Cost of Discipleship* as the end of that path. Today I can see the dangers of that book, though I still stand by what I wrote.

I discovered later, and I'm still discovering right up to this moment, that it is only by living completely in this world that one learns to have faith. One must completely abandon any attempt to make something of oneself, whether it be a saint, or a converted sinner, or a churchman (a so-called priestly type!), a righteous man or an unrighteous one, a sick man or a healthy one. By this-worldliness I mean living unreservedly in life's duties, problems, successes and failures, experiences and perplexities. In so doing we throw ourselves completely into the arms of God, taking seriously, not our own sufferings, but those of God in the world—watching with Christ in Gethsemane. That, I think, is faith; that is *metanoia;* and that is how one becomes a man and a Christian (cf. Jeremiah 45!). How can success make us arrogant, or failure lead us astray, when we share in God's sufferings through a life of this kind?

I think you see what I mean, even though I put it so briefly. I'm glad to have been able to learn this, and I know I've been able to do so only along the road that I've traveled. So I'm grateful for the past and present, and content with them.

You may be surprised at such a personal letter; but if for once I want to say this kind of thing, to whom should I say it? Perhaps the time will come one day when I can talk to Maria like this; I very much hope so. But I can't expect it of her yet.

May God in his mercy lead us through these times; but above all, may he lead us to himself.

I was delighted to hear from you, and am glad you're not finding it too hot. There must be a good many letters from me on the way. Didn't we go more or less along that way in 1936?

Good bye. Keep well, and don't lose hope that we shall all meet again soon. I always think of you in faithfulness and gratitude.

Your Dietrich

[21 August 1944]

Dear Eberhard,

It's your birthday in a week's time. Once again I've taken up the readings and meditated on them. The key to everything is the "in him." All that we may rightly expect from God, and ask him for, is to be found in Jesus Christ. The God of Jesus Christ has nothing to do with what God, as we imagine him, could do and ought to do. If we are to learn what God promises, and what he fulfils, we must persevere in quiet meditation on the life, sayings, deeds, sufferings, and death of Jesus. It is certain that we may al-ways live close to God and in the light of his presence, and that such living is an entirely new life for us; that nothing is then impossible for us, because all things are possible with God; that no earthly power can touch us without his will, and that danger and distress can only drive us closer to him. It is certain that we can claim nothing for ourselves, and may yet pray for everything; it is certain that our joy is hidden in suffering, and our life in death; it is certain that in all this we are in a fellowship that sustains us. In Jesus God has said Yes and Amen to it all, and that Yes and Amen is the firm ground on which we stand.

In these turbulent times we repeatedly lose sight of what really makes life worth living. We think that, because this or that person is living, it makes sense for us to live too. But the truth is that if this earth was good enough for the man Jesus Christ, if such a man as Jesus lived, then, and only then, has life a meaning for us. If Jesus had not lived, then our life would be meaningless, in spite of all the other people whom we know and honor and love. Perhaps we now sometimes forget the meaning and purpose of our profession. But isn't this the simplest way of putting it? The unbiblical idea of "meaning" is indeed only a translation of what the Bible calls "promise."

I feel how inadequate these words are to express my wish, namely to give you steadfastness and joy and certainty in your loneliness. This lonely birthday need not be a lost day, if it helps to determine more clearly the convictions on which you will base your life in time to come. I've often found it a great help to think in the evening of all those who I know are praying for me, children as well as grown-ups. I think I owe it to the prayers of others, both known and unknown, that I have often been kept in safety.

Another point: we are often told in the New Testament to "be strong" (1 Corinthians 16:13; Ephesians 6:10; 2 Timothy 2:1; 1 John 2:14). Isn't people's weakness (stupidity, lack of independence, forgetfulness, cowardice, vanity, corruptibility, temptability, etc.) a greater danger than evil? Christ not only makes people "good"; he makes them strong, too. The sins of weakness are the really human sins, whereas the willful sins are diabolical (and no doubt "strong," too!). I must think about this again. Good bye; keep well, and don't lose confidence. I hope we shall celebrate Renate's birthday together again. Thank you for everything. I keep thinking faithfully of you.

Your Dietrich

Christianity and Non-Christian Religions

Dietrich Bonhoeffer, a Christian, died in Flossenbürg, an extermination camp for Jews. Although millions of Christians, particularly the Slavic peoples from Eastern Europe, died in the camps, the German gas chambers are best known as the places where 6 million Jews were slaughtered. Animosity toward Jews certainly did not begin in the twentieth century, nor was it particularly a Christian passion. Nazis based their hatred of Jews on the claim that the Aryan race was superior, arguing that Jewish blood contaminated the purity of Aryanism. Yet Christian scholars examining the causes of the Holocaust found that centuries of Christian denigration of, discrimination against, and hatred of Jews did play some role in the twentieth-century atrocities suffered by the Jews.

For centuries, Christians used the Bible to attack the Jews for "killing Christ" and for being unfaithful to God. Since the Romans executed Jesus, and since all of his early followers were Jewish, it is inaccurate to say that the Jews killed Christ, or worse, killed God, as the charge was enlarged during the Middle Ages. Although official church policy over the centuries never encouraged killing Jews, unofficial policy condoned harassment, segregation, and imprisonment. Medieval Christians on their way to crusades against Muslims in the Holy Land stopped along the way in the Rhineland of Europe to massacre Jews. Martin Luther's tract *On the Jews and Their Lies* advocated burning Jews' books, confiscating their businesses, and sending them to work camps. Although Luther's intent was to force Jewish assimilation into Christian society, we can see how the Nazis interpreted Luther.

Recognition of the Christian contribution to the ongoing hatred and persecution of Jews has come only recently in history, and in large part because of the Holocaust. Christians and Jews both asked themselves how God could have let such a terrible thing happen to the Chosen People. While it remains to be seen whether the Holocaust becomes a major theological event in the self-understanding of Jews and in the history of Judaism, it was a turning point in the life of Christians and their attitude toward Jews. Christians began to examine their liturgies and educational materials to identify what might contribute to Jew hatred. Among the most significant events was Pope John XXIII's decision early in his pontificate (p. 1958–1963) to delete the prayer for the "perfidious" (faithless) Jews from the Catholic Good Friday liturgy.

The Readings

Church leaders at Vatican Council II met over a period of years, reading and discussing drafts of a statement about Christianity's view of non-Christian religions. The council as a whole adopted the "Declaration on the Relation of the Church to Non-Christian Religions," known as *Nostra Aetate,* in October 1965. This document is a political statement, one that was carefully crafted to reflect the sentiments of hundreds of Catholic leaders. It had to express Christian doctrine accurately while at the same time stating principles and opinions about other world religions. Catholics coming to Vatican II from outside Europe already were working in countries with a number of different faiths. Indeed, Catholics in Asia were a minority religion, while Catholics in Africa could be considered a minority against the backdrop of thousands of tribal beliefs and practices. Moreover, immigrants from Africa and Asia were bringing their traditions to Europe and North America, and attracting adherents

▨ Vatican Council II

John XXIII, like his namesake the antipope John XXIII in the fifteenth century, called for an ecumenical council of all Catholic Church leaders. At the height of church power, stability, and security in the twentieth century, John assembled Catholic cardinals, bishops, and theologians from around the world in order to update church teachings and practices. He convened the council not to refute previous doctrine, but rather to reinterpret it for the modern age. Known as Vatican II, the council convened in 1962 and concluded in 1965, two years after the pope's death.

The changes that resulted from Vatican II were far-reaching and enormous: everything from widening the role of laypeople in church life, to saying Mass in the vernacular—or language of the people—to requesting that all religious orders reexamine their roots and renew their organizations in order to respond to the "signs of the times." John himself knew that the "times, they are a changin'," before his pastoral and academic colleagues did, and the reforms enacted at Vatican II continue to reverberate within Catholicism today. They can be seen in the fact that priests now face the congregation rather than the altar. They can be seen in the increased presence of women in church leadership and teaching roles (although this has not been as extensive as many Catholic women would like). They can even be seen in the design of churches built since the 1960s, frequently locating the altar in the center of the sanctuary so that members of the congregation face each other in celebration of the Mass.

Vatican II set the stage for the rise of liberation theology (see below), which engaged bishops, priests, nuns, and laypeople in the struggle for economic, social, and political justice in Central America throughout the 1970s and 1980s. It issued guidelines on religious liberty aimed at protecting civil society from "abuses carried out in the name of religion," as well as at protecting the religious rights of individuals. It also opened the door to increased dialogue with other Christians and to engagement with people of other faiths in dynamic new ways.

A number of Catholics, young as well as old, have begun to resist the changes wrought by Vatican II, however, preferring to say the Mass in Latin and refusing to have female acolytes or communion servers. Other Catholics believe that the changes did not go far enough and argue that Pope John Paul II (p. 1978–2005) turned his back on the spirit of renewal that Vatican II generated. It will be interesting to see how future popes deal with the truly dramatic reforms promulgated by Vatican II.

among young people or those who were dispossessed in their own country. Thus, Christians could no longer ignore the challenges other faiths brought to Christianity.

Almost a decade after Vatican II, the Catholic Secretariat for the Promotion of the Unity of Christians, and the Committee for Religious Relations with the Jews issued "Guidelines on Religious Relations with the Jews." These guidelines presented specific advice on how to avoid anti-Jewish teachings in church liturgy, education, and doctrine. They also recommended ongoing dialogue between Christians and Jews, and joint social action projects, as ways to promote healing and understanding. Unlike *Nostra Aetate,* the guidelines were adopted by a relatively small group of Catholic leaders interested in and committed to Catholic Christian and Jewish harmony. In other words, the guidelines were an internal document for Catholic believers to use in practice, while *Nostra Aetate* was a statement of philosophy, or theory, in which the Catholic Church took an official, and public, position on world religions.

Questions to Consider

1. What are the implications for Christian missions in the statement from *Nostra Aetate* that "the Catholic Church rejects nothing of what is true and holy in these [other] religions"?

2. What is the church's position on Muslims? On Jews? On Hindus and Buddhists?

3. What is the church's position on Jesus Christ and Christianity?

4. What do you think the Catholic Church's position is regarding proselytizing Jews (that is, trying to convert Jews to Christianity)?

5. What changes in Catholic teaching and education does the Committee for Religious Relations with the Jews advise?

6. What specific projects can Christians and Jews work on together?

Declaration on the Relation of the Church to Non-Christian Religions (*Nostra Aetate*)

VATICAN COUNCIL II, 28 OCTOBER 1965

1. In this age of ours, when men are drawing more closely together and the bonds of friendship between different peoples are being strengthened, the Church examines with greater care the relation which she has to non-Christian religions. Ever aware of her duty to foster unity and charity among individuals, and even among nations, she reflects at the outset on what men have in common and what tends to promote fellowship among them.

All men form but one community. This is so because all stem from the one stock which God created to people the entire earth (cf. Acts 17:26), and also because all share a common destiny, namely God. His providence, evident goodness, and saving designs extend to all men (cf. Wisdom 8:1; Acts 14:17; Romans 2:6–7; 1 Timothy 2:4) against the day when the elect are gathered together in the holy city which is illumined by the glory of God, and in whose splendor all peoples will walk (cf. Revelation 21:23 ff.).

Men look to their different religions for an answer to the unsolved riddles of human existence. The problems that weigh heavily on the hearts of men are the same today as in the ages past. What is man? What is the meaning and purpose of life? What is upright behavior, and what is sinful? Where does suffering originate, and what end does it serve? How can genuine happiness be found? What happens at death? What is judgment? What reward follows death? And finally, what is the ultimate mystery, beyond human explanation, which embraces our entire existence, from which we take our origin and towards which we tend?

2. Throughout history even to the present day, there is found among different peoples a certain awareness of a hidden power, which lies behind the course of nature and the events of human life. At times there is present even a recognition of a supreme being, or still more of a Father. This awareness and recognition results in a way of life that is imbued with a deep religious sense. The religions which are found in more advanced civilizations endeavor by way of well-defined concepts and exact language to answer these questions. Thus, in Hinduism men explore the divine mystery and express it both in the limitless riches of myth and the accurately defined insights of philosophy. They seek release from the trials of the present life by ascetical practices, profound meditation and recourse to God in confidence and love. Buddhism in its various forms testifies to the essential inadequacy of this changing world. It proposes a way of life by which men can, with confidence and trust, attain a state of perfect liberation and reach supreme illumination either through their own efforts or by the aid of divine help. So, too, other religions which are found throughout the world attempt in their own ways to calm the hearts of men by outlining a program of life covering doctrine, moral precepts and sacred rites.

The Catholic Church rejects nothing of what is true and holy in these religions. She has a high regard for the manner of life and conduct, the precepts and doctrines which, although differing in many ways from her own teaching, nevertheless often reflect a ray of that truth which enlightens all men. Yet she proclaims and is in duty bound to proclaim without fail, Christ who is the way, the truth and the life (John

14:6). In him, in whom God reconciled all things to himself (2 Corinthians 5:18–19), men find the fullness of their religious life.

The Church, therefore, urges her sons to enter with prudence and charity into discussion and collaboration with members of other religions. Let Christians, while witnessing to their own faith and way of life, acknowledge, preserve and encourage the spiritual and moral truths found among non-Christians, also their social life and culture.

3. The Church has also a high regard for the Muslims. They worship God, who is one, living and subsistent, merciful and almighty, the Creator of heaven and earth, who has also spoken to men. They strive to submit themselves without reserve to the hidden decrees of God, just as Abraham submitted himself to God's plan, to whose faith Muslims eagerly link their own. Although not acknowledging him as God, they venerate Jesus as a prophet, his virgin Mother they also honor, and even at times devoutly invoke. Further, they await the day of judgment and the reward of God following the resurrection of the dead. For this reason they highly esteem an upright life and worship God, especially by way of prayer, alms-deeds and fasting.

Over the centuries many quarrels and dissensions have arisen between Christians and Muslims. The sacred Council now pleads with all to forget the past, and urges that a sincere effort be made to achieve mutual understanding; for the benefit of all men, let them together preserve and promote peace, liberty, social justice and moral values.

4. Sounding the depths of the mystery which is the Church, this sacred Council remembers the spiritual ties which link the people of the New Covenant to the stock of Abraham.

The Church of Christ acknowledges that in God's plan of salvation the beginning of her faith and election is to be found in the patriarchs, Moses and the prophets. She professes that all Christ's faithful, who as men of faith are sons of Abraham (cf. Galatians 3:7), are included in the same patriarch's call and that the salvation of the Church is mystically prefigured in the exodus of God's chosen people from the land of bondage. On this account the Church cannot forget that she received the revelation of the Old Testament by way of that people with whom God in his inexpressible mercy established the ancient covenant. Nor can she forget that she draws nourishment from that good olive tree onto which the wild olive branches of the Gentiles have been grafted (cf. Romans 11:17–24).

The Church believes that Christ who is our peace has through his cross reconciled Jews and Gentiles and made them one in himself (cf. Ephesians 2:14–16).

Likewise, the Church keeps ever before her mind the words of the apostle Paul about his kinsmen: "they are Israelites, and to them belong the sonship, the glory, the covenants, the giving of the law, the worship, and the promises; to them belong the patriarchs, and of their race according to the flesh, is the Christ" (Romans 9:4–5), the son of the virgin Mary. She is mindful, moreover, that the apostles, the pillars on which the Church stands, are of Jewish descent, as are many of those early disciples who proclaimed the Gospel of Christ to the world.

As holy Scripture testifies, Jerusalem did not recognize God's moment when it came (cf. Luke 19:42). Jews for the most part did not accept the Gospel; on the contrary, many opposed the spreading of it (cf. Romans 11:28). Even so, the apostle Paul maintains that the Jews remain very dear to God, for the sake of the patriarchs, since God does not take back the gifts he bestowed or the choice he made. Together with the prophets and that same apostle, the Church awaits the day, known to God alone, when all peoples will call on God with one voice and "serve him shoulder to shoulder" (Wisdom 3:9; cf. Isaiah 66:23; Psalm 65:4; Romans 11:11–32).

Since Christians and Jews have such a common spiritual heritage, this sacred Council wishes to encourage and further mutual understanding and appreciation. This can be obtained, especially, by way of biblical and theological enquiry and through friendly discussions.

Even though the Jewish authorities and those who followed their lead pressed for the death of Christ (cf. John 19:6), neither all Jews indiscriminately at that time, nor Jews today, can be charged with the crimes committed during his passion. It is true that the Church is the new people of God, yet the Jews should not be spoken of as rejected or accursed as if this followed from holy Scripture. Consequently, all must take care, lest in catechizing or in preaching the Word of God, they teach anything which is not in accord with the truth of the Gospel message or the spirit of Christ.

Indeed, the Church reproves every form of persecution against whomsoever it may be directed. Remembering, then, her common heritage with the Jews and moved not by any political consideration, but solely by the religious motivation of Christian charity, she deplores all hatreds, persecutions, displays of antisemitism leveled at any time or from any source against the Jews.

The Church always held and continues to hold that Christ out of infinite love freely underwent suffering and death because of the sins of all men, so that all might attain salvation. It is the duty of the Church, therefore, in her preaching to proclaim the cross of Christ as the sign of God's universal love and the source of all grace.

5. We cannot truly pray to God the Father of all if we treat any people in other than brotherly fashion, for all men are created in God's image. Man's relation to God the Father and man's relation to his fellowmen are so dependent on each other that the Scripture says "he who does not love, does not know God" (1 John 4:8).

There is no basis therefore, either in theory or in practice for any discrimination between individual and individual, or between people and people arising either from human dignity or from the rights which flow from it.

Therefore, the Church reproves, as foreign to the mind of Christ, any discrimination against people or any harassment of them on the basis of their race, color, condition in life or religion. Accordingly, following the footsteps of the holy apostles Peter and Paul the sacred Council earnestly begs the Christian faithful to "conduct themselves well among the Gentiles" (1 Peter 2:12) and if possible, as far as depends on them, to be at peace with all men (cf. Romans 12:18) and in that way to be true sons of the Father who is in heaven (cf. Matthew 5:45).

Guidelines on Religious Relations with the Jews (1 December 1974)

CATHOLIC SECRETARIAT FOR THE PROMOTION OF THE UNITY OF CHRISTIANS

The Declaration *Nostra Aetate,* issued by the Second Vatican Council on 28 October 1965, "on the relationship of the Church to non-Christian religions," marks an important milestone in the history of Jewish-Christian relations.

Moreover, the step taken by the Council finds its historical setting in circumstances deeply affected by the memory of the persecution and massacre of Jews which took place in Europe just before and during the Second World War.

Although Christianity sprang from Judaism, taking from it certain essential elements of its faith and divine worship, the gap dividing them was deepened more and more, to such an extent that Christian and Jew hardly knew each other.

After two thousand years, too often marked by mutual ignorance and frequent confrontation, the Declaration *Nostra Aetate* provides an opportunity to open or to continue a dialogue with a view to better mutual understanding. Over the past nine years, many steps in this direction have been taken in various countries. As a result, it is easier to define the conditions under which a new relationship between Jews and Christians may be worked out and developed. This seems the right moment to propose, following the guidelines of the Council, some concrete suggestions born of experience, hoping that they will help to bring into actual existence in the life of the Church the intentions expressed in the conciliar document.

While referring the reader back to this document, we may simply restate here that the spiritual bonds and historical links binding the Church to Judaism condemn (as opposed to the very spirit of Christianity) all forms of antisemitism and discrimination, which in any case the dignity of the human person alone would suffice to condemn. Further still, these links and relationships render obligatory a better mutual understanding and renewed mutual esteem. On the practical level in particular, Christians must therefore strive to acquire a better knowledge of the basic components of the religious tradition of Judaism; they must strive to learn by what essential traits the Jews define themselves in the light of their own religious experience.

With due respect for such matters of principle, we simply propose some first practical applications in different essential areas of the Church's life, with a view to launching or developing sound relations between Catholics and their Jewish brothers.

I. DIALOGUE

To tell the truth, such relations as there have been between Jew and Christian have scarcely ever risen above the level of monologue. From now on, real dialogue must be established.

Dialogue presupposes that each side wishes to know the other, and wishes to increase and deepen its knowledge of the other. It constitutes a particularly suitable means of favoring a better mutual knowledge and, especially in the case of dialogue between Jews and Christians, of probing the riches of one's own tradition. Dialogue demands respect for the other as he is; above all, respect for his faith and his religious convictions.

In virtue of her divine mission, and her very nature, the Church must preach Jesus Christ to the world (*Ad Gentes*). Lest the witness of Catholics to Jesus Christ should give offence to Jews, they must take care to live and spread their Christian faith while maintaining the strictest respect for religious liberty in line with the teaching of the Second Vatican Council (Declaration *Dignitatis Humanae*). They will likewise strive to understand the difficulties which arise for the Jewish soul—rightly imbued with an extremely high, pure notion of the divine transcendence—when faced with the mystery of the incarnate Word.

While it is true that a widespread air of suspicion, inspired by an unfortunate past, is still dominant in this particular area, Christians, for their part, will be able to see to what extent the responsibility is theirs and deduce practical conclusions for the future.

In addition to friendly talks, competent people will be encouraged to meet and to study together the many problems deriving from the fundamental convictions of Judaism and of Christianity. In order not to hurt (even involuntarily) those taking part, it will be vital to guarantee, not only tact, but a great openness of spirit and diffidence with respect to one's own prejudices.

In whatever circumstances as shall prove possible and mutually acceptable, one might encourage a common meeting in the presence of God, in prayer and silent meditation—a highly efficacious way of finding that humility, that openness of heart and mind, necessary prerequisites for a deep knowledge of oneself and of others. In particular, that will be done in connection with great causes such as the struggle for peace and justice.

II. LITURGY

The existing links between the Christian liturgy and the Jewish liturgy will be borne in mind. The idea of a living community in the service of God, and in the service of men for the love of God, such as it is realized in the liturgy, is just as characteristic of the Jewish liturgy as it is of the Christian one. To improve Jewish-Christian relations, it is important to take cognizance of those common elements of the liturgical life (formulas, feasts, rites, etc.) in which the Bible holds an essential place.

An effort will be made to acquire a better understanding of whatever in the Old Testament retains its own perpetual value (cf. *Dei Verbum*), since that has not been cancelled by the later interpretation of the New Testament. Rather, the New Testament brings out the full meaning of the Old, while both Old and New illumine and explain each other. This is all the more important since liturgical reform is now bringing the text of the Old Testament ever more frequently to the attention of Christians.

When commenting on biblical texts, emphasis will be laid on the continuity of our faith with that of the earlier Covenant, in the perspective of the promises, without minimizing those elements of Christianity which are original. We believe that those promises were fulfilled with the first coming of Christ. But it is none the less true that we still await their perfect fulfillment in his glorious return at the end of time.

With respect to liturgical readings, care will be taken to see that homilies based on them will not distort their meaning, especially when it is a question of passages which seem to show the Jewish people as such in an unfavorable light. Efforts will be made so to instruct the Christian people that they will understand the true interpretation of all the texts and their meaning for the contemporary believer.

Commissions entrusted with the task of liturgical translation will pay particular attention to the way in which they express those phrases and passages which Christians, if not well informed, might misunderstand because of prejudice. Obviously, one cannot alter the text of the Bible. The point is that, with a version destined for liturgical use, there should be an overriding preoccupation to bring out explicitly the meaning of a text,* while taking scriptural studies into account.

The preceding remarks also apply to introductions to biblical readings, to the Prayer of the Faithful, and to commentaries printed in missals used by the laity.

III. TEACHING AND EDUCATION

Although there is still a great deal of work to be done, a better understanding of Judaism itself and its relationship to Christianity has been achieved in recent years thanks to the teaching of the Church, the study and research of scholars, and also to the beginning of dialogue. In this respect, the following facts deserve to be recalled.

It is the same God, "inspirer and author of the books of both Testaments" (*Dei Verbum*), who speaks both in the old and new Covenants.

Judaism in the time of Christ and the Apostles was a complex reality, embracing many different trends, many spiritual, religious, social and cultural values.

The Old Testament and the Jewish tradition founded upon it must not be set against the New Testament in such a way that the former seems to constitute a religion of only justice, fear and legalism, with no appeal to the love of God and neighbor (cf. Deuteronomy 6:5, Leviticus 19:18, Matthew 22:34–40).

Jesus was born of the Jewish people, as were his Apostles and a large number of his first disciples. When he revealed himself as the Messiah and Son of God (cf. Matt. 16:16), the bearer of the new Gospel message, he did so at the fulfillment and perfection of the earlier Revelation. And, although his teaching had

---

* Thus the formula "the Jews," in St. John, sometimes according to the context means "the leaders of the Jews," or "the adversaries of Jesus," terms which express better the thought of the evangelist and avoid appearing to arraign the Jewish people as such. Another example is the use of the words "pharisee" and "pharisaism," which have taken on a largely pejorative meaning.

a profoundly new character, Christ nevertheless, in many instances, took his stand on the teaching of the Old Testament. The New Testament is profoundly marked by its relation to the Old. As the Second Vatican Council declared: "God, the inspirer and author of the books of both Testaments, wisely arranged that the New Testament be hidden in the Old and the Old be made manifest in the New" (*Dei Verbum*). Jesus also used teaching methods similar to those employed by the rabbis of his time.

With regard to the trial and death of Jesus, the Council recalled that "what happened in his passion cannot be blamed upon all the Jews then living, without distinction, nor upon the Jews of today" (*Nostra Aetate*).

The history of Judaism did not end with the destruction of Jerusalem, but rather went on to develop a religious tradition. And, although we believe that the importance and meaning of that tradition were deeply affected by the coming of Christ, it is still nonetheless rich in religious values.

With the prophets and the apostle Paul, "the Church awaits the day, known to God alone, on which all peoples will address the Lord in a single voice and 'serve him with one accord'" (Wisdom 3:9) (*Nostra Aetate*).

Information concerning these questions is important at all levels of Christian instruction and education. Among sources of information, special attention should be paid to the following:

> catechisms and religious textbooks
> history books
> the mass-media (press, radio, cinema, television)

The effective use of these means presupposes the thorough formation of instructors and educators in training schools, seminaries and universities.

Research into the problems bearing on Judaism and Jewish-Christian relations will be encouraged among specialists, particularly in the fields of exegesis, theology, history and sociology. Higher institutions of Catholic research, in association if possible with other similar Christian institutions and experts, are invited to contribute to the solution of such problems. Wherever possible, chairs of Jewish studies will be created, and collaboration with Jewish scholars encouraged.

IV. JOINT SOCIAL ACTION

Jewish and Christian tradition, founded on the Word of God, is aware of the value of the human person, the image of God. Love of the same God must show itself in effective action for the good of mankind. In the spirit of the prophets, Jews and Christians will work willingly together, seeking social justice and peace at every level—local, national and international.

At the same time, such collaboration can do much to foster mutual understanding and esteem.

CONCLUSION

The Second Vatican Council has pointed out the path to follow in promoting deep fellowship between Jews and Christians. But there is still a long road ahead.

The problem of Jewish-Christian relations concerns the Church as such, since it is when "pondering her own mystery" that she encounters the mystery of Israel. Therefore, even in areas where no Jewish communities exist, this remains an important problem. There is also an ecumenical aspect to the question: the very return of Christians to the sources and origins of their faith, grafted on to the earlier Covenant, helps the search for unity in Christ, the cornerstone.

In this field, the bishops will know what best to do on the pastoral level, within the general disciplinary framework of the Church and in line with the common teaching of her magisterium. For example, they will create some suitable commissions or secretariats on a national or regional level, or appoint some competent person to promote the implementation of the conciliar directives and the suggestions made above.

On 22 October 1974, the Holy Father instituted for the universal Church this Commission for Religious Relations with the Jews, joined to the Secretariat for Promoting Christian Unity. This special Commission, created to encourage and foster religious relations between Jews and Catholics—and to do so eventually in collaboration with other Christians—will be, within the limits of its competence, at the service of all interested organizations, providing information for them, and helping them to pursue their task in conformity with the instructions of the Holy See. The Commission wishes to develop this collaboration in order to implement, correctly and effectively, the express intentions of the Council.

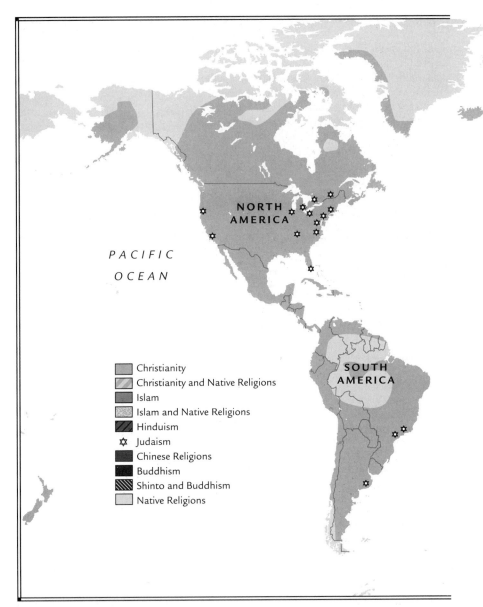

Distribution of the world's religions, 2005.

The Ecumenical Movement

In addition to considering Catholic relations with Jews and other non-Christians, the participants of Vatican II looked at Catholicism and its ties to members of the immediate family, that is, other Christians. Christians had worked together on various social issues in the past. For example, in the United States, Catholics and Protestants joined forces in support of progressive legislation as part of the Social Gospel move-

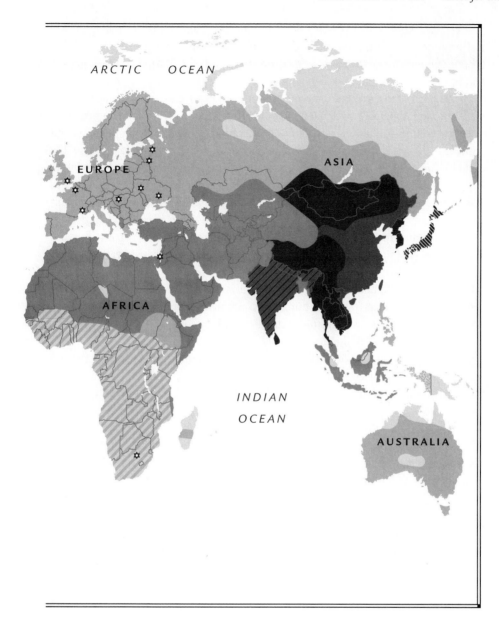

ment. Protestants formed first the Federal Council of Churches and then the National Council of Churches, which also promoted unity on social policies of interest to Christians, such as civil rights, pacifism, labor organizing, and women's rights. Prior to World War II, however, few denominations participated in ecumenical dialogue that explicitly deliberated church union, or rather, reunion. Orthodox and Anglican Christianity are the exceptions, meeting several times in the period between two world wars to discuss issues of agreement and of disagreement. Of special importance was the mutual recognition of the ordination of priests by each other's denomination. Progress seemed ongoing until the 1970s, when Anglicans and Episcopalians began to ordain women.

This type of interdenominational dialogue is known as the ecumenical movement, another hopeful development in twentieth-century Christianity. Ecumenism is the effort to find common ground among the various Christian denominations and churches. It pays particular attention to the Nicene Creed's affirmation that the church is *one,* holy, apostolic, and universal. But if the church really is one, why do Christians disagree on so many issues? On what is it possible to agree? In addition to Anglican-Orthodox dialogue, as well as Orthodox-Lutheran and Orthodox-Reformed conversations, Catholics and Lutherans have also engaged in important discussions, and in 1999 came to an agreement on the doctrine of justification. Within the past few years, Anglicans—including Episcopalians in the United States—and Lutherans have agreed to recognize and accept the ordination of each other's ministers. Mutual recognition of the legitimacy of each other's ordination is a significant achievement. Those committed to ecumenism argue that most divisions among Christians arise from misunderstanding and miscommunication, rather than from real differences of opinion.

A few years after World War II, the World Council of Churches (WCC) formed. This body meets in assemblies—rather than councils, which might give the meetings a significance no one is yet willing to concede—every seven years, and includes representatives from Protestant and Orthodox denominations. Although Catholics do not participate officially, representatives from the Catholic Church take part in almost all WCC programs. The first assembly met in Amsterdam in 1948 and adopted a simple foundational statement: "The World Council of Churches is a fellowship of churches which accept our Lord Jesus Christ as God and Savior." At its third assembly, in New Delhi, India, in 1961, the WCC amended its statement of principles to read: "The World Council of Churches is a fellowship of churches which confess the Lord Jesus Christ as God and Savior according to the scriptures and therefore seek to fulfill together their common calling to the glory of the one God, Father, Son and Holy Spirit." These statements, in effect, provide the bare minimum for a denomination to gain admittance into the WCC; in other words, they seem to provide a definition for what constitutes a Christian church.

At its fiftieth-anniversary assembly, in Harare, Zimbabwe, in 1998, these affirmations were put to the test when the Celestial Church of Christ of Nigeria requested admission into the WCC. Some of the older ministers in the Celestial Church practiced polygamy, although the practice had been outlawed by that church in 1986, and its younger ministers were not polygamous. While delegates to the assembly recognized that the Celestial Church accepted the WCC's faith statement, they questioned its ethical practices and did not accept its membership application.

Ongoing tension with its Orthodox members also characterizes WCC deliberations, especially in the body's consideration of topics like women's ordination and same-sex marriage. Although Orthodox churches have 37 seats on the 158-member Central Committee, more than any other single denomination, they are outnumbered by non-Orthodox members: 24 seats to African churches, 24 to Asian churches, 27 to European churches, and 22 to North American churches. Moreover, 81 percent of the WCC's funding comes from Europe, with German churches providing half that amount. The Russian Orthodox Church has threatened to leave the body several times, concerned especially about the name—World Council of *Churches*—because Orthodox Christians believe there is only a single church, namely, the Orthodox Church. Debate and conflict notwithstanding, the WCC continues to offer a forum for intra-Christian dialogue.

As the following documents indicate, Christian unity is more of an ideal than a reality, at least on some issues. Differences run deep, and ancient grievances remain fresh. For example, Orthodox Christians—who live primarily in Eastern Europe, Russia, East Africa, the Middle East, and the coastal Mediterranean—blame western Christians for a number of military and theological disasters, including the addition of the filioque to the Nicene Creed and the sack of Constantinople in 1204. Orthodoxy poses a constant reminder to western Christianity—as embodied in Catholicism and Protestantism—that more than 250 million Christians emphasize different doctrinal issues. These include the nature of salvation, the role of prayer, the practice of communion, and the importance of the mystical life for all believers. More and more Christians in the West are looking at Orthodoxy with a new appreciation for its upholding of ancient traditions and its rich liturgical practices. Conflict sometimes accompanies this interest, however, with competing claims about which branch of Christianity remains most faithful to its origins, which teaches correct doctrine, and which has the strongest claim to being called the "true" church.

The Readings

Four documents reveal the challenges the ecumenical movement faces, as well as the promise that continued dialogue holds for all Christians. Each emerges from a different context and was written for a different purpose. Sergius Bulgakov's chapter on "Orthodoxy and Other Christian Confessions" comes from his 1935 book *The Orthodox Church*. For decades, this was the major introduction to Orthodox Christianity that western Christians relied on for their understanding of the eastern church. Bulgakov, a Russian Orthodox priest, wrote his book for a Western audience that had little knowledge of Orthodoxy.

An important question to consider when reading Bulgakov is whether his views remain normative for Orthodoxy today. After all, much has happened since he wrote his book: a major world war, the Cold War and the fall of communism, and the rise of Islam in nations with large Orthodox populations. Despite all this, Bulgakov's position appears consistent within contemporary Orthodoxy. For example, Archbishop Timothy Ware—a professor at Oxford University and a current interpreter of Orthodox Christianity—affirms that "the Orthodox Church in all humility believes itself to be the 'one, holy, Catholic and Apostolic Church'." Ware admits that though this may sound exclusive, it does not mean that other Christians must submit to Orthodox power and jurisdiction; instead, the sole desire of the church is to reconcile all Christians to Orthodoxy.

The next two documents come from general assemblies of the World Council of Churches, including a message from the first assembly, meeting in Amsterdam, and the second, gathering in Evanston, Illinois. Like the documents from Vatican II, these are political documents, carefully worded to be acceptable to the majority of voting members.

The final document is an excerpt from Pope John Paul II's 1995 encyclical *Ut unum sint [That they may be one]: On Commitment to Ecumenism.* Pope John Paul II (p. 1978–2005) saw the Roman Catholic Church through more than twenty-five years of internal and external changes. The first Polish pope, Karol Jozef Wojtyla, helped the people of Poland end communist rule in their country. He traveled more widely than any other pope, visiting more than 115 countries on 170 trips, and survived an assassination attempt in 1981. His pontificate was one of the most influential in the history of Christianity. John Paul II criticized capitalism and communism alike; he promoted peace and justice; he opposed abortion and the death penalty.

Ut unum sint reproduces some of the language in the 1964 Vatican II document on church unity, titled the "Dogmatic Constitution on the Church," also known as *Lumen Gentium.* The pope goes on to explain what he understands *Lumen Gentium* [*Light of the World*] to mean some thirty years later.

Note: Sergius Bulgakov refers to Esperanto in his article. Esperanto was a language that combined English and various Romance languages (Spanish, French, Italian). Some hoped it would replace various languages, but it never caught on. He also mentions pharisaism, a reference to New Testament Pharisees and a way of saying that people are legalistic or concerned with the purity of their own beliefs.

Questions to Consider

1. How would you summarize or restate the positions of Bulgakov, the two assemblies of the World Council of Churches, and John Paul II on church union?

2. How do you think the competing claims of the Roman Catholic Church, with its single head identified as the pope (who is also the bishop of Rome), and of the Orthodox Church, which consists of autocephalous (independently headed) national churches, will be resolved? Can you come up with a solution in which "everybody wins"?

3. What difficulties do you perceive there to be in achieving church union? In other words, what are some of the major obstacles that stand in the way of Christian unity?

4. What do you think are the most hopeful signs that can be identified in the documents?

5. Are there potential threats to the integrity of various church bodies in the ecumenical movement? What might they be? Can they be overcome?

Orthodoxy and Other Christian Confessions

SERGIUS BULGAKOV

All the foregoing may give some idea of the relationship between Orthodoxy and other Christian confessions. Note at once that the Orthodox Church is aware that she is the true Church, possessing the plenitude and purity of the truth in the Holy Spirit. Hence proceeds the attitude of the Orthodox Church toward other confessions, separated, immediately or not, from the unity of the Church; it can desire but one thing, that is to make Orthodox the entire Christian world, so that all confessions, may be grounded in universal Orthodoxy. This is not a spirit of proselytism or imperialism; it is the inherent logic of the situation, for the truth is one and cannot be measured by half-truths. Neither is it a mark of pride, for the guardianship of the truth is entrusted to a recipient, not for its merits, but by election, and the history of the chosen people, as well as that of Orthodoxy, shows that the guardians of the truth may be little worthy of their calling. But truth is inflexible and inexorable, and will not suffer compromise.

Thus the Christian world should become Orthodox; but just what does this mean? Does it mean that everyone should become a member of a certain church organization? Is it a conquest of ecclesiastical imperialism? There does not even exist in Orthodoxy a single ecclesiastical organization which could be entered; the Orthodox Church is a system of national, autocephalous Churches, allied one with another. It is true that individuals often join themselves to Orthodoxy by becoming members of one of the national Churches, but this fact offers no solution for the question of the relationship between ecclesiastical communities or confessions. The only solution would

be the following: these communities, while preserving intact their historical, national, and local characters, would draw near to Orthodox doctrine and life and would become capable of joining forces in the unity of the ecumenical Church, as autonomous or autocephalous churches. Such an exterior reunion presupposes, of course, a corresponding interior movement. But such a movement is not impossible, for all ecclesiastical communities, even those whose road is farthest from that of the Orthodox Church, preserve a considerable part of the universal tradition, and, as a result of this, share in Orthodoxy. They all have "a grain" of Orthodoxy.

This Orthodox spirit, which lives in the universal Church, is more apparent to the eye of God than to that of man. In the first place all baptized persons are Christians, hence, in a certain sense, Orthodox. For Orthodoxy is composed, so to speak, of two circles: a large circle, the court of the temple, and a narrow circle, the temple itself and the holy of holies. Orthodoxy does not desire the submission of any person or group; it wishes to make each one understand. This is a field for the operation of the Holy Spirit which lives in the Church, beyond the direct efforts of men. Note here the sharp distinction between the attitude of Orthodoxy and that of Roman Catholicism. For the latter, reunion means, first of all, submission to the papal authority. Orthodoxy does not value exterior submission. And if such submission is necessary, it is only for the purpose of settling matters of the canonical organization of the community joining in ecumenical unity, or to guard against the ambitious pretensions of a local church, of which history affords examples. The ideal of the "union of the Churches" in its contemporary form would be realized by the entry of all Christian communities into the heart of Orthodoxy, but only if the maximum and not the minimum of the common heritage of the Churches forms the basis of reunion. By setting aside an abstract minimum on which all ecclesiastical societies would agree, unity could by no means be attained; this could only be the one first step on the road.

Only an agreement between the Churches, founded on the maximum of their common inheritance, can lead the Christian world to real union. This maximum is Orthodoxy. It cannot be a sort of amalgam or compromise, like a religious Esperanto, still less indifference to all dogmatic questions. Neither can it be something quite new in the history of the Church; then all the earlier life of the Church would have been a mistake, a misunderstanding, non-being. Orthodoxy is the interior way, the interior necessity for the universal Church on its way towards unity; it is only in Orthodoxy that the problems raised by the Christian confessions find a solution and an end, for it possesses the truth. Orthodoxy is not one of the historic confessions, it is the Church itself in its verity. It may even be added that, by becoming a confession, Orthodoxy fails to manifest all its force and its universal glory; it hides, one might say, in the catacombs.

The movement towards the reconstitution of universal Orthodoxy is steadily gaining force. In the same measure that the tendency of the sects toward isolation ceases, in the same measure that the ecumenical spirit is triumphing over sectarian pharisaism—this movement is pressing forward irresistibly, before our eyes today. It is not the result of Orthodox proselytizing, since there is no such thing. Contemporary Orthodoxy would probably not be able to muster strength sufficient for such a task, even if it wished. It is the Spirit of God Who leads the peoples toward Orthodoxy, in spite of human frailty and narrowness. As a matter of fact, what is the most important phenomenon of the spiritual life of the Christian world today? The search for the ecumenical Church, for integral unity. This unity may be realized only in two ways: by Orthodox conciliarity, "sobornost," or by the authoritarian monarchy of Catholicism. The success and the conquests of ecclesiastical authoritarianism may be considerable now, and perhaps even greater in the future. Still, it may confidently be affirmed that the conquest of the Christian world by a religion of authority is an aim which cannot hope to be realized; if that should happen it would be a proof of reaction and of spiritual decadence. The world will not become Catholic; on the other hand, we ob-

serve that papalism is becoming more and more isolated in the Christian world. This fact became very clear with the appearance of the encyclical "Mortalium Animos" after the Conference of Lausanne [1927]. It must be noted, however, that Catholicism is something greater than papalism. It may well be said that the Monarchy of the Vatican is a sort of shell, beneath which is the living body of the Church. And against the poisons of "statehood," of judicial authority, or ecclesiastical monarchy, which have affected that body, the everliving organism of the Church is constantly manufacturing anti-toxins. In spite of the triumph of authority in any Christian confession, the integral conscience of the ecumenical Church continues to live in the depths and naturally tends to another—an interior unity. This is witnessed by all the living holiness so plentiful in Catholicism, not because of papalism, but in spite of it. This is witnessed again by the purely religious movements in Catholicism, such as the liturgical movement among the Benedictines or the "Union" movement of the Priory of Amay (Belgium).

The same tendency is much more clearly evident in the Protestant world. The two names of Stockholm and Lausanne symbolize the movement toward reunion, which has begun in the heart of the Christian world, and which is already bearing fruit. But this movement brings with it a reexamination and revaluation of the spiritual basis of the Christian communities. By the very force of circumstances, it leads irresistibly to more profound consideration of questions concerning ecclesiastical tradition, and in consequence, it leads to a return, at first almost imperceptible, towards Orthodoxy. This return is already evident in the advanced movements of the Protestant world, which designate themselves as "Hochkirchliche Bewegung." Thanks to the modern tendency to restore the plenitude of tradition, thanks to certain movements which are leading to the liberation of Catholicism from the Roman system, an important rapprochement in regard to Orthodoxy is becoming outlined. But the decisive act, perhaps still far distant, would consist in the reestablishment of the hierarchy of the Apostolic Succession in those bodies where it was abolished.

A special place in this movement is occupied by the Episcopal Church of England, America and other countries. I shall not touch, here, the subject of the validity of Anglican orders, merely a canonical and not a dogmatic question, which can be decided for the Orthodox Church only by a competent ecclesiastical authority. In any case, the Episcopal Church is, of all the Protestant world, the nearest to Orthodoxy. Among the many tendencies in Anglicanism the Anglo-Catholic movement becomes more and more important; it is persistently devoted to reestablishment of ancient tradition and thus flows into the stream of Orthodoxy. We may hope that the reunion of Orthodoxy and of the Episcopal Churches of England and America will be an accomplishment of the not too distant future, and that this movement will be a decisive phase in the reestablishment of the unity lost to the Church, and of peace between the East and the West.

The Orthodox Church takes part in the interconfessional, "ecumenical" movements of our day in which Catholicism refuses to participate. Whence comes such a difference between the two parts of the separated Church? The participation of Orthodoxy in this movement does not all signify that it can renounce any portion whatever of its tradition or that it can accept a compromise or reconsideration. On the other hand, relations with heterodox confessions may aid the Orthodox Church to attain greater plenitude and breadth. Orthodoxy is present at such conferences to testify to the truth. These conferences are not councils, they are only preliminary assemblies, they are "conciliation." There are no reasons why Orthodoxy should avoid conferences. On the contrary, Christian love demands that the faith be testified to, that one be "all things to all men," as the Apostle said, "in order that by all means I might save some" (1 Corinthians 9:22). Orthodoxy is not separated from the rest of the Christian world by a wall of absolute power, the papacy, whose preliminary recognition is imposed. Since this obstacle does not exist for Orthodoxy, it can enter into relations, in all liberty and sincerity, with the whole Christian world, remaining always that which it is itself. The Orthodox Church does not put its hopes on human efforts and the missionary zeal of its members, but it hopes in the power of the Spirit of God, Who lives in the Church and Who is leading the peoples toward unity. This unity may be found only in Orthodoxy. The Christian peoples of the world are now seeking Orthodoxy, often without knowing it. And they will find it, for it is said: "Seek and ye shall find."

Message of the First Assembly (1948), Amsterdam, The Netherlands

WORLD COUNCIL OF CHURCHES

The World Council of Churches, meeting at Amsterdam, sends this message of greeting to all who are in Christ, and to all who are willing to hear.

We bless God our Father, and our Lord Jesus Christ Who gathers together in one the children of God that are scattered abroad. He has brought us here together at Amsterdam. We are one in acknowledging Him as our God and Savior. We are divided from one another not only in matters of faith, order and tradition, but also by pride of nation, class and race. But Christ has made us His own, and He is not divided. In seeking Him we find one another. Here at Amsterdam we have committed ourselves afresh to Him, and have covenanted with one another in constituting this World Council of Churches. We intend to stay together. We call upon Christian congregations everywhere to endorse and fulfill this covenant in their relations one with another. In thankfulness to God we commit the future to Him.

When we look to Christ, we see the world as it is—His world, to which He came and for which He died. It is filled both with great hopes and also with disillusionment and despair. Some nations are rejoicing in new freedom and power, some are bitter because freedom is denied them, some are paralyzed by division, and everywhere there is an undertone of fear. There are millions who are hungry, millions who have no home, no country and no hope. Over all mankind hangs the peril of total war. We have to accept God's judgment upon us for our share in the world's guilt. Often we have tried to serve God and mammon, put other loyalties before loyalty to Christ, confused the Gospel with our own economic or national or racial interests, and feared war more than we have hated it. As we have talked with one another here, we have begun to understand how our separation has prevented us from receiving correction from one another in Christ. And because we lacked this correction, the world has often heard from us not the Word of God but the words of men.

But there is a word of God for our world. It is that the world is in the hands of the living God, Whose will for it is wholly good; that in Christ Jesus, His incarnate Word, Who lived and died and rose from the dead, God has broken the power of evil once for all, and opened for everyone the gate into freedom and joy in the Holy Spirit; that the final judgment on all human history and on every human deed is the judgment of the merciful Christ; and that the end of history will be the triumph of His Kingdom, where alone we shall understand how much God has loved the world. This is God's unchanging word to the world. Millions of our fellow men have never heard it. As we are met here from many lands, we pray God to stir up His whole Church to make this Gospel known to the whole world, and to call on all men to believe in Christ, to live in His love and to hope for His coming.

Our coming together to form a World Council will be vain unless Christians and Christian congregations everywhere commit themselves to the Lord of the Church in a new effort to seek together, where they live, to be His witnesses and servants among their neighbors. We have to remind ourselves and all men that God has put down the mighty from their seats and exalted the humble and meek. We have to learn afresh together to speak boldly in Christ's name both to those in power and to the people, to oppose terror, cruelty and race discrimination, to stand by the outcast, the prisoner and the refugee. We have to make of the Church in every place a voice for those who have no voice, and a home where every man will be at home. We have to learn afresh together what is the duty of the Christian man or woman in industry, in agriculture, in politics, in the professions and in the home. We have to ask God to teach us together to say No and to say Yes in truth. No to all that flouts the love of Christ, to every system, every program and every person that treats any man as though he were an irresponsible thing or a means of profit, to the defenders of injustice in the name of order, to those who sow the seeds of war or urge war as inevitable; Yes, to all that conforms to the love of Christ, to all who seek for justice, to the peacemakers, to all who hope, fight and suffer for the cause of man, to all who—even without knowing it—look for new heavens and a new earth wherein dwelleth righteousness.

It is not in man's power to banish sin and death from the earth, to create the unity of the Holy Catholic Church, to conquer the hosts of Satan. But it is within the power of God. He has given us at Easter the certainty that His purpose will be accomplished. But, by our acts of obedience and faith, we can on earth set up signs which point to the coming victory. Till the day of that victory our lives are hid with Christ in God, and no earthly disillusion or distress or power of hell can separate us from Him. As those who wait in confidence and joy for their deliverance, let us give ourselves to those tasks which lie to our hands and so set up signs that men may see.

Now unto Him that is able to do exceeding abundantly above all that we ask or think, according to the power that worketh in us, unto Him be glory in the Church by Christ Jesus, throughout all ages, world without end.

Message From the Second Assembly (1954), Evanston, Illinois

WORLD COUNCIL OF CHURCHES

To all our fellow Christians, and to our fellowmen everywhere, we send greetings in the name of Jesus Christ. We affirm our faith in Jesus Christ as the hope of the world, and desire to share that faith with all men. May God forgive us that by our sin we have often hidden this hope from the world.

In the ferment of our time there are both hopes and fears. It is indeed good to hope for freedom, justice and peace, and it is God's will that we should have these things. But He has made us for a higher end. He has made us for Himself, that we might know and love Him, worship and serve Him. Nothing other than God can ever satisfy the heart of man. Forgetting this, man becomes his own enemy. He seeks justice but creates oppression. He wants peace, but drifts towards war. His very mastery of nature threatens him with ruin. Whether he acknowledges it or not, he stands under the judgment of God and in the shadow of death.

Here where we stand, Jesus Christ stood with us. He came to us, true God and true Man, to seek and to save. Though we were the enemies of God, Christ died for us. We crucified Him, but God raised Him from the dead. He is risen. He has overcome the powers of sin and death. A new life has begun. And in His risen and ascended power, He has sent forth into the world a new community, bound together by His Spirit, sharing His divine life, and commissioned to make Him known throughout the world. He will come again as Judge and King to bring all things to their consummation. Then we shall see Him as He is and know as we are known. Together with the whole creation we wait for this with eager hope, knowing that God is faithful and that even now He holds all things in His hand.

This is the hope of God's people in every age, and we commend it afresh today to all who will listen. To accept it is to turn from our ways to God's way. It is to live as forgiven sinners, as children growing in His love. It is to have our citizenship in that Kingdom which all man's sin is impotent to destroy, that realm of love and joy and peace which lies about all men, though unseen. It is to enter with Christ into the suffering and despair of men, sharing with them the great secret of that Kingdom which they do not expect. It is to know that whatever men may do, Jesus reigns and shall reign.

With this assurance we can face the powers of evil and the threat of death with a good courage. Delivered from fear we are made free to love. For beyond the judgment of men and the judgment of history lies the judgment of the King who died for all men, and who will judge us according to what we have done to the least of His brethren. Thus our Christian hope directs us towards our neighbor. It constrains us to pray daily, "Thy will be done on earth as it is in heaven," and to act as we pray in every area of life. It begets a life of believing prayer and expectant action, looking to Jesus and pressing forward to the day of His return in glory.

Now we would speak through our member churches directly to each congregation. Six years ago our churches entered into a covenant to form this Council, and affirmed their intention to stay together. We thank God for His blessing on our work and fellowship during these six years. We enter now upon a second stage. To stay together is not enough. We must go forward. As we learn more of our unity in Christ, it becomes the more intolerable that we should be divided. We therefore ask you: Is your church seriously considering its relation to other churches in the light of our Lord's prayer that we may be sanctified in the truth and that we may all be one? Is your congregation, in fellowship with sister congregations around you, doing all it can to ensure that your neighbors shall hear the voice of the one Shepherd calling all men into one flock?

The forces that separate men from one another are strong. At our meeting here we have missed the presence of Chinese churches which were with us at Amsterdam. There are other lands and churches unrepresented in our Council, and we long ardently for their fellowship. But we are thankful that, separated as we are by the deepest political divisions of our time, here at Evanston we are united in Christ. And we rejoice also that, in the bond of prayer and a common hope, we maintain communion with our Christian brethren everywhere.

It is from within this communion that we have to speak about the fear and distrust which at present divide our world. Only at the Cross of Christ, where men know themselves as forgiven sinners, can they be made one. It is there that Christians must pray daily for their enemies. It is there that we must seek deliverance from self-righteousness, impatience and fear. And those who know that Christ is risen should have the courage to expect new power to break through every human barrier.

It is not enough that Christians should seek peace for themselves. They must seek justice for others. Great masses of people in many parts of the world are hungry for bread, and are compelled to live in conditions which mock their human worth. Does your church speak and act against such injustice? Millions of men and women are suffering segregation and discrimination on the ground of race. Is your church willing to declare, as this Assembly has declared, that this is contrary to the will of God and to act on that declaration? Do you pray regularly for those who suffer unjust discrimination on grounds of race, religion or political conviction?

The Church of Christ is today a world-wide fellowship, yet there are countless people to whom He is unknown. How much do you care about this? Does your congregation live for itself, or for the world around it and beyond it? Does its common life, and does the daily work of its members in the world, affirm the Lordship of Christ or deny it?

God does not leave any of us to stand alone. In every place He has gathered us together to be His family, in which His gifts and His forgiveness are received. Do you forgive one another as Christ forgave you? Is your congregation a true family of God, where every man can find a home and know that God loves him without limit?

We are not sufficient for these things. But Christ is sufficient. We do not know what is coming to us. But we know Who is coming. It is He who meets us every day and who will meet us at the end—Jesus Christ our Lord.

Therefore we say to you: Rejoice in hope.

Ut Unum Sint: On Commitment to Ecumenism

POPE JOHN PAUL II

CHAPTER I—THE CATHOLIC CHURCH'S COMMITMENT TO ECUMENISM

God's Plan and Communion

5. Together with all Christ's disciples, the Catholic Church bases upon God's plan her ecumenical commitment to gather all Christians into unity. Indeed, "the Church is not a reality closed in on herself. Rather, she is permanently open to missionary and ecumenical endeavor, for she is sent to the world to announce and witness, to make present and spread the mystery of communion which is essential to her, and to gather all people and all things into Christ, so as to be for all an 'inseparable sacrament of unity'" [Congregation for the Doctrine of the Faith].

Already in the Old Testament, the Prophet Ezekiel, referring to the situation of God's People at that time, and using the simple sign of two broken sticks which are first divided and then joined together, expressed the divine will to "gather from all sides" the members of his scattered people. "I will be their God, and they shall be my people. Then the nations will know that I the Lord sanctify Israel" (cf. 37:16–28). The Gospel of John, for its part, considering the situation of the People of God at the time it was written, sees in Jesus' death the reason for the unity of God's children: "Jesus would die for the nation, and not for the nation only, but to gather into one the children of God who are scattered abroad" (11:51–52). Indeed, as the Letter to the Ephesians explains, Jesus "broke down the dividing wall of hostility . . . through the Cross, thereby bringing the hostility to an end"; in place of what was divided he brought about unity (cf. 2:14–16).

6. The unity of all divided humanity is the will of God. For this reason he sent his Son, so that by dying and rising for us he might bestow on us the Spirit of love. On the eve of his sacrifice on the Cross, Jesus himself prayed to the Father for his disciples and for all those who believe in him, that they *might be one,* a living communion. This is the basis not only of the duty, but also of the responsibility before God and his plan, which falls to those who through Baptism become members of the Body of Christ, a Body in which the fullness of reconciliation and communion must be made present. How is it possible to remain divided, if we have been "buried" through Baptism in the Lord's death, in the very act by which God, through the death of his Son, has broken down the walls of division? Division "openly contradicts the will of Christ, provides a stumbling block to the world, and inflicts damage on the most holy cause of proclaiming the Good News to every creature" [*Unitas Redintegratio*].

The Way of Ecumenism: The Way of the Church

7. "The Lord of the Ages wisely and patiently follows out the plan of his grace on behalf of us sinners. In recent times he has begun to bestow more generously upon divided Christians remorse over their divisions and a longing for unity. Everywhere, large numbers have felt the impulse of this grace, and among our separated brethren also *there increases from day to day a movement,* fostered by the grace of the Holy Spirit, *for the restoration of unity among all Christians.* Taking part in this movement, which is called ecumenical,

are those who invoke the Triune God and confess Jesus as Lord and Savior. They join in not merely as individuals but also as members of the corporate groups in which they have heard the Gospel, and which each regards as his Church and, indeed, God's. And yet almost everyone, though in different ways, *longs that there may be one visible Church of God,* a Church truly universal and sent forth to the whole world that the world may be converted to the Gospel and so be saved, to the glory of God."

8. This statement of the Decree *Unitatis Redintegratio* is to be read in the context of the complete teaching of the Second Vatican Council. The Council expresses the Church's decision to take up the ecumenical task of working for Christian unity and to propose it with conviction and vigor: "This sacred Synod exhorts all the Catholic faithful to recognize the signs of the times and to participate actively in the work of ecumenism."

In indicating the Catholic principles of ecumenism, the Decree *Unitatis Redintegratio* recalls above all the teaching on the Church set forth in the Dogmatic Constitution *Lumen Gentium* in its chapter on the People of God. At the same time, it takes into account everything affirmed in the Council's Declaration on Religious Freedom *Dignitatis Humanae.*

The Catholic Church embraces with hope the commitment to ecumenism as a duty of the Christian conscience enlightened by faith and guided by love. Here too we can apply the words of Saint Paul to the first Christians of Rome: "God's love has been poured into our hearts through the Holy Spirit"; thus our "hope does not disappoint us" (Romans 5:5). This is the hope of Christian unity, which has its divine source in the Trinitarian unity of the Father, the Son and the Holy Spirit.

9. Jesus himself, at the hour of his Passion, prayed "that they may all be one" (John 17:21). This unity, which the Lord has bestowed on his Church and in which he wishes to embrace all people, is not something added on, but stands at the very heart of Christ's mission. Nor is it some secondary attribute of the community of his disciples. Rather, it belongs to the very essence of this community. God wills the Church, because he wills unity, and unity is an expression of the whole depth of his *agape.*

In effect, this unity bestowed by the Holy Spirit does not merely consist in the gathering of people as a collection of individuals. It is a unity constituted by the bonds of the profession of faith, the sacraments and hierarchical communion. The faithful are *one* be-cause, in the Spirit, they are in *communion* with the Son and, in him, share in his *communion* with the Father: "Our fellowship is with the Father and with his Son Jesus Christ" (1 John 1:3). For the Catholic Church, then, the *communion* of Christians is none other than the manifestation in them of the grace by which God makes them sharers in his own *communion,* which is his eternal life. Christ's words "that they may be one" are thus his prayer to the Father that the Father's plan may be fully accomplished, in such a way that everyone may clearly see "what is the plan of the mystery hidden for ages in God who created all things" (Ephesians 3:9). To believe in Christ means to desire unity; to desire unity means to desire the Church; to desire the Church means to desire the communion of grace which corresponds to the Father's plan from all eternity. Such is the meaning of Christ's prayer: *"Ut unum sint."*

10. In the present situation of the lack of unity among Christians and of the confident quest for full communion, the Catholic faithful are conscious of being deeply challenged by the Lord of the Church. The Second Vatican Council strengthened their commitment with a clear ecclesiological vision, open to all the ecclesial values present among other Christians. The Catholic faithful face the ecumenical question in a spirit of faith.

The Council states that the Church of Christ "subsists in the Catholic Church, which is governed by the Successor of Peter and by the Bishops in communion with him," and at the same time acknowledges that "many elements of sanctification and of truth can be found outside her visible structure. These elements, however, as gifts properly belonging to the Church of Christ, possess an inner dynamism towards Catholic unity" [*Lumen Gentium*].

"It follows that these separated Churches and Communities, though we believe that they suffer from defects, have by no means been deprived of significance and value in the mystery of salvation. For the Spirit of Christ has not refrained from using them as means of salvation which derive their efficacy from the very fullness of grace and truth entrusted to the Catholic Church" [*Unitas Redintegratio*].

11. The Catholic Church thus affirms that during the two thousand years of her history she has been preserved in unity, with all the means with which God wishes to endow his Church, and this despite the often grave crises which have shaken her, the infidelity of some of her ministers, and the faults into

which her members daily fall. The Catholic Church knows that, by virtue of the strength which comes to her from the Spirit, the weaknesses, mediocrity, sins and at times the betrayals of some of her children cannot destroy what God has bestowed on her as part of his plan of grace. Moreover, "the powers of death shall not prevail against it" (Matthew 16:18). Even so, the Catholic Church does not forget that many among her members cause God's plan to be discernible only with difficulty. Speaking of the lack of unity among Christians, the Decree on Ecumenism does not ignore the fact that "people of both sides were to blame," and acknowledges that responsibility cannot be attributed only to the "other side." By God's grace, however, neither what belongs to the structure of the Church of Christ nor that communion which still exists with the other Churches and Ecclesial Communities has been destroyed.

Indeed, the elements of sanctification and truth present in the other Christian Communities, in a degree which varies from one to the other, constitute the objective basis of the communion, albeit imperfect, which exists between them and the Catholic Church.

To the extent that these elements are found in other Christian Communities, the one Church of Christ is effectively present in them. For this reason the Second Vatican Council speaks of a certain, though imperfect communion. The Dogmatic Constitution *Lumen Gentium* stresses that the Catholic Church "recognizes that in many ways she is linked" with these Communities by a true union in the Holy Spirit.

12. The same Dogmatic Constitution listed at length "the elements of sanctification and truth" which in various ways are present and operative beyond the visible boundaries of the Catholic Church: "For there are many who honor Sacred Scripture, taking it as a norm of belief and of action, and who show a true religious zeal. They lovingly believe in God the Father Almighty and in Christ, Son of God and Savior. They are consecrated by Baptism, through which they are united with Christ. They also recognize and receive other sacraments within their own Churches or Ecclesial Communities. Many of them rejoice in the episcopate, celebrate the Holy Eucharist, and cultivate devotion towards the Virgin Mother of God. They also share with us in prayer and other spiritual benefits. Likewise, we can say that in some real way they are joined with us in the Holy Spirit, for to them

also he gives his gifts and graces, and is thereby operative among them with his sanctifying power. Some indeed he has strengthened to the extent of the shedding of their blood. In all of Christ's disciples the Spirit arouses the desire to be peacefully united, in the manner determined by Christ, as one flock under one shepherd."

The Council's Decree on Ecumenism, referring to the Orthodox Churches, went so far as to declare that "through the celebration of the Eucharist of the Lord in each of these Churches, the Church of God is built up and grows in stature." Truth demands that all this be recognized.

13. The same Document carefully draws out the doctrinal implications of this situation. Speaking of the members of these Communities, it declares: "All those justified by faith through Baptism are incorporated into Christ. They therefore have a right to be honored by the title of Christian, and are properly regarded as brothers and sisters in the Lord by the sons and daughters of the Catholic Church."

With reference to the many positive elements present in the other Churches and Ecclesial Communities, the Decree adds: "All of these, which come from Christ and lead back to him, belong by right to the one Church of Christ. The separated brethren also carry out many of the sacred actions of the Christian religion. Undoubtedly, in many ways that vary according to the condition of each Church or Community, these actions can truly engender a life of grace, and can be rightly described as capable of providing access to the community of salvation."

These are extremely important texts for ecumenism. It is not that beyond the boundaries of the Catholic community there is an ecclesial vacuum. Many elements of great value (*eximia*), which in the Catholic Church are part of the fullness of the means of salvation and of the gifts of grace which make up the Church, are also found in the other Christian Communities.

14. All these elements bear within themselves a tendency towards unity, having their fullness in that unity. It is not a matter of adding together all the riches scattered throughout the various Christian Communities in order to arrive at a Church which God has in mind for the future. In accordance with the great Tradition, attested to by the Fathers of the East and of the West, the Catholic Church believes that in the Pentecost Event God has *already* manifested the Church in her eschatological reality, which he had prepared "from

the time of Abel, the just one." This reality is something already given. Consequently we are even now in the last times. The elements of this already-given Church exist, found in their fullness in the Catholic Church and, without this fullness, in the other Communities, where certain features of the Christian mystery have at times been more effectively emphasized. Ecumenism is directed precisely to making the partial communion existing between Christians grow towards full communion in truth and charity.

Pentecostal Christianity

Philip Jenkins writes about a "new Christendom" that is currently in the process of development. This Christendom—or Christian world order—has shifted the center of Christianity from Europe and North America southward, to Latin America, and Africa, and eastward to Asia. Evidence of this paradigm shift is everywhere: from record numbers of new churches and new denominations in these parts of the world, to the changing face and complexion of Christians at international meetings and assemblies. Here is but one example: in 1990, 10 million Christians were living in Africa; by 2000, the number had jumped to 360 million. Jenkins claims that these growing branches of Christianity tend to focus on miracles, the supernatural, healing, exorcism, dreams and visions, and biblical literalism. In other words, the new Christians are decidedly more conservative than their fellow Christians in the North. Yet there is more to it than that. While it is possible to differentiate between liberal and conservative Christians, it may be more helpful, according to Harvey Cox, to distinguish between fundamentalist and experientialist Christians.

Fundamentalists turn to scripture and to tradition as their primary sources of authority, claiming that both are closed and unchanging, impervious to interpretation or innovation. At times, fundamentalists seem to be locked into a dualistic worldview that can create an us-versus-them attitude. What is surprising is that fundamentalists, who seem antimodern in their attacks on certain contemporary values, are true children of the modern era in that they are concerned with literal history and factual truth. Thus, fundamentalism has broader appeal during times of stress, change, and uncertainty because of its claim to clarity and righteousness. This was apparent in the rise of the religious right in the United States during the 1980s, when conservative Christians and other groups banded together to organize against abortion, sex education, gay rights, and other moral issues.

On the other hand, experientialists are somewhat less concerned with scripture and tradition, and more concerned with their personal experience of the holy. This may lead some away from Christianity and to other religions, such as Buddhism and the practice of Zen meditation, or Hinduism and the contemplation of the divine in its various forms. It may lead some into Christian centering prayer, a new movement that recovers an ancient tradition, in which small groups of Christians gather and meditate on a single word in order to hear the voice of God. It may lead some to Orthodox Christianity, with its long history of mystical communion during the liturgy and its heritage of asceticism and prayer. Or it may lead some into ecstatic worship experiences in which the Holy Spirit seems a present reality, moving swiftly among a congregation that is open to the revelatory experience of the Spirit's presence. One of the fastest-growing forms of Christianity worldwide is Pentecostalism, a type of Spirit-filled Christianity. At its present growth rate, there will be a billion Pentecostals by 2050. Already Pentecostals and charismatics make up one-fourth of the world's Christians.

Pentecostalism began at the end of the nineteenth century and became widely known at revivals in Los Angeles, California, in the early twentieth. Pentecostalism has its roots in Acts 2 in the New Testament, where the Holy Spirit descends upon Jesus' followers, and all speak in their own languages—yet can be understood by witnesses. This gift of the Spirit, known as speaking in tongues (glossolalia), is the hallmark of Pentecostal Christianity. In addition, however, Pentecostalism embraces an ecstatic worship style, lively singing, adult baptism, and an intense group identity. At Pentecostalism's start in the early twentieth century, missionaries traveled throughout the world, and the movement took root in places as diverse as Chile and Korea. Today, hundreds of millions of Christians outside of the United States and Europe celebrate a Pentecostal faith, though regional and ethnic differences help give it a different flavor wherever it emerges. For example, Brazilian Pentecostalism wages (spiritual) war against Afro-Brazilian religions such as Macumba, Umbanda, and Candomble, which are seen as products of Satan. Sociologically speaking, however, all of these groups, including Pentecostals, are competing for the same believers, from the poorest of the poor, to the working classes, to the middle classes. Few in Latin America come from the ruling classes, which remain firmly committed to the historical Catholic faith, the majority religion in Latin America by far. Nonetheless, a charismatic movement has arisen among Catholics that presents an alternative to Protestant varieties of Pentecostalism. Charismatic Catholicism shares many characteristics with traditional Pentecostalism—ecstatic worship, singing, Bible study—yet maintains ties with traditional Catholicism.

Many, though by no means all, of the Pentecostal churches initiated in Africa and Latin America sanction a message that blesses material wealth and prosperity. Called "Prosperity Christianity," these churches claim that when believers give tithes and offerings to God, God blesses them with riches. The contemporary song "When Praises Go Up, Blessings Come Down" illustrates this form of Christianity, as does the popular "Prayer of Jabez":

> Jabez called on the God of Israel, saying, "Oh that you would bless me and enlarge my border, and that your hand might be with me, and that you would keep me from hurt and harm!" And God granted what he asked. (1 Chronicles 4:10, NRSV)

Gospel singers in the United States have made this prayer popular, emphasizing the idea of "enlargement" and expansion of one's material well-being.

Physical and spiritual healing, however, usually take precedence over prosperity in the new Pentecostal churches. Cox likens the role of pastors to that of shamans, who act as intermediaries between the spirit world and our own. Believers call upon the Holy Spirit for help, guidance, healing, deliverance, presence, gifts, and other practical—and not so practical—benefits.

The Reading

One of the most interesting, and probably the largest, of the Pentecostal churches in the world is the Yoido Full Gospel Church in Seoul, Korea. Headed by Dr. David Yonggi Cho, the Yoido Church boasts 800,000 members and counting. Its success, however, comes from the fact that members belong to "home cells," that is, small groups that meet at least weekly on an intimate and social basis. Cho says that the Yoido Church has 25,000 such cells. These small groups, which appear somewhat similar to the house churches started by Paul in the first century, are the source of Pentecostalism's strength in the world outside Europe and North America. People might feel lost in a church of 1000, let alone 100,000; but the cells promote Bible study, discussion, self-help, and face-to-face interaction with other believers in an informal and friendly setting.

Dr. Cho describes the home cell strategy and its advantages in the following selection, which comes from a church growth manual called *Successful Home Cell Groups*. These guidelines for modern evangelists and missionaries are based on a theology of evangelism. According to Cho, the primary task of the Christian is to spread the good news, and so he uses home cells to promote one-on-one contact in large urban areas where traditional proselytizing might be difficult. The reading gives an inside look at one successful method Christians now use to advance their message. It also provides a glimpse into Pentecostalism: its style of worship and its vocabulary of belief.

Questions to Consider

1. What is the purpose of the home cell method? How does the method work?

2. What are the advantages of the home cell method of evangelization, according to Cho?

3. Why do you think this method works? What do you think of this method?

4. What is the ecclesiology of this approach? In other words, what is the nature of the church?

5. What type of Christian identity does the home cell method create?

6. What is Cho's message? What is Cho saying about the essence of Christianity?

Home Cell Groups: A Key to Evangelism

DAVID YONGGI CHO

The human body needs to renew and replenish itself constantly or it will die. That requirement is just as true for the Church, the body of Christ. Therefore, one of the needs of a dynamic and growing church life is evangelism. If a church is not involved in serious evangelism, it will either remain stagnant or it will begin to die.

But more than that, it is the command of our Lord Jesus Christ to evangelize—to go into all the world and preach the gospel and make disciples.

When Jesus told His disciples that they would be His witnesses after the Holy Spirit came upon them, He said they would first be witnesses right there in their own hometown—in Jerusalem. It was only after they evangelized Jerusalem that they spread out into Judea and Samaria and, finally, to the ends of the earth.

Each of our churches needs to be involved in evangelism like that. We need evangelism that begins right in our own neighborhoods, in our cities and villages, wherever the Lord has planted us. That is the kind of evangelism we practice at Full Gospel Central Church in Seoul, and that is the reason for the tremendous growth we have experienced.

But our church does not follow the familiar pattern of door-to-door evangelism. In many respects that is a confrontation type of evangelism; it invites resistance. It's the same kind of resistance that a Christian puts up when a member of the Jehovah's Witnesses or the Mormons calls on him. It's true that many people are saved through door-to-door Christian witnessing, and the Holy Spirit will sometimes motivate Christians to undertake that kind of evangelism in areas where He has already prepared the hearts of the unbelievers. But in general, door-to-door evangelism becomes frustrating for the Christian witness because he sees such a low rate of productivity.

Our church, however, carries out evangelism primarily through the home cell group system. Each cell group becomes a nucleus of revival in its neighborhood, because the cell group is where real life is to be found in that neighborhood. When a home cell meeting is full of life, and when people are happy and

sharing their faith and witnessing to what the Lord has done in their lives, other people are drawn to them. Unbelievers become curious. They want to know why this little group of Christians is so joyful when all around them there are so many troubles.

Now, even though such groups become magnets in their neighborhoods, our members still have to work at evangelizing. Unbelievers infrequently come beating on the doors to find out what is happening. Our members have to go out looking for prospective converts. But we have other ways of helping them to become caring evangelists.

One way is through what we call "holy eavesdropping." Our cell leaders instruct the members of their group to be on the lookout for anyone who is having troubles. Many of us overhear conversations every day in which someone is speaking about the problems in his life. Whenever we overhear such conversations, we should immediately ask the Holy Spirit, "Is there some way I can witness to this person? Is there some way I can introduce him to Jesus, who can really solve his problems?"

In one case that was related to me, a woman from our congregation witnessed to a woman she had met at the neighborhood supermarket. She had overheard the woman, an unbeliever, telling a friend about problems with her marriage. She was on the verge of divorce. It turned out that our member had had some very similar problems, but the Lord Jesus had saved her marriage through prayer and through the ministry of the home fellowship.

Outside the market our member caught up with the other woman and said, "I couldn't help overhearing you discussing your problem with your friend. I had a very similar problem. Would you like to come over for tea while I tell you how I overcame that problem and saved my marriage?"

To her surprise, the woman accepted on the spot. During the time of sharing, our member told how she and her husband had been at the point of almost agreeing to a divorce, when they met the Lord and their lives were turned around. She did not immediately urge the woman to accept Christ as her Savior, but she did relate how much the home cell group meetings meant and invited the woman to the next one. She assured her that there were a lot of understanding neighborhood women in the group who would be able to identify with this woman's problems.

When she attended the cell meeting for the first time, the woman was immediately impressed. Although she did have a little difficulty with the enthusiastic singing, the hand-clapping and so on, she saw that the women were all much like she was. Yet there was a serenity about them that she longed to have. She did not give her heart to Jesus that first meeting, but she was drawn back. Then a few meetings later she surrendered her life to the Lord, and she soon joined the church. Not long afterward her husband began to come to church too. Eventually he met the Lord, and the marriage was saved.

This story illustrates the fact that woman-to-woman evangelism is very important in our church. We have more women than men, which is characteristic of most Christian churches, but that is not the reason we stress woman-to-woman evangelism. We have found that, when a woman becomes a Christian and is drawn into the fellowship of the church, her children will soon follow. This is almost a natural law. Where the women go for spiritual nourishment, they will take their children.

I realize that men are to be the spiritual leaders of their households, but men are not usually the first among the unbelievers to become interested in spiritual things. More often than not, the wife is the first one to be open to evangelism, and she is usually the first to commit her life to Jesus Christ. Frequently the husband is the last to come. He sees his wife and children going to church, and he sees they are getting something out of it. Usually he will go with them eventually, if only to find out what it's all about. If he then also can be drawn into a home cell meeting, we have found in our church that he will soon become caught up in the enthusiasm just as much as the rest of the family.

Today one of the greatest needs in the church is to evangelize our cities. It is not true that churches have to die in the central cities. I realize that materialism keeps many people away from the church and prevents them from opening their hearts and minds to the gospel. But our church is very successful in evangelism in the center of one of the world's largest cities. Seoul has more than eight million inhabitants. Yet in the past seven years we have gained 140,000 members, and we have also won thousands of others to the Lord and sent them to other churches. Our membership is now fifteen times larger than it was in 1973, when we moved to Yoido Island.

We have the same problems in trying to evangelize Seoul that any urban church has. There are many high-rise apartment buildings. It becomes difficult to meet new people in such circumstances. Christians just cannot go knocking on doors in an apartment building. (And besides, that is not our style of evangelism.)

However, one of our home cell leaders came up with a method. Every Saturday she began to spend a few hours riding up and down in the elevator of her apartment building. On many of those elevator rides she found opportunities to help people. One mother needed someone to carry her baby; an older woman needed help in carrying her groceries to the apartment. Always our cell leader was right there to offer help.

Little by little this enterprising leader became friends with many of the people she helped in the elevator. All the while she was secretly "planting" a home cell group meeting in her apartment building. While she was helping these people and making friends, she was silently praying for them. Eventually she obtained their telephone numbers from them, and she called them to invite them to a cell group meeting in her apartment.

She was so successful that today, if you go to any of the high-rise apartment buildings near our church on a Saturday afternoon, you will find our cell leaders in the elevators, riding up and down, up and down . . .

"Would you like me to help you carry your groceries?"

"Oh, please allow me to hold the door for you."

"Your faucet is leaking? My husband is very good at fixing faucets."

And so it goes; all the while seeds are being planted for home cell groups.

Our people are so enthusiastic about this kind of evangelism that even when they move away from Seoul they don't want to leave our church and our cell system. Four years ago one couple moved to Inchon, which is about twenty miles outside of Seoul. The wife was one of our cell leaders. When we talked, I said, "Well, I think you should join up with a good church in Inchon.

"Oh, no, Pastor Cho, that isn't what we want to do at all," the woman replied. "I think we will open our house for a cell meeting. Then on Sunday we will all get together and come to Seoul for church."

She had already begun to dream of the successful home cell group she would have in Inchon.

"Well, it's up to you," I said, and I gave her my blessing.

After that couple moved to Inchon, they did exactly as planned. Within a very short time they had a thriving home cell group, and on Sunday mornings they and their group would all come to church on a chartered bus! That was four years ago. Today that cell group has grown to 130 cells with 2,000 members in Inchon. Every Sunday they all charter buses to come to church.

One cell began to propagate and divide. Today Inchon is a full-fledged district of our church, with a licensed minister shepherding it.

That is quite remarkable. Without any evangelistic campaign, without any "revival meetings," without any fanfare, but with just the enthusiasm of a young Korean couple, we have 2,000 members in Inchon. In all that time I did not go once to Inchon to preach; the members all came to Seoul to hear me. These were 2,000 men, women, young people and children who met the Lord Jesus Christ through the zeal of that one couple.

Nowadays there are as many as 100 buses bringing members to our church every Sunday. Many visitors to Seoul look at that and say, "Oh, Yonggi Cho has a busing ministry. That must be the secret of his success. Look at how many buses he has!"

No, I do not charter a single bus. All of the home cell groups do this strictly on their own—to bring both members and newcomers to church. I have absolutely nothing to do with it. But I admit I'm happy it is taking place.

This is evangelism. This is church growth. By the end of 1980 we had 10,000 home cell groups. I firmly believe that when any church adopts this system of home cell groups, it is going to grow. If the church is already a large one, home cell groups are a real necessity for the members already in it; otherwise the pastor will have a nervous breakdown just trying to take care of the needs of his congregation, especially if he has more than 2,000 members.

In fact, I've been asked how many members I feel I could pastor successfully without a cell system. I don't think I could take care of more than 500. As it is now, I have to relate only to a relatively small number of leaders. Those leaders have others under them who shepherd the cell leaders, and it is the cell lead-

ers who perform the bulk of the ministry in our church.

Full Gospel Central Church is not simply in the building that houses its offices and sanctuary; our church is out in the houses and apartment buildings, in the offices and factories of Seoul and its suburbs. The ministry is taking place out there. Evangelism is taking place out there. The central church building is the worship center where people come on Sundays and at other times to celebrate and worship, and to receive encouragement, education and edification.

Our church has become a living organism. The home cell groups are living cells, and they function much like the cells in the human body. In a living organism, the cells grow and divide. Where once there was one cell, there become two. Then there are four, then eight, then sixteen, and so forth. Cells are not simply added to the body; they are multiplied by geometric progression.

This is exactly what is happening with our home cell groups. When a home cell group reaches a membership of more than fifteen families, it divides into two. After that, the two new cells invite new people until they both exceed fifteen families again, and then they divide into four.

I already mentioned that in the beginning of our cell group ministry many people were reluctant to divide. Division had to be forced. That still happens occasionally, but most of the members of Full Gospel Central Church realize that the life of the group and of the church depends on constant cell division. Occasionally we have to send one of the pastors to persuade a cell group to divide, but generally the division takes place spontaneously when the group exceeds fifteen families. That is the rule in our church, and most of the members obey it without complaining.

Yes, there are often tears when friends have to separate to attend different meetings, but it is not a life or death situation. All of the cell groups are limited to specific geographical areas. If friends are no longer able to see one another in the cell meeting, they still get together at other times during the week, as all friends do, naturally. In addition, there are frequent district activities, where a number of cell groups get together for a picnic, a big prayer meeting or some other event.

There is one more thing that needs to be said about evangelism. The other side of evangelism is the back door of the church. Many churches complain that as many people are lost from the congregation through the back door as are won in revival meetings, and those churches are not growing. Well, there is practically no back door to our church. The reason is that each home cell group is like a family circle. Through these family circles people feel a sense of belonging, and they are kept in the church. On top of that, each cell leader watches over his or her little flock, just as a hen watches over her chicks. He is constantly caring for the needs of his flock. But at the same time, if one member of his cell group "plays hooky" from church, the following day the leader calls to find out if anything is wrong. If anything is, he can go and attend to it right away. Perhaps the person is ill or having some other problem that can be handled through prayer and ministry. And if he is really backsliding, the leader can determine the source of the problem and discuss it with him.

Therefore, once a person comes into our church through the cell system, we are not likely to lose him. Someone is always watching out for him, caring for him, helping him.

One day a man and his wife came into my office. They introduced themselves as new members of the church. Then the husband laughed, shook his head and said, "It is impossible to escape this church."

"What do you mean?" I asked.

The husband began to tell me the story of how his son had become a hippie. "We were very much worried about him," he said. "But then a very nice lady from this church came to our house. She was one of our neighbors. Well, she began to deal with my son. She talked with him and prayed with him, and after a while my son was completely changed.

"We really appreciated what she had done. She was so kind and nice.

"Then she invited us to come to her house for a visit, saying, 'We have a wonderful weekly meeting in our house. It is a wonderful time of fellowship, and we serve tea and cookies, and talk about religion. Would you come, please?'

"So out of appreciation we went. I must admit that we really did enjoy ourselves too. We listened to the singing, and the testimonies were very exciting. The message was good, and we even appreciated the concern of the people when they prayed for us and our son.

"But after the meeting was over, we didn't think too much more about it. We didn't think it was anything more than a nice evening with some of our neighbors.

"But then the next week this lady invited us again So we thought it would be all right to go again, because we did enjoy ourselves the first time. But we never considered committing ourselves to anything on a regular basis.

"Then on Saturday she called us again and said, 'Tomorrow is Sunday. Won't you come with me to our mother church? We have a wonderful pastor. He always has a good message. Let's go!'

"The next day she came in her car and honked the horn. So we went.

"I have to tell you in all honesty that we were shocked when we arrived at the church. We had never seen such a place! It was overwhelming, so big! But what really shocked us even more was how noisy it was. We had never seen people praying out loud like that before, and praising God and clapping their hands.

"After it was all over and we were home again, I said to my wife, 'Well, that was a fine church, I guess, but it was too noisy. I think some of those people were hysterical. I don't think we should go there anymore.'"

They didn't realize it at the time, but they had already been hooked by our cell system. The next week the cell leader went over and invited them again to come to the meeting. After that she said, "I will pick you up again next Sunday for church."

"We tried to make excuses," the husband said, "but she very politely refused to accept them. So week after week we found ourselves going to the cell meetings and coming to church with the leader. Yet all the while we felt trapped and uncomfortable. We felt so harassed that we decided to sell the house and moved!"

They called a real estate broker, sold their house and left the neighborhood, all without the knowledge of the cell leader. They took up residence in a distant part of the city, and the husband said to his wife, "At last we are free of that lady!"

So the next week when the leader went to invite them to the cell meeting, she found an empty house. But she was not ready to give up on them. She went down to the town hall and found their new address, wrote it down and brought it to the pastoral department of the church. There the clerks looked up the new address and turned it over to the cell leader for that area.

"I couldn't believe it," the husband told me. "There we were on Friday evening enjoying our freedom, when there came a knock on the door. I opened it, and there was this lady who said, 'Welcome to our area! I am the cell leader for Full Gospel Central Church, and you have been transferred to my section. Tonight we are coming to your house to celebrate!'

"So they came and held a service in our home. Again we sang and we prayed, and the group prayed for us in our new home. After it was over and everybody had left, I said to my wife, 'What are we going to do? To avoid this church we are either going to have to emigrate to America, or to heaven!'

"Then my wife said, 'Well, if we cannot avoid them I guess the only thing to do is join them.'

"So the next Sunday we came to church, and we clapped and shouted just like everybody else. Now we have even become full members of the church."

Since then that couple has become an outstanding family in our congregation. It was all because of the persistence of the cell leaders. (I must add that it was all done in a very nice way, and the people were not in the least bit offended. In fact, I am convinced that all along they were under conviction by the Holy Spirit. They were not just trying to run from our church or our cell leader; they were really trying to run from God. When they found they could not escape Him, they surrendered.)

Not all of our leaders are so persistent, of course, and not all of them are as successful in persuading unbelievers to come to the meetings. But there is enough success that our church is really growing.

We need to let the sinners come to our churches and meet Jesus Christ; we need them to be saved. Then we should never let them leave. The only way a member should leave the church is either to transfer to a new church or to be buried in a casket.

In our church it is impossible for me to have personal contact with all 150,000 members. But through the cell leaders I do have contact in a secondary way with them. I am assured that our members are properly cared for, properly discipled, properly fed and properly corrected when needed.

That is why we have real evangelism in our church! Our enthusiastic leaders are constantly bringing in unbelievers, and after they have them, they are meeting their needs so well that very few are lost out the back door.

Liberation Theology in Latin America

Another global movement within Christianity has arisen alongside Pentecostalism. Though its style and theology differ, its message also appeals to the poor and the marginalized. Liberation theology exists wherever Christians come together, read the Bible, and understand it to be speaking a message of freedom from current conditions of both social and personal sin. In other words, salvation is not postponed until the afterlife, but instead is realized in part within the current reality. It will be fulfilled completely when Jesus returns, but in the meantime, Christians are called to build the reign of God in the present age. This was Jesus' message, say the liberation theologians, pointing to his ministry to society's outcasts. Jesus Christ is the liberator, not just from personal sin, but from the social sins of injustice, inequality, and oppression.

Many types of liberation theology exist. Historically, it arose during the 1960s, when anti-colonial movements emerged around the world. Vatican II helped pave the way for Catholics by redefining the nature of the church as a "pilgrim people of God," en route to glory and fulfillment but not yet arrived. The council encouraged the Catholic faithful to address the pressing issues of the day, and unquestionably poverty and underdevelopment were major problems for the majority of those in the world. Laypeople, priests, and bishops in Latin America responded by developing a theology of liberation which claimed that the Bible showed that God had a preferential option for the poor—that is, God sided with the poor—and that the church and the faithful must be present to the poor in their suffering. In addition, the church must act to eliminate the problems the poor face. The bishop of Recifé, Brazil, Dom Helder Camara, is known for saying that when he fed the poor, he was called a saint; but when he asked why there were poor people, he was called a communist. The charge of communism, or Marxism, was one that liberation theologians frequently confronted, since a small minority seemed to advocate armed resistance to oppression. The vast majority advocated radical social change, but pressed for peaceful transformation.

The liberation movement spread throughout Latin America primarily through the institution of Christian base communities. These were, in effect, Bible study groups in tiny villages and outposts, far removed from the large cathedrals and churches of the cities and towns. Led by lay catechists, or teachers, Christians in these base communities read the Bible for themselves and identified its revolutionary message:

> He has brought down the powerful from their thrones, and lifted up the lowly;
> He has filled the hungry with good things, and sent the rich away empty.
> (Luke 1:5 2–53, NRSV)

Those in power recognized the subversive implications such texts might hold for peasants and factory workers. The fact that priests and laypeople were involved in political resistance to brutal dictatorships made them targets of military and paramilitary operations. This was true in El Salvador during its 12-year civil war in which Archbishop Oscar Romero was assassinated (d. 1980); and it was true in Guatemala during its 36-year civil war (1960–1996), as the government attempted to root out opponents by relocating, removing, or "disappearing" sympathetic villages and villagers. "The army itself admits that 440 villages were destroyed," according to Phillip Berryman. As recently as 1998, Bishop Juan Gerardi was beaten to death in Guatemala City two days after he criticized the role that the military played during the civil war.

The Readings

The next two selections provide voices from Latin American Christianity on the subject of liberation theology. The first is a series of *testimonios* (testimonies) presented by Fernando Bermúdez, a Catholic priest in Guatemala, who witnessed atrocities and spoke with dozens of people who reported on the violence perpetrated against indigenous peoples—many of whom were Catholic believers—in Guatemala. These testimonies report outrageous brutalities and highlight the dangers Christians faced when they attempted to practice their religion despite government repression. They show that martyrdom is not ancient history for Christians.

The testimonies provide the backdrop for the second selection, which comes from Gustavo Gutiérrez, a Peruvian theologian and one of the premier theoreticians to develop and define liberation theology. This reading comes from his major work on the subject, *A Theology of Liberation,* in which he provides a scriptural and historical rationale for liberation theology. It is a work of theory and argument that scholars call "systematic theology" because the writer systematically considers the issues and makes an argument based on scripture, tradition, experience, and reason. Frequently, systematic theologians deal with two key events in the theological history of Christianity: creation and redemption. Creation, as we know from Genesis 1, was God's gracious act of love for all: plants, animals, and humans. But since humans "fell" (Genesis 2–3), God also has provided the means of redemption throughout history: from Moses to Christ. Gutiérrez addresses these two aspects of traditional Christian theology. His chapter complements the testimonies by going beyond the outrage they occasion and showing why biblical tradition reveals that salvation always occurs concretely in history. Just as Augustine tried to address the theological and historical question posed by the fall of the Roman Empire in the fifth century, Gutiérrez is trying to address the theological and historical questions posed by the problems facing Christians in the twentieth century.

Questions to Consider

1. What is your response, your gut reaction, after reading the *testimonios* of those brutalized by the Guatemalan army?

2. How do these *testimonios* compare with the description provided in the narrative of Perpetua and Felicity in Chapter Two? How is martyrdom the same? How is it different?

3. How do the *testimonios* relate to the essay by Gutiérrez?

4. What is the difference between quantitative and qualitative salvation, according to Gutiérrez?

5. What does Gutiérrez think is the relationship between creation and salvation?

6. What biblical examples does he use to argue that salvation occurs in history, not outside of it? How does Gutiérrez use the Bible to build his argument? Is he a fundamentalist? A liberal? Something else?

7. Compare and contrast the christology and ecclesiology of Gutiérrez with that of David Yonggi Cho. How are their views of Christ and the church similar? How are they different? Are there other examples in history (from our readings) that support or oppose Gutiérrez' views?

8. How does Gutiérrez' description of the liberation of biblical Israel compare with that of Steve Charleston in Chapter Six? Can you think of points of contact between the two essays?

Persecution and Martyrdom: Testimonials

FERNANDO BERMÚDEZ

The time was November 1980. The persecution and repression of catechists and Christian communities had grown very harsh. Catechists could no longer attend their meetings or carry Holy Communion to their communities without risking discovery by the Army and possible death. So they had to work under cover, pretending that they were only on shopping trips to the departmental capital. One said, "Now we need the Body of Christ more than ever to gain fortitude and strength to struggle side by side with our people."

They would carry the consecrated wafers hidden among ears of corn or in baskets of beans. One morning, as I was vesting for Mass, a catechist appeared out of nowhere and began, timidly, "I beg your pardon, Father . . . but you know we're having a hard time in our community. We want to receive Holy Communion, but if the Army or the Secret Service finds me I'm a goner. So I've got these tortillas here— if possible I'd like to push the Sacred Hosts down inside here." And he opened the napkin covering the tortillas. The faith and simplicity of this person gave me such a lump in my throat I couldn't answer him.

I took the tortillas from my friend and carried them to the altar. After Mass I stuffed a half-dozen hosts down alongside each tortilla. Then I wrapped everything all up in a big cloth and gave it back to the catechist. With the greatest respect and reverence, this good person took the Body of Christ from me and put it in his knapsack. Then he said goodbye and started off back to his community—a two days' walk away, on the other side of the River Chixoy. O Quiché, land of heroes and martyrs!

Because of the leadership they exercise in their communities, Delegates of the Word of God are especially sought out and persecuted by the Army, the Secret Service, and the death squads. They have contributed the greatest number of martyrs among all the pastoral ministers.

On 12 November 1980, government agents entered a village of Chicaman by night. They called at the door of catechist Nicolas Tum Quixtan. He failed to respond. So the agents kicked the door in, entered the house, and found Nicolas by using a flashlight.

They attempted to make off with him, but he defended himself as best he could, intent on staying in the house, as he knew that if he were abducted he would be tortured to make him betray the names of the other catechists of the region. As the agents were unable to drag him away, one of them shot him three times. Off went the agents. He fell to the floor and lay in a widening pool of blood. Beside themselves and in tears, Nicolas' wife and mother did not know which way to turn. But Nicolas, his voice distorted with pain, told them: "Kneel down and pray to God for yourselves! You're going to have to suffer a lot. I'm going to die, but I know I'll rise again . . . and take good care of the kids." A few minutes later he was dead.

In the Reina region, on 19 November 1980, some seventy Kaibiles—counterinsurgency specialists of the Guatemalan Army—entered a village by night, in the company of a number of their spies (or "ears," as they are called in Guatemala), used axes to break down the door of the parish church, and tossed a grenade inside. Then they set fire to the houses of five catechists and made off with three of them: Isaias Hernandez, his son Monico, and Manuel Choc. The three were never heard from again. There can be no doubt that they were tortured and killed. A catechist-trainer who had hidden in the mountains saw his little house reduced to ashes—saw the work of so many years disappear in minutes—saw his fourteen-year-old daughter raped, and saw the Kaibiles throw his son to the floor, kick him till he screamed, tie him up, and drag him off. He saw his wife, weeping in the street in helplessness and desperation, protecting her small children from those fiends.

The soldiers went out after this catechist, too, but he succeeded in eluding them. For several days and nights he wandered barefoot in the mountains, with nothing to eat, darting from tree to tree to avoid detection. One evening he appeared in our community, pale and drawn, full of scratches, hungry, despairing, his eyes filled with tears. His face looked as Christ must have looked on the cross. We could only stare at him wordlessly. This was the first time I had ever seen an Amerindian weeping. We did our best to comfort him, then we fed him, and celebrated the Eucharist in company with two more of the brothers who happened to be present. The blood and sorrow of our people were consecrated in the Eucharist that day.

In many regions of Guatemala it is no longer permitted to celebrate the Word. The Bible is considered a subversive book. The Army and the Police send search parties into the villages constantly. If they find a Bible, especially the *Latinoamericana* edition, not only do they take it with them to destroy it, but they make off with the owner as well, whom they accuse of being a communist. Then they kill the person.

Here is what one young catechist had to report:

> The soldiers came to our village and searched the houses. When they found Bibles, they ripped them up, stomped on them, and burned them on the spot, before the eyes of their owners and the other catechists. They told them, "If we catch you with one of these again you'll be killed. Get rid of your Bibles."

But the people do not lose their faith that easily. They continue to meet. The young catechist went on:

> What some do is bury their Bible and their hymnals. This way they stay out of trouble, and only they know where the books are. Others have to work underground, meeting in little groups so as not to make the government suspicious. They figure it won't make any difference if they're killed as long as they give witness to the Christian faith. They don't care if they're tortured to death; they keep at their work in the community; they keep organizing. They work like priests or sisters—they're the ones who baptize the babies and give communion.

Another catechist:

> You wonder why the government's against the Christians? Because we've caught on to what the Bible's trying to tell us. We see the example of Moses, who led his people out of their slavery. We see the example of Jesus, who was persecuted even as a baby. We compare everything our communities are going through to what went on in those times or to when Jesus was persecuted. Jesus was persecuted by a government. The persecution of the Christians here is so strong because the government knows we're waking up with the Bible and that we're going to keep on waking up. In the Bible we find out what we're supposed to do.

I made a trip to a village in Baja Verapaz, in the township of Rabinal. After the Eucharist a catechist invited me to lunch in his home. There in a corner of his poor little hut on the floor some vigil lamps were burning. I paid no special attention to them, supposing that this was a native custom. But no, those lamps were burning over the hiding place in which the family Bible was buried. This family, like so many others, prayed every day over the Word of God buried under the floor of their house, recalling various passages from memory. If you saw lamps or flowers on the dirt floor of a house, that was a sign that the Holy Book was buried there.

In this same department of Baja Verapaz, one evening a community was gathered for a Celebration of the Word in a chapel near the village of Rabinal—not without fear that the Army might turn up. And so it happened. Some fifty soldiers came and surrounded the chapel. An officer entered, most irreverently, climbed onto the altar, kicked the Bible to the floor, and shouted that this book was "all a pack of lies." Then he gave orders to a soldier to burn it. The soldier strode up, tore the pages out of the Bible with a great show of irreverence, and set fire to them.

The whole community was terrified. In the deathly silence, which was broken only by the sardonic laughter of the troops, the officer read a list of names of twenty-three members of the community, who were also present. These were dragged from the chapel and taken to a house where, without any explanation, they were machine-gunned.

The families of these unlucky ones, crying with anguish and helplessness, did all they could to remain at the victims' sides, but to no avail—the soldiers thrust them back at every turn. It all happened at about midnight. This is from the account of an Amerindian catechist who witnessed the massacre and is presently a refugee in Mexico.

In early January of 1981, the Army entered the village of Macalajou, in Uspantan. The community prepared to flee, and many escaped to the mountains. But the Delegate of the Eucharist, with his wife, headed for the chapel, to rescue the Blessed Sacrament lest the soldiers profane it. They hid it in an earthen vessel, placed the whole thing in a plastic bag, dug a hole in the earth behind the chapel with a machete, and buried it. "They'll kill us," he said. "But Christ will always be in this village."

The catechist was seized and carried off, along with a number of others. Before leaving the village the soldiers put it to the torch, all of the houses and the chapel. They killed the animals, even the dogs. Some women died after being raped. Others, widowed and homeless, wandered with their children to the town of Uspantan. They installed themselves next to the market. It was cold, as it had been raining for days. The Army told the people of Uspantan: "These women are guerrillas—anyone giving them any assistance will be considered to be working for the guerrillas."

Cold and hungry, agonizing and desperate, many of these women, with their children, headed off in various directions, whither they knew not. Several days later fifteen of them were found along a road with their heads cut off. Others reached Alta Verapaz, where one of them told this story:

> There were five of us living in the house—my husband, my three children, and I. I'm the only one left. One evening government soldiers came in, dressed as peasants. They came in unmarked trucks, firing their machine guns. They dragged us all out of our houses. They tied the men to trees, then they raped the women, even little girls nine years old. They said they were guerrillas. Some of the men were dragged away; others were killed on the spot. They slit open the abdomen of a seven-months-pregnant woman with a knife and pulled out the fetus. Then they put her husband's head in her belly. There's nobody left in the village. We're afraid. We're running. We're afraid the Army will come back.

The Army entered the village of Lancetillo during the last week of May 1981. They took Tino Salazar from his home. His daughter Olivia, seeing that the worst was about to happen, asked the soldiers to explain why they were doing this to her father. Unable to help him in any way and desperate, she cried out for help, whereupon a soldier shot her in the head. She collapsed, killed instantly, still clutching her one-year-old daughter to her breast. The baby did not die. Olivia was nineteen. The soldiers burned her hut and seven others. Luckily, most of the people had already fled to the mountains. Some of them managed to get to the rectory in Coban and report what had happened.

In January 1982, the Army went to San Cristobal Verapaz. They arrested several catechists, good persons who had chosen to work for the liberation of their people. Four months later, three villages of this township were bombed, and people were massacred in Najtilabaj, Chirexquiche, Las Pacayas, Chituj, and Chisiram—men, women, and children. One hundred twenty bodies were counted.

After the massacres the remaining population fled to the mountains to hide in the forests there. But the Army was not satisfied. They sprayed the mountains with poison gases to exterminate the population, and the Civil Patrol (a military body) poisoned the waters of the wells and streams.

Poor, good people—men and women, young and old—all murdered! Why? You have only to look the people in the eye to discover how much they have suffered. Before it was exploitation, hunger, disease. Now, besides all this, comes repression, fear, anguish, and death.

These massacres are the result of a cold-blooded decision to depopulate certain zones in order to rid them of supposed Guatemalan guerrilla bases. The massacres have caused the flight of two hundred thousand refugees abroad and more than a million to the interior of the country. These massacres are the Army's response to our people's cry for justice and freedom.

Liberation and Salvation

GUSTAVO GUTIÉRREZ

What is the relationship between salvation and the process of human liberation throughout history? Or more precisely, what is the meaning of the struggle against an unjust society and the creation of a new humanity in the light of the Word? A response to these questions presupposes an attempt to define what is meant by salvation, a concept central to the Christian mystery. This is a complex and difficult task which leads to reflection on the meaning of the saving action of the Lord in history. The salvation of the whole man is centered upon Christ the Liberator.

SALVATION: CENTRAL THEME
OF THE CHRISTIAN MYSTERY

One of the great deficiencies of contemporary theology is the absence of a profound and lucid reflection on the theme of salvation. On a superficial level this might seem surprising, but actually it is what often happens with difficult matters: people are afraid to tackle them. It is taken for granted that they are understood. Meanwhile, new edifices are raised on old foundations established in the past on untested assumptions and vague generalities. The moment comes, however, when the whole building totters; this is the time to look again to the foundations. This hour has arrived for the notion of salvation. Recently various works have appeared attempting to revise and deepen our understanding of this idea. These are only a beginning.

We will not attempt to study this criticism in detail, but will only note that a consideration of this question has revealed two focal points; one follows the other in the manner of two closely linked stages.

From the Quantitative . . .

The questions raised by the notion of salvation have for a long time been considered under and limited by the classical question of the "salvation of the pagans." This is the quantitative, extensive aspect of salvation; it is the problem of the number of persons saved, the possibility of being saved, and the role which the Church plays in this process. The terms of the problem are, on the one hand, the universality of salva-tion, and on the other, the visible Church as the mediator of salvation.

The evolution of the question has been complex and fatiguing. Today we can say that in a way this evolution has ended. The idea of the universality of the salvific will of God, clearly enunciated by Paul in his letter to Timothy, has been established. It has overcome the difficulties posed by various ways of understanding the mission of the Church and has attained definite acceptance. All that is left to do is to consider the ramifications, which are many.

Here we will briefly consider one important point and leave for later a treatment of the repercussions of this idea on ecclesiological matters. The notion of salvation implied in this point of view has two very well-defined characteristics: it is a cure for sin in this life; and this cure is in virtue of a salvation to be attained beyond this life. What is important, therefore, is to know how a person outside the normal pale of grace, which resides in the institutional Church, can attain salvation. Multiple explanations have attempted to show the extraordinary ways by which a person could be assured of salvation, understood above all as life beyond this one. The present life is considered to be a test: one's actions are judged and assessed in relation to the transcendent end. The perspective here is moralistic, and the spirituality is one of flight from this world. Normally, only contact with the channels of grace instituted by God can eliminate sin, the obstacle which stands in the way of reaching that life beyond. This approach is very understandable if we remember that the question of "the salvation of the pagans" was raised at the time of the discovery of people belonging to other religions and living in areas far from those where the Church had been traditionally rooted.

. . . to the Qualitative

As the idea of the universality of salvation and the possibility of reaching it gained ground in Christian consciousness and as the quantitative question was resolved and decreased in interest, the whole problem of salvation made a qualitative leap and began to be perceived differently. Indeed, there is more to the idea of the universality of salvation than simply asserting the possibility of reaching it while outside the visible frontiers of the Church. The very heart of the question was touched in the search for a means to widen the scope of the possibility of salvation: persons are saved if they open themselves to God and to others, even if they are not clearly aware that they are doing so. This is valid for Christians and non-Christians alike—for all people. To speak about the presence of grace—whether accepted or rejected—in all people implies, on the other hand, to value from a Christian standpoint the very roots of human activity. We can no longer speak properly of a profane world. A qualitative and intensive approach replaces a quantitative and extensive one. Human existence, in the last instance, is nothing but a yes or a no to the Lord: "Persons already partly accept communion with God, although they do not explicitly confess Christ as their Lord, insofar as they are moved by grace (*Lumen gentium*), sometimes secretly (*Gaudium et spes*), renounce their selfishness, and seek to create an authentic fellowship among human beings. They reject union with God insofar as they turn away from the building up of this world, do not open themselves to others, and culpably withdraw into themselves (Matthew 25: 31–46)."[1]

From this point of view the notion of salvation appears in a different light. Salvation is not something otherworldly, in regard to which the present life is merely a test. Salvation—the communion of human beings with God and among themselves—is something which embraces all human reality, transforms it, and leads it to its fullness in Christ: "Thus the center of God's salvific design is Jesus Christ, who by his death and resurrection transforms the universe and makes it possible for the person to reach fulfillment as a human being. This fulfillment embraces every aspect of humanity: body and spirit, individual and society, person and cosmos, time and eternity. Christ, the image of the Father and the perfect God-Man, takes on all the dimensions of human existence."

Therefore, sin is not only an impediment to salvation in the afterlife. Insofar as it constitutes a break with God, sin is a historical reality, it is a breach of the communion of persons with each other, it is a turning in of individuals on themselves which manifests itself in a multifaceted withdrawal from others. And because sin is a personal and social intrahistorical real-

ity, a part of the daily events of human life, it is also, and above all, an obstacle to life's reaching the fullness we call salvation.

The idea of a universal salvation, which was accepted only with great difficulty and was based on the desire to expand the possibilities of achieving salvation, leads to the question of the intensity of the presence of the Lord and therefore of the religious significance of human action in history. One looks then to this world, and now sees in the world beyond not the "true life," but rather the transformation and fulfillment of the present life. The absolute value of salvation—far from devaluing this world—gives it its authentic meaning and its own autonomy, because salvation is already latently there. To express the idea in terms of Biblical theology: the prophetic perspective (in which the Kingdom takes on the present life, transforming it) is vindicated before the sapiential outlook (which stresses the life beyond).

This qualitative, intensive approach has undoubtedly been influenced by the factor which marked the last push toward the unequivocal assertion of the universality of salvation, that is, the appearance of atheism, especially in the heart of Christian countries. Nonbelievers are not interested in an otherworldly salvation, as are believers in other religions; rather they consider it an evasion of the only question they wish to deal with: the value of earthly existence. The qualitative approach to the notion of salvation attempts to respond to this problem.

The developments which we have reviewed here have allowed us definitively to recover an essential element of the notion of salvation which had been overshadowed for a long time by the question of the possibility of reaching it. We have recovered the idea that salvation is an intrahistorical reality. Furthermore, salvation—the communion of human beings with God and among themselves—orients, transforms, and guides history to its fulfillment.

HISTORY IS ONE

What we have recalled in the preceding paragraph leads us to affirm that, in fact, there are not two histories, one profane and one sacred, "juxtaposed" or "closely linked." Rather there is only one human destiny, irreversibly assumed by Christ, the Lord of history. His redemptive work embraces all the dimensions of existence and brings them to their fullness. The history of salvation is the very heart of human history. Christian consciousness arrived at this unified view after an evolution parallel to that experienced regarding the notion of salvation. The conclusions converge. From an abstract, essentialist approach we moved to an existential, historical, and concrete view which holds that the only human being we know has been efficaciously called to a gratuitous communion with God. All reflection, any distinctions which one wishes to treat, must be based on this fact: the salvific action of God underlies all human existence. The historical destiny of humanity must be placed definitively in the salvific horizon. Only thus will its true dimensions emerge and its deepest meaning be apparent. It seems, however, that contemporary theology has not yet fashioned the categories which would allow us to think through and express adequately this unified approach to history. We work, on the one hand, under the fear of falling back again into the old dualities, and, on the other, under the permanent suspicion of not sufficiently safeguarding divine gratuitousness or the unique dimension of Christianity. Although there may be different approaches to understanding it, the fundamental affirmation is clear: there is only one history—a "Christo-finalized" history.

The study of two great Biblical themes will allow us to illustrate this point of view and to understand better its scope. The themes are the relationship between creation and salvation and the eschatological promises.

Creation and Salvation

The Bible establishes a close link between creation and salvation. But the link is based on the historical and liberating experience of the Exodus. To forget this perspective is to run the risk of merely juxtaposing these two ideas and therefore losing the rich meaning which this relationship has for understanding the recapitulating work of Christ.

Creation: The First Salvific Act

The Bible does not deal with creation in order to satisfy philosophic concerns regarding the origin of the world. Its point of view is quite diverse.

Biblical faith is, above all, faith in a God who gives self-revelation through historical events, a God who saves in history. Creation is presented in the Bible, not as a stage previous to salvation, but as a part of the salvific process: "Praise be to God the Father of our Lord Jesus Christ. . . . In Christ he chose us before the world was founded, to be dedicated, to be without blemish in his sight, to be full of love; and he destined us—such was his will and pleas-

ure—to be accepted as his sons through Jesus Christ" (Ephesians 1 :3–5). God did not create only in the beginning; he also had an end in mind. God creates all to be his children. Moreover, creation appears as the first salvific act: "Creation," writes Von Rad, "is regarded as a work of Yahweh in history, a work within time. This means that there is a real and true opening up of historical prospect. No doubt, creation as the first of Yahweh's works stands at the very remotest beginnings—only, it does not stand alone, other works are to follow."[2] The creation of the world initiates history, the human struggle, and the salvific adventure of Yahweh. Faith in creation does away with its mythical and supernatural character. It is the work of a God who saves and acts in history; since humankind is the center of creation, it is integrated into the history which is being built by human efforts.

Second Isaiah—"the best theologian among Old Testament writers"—is an excellent witness in this respect. His texts are frequently cited as one of the richest and clearest expressions of the faith of Israel in creation. The stress, however, is on the saving action of Yahweh; the work of creation is regarded and understood only in this context: "But now this is the word of the Lord, the word of your creator, O Jacob, of him who fashioned you, Israel: Have no fear; for I have paid your ransom; I have called you by name and you are my own" (43:1; cf. 42:5–6). The assertion is centered on the redemption (or the Covenant). Yahweh is at one and the same time Creator and Redeemer: "For your husband is your maker, whose name is the Lord of Hosts; your ransomer is the Holy One of Israel who is called God of all the earth" (54:5). Numerous psalms sing praise to Yahweh simultaneously as Creator and Savior (cf. Psalms 74, 89, 93, 95, 135, 136). But this is because creation itself is a saving action: "Thus says the Lord, your ransomer, who fashioned you from birth: I am the Lord who made all things, by myself I stretched out the skies, alone I hammered out the floor of the earth" (Isaiah 44:24; cf. also Amos 4:12ff.; 5:8ff.; Jeremiah 33:25ff.; 10:16; 27:5; 32: 17; Malachi 2:10). Creation is the work of the Redeemer. Rendtorff says: "A more complete fusion between faith in creation and salvific faith is unimaginable."[3]

Political Liberation: Human Self-Creation

The liberation from Egypt—both a historical fact and at the same time a fertile Biblical theme—enriches this vision and is moreover its true source. The creative act is linked, almost identified with, the act which freed Israel from slavery in Egypt. Second Isaiah, who writes in exile, is likewise the best witness to this idea: "Awake, awake, put on your strength, O arm of the Lord, awake as you did long ago, in days gone by. Was it not you who hacked the Rahab in pieces and ran the dragon through? Was it not you who dried up the sea, the waters of the great abyss, and made the ocean depths a path for the ransomed?" (Isaiah 51:9–10). The words and images refer simultaneously to two events: creation and liberation from Egypt. Rahab, which for Isaiah symbolizes Egypt (cf. 30:7; cf. also Psalm 87:4), likewise symbolizes the chaos Yahweh had to overcome to create the world (cf. Psalms 74:14; 89:11). The "waters of the great abyss" are those which enveloped the world and from which creation arose, but they are also the Red Sea which the Jews crossed to begin the Exodus. Creation and liberation from Egypt are but one salvific act. It is significant, furthermore, that the technical term *bara*, designating the original creation, was used for the first time by Second Isaiah (43:1, 15; cf. Deuteronomy 32:6) to refer to the creation of Israel. Yahweh's historical actions on behalf of the people are considered creative (41:20; 43:7; 45:8; 48:7). The God who frees Israel is the Creator of the world.

The liberation of Israel is a political action. It is the breaking away from a situation of despoliation and misery and the beginning of the construction of a just and comradely society. It is the suppression of disorder and the creation of a new order. The initial chapters of Exodus describe the oppression in which the Jewish people lived in Egypt, in that "land of slavery" (13:3; 20:2; Deuteronomy 5:6): repression (Exodus 1:10–11), alienated work (5:6–14), humiliations (1:13–14), enforced birth control policy (1:15–22). Yahweh then awakens the vocation of a liberator: Moses. "I have indeed seen the misery of my people in Egypt. I have heard their outcry against their slavemasters. I have taken heed of their sufferings, and have come down to rescue them from the power of Egypt. . . . I have seen the brutality of the Egyptians towards them. Come now; I will send you to Pharaoh and you shall bring my people Israel out of Egypt" (3:7–10).

Sent by Yahweh, Moses began a long, hard struggle for the liberation of the people. The alienation of the children of Israel was such that at first "they did not listen to him; they had become impatient because of their cruel slavery" (6:9). And even after they had left Egypt, when they were threatened by Pharaoh's armies, they complained to Moses: "Were there no graves in Egypt, that you should have brought us here to die in the wilderness? See what you have done to us by bringing us out of Egypt! Is not this just what we meant when we said in Egypt, 'Leave us alone; let us be slaves to the Egyptians'? We would rather be slaves to the Egyptians than die here in the wilderness" (14:11–12). And in the midst of the desert, faced with the first difficulties, they told him that they preferred the security of slavery—whose cruelty they were beginning to forget—to the uncertainties of a liberation in process: "If only we had died at the Lord's hand in Egypt, where we sat round the fleshpots and had plenty of bread to eat" (16:3). A gradual pedagogy of successes and failures would be necessary for the Jewish people to become aware of the roots of their oppression, to struggle against it, and to perceive the profound sense of the liberation to which they were called. The Creator of the world is the Creator and Liberator of Israel, to whom is entrusted the mission of establishing justice: "Thus speaks the Lord who is God, he who created the skies, . . . who fashioned the earth. . . . I, the Lord, have called you with righteous purpose and taken you by the hand; I have formed you, and appointed you . . . to open eyes that are blind, to bring captives out of prison, out of the dungeons where they lie in darkness" (Isaiah 42:5–7).

Creation, as we have mentioned above, is regarded in terms of the Exodus, a historical-salvific fact which structures the faith of Israel. And this fact is a political liberation through which Yahweh expresses love for the people and the gift of total liberation is received.

Salvation: Re-Creation and Complete Fulfillment

Yahweh summons Israel not only to leave Egypt but also and above all to "bring them up out of that country into a fine, broad land; it is a land flowing with milk and honey" (3:8). The Exodus is the long march towards the promised land in which Israel can establish a society free from misery and alienation. Throughout the whole process, the religious event is not set apart. It is placed in the context of the entire narrative, or more precisely, it is its deepest meaning. It is the root of the situation. In the last instance, it is in this event that the dislocation introduced by sin is resolved and justice and injustice, oppression and liberation, are determined. Yahweh liberates the Jewish people politically in order to make them a holy nation: "You have seen with your own eyes what I did to Egypt. . . . If only you will now listen to me and keep my covenant, then out of all peoples you shall become my special possession; for the whole earth is mine. You shall be my kingdom of priests, my holy nation" (19:4–6). The God of Exodus is the God of history and of political liberation more than the God of nature. Yahweh is the Liberator, the *goel* of Israel (Isaiah 43:14; 47:4; Jeremiah 50:34). The Covenant gives full meaning to the liberation from Egypt; one makes no sense without the other: "The Covenant was a historical event," asserts Gelin, "which occurred in a moment of disruption, in an atmosphere of liberation; the revolutionary climate still prevailed: an intense spiritual impulse would arise from it, as often happens in history."[4] The Covenant and the liberation from Egypt were different aspects of the same movement, a movement which led to encounter with God. The eschatological horizon is present in the heart of the Exodus. Casalis rightly notes that "the heart of the Old Testament is the Exodus from the servitude of Egypt and the journey towards the promised land. . . . The hope of the people of God is not to return to the mythological primitive garden, to regain paradise lost, but to march forward towards a new city, a human and comradely city whose heart is Christ."[5]

Yahweh will be remembered throughout the history of Israel by this act which inaugurates its history, a history which is a re-creation. The God who makes the cosmos from chaos is the same God who leads Israel from alienation to liberation. This is what is celebrated in the Jewish Passover. Andre Neher writes: "The first thing that is expressed in the Jewish Passover is the certainty of freedom. With the Exodus a new age has struck for humanity: redemption from misery. If the Exodus had not taken place, marked as it was by the twofold sign of the overriding will of God and the free and conscious assent of men, the historical destiny of humanity would have followed another course. This course would have been radically different, as the redemption, the *geulah* of the Exodus from Egypt, would not have been its foundation. . . . All constraint is accidental; all misery is only provisional. The breath of freedom which has blown over the world since the Exodus can dispel them this very day."[6] The memory of the Exodus pervades the pages of the Bible and inspires one to reread often the Old as well as the New Testament.

The work of Christ forms a part of this movement and brings it to complete fulfillment. The redemptive action of Christ, the foundation of all that exists, is also conceived as a re-creation and presented in a context of creation (cf. Colossians 1:15–20; 1 Corinthians 8:6; Hebrews 1:2; Ephesians 1:1–23). This idea is particularly clear in the prologue to the Gospel of St. John. According to some exegetes it constitutes the foundation of this whole Gospel.

The work of Christ is a new creation. In this sense, Paul speaks of a "new creation" in Christ (Galatians 6:15; 2 Corinthians 5:17). Moreover, it is through this "new creation," that is to say, through the salvation which Christ affords, that creation acquires its full meaning (cf. Romans 8). But the work of Christ is presented simultaneously as a liberation from sin and from all its consequences: despoliation, injustice, hatred. This liberation fulfills in an unexpected way the promises of the prophets and creates a new chosen people, which this time includes all humanity. Creation and salvation therefore have, in the first place, a Christological sense: all things have been created in Christ, all things have been saved in him (cf. Colossians 1:15–20).

Humankind is the crown and center of the work of creation and is called to continue it through its labor (cf. Genesis 1:28)—and not only through its labor. The liberation from Egypt, linked to and even coinciding with creation, adds an element of capital importance: the need and the place for human active participation in the building of society. If faith "desacralizes" creation, making it the area proper for human work, the Exodus from Egypt, the home of a sacred monarchy, reinforces this idea: it is the "desacralization" of social praxis, which from that time on will be the work of humankind. By working, transforming the world, breaking out of servitude, building a just society, and assuming its destiny in history, humankind forges itself. In Egypt, work is alienated and, far from building a just society, contributes rather to increasing injustice and to widening the gap between exploiters and exploited.

To dominate the earth as Genesis prescribed, to continue creation, is worth nothing if it is not done for the good of humanity, if it does not contribute to human liberation, in solidarity with all, in history. The liberating initiative of Yahweh responds to this need by stirring up Moses' vocation. Only the mediation of this self-creation—first revealed by the liberation from Egypt—allows us to rise above poetic expressions and general categories and to understand in a profound and synthesizing way the relationship between creation and salvation so vigorously proclaimed by the Bible.

The Exodus experience is paradigmatic. It remains vital and contemporary due to similar historical experiences which the People of God undergo. As Neher writes, it is characterized "by the twofold sign of the overriding will of God and the free and conscious consent of humans." And it structures our faith in the gift of the Father's love. In Christ and through the Spirit, persons are becoming one in the very heart of history, as they confront and struggle against all that divides and opposes them. But the true agents of this quest for unity are those who today are oppressed (economically, politically, culturally) and struggle to become free. Salvation—totally and freely given by God, the communion of human beings with God and among themselves—is the inner force and the fullness of this movement of human self-generation initiated by the work of creation.

Consequently, when we assert that humanity fulfills itself by continuing the work of creation by means of its labor, we are saying that it places itself, by this very fact, within an all-embracing salvific process. To work, to transform this world, is to become a man and to build the human community; it is also to save. Likewise, to struggle against misery and exploitation and to build a just society is already to be part of the saving action, which is moving towards its complete fulfillment. All this means that building the

temporal city is not simply a stage of "humanization" or "pre-evangelization" as was held in theology until a few years ago. Rather it is to become part of a saving process which embraces the whole of humanity and all human history. Any theological reflection on human work and social praxis ought to be rooted in this fundamental affirmation.

NOTES

1. This quotation and the next come from *Las pastoral en las misiones de América Latina,* Conclusions of the meeting of Melgar organized by the Department of Missions of CELAM [Latin American Bishops Conference] (Bogotá, 1968), 16–17.

2. Gerhard Von Rad, *Old Testament Theology,* trans. D. M. G. Stalker (New York: Harper and Brothers, 1962), 1:139; see also Von Rad's, *Genesis,* trans. John H. Marks (London: SCM Press Ltd., 1961).

3. *Mysterium Salutis* (Einseideln, Zurich, Cologne: Benziger Verlag, 1967).

4. Albert Gelin, "Moise dans l"Ancien Testament," in *Moïse, L'homme de l'Alliance* (Paris: Desclée & Cie, Éditeurs, 1955), 39.

5. Cited by Yves Congar in "Christianism et libération de l'homme," *Masses Ouvrières,* no. 258 (December 1969), 8.

6. Andre Neher, *Moses and the Vocation of the Jewish People,* trans. Irene Marinoff (New York: Harper Torchbooks, 1959), 136–137.

Liberation Theology in North America

Just as liberation movements were occurring in Latin America, Africa, and Asia, they were happening in the United States at the same time. Indeed, the theologians of the civil rights movement, which began in the 1950s, predate their foreign counterparts by a decade. Although civil rights are a political matter, the battle for their realization in U.S. society was fought in the courts and in the streets with the support of black churches. The movement would not have succeeded were it not for the financial, logistical, organizational, and spiritual backing of hundreds of black pastors and thousands of laypeople throughout the U.S. South and North. Certainly, white Christians helped to sustain the struggle, but by far the bulk of support came directly from the pews of black churches.

Black theology emerged from this political movement. Like its global counterpart, liberation theology, black theology offered a clear theoretical justification of its principles. God could never side with the oppressor, according to a number of black theologians writing in the 1960s and 1970s. While the divine was a God of love, the divine was also a God of justice. Thus, righteousness—and more importantly, unrighteousness—would be judged.

The African American civil rights movement raised the consciousness of others who had been exploited or denied justice: Native Americans, women, gays and lesbians, and black women. New forms of liberation theologies emerged. Two key concepts dominated theological discussions: inclusion and diversity. Inclusion meant welcoming *all* Christians in the church. For feminists, this meant reviewing biblical translations that inaccurately used masculine-gendered nouns where neutral nouns would better reflect the biblical languages. For Native Americans, it meant incorporating native elements in worship, such as eagle feathers or sage. For gays and les-

▨ Feminist Theology

One of the most important movements in North American liberation theology involved feminist theologians who critically analyzed the Bible and subsequent Christian theology, and recovered voices and histories long obscured by the dominant (male) church hierarchy. In fact, the writings in this very textbook come out of the process in which women studied women's roles in Christianity and amplified lost voices from the past and present: the martyrdom of Perpetua and Felicity, for example, and Julian of Norwich's *Showings*. The essay by Mercy Amba Oduyoye in Chapter Six is a good example of the analysis being conducted by feminist theologians today.

In the 1960s and 1970s, however, feminist scholars felt silenced both in academia and in the church. They sought to retrieve voices that had been silenced or suppressed: the biblical figures, the debates in the early church, the women leaders, martyrs, and writers. In addition, they critically assessed various church teachings that related to women's roles at home, at church, and in society. Some, like Mary Daly, eventually left Christianity altogether. It was hopelessly patriarchal, they felt, and could not be salvaged. Others, like Rosemary Radford Ruether, reclaimed Christian teachings that celebrated the divine feminine, gender equality, and women's active participation in the life and thought of Christianity. Feminist scholars examined Christian history to learn how certain beliefs had arisen; and they turned to the New Testament as a source of liberative, rather than oppressive, teachings.

The list of feminist scholars is long and still growing. By considering women and their place in the history of Christianity, they have enriched our understanding of how Christianity developed over the centuries. They have asked different questions than traditional scholarship has. As a result, they have come up with new, and enlightening, answers that deepen our appreciation of the involvement of women and men—families, children, households, and all sorts of Christians—who have been neglected and overlooked.

bians, it meant being allowed and encouraged to be Christians, and being affirmed in their sexuality. For all groups, diversity of being and expression suggested that Christianity would look as varied as the colors of the rainbow, to deliberately select the image chosen by gays and lesbians to indicate their diversity.

One voice stands out amidst all the diversity that exists within liberation theologies in the United States. Although he was a pastoral theologian, and not a systematician—and though he preceded the more militant theoreticians of black theology—Martin Luther King Jr. preached and lived a prophetic message that exemplified the meaning of Christianity for millions of people in the twentieth century. The son and grandson of preachers, King went to seminary for a divinity degree and then on to Boston University for a doctorate. His first pastoral appointment took him to Dexter Avenue Baptist Church in Montgomery, Alabama. It was there that the young preacher came to national prominence as the voice of the Montgomery bus boycott in 1955. Many were involved in the boycott, which brought great hardships to the African Americans of the city, but King's charisma and oratory set the tone for the civil rights movement for more than a decade.

As noted previously, King had been attracted to liberal theology, to neo-orthodoxy, to the Social Gospel, and even to existentialism. But it was the teachings of Mohandas K. Gandhi, the Hindu leader who led the peoples of India to liberation from British colonial rule in the 1940s, coupled with the message of Jesus, that most influenced the young King. He saw in Gandhi's nonviolent resistance to unjust authority a powerful tool for raising the consciousness of Americans and the world to the inhumanity of segregation, discrimination, and repression in the United States. Even before King was assassinated in 1968, just as Gandhi had been twenty years earlier, however, the civil rights movement had fragmented, with young people abandoning the commitment to nonviolence and taking a more militant stance. King gave Gandhi's *satyagraha* (soul force), a distinctly American and Christian twist. He saw in the Hindu's philosophy a restatement of the values and principles taught by Jesus of Nazareth in the Sermon on the Mount (Matthew 5–7). Nowhere is this more apparent than in the sermon "Loving Your Enemies," which King first preached in 1954 to his Montgomery congregation.

The Reading

Sermons make up a particular genre and generally follow a clear formula. First, there is the scripture upon which the sermon is based. A discussion of the context of the passage usually follows, setting the historical stage for what is to come. Then the sermon addresses the theological issues implied in the biblical quotation: What does the passage mean theologically? How does it relate to Christian teaching and doctrine? Finally, the sermon usually addresses what is known as application, that is, how the Bible applies to the life of the believer: What lessons can be learned? Sermons are meant to be heard, not read, and thus, to get the full flavor of King's sermon "Loving Your Enemies," it would be a good idea to read a few sections out loud to hear the rhythm and style he uses. Audiotapes of his sermons and speeches also bring the words on the page to life.

Questions to Consider

1. What is King's philosophy of love?

2. How can love be a political force in the world today, according to King?

3. Does King follow the sermon format outlined above? How would you outline or describe the content?

4. What specific examples of the three types of love King discusses can you come up with?

5. What do you think about this philosophy? How easy is it to put into practice? What are the risks and benefits?

6. How does King's sermon differ from Gutiérrez' essay? Can we attribute differences to genre, outlook, style, or some other qualities or characteristics?

7. How does King use the Bible to comment upon current events? How does this compare to Gutiérrez? What are their views on history?

Loving Your Enemies

MARTIN LUTHER KING JR.

Ye have heard that it hath been said, Thou shalt love thy neighbor, and hate thine enemy. But I say unto you, Love your enemies, bless them that curse you, do good to them that hate you, and pray for them which despitefully use you, and persecute you; that ye may be children of your Father which is in heaven. (Matthew 5:43-45, KJV)

Probably no admonition of Jesus has been more difficult to follow than the command to "love your enemies." Some men have sincerely felt that its actual practice is not possible. It is easy, they say, to love those who love you, but how can one love those who openly and insidiously seek to defeat you? Others, like the philosopher Nietzsche, contend that Jesus' exhortation to love one's enemies is testimony to the fact that the Christian ethic is de-

signed for the weak and cowardly, and not for the strong and courageous. Jesus, they say, was an impractical idealist.

In spite of these insistent questions and persistent objections, this command of Jesus challenges us with new urgency. Upheaval after upheaval has reminded us that modern man is traveling along a road called hate, in a journey that will bring us to destruction and damnation. Far from being the pious injunction of a Utopian dreamer, the command to love one's enemy is an absolute necessity for our survival. Love even for enemies is the key to the solution of the problems of our world. Jesus is not an impractical idealist: he is the practical realist.

I am certain that Jesus understood the difficulty inherent in the act of loving one's enemy. He never joined the ranks of those who talk glibly about the easiness of the moral life. He realized that every genuine expression of love grows out of a consistent and total surrender to God. So when Jesus said "Love your enemy," he was not unmindful of its stringent qualities. Yet he meant every word of it. Our responsibility as Christians is to discover the meaning of this command and seek passionately to live it out in our daily lives.

Let us be practical and ask the question, *How do we love our enemies?*

First, we must develop and maintain the capacity to forgive. He who is devoid of the power to forgive is devoid of the power to love. It is impossible even to begin the act of loving one's enemies without the prior acceptance of the necessity, over and over again, of forgiving those who inflict evil and injury upon us. It is also necessary to realize that the forgiving act must always be initiated by the person who has been wronged, the victim of some great hurt, the recipient of some tortuous injustice, the absorber of some terrible act of oppression. The wrongdoer may request forgiveness. He may come to himself, and, like the prodigal son, move up some dusty road, his heart palpitating with the desire for forgiveness. But only the injured neighbor, the loving father back home, can really pour out the warm waters of forgiveness.

Forgiveness does not mean ignoring what has been done or putting a false label on an evil act. It means, rather, that the evil act no longer remains as a barrier to the relationship. Forgiveness is a catalyst creating the atmosphere necessary for a fresh start and a new beginning. It is the lifting of a burden or the canceling of a debt. The words "I will forgive you, but I'll never forget what you've done" never explain the real nature of forgiveness. Certainly one can never forget, if that means erasing it totally from his mind. But when we forgive, we forget in the sense that the evil deed is no longer a mental block impeding a new relationship. Likewise, we can never say, "I will forgive you, but I won't have anything further to do with you." Forgiveness means reconciliation, a coming together again. Without this, no man can love his enemies. The degree to which we are able to forgive determines the degree to which we are able to love our enemies.

Second, we must recognize that the evil deed of the enemy-neighbor, the thing that hurts, never quite expresses all that he is. An element of goodness may be found even in our worst enemy. Each of us is something of a schizophrenic personality, tragically divided against ourselves. A persistent civil war rages within all of our lives. Something within us causes us to lament with Ovid, the Latin poet, "I see and approve the better things, but follow worse," or to agree with Plato that human personality is like a charioteer having two headstrong horses, each wanting to go in a different direction, or to repeat with the Apostle Paul, "The good that I would I do not: but the evil which I would not, that I do."

This simply means that there is some good in the worst of us and some evil in the best of us. When we discover this, we are less prone to hate our enemies. When we look beneath the surface, beneath the impulsive evil deed, we see within our enemy-neighbor a measure of goodness and know that the viciousness and evilness of his acts are not quite representative of all that he is. We see him in a new light. We recognize that his hate grows out of fear, pride, ignorance, prejudice, and misunderstanding, but in spite of this, we know God's image is ineffably etched in his being. Then we love our enemies by realizing that they are not totally bad and that they are not beyond the reach of God's redemptive love.

Third, we must not seek to defeat or humiliate the enemy but to win his friendship and understanding. At times we are able to humiliate our worst enemy. Inevitably, his weak moments come and we are able to thrust in his side the spear of defeat. But this we must not do. Every word and deed must contribute to an understanding with the enemy and release those vast reservoirs of goodwill which have been blocked by impenetrable walls of hate.

The meaning of love is not to be confused with some sentimental outpouring. Love is something much deeper than emotional bosh. Perhaps the Greek language can clear our confusion at this point. In the Greek New Testament are three words for love. The word *eros* is a sort of aesthetic or romantic love. In the Platonic dialogues *eros* is a yearning of the soul for the realm of the divine. The second word is *philia,* a reciprocal love and the intimate affection and friendship between friends. We love those whom we like, and we love because we are loved. The third word is *agape,* understanding and creative, redemptive goodwill for all men. An overflowing love which seeks nothing in return, *agape* is the love of God operating in the human heart. At this level, we love men not because we like them, nor because their ways appeal to us, nor even because they possess some type of divine spark; we love every man because God loves him. At this level, we love the person who does an evil deed, although we hate the deed that he does.

Now we can see what Jesus meant when he said, "Love your enemies." We should be happy that he did not say, "Like your enemies." It is almost impossible to like some people. "Like" is a sentimental and affectionate word. How can we be affectionate toward a person whose avowed aim is to crush our very being and place innumerable stumbling blocks in our path? How can we like a person who is threatening our children and bombing our homes? That is impossible. But Jesus recognized that *love* is greater than *like.* When Jesus bids us to love our enemies, he is speaking neither of *eros* nor *philia;* he is speaking of *agape,* understanding and creative, redemptive goodwill for all men. Only by following this way and responding with this type of love are we able to be children of our Father who is in heaven.

Let us move now from the practical *how* to the theoretical *why: Why should we love our enemies?* The first reason is fairly obvious. Returning hate for hate multiplies hate, adding deeper darkness to a night already devoid of stars. Darkness cannot drive out darkness; only light can do that. Hate cannot drive out hate; only love can do that. Hate multiplies hate, violence multiplies violence, and toughness multiplies toughness in a descending spiral of destruction. So when Jesus says "Love your enemies," he is setting forth a profound and ultimately inescapable admonition. Have we not come to such an impasse in the modern world that we must love our enemies—or else? The chain reaction of evil—hate begetting hate, wars producing more wars—must be broken, or we shall be plunged into the dark abyss of annihilation.

Another reason why we must love our enemies is that hate scars the soul and distorts the personality. Mindful that hate is an evil and dangerous force, we too often think of what it does to the person hated. This is understandable, for hate brings irreparable damage to its victims. We have seen its ugly consequences in the ignominious deaths brought to six million Jews by a hate-obsessed madman named Hitler, in the unspeakable violence inflicted upon Negroes by bloodthirsty mobs, in the dark horrors of war, and in the terrible indignities and injustices perpetrated against millions of God's children by unconscionable oppressors.

But there is another side which we must never overlook. Hate is just as injurious to the person who hates. Like an unchecked cancer, hate corrodes the personality and eats away its vital unity. Hate destroys a man's sense of values and his objectivity. It causes him to describe the beautiful as ugly and the ugly as

beautiful, and to confuse the true with the false and the false with the true.

Dr. E. Franklin Frazier, in an interesting essay entitled "The Pathology of Race Prejudice," included several examples of white persons who were normal, amiable, and congenial in their day-to-day relationships with other white persons but when they were challenged to think of Negroes as equals or even to discuss the question of racial injustice, they reacted with unbelievable irrationality and an abnormal unbalance. This happens when hate lingers in our minds. Psychiatrists report that many of the strange things that happen in the subconscious, many of our inner conflicts, are rooted in hate. They say, "Love or perish." Modern psychology recognizes what Jesus taught centuries ago: hate divides the personality and love in an amazing and inexorable way unites it.

A third reason why we should love our enemies is that love is the only force capable of transforming an enemy into a friend We never get rid of an enemy by meeting hate with hate; we get rid of an enemy by getting rid of enmity. By its very nature, hate destroys and tears down; by its very nature, love creates and builds up. Love transforms with redemptive power.

Lincoln tried love and left for all history a magnificent drama of reconciliation. When he was campaigning for the presidency one of his arch-enemies was a man named Stanton. For some reason Stanton hated Lincoln. He used every ounce of his energy to degrade him in the eyes of the public. So deep rooted was Stanton's hate for Lincoln that he uttered unkind words about his physical appearance, and sought to embarrass him at every point with the bitterest diatribes. But in spite of this Lincoln was elected President of the United States. Then came the period when he had to select his cabinet which would consist of the persons who would be his most intimate associates in implementing his program. He started choosing men here and there for the various secretaryships. The day finally came for Lincoln to select a man to fill the all-important post of Secretary of War. Can you imagine whom Lincoln chose to fill this post? None other than the man named Stanton. There was an immediate uproar in the inner circle when the news began to spread. Adviser after adviser was heard saying, "Mr. President, you are making a mistake Do you know this man Stanton? Are you familiar with all of the ugly things he said about you? He is your enemy. He will seek to sabotage your program. Have you thought this through Mr. President?" Mr. Lincoln's answer was terse and to the point: "Yes, I know Mr. Stanton. I am aware of all the terrible things he has said about me. But after looking over the nation, I find he is the best man for the job." So Stanton became Abraham Lincoln's Secretary of War and rendered an invaluable service to his nation and his President. Not many years later Lincoln was assassinated. Many laudable things were said about him. Even today millions of people still adore him as the greatest of all Americans. H. G. Wells selected him as one of the six great men of history. But of all the great statements made about Abraham Lincoln, the words of Stanton remain among the greatest. Standing near the dead body of the man he once hated, Stanton referred to him as one of the greatest men that ever lived and said "he now belongs to the ages." If Lincoln had hated Stanton both men would have gone to their graves as bitter enemies. But through the power of love Lincoln transformed an enemy into a friend. It was this same attitude that made it possible for Lincoln to speak a kind word about the South during the Civil War when feeling was most bitter. Asked by a shocked bystander how he could do this, Lincoln said, "Madam, do I not destroy my enemies when I make them my friends?" This is the power of redemptive love.

We must hasten to say that these are not the ultimate reasons why we should love our enemies. An even more basic reason why we are commanded to love is expressed explicitly in Jesus' words, "Love your enemies . . . *that ye may be children of your Father which is in heaven.*" We are called to this difficult task in order to realize a unique relationship with God. We are potential sons of God. Through love that potentiality becomes actuality. We must love our enemies, because only by loving them can we know God and experience the beauty of his holiness.

The relevance of what I have said to the crisis in race relations should be readily apparent. There will be no permanent solution to the race problem until oppressed men develop the capacity to love their enemies. The darkness of racial injustice will be dispelled only by the light of forgiving love. For more than three centuries American Negroes have been battered by the iron rod of oppression, frustrated by day and bewildered by night by unbearable injustice, and burdened with the ugly weight of discrimination. Forced to live with these shameful conditions, we are tempted to become bitter and to retaliate with a corresponding hate. But if this happens, the new order

we seek will be little more than a duplicate of the old order. We must in strength and humility meet hate with love.

Of course, this is not *practical.* Life is a matter of getting even, of hitting back, of dog eat dog. Am I saying that Jesus commands us to love those who hurt and oppress us? Do I sound like most preachers—idealistic and impractical? Maybe in some distant Utopia, you say, that idea will work, but not in the hard, cold world in which we live.

My friends, we have followed the so-called practical way for too long a time now, and it has led inexorably to deeper confusion and chaos. Time is cluttered with the wreckage of communities which surrendered to hatred and violence. For the salvation of our nation and the salvation of mankind, we must follow another way. This does not mean that we abandon our righteous efforts. With every ounce of our energy we must continue to rid this nation of the incubus of segregation. But we shall not in the process relinquish our privilege and our obligation to love. While abhorring segregation, we shall love the segregationist. This is the only way to create the beloved community.

To our most bitter opponents we say: "We shall match your capacity to inflict suffering by our capacity to endure suffering. We shall meet your physical force with soul force. Do to us what you will, and we shall continue to love you. We cannot in all good conscience obey your unjust laws, because noncooperation with evil is as much a moral obligation as is cooperation with good. Throw us in jail, and we shall still love you. Send your hooded perpetrators of violence into our community at the midnight hour and beat us and leave us half dead, and we shall still love you. But be ye assured that we will wear you down by our capacity to suffer. One day we shall win freedom, but not only for ourselves. We shall so appeal to your heart and conscience that we shall win you in the process, and our victory will be a double victory."

Love is the most durable power in the world. This creative force, so beautifully exemplified in the life of our Christ, is the most potent instrument available in mankind's quest for peace and security. Napoleon Bonaparte, the great military genius, looking back over his years of conquest, is reported to have said: "Alexander, Caesar, Charlemagne and I have built great empires. But upon what did they depend? They depended on force. But centuries ago Jesus started an empire that was built on love, and even to this day millions will die for him." Who can doubt the veracity of these words? The great military leaders of the past have gone, and their empires have crumbled and burned to ashes. But the empire of Jesus, built solidly and majestically on the foundation of love, is still growing. It started with a small group of dedicated men, who, through the inspiration of their Lord, were able to shake the hinges from the gates of the Roman Empire, and carry the gospel into all the world. Today the vast earthly kingdom of Christ numbers more than 900,000,000 and covers every land and tribe. Today we hear again the promise of victory:

> Jesus shall reign where'er the sun
> Does his successive journeys run;
> His kingdom stretch from shore to shore,
> Till moon shall wax and wane no more.

Another choir joyously responds:

> In Christ there is no East or West,
> In Him no South or North,
> But one great Fellowship of Love
> Throughout the whole wide earth.

Jesus is eternally right. History is replete with the bleached bones of nations that refused to listen to him. May we in the twentieth century hear and follow his words—before it is too late. May we solemnly realize that we shall never be true sons of our heavenly Father until we love our enemies and pray for those who persecute us.

Liberating the Planet

The decades following World War II were ones in which Christian concern for human liberation—both spiritual and material—dominated theological discussions. Some saw the solution to the multiplicity of problems as one of individual salvation. If individuals turned to Christ, then society would change through the efforts of those transformed. The Greek term for this transformation is *metanoia,* which suggests a 180-degree turnaround. Such a radical shift would ripple throughout society; better people, better Christians, would make for a better society. Other Christians, however, saw the solution to the world's problems as one of collective salvation. Because we all live in structures of sin, they argued, those structures must be rebuilt before individuals can change. If poverty and injustice were woven into the very fabric of society, there was no way a single person could be "saved"; society had to be transformed, and only then could the kingdom of God truly be established on the earth. Despite the differences between these two views, both focused on the problem of human salvation.

With the celebration of the first Earth Day in April 1970, and the subsequent growth in environmental consciousness, Christian interest in salvation expanded to include the earth itself: its plants, animals, oceans, and lands. The possibility of nuclear annihilation—somewhat distant from us today, but an ever-present reality for those living in the second half of the twentieth century—posed a real threat to the planet's very survival, not just to human survival. In addition, environmental problems ranging from air and water pollution, to global warming, to the daily loss of plant and animal species and the dramatic disappearance of fish from the oceans also created a new consciousness about the responsibility Christians had for saving the earth. The biblical injunction from Genesis 1:27 to "fill the earth and subdue it; and have dominion over the fish of the sea and over the birds of the air and over every living thing that moves upon the earth" seemed to have justified exploitation of the earth's resources. At the close of the twentieth century, however, Christians and

Jews reinterpreted it as a statement of responsibility: God wanted humans to be good stewards of the earth, and to take care, and manage, the precious creation which God had given humanity.

More than two decades before the first Earth Day, a French Jesuit analyzed the earth's ecosystem and wrote that it was a single organism, which he called the "noö-sphere." Pierre Teilhard de Chardin (1881–1955) was a paleontologist, biologist, and philosopher who is best known for his idea that the earth, and all that is in it, is slowly evolving into a higher form of consciousness. Human and planetary consciousness is converging into an omega point—an end point—that is ultimately divine. Thus, evolution was God's plan from the start, though Teilhard de Chardin did not limit it to humans but included the earth itself. In the "Hymn of the Universe," he wrote:

> Bathe yourself in the ocean of matter; plunge into it where it is deepest and most violent; struggle in its currents and drink its water, for it cradled you long ago in your preconcious existence; and it is that ocean that will raise you up to God.

A number of his works were published posthumously, and at times he was in danger of being excommunicated because of his belief in evolution. Although Pope John Paul II declared in the 1990s that Darwin's theory of evolution was not incompatible with Christian teachings, in the mid-twentieth century this seemed clear only to Teilhard de Chardin. His attempt to integrate natural science, especially evolution, and theology, however, set the stage for future eco-theologians.

Christians examined their historical role as caretakers and noted a number of different trends. Liberation theologians from Latin America found a connection between exploitation of the earth and exploitation of the poor. The two were inextricably linked. Leonardo Boff, for example, related the destruction of the Amazon rain forests to the destruction of indigenous peoples living in those forests, as well as the destruction of small-scale agriculture and sustainable economies. Evangelical Christians, working with Jews and mainline Protestants, launched an ad campaign that featured the acronym WWJD—"What would Jesus do?"—and asked, "What would Jesus drive?" The campaign targeted gas-guzzling sport-utility vehicles and other large-size cars and trucks.

Feminist theologians identified a link between patriarchy, and patriarchal language for the divine, and environmental disaster. They saw in patriarchy the will to dominance, not just over women but over all of nature. The language Christians used for God helped to justify and defend this system. If God is called "king," for example, then our relationship to God is one of subjects. We have to do what God, the heavenly king, says; and since earth is a microcosm of the heavenly realm, that means we also have to do what an earthly human king says. As a result, as individuals, we have little say in or responsibility for what happens to the planet. Or, if God is Father, and we are God's children, then we have to obey God and our fathers. Feminists asked the profound question "Is 'Father' the actual name for God, or is it a metaphor for God?" They claimed that the father-son language Christians inherited from the Bible and from Christian tradition was always intended as a metaphor for the inexplicable divine mystery. Other Christians vehemently disagreed, and continue to disagree, arguing that "Father" is the only appropriate name for God the creator of the world and the parent of Jesus Christ.

If Christians use different language, or different metaphors, for God, will their attitude toward each other and toward the planet change? Feminists and others have said yes, and have suggested a number of alternatives for traditional Trinitarian language, such as Creator, Redeemer, and Sustainer, for Father, Son, and Holy Spirit; or Abba (Papa), Servant, and Advocate. Sallie McFague, a feminist theologian who attempted to work out life-sustaining theologies in the face of potential environmental and nuclear disasters, developed a number of models of God. McFague asserted that all language about God is metaphorical; it merely attempts to state in human terms what is utterly inexpressible. If language about God is not literal, but rather figurative, then Christians can come up with some new models that might create a healthier approach to caring for the planet on which we live. In her view, instead of thinking of the earth as God's kingdom, it might be better to think of it as God's body: Would we throw litter on God's body? Would we tear it up with bulldozers and chainsaws? Further, our understanding of God might be enhanced if we tried some new metaphors for the divine. McFague suggested thinking of God as mother: What might be our relationship to a mother, rather than to a king? She also proposed thinking of God as lover and as friend. Each of these models implies different relationships, different modes of being with the divine.

The Reading

The selection that closes this reader comes from the conclusion of Sallie McFague's book *Models of God: Theology for an Ecological, Nuclear Age*. The theologian has carefully constructed her arguments up to this point. She has tried to make the case for thinking about our God-talk as metaphorical, rather than literal, and has proposed three alternative models: mother, lover, and friend. The conclusion presupposes our knowledge of her arguments. This selection exemplifies systematic theology. Like Gutiérrez' argument for understanding liberation as a this-worldly phenomenon, McFague's book presents a step-by-step analysis to make her case for using alternative metaphors for God. Although she claims to be writing a "heuristic theology," meaning it is experimental and tentative, McFague nevertheless believes that her approach leads to a helpful and constructive conception of the divine.

Note: McFague mentions "agapic love," which refers to *agape* (pronounced AH-gah-pay), a Greek word that describes divine, rather than human, love.

Questions to Consider

1. What do you think about the claim that God has many names?

2. What does it mean to say that we are "addressing" God rather than "describing" God?

3. Can McFague's language for the divine be reconciled with the affirmations of the Nicene Creed and the Definition of Chalcedon we studied in Chapter Two? Why or why not?

4. What does McFague mean by God's immanence and transcendence? What examples does she give of each concept?

5. McFague asks what her experiment says about God's immanence and transcendence. What are her answers?

6. Do you think contemporary Christianity can accept the language McFague proposes? Why or why not? Do you think modern Christians should consider updating historical creeds and language to describe the eternal in modern terms?

7. What do you think would happen if Christians began to think of the world as God's body rather than as God's kingdom?

Models of God: Conclusion

SALLIE McFAGUE

When we pray, we know we are addressing, not describing, God. When in prayer we add a noun to the Thou, the You, we are addressing, we know it does not define or in any way limit God. When we address God as mother, father, lover, friend, or as judge, healer, liberator, companion, or yet again as sun, ocean, fortress, shield, or even as creator, redeemer, and sustainer, we know that these terms are not descriptions of God. When we speak to God we are most conscious of how inadequate our language is for God, something we more easily forget when we speak about God—that is, when we are doing theology.

And of this profound and permanent inadequacy we need to remind ourselves as we come to the close of our thought experiment with a few models of the relationship between God and the world in an ecological, nuclear age. Even a metaphorical, heuristic theology that believes itself to be skeptical, open-ended, and pluralistic can become enamored of its experiment, finding its new models a sufficient improvement on alternatives that they become subtly elevated to a new trinity with a position of authority. Is it mere coincidence that we dealt principally with *three* models—mother, lover, and friend—and that they conveniently fell into the categories of creator,

savior, and sustainer, thus taking the place, as it were, of the most ancient and hallowed names of the Trinitarian God—Father, Son, and Holy Spirit?

It was not a coincidence but a deliberate attempt to unseat those names as descriptions of God which will allow no supplements or alternatives. That objective was certainly not the central concern of these pages, but it is an important byproduct of the experiment attempted here. That is to say, if it can be shown that models other than the traditional ones are appropriate and illuminating for expressing the Christian gospel in our time, an important admission will have been made: *God has many names.* The attempt to unseat both monarchical and traditional Trinitarian language, however, is not a subterfuge to establish a new trinity using different names. To do so would be to fall into the "tyranny of the absolutizing imagination," which we have all along tried to avoid. There are, however, two moves being made here: one disorienting, the other reorienting. The disorienting move is the introduction of alternative models for God and the world, and the experiment with them to try out their possibilities in relationship to an understanding of the gospel as destabilizing, inclusive, nonhierarchical fulfillment. In this experiment I attempted to see if they could, in their own way, address many of the traditional formal theological categories of creation, salvation, and preservation; revelation and incarnation; the nature of human existence; sin and evil; the character of Christian life; church and sacraments; and so forth. Part of their power, I believed, was to show how they would do the job that the traditional models have done. So although the stress in these pages has been on an imaginative picture to undergird the new holistic sensibility needed in our time, of substantial importance as well—in order to make this picture persuasive—is its ability to deal with traditional Christian themes. Hence, a reorienting move is also intended. The alternative models we have considered are not a trinity in the old sense of hallowed names for God intended to discourage experimentation and insure orthodoxy; nevertheless, a modest proposal is advanced: for our time the new models are illuminating, helpful, and appropriate ways in which to think about the relationship between God and the world. And that is all that is being advanced, inasmuch as metaphorical, heuristic theology says much but means little. It is mostly fiction, mainly fleshing out a few basic metaphors in as deep and comprehensive a fashion as possible to see what their implications might be. Perhaps the imaginative picture that has been painted provides a habitable house in which to live for a while, with doors open and windows ajar, and with the promise that additions and renovations are desired and needed.

One matter of importance remains, however. In one sense the entire essay has been about God, but the seriatim fashion in which we have considered our models—the world as God's body, and God as mother, lover, and friend—has not allowed us to address in a unified way one of the central issues of the Christian doctrine of God, and what I believe the doctrine of the trinity expresses—namely, the transcendence and immanence of God. I have no intentions of embarking on a historical overview of the myriad ways theologians and church councils have interpreted this doctrine or of the conundrums it has presented, but from the point of view of our models, the doctrine or something like it is appropriate. For what it says in light of our models is that God is not a solitary deity distant from and unrelated to the world, nor a God submerged into the world and undifferentiated from it. Rather, God as mother, lover, and friend of the world as God's body is both transcendent to the world (even as we are transcendent to our bodies) and profoundly immanent in the world (even as we are at one with our bodies). We have seen God's transcendence in agapic love that is the source of all life and that wills existence to all; we have seen God's immanence in erotic love that finds the world valuable and that identifies with it in the incarnation—both in the world as the body of God and in paradigmatic individuals, most notably, Jesus of Nazareth. Is more needed? What of the "third" in the trinity? Is there something sacred about three? I do not think so. But the vision of salvation we have attempted to picture, in which an original unity is divided and separated by sin and evil to be healed and made whole again, a unity symbolized by the festive meal of friends where all are included, is, I believe, enriched and filled out by the third. In our understanding of the work of God in relation to the world, it is all of one piece: the creator says that it is good that you exist; the savior, that you are valuable beyond all imagining; the sustainer, that we shall all eat together, even the outsider. Yet in this one piece there are different emphases, providing a picture too rich and varied to be compassed in a single mode of speaking of the way God and the world are related. To be sure, any one of the models of God as mother, lover, and friend of the world as God's body projects an image of God as both transcendent and immanent; moreover, as we have emphasized many times, neither these names nor any others describe, define, or limit the divine nature. In view of the theology presented here, a trinity is not a necessity nor should the divine nature be in any way circumscribed by it. All the same, a trinity fits well with the models of our experiment, and even more important, as other monistic theologians have pointed out, the pattern of three is appropriate for expressing the unity, separation, and reunification that have been the central theme of this experiment. Admittedly, there are other ways besides the trinity to express the transcendence and immanence of God; nonetheless, it is a valuable, rich way. It suggests the profound immanence of God in the world through its dialectical pattern; it underscores the plurality of names for God; it provides a rich context for speaking of the variety of God's activities in relation to the world. In other words, it helps us to talk of God in an economical yet ample way: it is neither too little nor too much, neither the dull limitation of the unitary nor the riotous confusion of uncontrolled numbers. There is, then, a kind of pragmatism in settling for three: it has proved fruitful and illuminating.

But what, more specifically, does our experiment say about the transcendence and immanence of God to and in the world? The central picture we have been developing is of the world as God's body, which God—and we—mother, love, and befriend. God is incarnated or embodied in our world, in both cosmological and anthropological ways. The implication of this picture is that we never meet God unmediated or unembodied. The transcendence of God in our picture, whatever it does mean, cannot be understood apart from the world, or to phrase it more precisely, what we can know of God's transcendence is neither above nor beneath but in and through the world. We meet God in the body of the world. What, then, do we say of God's immanence and transcendence? We have already considered some of the classic theological issues surrounding these themes in our treatment of the world as God's body, but now, in closing, we need to reflect on how we become aware of God's immanence and transcendence. If we understand our contact with God always to be a mediated, embodied one with the body of our world, our universe, as the place where we meet God—what does this imply about divine immanence and transcendence in an ecological, nuclear age? It implies that we perceive or become aware of God not as solitary individuals who meet God in moments of religious ecstasy but as workers—parents, lovers, and friends—in the world. The world is our meeting place with God, and this means that God's immanence will be "universal" and God's transcendence will be "worldly."

To say that God's presence to us, God's immanence, is universal means that it is not limited to special times or places or to particular people or institutions, although special times and places, as well as particular people or institutions, may have paradigmatic importance. If the world, the cosmos, is our point of contact with God, the place where we join God to work on a project of mutual importance—the well-being of the body for which we have been given special responsibility—then it is here that we find God, become aware of God. This means we look at the world, all parts and aspects of it, differently: it is the body of God, and hence we revere it, find it special and precious, not as God but as the way God has chosen to be visible, available, to us. In addition, then, to special, paradigmatic individuals and to the church as the fellowship of friends, both of which are illuminating places where God is immanent, there is also the world that belongs to God in so

intimate and special a way that we call it God's body. It is not, then, mere earth or dead matter; it is "consecrated," formally dedicated to a divine purpose. We do not know in all ways or even in many ways what this purpose is, but the world is not *ours* to manipulate for *our* purposes. If we see it as God's body, the way God is present to us, we will indeed know we tread on sacred ground. God's immanence, then, being universal, undergirds a sensibility that is open to the world, both to other people and to other forms of life, as the way one meets God. In this picture we do not meet God vis-à-vis, but we meet God only and always as mediated, as embodied.

Such universal immanence is but one side of God's presence: the other is worldly transcendence. We have said much in these pages concerning divine immanence, and in fact the experiment was conducted in part to counter the overly transcendent tradition of historical Christianity, with its emphasis on monarchical, triumphalist models of God. Less has been said about how, in our model, one perceives divine transcendence. What does it mean to call divine transcendence worldly? It means that we look to the universe as God's body for images of transcendence, and not to the political realm with its models of lord, king, and patriarch, as the tradition has done. And in fact, does not the universe provide us with far more awesome images of transcendence that the political arena? An ecological evolutionary sensibility is aware of what one sees through telescope and microscope: the vast, unending space that is beyond all human comprehension, as well as the intricate pattern on an insect's wing that is likewise beyond our grasp. If one can say that the basic religious apprehension is the wonder at being, wondering that there is something rather than nothing, then the ecological, evolutionary sensibility is in this sense religious, for it avoids the "middle vision" we conventionally use in looking at our world and focuses on the very small and the very large. Both are awesome and wondrous: studying the bark of a tree or reflecting on the eons of geological time brings about the same awareness—that our universe is, in its age and size, its variety and richness, its intricacy and order, its detail and beauty, beyond all comprehension, all imagining. Is this a revival of the old argument from design for the existence of God? Hardly. It is, however, a context for imaging the transcendence of God in a worldly way, not through political images or, like the usual alternative to political models, in abstract terms of infinity, eternality, omniscience, omnipresence, and so forth, but in the mythology or images of our own day that inspire feelings of awe, reverence, wonder. These are the images, and many of them will be naturalistic, springing from the ecological, evolutionary sensibility that sees the universe, the body of God, with eyes of wonder. These as yet unknown, unplumbed metaphors have not been the focus of this essay; we have concentrated on immanental rather than transcendent models, on anthropological rather than naturalistic ones. But much remains for other experiments with alternative models of God, and a rich resource for metaphors of God's worldly transcendence is surely what we perceive through the microscope and the telescope that overturns our conventional middle vision of the world as a comfortable, comprehensible place. As the body of God, it is wondrously, awesomely, divinely mysterious.

We come to perceive our world in this way most immediately and painfully when we think of its end or its desecration. What the ecological, evolutionary sensibility brings to consciousness in a positive way—the wonder of being—awareness of a possible nuclear holocaust does in a negative way. And in this case, it is more effective to "think small." Middle vision, of course, can here also be overcome by thinking big, and that is the direction most consciousness-raising efforts on nuclear war have taken: they have painted a picture of nuclear winter or the extent of death and destruction that will occur after such an event. But it is even more telling in terms of our perception of the world, of how wondrous it is and how much we do in fact care for it, to think small. This demands a new form of meditation in which we call up concrete images of events, people, plants and animals, objects, places, whatever—as long as they are particular, cherished aspects of our world—and dwell upon their specialness, their distinctiveness, their value, until the pain of contemplating their permanent loss not just to you or me, but to all for all time, becomes unbearable. This is a form of prayer for the world as the body of God which we, as mothers and fathers, lovers, and friends of the world, are summoned to practice. This prayer, though not the only one in an ecological, nuclear age, is a necessary and permanent one. The prayer we *wish* to pray, the prayer of thanksgiving for the joyful feast of all in the presence of God, depends upon accepting responsibility for our beautiful, fragile earth, without which there will be no bread and no wine.

Conclusions

Dietrich Bonhoeffer asked what Christians have to say about God in a world come of age. We see that they provide a number of different answers to his question. Ecumenism and interfaith dialogue examine what divides Christians from each other and from believers of different faiths. But the dialogue also lifts up what they have in common. Although many Christians believe that Jesus is the one and only way to God, many others question this claim; both sides use the Bible in support of their argument. Liberation theologians, like Bonhoeffer himself, chose to understand God as working in the concrete realities of history. Their answer has been to walk with the poor, to suffer and die with them, just as Jesus walked with those whom his society had marginalized. Still other Christians have responded to Bonhoeffer's question by energetically evangelizing their neighbors at home and abroad, in the belief that spreading the word of God would bring eternal life and hope to one and all. Finally, some Christians have answered Bonhoeffer by changing the very terms by which they discuss Jesus and God.

These voices for the future all point to the different directions that Christianity has taken the past hundred years and is likely to take in the future. As in its very beginnings, which we can see as early as the New Testament record, Christianity remains diverse, with disagreement as to practices and priorities. In the first century, as well as in our own, Christianity has had to face the challenge of competing truth claims from other religions and from within its own communion of churches. Yet it has also remained constant in its belief that the lordship of Jesus Christ transformed the world and its people forever. This belief is as strong today as it was 2000 years ago.

Sources of Selections

Bermúdez, Fernando. *Death and Resurrection in Guatemala.* Introduction by Phillip Berryman. Trans. Robert R. Barr. Maryknoll, N.Y.: Orbis Books, 1986.

Bonhoeffer, Dietrich. *Letters and Papers from Prison.* Enlarged ed. Ed. Eberhard Bethge, trans. Reginald Fuller, Frank Clarke, John Bowden, and others. New York: Macmillan, 1971.

Bulgakov, Sergius. *The Orthodox Church.* Trans. Lydia Kesich. Crestwood, N.Y.: St. Vladimir's Seminary Press, 1988.

Cho, David Yonggi, with Harold Hostetler. *Successful Home Cell Groups.* Gainesville, Fla.: Bridge-Logos, 1981, 2001.

Flannery, O.P., Austin ed. *Vatican Council II. The Conciliar and Post Conciliar Documents.* New rev. ed. Vol. I. Northport, N.Y.: Costello, 1992.

Gutiérrez, Gustavo. *A Theology of Liberation: History, Politics, and Salvation.* Rev. ed. with new Introduction. Trans. and ed. Sister Caridad Inda and John Eagleson. Maryknoll, N.Y.: Orbis Books, 2001.

John Paul II. *Ut unum sint: On Commitment to Ecumenism.* 25 May 1995. <http://www.vatican .va/holy_father/john_paul_ii/encyclicals/documents/hf_jpii_enc_25051995 _ut-unum-sint_en.html>

King Jr., Martin Luther. *A Testament of Hope: The Essential Writings and Speeches of Martin Luther King, Jr.* San Francisco: HarperSanFrancisco, 1986.

————. *Strength to Love.* Philadelphia: Fortress, 1981.

Leith, John H., ed. *Creeds of the Churches,* 3d ed. Louisville, Ky.: Knox, 1982.

McFague, Sallie. *Models of God: Theology for an Ecological, Nuclear Age.* Philadelphia: Fortress Press, 1987.

Additional Resources

Anderson, Allan H., and Walter J. Hollenweger, eds. *Pentecostals After a Century: Global Perspectives on a Movement in Transition.* Sheffield, U.K.: Sheffield Academic Press, 1999.

Bediako, Kwame. *Christianity in Africa: The Renewal of a Non-Western Religion.* Edinburgh: Edinburgh University Press and Orbis Books, 1995.

Boff, Leonard. *Cry of the Earth, Cry of the Poor.* Trans. Phillip Berryman. Maryknoll, N.Y.: Orbis Books, 1997.

Boff, Leonardo, and Clodovis Boff. *Introducing Liberation Theology.* Trans. Paul Burns. Maryknoll, N.Y.: Orbis Books, 1997.

Bonino, José Míguez. *Faces of Latin American Protestantism: 1993 Carnahan Lectures.* Trans. Eugene L. Stockwell. Grand Rapids, Mich.: Eerdmans, 1995.

Carson, Clayborne, and Peter Holloran. *A Knock at Midnight: Inspiration from the Great Sermons of Reverend Martin Luther King, Jr.* New York: Warner Books, 1998.

Corten, André, and Ruth Marshall-Fratani, eds. *Between Babel and Pentecost: Transnational Pentecostalism in Africa and Latin America.* Bloomington: Indiana University Press, 2001.

Cox, Harvey. *Fire from Heaven: The Rise of Pentecostal Spirituality and the Reshaping of Religion in the Twenty-First Century.* New York: Addison-Wesley, 1995.

Ellacuría, Ignacio, and Jon Sobrino, eds. *Mysterium Liberationis: Fundamental Concepts of Liberation Theology.* Maryknoll, N.Y.: Orbis Books, 1993.

Fiorenza, Francis Schüssler, and John P. Galvin, eds. *Systematic Theology: Roman Catholic Perspectives.* 2 vols. Minneapolis: Fortress Press, 1991.

Jenkins, Philip. *The Next Christendom: The Coming of Global Christianity.* New York: Oxford University Press, 2002.

Keating, Thomas. *Open Mind, Open Heart: The Contemplative Dimension of the Gospel.* Rockport, Mass.: Element, 1992.

Kinnamon, Michael, and Brian E. Cope, eds. *The Ecumenical Movement: An Anthology of Key Texts and Voices.* Geneva, Switzerland, and Grand Rapids, Mich.: WCC Publications and Eerdmans, 1997.

Meyendorff, John. *The Orthodox Church: Its Past and Its Role in the World Today.* 3d rev. ed. Trans. John Chapin. Crestwood, N.Y.: St. Vladimir's Seminary Press, 1981.

Ouspensky, Leonid. *Theology of the Icon.* Vol. II. Trans. Anthony Gythiel. Crestwood, N.Y.: St. Vladimir's Seminary Press, 1992.

Ruether, Rosemary Radford. *Gaia and God: An Ecofeminist Theology of Earth Healing.* San Francisco: HarperSanFrancisco, 1992.

Sundkler, Bengt, and Christopher Steed. *A History of the Church in Africa.* Cambridge, U.K.: Cambridge University Press, 2000.

Ware, Timothy. *The Orthodox Church.* Rev. ed. Baltimore: Penguin Books, 1993.

Films

Four Little Girls. Directed by Spike Lee, 1997.

Hotel Rwanda. Directed by Terry George, 2004.

The Killing Fields. Directed by Roland Joffe, 1984.

No Man's Land. Directed by Danis Tanovic, 2001.

Romero. Directed by John Duigan, 1989.

Schindler's List. Directed by Steven Spielberg, 1993.

Testament. Directed by Lynne Littman, 1983.

The Wannsee Conference. Directed by Heinz Schirk, 1984.

Credits

p. 11, 28, 38: Excerpts from *New Revised Standard Version Bible.* Copyright © 1989 by the Division of Christian Education of the National Council of the Churches of Christ in the United States of America. Used by permission. All rights reserved.

p. 17: Geza Vermes (trans.), "Community Rule, IX ≅ from *The Dead Sea Scrolls, Third Edition.* Copyright 8 1962, 1965, 1968, 1975, 1987 by G. Vermes. Reprinted with the permission of Penguin Books, Ltd.

p. 54: Willis Barnstone (trans.), Mark 1:1-20 from *The Holy Covenant, Commonly Called the New Testament, Volume I.* Copyright © 2002 by Willis Barnstone. Reprinted with the permission of Riverhead Books, a division of Penguin Group (USA) Inc.

p. 71, 75: Cyril of Jerusalem, excerpts from *St. Cyril of Jerusalem's Lectures on the Christian Sacraments: The Procatechesis and the Five Mystagogical Catecheses,* edited by F.L. Cross. Reprinted with the permission of SPCK, London.

p. 73: R.A. Kraft (trans.), from "The Didache (The Teaching of the Lord to the Gentiles by the Twelve Apostles)" in *The Apostolic Fathers,* edited by Jack N. Sparks. Copyright © 1978 by R.A. Kraft. Reprinted with the permission of Thomas Nelson, Inc.

p. 78: M.R. James (trans.), excerpt from "The Acts of Thomas" from *The Apocryphal New Testament.* Reprinted with the permission of Clarendon Press/Oxford University Press, Ltd.

p. 93: Athanasius of Alexandria, 11-18 from "The Divine Dilemma and Its Solution in the Incarnation" from *St. Athanasius on the Incarnation: The Treatise* De Incarnatione Verbi Dei, translated and edited by a Religious of CSMV. Reprinted with the permission of St. Vladimir's Seminary Press, 575 Scarsdale Road, Crestwood, NY 10707, www.svspress.com.

p. 98: Eusebius, from *Life of Constantine,* translated by Averil Cameron and Stuart G. Hall. Copyright © 1999 by Averil Cameron and Stuart G. Hall. Reprinted with the permission of Oxford University Press.

p. 101: Augustine of Hippo, Book XIV, sections IV, XI-XV, and XXVIII from *The City of God Against the Pagans,* from *Augustine: Volume IV,* Loeb Classical Library 7 Volume 414, translated by Philip Levine. Copyright © 1966 by the President and Fellows of Harvard College. Reprinted with the

permission of Harvard University Press and the Trustees of the Loeb Classical Library. The Loeb Classical Library 7 is a registered trademark of the President and Fellows of Harvard College..

p. 121: Hildegard of Bingen, excerpt from *Hildegard of Bingen's "Book of Divine Works" with Letters and Songs,* edited by Matthew Fox. Reprinted with the permission of Bear & Company/Inner Traditions.

p. 123: Julian of Norwich, Chapters 57-60 from *Revelations of Divine Love,* translated by Clifton Wolters (London: Penguin Books, 1966). Copyright © 1966 by Clifton Wolters. Reprinted with the permission of John Clifton Wolters.

p. 131: Haimo of Auxerre, Prologue and Chapter 1 from *Commentary on the Book of Jonah,* translated by Deborah Everhart. Copyright © 1993 by the Board of the Medieval Institute. Reprinted with the permission of Medieval Institute Publications, Western Michigan University.

p. 146: St. Francis of Assisi, "Canticle of the Sun," translated by Bill Barrett, from http://www.webster.edu/~barrettb/canticle.htm. Reprinted with the permission of the translator.

p. 146: St. Francis of Assisi, "All Creatures of Our God and King," translated by William H. Draper. Copyright © 1989 by The United Methodist Publishing House (Administered by The Copyright Company c/o The Copyright Company, Nashville, TN). All rights reserved. International Copyright Secured. Used By Permission.

p. 150: St. John of Damascus, from "Third Apology of Saint John of Damascus Against Those Who Attack the Divine Images" from *On the Divine Images: Three Apologies Against Those Who Attack the Divine Images,* translated by David Anderson. Reprinted with the permission of St. Vladimir's Seminary Press, 575 Scarsdale Road, Crestwood, NY10707, www.svspress.com.

p. 159: Gregory Palamas, from *The Triads,* edited by John Meyendorff, translated by Nicholas Gendle, preface by Jaroslav Pelikan. Copyright © 1983 by Paulist Press, Inc., New York/Mahwah, NJ. Reprinted with the permission of Paulist Press, www.paulistpress.com.

p. 169: William of Ockham, from "Eight Questions on the Power of the Pope" from *A Letter to the Friars Minor and Other Writings,* translated by John Kilcullen. Copyright ©

449

Biblical Index

Subject Index